D1443620

# Homeland
# Security

# Homeland Security

## A Documentary History

Bruce Maxwell

LAS POSITAS COLLEGE LIBRARY
3033 COLLIER CANYON RD.
LIVERMORE, CA 94551-9797

CQ PRESS

A Division of Congressional Quarterly Inc.
Washington, D.C.

111.89

Ref
UA
921
H657
2004

CQ Press
1255 22nd Street, N.W., Suite 400
Washington, D.C. 20037

202-729-1900; toll-free, 1-866-4CQ-PRESS (1-866-427-7737)

www.cqpress.com

Copyright © 2004 by CQ Press, a Division of Congressional Quarterly Inc.

All rights reserved. No part of this publication may be reproduced or transmitted in any form or by any means, electronic or mechanical, including photocopy, recording, or any information storage and retrieval system, without permission in writing from the publisher.

♾ The paper used in this publication exceeds the requirements of the American National Standard for Information Sciences—Permanence of Paper for Printed Library Materials, ANSI Z39.48-1992.

Printed and bound in the United States of America

08   07   06   05   04        5   4   3   2   1

CQ Press gratefully acknowledges the permission to reprint on page 361 "The Congress: Preserving Our Institutions," copyright © 2003 by the American Enterprise Institute for Public Policy Research. Reprinted with the permission of the American Enterprise Institute for Public Policy Research, Washington, D.C., and on page 445 "Emergency Responders: Drastically Underfunded, Dangerously Unprepared," copyright © 2003 by the Council on Foreign Relations. Reprinted with the permission of the Council on Foreign Relations, New York, N.Y.

Cover design by Naylor Design Inc.
Composition by Auburn Associates, Inc.

Cover photos: *Top left,* Transportation Security Administration inspectors check airport baggage, NewsCom; *Bottom left,* House representatives Mike Pence, R-Ind. (left), Carolyn B. Maloney, D-N.Y., and Christopher Shays, R-Conn. (right), part of a bipartisan group pushing for a quick response to the 9/11 Commission recommendations, Scott J. Ferrell, CQ; *Center,* onlookers peer across the Hudson River from New Jersey at the burning World Trade Center on September 11, 2001, AFP Photos/Michael Boesl; *Top right,* Sen. Joseph McCarthy, Library of Congress; *Bottom right,* Manzanar War Relocation Center, Library of Congress.

Library of Congress Cataloging-in-Publication Data

Library of Congress Catalog Number: 2004026831

ISBN: 1-56802-884-9

*For Barbara, with love*

# Contents

# Preface

The phrase "homeland security" was not part of the general lexicon before the terrorist attacks of September 11, 2001. Yet threats to homeland security—real and imagined—have regularly occurred throughout the nation's history. *Homeland Security: A Documentary History* presents more than 140 documents to allow the reader to trace the history, issues, and impact of homeland security concerns from the Alien and Sedition Acts of 1798 to the present. The documents include presidential orders and directives, reports by government watchdogs, transcripts of congressional hearings, congressional resolutions, studies conducted by commissions appointed by the president or Congress, Supreme Court decisions, rules published in the *Federal Register,* transcripts of speeches by federal officials, resolutions adopted by state and local governments, statements by the staff of the 9/11 Commission, and the commission's final report, among others.

The book opens with an introduction that explains the crucial distinction between "homeland security" and "homeland defense," describes some of the earliest homeland security incidents, and discusses some links between historic events and efforts since September 11, 2001, to improve homeland security.

The thirty-four chapters discuss and reproduce multiple, thematically related documents. This rich structure provides a deeper understanding by tracing individual issues through a variety of government reports, independent studies, speeches, and other documents. The chapters are arranged chronologically based on the date of the first document reprinted in each one. All documents within a chapter are arranged chronologically as well, except Documents 26 and 27, which are discussed in the order most helpful to the reader.

The editor reviewed more than 1,000 documents to select the 142 that are reprinted. Instead of trying to cover every issue related to homeland security, the editor chose documents that trace concerns about specific homeland security issues that emerged long before the September 2001 attacks, show patterns in attempts to address particular homeland security issues, illustrate parallels between historical and current events, or are historically significant.

Each chapter includes a list of documents, an introduction that provides context, and then the documents themselves, along with full source citations. In addition to the Alien and Sedition Acts, early documents explore President Abraham Lincoln's suspension of the writ of habeas corpus during the Civil War; laws passed during World War I that limited the movement of aliens within the United States and punished citizens such as labor leader Eugene Debs for speaking or writing in opposition to the war; the internment of more than 120,000 people of Japanese descent—citizen and noncitizen alike—during World War II; and the "Red Scare" during the 1950s that was fueled in part by Sen. Joseph McCarthy of Wisconsin and resulted in Congress approving the construction of detention camps and requiring communists to register with the government.

Some of these government actions, such as Lincoln's suspension of the writ of habeas corpus and the Japanese internment, were responses to attacks on American soil. Others, such as the Alien and Sedition Acts of 1798, used war fears to silence political dissent. Still others, such as the rise of McCarthyism and passage of the Internal Security Act of 1950, occurred because of hysterical reactions to events at the time.

Moving to the modern era, the documents explore questions in the 1970s and 1990s about the capabilities and organization of U.S. intelligence agencies; warnings dating from 1987 about serious vulnerabilities in aviation security; the 1993 bombing of the World Trade Center in New York City and the 1995 bombing of the Alfred P. Murrah Federal Building in Oklahoma City; concerns that terrorists could obtain biological, chemical, radioactive, or nuclear weapons and unleash them on the United States; studies that found widespread vulnerabilities in government computer systems; the government's changing view of the threat posed by Osama bin Laden; and warnings in the 1990s from several government commissions that terrorists could and would attack the United States, among other topics.

The book then turns to the terrorist attacks on September 11, 2001, and their aftermath. The documents examine the creation of the Office of Homeland Security and later the Department of Homeland Security to improve counterterrorism coordination among government agencies; the launching of the war in Afghanistan; the government's jailing of more than 1,200 men of Middle Eastern and South Asian descent in almost total secrecy; the USA Patriot Act; the tightening of the nation's borders; attempts to block terrorist financing; the impact on "first responders" at the state and local levels; changes within the Federal Bureau of Investigation (FBI); efforts to ensure government continuity if terrorists attacked Washington, D.C.; and investigations of the 2001 terrorist attacks by congressional committees and the 9/11 Commission, along with other subjects.

This volume is designed to provide a broad-based overview of homeland security that serves as a springboard for reflection, discussion, and study. Numerous recommendations for further study are listed in the bibliography. Many of the articles, books, government documents, and reports are available on the Internet, and URLs are listed for items that can be accessed online. The bibliography also briefly describes dozens of selected Web sites about homeland security.

The most important item listed in the bibliography is *The 9/11 Commission Report: Final Report of the National Commission on Terrorist Attacks Upon the United States*. In gripping detail, the report describes minute-by-minute what happened on September 11, 2001, why the nation was unprepared, and what the commission believes must be done to prevent further attacks. The 567-page book is so compelling that it was named a finalist for a National Book Award, an honor rarely accorded to government documents.

A few notes about the reprinted documents in this book may be helpful to readers:

- Most of the documents, some of which are entire books themselves, are carefully excerpted to focus on the highlights and allow the inclusion of as many documents as possible. The customary ellipsis points indicate any omissions.
- The original spelling and punctuation have been retained for all documents.
- Capitalization of headings and the use of italic and boldface within documents have been stylized for volume consistency and do not necessarily match the original sources.
- Material in the document texts enclosed by brackets has been added by the editor to enhance clarity.
- The source note at the end of each document provides complete bibliographic information. The source note also includes a URL if the full text of the document is available online.
- The official title of every document is listed in its source note.
- Many documents originated with the investigative arm of Congress. This agency was called the General Accounting Office until July 7, 2004, when its name changed to the Government Accountability Office.

Even more so than with my previous books, I am indebted to many people who helped make this one possible. I have been extremely fortunate to work once again with the superb staff at CQ Press. Special thanks go to acquisitions editor Shana Wagger for believing in this book throughout its creation, being unwavering in her graciousness, and helping shape the book; to development editor January Layman-Wood for providing sound editorial suggestions, coordinating the electronic files, and constantly exuding cheerfulness; to production editor Joan Gossett for overseeing the paging of the book; to Circle Graphics for designing such a beautiful book; and to the excellent production staff for turning around the manuscript in record time. I would also like to recognize Jon Preimesberger, a former staff member at CQ Press, for his careful and thoughtful editing of the manuscript.

For assistance in obtaining documents, I am grateful to two people. Ron Sharp, a reference librarian at the Indiana State Library, helped track down some of the earliest documents in the book. Steven Aftergood at the Federation of American Scientists (FAS) works tirelessly to place government documents online—especially Congressional Research Service reports—that the government has decided for one reason or another should not be readily available to the public. Several reports in this book were obtained from the FAS Web site, as indicated in the source notes for individual documents.

Two other people deserve thanks for speedily and graciously granting permission to reprint copyrighted materials: Kim Spears at the American Enterprise Institute for Public Policy Research and Lisa Shields at the Council on Foreign Relations.

I am also extremely grateful to the staff of the Carmel Clay Public Library in Carmel, Indiana, for providing a most congenial place in which to write.

Finally and most importantly, my greatest thanks are reserved for my wife, Barbara. Without her love, support, and patience this book would not exist.

# Introduction

"Homeland defense" and "homeland security" can be easily confused or lumped together, but they are distinctly different concepts. Homeland defense involves protecting the United States against attack by the military forces of a foreign country, such as occurred during the War of 1812 and the Japanese attack on Pearl Harbor in 1941. The U.S. military has primary responsibility for homeland defense, although intelligence agencies such as the Central Intelligence Agency (CIA) also play roles. Homeland defense is largely reactive, a posture whereby U.S. military forces engage in "watchful waiting" so they can immediately repel any hostile action launched by a foreign nation.

By contrast, homeland security involves protecting the United States from attacks by individuals or small groups that are not part of a foreign nation's armed forces. The individuals or groups may receive support from a foreign nation, but they operate independently. Some are homegrown, such as Oklahoma City bomber Timothy McVeigh. Others, such as the hijackers on September 11, 2001, infiltrate the United States from other countries to carry out their attacks.

Homeland security emphasizes being proactive, although it also has a reactive component. The proactive piece focuses on preventing attacks through a variety of methods: using watch lists to prevent known terrorists from entering the country, screening airline passengers to ensure they are not carrying dangerous items, inspecting cargo containers that arrive on ships to intercept weapons of mass destruction, and conducting surveillance of citizens or visitors who may pose a threat to homeland security, among many others.

The reactive component of homeland security takes precedence when a terrorist attack occurs. The primary jobs then are to minimize casualties and damage, recover from the attacks, and neutralize any terrorists that may have survived.

Responsibility for homeland security is shared by a wide assortment of federal, state, and local government agencies and the private sector. At the federal level, primary responsibility rests with the Federal Bureau of Investigation

(FBI) and the Department of Homeland Security (DHS), which Congress and President George W. Bush created in late 2002. In early 2003 the new department merged all or parts of twenty-two agencies with homeland security duties, involving about 180,000 federal employees and joining together the Coast Guard, the Immigration and Naturalization Service, the Transportation Security Administration, the Federal Emergency Management Agency, the Border Patrol, the Customs Service, the Secret Service, and other agencies.

The Department of Health and Human Services (HHS) is responsible for preparing the U.S. health care system to handle mass casualties from a terrorist attack or other major disaster. Two of its agencies, the National Institutes of Health (NIH) and the Centers for Disease Control and Prevention (CDC), also have important homeland security duties. NIH is charged with developing vaccines and other drugs to protect Americans from biological or chemical weapons. If an attack with these weapons occurs—as it did when anthrax was mailed to major media and political figures shortly after the 2001 hijackings—the CDC is responsible for identifying the biological or chemical agent used and helping track its source. Outside the United States, the CIA and State Department offices that issue visas to aliens work to keep terrorists out of the country.

The Defense Department plays an increasingly important role in homeland security. One of the purposes of the wars in Afghanistan and Iraq has been to root out and neutralize terrorists who might pose a threat to the United States. At home, after the 2001 hijackings, the Defense Department provided combat air patrols over major cities, troops to temporarily beef up security around Washington, D.C., and members of the National Guard to patrol airports. The Defense Department also operates antiaircraft missile batteries around the nation's capital when the terrorist threat is perceived to be high, supports other agencies that have the lead in providing security at events such as the Olympics, and stands ready with units that are specially trained to handle and contain weapons of mass destruction.

Many states now have homeland security departments, which typically have the lead role in coordinating state efforts. Other agencies, such as the state police and the state health department, frequently contribute to state homeland security efforts as well.

At the local level, police departments play an important day-to-day role in monitoring activities in their communities and watching for anything unusual. If an attack occurs, first responders—police officers, firefighters, emergency medical technicians, public works personnel, and emergency management officials—are on the front lines. In some cases, local public health departments can help identify chemical or biological weapons that terrorists release. If an attack causes large numbers of casualties, hospitals and medical personnel have critical responsibilities for saving lives.

The private sector plays three major roles in homeland security. Most importantly, it controls 85 percent of the nation's critical infrastructure and must ensure that these systems are secure. The USA Patriot Act defines critical infrastructure as those "systems and assets, whether physical or virtual, so vital to the United States that the incapacity or destruction of such systems and assets would have a debilitating impact on security, national economic security, national public health or safety, or any combination of those matters." Some examples of critical infrastructures include information and telecommunications systems, banking and financial services, the agricultural system, and energy services.

On a smaller scale, the private sector also is responsible for securing its facilities—everything from office buildings to chemical plants. Finally, some parts of the private sector are developing products or services aimed at improving homeland security.

This list is nowhere near a complete record of all the government agencies and private-sector entities that are crucial to protecting homeland security. However, it should give some idea of the breadth of the homeland security issue.

It is important to note the changing balance between homeland defense and homeland security in recent decades. During the cold war, homeland defense was far more important primarily because one nation—the Soviet Union—presented the greatest potential danger to the United States. The Soviet Union had enough nuclear missiles aimed at the United States to destroy it many times over. Homeland defense efforts focused on ensuring those missiles were never launched and creating technologies that would immediately detect any launch so the United States could retaliate. The breakup of the Soviet Union has left the United States as the world's sole military superpower. Any nation that tried to attack the American homeland would only assure its own destruction by overwhelming military power.

Today, terrorists pose the greatest threat to the United States, thus tipping the scale toward homeland security. Homeland defense efforts continue because some nations are steadily increasing their military capabilities, but the greatest focus is on homeland security.

## The National Strategy for Homeland Security

On July 16, 2002, the White House released the *National Strategy for Homeland Security*. It was the first such document in the nation's history, although for years earlier expert commissions and government watchdogs such as the General Accounting Office (GAO), the investigative arm of Congress, had repeatedly cited the critical need for a homeland security strategy.

The ninety-page report officially defined homeland security as "a concerted national effort to prevent terrorist attacks within the United States, reduce America's vulnerability to terrorism, and minimize the damage and recover from attacks that do occur." The report divided homeland security functions into six areas:

- Intelligence and warning;
- Border and transportation security;
- Domestic counterterrorism;
- Protecting critical infrastructure;
- Defending against catastrophic terrorism; and
- Emergency preparedness and response.

"The first three mission areas focus primarily on preventing terrorist attacks; the next two on reducing our Nation's vulnerabilities; and the final one on minimizing the damage and recovering from attacks that do occur," the report said.

For each area, the report identified a number of major initiatives. Some of the highlights include:

- Enhance the analytic capabilities of the FBI;
- Employ "red team" techniques to test defenses;
- Ensure accountability in border and transportation security;
- Increase the security of international shipping containers;
- Reform immigration services;
- Improve intergovernmental law enforcement coordination;
- Complete FBI restructuring to emphasize prevention of terrorist attacks;
- Build and maintain a complete and accurate assessment of America's critical infrastructure and key assets;
- Develop a national infrastructure protection plan;
- Secure cyberspace;
- Prevent terrorist use of nuclear weapons through better sensors and procedures;
- Improve chemical sensors and decontamination techniques;
- Develop broad spectrum vaccines, antimicrobials, and antidotes;
- Integrate separate federal response plans into a single all-discipline incident management plan;
- Improve tactical counterterrorist capabilities;
- Enable seamless communication among all responders;
- Prepare health care providers for catastrophic terrorism; and
- Plan for military support to civil authorities.

Once again, the list indicates the huge range of issues that fall under the homeland security umbrella.

## Early Homeland Security Incidents

The first recorded homeland security incident in what later became the United States occurred in 1607, only months after the first permanent English settlers arrived in the New World and created a colony at Jamestown. James Kendall, one of the settlement's appointed leaders, was arrested. History books disagree about the exact charge against Kendall—it may have been mutiny, spying for Spain, or "sowing discord" among the settlers. He was tried, convicted, and shot to death. Kendall was executed because the jury believed that he threatened the security of the precarious "homeland" established at Jamestown.

Conflicts quickly erupted between the English settlers and the Native American tribes who had inhabited the land for centuries. Many of these "First Americans," as the Smithsonian Institution calls them, viewed the settlers as invaders of their homeland and a dangerous threat to their security, especially as the settlers kept pressing westward. To the settlers from England, and later from other European nations, the Native Americans threatened the security of the new homeland they were trying to establish. Each side repeatedly attacked the other, marking the first chapter in a bloodthirsty war that gradually spread across the United States and lasted for more than 250 years. The conflict nearly wiped out the tribes, who lost almost all of the territories they considered their ancestral homelands.

Meanwhile, in the early 1770s citizens in the colonies that later became the United States were growing increasingly unhappy about British authority and taxes. When the British-appointed governor of Massachusetts learned that the colonists had stored a cache of arms at Concord, on April 18, 1775, he dispatched British troops to destroy it. In the early morning hours the next day, the troops were confronted at Lexington by a small, disorganized group of militiamen, and some shots were fired. When the troops marched a few more miles to Concord, a much larger group of militiamen met them. Firing erupted, but the British troops quickly determined they were outnumbered and retreated. Thus started the Revolutionary War, in which the colonists fought to protect their homeland from what they saw as oppressive British rule.

Some colonists, however, were perfectly content under British rule. The Loyalists, who numbered in the tens or perhaps hundreds of thousands among a total population of 2.5 million, opposed the war. Many suffered rough treatment at the hands of the revolutionaries, saw their property confiscated or destroyed, and were banished. Seeing that their personal safety and the security of their homeland were seriously threatened, between 60,000 and 80,000 Loyalists fled during and after the Revolutionary War, according to *The Reader's Companion to American History.* Most went to Canada.

## Historical Parallels

Some of the parallels between historical and current events are striking. For example, the Alien and Sedition Acts that Congress passed in 1798 greatly expanded the executive branch's power and made it a crime to "write, print, utter or publish . . . any false, scandalous and malicious writing" about the government. In response, the Kentucky and Virginia legislatures passed resolutions saying the laws should be repealed because they concentrated too much power in the executive branch and violated civil liberties protections. Since Congress passed the USA Patriot Act in October 2001, several state legislatures and hundreds of local governmental bodies have adopted resolutions challenging the USA Patriot Act on virtually the same grounds as those cited in 1798.

Some intriguing linkages between historical and current events also emerge from the documents. In 1976, for example, a Senate committee headed by Sen. Frank Church, D-Idaho, completed a fifteen-month investigation that revealed U.S. intelligence agencies had routinely and wantonly violated the civil liberties of Americans during domestic intelligence investigations. The FBI was one of the main culprits. The attorney general responded to the resulting public outcry by issuing guidelines that limited the FBI's ability to monitor Americans. On May 30, 2002, Attorney General John Ashcroft—reacting to the terrorist attacks eight months earlier—announced new investigative guidelines for the FBI that largely overturned the restrictions on domestic surveillance imposed in the 1970s. Ashcroft said the old rules hampered the FBI's ability to prevent terrorism.

These historical parallels and linkages are particularly relevant today as the nation engages in a "war on terrorism" that seems unlikely to end. During an interview with the British Broadcasting Corporation slightly more than a week after the terrorist attacks on September 11, 2001, Secretary of State Colin Powell was asked how long the war on terrorism would last. "I can't predict that," Powell said. "I think it will certainly be years and I think it's a campaign that will probably continue as long as I can imagine."

Given this environment, what is the best way to judge a governmental request for more power, such as authority to increase the surveillance of Americans? The National Commission on Terrorist Attacks Upon the United States—usually referred to as the 9/11 Commission—tackled this question in its final report:

> In wartime, government calls for greater powers, and then the need for those powers recedes after the war ends. This struggle [against terrorism] will go on. Therefore, while protecting our homeland, Americans should be mindful of threats to vital personal and civil liberties. This balancing is no easy task, but we must constantly strive to keep it right.

The commission also said a power could be revoked:

> The burden of proof for retaining a particular governmental power should be on the executive, to explain (a) that the power actually materially enhances security and (b) that there is adequate supervision of the executive's use of the powers to ensure protection of civil liberties. If the power is granted, there must be adequate guidelines and oversight to properly confine its use.

# Laws Provide Broad Powers to Deport Aliens and Penalize Speech

1. The Alien Act, June 25, 1798

2. The Alien Enemies Act, July 6, 1798

3. The Sedition Act, July 14, 1798

4. Kentucky Resolutions of 1798, November 13, 1798

5. Virginia Resolutions of 1798, December 21, 1798

6. Address to the People of Virginia, January 23, 1799

## INTRODUCTION

Using the pretext of a possibly imminent war with France, President John Adams and his Federalist colleagues who controlled both houses of Congress passed a series of laws in June and July 1798 that collectively became known as the Alien and Sedition Acts. The real purpose of the laws was to silence critics of the Federalists and the Adams administration—especially the highly partisan newspapers of the period.

One bill, the Alien Act, empowered the president to deport all aliens whom he judged were "dangerous to the peace and safety of the United States." Although aliens could appeal, the president's ultimate decision was final. A number of recent immigrants published newspapers or pamphlets. The law effectively let Adams deport anyone who published anything he did not like [Document 1].

The second measure, the Alien Enemies Act, said that at any time of actual or threatened war, alien males above age fourteen from the hostile nation who were not naturalized were "liable to be apprehended, restrained, secured and removed, as alien enemies. . . ." Again, all decisions were left to the president's sole discretion [Document 2].

The third bill, the Sedition Act, was the most onerous. One section of the bill made it a crime to "write, print, utter or publish . . . any false, scandalous and malicious writing or writings against the government of the United States, or either house of the Congress . . . or the President . . . with intent to defame the said government, or either house of the said Congress, or the said President, or to bring them . . . into contempt or disrepute; or to excite against them . . . the hatred of the good people of the United States, or to stir up sedition within the United States. . . ." Violators faced a maximum penalty of two years in prison and a $2,000 fine [Document 3].

The Sedition Act was aimed at silencing newspaper publishers such as Benjamin Franklin Bache, the grandson of Benjamin Franklin, whose *Aurora* was the leading Republican newspaper of the day and a constant thorn in the side of Adams and other Federalists. The day after the House of Representatives passed the Sedition Act, Bache wrote in his newspaper: "[T]he good citizens of these States had better hold their tongues and make tooth picks of their pens." Bache's advice came too late to save himself. He was arrested only days before Adams signed the Sedition Act and charged under the common law with libeling the president and the government. Bache died in a yellow fever epidemic in September 1798 before he could be tried.

Bache was far from the only critic of the Alien and Sedition Acts. One of the most prominent opponents was Vice President Thomas Jefferson, a Republican. Under the election law of the time, the presidential candidate who received the second highest number of votes became vice president, allowing situations where the president and vice president could be from opposing political parties. Such was the case with Adams and Jefferson.

Opponents could not challenge the acts in court, because the Supreme Court did not yet have authority to rule on the constitutionality of laws passed by Congress. Instead, opponents of the acts tried to convince legislatures in each state to demand that Congress rescind the laws.

Their vehicles were measures passed by the state legislatures in Kentucky and Virginia. Jefferson wrote the Kentucky resolutions, and James Madison wrote the Virginia resolutions. Resolutions in both states primarily argued that the new laws usurped rights reserved to the states. But Jefferson and Madison also criticized the laws for giving the president unchecked powers and for violating the right to free speech guaranteed by the First Amendment [Kentucky resolutions, Document 4; Virginia resolutions, Document 5].

The Virginia legislature took the additional step of writing an open letter to the state's citizens, warning that the Federalists were using the cover of a possible war with France to unconstitutionally seize more power [Document 6]:

> Exhortations to disregard domestic usurpation, until foreign danger shall have passed, is an artifice which may be forever used; because the possessors of power, who are the advocates for its extension, can ever create national embarrassments, to be successively employed to soothe the people into sleep, whilst that power is swelling, silent, secretly, and fatally. Of the same character are insinuations of a foreign influence, which seize upon a laudable enthusiasm against danger from abroad, and distort it by an unnatural application, so as to blind your eyes against danger at home. . . .

The argument is similar to one made today by opponents of the Patriot Act and other laws passed in the wake of the terrorist attacks on September 11, 2001. Critics contend that the administration of George W. Bush used the pretense of the war on terrorism to take actions and pass laws that unconstitutionally enhance the power of the executive office and restrict civil liberties. The Kentucky and Virginia resolutions themselves have been compared to resolutions passed since late 2001 by more than 330 state legislatures and local governments opposing the Patriot Act.

The Kentucky and Virginia legislatures sent their resolutions to legislatures in other states, looking for support. None was forthcoming. A resolution approved by the Delaware legislature was a typical response:

> *Resolved,* By the Senate and House of Representatives of the state of Delaware, in General Assembly met, that they consider the resolutions from the state of Virginia as a very unjustifiable interference with the general government and constituted authorities of the United States, and of dangerous tendency, and therefore not fit subject for the further consideration of the General Assembly.

Ironically, Adams never deported any aliens under the authority granted to him by the two alien acts. However, the acts provided precedents for similar measures in later years. For example, current federal law contains a provision that uses some of the exact language from the 1798 alien enemies law to authorize the president to deport alien enemies in the event of a threatened or actual war.

Unlike its enforcement of the alien acts, the Adams administration strictly enforced the Sedition Act against some of its fiercest opponents. Editors at eight major anti-Federalist newspapers were indicted, and four of the newspapers folded because of the prosecutions. A few leading anti-Federalist politicians also were indicted. Although the total number of indictments and convictions was small, they had a chilling effect on domestic dissent and, together with the alien acts, aroused great public anger toward the Adams administration. "No Federalist legislation passed since the adoption of the Constitution more inflamed political passions than the Alien and Sedition Acts," historian Saul Cornell wrote in *The Other Founders,* "and the Sedition Act precipitated the most serious constitutional crisis in the period after ratification."

Historians generally agree that anger over the Alien and Sedition Acts was a major factor in Jefferson being elected president in 1800. The Sedition Act expired the day before he took office, and he quickly pardoned everyone convicted under the law.

In the classic First Amendment case of *New York Times Co. v. Sullivan,* U.S. Supreme Court Justice William Brennan wrote in 1964 that the 1798 Sedition Act "first crystallized a national awareness of the central meaning of the First Amendment." Although the Court never ruled on the constitutionality of the 1798 law, Brennan wrote, "the attack upon its validity has carried the day in the court of history." Nevertheless, in the intervening years Congress repeatedly passed new variations of the Alien and Sedition Acts (*see* World War I Laws Limit Speech and Movement, p. 17; Japanese Internment During World War II, p. 27; and Bill Authorizes Detention Camps and Requires Communist Registration, p. 52).

# 1. The Alien Act

*June 25, 1798*

SECTION 1. *Be it enacted by the Senate and House of Representatives of the United States of America in Congress assembled,* That it shall be lawful for the President of the United States at any time during the continuance of this act, to *order* all such *aliens* as he shall judge dangerous to the peace and safety of the United States, or shall have reasonable grounds to suspect are concerned in any treasonable or secret machinations against the government thereof, to depart out of the territory of the United States, within such time as shall be expressed in such order. . . . And in case any alien, so ordered to depart, shall be found at large within the United States after the time limited in such order for his departure, and not having obtained a *license* from the President to reside therein, or having obtained such *license* shall not have conformed thereto, every such alien shall, on conviction thereof, be imprisoned for a term not exceeding three years, and shall never after be admitted to become a citizen of the United States. *Provided always, and be it further enacted,* that if any alien so ordered to depart shall prove to the satisfaction of the President, by evidence to be taken before such person or persons as the President shall direct, who are for that purpose hereby authorized to administer oaths, that no injury or danger to the United States will arise from suffering such alien to reside therein, the President may grant a *license* to such alien to remain within the United States for such time as he shall judge proper, and at such place as he may designate. And the President may also require of such alien to enter into a bond to the United States, in such penal sum as he may direct, with one or more sufficient sureties to the satisfaction of the person authorized by the President to take the same, conditioned for the good behavior of such alien during his residence in the United States, and not violating his license, which license the President may revoke, whenever he shall think proper.

SEC. 2. *And be it further enacted,* That . . . if any alien . . . removed or sent out of the United States by the President shall voluntarily return thereto, unless by permission of the President of the United States, such alien on conviction thereof, shall be imprisoned so long as, in the opinion of the President, the public safety may require.

Excerpted from U.S. Congress. *An Act Concerning Aliens.* 5th Cong., 2nd sess., June 25, 1798. *United States Statutes at Large* 1:570–572. http://memory.loc.gov/ammem/amlaw/lwsl.html (accessed September 1, 2004).

## 2. The Alien Enemies Act

*July 6, 1798*

SECTION 1. *Be it enacted by the Senate and House of Representatives of the United States of America in Congress assembled,* That whenever there shall be a declared war between the United States and any foreign nation or government, or any invasion or predatory incursion shall be perpetrated, attempted, or threatened against the territory of the United States, by any foreign nation or government, and the President of the United States shall make public proclamation of the event, all natives, citizens, denizens, or subjects of the hostile nation or government, being males of the age of fourteen years and upwards, who shall be within the United States, and not actually naturalized, shall be liable to be apprehended, restrained, secured and removed, as alien enemies. . . .

> Excerpted from U.S. Congress. *An Act Respecting Alien Enemies.*
> 5th Cong., 2nd sess., July 6, 1798. *United States Statutes at Large*
> 1:577–578. http://memory.loc.gov/ammem/amlaw/lwsl.html (accessed
> September 1, 2004).

## 3. The Sedition Act

*July 14, 1798*

SECTION 1. *Be it enacted by the Senate and House of Representatives of the United States of America, in Congress assembled,* That if any persons shall unlawfully combine or conspire together, with intent to oppose any measure or measures of the government of the United States, which are or shall be directed by proper authority, or to impede the operation of any law of the United States, or to intimidate or prevent any person holding a place or office in or under the government of the United States, from undertaking, performing or executing his trust or duty; and if any person or persons, with intent as aforesaid, shall counsel, advise, or attempt to procure any insurrection, riot, unlawful assembly, or combination, which such conspiracy, threatening, counsel, advice, or attempt shall have the proposed effect or not, he or they shall be deemed guilty of a high misdemeanor, and on conviction, before any court of the United States having jurisdiction thereof, shall be punished by a fine not exceeding five thousand dollars, and by imprisonment during a term not less than six months nor exceeding five years; and further, at the discretion of the court may be holden to find sureties for his good behavior in such sum, and for such time, as the said court may direct.

SEC. 2. *And be it further enacted,* That if any person shall write, print, utter or publish, or shall cause or procure to be written, printed, uttered or published, or shall knowingly and willingly assist or aid in writing, printing, uttering or publishing any false, scandalous and malicious writing or writings against the government of the United States, or either house of the Congress of the United States, or the President of the United States, with intent to defame the said government, or either house of the said Congress, or the said President, or to bring them, or either of them, into contempt or disrepute; or to excite against them, or either or any of them, the hatred of the good people of the United States, or to stir up sedition within the United States . . . then such person, being thereof convicted before any court of the United States having jurisdiction thereof, shall be punished by a fine not exceeding two thousand dollars, and by imprisonment not exceeding two years.

SEC. 3. *And be it further enacted and declared,* That if any person shall be prosecuted under this act, for the writing or publishing any libel aforesaid, it shall be lawful for the defendant, upon the trial of the cause, to give in evidence in his defence, the truth of the matter contained in the publication charged as a libel. And the jury who shall try the cause, shall have a right to determine the law and the fact, under the direction of the court, as in other cases. . . .

Excerpted from U.S. Congress. *An Act in Addition to the Act, Entitled "An Act for the Punishment of Certain Crimes Against the United States."* 5th Cong., 2nd sess., July 14, 1798. *United States Statutes at Large* 1:596–597. http://memory.loc.gov/ammem/amlaw/lwsl.html (accessed September 1, 2004).

# 4. Kentucky Resolutions of 1798
*November 13, 1798*

1. *Resolved,* That the several states composing the United States of America are not united on the principle of unlimited submission to their general government; but that, by compact, under the style and title of a Constitution for the United States, and of amendments thereto, they constituted a general government for special purposes, delegated to that government certain definite powers, reserving, each state to itself, the residuary mass of right to their own self-government; and that whensoever the general gov-

ernment assumes undelegated powers, its acts are unauthoritative, void, and of no force. . . .

3. *Resolved,* That it is true, as a general principle, and is also expressly declared by one of the amendments to the Constitution, that "the powers not delegated to the United States by the Constitution, nor prohibited by it to the states, are reserved to the states respectively, or to the people;" and that, no power over the freedom of religion, freedom of speech, or freedom of the press, being delegated to the United States by the Constitution, nor prohibited by it to the states, all lawful powers respecting the same did of right remain, and were reserved to the states, or to the people; that thus was manifested their determination to retain to themselves the right of judging how far the licentiousness of speech, and of the press, may be abridged without lessening their useful freedom, and how far those abuses which cannot be separated from their use, should be tolerated rather than the use be destroyed . . . another and more special provision has been made by one of the amendments to the Constitution, which expressly declares, that "Congress shall make no laws respecting an establishment of religion, or prohibiting the free exercise thereof, or abridging the freedom of speech, or of the press," thereby guarding, in the same sentence, and under the same words, the freedom of religion, of speech, and of the press, insomuch that whatever violates either throws down the sanctuary which covers the others,—and that libels, falsehood, and defamation, equally with heresy and false religion, are withheld from the cognizance of federal tribunals. That therefore the act of the Congress of the United States, passed on the 14th of July, 1798, entitled "An Act in Addition to the Act entitled 'An Act for the Punishment of Certain Crimes Against the United States,' " which does abridge the freedom of the press, is not law, but is altogether void, and of no force. . . .

6. *Resolved,* That the imprisonment of a person under the protection of the laws of this commonwealth, on his failure to obey the simple order of the President to depart out of the United States, as is undertaken by the said act, entitled, "An Act Concerning Aliens," is contrary to the Constitution, one amendment in which has provided, that "no person shall be deprived of liberty without due process of law;" and that another having provided, "that, in all criminal prosecutions, the accused shall enjoy the right of a public trial by an impartial jury, to be informed as to the nature and cause of the accusation, to be confronted with the witnesses against him, to have compulsory process for obtaining witnesses in his favor, and to have assistance of counsel for his defence," the same act undertaking to authorize the President to remove a person out of the United States who is under the protection of the law, on his own suspicion, without jury, without public trial, without confrontation of the witnesses against him, without having witnesses in his favor, without defence, without counsel— contrary to these provisions also of the Constitution—is therefore not law, but utterly void, and of no force.

That transferring the power of judging any person who is under the protection of the laws, from the courts to the President of the United States, as is undertaken by the same act concerning aliens, is against the article of the Constitution which provides, that "the judicial power of the United States shall be vested in the courts, the judges of which shall hold their office during good behavior," and that the said act is void for that reason also; and it is further to be noted that this transfer of judiciary power is to that magistrate of the general government who already possesses all the executive, and a qualified negative in all the legislative powers. . . .

8. *Resolved,* That the preceding resolutions be transmitted to the senators and representatives in Congress from this commonwealth, who are enjoined to present the same to their respective houses, and to use their best endeavors to procure, at the next session of Congress, a repeal of the aforesaid unconstitutional and obnoxious acts.

9. *Resolved,* . . . [T]hat, if the acts before specified should stand, these conclusions would flow from them—that the general government . . . may transfer its cognizance to the President, or any other person, who may himself be the accuser, counsel, judge, and jury, whose suspicions may be the evidence, his order the sentence, his officer the executioner, and his breast the sole record of the transaction; that a very numerous and valuable description of the inhabitants of these states [aliens], being, by this precedent, reduced, as outlaws, to absolute dominion of one man, and the barriers of the Constitution thus swept from us all, no rampart now remains against the passions and the power of a majority of Congress, to protect from a like exportation, or other grievous punishment, the minority of the same body, the legislatures, judges, governors, and counselors of the states, nor their other peaceable inhabitants, who may venture to reclaim the constitutional rights and liberties of the states and people, or who, for other causes, good or bad, may be obnoxious to the view, or marked by the suspicions, of the President, or be thought dangerous to his or their elections, or other interests, public or personal; that the friendless alien has been selected as the safest subject of a first experiment; but the citizen will soon follow, or rather has already followed; for already has a Sedition Act marked him as a prey. . . .

Excerpted from Elliot, Jonathan, ed., *The Debates in the Several State Conventions on the Adoption of the Federal Constitution.* . . . Vol. 4 (Philadelphia: J. B. Lippincott & Co./Washington, D.C.: Taylor & Maury, 1836–1859), 540–544. http://memory.loc.gov/ammem/amlaw/lwed.html (accessed September 1, 2004).

# 5. Virginia Resolutions of 1798

*December 21, 1798*

*Resolved,* That the General Assembly of Virginia doth unequivocally express a firm resolution to maintain and defend the Constitution of the United States, and the Constitution of this state, against every aggression, either foreign or domestic; and that they will support the government of the United States in all measures warranted by the former. . . .

That this Assembly doth explicitly and peremptorily declare, that it views the powers of the federal government as resulting from the compact to which the states are parties, as limited by the plain sense and intention of the instrument constituting that compact. . . .

*That the General Assembly doth particularly PROTEST against the palpable and alarming infractions of the Constitution, in the two late cases of the "Alien and Sedition Acts," passed at the last session of Congress; the first of which exercises a power nowhere delegated to the federal government, and which, by uniting legislative and judicial powers to those of executive, subverts the general principles of free government, as well as the particular organization and positive provisions of the Federal Constitution; and the other of which acts exercises, in like manner, a power not delegated by the Constitution, but, on the contrary, expressly and positively forbidden by one of the amendments thereto,—a power which, more than any other, ought to produce universal alarm, because it is leveled against the right of freely examining public characters and measures, and of free communication among the people thereon, which has ever been justly deemed the only effectual guardian of every other right.*

That this state having, by its Convention, which ratified the Federal Constitution, expressly declared that, among other essential rights, "the liberty of conscience and the press cannot be cancelled, abridged, restrained, or modified, by any authority of the United States," and from its extreme anxiety to guard these rights from every possible attack of sophistry and ambition, having, with other states, recommended an amendment for that purpose, which amendment was, in due time, annexed to the Constitution,—it would mark a reproachful inconsistency, and criminal degeneracy, if an indifference were now shown to the most palpable violation of one of the rights thus declared and secured, and to the establishment of a precedent which may be fatal to the other. . . .

That the governor be desired to transmit a copy of the foregoing resolutions to the executive authority of each of the other states, with a request that the same may be communicated to the legislature thereof, and that a copy be furnished to each of the senators and representatives representing this state in the Congress of the United States.

Excerpted from Elliot, Jonathan, ed., *The Debates in the Several State Conventions on the Adoption of the Federal Constitution. . . .* Vol. 4 (Philadelphia: J. B. Lippincott & Co./Washington, D.C.: Taylor & Maury, 1836–1859), 528–529. http://memory.loc.gov/ammem/amlaw/lwed.html (accessed September 1, 2004).

# 6. Address to the People of Virginia
## *January 23, 1799*

Fellow-citizens: Unwilling to shrink from our representative responsibilities, conscious of the purity of our motives, but acknowledging your right to supervise our conduct, we invite your serious attention to the emergency which dictated the subjoined resolutions. . . .

It would be perfidious in those intrusted with the GUARDIANSHIP OF THE STATE SOVEREIGNTY, and acting under the solemn obligation of the following oath,—"I do swear that I will support the Constitution of the United States,"—not to warn you of encroachments, which, though clothed with the pretext of necessity, or disguised by arguments of expediency, may yet establish precedents which may ultimately devote a generous and unsuspicious people to all the consequences of usurped power. . . .

Exhortations to disregard domestic usurpation, until foreign danger shall have passed, is an artifice which may be forever used; because the possessors of power, who are the advocates for its extension, can ever create national embarrassments, to be successively employed to soothe the people into sleep, whilst that power is swelling, silent, secretly, and fatally. Of the same character are insinuations of a foreign influence, which seize upon a laudable enthusiasm against danger from abroad, and distort it by an unnatural application, so as to blind your eyes against danger at home. . . .

Excerpted from Elliot, Jonathan, ed., *The Debates in the Several State Conventions on the Adoption of the Federal Constitution. . . .* Vol. 4 (Philadelphia: J. B. Lippincott & Co./Washington, D.C.: Taylor & Maury, 1836–1859), 529–532. http://memory.loc.gov/ammem/amlaw/lwed.html (accessed September 1, 2004).

# President Abraham Lincoln Suspends the Writ of Habeas Corpus

## INTRODUCTION

On April 12, 1861, the Civil War began when Confederate forces started shelling Fort Sumter, a Union military post perched on an island in the harbor at Charleston, South Carolina. The fort surrendered the next day. On April 19, four Union soldiers and nine civilians were killed during a riot in Baltimore, a hotbed of Confederate sympathizers, as Union troops marched through the city on their way to Washington, D.C. With Virginia already seceded and Maryland seemingly poised to follow suit, President Abraham Lincoln faced the possibility that Washington might be cut off from the rest of the United States.

In an effort to keep transportation open between Washington and loyal states, on April 27, 1861, Lincoln signed an executive order granting military officials authority to suspend the writ of habeas corpus anywhere near a railroad line between Washington and Philadelphia. Suspending the writ of habeas corpus allowed soldiers to arrest any civilians in the area who offered "resistance" and imprison them indefinitely without charges or trial [Document 7].

Lincoln's action was momentous. The writ of habeas corpus was known as "the great writ" because it protected citizens from illegal imprisonment. A prisoner could appeal to a judge for a writ, a legal order that required his jailer to appear in court with the prisoner and explain why he was being held. If the judge decided the prisoner was jailed illegally, he was freed.

In 1833 Joseph Story, a prominent Harvard law professor, wrote in *Commentaries on the Constitution of the United States* that the writ of habeas corpus was "justly esteemed the great bulwark of personal liberty." He then approvingly quoted Sir William Blackstone, widely regarded as one of the leading British legal scholars in history:

Mr. Justice Blackstone has remarked with great force, that "to bereave a man of life, or by violence to confiscate his estate without accusation or trial, would be so gross and notorious an act of despotism, as must at once convey the alarm of tyranny throughout the whole kingdom. But confinement of the person by secretly hurrying him to jail, where his sufferings are unknown or forgotten, is a less public, a less striking, and therefore a more dangerous engine of arbitrary force."

The U.S. Constitution mentions the writ of habeas corpus only once, in Article 1, Section 9, Clause 2: "The Privilege of the Writ of Habeas Corpus shall not be suspended, unless when in Cases of Rebellion or Invasion the public Safety may require it." But the document is silent about who can suspend the writ.

In 1861 Democratic opponents of the Republican Lincoln (supported then and since by many legal scholars) protested loudly that Lincoln's suspension of the writ of habeas corpus was illegal because the Constitution's authors meant for Congress—not the president—to have sole authority in the matter. In a speech to a special session of Congress on July 4, 1861, Lincoln basically justified his action on the grounds of expediency. Noting his oath to "take care that the laws be faithfully executed," Lincoln asked: "Are all the laws *but one* to go unexecuted, and the government itself go to pieces, lest that one be violated?" [Document 8].

Jefferson Davis, president of the Confederate States of America, ridiculed Lincoln in his second inaugural address on February 22, 1862:

Bastiles filled with prisoners, arrested without civil process or indictment duly found; the writ of *habeas corpus* suspended by Executive mandate; a State Legislature controlled by the imprisonment of members whose avowed principles suggested to the Federal Executive that there might be another added to the list of seceded States; elections held under threats of a military power; civil officers, peaceful citizens, and gentlewomen incarcerated for opinion's sake—proclaimed the incapacity of our late associates to administer a Government as free, liberal, and humane as that established for our common use.

Lincoln continued issuing orders expanding the areas where the writ of habeas corpus was suspended. On September 24, 1862, Lincoln finally suspended the writ across the entire nation. His new order also permitted trials of civilians by military commissions [Document 9].

On March 3, 1863, Congress passed the Habeas Corpus Act, which explicitly authorized Lincoln to suspend the writ when necessary to protect public safety. This ended constitutional arguments over Lincoln's action.

Despite great efforts, historians have been unable to accurately determine how many civilians military authorities arrested and tried during the Civil War. Estimates range from about 13,000 to 38,000. Some were arrested for political reasons such as expressing joy at a Confederate victory or having a close friend who was arrested for being disloyal. But in his Pulitzer Prize–winning book *The Fate of Liberty,* historian Mark E. Neely Jr. said the vast majority of arrests were for common crimes that had no connection to civil liberties.

The Supreme Court never directly addressed Lincoln's suspension of the writ of habeas corpus, although in 1866—a year after the Civil War ended—it ruled that constitutional rights could not be suspended except in areas where war made it impossible for regular law enforcement authorities and courts to function. The Court's decision in *Ex parte Milligan* contains a classic quotation about civil liberties in times of war or other national crisis:

> The Constitution of the United States is a law for rulers and people, equally in war and in peace, and covers with the shield of its protection all classes of men, at all times, and under all circumstances. No doctrine, involving more pernicious consequences, was ever invented by the wit of man than that any of its provisions can be suspended during any of the great exigencies of government. Such a doctrine leads directly to anarchy or despotism, but the theory of necessity on which it is based is false; for the government, within the Constitution, has all the powers granted to it, which are necessary to preserve its existence; as has been happily proved by the result of the great effort to throw off its just authority.

Controversy over the writ of habeas corpus erupted again after the terrorist attacks of September 11, 2001, in several cases where the government indefinitely jailed people and denied them access to the courts:

- In the months after the attacks, law enforcement officials arrested more than 1,200 people—almost all of Middle Eastern or South Asian descent—on suspicions they were terrorists or knew about terrorist activities. The government refused to release the detainees' names and tried their cases in secret. No one arrested after September 11 was charged in connection with the attacks, but most were deported for immigration violations—sometimes after being held for months or even years.
- At the U.S. naval base at Guantánamo Bay, Cuba, the U.S. military held nearly 600 people it said were terrorists or fighters for the Taliban regime in Afghanistan. On June 28, 2004, the U.S. Supreme Court ruled that the prisoners could challenge their detentions, but the Court did not spell out what procedures were required. The government responded by convening military tribunals to examine the status of each prisoner, but the rules of evidence did not apply and the prisoners did not have attorneys. Lawyers for some of the prisoners filed suits contending the prisoners must receive hearings in federal courts under the Court's ruling.
- U.S. citizens whom the president designated as "enemy combatants" were held in military prisons. One such person was Yaser Hamdi, who was captured with Taliban forces in Afghanistan in 2001 and held in solitary confinement. On June 28, 2004, the U.S. Supreme Court ruled that Hamdi

must have access to a lawyer and the opportunity to challenge his detention "before a neutral decision maker." Hamdi's lawyers ultimately negotiated his release in October 2004, precluding his appearance before a court and leaving many questions unresolved. Hamdi was permitted to return to Saudi Arabia, but he agreed to renounce his U.S. citizenship and to restrictions limiting his travel. He also renounced terrorism and violent jihad and agreed that he would not aid or "affiliate with" the Taliban or any terrorist organization.

# 7. President Lincoln's Letter to General Winfield Scott

*April 27, 1861*

The COMMANDING GENERAL ARMY OF THE UNITED STATES:

You are engaged in repressing an insurrection against the laws of the United States. If at any point on or in the vicinity of any military line which is now or which shall be used between the city of Philadelphia and the city of Washington you find resistance which renders it necessary to suspend the writ of habeas corpus for the public safety, you personally or through the officer in command at the point where resistance occurs are authorized to suspend that writ.

Given under my hand and the seal of the United States, at the city of Washington, this 27th day of April, 1861, and of the Independence of the United States the eighty-fifth.

ABRAHAM LINCOLN

U.S. War Department, Record and Pension Office, War Records Office, et al. *The War of the Rebellion: A Compilation of the Official Records of the United and Confederate Armies.* Series 2, Vol. 2 (Washington, D.C.: Government Printing Office, 1897). http://cdl.library.cornell.edu/cgi-bin/moa/sgml/moa-idx?notisid=ANU4519-0115 (accessed September 1, 2004).

# 8. President Lincoln's Message to Congress
*July 4, 1861*

. . . Soon after the first call for militia, it was considered a duty to authorize the commanding general, in proper cases, according to his discretion, to
suspend the privilege of the writ of habeas corpus; or, in other words, to
arrest and detain, without resort to the ordinary processes and forms of law,
such individuals as he might deem dangerous to the public safety. This
authority has purposely been exercised but very sparingly. Nevertheless, the
legality and propriety of what has been done under it are questioned, and
the attention of the country has been called to the proposition that one who
is sworn to "take care that the laws be faithfully executed," should not himself violate them. Of course some consideration was given to the questions
of power, and propriety, before this matter was acted upon. The whole of
the laws which were required to be faithfully executed, were being resisted,
and failing of execution in nearly one-third of the States. Must they be
allowed to finally fail of execution, even had it been perfectly clear, that by
the use of the means necessary to their execution, some single law, made in
such extreme tenderness of the citizen's liberty, that practically, it relieves
more of the guilty, than of the innocent, should, to a very limited extent, be
violated? To state the question more directly, are all the laws *but one* to go
unexecuted, and the government itself go to pieces, lest that one be violated? Even in such a case, would not the official oath be broken, if the government should be overthrown, when it was believed that disregarding the
single law, would tend to preserve it? But it was not believed that this question was presented. It was not believed that any law was violated. The provision of the Constitution that "the privilege of the writ of habeas corpus
shall not be suspended unless when, in cases of rebellion or invasion, the
public safety may require it," is equivalent to a provision—is a provision—
that such privilege may be suspended when, in cases of rebellion or invasion, the public safety *does* require it. It was decided that we have a case of
rebellion, and that the public safety does require the qualified suspension of
the privilege of the writ which was authorized to be made. Now it is insisted
that Congress, and not the Executive, is vested with this power. But the
Constitution itself is silent as to which, or who, is to exercise the power; and
as the provision was plainly made for a dangerous emergency, it cannot be
believed the framers of the instrument intended, that in every case, the danger should run its course, until Congress could be called together; the very
assembling of which might be prevented, as was intended in this case, by
the rebellion. . . .

Excerpted from U.S. Executive Office of the President. *Abraham Lincoln Message to Congress, Second Printed Draft with Changes in Lincoln's Hand.* July 4, 1861. Transcribed and annotated by the Lincoln Studies Center, Knox College, Galesburg, Illinois. *Abraham Lincoln Papers at the Library of Congress.* http://memory.loc.gov/ammem/alhtml/alhome.html (accessed September 1, 2004).

## 9. President Lincoln's Proclamation Suspending Habeas Corpus Nationwide

*September 24, 1862*

WHEREAS, it has become necessary to call into service not only volunteers but also portions of the militia of the states by draft in order to suppress the insurrection existing in the United States, and disloyal persons are not adequately restrained by the ordinary processes of law from hindering this measure and from giving aid and comfort in various ways to the insurrection:

Now, therefore, be it ordered, First.—That during the existing insurrection and as a necessary measure for suppressing the same, all rebels and insurgents, their aiders and abettors within the United States, and all persons discouraging volunteer enlistments, resisting militia drafts, or guilty of any disloyal practice, affording aid and comfort to rebels against the authority of the United States, shall be subject to martial law and liable to trial and punishment by courts-martial or military commissions;

Second.—That the writ of habeas corpus is suspended in respect to all persons arrested, or who are now, or hereafter during the rebellion shall be, imprisoned in any fort, camp, arsenal, military prison, or other place of confinement by any military authority or by the sentences of any court-martial or military commission.

In witness whereof, I have hereunto set my hand, and caused the seal of the United States to be affixed.

Done at the city of Washington, this twenty-fourth day of September, in the year of our Lord one thousand eight hundred and sixty-two, and of the Independence of the United States the eighty-seventh.

ABRAHAM LINCOLN

U.S. Executive Office of the President. *By the President of the United States of America: A Proclamation.* September 24, 1862. *United States Statutes at Large* 13:730. http://memory.loc.gov/ammem/amlaw/lwsl.html (accessed September 1, 2004).

# World War I Laws Limit Speech and Movement

## INTRODUCTION

During the years immediately preceding American entry into World War I in 1917, fears about homeland security were rampant. These fears were fueled by a large influx of immigrants, the rising militancy of labor unions, growth in political groups that championed foreign political ideas such as socialism or communism, widespread opposition to the United States getting involved in the growing European war, and strong opposition to the draft once the United States entered World War I, among other factors.

The federal government responded by launching the nation's first domestic intelligence programs. Agents initially targeted German agents who might engage in sabotage or espionage but soon turned their attention to critics of the war, labor leaders, radical and anarchist groups, and, ultimately, anyone who criticized the government at all.

In the mid-1970s a Senate committee compiled a massive history of federal intelligence efforts stretching back to World War I. The report by the Senate Select Committee to Study Governmental Operations with Respect to Intelligence Activities quoted John Lord O'Brien, special assistant to the attorney general during World War I, as recalling there was an "immense pressure brought to bear throughout the war upon the Department of Justice in all parts of the country for indiscriminate prosecution demanded in behalf of a policy of wholesale repression and restraint of public opinion."

The administration of President Woodrow Wilson "quickly embarked upon a program of repression that matched or exceeded wartime repression even in clearly totalitarian countries such as Germany and Russia," political science professor Robert Justin Goldstein wrote in *Political Repression in Modern America: From 1870 to 1976*. Wilson's first act was to issue a proclamation on April 6, 1917, the day the United States entered World War I, restricting the movements and activities of "alien enemies." Wilson's order required alien enemies to stay at least one-half mile away from any facilities related to the war effort, made it illegal for them to "write, print, or publish any attack or threats against the Government or Congress of the United States," and authorized Wilson to deport any alien enemy he decided posed a "danger" to "the public peace or safety of the United States" [Document 10].

Two months later, Congress passed the Espionage Act of 1917. Among other provisions, the law made it illegal to "cause or attempt to cause insubordination, disloyalty, mutiny, or refusal of duty" in the armed forces or "obstruct the recruiting or enlistment service of the United States." Offenders faced a maximum penalty of twenty years in prison and a $10,000 fine [Document 11].

Some people thought prison was too good for anyone who opposed the war. After naming the six senators who had voted against going to war, a federal judge in Texas said they should be shot to death. "If any man deserves death, it is a traitor," said Judge Waller T. Burns. "I wish that I could pay for the ammunition" [Document 12].

On November 16, 1917, Wilson issued a proclamation that placed additional restrictions on alien enemies. One provision ordered alien enemies to register with the federal government, and another barred them from entering the District of Columbia. Between them, Wilson's two declarations resulted in 2,300 alien enemies being interned during the war [Document 13].

Deciding that the Espionage Act it passed in 1917 was insufficient, Congress on May 16, 1918, approved amendments that became known as the Sedition Act of 1918. The most prominent provision made it illegal to "utter, print, write, or publish any disloyal, profane, scurrilous, or abusive language" about the United States when the nation was at war. Congress set the maximum penalty for violators at twenty years in prison and a $10,000 fine. The Sedition Act "outlawed virtually all criticism of the war or the government," Goldstein wrote [Document 14].

Germany formally surrendered on November 11, 1918, but by then civil liberties in the United States had suffered serious damage. "Altogether, over twenty-one hundred were indicted under the Espionage and Sedition laws, invariably for statements of opposition to the war rather than for any overt acts, and over one thousand persons were convicted," Goldstein wrote. "Over one hundred persons were sentenced to jail terms of ten years or more. Not a single person was ever convicted for actual spy activities."

The Supreme Court heard appeals in six cases involving the Espionage and Sedition Acts and upheld the convictions in every case. In one of the most prominent cases, the court on March 3, 1919, unanimously upheld the conviction of Charles Schenck for printing a pamphlet opposing the draft. Justice

Oliver Wendell Holmes wrote that although the pamphlet's language would be constitutional in times of peace, the words presented "a clear and present danger" in wartime that trumped the First Amendment. Holmes wrote: "When a nation is at war many things that might be said in time of peace are such a hindrance to its efforts that their utterance will not be endured so long as men fight. . . ." [Document 15].

A week later, the Court considered an appeal by the prominent socialist and labor leader Eugene Debs. He had been convicted of giving a speech in Canton, Ohio, that incited insubordination in the military and obstructed recruitment and enlistment services. Debs focused most of his remarks on socialism but apparently ran into trouble when he said: "You need to know that you are fit for something better than slavery and cannon fodder." The Supreme Court unanimously upheld Debs's conviction and ten-year prison sentence [Document 16].

The fear in the United States of foreign people and foreign ideas did not end with Germany's surrender. The Russian revolution in November 1917, coupled with increases in activities by radicals inside and outside the labor movement, helped create a "Red Scare" in 1919. Public fears soared during a wave of terrorist mail bombings in 1919, including an explosion at the home of Attorney General A. Mitchell Palmer (he was not injured).

Federal officials launched a series of raids that became known as the "Palmer raids." The largest action occurred on the night of January 2, 1920, when federal agents in thirty-three cities arrested 10,000 people who were suspected of being communists. Many of those arrested were not communists; the authorities frequently made arrests without search or arrest warrants; and the civil liberties of those arrested—such as the right to counsel—were routinely violated. But the public considered the raids an unqualified success by law enforcement.

"Perhaps the most important factor leading to the decline of the red scare after early 1920 was simply that it had accomplished its purpose—the intimidation of the labor movement and the decimation of the radical movement in the U.S.," Goldstein concluded.

---

# 10. President Woodrow Wilson's First Proclamation Regarding Alien Enemies

*April 6, 1917*

WHEREAS the Congress of the United States in the exercise of the constitutional authority vested in them have resolved, by joint resolution of the

Senate and House of Representatives bearing date this day "That the state of war between the United States and the Imperial German Government which has . . . been thrust upon the United States is hereby formally declared. . . ."

Pursuant to the authority vested in me, I hereby declare and establish the following regulations, which I find necessary in the premises and for the public safety:

(1) An alien enemy shall not have in his possession, at any time or place, any fire-arm, weapon or implement of war, or component part thereof, ammunition, maxim or other silencer, bomb or explosive or material used in the manufacture of explosives;

(2) An alien enemy shall not have in his possession at any time or place, or use or operate any aircraft or wireless apparatus, or any form of signalling device or any form of cipher code, or any paper, document or book written or printed in cipher or in which there may be invisible writing. . . .

(4) An alien enemy shall not approach or be found within one-half mile of any Federal or State fort, camp, arsenal, aircraft station, Government or naval vessel, navy yard, factory, or workshop for the manufacture of munitions of war or of any products for the use of the Army or Navy;

(5) An alien enemy shall not write, print, or publish any attack or threats against the Government or Congress of the United States, or either branch thereof, or against the measures or policy of the United States, or against the person or property of any person in the military, naval, or civil service of the United States, or of the States or Territories, or of the District of Columbia, or of the municipal governments therein. . . .

(8) An alien enemy whom the President shall have reasonable cause to believe to be aiding or about to aid the enemy, or to be at large to the danger of the public peace or safety of the United States, or to have violated or to be about to violate any of these regulations, shall remove to any location designated by the President by Executive Order, and shall not remove therefrom without a permit, or shall depart from the United States if so required by the President. . . .

Excerpted from U.S. Executive Office of the President. *By the President of the United States of America: A Proclamation.* April 6, 1917. *United States Statutes at Large* 40:1650. A partial transcript of this document is available at https://netfiles.uiuc.edu/rcunning/www/presproc.htm (accessed July 15, 2004).

# 11. The Espionage Act of 1917

*June 15, 1917*

SECTION 1. That (a) whoever, for the purpose of obtaining information respecting the national defense with intent or reason to believe that the information . . . is to be used to the injury of the United States, or to the advantage of any foreign nation, goes upon, enters, flies over, or otherwise obtains information concerning any vessel, aircraft, work of defense, navy yard, naval station, submarine base, coaling station, battery, torpedo station, dockyard, canal, railroad, arsenal, camp, factory, mine, telegraph, telephone, wireless, or signal station, building, office, or other place connected with the national defense . . . or any place in which any vessel, aircraft, arms, munitions, or other materials or instruments for use in time of war are being made, prepared, repaired, or stored . . . or (b) whoever for the purpose aforesaid, and with like intent or reason to believe, copies, takes, makes, or obtains, or attempts, or induces or aids another to copy, take, make or obtain, any sketch, photograph, photographic negative, blue print, plan, map, model, instrument, appliance, document, writing, or note of anything connected with the national defense . . . shall be punished by a fine of not more than $10,000, or by imprisonment for not more than two years, or both.

SEC. 2. (a) Whoever, with intent or reason to believe that it is to be used to the injury of the United States or to the advantage of a foreign nation, communicates, delivers, or transmits, or attempts to, or aids or induces another to, communicate, deliver, or transmit, to any foreign government, or to any faction or party or military or naval force within a foreign country, whether recognized or unrecognized by the United States, or to any representative, officer, agent, employee, subject, or citizen thereof, either directly or indirectly, any document, writing, code book, signal book, sketch, photograph, photographic negative, blue print, plan, map, model, note, instrument, appliance, or information relating to the national defense, shall be punished by imprisonment for not more than twenty years: *Provided,* That whoever shall violate . . . this section in time of war shall be punished by death or by imprisonment for not more than thirty years. . . .

SEC. 3. Whoever, when the United States is at war, shall willfully make or convey false reports or false statements with intent to interfere with the operation or success of the military or naval forces of the United States or to promote the success of its enemies and whoever, when the United States is at war, shall willfully cause or attempt to cause insubordination, disloyalty, mutiny, or refusal of duty, in the military or naval forces of the United States, or shall willfully obstruct the recruiting or enlistment service of the United States, to the injury of the service or of the United States, shall be punished by a fine of not more than $10,000 or imprisonment for not more than twenty years or both. . . .

Excerpted from U.S. Congress. *An Act To Punish Acts of Interference With the Foreign Relations, the Neutrality, and the Foreign Commerce of the United States, to Punish Espionage, and Better to Enforce the Criminal Laws of the United States, and for Other Purposes.* 65th Cong., 1st sess., June 15, 1917. *United States Statutes at Large* 40:217.

## 12.  District Judge Would Like to Take Shot at Traitors in Congress
### *October 1, 1917*

Houston, Texas

Judge Waller T. Burns, of the United States district court in charging a Federal grand jury at the beginning of the October term to-day, after calling by name Senators STONE of Missouri, HARDWICK of Georgia, VARDAMAN of Mississippi, GRONNA of North Dakota, GORE of Oklahoma, and LA FOLLETTE of Wisconsin, said:

"If I had a wish, I would wish that you men had jurisdiction to return bills of indictment against these men. They ought to be tried promptly and fairly, and I believe this court could administer the law fairly; but I have a conviction, as strong as life, that this country should stand them up against an adobe wall to-morrow and give them what they deserve. If any man deserves death, it is a traitor. I wish that I could pay for the ammunition. I would like to attend the execution, and if I were in the firing squad, I would not want to be the marksman who had the blank shell."

U.S. Congress. Senate. Newspaper article quoted in *Free Speech and the Right of Congress to Declare the Objects of the War,* a speech by Sen. Robert La Follette. *Congressional Record.* 65th Cong., 1st sess., October 6, 1917: 7878. A partial transcript of the speech is available at http://www.pbs. org/greatspeeches/timeline/r_lafollette_s2.html (accessed July 15, 2004).

# 13. President Wilson's Second Proclamation Regarding Alien Enemies

*November 16, 1917*

. . . 13. An alien enemy shall not approach or be found within one hundred yards of any canal; nor within one hundred yards of any wharf, pier or dock used directly by or by means of lighters by any vessel or vessels of over five hundred (500) tons gross engaged in foreign or domestic trade other than fishing; nor within one hundred yards of any warehouse, shed, elevator, railroad terminal or other terminal, storage or transfer facility adjacent to or operated in connection with any such wharf, pier or dock. . . .

15. An alien enemy shall not, except on public ferries, be found on any ocean, bay, river, or other waters within three miles of the shore line of the United States or its territorial possessions. . . .

16. No alien enemy shall ascend into the air in any airplane, balloon, airship, or flying machine.

17. An alien enemy shall not enter or be found within the District of Columbia. . . .

19. All alien enemies are hereby required to register at such times and places and in such manner as may be fixed by the Attorney General of the United States. . . .

20. An alien enemy shall not change his place of abode or occupation or otherwise travel or move from place to place without full compliance with any such regulations as the Attorney General of the United States may, from time to time, make and declare; and the Attorney General is hereby authorized to make and declare, from time to time, such regulations concerning the movements of alien enemies as he may deem necessary in the premises and for the public safety, and to provide in such regulations for monthly, weekly, or other periodical report by alien enemies to federal, state or local authorities; and all alien enemies shall report at the times and places and to the authorities specified in such regulations. . . .

Excerpted from U.S. Executive Office of the President. *By the President of the United States of America: A Proclamation.* November 16, 1917. *United States Statutes at Large* 40:1716. A partial transcript of this document is available at https://netfiles.uiuc.edu/rcunning/www/presproc.htm (accessed July 15, 2004).

# 14. The Sedition Act of 1918
## *May 16, 1918*

. . . SEC. 3. Whoever, when the United States is at war . . . shall willfully utter, print, write, or publish any disloyal, profane, scurrilous, or abusive language about the form of government of the United States, or the Constitution of the United States, or the military or naval forces of the United States, or the flag of the United States, or the uniform of the Army or Navy of the United States, or any language intended to bring the form of government of the United States, or the constitution of the United States, or the military or naval forces of the United States, or the flag of the United States, or the uniform of the Army or Navy of the United States into contempt, scorn, contumely, or disrepute, or shall willfully utter, print, write, or publish any language intended to incite, provoke, or encourage resistance to the United States, or to promote the cause of its enemies, or shall willfully display the flag of any foreign enemy, or shall willfully by utterance, writing, printing, publication, or language spoken, urge, incite, or advocate any curtailment of production in this country of any thing or things, product or products, necessary or essential to the prosecution of the war in which the United States may be engaged, with intent by such curtailment to cripple or hinder the United States in the prosecution of the war, and whoever shall willfully advocate, teach, defend, or suggest the doing of any of the acts or things in this section enumerated, and whoever shall by word or act support or favor the cause of any country with which the United States is at war or by word or act oppose the cause of the United States therein, shall be punished by a fine of not more than $10,000 or imprisonment for not more than twenty years, or both. . . .

SEC. 4. When the United States is at war, the Postmaster General may, upon evidence satisfactory to him that any person or concern is using the mails in violation of any of the provisions of this Act, instruct the postmaster at any post office at which mail is received addressed to such person or concern to return to the postmaster at the office at which they were originally mailed all letters or other matter so addressed, with the words, 'Mail to this address undeliverable under Espionage Act' plainly written or stamped upon the outside thereof. . . .

Excerpted from U.S. Congress. *An Act to Amend Section Three, Title One, of the Act Entitled "An Act to Punish Acts of Interference With the Foreign Relations, the Neutrality, and the Foreign Commerce of the United States, to Punish Espionage, and Better to Enforce the Criminal Laws of the United States, and For Other Purposes," Approved June Fifteenth, Nineteen Hundred and Seventeen, and for Other Purposes.* 65th Cong., 2nd sess., May 16, 1918. *United States Statutes at Large* 40:553.

# 15. *Schenck v. U.S.*

*March 3, 1919*

. . . The document in question upon its first printed side recited the first section of the Thirteenth Amendment, said that the idea embodied in it was violated by the conscription act and that a conscript is little better than a convict. In impassioned language it intimated that conscription was despotism in its worst form and a monstrous wrong against humanity in the interest of Wall Street's chosen few. It said, 'Do not submit to intimidation,' but in form at least confined itself to peaceful measures such as a petition for the repeal of the act. The other and later printed side of the sheet was headed 'Assert Your Rights.' It stated reasons for alleging that any one violated the Constitution when he refused to recognize 'your right to assert your opposition to the draft,' and went on, 'If you do not assert and support your rights, you are helping to deny or disparage rights which it is the solemn duty of all citizens and residents of the United States to retain.' It described the arguments on the other side as coming from cunning politicians and a mercenary capitalist press, and even silent consent to the conscription law as helping to support an infamous conspiracy. It denied the power to send our citizens away to foreign shores to shoot up the people of other lands, and added that words could not express the condemnation such cold-blooded ruthlessness deserves, &c., &c., winding up, 'You must do your share to maintain, support and uphold the rights of the people of this country.' Of course the document would not have been sent unless it had been intended to have some effect, and we do not see what effect it could be expected to have upon persons subject to the draft except to influence them to obstruct the carrying of it out. The defendants do not deny that the jury might find against them on this point. . . .

. . . We admit that in many places and in ordinary times the defendants in saying all that was said in the circular would have been within their constitutional rights. But the character of every act depends upon the circumstances in which it is done. The most stringent protection of free speech would not protect a man in falsely shouting fire in a theatre and causing a panic. . . . The question in every case is whether the words used are used in such circumstances and are of such a nature as to create a clear and present danger that they will bring about the substantive evils that Congress has a right to prevent. It is a question of proximity and degree. When a nation is at war many things that might be said in time of peace are such a hindrance to its efforts that their utterance will not be endured so long as men fight and that no Court could regard them as protected by any constitutional right. . . .

Excerpted from U.S. Supreme Court. *Schenck v. U.S.* 249 U.S. 47. March 3, 1919. http://caselaw.lp.findlaw.com/scripts/getcase.pl?navby=case&court= us&vol=249&page=47 (accessed July 15, 2004).

# 16. *Debs v. U.S.*

## *March 10, 1919*

. . . The [first count] alleges that on or about June 16, 1918, at Canton, Ohio, the defendant caused and incited and attempted to cause and incite insubordination, disloyalty, mutiny and refusal of duty in the military and naval forces of the United States and with intent so to do delivered, to an assembly of people, a public speech, set forth. The [other count] alleges that he obstructed and attempted to obstruct the recruiting and enlistment service of the United States and to that end and with that intent delivered the same speech. . . .

The main theme of the speech was Socialism, its growth, and a prophecy of its ultimate success. With that we have nothing to do, but if a part or the manifest intent of the more general utterances was to encourage those present to obstruct the recruiting service and if in passages such encouragement was directly given, the immunity of the general theme may not be enough to protect the speech. . . .

The defendant . . . said that the master class has always declared the war and the subject class has always fought the battles—that the subject class has had nothing to gain and all to lose, including their lives; that the working class, who furnish the corpses, have never yet had a voice in declaring war and never yet had a voice in declaring peace. 'You have your lives to lose; you certainly ought to have the right to declare war if you consider a war necessary. . . .'

There followed personal experiences and illustrations of the growth of Socialism, a glorification of minorities, and a prophecy of the success of the international Socialist crusade, with the interjection that 'you need to know that you are fit for something better than slavery and cannon fodder.' The rest of the discourse had . . . a final exhortation, 'Don't worry about the charge of treason to your masters; but be concerned about the treason that involves yourselves. . . .'

. . . We should add that the jury were most carefully instructed that they could not find the defendant guilty for advocacy of any of his opinions unless the words used had as their natural tendency and reasonably probable effect to obstruct the recruiting service, &c., and unless the defendant had the specific intent to do so in his mind. . . .

Excerpted from U.S. Supreme Court. *Debs v. U.S.* 249 U.S. 211. March 10, 1919. http://caselaw.lp.findlaw.com/scripts/getcase.pl?navby=case& court=us&vol=249&page=212 (accessed July 15, 2004).

# Japanese Internment during World War II

## INTRODUCTION

One of the darkest chapters in American history occurred when, in the name of homeland security, the federal government forced nearly 120,000 people of Japanese ancestry—U.S. citizens and noncitizens alike—to leave their homes on the West Coast and interned them in camps during World War II.

The internment arose from Japan's sneak bombing attack at Pearl Harbor, Hawaii, on December 7, 1941. Suddenly, people of Japanese descent were widely viewed as potential saboteurs and terrorists. On February 19, 1942—just ten weeks after Pearl Harbor—President Franklin D. Roosevelt signed Executive Order No. 9066. It authorized the secretary of war and military commanders under him to designate military areas from which "any or all persons" could be excluded [Document 17].

Within weeks military officials issued a series of orders barring anyone of Japanese descent from living or traveling on the West Coast. One such order, issued May 3, 1942, required all people of Japanese ancestry living in Los Angeles to go to "civil control stations" by May 5, 1942. From there the government transported them to desolate camps that were surrounded by barbed wire and guarded by soldiers. The internees were allowed to take only those possessions that they could personally carry [Document 18].

The Supreme Court upheld the detentions in a case decided December 18, 1944. The majority said that "exclusion from a threatened area . . . has a definite and close relationship to the prevention of espionage and sabotage" and that military authorities did not have enough time to segregate loyal people of Japanese descent from the disloyal. In a stinging dissent, Justice Frank Murphy attacked what he called the "legalization of racism." He said there was no evidence of imminent or impending public danger "to support this racial restriction which is one of the most sweeping and complete deprivations of constitutional rights in the history of this nation in the absence of martial law" [Document 19].

Although some of the internees were allowed to leave the camps to join the Army, attend college away from the West Coast, or find employment, many remained in the camps until the prohibition against returning to their homes was lifted in January 1945. The last camp closed on March 20, 1946.

On February 24, 1983, a panel created by Congress to investigate the internments concluded that a "grave injustice" had been done to the internees. "The record does not permit the conclusion that military necessity warranted the exclusion of ethnic Japanese from the West Coast," the Commission on Wartime Relocation and Internment of Civilians said in a 467-page report titled "Personal Justice Denied." Shortly after issuing the report, the commission recommended that the government pay $20,000 to each of the 60,000 internees who were still alive "as an act of national apology" [Document 20].

Another five years passed before Congress on August 10, 1988, passed the Civil Liberties Act of 1988, which authorized the payments. The bill also apologized "on behalf of the Nation" for the "fundamental violations of the basic civil liberties and constitutional rights" that the internees suffered [Document 21].

---

# 17. President Franklin D. Roosevelt's Executive Order No. 9066: Authorizing the Secretary of War to Prescribe Military Areas
*February 19, 1942*

Whereas the successful prosecution of the war requires every possible protection against espionage and against sabotage to national-defense material, national-defense premises, and national-defense utilities. . . .

Now, therefore, by virtue of the authority vested in me as President of the United States, and Commander in Chief of the Army and Navy, I hereby authorize and direct the Secretary of War, and the Military Commanders whom he may from time to time designate, whenever he or any designated Commander deems such action necessary or desirable, to prescribe military areas in such places and of such extent as he or the appropriate Military Commander may determine, from which any or all persons may be excluded, and with respect to which, the right of any person to enter, remain in, or leave shall be subject to whatever restrictions the Secretary of War or the appropriate Military Commander may impose in his discretion. The Secretary of War is hereby authorized to provide for residents of any such area who are excluded therefrom, such transportation, food, shelter, and other accommodations as may be necessary, in the judgment of the Secretary of War or the said Military Commander, and until other arrangements are made, to accomplish the purpose of this order. . . .

I hereby further authorize and direct the Secretary of War and the said Military Commanders to take such other steps as he or the appropriate Military Commander may deem advisable to enforce compliance with the restrictions applicable to each Military area hereinabove authorized to be designated, including the use of Federal troops and other Federal Agencies, with authority to accept assistance of state and local agencies.

I hereby further authorize and direct all Executive Departments, independent establishments and other Federal Agencies, to assist the Secretary of War or the said Military Commanders in carrying out this Executive Order, including the furnishing of medical aid, hospitalization, food, clothing, transportation, use of land, shelter, and other supplies, equipment, utilities, facilities, and services. . . .

Franklin D. Roosevelt
The White House
February 19, 1942

Excerpted from U.S. Executive Office of the President. Executive Order No. 9066: Authorizing the Secretary of War to Prescribe Military Areas. February 19, 1942. *Federal Register* 7:1407. http://www.ourdocuments. gov/doc.php?doc=74&page=transcript (accessed July 15, 2004).

# 18. Instructions to All Persons of Japanese Ancestry, Issued by Lt. Gen. John L. DeWitt, Commander of the Western Defense Command and Fourth Army

*May 3, 1942*

WESTERN DEFENSE COMMAND AND FOURTH ARMY
WARTIME CIVIL CONTROL ADMINISTRATION
Presidio of San Francisco, California
May 3, 1942

## Instructions to all Persons of Japanese Ancestry Living in the Following Area:

All of that portion of the City of Los Angeles, State of California, within that boundary beginning at the point at which North Figueroa Street meets a line following the middle of the Los Angeles River; thence southerly and following the said line to East First Street; then westerly on East First Street to Alameda Street; thence southerly on Alameda Street to East Third Street; thence northwesterly on East Third Street to Main Street; thence northerly on Main Street to First Street; thence northwesterly on First Street to Figueroa Street; thence northeasterly on Figueroa Street to the point of beginning.

Pursuant to the provisions of Civilian Exclusion Order No. 33, this Headquarters, dated May 3, 1942, all persons of Japanese ancestry, both alien and non-alien, will be evacuated from the above area by 12 o'clock noon, P.W.T., Saturday, May 9, 1942.

No Japanese person living in the above area will be permitted to change residence after 12 o'clock noon, P.W.T., Sunday, May 3, 1942, without obtaining special permission from the representative of the Commanding General, Southern California Sector, at the Civil Control Station located at:

Japanese Union Church
120 North San Pedro Street
Los Angeles, California

Such permits will only be granted for the purpose of uniting members of a family, or in cases of grave emergency.

The Civil Control Station is equipped to assist the Japanese population affected by this evacuation in the following ways:

1. Give advice and instructions on the evacuation.
2. Provide services with respect to the management, leasing, sale, storage or other disposition of most kinds of property, such as real estate, business and professional equipment, household goods, boats, automobiles and livestock.
3. Provide temporary residence elsewhere for all Japanese in family groups.
4. Transport persons and a limited amount of clothing and equipment to their new residence.

### *The Following Instructions Must Be Observed:*
1. A responsible member of each family, preferably the head of the family, or the person in whose name most of the property is held, and each individual living alone, will report to the Civil Control Station to receive further instructions. This must be done between 8:00 A.M. and 5:00 P.M. on Monday, May 4, 1942, or between 8:00 A.M. and 5:00 P.M. on Tuesday, May 5, 1942.
2. Evacuees must carry with them on departure for the Assembly Center, the following property:
   (a) Bedding and linens (no mattress) for each member of the family;
   (b) Toilet articles for each member of the family;
   (c) Extra clothing for each member of the family;
   (d) Sufficient knives, forks, spoons, plates, bowls and cups for each member of the family;
   (e) Essential personal effects for each member of the family.
   All items carried will be securely packaged, tied and plainly marked with the name of the owner and number in accordance with instructions obtained at the Civil Control Station. The size and number of packages is limited to that which can be carried by the individual or family group.
3. No pets of any kind will be permitted.
4. No personal items and no household goods will be shipped to the Assembly Center.
5. The United States Government through its agencies will provide for the storage, at the sole risk of the owner, of the more substantial household items, such as iceboxes, washing machines, pianos and other heavy furniture. Cooking utensils and other small items will be accepted for storage if crated, packed and plainly marked with the name and address of the owner. Only one name and address will be used by a given family.
6. Each family, and individual living alone, will be furnished transportation to the Assembly Center or will be authorized to travel by private automobile in a supervised group. All instructions pertaining to the movement will be obtained at the Civil Control Station. . . .

Excerpted from U.S. Western Defense Command and Fourth Army.
Wartime Civil Control Administration. Presidio of San Francisco, California.
*Instructions to all Persons of Japanese Ancestry* . . . (poster). May 3, 1942.
http://www.nps.gov/manz/evacposter.htm (accessed July 15, 2004).

## 19. *Korematsu v. United States*
### December 18, 1944

Mr. Justice BLACK delivered the opinion of the Court.

The petitioner, an American citizen of Japanese descent, was convicted in a federal district court for remaining in San Leandro, California, a 'Military Area,' contrary to Civilian Exclusion Order No. 34 of the Commanding General of the Western Command, U.S. Army, which directed that after May 9, 1942, all persons of Japanese ancestry should be excluded from that area. No question was raised as to petitioner's loyalty to the United States. . . .

It should be noted, to begin with, that all legal restrictions which curtail the civil rights of a single racial group are immediately suspect. That is not to say that all such restrictions are unconstitutional. It is to say that courts must subject them to the most rigid scrutiny. Pressing public necessity may sometimes justify the existence of such restrictions; racial antagonism never can. . . .

In the light of the principles we announced in [an earlier case involving a curfew for people of Japanese ancestry], we are unable to conclude that it was beyond the war power of Congress and the Executive to exclude those of Japanese ancestry from the West Coast war area at the time they did. True, exclusion from the area in which one's home is located is a far greater deprivation than constant confinement to the home from 8 p.m. to 6 a.m. Nothing short of apprehension by the proper military authorities of the gravest imminent danger to the public safety can constitutionally justify either. But exclusion from a threatened area, no less than curfew, has a definite and close relationship to the prevention of espionage and sabotage. The military authorities, charged with the primary responsibility of defending our shores, concluded that curfew provided inadequate protection and ordered exclusion. They did so . . . in accordance with Congressional authority to the military to say who should, and who should not, remain in the threatened areas. . . .

Here, as in the [earlier] case, '. . . we cannot reject as unfounded the judgment of the military authorities and of Congress that there were disloyal members of that population, whose number and strength could not be precisely and quickly ascertained. We cannot say that the war-making branches of the Government did not have ground for believing that in a critical hour such persons could not readily be isolated and separately dealt with, and constituted a menace to the national defense and safety, which demanded that prompt and adequate measures be taken to guard against it.'

Like curfew, exclusion of those of Japanese origin was deemed necessary because of the presence of an unascertained number of disloyal members of the group, most of whom we have no doubt were loyal to this country. It was because we could not reject the finding of the military authorities that it was impossible to bring about an immediate segregation of the disloyal from the loyal that we sustained the validity of the curfew order as applying to the whole group. In the instant case, temporary exclusion of the entire group was rested by the military on the same ground. The judgment that exclusion of the whole group was for the same reason a military imperative answers the contention that the exclusion was in the nature of group punishment based on antagonism to those of Japanese origin. That there were members of the group who retained loyalties in Japan has been confirmed by investigations made subsequent to the exclusion. Approximately five thousand American citizens of Japanese ancestry refused to swear unqualified allegiance to the United States and to renounce allegiance to the Japanese Emperor, and several thousand evacuees requested repatriation to Japan.

We uphold the exclusion order as of the time it was made and when the petitioner violated it. . . . In doing so, we are not unmindful of the hardships imposed by it upon a large group of American citizens. . . . But hardships are part of war, and war is an aggregation of hardships. All citizens alike, both in and out of uniform, feel the impact of war in greater or lesser measure. Citizenship has its responsibilities as well as its privileges, and in time of war the burden is always heavier. Compulsory exclusion of large groups of citizens from their homes, except under circumstances of direct emergency and peril, is inconsistent with our basic governmental institutions. But when under conditions of modern warfare our shores are threatened by hostile forces, the power to protect must be commensurate with the threatened danger. . . .

It is said that we are dealing here with the case of imprisonment of a citizen in a concentration camp solely because of his ancestry, without evidence or inquiry concerning his loyalty and good disposition towards the United States. Our task would be simple, our duty clear, were this a case involving the imprisonment of a loyal citizen in a concentration camp because of racial prejudice. Regardless of the true nature of the assembly and relocation centers—and we deem it unjustifiable to call them concentration camps with all the ugly connotations that term implies—we are dealing specifically with nothing but an exclusion order. To cast this case into outlines of racial prejudice, without reference to the real military dangers which were presented, merely confuses the issue. Korematsu was not excluded from the Military Area because of hostility to him or his race. He was excluded because we are at war with the Japanese Empire, because the properly constituted military authorities feared an invasion of our West Coast and felt constrained to take proper security measures, because they decided that the military urgency of the situation demanded that all citizens of Japanese ancestry be segregated from the West Coast temporarily, and finally, because Congress, reposing its confidence in this time of war in our military leaders—as inevitably it must—determined that they should have the power to do just this. There was evidence of disloyalty on the part of some, the military authorities considered that the need for action was great, and time was short. We cannot—by availing ourselves of the calm perspective of hindsight—now say that at that time these actions were unjustified.

Mr. Justice MURPHY, dissenting.

This exclusion of 'all persons of Japanese ancestry, both alien and non-alien,' from the Pacific Coast area on a plea of military necessity in the absence of martial law ought not to be approved. Such exclusion goes over 'the very brink of constitutional power' and falls into the ugly abyss of racism.

In dealing with matters relating to the prosecution and progress of a war, we must accord great respect and consideration to the judgments of the military authorities who are on the scene and who have full knowledge of the military facts. The scope of their discretion must, as a matter of necessity and common sense, be wide. And their judgments ought not to be overruled lightly by those whose training and duties ill-equip them to deal intelligently with matters so vital to the physical security of the nation.

At the same time, however, it is essential that there be definite limits to military discretion, especially where marital law has not been declared. Individuals must not be left impoverished of their constitutional rights on plea of military necessity that has neither substance nor support. . . .

Being an obvious racial discrimination, the order deprives all those within its scope of the equal protection of the laws as guaranteed by the Fifth Amendment. It further deprives these individuals of their constitutional rights to live and work where they will, to establish a home where they choose and to move about freely. In excommunicating them without benefit of hearings, this order also deprives them of all their constitutional rights to procedural due process. Yet no reasonable relation to an 'immediate, imminent, and impending' public danger is evident to support this racial restriction which is one of the most sweeping and complete deprivations of constitutional rights in the history of this nation in the absence of martial law.

It must be conceded that the military and naval situation in the spring of 1942 was such as to generate a very real fear of invasion of the Pacific Coast, accompanied by fears of sabotage and espionage in that area. The military command was therefore justified in adopting all reasonable means necessary to combat these dangers. In adjudging the military action taken in light of the then apparent dangers, we must not erect too high or too meticulous standards; it is necessary only that the action have some reasonable relation to the removal of the dangers of invasion, sabotage and espionage. But the exclusion, either temporarily or permanently, of all persons with Japanese blood in their veins has no such reasonable relation. And that relation is lacking because the exclusion order necessarily must rely for its reasonableness upon the assumption that all persons of Japanese ancestry may have a dangerous tendency to commit sabotage and espionage and to aid our Japanese enemy in other ways. It is difficult to believe that reason, logic or experience could be marshaled in support of such an assumption.

That this forced exclusion was the result in good measure of this erroneous assumption of racial guilt rather than bona fide military necessity is evidenced by the Commanding General's Final Report on the evacuation from the Pacific Coast area. In it he refers to all individuals of Japanese descents as 'subversive,' as belonging to 'an enemy race' whose 'racial strains are undiluted,' and as constituting 'over 112,000 potential enemies . . . at large today' along the Pacific Coast. In support of this blanket condemnation of all persons of Japanese descent, however, no reliable evidence is cited to show that such individuals were generally disloyal, or had generally so conducted themselves in this area as to constitute a special menace to defense installations or war industries, or had otherwise by their behavior furnished reasonable ground for their exclusion as a group.

Justification for the exclusion is sought, instead, mainly upon questionable racial and sociological grounds not ordinarily within the realm of expert military judgment, supplemented by certain semi-military conclusions drawn from an unwarranted use of circumstantial evidence. . . .

No one denies, of course, that there were some disloyal persons of Japanese descent on the Pacific Coast who did all in their power to aid their ancestral land. Similar disloyal activities have been engaged in by many persons of German, Italian and even more pioneer stock in our country. But to infer that examples of individual disloyalty prove group disloyalty and justify discriminatory action against the entire group is to deny that under our system of law individual guilt is the sole basis for deprivation of rights. Moreover, this inference, which is at the very heart of the evacuation orders, has been used in support of the abhorrent and despicable treatment of minority groups by the dictatorial tyrannies which this nation is now pledged to destroy. To give constitutional sanction to that inference in this case, however well-intentioned may have been the military command on the Pacific Coast, is to adopt one of the cruelest of the rationales used by our enemies to destroy the dignity of the individual and to encourage and open the door to discriminatory actions against other minority groups in the passions of tomorrow. . . .

I dissent, therefore, from this legalization of racism. Racial discrimination in any form and in any degree has no justifiable part whatever in our democratic way of life. It is unattractive in any setting but it is utterly revolting among a free people who have embraced the principles set forth in the Constitution of the United States. All residents of this nation are kin in some way by blood or culture to a foreign land. Yet they are primarily and necessarily a part of the new and distinct civilization of the United States. They must accordingly be treated at all times as the heirs of the American experiment and as entitled to all the rights and freedoms guaranteed by the Constitution.

Excerpted from U.S. Supreme Court. *Korematsu v. United States.* 323 U.S. 214. December 18, 1944. Available at http://www.access.gpo.gov/su_docs/supcrt/index.html (accessed July 15, 2004).

# 20. Personal Justice Denied: Report of the Commission on Wartime Relocation and Internment of Civilians

*February 24, 1983*

On February 19, 1942, ten weeks after the Pearl Harbor attack, President Franklin D. Roosevelt signed Executive Order 9066, which gave to the Secretary of War and the military commanders to whom he delegated authority, the power to exclude any and all persons, citizens and aliens, from designated areas in order to provide security against sabotage, espionage and fifth column activity. Shortly thereafter, all American citizens of Japanese descent were prohibited from living, working or traveling on the West Coast of the United States. The same prohibition applied to the generation of Japanese immigrants who, pursuant to federal law and despite long residence in the United States, were not permitted to become American citizens. Initially, this exclusion was to be carried out by "voluntary" relocation. That policy inevitably failed, and these American citizens and their alien parents were removed by the Army, first to "assembly centers"— temporary quarters at racetracks and fairgrounds—and then to "relocation centers"—bleak barrack camps mostly in desolate areas of the West. The camps were surrounded by barbed wire and guarded by military police. . . .

All this was done despite the fact that not a single documented act of espionage, sabotage or fifth column activity was committed by an American citizen of Japanese ancestry or by a resident Japanese alien on the West Coast.

No mass exclusion or detention, in any part of the country, was ordered against American citizens of German or Italian descent. Official actions against enemy aliens of other nationalities were much more individualized and selective than those imposed on the ethnic Japanese.

The exclusion, removal and detention inflicted tremendous human cost. There was the obvious cost of homes and businesses sold or abandoned under circumstances of great distress, as well as injury to careers and professional advancement. But, most important, there was the loss of liberty and the personal stigma of suspected disloyalty for thousands of people who knew themselves to be devoted to their country's cause and to its ideals but whose repeated protestations of loyalty were discounted—only to be demonstrated beyond any doubt by the record of Nisei [the first generation of ethnic Japanese born in the United States] solders, who returned from the battlefields of Europe as the most decorated and distinguished combat unit of World War II, and by the thousands of other Nisei who served against the enemy in the Pacific, mostly in military intelligence. The wounds of the exclusion and detention have healed in some respects, but the scars of that experience remain, painfully real in the minds of those who lived through the suffering and deprivation of the camps. . . .

The exclusion and removal were attacks on the ethnic Japanese which followed a long and ugly history of West Coast anti-Japanese agitation and legislation. Antipathy and hostility toward the ethnic Japanese was a major factor of the public life of the West Coast states for more than forty years before Pearl Harbor. . . .

Contrary to the facts, there was a widespread belief, supported by a statement by Frank Knox, Secretary of the Navy, that the Pearl Harbor attack had been aided by sabotage and fifth column activity by ethnic Japanese in Hawaii. Shortly after Pearl Harbor the government knew that this was not true, but took no effective measures to disabuse public belief that disloyalty had contributed to massive American losses on December 7, 1941. Thus the country was unfairly led to believe that both American citizens of Japanese descent and resident Japanese aliens threatened American security. . . .

Having concluded that no military necessity supported the exclusion, the Commission has attempted to determine how the decision came to be made.

First, General DeWitt [Lieutenant General John L. DeWitt, commanding general of the western defense command] apparently believed what he told Secretary Stimson [Secretary of War Henry L. Stimson]: ethnicity determined loyalty. Moreover, he believed that the ethnic Japanese were so alien to the thought processes of white Americans that it was impossible to distinguish the loyal from the disloyal. On this basis he believed them to be potential enemies among whom loyalty could not be determined.

Second, the FBI and members of Naval Intelligence who had relevant intelligence responsibility were ignored when they stated that nothing more than careful watching of suspicious individuals or individual reviews of loyalty were called for by existing circumstances. In addition, the opinions of the Army General Staff that no sustained Japanese attack on the West Coast was possible were ignored.

Third, General DeWitt relied heavily on civilian politicians rather than informed military judgments in reaching his conclusions as to what actions were necessary, and civilian politicians largely repeated the prejudiced, unfounded themes of anti-Japanese factions and interest groups on the West Coast.

Fourth, no effective measures were taken by President Roosevelt to calm the West Coast public and refute the rumors of sabotage and fifth column activity at Pearl Harbor.

Fifth, General DeWitt was temperamentally disposed to exaggerate the measures necessary to maintain security and placed security far ahead of any concern for the liberty of citizens. . . .

Excerpted from U.S. Commission on Wartime Relocation and Internment of Civilians. *Personal Justice Denied: Report of the Commission on Wartime Relocation and Internment of Civilians.* The Commission, 1983.

# 21.  The Civil Liberties Act of 1988
*August 10, 1988*

## SECTION 1. PURPOSES

The purposes of this Act are to—

(1) acknowledge the fundamental injustice of the evacuation, relocation, and internment of United States citizens and permanent resident aliens of Japanese ancestry during World War II;

(2) apologize on behalf of the people of the United States for the evacuation, relocation, and internment of such individuals so as to prevent the recurrence of any similar event;

(3) provide for a public education fund to finance efforts to inform the public about the internment of such individuals so as to prevent the recurrence of any similar event;

(4) make restitution to those individuals of Japanese ancestry who were interned. . . .

(6) discourage the occurrence of similar injustices and violations of civil liberties in the future; and

(7) make more credible and sincere any declaration of concern by the United States over violations of human rights committed by other nations.

# SEC. 2. STATEMENT OF THE CONGRESS

(a) WITH REGARD TO INDIVIDUALS OF JAPANESE ANCESTRY.—The Congress recognizes that, as described by the Commission on Wartime Relocation and Internment of Civilians, a grave injustice was done to both citizens and permanent resident aliens of Japanese ancestry by the evacuation, relocation, and internment of civilians during World War II. As the Commission documents, these actions were carried out without adequate security reasons and without any acts of espionage or sabotage documented by the Commission, and were motivated largely by racial prejudice, wartime hysteria, and a failure of political leadership. The excluded individuals of Japanese ancestry suffered enormous damages, both material and intangible, and there are incalculable losses in education and job training, all of which resulted in significant human suffering for which appropriate compensation has not been made. For these fundamental violations of the basic civil liberties and constitutional rights of these individuals of Japanese ancestry, the Congress apologizes on behalf of the Nation. . . .

U.S. Congress. *An Act to Implement Recommendations of the Commission on Wartime Relocation and Internment of Civilians.* 100th Cong., 2nd sess., August 10, 1988. *United States Statutes at Large* 102:903. http://thomas. loc.gov/cgi-bin/bdquery/z?d100:HR00442:ITOM:/bss/d100query.html (accessed July 15, 2004).

# McCarthy Charges That Communists Infest the State Department

## INTRODUCTION

In the years immediately following the end of World War II, a fear of communism swept across the United States. There were many reasons:

- The Soviet Union was expanding its influence across Eastern Europe.
- In 1947 the House Un-American Activities Committee held celebrated hearings on communist penetration of Hollywood, and movie studios responded by creating a "blacklist" of directors, actors, and writers whose careers were effectively ended; President Harry S. Truman established by executive order a Federal Employee Loyalty Program designed to ferret out any communist spies in the government; and the United States Chamber of Commerce alleged that large numbers of communists had infiltrated the federal government and labor unions.
- In 1948 former State Department official Alger Hiss was accused of spying for the Soviet Union (he was convicted of perjury in 1950), and communists gained control of the government in Czechoslovakia.
- In 1949 communists won the civil war in China (some claimed this happened because the State Department was "soft" on communism), and the Soviet Union surprised the world by exploding its first atomic bomb.
- In June 1950 communist North Korea invaded South Korea.

Into this environment stepped a little-known Republican senator from Wisconsin named Joseph R. McCarthy. On February 9, 1950, he gave a speech to the Ohio County Republican Women's Club in Wheeling, West Virginia, that quickly created a national sensation. According to a report the next day in the *Wheeling Intelligencer,* McCarthy said:

> While I cannot take the time to name all of the men in the State Department who have been named as members of the Communist Party and members of a spy ring, I have here in my hand a list of 205 that were known to the Secretary of State as being members of the Communist Party and who, nevertheless, are still working and shaping the policy in the State Department [Document 22].

Exactly what McCarthy said remains unknown. The senator's appearance drew scant media coverage, and McCarthy said he did not use a written speech. Eleven days later, he read a version of the speech on the Senate floor that he said was taken from a recording. In this version, however, the number of communists at the State Department dropped to fifty-seven. His fellow senators asked McCarthy which number was correct, but he dodged their questions. Wildly throwing around numbers and accusations, some of which contradicted each other, became a McCarthy trademark. He also had a ready response for those who challenged him: they were members of the communist conspiracy.

A committee in the Democratic-controlled Senate found the charges groundless. So did Sen. Margaret Chase Smith, R-Maine, who initially supported McCarthy until she examined the documents that supposedly proved his claims. Chase, the only woman in the Senate, became one of the first major figures to challenge McCarthy when she rose on the Senate floor on June 1, 1950, to give a speech titled "A Declaration of Conscience":

> The American people are sick and tired of being afraid to speak their minds lest they be politically smeared as "Communists" or "Fascists" by their opponents. Freedom of speech is not what it used to be in America. It has been so abused by some that it is not exercised by others [Document 23].

McCarthy continued his attacks on the Senate floor and in the media. The national hysteria that McCarthy stirred up caused many people inside and outside government who were said to have "leftist" or "radical" tendencies to lose their jobs.

McCarthy gained a much larger platform for his charges after Republicans won control of the Senate in 1952—partially because of McCarthy's smears against many Democratic senators and candidates. The Republican leadership rewarded him with chairmanship of the Special Subcommittee on Investigations, and he started issuing subpoenas to hundreds of people in his crusade to find communists in government.

The Democratic members of the subcommittee quit, and Republican members frequently did not attend hearings because McCarthy called them with little notice or held them outside Washington, D.C. This left McCarthy and Roy Cohn, his chief counsel, with almost free reign to bully and intimidate witnesses, often in closed hearings. Some of the witnesses had left the Communist Party years earlier, but McCarthy did not care. Witnesses quickly learned that the only way to save themselves was to name other people in the party. The fact that McCarthy's "evidence" was old, garbled, or totally fictitious made no difference.

In late 1953 and early 1954, McCarthy started investigating alleged communist infiltration of the military up to the highest ranks. The "Army-McCarthy" hearings started on April 22, 1954, and continued for fifty-five days. The hearings were broadcast live on television, and many newspapers printed transcripts of the proceedings.

The climax came on June 9, 1954, when Boston lawyer Joseph Welch, who represented the army, questioned Cohn. McCarthy had temporarily stepped down as chairman in anticipation of testifying himself.

Welch badgered Cohn about the need to get all communists out of government "by sundown," a tactic he knew would enrage McCarthy. The Wisconsin senator fell into the trap, denouncing Welch and naming a man at Welch's law firm who McCarthy claimed was a known communist. As McCarthy continued, Welch interrupted him with the famous line: "Have you no sense of decency, sir, at long last? Have you left no sense of decency?" [Document 24].

The hearings continued, but the national exposure of McCarthy's tactics effectively ruined him. On December 2, 1954, by a 67–22 vote the Senate passed a resolution censuring McCarthy for conduct that "tended to bring the Senate into dishonor and disrepute." McCarthy remained in the Senate, but his previous heavy drinking turned to alcoholism and he died in 1957 at age forty-eight [Document 25].

McCarthy "was in many ways the most gifted demagogue ever bred on these shores," biographer Richard H. Rovere wrote years later. "No bolder seditionist ever moved among us—nor any politician with a surer, swifter access to the dark places of the American mind."

---

# 22. Senator Joe McCarthy's Speech in Wheeling, West Virginia

*February 9, 1950*

[The version that McCarthy read on the Senate floor on February 20, 1950]

Ladies and gentlemen, tonight as we celebrate the one hundred and forty-first birthday of one of the greatest men in American history, I would like to be able to talk about what a glorious day today is in the history of the world. As we celebrate the birth of this man who with his whole heart and soul hated war, I would like to be able to speak of peace in our time, of war being outlawed, and of world-wide disarmament. These would be truly appropriate things to be able to mention as we celebrate the birthday of Abraham Lincoln.

Five years after a world war has been won, men's hearts should anticipate a long peace, and men's minds should be free from the heavy weight that comes with war. But this is not such a period—for this is not a period of peace. This is a time of the "cold war." This is a time when all the world is split into two vast, increasingly hostile armed camps—a time of a great armaments race. . . .

The one encouraging thing is that the "mad moment" has not yet arrived for the firing of the gun or the exploding of the bomb which will set civilization about the final task of destroying itself. There is still a hope for peace if we finally decide that no longer can we safely blind our eyes and close our ears to those facts which are shaping up more and more clearly. And that is that we are now engaged in a show-down fight—not the usual war between nations for land areas or other material gains, but a war between two diametrically opposed ideologies. . . .

Today we are engaged in a final, all-out battle between communistic atheism and Christianity. The modern champions of communism have selected this as the time. And ladies and gentlemen, the chips are down—they are truly down.

Lest there be any doubt that the time has been chosen, let us go directly to the leader of communism today—Joseph Stalin. Here is what he said—not back in 1928, not before the war, not during the war—but 2 years after the last war ended: "To think that the Communist revolution can be carried out peacefully, within the framework of a Christian democracy, means one has either gone out of one's mind and lost all normal understanding, or has grossly and openly repudiated the Communist revolution.". . .

Six years ago, at the time of the first conference to map out the peace—Dumbarton Oaks—there was within the Soviet orbit 180,000,000 people. Lined up on the antitotalitarian side there were in the world at that time roughly 1,625,000,000 people. Today, only 6 years later, there are 800,000,000 people under the absolute domination of Soviet Russia—an increase of over 400 percent. On our side, the figure has shrunk to around 500,000,000. In other words, in less than 6 years the odds have changed from 9 to 1 in our favor to 8 to 5 against us. This indicates the swiftness of the tempo of Communist victories and American defeats in the cold war. As one of our outstanding historical figures once said, "When a great democracy is destroyed it will not be because of enemies from without, but rather because of enemies from within."

The truth of this statement is becoming terrifyingly clear as we see this country each day losing on every front. . . .

The reason why we find ourselves in a position of impotency is not because our only powerful potential enemy has sent men to invade our shores, but rather because of the traitorous actions of those who have been treated so well by this Nation. It has not been the less fortunate or members of minority groups who have been selling this Nation out, but rather those who have had all the benefits that the wealthiest nation on earth has had to offer—the finest homes, the finest college education, and the finest jobs in Government we can give.

This is glaringly true in the State Department. There the bright young men who are born with silver spoons in their mouths are the ones who have been the worst. . . .

. . . In my opinion the State Department, which is one of the most important government departments, is thoroughly infested with Communists.

I have in my hand 57 cases of individuals who would appear to be either card carrying members or certainly loyal to the Communist Party, but who nevertheless are still helping to shape our foreign policy.

One thing to remember in discussing the Communists in our Government is that we are not dealing with spies who get 30 pieces of silver to steal the blueprints of a new weapon. We are dealing with a far more sinister type of activity because it permits the enemy to guide and shape our policy. . . .

As you hear this story of high treason, I know that you are saying to yourself, "Well, why doesn't the Congress do something about it?" Actually, ladies and gentlemen, one of the important reasons for the graft, the corruption, the dishonesty, the disloyalty, the treason in high Government positions—one of the most important reasons why this continues is a lack of moral uprising on the part of the 140,000,000 American people. . . .

Excerpted from U.S. Congress. Senate. Speech by Senator Joe McCarthy Delivered in Wheeling, West Virginia. *Congressional Record*, 81st Cong., 2nd sess., February 20, 1950. Vol. 96, pt 2: 1954–1957.

---

# 23. A Declaration of Conscience, Senator Margaret Chase Smith's Speech on the Senate Floor
*June 1, 1950*

Mr. President, I would like to speak briefly and simply about a serious national condition. It is a national feeling of fear and frustration that could result in national suicide and the end of everything that we Americans hold dear. It is a condition that comes from the lack of effective leadership either in the legislative branch or the executive branch of government. . . .

I speak as briefly as possible because too much harm has already been done with irresponsible words of bitterness and selfish political opportunism. I speak as simply as possible because the issue is too great to be obscured by eloquence. I speak simply and briefly in the hope that my words will be taken to heart.

Mr. President, I speak as a Republican. I speak as a woman. I speak as a United States senator. I speak as an American.

The United States Senate has long enjoyed worldwide respect as the greatest deliberative body in the world. But recently that deliberative character has too often been debased to the level of a forum of hate and character assassination sheltered by the shield of congressional immunity.

It is ironical that we senators can in debate in the Senate, directly or indirectly, by any form of words, impute to any American who is not a senator any conduct or motive unworthy or unbecoming an American—and without that non-senator American having any legal redress against us—yet if we say the same thing in the Senate about our colleagues we can be stopped on the grounds of being out of order. . . .

I think that it is high time for the United States Senate and its members to do some real soul searching and to weigh our consciences as to the manner in which we are performing our duty to the people of America and the manner in which we are using or abusing our individual powers and privileges.

I think that it is high time that we remembered that we have sworn to uphold and defend the Constitution. I think it is high time that we remembered that the Constitution, as amended, speaks not only of the freedom of speech but also of trial by jury instead of trial by accusation.

Whether it be a criminal prosecution in court or a character prosecution in the Senate, there is little practical distinction when the life of a person has been ruined.

Those of us who shout the loudest about Americanism in making character assassinations are all too frequently those who, by our own words and acts, ignore some of the basic principles of Americanism—

The right to criticize.

The right to hold unpopular beliefs.

The right to protest.

The right of independent thought.

The exercise of these rights should not cost one single American citizen his reputation or his right to a livelihood nor should he be in danger of losing his reputation or livelihood merely because he happens to know someone who holds unpopular beliefs. Who of us does not? Otherwise none of us could call our souls our own. Otherwise thought control would have set in.

The American people are sick and tired of being afraid to speak their minds lest they be politically smeared as "Communists" or "Fascists" by their opponents. Freedom of speech is not what it used to be in America. It has been so abused by some that it is not exercised by others. . . .

Today our country is being psychologically divided by the confusion and the suspicions that are bred in the United States Senate to spread like cancerous tentacles of "know nothing, suspect everything" attitudes. . . .

The Democratic administration has greatly lost the confidence of the American people by its complacency to the threat of communism here at home and the leak of vital secrets to Russia through key officials of the Democratic administration. There are enough proved cases to make this point without diluting our criticism with unproved charges. . . .

As a woman, I wonder how the mothers, wives, sisters, and daughters feel about the way in which members of their families have been politically mangled in Senate debate—and I use the word "debate" advisedly.

As a United States senator, I am not proud of the way in which the Senate has been made a publicity platform for irresponsible sensationalism. I am not proud of the reckless abandon in which unproved charges have been hurled from this side of the aisle. I am not proud of the obviously staged, undignified countercharges which have been attempted in retaliation from the other side of the aisle.

I do not like the way the Senate has been made a rendezvous for vilification, for selfish political gain at the sacrifice of individual reputations and national unity. I am not proud of the way we smear outsiders from the floor of the Senate and hide behind the cloak of congressional immunity and still place ourselves beyond criticism on the floor of the Senate.

As an American, I am shocked at the way Republicans and Democrats alike are playing directly into the Communist design of "confuse, divide, and conquer." As an American, I do not want a Democratic administration "whitewash" or "coverup" any more than I want a Republican smear or witch hunt.

As an American, I condemn a Republican Fascist just as much as I condemn a Democrat Communist. I condemn a Democrat Fascist just as much as I condemn a Republican Communist. They are equally dangerous to you and me and to our country. As an American, I want to see our nation recapture the strength and unity it once had when we fought the enemy instead of ourselves. . . .

Excerpted from U.S. Congress. Senate. *A Declaration of Conscience.* Speech by Sen. Margaret Chase Smith, June 1, 1950. *Congressional Record,* 81st Cong., 2nd sess.: 7894-7895. http://www.mcslibrary.org/program/library/declaration.htm (accessed July 15, 2004).

# 24. The Army-McCarthy Hearings
## June 9, 1954

[Questioning of Roy Cohn, counsel for the Senate Special Subcommittee on Investigations, by Joseph Welch, chief attorney for the U.S. Army]

Mr. WELCH: Mr. Cohn, tell me once more: Every time you learn of a Communist or a spy anywhere, is it your policy to get them out as fast as possible?

Mr. COHN: Surely, we want them out as fast as possible, sir.

Mr. WELCH: And whenever you learn of one from now on, Mr. Cohn, I beg of you, will you tell somebody about them quick?

Mr. COHN: Mr. Welch, with great respect, I work for the committee here. They know how we go about handling situations of Communist infiltration and failure to act on FBI information about Communist infiltration. If they are displeased with the speed with which I and the group of men who work with me proceed, if they are displeased with the order in which we move, I am sure, they will give me appropriate instructions along those lines, and I will follow any which they give me.

Mr. WELCH: May I add my small voice, sir, and say whenever you know about a subversive or a Communist or a spy, please hurry. Will you remember those words?

Senator McCARTHY: Mr. Chairman.

Mr. COHN: Mr. Welch, I can assure you, sir, as far as I am concerned, and certainly as far as the chairman of this committee and the members, and the members of the staff, are concerned, we are a small group, but we proceed as expeditiously as is humanly possible to get out Communists and traitors and to bring to light the mechanism by which they have been permitted to remain where they were for so long a period of time.

Senator McCARTHY: Mr. Chairman, in view of that question—

Senator MUNDT: Have you a point of order?

Senator McCARTHY: Not exactly, Mr. Chairman, but in view of Mr. Welch's request that the information be given once we know of anyone who might be performing any work for the Communist Party, I think we should tell him that he has in his law firm a young man named Fisher whom he recommended, incidentally, to do work on this committee, who has been for a number of years a member of an organization [the Lawyers Guild] which was named, oh, years and years ago, as the legal bulwark of the Communist Party. . . . I certainly assume that Mr. Welch did not know of this young man at the time he recommended him as the assistant counsel for this committee, but he has such terror and such a great desire to know where anyone is located who may be serving the Communist cause, Mr.

Welch, that I thought we should just call to your attention the fact that your Mr. Fisher, who is still in your law firm today, whom you asked to have down here looking over the secret and classified material, is a member of an organization, not named by me but named by various committees, named by the Attorney General, as I recall, and I think I quote this verbatim, as "the legal bulwark of the Communist Party." He belonged to that for a sizable number of years, according to his own admission, and he belonged to it long after it has been exposed as the legal arm of the Communist Party. . . .

I don't think you can find anyplace, anywhere, an organization which has done more to defend Communists—I am again quoting the report—to defend Communists, to defend espionage agents, and to aid the Communist cause, than the man whom you originally wanted down here at your right hand instead of Mr. St. Clair.

I have hesitated bringing that up, but I have been rather bored with your phony requests to Mr. Cohn here that he personally get every Communist out of government before sundown. Therefore, we will give you information about the young man in your own organization.

I am not asking you at this time to explain why you tried to foist him on this committee. Whether you knew he was a member of that Communist organization or not, I don't know. I assume you did not, Mr. Welch, because I get the impression that, while you are quite an actor, you play for a laugh, I don't think you have any conception of the danger of the Communist Party. I don't think you yourself would ever knowingly aid the Communist cause. I think you are unknowingly aiding it when you try to burlesque this hearing in which we are attempting to bring out the facts, however.

Mr. WELCH: Mr. Chairman.

Senator MUNDT: Mr. Welch, the Chair should say he has no recognition or no memory of Mr. Welch's recommending either Mr. Fisher or anybody else as counsel for this committee.

I will recognize Mr. Welch.

Senator McCARTHY: Mr. Chairman, I will give you the news story on that.

Mr. WELCH: Mr. Chairman, under these circumstances I must have something approaching a personal privilege.

Senator MUNDT: You may have it, sir. It will not be taken out of your time.

Mr. WELCH: Senator McCarthy, I did not know—Senator, sometimes you say "May I have your attention?"

Senator McCARTHY: I am listening to you. I can listen with one ear.

Mr. WELCH: This time I want you to listen with both.

Senator McCARTHY: Yes.

Mr. WELCH: Senator McCarthy, I think until this moment—

Senator McCARTHY: Jim, will you get the news story to the effect that this man belonged to this Communist-front organization? Will you get the citations showing that this was the legal arm of the Communist Party, and the length of time that he belonged, and the fact that he was recommended by Mr. Welch? I think that should be in the record.

Mr. WELCH: You won't need anything in the record when I have finished telling you this.

Until this moment, Senator, I think I never really gauged your cruelty or your recklessness. Fred Fisher is a young man who went to the Harvard Law School and came into my firm and is starting what looks to be a brilliant career with us.

When I decided to work for this committee, I asked Mr. Jim St. Clair, who sits on my right, to be my first assistant. I said to Jim, "Pick somebody in the firm who works under you that you would like." He chose Fred Fisher and they came down here on an afternoon plane. That night, when he had taken a little stab at trying to see what the case was about, Fred Fisher and Jim St. Clair and I went to dinner together. I then said to these two young men, "Boys, I don't know anything about you except I have always liked you, but if there is anything funny in the life of either one of you that would hurt anybody in this case you speak up quick."

Fred Fisher said, "Mr. Welch, when I was in law school and for a period of months after, I belonged to the Lawyers Guild," as you have suggested, Senator. He went on to say, "I am secretary of the Young Republicans League in Newton with the son of Massachusetts' Governor, and I have the respect and admiration of my community and I am sure I have the respect and admiration of the 25 lawyers or so in Hale & Dorr."

I said, "Fred, I just don't think I am going to ask you to work on the case. If I do, one of these days that will come out and go over national television and it will just hurt like the dickens."

So, Senator, I asked him to go back to Boston.

Little did I dream you could be so reckless and so cruel as to do an injury to that lad. It is true he is still with Hale & Dorr. It is true that he will continue to be with Hale & Dorr. It is, I regret to say, equally true that I fear he shall always bear a scar needlessly inflicted by you. If it were in my power to forgive you for your reckless cruelty, I will do so. I like to think I am a gentleman, but your forgiveness will have to come from someone other than me. . . .

Senator MCCARTHY: I just give this man's record, and I want to say, Mr. Welch, that it has been labeled long before he became a member, as early as 1944—

Mr. WELCH: Senator, may we not drop this? We know he belonged to the Lawyers Guild. . . . Let us not assassinate this lad further, Senator. You have done enough. Have you no sense of decency, sir, at long last? Have you left no sense of decency?

Senator McCARTHY: I know this hurts you, Mr. Welch. But I may say, Mr. Chairman, on the point of personal privilege, and I would like to finish it—

Mr. WELCH: Senator, I think it hurts you, too, sir.

Senator McCARTHY: I would like to finish this.

Mr. Welch has been filibustering this hearing, he has been talking day after day about how he wants to get anyone tainted with communism out before sundown. I know Mr. Cohn would rather not have me go into this. I intend to, however. Mr. Welch talks about any sense of decency. If I say anything which is not the truth, then I would like to know about it. . . .

And, Mr. Welch . . . I have heard you and every one else talk so much about laying the truth upon the table that when I hear—and it is completely phony, Mr. Welch, I have listened to you for a long time—when you say "Now, before sundown, you must get these people out of Government," I want to have it very clear, very clear that you were not so serious about that when you tried to recommend this young man for this committee.

And may I say, Mr. Welch, in fairness to you, I have reason to believe that you did not know about his Communist-front record at the time you recommended him. I don't think you would have recommended him to the committee if you knew that.

I think it is entirely possible you learned that after you recommended him.

Senator MUNDT: The Chair would like to say again that he does not believe that Mr. Welch recommended Mr. Fisher as counsel for this committee, because he has through his office all the recommendations that were made. He does not recall any that came from Mr. Welch, and that would include Mr. Fisher.

Senator McCARTHY: Let me ask Mr. Welch. You brought him down, did you not, to act as your assistant?

Mr. WELCH: Mr. McCarthy, I will not discuss this with you further. You have sat within 6 feet of me, and could have asked me about Fred Fisher. You have brought it out. If there is a God in heaven, it will do neither you nor your cause any good. I will not discuss it further. . . .

Excerpted from U.S. Congress. Senate. Committee on Government Operations. *Special Senate Investigation on Charges and Countercharges Involving: Secretary of the Army Robert T. Stevens, John G. Adams, H. Struve Hensel and Senator Joe McCarthy, Roy M. Cohn, and Francis P. Carr. Hearing Before the Special Subcommittee on Investigations, Pursuant to S. Res. 189, Part 59.* 83rd Cong., 2nd sess., June 9, 1954.

# 25. The Censure of Senator McCarthy
## *December 2, 1954*

*Resolved,* That the Senator from Wisconsin, Mr. McCARTHY, failed to cooperate with the Subcommittee on Privileges and Elections of the Senate Committee on Rules and Administration in clearing up matters referred to that subcommittee which concerned his conduct as a Senator and affected the honor of the Senate and, instead, repeatedly abused the subcommittee and its members who were trying to carry out assigned duties, thereby obstructing the constitutional processes of the Senate, and that this conduct of the Senator from Wisconsin, Mr. McCARTHY, is contrary to senatorial traditions and is hereby condemned.

SEC. 2. The Senator from Wisconsin, Mr. McCARTHY, in writing to the chairman of the Select Committee To Study Censure Charges (Mr. WATKINS) after the select committee had issued its report and before the report was presented to the Senate charging three members of the Select Committee with "deliberate deception" and "fraud" for failure to disqualify themselves; in stating to the press on November 4, 1954, that the special Senate session that was to begin November 8, 1954, was a "lynch-party"; in repeatedly describing this special Senate session as a "lynch bee" in a nation-wide television and radio show on November 7, 1954; in stating to the public press on November 13, 1954, that the chairman of the select committee (Mr. WATKINS) was guilty of "the most unusual, most cowardly things I've ever heard of" and stating further: "I expected he would be afraid to answer the questions, but didn't think he'd be stupid enough to make a public statement"; and in characterizing the said committee as the "unwitting handmaiden," "involuntary agent" and "attorneys-in-fact" of the Communist Party and in charging that the said committee in writing its report "imitated Communist methods—that it distorted, misrepresented, and omitted in its effort to manufacture a plausible rationalization" in support of its recommendations to the Senate, which characterizations and charges were contained in a statement released to the press and inserted in the CONGRESSIONAL RECORD of November 10, 1954, acted contrary to senatorial ethics and tended to bring the Senate into dishonor and disrepute, to obstruct the constitutional processes of the Senate, and to impair its dignity; and such conduct is hereby condemned.

U.S. Congress. Senate. *Senate Resolution 301.* 83rd Cong., 2nd sess. *Congressional Record,* December 2, 1954: 16392. http://usinfo.state.gov/usa/infousa/facts/democrac/60.htm (accessed July 15, 2004).

# Bill Authorizes Detention Camps and Requires Communist Registration

26. Internal Security Act of 1950, Passed by Congress over President Harry S. Truman's Veto on September 23, 1950

27. President Harry S. Truman's Veto of the Internal Security Act, September 22, 1950

## INTRODUCTION

Just five years after more than 100,000 people of Japanese ancestry—many of them American citizens—were released from detention camps and allowed to return to their homes on the West Coast, in 1950 Congress passed a new law allowing detention without charges in certain circumstances (*see* Japanese Internment During World War II, p. 27).

The law, the Emergency Detention Act of 1950, was part of a larger measure known overall as the Internal Security Act of 1950. The detention law authorized the president to declare an "Internal Security Emergency" if the United States was invaded, Congress declared war, or an insurrection occurred within the United States "in aid of a foreign enemy."

The bill provided that during an emergency, "the President, acting through the Attorney General, is hereby authorized to apprehend and by order detain . . . each person as to whom there is reasonable ground to believe that such person probably will engage in, or probably will conspire with others to engage in, acts of espionage or of sabotage." The measure required no court order before a person was detained and permitted only limited judicial review after detainment.

Congress approved the bill amid a huge "Red Scare" that swept across the United States. The bill came on the heels of charges by Sen. Joseph R. McCarthy, R-Wis., that communists had infiltrated the State Department. Millions of Americans believed that communists both within and outside the federal government threatened homeland security (*see* McCarthy Charges That Communists Infest the State Department, p. 40).

A second major provision in the overall bill required "communist-action organizations" and "communist-front organizations" to register with the attorney general. The law required both types of groups to provide the names and addresses of all officers and an accounting of all money received and spent.

Communist-front organizations were further required to provide the name and address of every member. All members of communist organizations were also barred from obtaining or using U.S. passports, and certain aliens were barred from entering the United States. Other provisions placed further restrictions on members of communist organizations [Document 26].

President Harry S. Truman vetoed the bill on September 22, 1950, contending that it was unconstitutional and would actually help communists instead of hurting them. "We can and we will prevent espionage, sabotage, or other actions endangering our national security," Truman wrote in a lengthy veto message. "But we would betray our finest traditions if we attempted, as this bill would attempt, to curb the simple expression of opinion. This we should never do, no matter how distasteful the opinion may be to the vast majority of our people. The course proposed by this bill would delight the communists, for it would make a mockery of the Bill of Rights and of our claims to stand for freedom in the world" [Document 27].

Nonetheless, the next day—September 23, 1950—the House and Senate overrode Truman's veto and the Internal Security Act of 1950 became law.

In 1951 Congress appropriated $1.5 million to place six detention camps on a standby basis. Years earlier, the FBI had started compiling a list of people who should be immediately detained during any national emergency. By the time Congress passed the Emergency Detention Act, the list included almost 12,000 names. Nearly all of those listed were members of the Communist Party.

"The United States could intern 5,000 spies and saboteurs almost immediately in the event of war, an invasion or an insurrection," a *New York Times* reporter who visited three of the detention camps wrote on December 27, 1955. "Thousands more could be put in detention camp as fast as they were rounded up."

No one was ever detained under the Emergency Detention Act of 1950. The camps were apparently maintained until the late 1950s, when they were turned over to other uses. But in his classic 1970 book *The System of Freedom of Expression,* Yale Law School professor Thomas I. Emerson argued that the camps themselves were unimportant. "The significant issue is not whether detention camps are ready for immediate occupancy; the government could always improvise physical facilities," Emerson wrote. "The question is whether the very existence of the detention camp provisions in [the Emergency Detention Act of 1950] has a depressant effect upon the system of freedom of expression. There can hardly be any doubt that they have."

Congress finally repealed the Emergency Detention Act of 1950 on September 25, 1971. To make its intention absolutely clear, Congress added a provision to the repeal measure: "No citizen shall be imprisoned or otherwise detained by the United States except pursuant to an Act of Congress." The provision remains law today. Nonetheless, in the war on terrorism President George W. Bush has authorized detention of some American citizens as "enemy combatants" without congressional approval and has denied them access to the legal system.

Meanwhile, a number of legal cases involving the communist registration provisions of the Internal Security Act of 1950 wound their way through the courts for fifteen years. Ultimately, no group was ever forced to register.

Nonetheless, Emerson wrote that the provisions unconstitutionally stifled the right to freedom of association. "There was no question but that the Communist Party, like other political parties, was engaging in conduct that constituted expression within the meaning of the First Amendment," he wrote. "Nor can it be seriously doubted that the restrictions imposed by the registration provisions were intended to and would in fact have seriously crippled the organization and probably forced it wholly underground. To treat the statute as one that simply required disclosure for purposes of informing the public and thereby facilitating operation of the system of freedom of expression was pure fiction. . . . [In addition], the statute did not require a showing of advocacy of force or violence . . . or any other illegal conduct, as a precondition to ordering registration."

---

# 26. Internal Security Act of 1950, Passed by Congress over President Harry S. Truman's Veto

*September 23, 1950*

## Title I—Subversive Activities Control

### *. . . Necessity for Legislation*

SEC. 2. As a result of evidence adduced before various committees of the Senate and House of Representatives, the Congress hereby finds that—

(1) There exists a world Communist movement which, in its origins, its development, and its present practice, is a worldwide revolutionary movement whose purpose it is, by treachery, deceit, infiltration into other groups (governmental and otherwise), espionage, sabotage, terrorism, and any other means deemed necessary, to establish a Communist totalitarian dictatorship in the countries throughout the world through the medium of a world-wide Communist organization. . . .

(4) The direction and control of the world Communist movement is vested in and exercised by the Communist dictatorship of a foreign country [Soviet Union].

(5) The Communist dictatorship of such foreign country, in exercising such direction and control and in furthering the purposes of the world Communist movement, establishes or causes the establishment of, and utilizes, in various countries, action organizations which are not free and independent organizations, but are sections of a world-wide Communist organization and are controlled, directed, and subject to the discipline of the Communist dictatorship of such foreign country.

(6) The Communist action organizations so established and utilized in various countries, acting under such control, direction, and discipline, endeavor to carry out the objectives of the world Communist movement by bringing about the overthrow of existing governments by any available means, including force if necessary, and setting up Communist totalitarian dictatorships which will be subservient to the most powerful existing Communist totalitarian dictatorship. Although such organizations usually designate themselves as political parties, they are in fact constituent elements of the world-wide Communist movement and promote the objectives of such movement by conspiratorial and coercive tactics. . . .

(7) In carrying on the activities referred to in paragraph (6), such Communist organizations in various countries are organized on a secret, conspiratorial basis and operate to a substantial extent through organizations, commonly known as "Communist fronts," which in most instances are created and maintained, or used, in such manner as to conceal the facts as to their true character and purposes and their membership. . . .

(9) In the United States those individuals who knowingly and willfully participate in the world Communist movement, when they so participate, in effect repudiate their allegiance to the United States, and in effect transfer their allegiance to the foreign country in which is vested the direction and control of the world Communist movement. . . .

(11) The agents of communism have devised clever and ruthless espionage and sabotage tactics which are carried out in many instances in form or manner successfully evasive of existing law. . . .

(13) There are, under our present immigration laws, numerous aliens who have been found to be deportable, many of whom are in the subversive, criminal, or immoral classes who are free to roam the country at will without supervision or control. . . .

(15) The Communist movement in the United States is an organization numbering thousands of adherents, rigidly and ruthlessly disciplined. Awaiting and seeking to advance a moment when the United States may be so far extended by foreign engagements, so far divided in counsel, or so far in industrial or financial straits, that overthrow of the Government of the United States by force and violence may seem possible of achievement, it seeks converts far and wide by an extensive system of schooling and indoctrination. . . .

## Certain Prohibited Acts

SEC. 4. (a) It shall be unlawful for any person knowingly to combine, conspire, or agree with any other person to perform any act which would substantially contribute to the establishment within the United States of a totalitarian dictatorship . . . the direction and control of which is to be vested in, or exercised by or under the domination or control of, any foreign government, foreign organization, or foreign individual; *Provided, however,* That this subsection shall not apply to the proposal of a constitutional amendment. . . .

### *Registration and Annual Reports of Communist Organizations*

SEC. 7. (a) Each Communist-action organization . . . shall, within the time specified . . . register with the Attorney General, on a form prescribed by him by regulations, as a Communist-action organization.

(b) Each Communist-front organization . . . shall, within the time specified . . . register with the Attorney General, on a form prescribed by him by regulations, as a Communist-front organization. . . .

(d) The registration made under subsection (a) or (b) shall be accompanied by a registration statement, to be prepared and filed in such manner and form as the Attorney General shall by regulations prescribe, containing the following information:

(1) The name of the organization and the address of its principal office.

(2) The name and last-known address of each individual who is . . . an officer of the organization, with the designation or title of the office so held, and with a brief statement of the duties and functions of such individual or such officer.

(3) An accounting . . . of all moneys received and expended (including the sources from which received and the purposes for which expended) by the organization. . . .

(4) In the case of a Communist-action organization, the name and last-known address of each individual who was a member of the organization at any time during the period of twelve full calendar months preceding the filing of such statement. . . .

## Amending Act of October 16, 1918

SEC. 22. The Act of October 16, 1918 . . . is amended to read as follows: "That any alien who is a member of any one of the following classes shall be excluded from admission into the United States:

"(1) Aliens who seek to enter the United States whether solely, principally, or incidentally, to engage in activities which would be prejudicial to the public interest, or would endanger the welfare or safety of the United States;

"(2) Aliens who, at any time, shall be or shall have been members of any of the following classes:

"(A) Aliens who are anarchists;

"(B) Aliens who advocate or teach, or who are members of or affiliated with any organization that advocates or teaches, opposition to all organized government. . . .

"(G) Aliens who write or publish . . . any written or printed matter, advocating or teaching opposition to all organized government, or advocating (i) the overthrow by force or violence or other unconstitutional means of the Government of the United States or of all forms of law; or . . . (v) the economic, international, and governmental doctrines of world communism or the economic and governmental doctrines of any other form of totalitarianism.

"(3) Aliens with respect to whom there is reason to believe that such aliens would, after entry, be likely to (A) engage in activities which would be prohibited by the laws of the United States relating to espionage, sabotage, public disorder, or in other activity subversive to the national security. . . .

## Title II—Emergency Detention

### *Findings of Fact and Declaration of Purpose*

SEC. 101. As a result of evidence adduced before various committees of the Senate and the House of Representatives, the Congress hereby finds that—. . . .

(14) The detention of persons who there is reasonable ground to believe probably will commit or conspire with others to commit espionage or sabotage is, in a time of internal security emergency, essential to the common defense and to the safety and security of the territory, the people and the Constitution of the United States.

(15) It is also essential that such detention in an emergency involving the internal security of the Nation shall be so authorized, executed, restricted and reviewed as to prevent any interference with the constitutional rights and privileges of any persons, and at the same time shall be sufficiently effective to permit the performance by the Congress and the President of their constitutional duties to preserve, protect and defend the Constitution, the Government and the people of the United States.

## Declaration of "Internal Security Emergency"

SEC. 102. (a) In the event of any one of the following:

(1) Invasion of the territory of the United States or its possessions,

(2) Declaration of war by Congress, or

(3) Insurrection within the United States in aid of a foreign enemy,

and if, upon the occurrence of one or more of the above, the President shall find that the proclamation of an emergency pursuant to this section is essential to the preservation, protection and defense of the Constitution, and to the common defense and safety of the territory and people of the United States, the President is authorized to make public proclamation of the existence of an "Internal Security Emergency". . . .

SEC. 103. (a) Whenever there shall be in existence such an emergency, the President, acting through the Attorney General, is hereby authorized to apprehend and by order detain, pursuant to the provisions of this title, each person as to whom there is reasonable ground to believe that such person probably will engage in, or probably will conspire with others to engage in, acts of espionage or of sabotage. . . .

SEC. 109. . . .

(h) In deciding the question of the existence of reasonable ground to believe a person probably will engage in or conspire with others to engage in espionage or sabotage, the Attorney General, any preliminary hearing officer, and the Board of Detention Review are authorized to consider evidence of the following:

(1) Whether such person has knowledge of or has received or given instruction or assignment in the espionage, counterespionage, or sabotage service or procedures of a government or political party of a foreign country, or in the espionage, counterespionage, or sabotage service or procedures of the Communist Party of the United States or of any other organization or political party which seeks to overthrow or destroy by force and violence the Government of the United States or any of its subdivisions and to substitute therefor a totalitarian dictatorship controlled by a foreign government. . . .

(2) Any past act or acts of espionage or sabotage committed by such person, or any past participation by such person in any attempt or conspiracy to commit any act of espionage or sabotage, against the United States, any agency or instrumentality thereof, or any public or private national defense facility within the United States;

(3) Activity in the espionage or sabotage operations of, or the holding at any time after January 1, 1949, of membership in, the Communist Party of the United States or any other organization or political party which seeks to overthrow or destroy by force and violence the Government of the United States. . . .

Excerpted from U.S. Congress. *An Act to Protect the United States Against Certain Un-American and Subversive Activities by Requiring Registration of Communist Organizations, and for Other Purposes.* 81st Cong., 2nd sess. *Congressional Record,* daily ed. (September 23, 1950): 987–1031.

# 27. President Harry S. Truman's Veto of the Internal Security Act

*September 22, 1950*

I return herewith, without my approval, H.R. 9490, the proposed "Internal Security Act of 1950."

I am taking this action only after the most serious study and reflection and after consultation with the security and intelligence agencies of the Government. The Department of Justice, the Department of Defense, the Central Intelligence Agency, and the Department of State have all advised me that the bill would seriously damage the security and the intelligence operations for which they are responsible. They have strongly expressed the hope that the bill would not become law.

This is an omnibus bill containing many different legislative proposals with only one thing in common: they are all represented to be "anti-communist." But when the many complicated pieces of the bill are analyzed in detail, a startling result appears.

H.R. 9490 would not hurt the communists. Instead, it would help them. Specifically, some of the principal objections to the bill are as follows:

1. It would aid potential enemies by requiring the publication of a complete list of vital defense plants, laboratories, and other installations.
2. It would require the Department of Justice and its Federal Bureau of Investigation to waste immense amounts of time and energy attempting to carry out its unworkable registration provisions.
3. It would deprive us of the great assistance of many aliens in intelligence matters.
4. It would antagonize friendly governments.
5. It would put the Government of the United States in the thought control business.
6. It would make it easier for subversive aliens to become naturalized as United States citizens.
7. It would give Government officials vast powers to harass all of our citizens in the exercise of their right of free speech.

Legislation with these consequences is not necessary to meet the real dangers which communism presents to our free society. Those dangers are serious, and must be met. But this bill would hinder us, not help us, in meeting them. Fortunately, we already have on the books strong laws which give us most of the protection we need from the real dangers of treason, espionage, sabotage, and actions looking to the overthrow of our Government by force and violence. Most of the provisions of this bill have no relation to these real dangers. . . .

Sections 1 through 17 are designed for two purposes. First, they are intended to force communist organizations to register and to divulge certain information about themselves—information on their officers, their finances, and, in some cases, their membership. These provisions would in practice be ineffective, and would result in obtaining no information about communists that the FBI and our other security agencies do not already have. But in trying to enforce these sections, we would have to spend a great deal of time, effort, and money—all to no good purpose.

Second, those provisions are intended to impose various penalties on communists and others covered by the terms of the bill. So far as communists are concerned, all these penalties which can be practicably enforced are already in effect under existing laws and procedures. But the language of the bill is so broad and vague that it might well result in penalizing the legitimate activities of people who are not communists at all, but loyal citizens. . . .

Sections 100 through 117 of this bill (Title II) are intended to give the Government power, in the event of invasion, war, or insurrection in the United States in aid of a foreign enemy, to seize and hold persons who could be expected to attempt acts of espionage or sabotage, even though they had as yet committed no crime. It may be that legislation of this type should be on the statute books. But the provisions in H.R. 9490 would very probably prove ineffective to achieve the objective sought, since they would not suspend the writ of habeas corpus, and under our legal system to detain a man not charged with a crime would raise serious constitutional questions unless the writ of habeas corpus were suspended. Furthermore, it may well be that other persons than those covered by these provisions would be more important to detain in the event of emergency. This whole problem, therefore, should clearly be studied more thoroughly before further legislative action along these lines is considered.

In brief, when all the provisions of H.R. 9490 are considered together, it is evident that the great bulk of them are not directed toward the real and present dangers that exist from communism. Instead of striking blows at communism, they would strike blows at our own liberties and at our position in the forefront of those working for freedom in the world. At a time when our young men are fighting for freedom in Korea, it would be tragic to advance the objectives of communism in this country, as this bill would do.

In so far as the bill would require registration by the Communist Party itself, it does not endanger our traditional liberties. However, the application of the registration requirements to so-called communist-front organizations can be the greatest danger to freedom of speech, press and assembly, since the Alien and Sedition Laws of 1798. This danger arises out of the criteria or standards to be applied in determining whether an organization is a communist-front organization.

There would be no serious problem if the bill required proof that an organization was controlled and financed by the Communist Party before it could be classified as a communist-front organization. However, recognizing the difficulty of proving those matters, the bill would permit such a determination to be based solely upon "the extent to which the positions taken or advanced by it from time to time on matters of policy do not deviate from those" of the communist movement. . . .

The basic error of these sections is that they move in the direction of suppressing opinion and belief. This would be a very dangerous course to take, not because we have any sympathy for communist opinions, but because any governmental stifling of the free expression of opinion is a long step toward totalitarianism.

There is no more fundamental axiom of American freedom than the familiar statement: In a free country, we punish men for the crimes they commit, but never for the opinions they have. And the reason this is so fundamental to freedom is not, as many suppose, that it protects the few unorthodox from suppression by the majority. To permit freedom of expression is primarily for the benefit of the majority, because it protects criticism, and criticism leads to progress.

We can and we will prevent espionage, sabotage, or other actions endangering our national security. But we would betray our finest traditions if we attempted, as this bill would attempt, to curb the simple expression of opinion. This we should never do, no matter how distasteful the opinion may be to the vast majority of our people. The course proposed by this bill would delight the communists, for it would make a mockery of the Bill of Rights and of our claims to stand for freedom in the world. . . .

Section 22 is so contrary to our national interests that it would actually put the Government into the business of thought control by requiring the deportation of any alien who distributes or publishes, or who is affiliated with an organization which distributes or publishes, any written or printed matter advocating (or merely expressing belief in) the economic and governmental doctrines of any form of totalitarianism. This provision does not require an evil intent or purpose on the part of the alien, as does a similar provision in the Smith Act. Thus, the Attorney General would be required to deport any alien operating or connected with a well-stocked bookshop containing books on economics or politics written by supporters of the present government of Spain, of Yugoslavia, or any one of a number of other countries. Section 25 would make the same aliens ineligible for citizenship. There should be no room in our laws for such hysterical provisions. The next logical step would be to "burn the books.". . .

No considerations of expediency can justify the enactment of such a bill as this, a bill which would so greatly weaken our liberties and give aid and comfort to those who would destroy us. I have, therefore, no alternative but to return this bill without my approval, and I earnestly request the Congress to reconsider its action.

HARRY S. TRUMAN

Excerpted from U.S. Executive Office of the President. *Veto of the Internal Security Bill.* September 22, 1950. *Public Papers of the Presidents of the United States: Harry S. Truman, 1945–1953.* Washington, D.C.: Government Printing Office, 1966. http://www.trumanlibrary.org/publicpapers/index.php?pid=883&st=Subversive&st1= (accessed September 1, 2004).

# Reviews of Intelligence Agencies

## INTRODUCTION

Every investigation of the terrorist attacks on September 11, 2001, has sharply criticized U.S. intelligence agencies, and some have called for sweeping changes in the organization and implementation of intelligence efforts. But concerns about the organization, coordination, and capabilities of U.S. intelligence programs existed for more than a half-century before the terrorist attacks.

The Central Intelligence Agency (CIA), the best known of the federal intelligence agencies, was created in 1947 as a direct result of World War II. "The surprise attack on Pearl Harbor by the Japanese on December 7, 1941, brought America into the war and revealed a significant failure on the part of the U.S. intelligence apparatus," the Commission on the Roles and Responsibilities of the United States Intelligence Community wrote in its March 1996 report, *Preparing for the 21st Century: An Appraisal of U.S. Intelligence.*

As subsequent investigations found, intelligence had been handled in a casual, uncoordinated manner, and there had been insufficient attention to certain collection requirements. The lack of coordination among agencies, principally the Army and the Navy, resulted in a failure to provide timely dissemination of relevant information to key decisionmakers. Moreover, intelligence analysts had grossly underestimated Japanese capabilities and intentions, revealing a tendency to misunderstand Japanese actions by looking at them with American cultural biases. After the war, the resolve of America's leaders "never again" to permit Pearl Harbor largely prompted the establishment of a centralized intelligence structure.

On July 27, 1947, President Harry S. Truman signed into law the National Security Act of 1947, which created the CIA to coordinate and centralize intelligence information gathered by a variety of federal agencies. It joined an "intelligence community" which today consists of fourteen agencies besides the CIA that have intelligence responsibilities: the Federal Bureau of Investigation, the Department of State, the Department of the Treasury, the Department of Homeland Security, the Department of Energy, the Defense Intelligence Agency, the Coast Guard, the National Security Agency, the National Geospatial-Intelligence Agency, the National Reconnaissance Office, and separate intelligence operations in the Army, Navy, Air Force, and Marine Corps.

Over time, the director of central intelligence was charged with three missions:

- Serving as the president's chief adviser on intelligence issues.
- Running the CIA, including its covert operations.
- Overseeing and coordinating efforts by all the other members of the intelligence community.

Although he was charged with coordinating the intelligence community, the director of central intelligence lacked the authority needed to actually do the job. The other agencies fiercely protected their turf, and some restricted the amount of information they would share with the CIA. The CIA received only about 15 percent of the overall intelligence budget, and its director had no authority over the remaining 85 percent that primarily went to the Defense Department.

The CIA had barely hired its first agents before various commissions and committees started examining its role, management, and interagency relations. The initial reviews were not flattering. The first report, released in January 1949 by a three-member panel appointed by the National Security Council, said the CIA was not coordinating intelligence activities among agencies, efforts to correlate and analyze intelligence data were poorly organized, and the director had insufficient contact with day-to-day CIA operations. Over subsequent years, many similar reviews of the CIA in particular and the intelligence community in general followed.

One of the harshest critiques was completed in March 1971 by James Schlesinger, who at the time was deputy director of the Office of Management and Budget. President Richard Nixon had asked Schlesinger to recommend structural changes in the intelligence community. "The operations of the intelligence community have produced two disturbing phenomena," Schlesinger wrote. "The first is an impressive rise in their size and cost. The second is an apparent inability to achieve a commensurate improvement in the scope and overall quality of intelligence products. . . ." [Document 28].

Schlesinger's scathing report remained classified until 1998, when most of it was released under the Freedom of Information Act. Ironically, Schlesinger later served as CIA director for six months in early 1973 and as secretary of defense from the later part of 1973 to 1975.

As part of an exhaustive investigation of the U.S. intelligence community in the mid-1970s, a Senate committee looked at the quality of intelligence reports produced by the CIA. The quality of the reports had improved but "much remains to be done," concluded the Select Committee to Study Governmental Operations with Respect to Intelligence Activities, better known as the Church Committee because its chairman was Sen. Frank Church, D-Idaho [Document 29].

The committee especially criticized the CIA's focus on "current events" research:

> The "current events" approach has fostered the problem of "incremental analysis," the tendency to focus myopically on the latest piece of information without systematic consideration of an accumulated body of integrated evidence. Analysts in their haste to compile the day's traffic, tend to lose sight of underlying factors and relationships. . . .

A 1993 report by the National Performance Review, an effort spearheaded by Vice President Al Gore that examined the entire federal government, foreshadowed one of the most significant criticisms of intelligence agencies following the September 2001 terrorist attacks. Each intelligence agency had developed its own computer system, the report found, and none of them could communicate with each other. "The [Intelligence] Community's business is information," the report said. "Without immediate and aggressive action, the status quo in its management of information will result in the equivalent of bankruptcy" [Document 30].

---

# 28. Schlesinger Report on the Intelligence Community
## March 10, 1971

### I. Introduction: The Costs and Benefits of Intelligence

The operations of the intelligence community have produced two disturbing phenomena. The first is an impressive rise in their size and cost. The second is an apparent inability to achieve a commensurate improvement in the scope and overall quality of intelligence products. . . .

The growth in raw intelligence . . . has come to serve as a proxy for improved analysis, inference, and estimation. . . .

## II. Cost Trends

1. The distribution of intelligence functions has become increasingly fragmented and disorganized. . . .
2. The community's activities are dominated by collection competition and have become unproductively duplicative. . . .
   - The blurring of traditional boundaries has encouraged community members to engage in a competitive struggle for survival and dominance, primarily through new technology, which has resulted in the redundant acquisition of data at virtually all levels. . . .
   - Collection capabilities remain in operation beyond their useful lives. As older systems lose their attractiveness at the national level, they are taken over at the command or tactical level where they duplicate higher level activities or collect data of little value.
   - Simultaneously, compartmentalization within various security systems has served to hide or obscure competitive capabilities from evaluation, comparison, and tradeoff analysis.
3. The community's growth is largely unplanned and unguided.
   - Serious forward planning is often lacking as decisions are made about the allocation of resources.
   - The consumer frequently fails to specify his product needs for the producer; the producer, uncertain about eventual demands, encourages the collector to provide data without selectivity or priority; and the collector emphasizes quantity rather than quality.
4. The community's activities have become exceedingly expensive. . . .
   - In the absence of planning and guidance, internally generated values predominate in the community's institutions. These values favor increasingly sophisticated and expensive collection technologies at the expense of analytical capabilities. . . .
   - While the budgetary process might be used to curb some of the more obvious excesses, it cannot substitute for centralized management of the community.

## III. Questions About the Product

In a world of perfect information, there would be no uncertainties about the present and future intentions, capabilities, and activities of foreign powers. Information, however, is bound to be imperfect for the most part. Consequently, the intelligence community can at best reduce the uncertainties and construct plausible hypotheses about these factors on the basis of what continues to be partial and often conflicting evidence.

Despite the richness of the data made available by modern methods of collection, and the rising costs of their acquisition, it is not at all clear that our hypotheses about foreign intentions, capabilities, and activities have improved commensurately in scope and quality. Nor can it be asserted with confidence that the intelligence community has shown much initiative in developing the full range of possible explanations in light of available data. . . .

Difficulties of this kind with the intelligence product are all the more disturbing because the need to explore and test a number of hypotheses will, if anything, expand. . . .

The community's heavy emphasis on collection is itself detrimental to correcting product problems. Because each organization sees the maintenance and expansion of its collection capabilities as the principal route to survival and strength within the community, there is a strong presumption in today's intelligence set-up that additional data collection rather than improved analysis will provide the answer to particular intelligence problems. It has become commonplace to translate product criticism into demands for enlarged collection efforts. . . .

The inevitable result is that production remains the stepchild of the community. It is a profession that lacks strong military and civilian career incentives, even within CIA. The analysts, with a heavy burden of responsibility, find themselves swamped with data. The consumers, at the same time, treat their product as a free good, so that demand exceeds supply, priorities are not established, the system becomes overloaded and the quality of the output suffers. . . . Under such difficult conditions, it is not surprising that hypotheses tend to harden into dogma, that their sensitivity to changed conditions is not articulated, and that new data are not sought to test them.


## IV. Organizational Dilemmas

Questions about cost and product might exist even if the intelligence community possessed strong leadership. It is noteworthy, however, that they have arisen under conditions the most marked of which is a lack of institutions governing the community with the authority and responsibility to resolve issues without excessive compromise, allocate resources according to criteria of effectiveness, and consider the relationship between cost and substantive output from a national perspective. . . .

There is another reason why the [bill creating the Central Intelligence Agency] did so little to provide strong leadership for the community: powerful interests in the Military Services and elsewhere opposed (and continue to oppose) more centralized management of intelligence activities. Partly, this opposition arises from the belief of the Services that direct control over intelligence programs is essential if they are to conduct successful military operations; partly, it results from bureaucratic concerns. The Services are reluctant to accept assurance that information from systems not controlled by them will be available as and when they require it. . . .

Realistically, it is clear that the DCI [Director of Central Intelligence], as his office is now constituted, cannot be expected to perform effectively the community-wide leadership role because:

- As an agency head he bears a number of weighty operational and advisory responsibilities which limit the effort he can devote to community-wide management.
- He bears a particularly heavy burden for the planning and conduct of covert operations.
- His multiple roles as community leader, agency head, and intelligence adviser to the President, and to a number of sensitive executive committees, are mutually conflicting.
- He is a competitor for resources within the community owing to his responsibilities as Director of CIA, which has large collection programs of its own; thus he cannot be wholly objective in providing guidance for community-wide collection.
- He controls only [redacted] percent of the community's resources and must therefore rely on persuasion to influence his colleagues regarding the allocation and management of the other [redacted] percent, which is appropriated to the Department of Defense. Since Defense is legally responsible for these very large resources, it feels that it cannot be bound by outside advice on how they should be used.
- The DCI is outranked by other departmental heads who report directly to the President and are his immediate supervisors on the National Security Council. . . .

Even within the Department of Defense, there is no centralized management of intelligence resources and activities. . . .

## IX. Toward Improvements in the Product

Much of the emphasis by the intelligence community and the bulk of its resources go to the high technology necessary to overcome barriers to information in the USSR and China. Yet this stress on the technology of collection—admittedly important—comes at a time when improved analysis is even more important. . . .

- Stronger incentives to attract good analysts, better career opportunities to hold them as analysts instead of forcing them to become supervisors to achieve promotion, and a more effective use of personnel already trained and experienced in intelligence [are needed]. . . .

Excerpted from U.S. Executive Office of the President. Office of Management and Budget. *A Review of the Intelligence Community*. March 10,

1971. Classified as Top Secret until a redacted version was released in 1998. http://www.fas.org/irp/cia/product/review1971.pdf (accessed September 1, 2004).

## 29. Church Committee Report on CIA Intelligence Activities
*April 26, 1976*

### XII. CIA Production of Finished Intelligence

The main purpose of the intelligence system of the United States is to provide the President, his chief advisers, and the Congress in appropriate ways with the best information about activities abroad that can be obtained. It is not surprising, therefore, that the quality of finished intelligence produced by the intelligence agencies has been a source of continuing concern and controversy. Policymakers are understandably seldom satisfied with the intelligence they receive, for they want and need intelligence which eliminates uncertainties and ensures successful policy decisions. Since such perfection is unattainable, however, the realistic question is how to evaluate and improve the quality of our finished intelligence. This is an extremely complicated and difficult area. The simple answer is that there are no objective criteria or standards that can be universally applied. In the end, the assessment by policymakers of the value and quality of our finished intelligence is necessarily subjective. There is a record of steadily improved quality over the years, but the need for a higher level of performance is accepted, both at the policy level and among the intelligence agencies of the U.S. Government. . . .

The CIA for its part has, in the view of the Committee, made creditable efforts to improve the quality of finished intelligence, although much remains to be done. . . .

Although the provision of intelligence analysis to policymakers is the major purpose of the intelligence mission, the production of intelligence has been referred to as the "stepchild of the community." It is an area which has been overshadowed by the glamour of clandestine activities and the lure of exotic technical collection systems. Yet the basic rationale for intelligence operations is the provision of information to the people who need it in order to do their jobs—the President and other senior officials responsible for the formulation and implementation of foreign policy.

The Pearl Harbor experience, which so heavily influenced the establishment of the Central Intelligence Agency in 1947, pointed to the need for the collection, coordination, and analysis of all national intelligence in a centralized fashion, so that policymakers could be assured of receiving all the information they needed, when they needed it. Finished intelligence represents the "payoff" of investment in the plethora of collection activities.

The CIA and its predecessor body, the Central Intelligence Group, were established to rectify the duplication and biases that existed in the intelligence production of the State Department and the military services. By reviewing and analyzing the data collected by these departments, the CIA was to provide senior government officials with high-quality, objective intelligence. In practice, however, the CIA has given precedence to independent collection and production, becoming a competing department in the dissemination of information.

Historically, the departments resisted providing their data to the Agency and thereby prevented the CIA from fulfilling its designated role in the production of "coordinated" intelligence. Moreover, individual Directors of Central Intelligence have not been consistent advocates of the Agency's intelligence production function. For the DCIs, the demands of administering an organization with thousands of employees and in particular, the requirements of supervising clandestine operations encroached on the intended priority of intelligence production. . . .

In recent years, however, and particularly with the introduction of advanced technical collection systems, the requirement for bringing together the vast quantities of information into useable analytic forms has become the primary concern of the intelligence community. . . .

### C. The Relationship Between Intelligence and Policy

The relationship between intelligence and policy is a delicate and carefully balanced one. One witness told the Select Committee that there is a "natural tension" between the two and that

> if the policy-intelligence relationship is to work, there must be mutual respect, trust, civility, and also a certain distance. Intelligence people must provide honest and best judgments and avoid intrusion on decisionmaking or attempts to influence it. Policymakers must assume the integrity of the intelligence provided and avoid attempts to get materials suited to their tastes. . . .

While intelligence analysts have a very good record in the area of technical assessment (e.g., hard data on foreign military hardware), the record is weaker in qualitative judgments, trend forecasting, and political estimating. . . .

Some policymakers feel that intelligence analysts have not been especially helpful to policymakers on the more subtle questions of political, economic, and military intentions of foreign groups and leaders. The view from the top is, of course, very different from the view held by analysts in the departments and agencies or in the field. Too often analysts are not willing to address such questions directly. Analysts tend to believe that policymakers want answers instead of insights. Some consumers argue that intelligence analysts lack sufficient awareness of the real nature of the national security decisonmaking process—how it really works, where and how intelligence fits in, and what kinds of information are important.

On the other hand, the Select Committee is concerned that analysts are not always kept sufficiently informed, in a timely fashion, of U.S. policies and activities which affect their analyses and estimates. The Committee is concerned that the secrecy and compartmentation surrounding security policy decisionmaking affects the relevance and quality of intelligence analysis. . . .

### E. The Personnel System

The Agency's promotion system is structured in such a way that the most outstanding lower-level people are singled out for advancement into managerial positions. Such a system works well for the purposes of the Directorate of Operations (DDO), where the skills necessary for good management are essentially the same as those required of a good case officer. But when applied to the DDI [Directorate for Intelligence], that system encourages the best analysts to assume supervisory positions, reducing the time available to utilize their analytical skills. . . .

Some analysts complain that the personnel system has fostered too much bureaucratic "layering," and that there are too many people writing reports *about* reports. The effects are predictable. In the words of former DCI and Secretary of Defense James Schlesinger, "If you've got too much specialization and pigeonholing of people, you get the kind of people in the intelligence game who don't mind being pigeonholed, and the entire U.S. intelligence establishment is too much bureaucratized." The Intelligence Community (IC) staff, in its post-mortems of major U.S. intelligence failures, has pointed in all cases to the shortage of talented personnel. . . .

### H. The Nature of the Production Process: Consensus Versus Competition

The nature of the production process can itself undermine the quality of the product. That process is consensus-oriented. . . . The coordination process, however necessary and desirable, may tend to produce a "reinforcing consensus," whereby divergent views of individual analysts can become "submerged in a sea of conventional collective wisdom," and doubts or disagreements can simply disappear in the face of mutually reinforcing agreements. . . .

Some consumers complain that finished intelligence frequently lacks clarity, especially clarity of judgment, and that it is often presented in waffly or "delphic" forms, without attribution of views. Opposing views are not always clearly articulated. Judgments on difficult subjects are sometimes hedged, or represent the outcome of compromise, and are couched in fuzzy, imprecise terms. Yet intelligence consumers increasingly maintain that they want a more clearly spelled out distinction between different interpretations, with judgments as to relative probabilities. . . .

### I. The "Current Events" Syndrome

The task of producing intelligence—analyzing day-to-day events for quick dissemination—today occupies much of the resources of the DDI. Responding to the growing demands for information of current concern by policymakers for more coverage of more topics, the DDI has of necessity resorted to a "current events" approach to much of its research. There is less interest in and fewer resources have been devoted to in-depth analysis of problems with long-range importance to policymakers. . . .

According to some observers, this syndrome has had an unfavorable impact on the quality of crisis warning and the recognition of longer term trends. The "current events" approach has fostered the problem of "incremental analysis," the tendency to focus myopically on the latest piece of information without systematic consideration of an accumulated body of integrated evidence. Analysts in their haste to compile the day's traffic, tend to lose sight of underlying factors and relationships. . . .

### K. Overload of Analysts and Consumers

Yet today the intelligence establishment remains structured in such a way that collection guides production, rather than vice versa; available data and "the impetus of technology" tend to govern what is produced. . . .

Consumers tend to treat the intelligence product as a free good. Instead of articulating priorities, they demand information about everything, and the demand exceeds the supply. And analysts, perhaps for fear of being accused of an "intelligence failure," feel that they *have* to cover every possible topic, with little regard for its relevance to U.S. foreign policy interests. . . .

Excerpted from U.S. Congress. Senate. *Foreign and Military Intelligence: Final Report of the Select Committee to Study Governmental Operations with Respect to Intelligence Activities, Book I.* 94th Cong., 2nd sess., S. Rep. 94-755. April 26, 1976. http://www.aarclibrary.org/publib/church/reports/book1/contents.htm (accessed September 1, 2004).

# 30. National Performance Review Report
*September 1993*

. . . Information management activities within the Intelligence Community (IC) lack system interoperability, do not adhere to a common set of standards, and operate without an integrated communications strategy. This environment leads to a proliferation of redundant efforts, inadequate support to IC customers, and a spiraling and unaffordable cost of doing business. The Community's business is information. Without immediate and aggressive action, the status quo in its management of information will result in the equivalent of bankruptcy.

The historical autonomy between elements of the Community has led it to the current crisis in interoperability and the lack of information integration throughout the Community. Operating under rules developed in the 1970s, managers bought non-integrated computers, developed non-integrated software, and were surprised during Operation JUST CAUSE in Panama, when these systems, purchased and developed independently, were not compatible. Moreover, there is no precise accounting of the amount the Community spends on information technology. Performance measurement, management decisions, and congressional oversight will continue to be extremely difficult until this situation can be remedied.

Acquisition rules must also be changed. An approach needs to be considered that emphasizes software libraries, portable to any architecture, and a design methodology that allows for purchase or lease of commercial equipment currently available. . . .

One of the objectives for Community information integration should be a common communications network that connects a global information grid accessible by all customers. This requires a close relationship between the information and communications suppliers to ensure that the communications architecture supports the data load and accommodates global access. . . .

## Implications

Whenever the term "integration" is used within the Intelligence Community, it immediately triggers alarm systems within the component activities. Implementing change in any culture is a difficult task at best. Any efforts to cross intelligence disciplines and agencies will face substantial resistance. It is essential to the Intelligence Community's survival to implement the recommended actions to integrate the Community into a smoothly functioning whole. . . .

Excerpted from U.S. Office of the Vice President. *The Intelligence Community: Accompanying Report of the National Performance Review.* September 1993. http://govinfo.library.unt.edu/npr/library/reports/intel04.html (accessed September 1, 2004).

# Supreme Court Limits Presidential Power Regarding Internal Security Cases

**31.** *United States v. United States District Court,* June 19, 1972

## INTRODUCTION

Ever since the terrorist attacks of September 11, 2001, much debate and many court cases have centered on the scope of the president's unilateral power to protect homeland security. The U.S. Supreme Court limited that power in a decision released on June 19, 1972.

The case arose from the bombing of the Central Intelligence Agency's recruiting office in Ann Arbor, Michigan, on September 29, 1968. The bombing occurred amid growing concern about protecting homeland security. Within the previous year the nation had been rocked by massive protests against the Vietnam War, racial rioting, and the assassinations of Sen. Robert F. Kennedy and Rev. Martin Luther King Jr.

As part of the bombing investigation, Attorney General John Mitchell authorized wiretapping the phone of one suspect who was among three people later charged with the crime. Normally, because of the Fourth Amendment's prohibition against unreasonable searches and seizures, law enforcement officers have to obtain a court order authorizing a wiretap before it can be installed. But in the Ann Arbor case no court order was obtained.

Attorneys for the defendants challenged the wiretap's legality. Government attorneys argued that the electronic surveillance was legal because it represented a reasonable exercise of the president's power, through the attorney general, to protect national security. In an affidavit, Mitchell said he had authorized the wiretaps "to gather intelligence information deemed necessary to protect the nation from attempts of domestic organizations to attack and subvert the existing structure of the Government."

The Supreme Court ruled unanimously that installing the wiretaps without a court order violated the Fourth Amendment. Justice Lewis F. Powell Jr., an appointee of President Richard Nixon who had a record of supporting wiretapping, wrote in the opinion that Fourth Amendment freedoms "cannot safely be guaranteed if domestic security surveillance may be conducted solely within the discretion of the executive branch."

In another section of the opinion Powell wrote: "The danger to political dissent is acute where the Government attempts to act under so vague a concept as the power to protect 'domestic security.'" That same argument is being made today by those challenging President George W. Bush's powers in the war on terrorism.

# 31. *United States v. United States District Court*

## June 19, 1972

The issue before us is an important one for the people of our country and their Government. It involves the delicate question of the President's power, acting through the Attorney General, to authorize electronic surveillance in internal security matters without prior judicial approval. Successive Presidents for more than one-quarter of a century have authorized such surveillance in varying degrees, without guidance from the Congress or a definitive decision of this Court. This case brings the issue here for the first time. Its resolution is a matter of national concern, requiring sensitivity both to the Government's right to protect itself from unlawful subversion and attack and to the citizen's right to be secure in his privacy against unreasonable Government intrusion. . . .

. . . [T]he United States charged three defendants with conspiracy to destroy Government property . . . . One of the defendants, Plamondon, was charged with the dynamite bombing of an office of the Central Intelligence Agency in Ann Arbor, Michigan.

During pretrial proceedings, the defendants moved to compel the United States to disclose certain electronic surveillance information and to conduct a hearing to determine whether this information "tainted" the evidence on which the indictment was based or which the Government intended to offer at trial. In response, the Government filed an affidavit of the Attorney General, acknowledging that its agents had overheard conversations in which Plamondon had participated. The affidavit also stated that the Attorney General approved the wiretaps "to gather intelligence information deemed necessary to protect the nation from attempts of domestic organizations to attack and subvert the existing structure of the Government." The logs of the surveillance were filed in a sealed exhibit . . . .

On the basis of the Attorney General's affidavit and the sealed exhibit, the Government asserted that the surveillance was lawful, though conducted without prior judicial approval, as a reasonable exercise of the President's power (exercised through the Attorney General) to protect the national security. . . .

It is important at the outset to emphasize the limited nature of the question before the Court. This case raises no constitutional challenge to electronic surveillance as specifically authorized by Title III of the Omnibus Crime Control and Safe Streets Act of 1968. Nor is there any question or doubt as to the necessity of obtaining a warrant in the surveillance of crimes unrelated to the national security interest. Further, the instant case requires no judgment on the scope of the President's surveillance power with respect to the activities of foreign powers, within or without this country. The Attorney General's affidavit in this case states that the surveillances were "deemed necessary to protect the nation from attempts of *domestic organizations* to attack and subvert the existing structure of Government" (emphasis supplied). There is no evidence of any involvement, directly or indirectly, of a foreign power.

Our present inquiry, though important, is therefore a narrow one. It addresses a question left open by *Katz* [*Katz v. United States* (1967)]: "Whether safeguards other than prior authorization by a magistrate would satisfy the Fourth Amendment in a situation involving the national security . . . ."

We begin the inquiry by noting that the President of the United States has the fundamental duty, under Art. II, 1, of the Constitution, "to preserve, protect, and defend the Constitution of the United States." Implicit in that duty is the power to protect our Government against those who would subvert or overthrow it by unlawful means. In the discharge of this duty, the President—through the Attorney General—may find it necessary to employ electronic surveillance to obtain intelligence information on the plans of those who plot unlawful acts against the Government. The use of such surveillance in internal security cases has been sanctioned more or less continuously by various Presidents and Attorneys General since July 1946. . . .

Though the Government and respondents debate their seriousness and magnitude, threats and acts of sabotage against the Government exist in sufficient number to justify investigative powers with respect to them. The covertness and complexity of potential unlawful conduct against the Government and the necessary dependency of many conspirators upon the telephone make electronic surveillance an effective investigatory instrument in certain circumstances. The marked acceleration in technological developments and sophistication in their use have resulted in new techniques for the planning, commission, and concealment of criminal activities. It would be contrary to the public interest for Government to deny to itself the prudent and lawful employment of those very techniques which are employed against the Government and its law-abiding citizens.

It has been said that "the most basic function of any government is to provide for the security of the individual and of his property" [quoting *Miranda v. Arizona* (1966)]. And unless Government safeguards its own capacity to function and to preserve the security of its people, society itself could become so disordered that all rights and liberties would be endangered. . . .

But a recognition of these elementary truths does not make the employment by Government of electronic surveillance a welcome development—even when employed with restraint and under judicial supervision. There is, understandably, a deep-seated uneasiness and apprehension that this capability will be used to intrude upon cherished privacy of law-abiding citizens. We look to the Bill of Rights to safeguard their privacy. Though physical entry of the home is the chief evil against which the wording of the Fourth Amendment is directed, its broader spirit now shields private speech from unreasonable surveillance. . . .

National security cases, moreover, often reflect a convergence of First and Fourth Amendment values not present in cases of "ordinary" crime. Though the investigative duty of the executive may be stronger in such cases, so also is there greater jeopardy to constitutionally protected speech. . . . History abundantly documents the tendency of Government—however benevolent and benign its motives—to view with suspicion those who most fervently dispute its policies. Fourth Amendment protections become the more necessary when the target of official surveillance may be those suspected of unorthodoxy in their political beliefs. The danger to political dissent is acute where the Government attempts to act under so vague a concept as the power to protect "domestic security." Given the difficulty of defining the domestic security interest, the danger of abuse in acting to protect that interest becomes apparent. . . .

The price of lawful public dissent must not be a dread of subjection to an unchecked surveillance power. Nor must the fear of unauthorized official eavesdropping deter vigorous citizen dissent and discussion of Government action in private conversation. For private dissent, no less than open public discourse, is essential to our free society. . . .

These Fourth Amendment freedoms cannot properly be guaranteed if domestic security surveillances may be conducted solely within the discretion of the Executive Branch. The Fourth Amendment does not contemplate the executive officers of Government as neutral and disinterested magistrates. Their duty and responsibility is to enforce the laws, to investigate and to prosecute. But those charged with this investigative and prosecutorial duty should not be the sole judges of when to utilize constitutionally sensitive means in pursuing their tasks. The historical judgment, which the Fourth Amendment accepts, is that unreviewed executive discretion may yield too readily to pressures to obtain incriminating evidence and overlook potential invasions of privacy and protected speech. . . .

The independent check upon executive discretion is not satisfied, as the Government argues, by "extremely limited" post-surveillance judicial review. Indeed, post-surveillance review would never reach the surveillances which failed to result in prosecutions. Prior review by a neutral and detached magistrate is the time-tested means of effectuating Fourth Amendment rights. . . .

Security surveillances are especially sensitive because of the inherent vagueness of the domestic security concept, the necessarily broad and continuing nature of intelligence gathering, and the temptation to utilize such surveillances to oversee political dissent. We recognize, as we have before, the constitutional basis of the President's domestic security role, but we think it must be exercised in a manner compatible with the Fourth Amendment. In this case we hold that this requires an appropriate prior warrant procedure.

We cannot accept the Government's argument that internal security matters are too subtle and complex for judicial evaluation. Courts regularly deal with the most difficult issues of our society. There is no reason to believe that federal judges will be insensitive to or uncomprehending of the issues involved in domestic security cases. Certainly courts can recognize that domestic security surveillance involves different considerations from the surveillance of "ordinary crime." If the threat is too subtle or complex for our senior law enforcement officers to convey its significance to a court, one may question whether there is probable cause for surveillance.

Nor do we believe prior judicial approval will fracture the secrecy essential to official intelligence gathering. The investigation of criminal activity has long involved imparting sensitive information to judicial officers who have respected the confidentialities involved. Judges may be counted upon to be especially conscious of security requirements in national security cases. . . .

Thus, we conclude that the Government's concerns do not justify departure in this case from the customary Fourth Amendment requirement of judicial approval prior to initiation of a search or surveillance. Although some added burden will be imposed upon the Attorney General, this inconvenience is justified in a free society to protect constitutional values. Nor do we think the Government's domestic surveillance powers will be impaired to any significant degree. A prior warrant establishes presumptive validity of the surveillance and will minimize the burden of justification in post-surveillance judicial review. By no means of least importance will be the reassurance of the public generally that indiscriminate wiretapping and bugging of law-abiding citizens cannot occur. . . .

Excerpted from U.S. Supreme Court. *United States v. United States District Court.* 407 U.S. 297. June 19, 1972. http://laws.findlaw.com/us/407/297.html (accessed September 1, 2004).

# Intelligence Agencies and Civil Liberties

## INTRODUCTION

The nation's intelligence agencies provide its chief defense against terrorism. Yet on several occasions before the attacks of September 2001, investigations found that the Central Intelligence Agency (CIA), the Federal Bureau of Investigation (FBI), and other agencies wantonly violated the law and the rights of Americans in the name of protecting homeland security.

In the early 1970s reporters started uncovering some of the intelligence abuses, many of which had targeted opponents of the Vietnam War. The news stories prompted several official investigations. The first study, by a commission chaired by Vice President Nelson A. Rockefeller, examined CIA activities within the United States. The 1947 law that created the CIA expressly barred it from having any "police, subpoena, law-enforcement powers, or internal security functions."

The Rockefeller panel found that some domestic CIA activities were "plainly unlawful and improper invasions of the rights of Americans." Although its report described numerous abuses by the CIA ranging from illegal mail intercepts to "black bag" burglaries, the Rockefeller commission concluded that the "great majority" of the agency's domestic activities were legal. The Rockefeller report was widely viewed as a whitewash [Document 32].

By far the most wide-ranging and important probe of American intelligence agencies during the period was conducted by the Senate Select Committee to Study Governmental Operations with Respect to Intelligence Agencies, widely known as the Church committee because Sen. Frank Church, D-Idaho, was its chairman. After fifteen months of hearings and study, the Church committee issued more than a dozen reports documenting a huge range of abuses conducted during domestic intelligence investigations. "We have seen segments of our Government, in their attitudes and action, adopt tactics unworthy of a democracy, and occasionally reminiscent of the tactics of totalitarian regimes," the committee said [Document 33].

In many cases, intelligence officials and agents knew their activities were illegal but went ahead anyway, the Church committee said. In other cases, officials and agents simply never considered whether their actions were proper. The committee quoted William C. Sullivan, who during his lengthy intelligence career served for a decade as the FBI's assistant director for intelligence, as saying he had never heard discussions about legal issues:

> We never gave any thought to this realm of reasoning, because we were just naturally pragmatists. The one thing we were concerned about was this: Will this course of action work, will it get us what we want, will we reach the objective that we desire to reach? As far as legality is concerned, morals, or ethics, [it] was never raised by myself or anybody else. . . . I think this suggests really in government that we are amoral. In government—I am not speaking for everybody—the general atmosphere is one of amorality.

The next major domestic intelligence scandal involving violations of the law and civil liberties occurred in the late 1980s. It involved an FBI probe of the Committee in Solidarity with the People of El Salvador (CISPES), an American group that strongly opposed Reagan administration policies in Central America. The FBI launched the investigation after an informant who it later determined never should have been trusted said CISPES was providing money to a foreign terrorist group and was preparing to conduct terrorist attacks in the United States. During its three-year investigation of CISPES, the FBI created files on 2,375 individuals and 1,330 groups, but it never filed any criminal charges. FBI headquarters closed the investigation in June 1985 after finding that "CISPES appears to be involved in political activities involving First Amendment activities but not international terrorism."

Two congressional committees examined the FBI's conduct in the CISPES case, and one asked the General Accounting Office (GAO)—the investigative arm of Congress—to review the FBI's international terrorism program. The GAO reported on September 7, 1990, that between January 1982 and June 1988 the FBI closed about 19,500 international terrorism investigations, but that only a tiny fraction resulted in arrests. The GAO also said that in about 12 percent of the cases the FBI appeared to monitor activities that were protected by the First Amendment [Document 34].

Ultimately, the CISPES case resulted in the FBI mildly disciplining six employees for "mistakes in judgment," changing nearly three dozen policies related to international terrorism investigations, deleting all records created during the CISPES investigation, and settling a lawsuit filed by CISPES in which it agreed to pay the group's legal costs of $190,000. The settlement also included a consent decree agreed to by the government that said in part: "The FBI, in investigating United States persons, shall not employ any techniques designed to impair their lawful and constitutionally protected political conduct or to defame the character or reputation of a United States person."

---

# 32. Rockefeller Commission Report on CIA Activities

*June 6, 1975*

## A. Summary of Charges and Findings

. . . A detailed analysis of the facts has convinced the Commission that the great majority of the CIA's domestic activities comply with its statutory authority.

Nevertheless, over the 28 years of its history, the CIA has engaged in some activities that should be criticized and not permitted to happen again—both in light of the limits imposed on the Agency by law and as a matter of public policy.

Some of these activities were initiated or ordered by Presidents, either directly or indirectly.

Some of them fall within the doubtful area between responsibilities delegated to the CIA by Congress and the National Security Council on the one hand and activities specifically prohibited to the Agency on the other.

Some of them were plainly unlawful and constituted improper invasions upon the rights of Americans.

The Agency's own recent actions, undertaken for the most part in 1973 and 1974, have gone far to terminate the activities upon which this investigation has focused. . . .

## D. Significant Areas of Investigation

### 1. The CIA's Mail Intercepts

*Findings*

At the time the CIA came into being, one of the highest national intelligence priorities was to gain an understanding of the Soviet Union and its worldwide activities affecting our national security.

In this context, the CIA began in 1952 a program of surveying mail between the United States and the Soviet Union as it passed through a New York postal facility. In 1953 it began opening some of this mail. The program was expanded over the following two decades and ultimately involved the opening of many letters and the analysis of envelopes, or "covers," of a great many more letters.

The New York mail intercept was designed to attempt to identify persons within the United States who were cooperating with the Soviet Union and its intelligence forces to harm the United States. It was also intended to determine technical communications procedures and mail censorship techniques used by the Soviets.

The Director of the Central Intelligence Agency approved commencement of the New York mail intercept in 1952. . . . Since 1958, the FBI was aware of this program and received 57,000 items from it.

A 1962 CIA memorandum indicates the Agency was aware that the mail openings would be viewed as violating federal criminal laws prohibiting obstruction or delay of the mails.

In the last year before the termination of this program, out of 4,350,000 items of mail sent to and from the Soviet Union, the New York intercept examined the outside of 2,300,000 items, photographed 33,000 envelopes, and opened 8,700.

The mail intercept was terminated in 1973 when the Chief Postal Inspector refused to allow its continuation without an up-to-date high-level approval. . . .

*Conclusions*

While in operation, the CIA's domestic mail opening programs were unlawful. United States statutes specifically forbid opening the mail.

The mail openings also raise Constitutional questions under the Fourth Amendment guarantees against unreasonable search, and the scope of the New York project poses possible difficulties with the First Amendment rights of speech and press.

Mail cover operations (examining and copying of envelopes only) are legal when carried out in compliance with postal regulations on a limited and selective basis involving matters of national security. The New York mail intercept did not meet these criteria.

The nature and degree of assistance given by the CIA to the FBI in the New York mail project indicate that the CIA's primary purpose eventually became participation with the FBI in internal security functions. Accordingly, the CIA's participation was prohibited under the National Security Act. . . .

### 3. Special Operations Group—"Operation CHAOS"

*Findings*

The late 1960's and early 1970's were marked by widespread violence and civil disorders. Demonstrations, marches and protest assemblies were frequent in a number of cities. Many universities and college campuses became places of disruption and unrest. . . .

Responding to Presidential requests made in the face of growing domestic disorder, the Director of Central Intelligence in August 1967 established a Special Operations Group within the CIA to collect, coordinate, evaluate and report on the extent of foreign influence on domestic dissidence.

The group's activities, which later came to be known as Operation CHAOS, led the CIA to collect information on dissident Americans from CIA field stations overseas and from the FBI. . . .

During six years, the Operation compiled some 13,000 different files, including files on 7,200 American citizens. The documents in these files and related materials included the names of more than 300,000 persons and organizations, which were entered into a computerized index.

This information was kept closely guarded within the CIA. Using this information, personnel of the Group prepared 3,500 memoranda for internal use; 3,000 memoranda for dissemination to the FBI; and 37 memoranda for distribution to White House and other top level officials in the government. . . .

Activity of the Operation decreased substantially by mid-1972. The Operation was formally terminated in March 1974.

*Conclusions*

Some domestic activities of Operation CHAOS unlawfully exceeded the CIA's statutory authority . . . .

Most significantly, the Operation became a repository for large quantities of information on the domestic activities of American citizens. This information was derived principally from FBI reports or from overt sources and not from clandestine collection by the CIA, and much of it was not directly related to the question of the existence of foreign connections. . . .

### 4. Protection of the Agency Against Threats of Violence—Office of Security

*Findings*

The CIA was not immune from the threats of violence and disruption during the period of domestic unrest between 1967 and 1972. The Office of Security was charged throughout this period with the responsibility of ensuring the continued functioning of the CIA. . . .

The Office was also responsible, with the approval of the Director of Central Intelligence, for a program from February 1967 to December 1968, which at first monitored, but later infiltrated, dissident organizations in the Washington, D.C., area to determine if the groups planned any activities against CIA or other government installations. . . . The project was terminated when the Washington Metropolitan Police Department developed its own intelligence capability. . . .

About 500 to 800 files were maintained on dissenting organizations and individuals. Thousands of names in the files were indexed. Report publication was ended in late 1972, and the entire project was ended in 1973.

*Conclusions*

. . . The Agency should not infiltrate a dissident group for security purposes unless there is a clear danger to Agency installations, operations or personnel, and investigative coverage of the threat by the FBI and local law enforcement authorities is inadequate. The Agency's infiltration of dissident groups in the Washington area went far beyond steps necessary to protect the Agency's own facilities, personnel and operations, and therefore exceeded the CIA's statutory authority.

In addition, the Agency undertook to protect other government departments and agencies—a police function prohibited to it by statute.

Intelligence activity directed toward learning from what sources a domestic dissident group receives its financial support within the United States, and how much income it has, is no part of the authorized security operations of the Agency. Neither is it the function of the Agency to compile records on who attends peaceful meetings of such dissident groups, or what each speaker has to say (unless it relates to disruptive or violent activities which may be directed against the Agency).

The Agency's actions in contributing funds, photographing people, activities and cars, and following people home were unreasonable under the circumstances and therefore exceeded the CIA's authority. . . .

## B. Investigations of Possible Breaches of Security

### 1. Persons Investigated

*Findings*

. . . A few investigations involving intrusions on personal privacy were directed at subjects with no relationship to the Agency. . . . Five were directed against newsmen, in an effort to determine their sources of leaked classified information, and nine were directed against other United States citizens.

The CIA's investigations of newsmen to determine their sources of classified information stemmed from pressures from the White House and were partly a result of the FBI's unwillingness to undertake such investigations. . . .

*Conclusions*

. . . The Director's responsibility to protect intelligence sources and methods is not so broad as to permit investigations of persons having no relationship whatever with the Agency. The CIA has no authority to investigate newsmen simply because they have published leaked classified information. . . .

## 2. Investigative Techniques

*Findings*

. . . Some investigations involved physical surveillance of the individuals concerned, possibly in conjunction with other methods of investigation. The last instance of physical surveillance by the Agency within the United States occurred in 1973.

The investigation disclosed the domestic use of 32 wiretaps, the last in 1965; 32 instances of bugging, the last in 1968; and 12 break-ins, the last in 1971. None of these activities was conducted under a judicial warrant, and only one with the written approval of the Attorney General. . . .

## 6. Involvement of the CIA in Improper Activities for the White House

*Findings*

During 1971, at the request of various members of the White House staff, the CIA provided alias documents and disguise material, a tape recorder, camera, film and film processing to E. Howard Hunt. It also prepared a psychological profile of Dr. Daniel Ellsberg.

Some of this equipment was later used without the knowledge of the CIA in connection with various improper activities, including the entry into the office of Dr. Lewis Fielding, Ellsberg's psychiatrist.

Some members of the CIA's medical staff who participated in the preparation of the Ellsberg profile knew that one of its purposes was to support a public attack on Ellsberg. . . .

President Nixon and his staff also insisted in this period that the CIA turn over to the President highly classified files relating to the Lebanon landings, the Bay of Pigs, the Cuban missile crisis, and the Vietnam War. The request was made on the ground that these files were needed by the President in the performance of his duties, but the record shows the purpose, undisclosed to the CIA, was to serve the President's personal political ends. . . .

*Conclusions*

Providing the assistance requested by the White House, including the alias and disguise materials, the camera and the psychological profile on Ellsberg, was not related to the performance by the Agency of its authorized intelligence functions and was therefore improper. . . .

The record does show, however, that individuals in the Agency failed to comply with the normal control procedures in providing assistance to E. Howard Hunt. It also shows that the Agency's failure to cooperate fully with ongoing investigations following Watergate was inconsistent with its obligations.

Finally, the Commission concludes that the requests for assistance by the White House reflect a pattern for actual and attempted misuse of the CIA by the Nixon administration. . . .

Excerpted from U.S. Commission on CIA Activities Within the United States. *Report to the President by the Commission on CIA Activities Within the United States.* June 6, 1975. http://www.aarclibrary.org/publib/church/rockcomm/contents.htm (accessed September 1, 2004).

# 33. Church Committee Report on Rights Violations by Intelligence Agencies
*April 26, 1976*

## I. Introduction and Summary

... The critical question before the Committee was to determine how the fundamental liberties of the people can be maintained in the course of the Government's effort to protect their security. The delicate balance between these basic goals of our system of government is often difficult to strike, but it can, and must, be achieved. We reject the view that the traditional American principles of justice and fair play have no place in our struggle against the enemies of freedom. Moreover, our investigation has established that the targets of intelligence activity have ranged far beyond persons who could properly be characterized as enemies of freedom and have extended to a wide array of citizens engaging in lawful activity.

Americans have rightfully been concerned since before World War II about the dangers of hostile foreign agents likely to commit acts of espionage. Similarly, the violent acts of political terrorists can seriously endanger the rights of Americans. Carefully focused intelligence investigations can help prevent such acts.

But too often intelligence has lost this focus and domestic intelligence activities have invaded individual privacy and violated the rights of lawful assembly and political expression. Unless new and tighter controls are established by legislation, domestic intelligence activities threaten to undermine our democratic society and fundamentally alter its nature. . . .

### A. Intelligence Activity: A New Form of Governmental Power to Impair Citizens' Rights
... We have seen segments of our Government, in their attitudes and action, adopt tactics unworthy of a democracy, and occasionally reminiscent of the tactics of totalitarian regimes. We have seen a consistent pattern

in which programs initiated with limited goals, such as preventing criminal violence or identifying foreign spies, were expanded to what witnesses characterized as "vacuum cleaners", sweeping in information about lawful activities of American citizens.

The tendency of intelligence activities to expand beyond their initial scope is a theme which runs through every aspect of our investigative findings. Intelligence collection programs naturally generate ever-increasing demands for new data. And once intelligence has been collected, there are strong pressures to use it against the target. . . .

### C. Summary of the Main Problems

. . . Too many people have been spied upon by too many Government agencies and too much information has been collected. The Government has often undertaken the secret surveillance of citizens on the basis of their political beliefs, even when those beliefs posed no threat of violence or illegal acts on behalf of a hostile foreign power. The Government, operating primarily through secret informants, but also using other intrusive techniques such as wiretaps, microphone "bugs," surreptitious mail opening, and break-ins, has swept in vast amounts of information about the personal lives, views, and associations of American citizens. Investigations of groups deemed potentially dangerous—and even of groups suspected of associating with potentially dangerous organizations—have continued for decades, despite the fact that those groups did not engage in unlawful activity. Groups and individuals have been harassed and disrupted because of their political views and their lifestyles. Investigations have been based upon vague standards whose breadth made excessive collection inevitable. Unsavory and vicious tactics have been employed—including anonymous attempts to break up marriages, disrupt meetings, ostracize persons from their professions, and provoke target groups into rivalries that might result in deaths. Intelligence agencies have served the political and personal objectives of presidents and other high officials. While the agencies often committed excesses in response to pressure from high officials in the Executive branch and Congress, they also occasionally initiated improper activities and then concealed them from officials whom they had a duty to inform.

Governmental officials—including those whose principal duty is to enforce the law—have violated or ignored the law over long periods of time and have advocated and defended their right to break the law.

The Constitutional system of checks and balances has not adequately controlled intelligence activities. Until recently the Executive branch has neither delineated the scope of permissible activities nor established procedures for supervising intelligence agencies. Congress has failed to exercise sufficient oversight, seldom questioning the use to which its appropriations were being put. Most domestic intelligence issues have not reached the courts, and in those cases when they have reached the courts, the judiciary has been reluctant to grapple with them. . . .

*1. The Number of People Affected by Domestic Intelligence Activity*

United States intelligence agencies have investigated a vast number of American citizens and domestic organizations. FBI headquarters alone has developed over 500,000 domestic intelligence files, and these have been augmented by additional files at FBI Field Offices. The FBI opened 65,000 of these domestic intelligence files in 1972 alone. In fact, substantially more individuals and groups are subject to intelligence scrutiny than the number of files would appear to indicate, since typically, each domestic intelligence file contains information on more than one individual or group, and this information is readily retrievable through the FBI General Name Index.

The number of Americans and domestic groups caught in the domestic intelligence net is further illustrated by the following statistics:

- Nearly a quarter of a million first class letters were opened and photographed in the United States by the CIA between 1953–1973, producing a CIA computerized index of nearly one and one-half million names.
- At least 130,000 first class letters were opened and photographed by the FBI between 1940–1966 in eight U.S. cities.
- Some 300,000 individuals were indexed in a CIA computer system and separate files were created on approximately 7,200 Americans and over 100 domestic groups during the course of CIA's Operation CHAOS (1967–1973).
- Millions of private telegrams sent from, to, or through the United States were obtained by the National Security Agency from 1947 to 1975 under a secret arrangement with three United States telegraph companies.
- An estimated 100,000 Americans were the subjects of United States Army intelligence files created between the mid-1960's and 1971.
- Intelligence files on more than 11,000 individuals and groups were created by the Internal Revenue Service between 1969 and 1973 and tax investigations were started on the basis of political rather than tax criteria.
- At least 26,000 individuals were at one point catalogued on an FBI list of persons to be rounded up in the event of a "national emergency. . . ."

*2. Too Much Information Is Collected for Too Long*

. . . (d) Some investigations of the lawful activities of peaceful groups have continued for decades. For example, the NAACP was investigated to determine whether it "had connections with" the Communist Party. The investigation lasted for over twenty-five years, although nothing was found to rebut a report during the first year of the investigation that the NAACP had a "strong tendency" to "steer clear of Communist activities. . . ."

(e) . . . In the 1960's President Johnson asked the FBI to compare various Senators' statements on Vietnam with the Communist Party line and to conduct name checks on leading antiwar Senators. . . .

(g) In the late 1960's and early 1970's, student groups were subjected to intense scrutiny. In 1970 the FBI ordered investigations of every member of the Students for a Democratic Society and of "every Black Student Union and similar group regardless of their past or present involvement in disorders." Files were opened on thousands of young men and women so that, as the former head of FBI intelligence explained, the information could be used if they applied for a government job. . . .

### 3. Covert Action and the Use of Illegal or Improper Means

(a) *Covert Action.*—Apart from uncovering excesses in the collection of intelligence, our investigation has disclosed covert actions directed against Americans, and the use of illegal and improper surveillance techniques to gather information. For example:

(i) The FBI's COINTELPRO—counterintelligence program—was designed to "disrupt" groups and "neutralize" individuals deemed to be threats to domestic security. The FBI resorted to counterintelligence tactics in part because its chief officials believed that the existing law could not control the activities of certain dissident groups, and that court decisions had tied the hands of the intelligence community. Whatever opinion one holds about the policies of the targeted groups, many of the tactics employed by the FBI were indisputably degrading to a free society. COINTELPRO tactics included:

- Anonymously attacking the political beliefs of targets in order to induce their employers to fire them;
- Anonymously mailing letters to the spouses of intelligence targets for the purpose of destroying their marriages;
- Obtaining from IRS the tax returns of a target and then attempting to provoke an IRS investigation for the express purpose of deterring a protest leader from attending the Democratic National Convention;
- Falsely and anonymously labeling as Government informants members of groups known to be violent, thereby exposing the falsely labelled member to expulsion or physical attack. . . .

(b) *Illegal or Improper Means.*—The surveillance which we investigated was not only vastly excessive in breadth and a basis for degrading counterintelligence actions, but was also often conducted by illegal or improper means. For example:

(1) For approximately 20 years the CIA carried out a program of indiscriminately opening citizens' first class mail. The Bureau also had a mail opening program, but cancelled it in 1966. The Bureau continued, how-

ever, to receive the illegal fruits of CIA's program. In 1970, the heads of both agencies signed a document for President Nixon, which correctly stated that mail opening was illegal, falsely stated that it had been discontinued, and proposed that the illegal opening of mail should be resumed because it would provide useful results. The President approved the program, but withdrew his approval five days later. The illegal opening continued nonetheless. Throughout this period CIA officials knew that mail opening was illegal, but expressed concern about the "flap potential" of exposure, not about the illegality of their activity.

(2) From 1947 until May 1975, NSA received from international cable companies millions of cables which had been sent by American citizens in the reasonable expectation that they would be kept private.

(3) Since the early 1930's, intelligence agencies have frequently wiretapped and bugged American citizens without the benefit of judicial warrant. Recent court decisions have curtailed the use of these techniques against domestic targets. But past subjects of these surveillances have included a United States Congressman, a Congressional staff member, journalists and newsmen, and numerous individuals and groups who engaged in no criminal activity and who posed no genuine threat to the national security, such as two White House domestic affairs advisers and an anti-Vietnam War protest group. While the prior written approval of the Attorney General has been required for all warrantless wiretaps since 1940, the record is replete with instances where this requirement was ignored and the Attorney General gave only after-the-fact authorization. . . .

(4) In several cases, purely political information (such as the reaction of Congress to an Administration's legislative proposal) and purely personal information (such as coverage of the extra-marital social activities of a high-level Executive official under surveillance) was obtained from electronic surveillance and disseminated to the highest levels of the federal government.

(5) Warrantless break-ins have been conducted by intelligence agencies since World War II. During the 1960's alone, the FBI and CIA conducted hundreds of break-ins, many against American citizens and domestic organizations. In some cases, these break-ins were to install microphones; in other cases, they were to steal such items as membership lists from organizations considered "subversive" by the Bureau. . . .

### 4. Ignoring the Law

Officials of the intelligence agencies occasionally recognized that certain activities were illegal, but expressed concern only for "flap potential." Even more disturbing was the frequent testimony that the law, and the Constitution were simply ignored. . . .

### 6. The Adverse Impact of Improper Intelligence Activity

*. . . (c) Distorting Data to Influence Government Policy and Public Perceptions*

. . . On certain crucial subjects the domestic intelligence agencies reported the "facts" in ways that gave rise to misleading impressions.

For example, the FBI's Domestic Intelligence Division initially discounted as an "obvious failure" the alleged attempts of Communists to influence the civil rights movement. Without any significant change in the factual situation, the Bureau moved from the Division's conclusion to Director Hoover's public congressional testimony characterizing Communist influence on the civil rights movement as "vitally important."

FBI reporting on protests against the Vietnam War provides another example of the manner in which the information provided to decision-makers can be skewed. In acquiescence with a judgment already expressed by President Johnson, the Bureau's reports on demonstrations against the War in Vietnam emphasized Communist efforts to influence the anti-war movement and underplayed the fact that the vast majority of demonstrators were not Communist controlled. . . .


*7. Cost and Value*

. . . Apart from the excesses described above, the usefulness of many domestic intelligence activities in serving the legitimate goal of protecting society has been questionable. Properly directed intelligence investigations concentrating upon hostile foreign agents and violent terrorists can produce valuable results. The committee has examined cases where the FBI uncovered "illegal" agents of a foreign power engaged in clandestine intelligence activities in violation of federal law. Information leading to the prevention of serious violence has been acquired by the FBI through its informant penetration of terrorist groups and through the inclusion in Bureau files of the names of persons actively involved with such groups. Nevertheless, the most sweeping domestic intelligence surveillance programs have produced surprisingly few useful returns in view of their extent. For example:

- Between 1960 and 1974, the FBI conducted over 500,000 separate investigations of persons and groups under the "subversive" category, predicated on the possibility that they might be likely to overthrow the government of the United States. Yet not a single individual or group has been prosecuted since 1957 under the laws which prohibit planning or advocating action to overthrow the government and which are the main alleged statutory basis for such FBI investigations.
- A recent study by the General Accounting Office has estimated that of some 17,528 FBI domestic intelligence investigations of individuals in 1974, only 1.3 percent resulted in prosecution and conviction, and in only "about 2 percent" of the cases was advance knowledge of any activity—legal or illegal—obtained. . . .

Excerpted from U.S. Congress. Senate. *Intelligence Activities and the Rights of Americans: Final Report of the Select Committee to Study Governmental Operations with Respect to Intelligence Activities, Book 2.* 94th Cong., 2nd sess., S. Rep. 94-755. April 26, 1976. http://www.aarclibrary. org/publib/church/reports/book2/contents.htm (accessed September 1, 2004).

# 34. General Accounting Office Report on FBI Terrorism Probes

*September 7, 1990*

## Purpose

In carrying out its responsibilities for investigating possible terrorist activities, the Federal Bureau of Investigation (FBI) must balance its investigative needs against the need to respect individuals' First Amendment rights, such as the freedom of speech and the right to peaceably assemble. The difficulties in trying to balance between the two was exemplified in an investigation of the Committee in Solidarity with the People of El Salvador (CISPES). According to the FBI, it opened an investigation on the basis of an informant's information that CISPES was involved in terrorist activities. CISPES alleged that the FBI investigated it because it opposed the Reagan administration's Central American policies. The release of documents obtained under the Freedom of Information Act raised questions about the FBI monitoring of American citizens exercising their First Amendment rights. . . .

## Background

The FBI is responsible for detecting, preventing, and reacting to international terrorism activities that involve the unlawful use of force or violence to try to intimidate a government or its civilian population for political or social objectives. The FBI maintains a general index system in support of its investigative matters. The FBI identifies various information it obtains during its investigations and enters it into the system for future retrieval. This process, known as indexing, records such information as individuals' and organizations' names, addresses, telephone numbers, and automobile license plate numbers. The FBI has policies governing indexing and the period of time indexed information is retained.

The allegations raised about the FBI's CISPES investigation prompted an internal FBI inquiry of that investigation. The internal study found that the FBI had properly opened the investigation, but the study also found that the FBI had substantially and unnecessarily broadened the scope of the investigation and had mismanaged the investigation. In response to the study's finding, the FBI Director implemented a number of policy and procedure changes regarding international terrorism investigations.

Between January 1982 and June 1988, the FBI closed about 19,500 international terrorism investigations. The FBI completed GAO questionnaires about various aspects of 1,003 cases randomly selected by GAO (e. g., the reasons cases were opened and closed, the subjects of investigations, the monitoring of First Amendment activities, and the use of indexing). GAO is generalizing the results of its questionnaire analyses to an adjusted universe of 18,144 closed international terrorism cases.

On the basis of the questionnaire responses, GAO randomly selected 150 cases for review. Eight more cases were added at the request of the Subcommittee. However, the FBI limited GAO's access to data by removing from the case files information it believed could potentially identify informants, ongoing investigations, and sensitive investigative techniques. The FBI also removed information it received from other agencies.

## Results in Brief

GAO estimates that about half of the 18,144 cases were opened because the FBI suspected that individuals or groups were involved in terrorist activities. U.S. citizens and permanent resident aliens were the subjects in 38.0 percent of the 18,144 cases. The FBI monitored First Amendment-type activities in about 11.5 percent of these 18,144 cases. The FBI indexed information about (1) individuals who were not the subjects of the investigations in about 47.8 percent of the cases and (2) groups not the subjects of the investigations in about 11.6 percent of the cases. The FBI closed about 67.5 percent of the cases because it did not develop evidence to indicate that the subjects were engaging in international terrorist activities.

The questionnaire and case file data show that the FBI did monitor First Amendment-type activities during some of its international terrorism investigations. Because of the limitations placed on its access to files, however, GAO cannot determine if the FBI abused individuals' First Amendment rights when it monitored these activities or if the FBI had a reasonable basis to monitor such activities.

## GAO's Analysis

### Reasons Cases Were Opened

From an adjusted universe of 18,144 closed international terrorism investigations from January 1982 to June 1988, GAO estimates that the FBI opened 9,507 cases (52.4 percent) because it had obtained information indicating that someone was engaged in or planning international terrorist activities.

The reasons cases were opened were essentially those stated in broad categories listed on GAO's questionnaires, which were completed by FBI personnel. To develop more detailed descriptions of the reasons cases were opened, GAO reviewed 158 cases and identified whether the information in the files indicated that the subject was or may have been (1) involved in or planned a terrorist act, (2) a leader or member of a terrorist group, or (3) associated with or linked to a terrorist group. The results of GAO's review showed that the FBI opened 70 of the 158 cases because of information indicating the subjects were associated with or linked to a terrorist group. For example, the information obtained may have indicated that the individual's phone number had been called by another person under investigation. Of these 70 cases, U.S. citizens and permanent resident aliens were the subjects in 37 cases.

### Monitoring of First Amendment Activities

The FBI observed First Amendment-type activities to obtain information about the subjects of investigations. Information on such activities was also obtained through informants or from other law enforcement agencies.

On the basis of its questionnaire results, GAO estimates that the FBI monitored or observed First Amendment activities in 2,080 (11.5 percent) of its international terrorism cases. Of these 2,080 cases, 951 were investigations of U.S. citizens or permanent resident aliens.

### Indexing of Names in Terrorism Investigations

On the basis of its questionnaire results, GAO estimates that the FBI indexed information about individuals, other than the subjects of investigations, in 8,671 (47.8 percent) of its international terrorism cases. Of these 8,671 cases, 3,354 were cases involving indexing of U.S. citizens or permanent resident aliens. Similarly, GAO estimates that 2,105 cases involved indexing of groups during the investigations. Of these 2,105 cases, 913 were cases involving indexing of groups with U.S. citizens or permanent resident aliens.

### Reasons Cases Were Closed

GAO estimates that the FBI closed 12,240 cases (67.5 percent) because it found no evidence linking the subject to international terrorist activities. Of the investigations, another 4,015 cases (22.1 percent) were closed because the subject moved or could not be located. The remaining 1,889 cases (10.4 percent) were closed for other reasons, such as the subject was arrested or the case was transferred to another FBI field office.

## Recommendations

The FBI removed information it considered sensitive from the closed case files before giving the files to GAO to review. Further, the FBI denied GAO access to open cases. Because of these limitations—information being removed from the files and no access to open cases—GAO is not making any recommendations. Also, GAO could not evaluate changes the FBI had made to its international terrorism program because of the lack of access to open cases. . . .

Excerpted from U.S. Congress. General Accounting Office. *International Terrorism: FBI Investigates Domestic Activities to Identify Terrorists.* GAO/GGD-90-112, September 7, 1990. http://www.gao.gov/docdblite/ summary.php?recflag=&accno=142382&rptno=GGD-90-112 (accessed September 1, 2004).

# Aviation Security before September 11, 2001

## INTRODUCTION

Federal agencies repeatedly detected gaping holes in U.S. aviation security for more than two decades before the terrorist hijackings on September 11, 2001. Problems ranging from poor performance by security screeners to inadequate control over access to airplanes were identified in studies conducted by the airline industry, the Federal Aviation Administration (FAA), the inspector general at the Department of Transportation, and the General Accounting Office (GAO), the investigative arm of Congress.

Following a string of airplane hijackings, in January 1973 the FAA started requiring airlines to screen all passengers and their carry-on baggage for guns, explosives, and other weapons. Passengers walked through metal detectors, and screeners operating x-ray machines scanned carry-on items. The number of hijackings fell sharply after screening started. However, in 1979 a joint study by the FAA and the airline industry identified numerous problems with security screeners, including high turnover, low wages, and inadequate training. The screeners typically worked for private security firms hired by the airlines.

FAA security tests where inspectors tried to get weapons past screeners turned up widely varying results, according to testimony before a congressional subcommittee on June 18, 1987, by Kenneth M. Mead, an associate director at the GAO. At major airports screeners detected weapons at rates from a low of 34 percent to a high of 99 percent, Mead said. Even those numbers were probably artificially high, he added, because the FAA's tests were too simple and were often conducted by FAA personnel known by the screeners. Mead recommended that the FAA establish performance standards for screeners and fine airlines that failed to meet them [Document 35].

Six months later, Mead returned to Capitol Hill to testify about problems at the sixteen airports deemed to have the highest security risk. Some of the problems he identified included ongoing issues with screeners, lack of control over badges that allowed access to restricted sections of airports, failure of airport and airline personnel to challenge unauthorized persons found in secure areas, and poor control over access to areas where airplanes loaded and unloaded passengers. "Deficiencies in aviation security are not just limited to the passenger screening process," Mead said. "In general, we believe that a heightened sensitivity to the importance of security is needed. . . ." [Document 36].

On December 21, 1988, a year after Mead's second appearance on Capitol Hill, Pan Am Flight 103 exploded at 30,000 feet over Lockerbie, Scotland. The blast, caused by a small amount of the plastic explosive Semtex hidden in a cassette player in a checked bag, killed all 259 people on board—including 189 Americans—and eleven people on the ground. A presidential commission appointed to investigate the bombing concluded it "may well have been preventable" if luggage had been screened properly at airports in Frankfurt and London. The commission's 182-page report, issued May 15, 1990, blasted Pan Am for lax security procedures and the FAA for failing to enforce its security regulations. Years later, a Libyan intelligence agent was convicted in the bombing [Document 37].

In a report issued January 27, 1994, the GAO warned the FAA to pay closer attention to dangers posed by terrorists. Government officials believed the terrorist threat was far greater overseas than in the United States, but the GAO pointedly noted that less than one year earlier—in February 1993—terrorists had bombed the World Trade Center in New York City, sending "a signal that it is possible for terrorists to operate in the United States." The

GAO noted that the FAA, airports, and airlines had taken steps to improve aviation security, but said that FAA and FBI officials "believe that airports and aircraft will remain an attractive target for terrorists well into the foreseeable future" [Document 38].

Less than five months later, on May 19, 1994, the GAO said the FAA had "made little progress" toward meeting a congressionally mandated deadline of November 1993 for installing improved explosive detection equipment in the nation's airports. Technical problems were slowing development of the new machines, the GAO said, but the agency also faulted the FAA for lacking an implementation strategy for the project [Document 39].

On September 11, 1996—exactly five years before terrorists hijacked four commercial airliners and killed nearly 3,000 people—a senior GAO official testified before a House subcommittee that protecting aviation against terrorism was an "urgent national issue" that required greater attention and funding. "Nearly every major aspect of the system—ranging from the screening of passengers, checked and carry-on baggage, mail, and cargo as well as access to secured areas within airports and aircraft—has weaknesses that terrorists could exploit," said Keith O. Fulz, an assistant comptroller general [Document 40].

Another warning about the growing threat that terrorists posed to aviation came just months later from the White House Commission on Aviation Safety and Security, which was directed by Vice President Al Gore. In a final report released February 12, 1997, the commission said the FBI and the Central Intelligence Agency both believed terrorists had targeted the United States and noted that current aviation security was based "in part on the defenses erected in the 1970s against hijackers. . . ." It made more than two dozen recommendations for improving aviation security and said greater cooperation was needed to implement them. "Improvements in aviation security have been complicated because government and industry often found themselves at odds, unable to resolve disputes over financing, effectiveness, technology, and potential impacts on operations and passengers," the commission said [Document 41].

The inspector general's office at the Department of Transportation issued one of the most damning reports on November 18, 1999. Investigators who tested access controls at eight major airports penetrated secure areas on 117 of 173 attempts, a success rate of 68 percent. The investigators boarded 117 aircraft, and in twelve cases were seated and ready for departure when they concluded their tests. Investigators usually gained access because airport and airline employees failed to follow required procedures, the study said. The report noted that the same access control weaknesses had been identified in an inspector general study released in 1993 [Document 42].

Ongoing problems with screeners were the subject when Gerald R. Dillingham, an associate director at the GAO, testified before the House Aviation Subcommittee on March 16, 2000. "The message I bring here today is not new," he said. "The performance problems affecting airport screeners are longstanding." Most major airports had screener turnover rates of more than 100 percent annually, and the rate at one airport topped 400 percent, Dillingham said. A major reason for the high turnover, Dillingham said, was that screeners were typically paid less than workers at airport fast-food restaurants [Document 43].

Some of the security screeners working at the Philadelphia airport were convicted felons, the Department of Transportation's inspector general announced on October 25, 2000. Their employer, Argenbright Holdings Limited, had failed to conduct required background checks on screeners between 1995 and 1999, according to the inspector general. Argenbright was fined $1 million, and the former district manager for the firm was sentenced to thirty months in prison for falsely certifying to the FAA that 1,300 security screeners had been properly checked and trained [Document 44].

Aviation security was improved after nineteen hijackers evaded the system's multiple layers on September 11, 2001, hijacked four commercial airliners, and crashed them into the World Trade Center, the Pentagon, and a field in Pennsylvania. Yet several years later, questions still remained about whether the improvements were sufficient to stop other terrorists from turning airliners filled with people into deadly missiles.

# 35. General Accounting Office Congressional Testimony on Passenger Screening
*June 18, 1987*

. . . FAA considers the passenger screening process effective in deterring criminal acts against civil aviation. According to FAA data, since 1973, over 38,000 firearms have been detected and at least 117 potential hijackings and related crimes may have been averted by FAA required security measures. Overall, we believe this aviation security program plays a significant deterrent role and promotes the safety of the traveling public. However, we believe the passenger screening process can be made more effective. We found that there are shortfalls in the passenger screening program and, based on FAA test results, wide variations in the frequency with which weapons are detected. FAA is working to improve preboard passenger screening, but the program continues to experience many of the personnel-related problems—high turnover, low wages, inadequate training—identified in a 1979 FAA/industry study. . . .

## Preboard Passenger Screening and How It Works

The current process for screening aircraft passengers and their carry-on baggage began in January 1973 following the issuance of an emergency regulation by FAA. FAA established the process to curb the growing number of aircraft hijackings that were occurring in the early 1970's and to insure safety. In 1974, the process was made statutory.

FAA prescribes screening regulations, provides overall guidance and direction for the program, and reports semi-annually to Congress on the effectiveness of screening procedures. The air carriers are responsible for screening passengers and their carry-on baggage; however, private security firms under contract to air carriers typically do the screening. Both the air carriers and FAA monitor a security firm's performance.

Screening personnel rely on equipment consisting primarily of walk-through metal detectors and x-ray inspection systems to screen carry-on items. Hand-held metal detection devices are used as backup support for the walk-through detectors. In addition, screening personnel may require physical searches for items in carry-on baggage that appear suspicious when x-rayed. Each of the components of the process—x-ray, metal detector, and physical search—are periodically tested by the airline and FAA. While there have been some technological improvements to screening equipment, for the most part the process operates essentially the same today as it did when implemented in 1973.

## FAA Test Results: Absence of Performance Standard

FAA has periodically tested preboard passenger screening and has not been satisfied with test results. However, the Air Carrier Standard Security Program, which establishes preboard passenger screening requirements and is approved by FAA, does not establish a performance standard for measuring the effectiveness of the process. FAA officials told us that they are considering incorporating such a standard in the Security Program. Without a standard, FAA cannot take enforcement actions, which range from warning letters to fines, when air carriers' screening stations fail to detect test weapons.

The results of about 700 tests of x-ray screening operations conducted during 1978 showed a detection rate of approximately 87 percent. The fact that 13 percent of the test weapons passed through the x-ray system were not detected was considered "significant and alarming" by both FAA and the airline industry. In 1981 and 1982, tests of both x-ray and metal detector screening operations showed an overall weapon detection rate of 89 and 83 percent, respectively.

In tests conducted by FAA from September through December 1986, screening personnel detected approximately 79 percent of the test weapons for x-ray tests, 82 percent for metal detector tests, and 81 percent for physical search tests. Detection rates varied significantly among FAA regions, ranging from a low of 63 percent to a high of 99 percent. For major airports, the detection rate ranged from a low of 34 percent to a high of 99 percent.

Moreover, our analysis shows that FAA test results may overstate the screening process' success in detecting weapons for at least two reasons: First, FAA test procedures are designed to favor detection of test weapons. For example, FAA inspectors are allowed to place only two or three objects such as a sweater, book, and shirt with a test weapon in the carry-on bag to be tested in an x-ray device. The tester cannot hide the test object among other objects in the carry-on bag or place other metal objects in the bag, as a saboteur might.

Second, screening personnel may be aware they are being tested. This is because FAA inspectors in some locations are well known to screening station personnel. FAA is aware of this problem and has acknowledged that high detection rates in certain locations may indicate the screeners recognized the FAA inspector.

## Personnel-Related Factors

Following the 1978 tests of the screening process, a task group of FAA and airline security personnel studied ways to improve performance at passenger screening checkpoints. This task group's report, referred to as the "Human Factors Study," recommended several actions which were endorsed by both FAA and the airlines. For the most part, these recommendations focused on the personnel-related aspects of the process such as high employee turnover rates, low pay, and inadequate training. Although FAA and the industry endorsed the study's recommendations, the air carriers have not yet fully implemented them.

We visited six major airports and found that many of the problems addressed in the human factors study still exist. For example, security firm managers said that screening employees are still being paid at or near minimum wage and that low pay contributes to high turnover—in some cases, about 100 percent annually—and problems in hiring capable people.

We found that training was generally provided as required by the Air Carrier Standard Security Program. However, we noted that problems continue to exist in the training area. For example, at one screening firm's training session, we were advised that instructors did not attend the training and that trainees simply viewed the 5-part FAA "Safety through Screening" series by themselves. They then signed a statement to attest that they had attended. As a result, no one was available to answer questions as recommended by the Human Factors study group. In another case, we observed that trainees were tested on the training they received but were not graded.

Thus, there was no measurement of the trainees' comprehension of the subject matter.

In addition, FAA's 1986 physical search test results show that screeners could not identify test weapons in 47 of 249 cases. During our work, we observed one case where the FAA test weapon—a mock pipe bomb—was initially identified as suspect by the x-ray operator. However, when the required physical search was made by another screener, the screener did not recognize the pipe bomb as a weapon and replaced it in the carry-on baggage. The screener then cleared the tester to proceed to the aircraft boarding gate. . . .

Excerpted from U.S. Congress. General Accounting Office. *FAA's Preboard Passenger Screening Process.* Prepared testimony of Kenneth M. Mead for a hearing by the Subcommittee on Government Activities and Transportation of the House Committee on Government Operations. GAO/T-RCED-87-34, June 18, 1987. http://161.203.16.4/d39t12/133425.pdf (accessed July 31, 2004).

## 36. General Accounting Office Congressional Testimony on Security at Highest-Risk Airports
*December 17, 1987*

. . . [W]e are testifying today on various security components, including passenger screening, at the nation's airports with the highest security risk—those designated "category X" by FAA. For security reasons, these airports will not be identified. Our testimony is based on our ongoing review of domestic aviation security. As part of this review, we conducted audit work at 6 of the nation's 16 category X airports, analyzed FAA security inspection reports for all 16 airports, and reviewed the series of reports on domestic aviation security by the Department of Transportation's (DOT) Safety Review Task Force.

Our work demonstrates the existence of security deficiencies at the nation's category X airports. FAA inspectors and the DOT Safety Review Task Force noted many of the same deficiencies. Chief among the problems we found were ineffective passenger screening and inadequate controls over personnel identification systems and over access to those parts of the airport where aircraft operate. . . .

## Security Measures Interrelated, but Deficiencies Create Potential for Unauthorized Access

In general terms, an airport is divided into two parts: (1) the air operations area which is the part of the airport where aircraft operate, load, and disembark cargo and passengers and (2) the rest of the airport, predominately the terminal, cargo and other buildings, and vehicle parking lots. A hallmark of FAA's aviation security program is redundancy, in that the security measures in place at our nation's airports are interrelated. Generally, if one measure fails, another measure is in place to support the first measure.

FAA regulations for the aviation security program mandate that access to the air operations area be controlled through various interrelated security features. The passenger screening process is one of the most visible features, well known to the traveling public. Other less obvious security features include:

- employee identification systems;
- the requirement that airport and air carrier employees "challenge" or question the presence of unauthorized persons in nonpublic areas; and
- perimeter barriers, such as fencing, vehicle gates, air cargo buildings, fire doors, and jetways. . . .

### Personnel Identification

In April 1987, FAA instituted new requirements to improve accountability and control over personnel identification systems. These requirements call for color coded badges which reflect access area authorization and include an expiration date. At category X airports, implementation of computerized identification systems is also required. FAA will consider these systems to be compromised when 5 percent of the issued badges at each airport cannot be properly accounted for.

During our review, we found that in general, airport officials were not properly accounting for and controlling personnel identification badges. Our verification of airport personnel identification cards for four aviation service companies located at one category X airport showed that three of the four companies had terminated employees and had reportedly returned badges to the airport officials. These officials, however, had no records of the badges being returned. At another category X airport, airport officials stated that approximately 16 percent of about 38,000 (or over 6,000) badges could not be accounted for. At this same airport, we visited three other service companies who were not tracking the retrieval of badges from terminated employees. These companies said they could only guess at the number of lost badges. . . .

### *"Challenging" Unauthorized Persons*

Airport and air carrier employees are required to challenge or question the presence of unauthorized persons in the air operations area as well as in baggage rooms, cargo areas, and other nonpublic areas. This challenge procedure has been referred to as a last line of defense; that is, if the other security features of an airport have been breached, the last security feature to be encountered before gaining access to the aircraft would be the airport or air carrier employee who is to challenge any unauthorized persons.

At most airports we visited, there were shortcomings in the effectiveness of the challenge procedures. With the full knowledge and cooperation of FAA inspectors, we gained access to air operations areas, including aircraft, without being challenged by the airport and air carrier employees who saw us. Without wearing identification, we entered open or unlocked cargo doors, walked through the buildings or gates and out onto the air operations area, and had access to cargo shipments or aircraft. In all cases, personnel were present who could have challenged us.

In addition to employees' not following proper challenge procedures, we found numerous instances at one airport in which air carrier employees were not displaying their identification badges as required. . . . Our tests also demonstrated that given the right clothing, an unauthorized person could easily go unnoticed. For example, we gained easy access to restricted areas while attired in clothing similar to that worn by one airline's flight attendants.

### *Perimeter Barriers*

To minimize the possibility of unauthorized entry, FAA regulations require that all openings in the perimeter should be controlled and that perimeter barriers such as fences and buildings be kept clear of trees, stowed equipment and material, and vehicles which could facilitate the climbing of such barriers. In some cases, control of certain exits, such as fire doors, is considered adequate if restricted area signs and challenge procedures are used during airport operational hours.

In general, we found that access to the air operations area could be gained by walking through perimeter buildings, including post office and air cargo buildings. Given the ineffectiveness of challenge procedures, we were able to walk through unalarmed fire doors and through jetways to gain access. . . .

In summary, deficiencies in aviation security are not just limited to the passenger screening process. In general, we believe that a heightened sensitivity to the importance of security is needed. . . .

Excerpted from U.S. Congress. General Accounting Office. *Security at Nation's Highest Risk Airports.* Prepared testimony of Kenneth M. Mead for a hearing by the Subcommittee on Government Activities and Transportation of the House Committee on Government Operations. GAO/T-RCED-88-

14, December 17, 1987. http://archive.gao.gov/d39t12/134666.pdf
(accessed July 31, 2004).

## 37. President's Commission on Aviation Security and Terrorism Report on the Bombing of Pan Am Flight 103

*May 15, 1990*

. . . The Commission's inquiry also finds that the U.S. civil aviation security system is seriously flawed and has failed to provide the proper level of protection for the traveling public. This system needs major reform.

The Commission found the Federal Aviation Administration to be a reactive agency—preoccupied with responses to events to the exclusion of adequate contingency planning in anticipation of future threats. The Commission recommends actions designed to change this focus at the FAA.

Pan Am's apparent security lapses and FAA's failure to enforce its own regulations followed a pattern that existed for months prior to Flight 103, during the day of the tragedy, and—notably—for nine months thereafter. . . .

The destruction of Flight 103 may well have been preventable. Stricter baggage reconciliation procedures could have stopped any unaccompanied checked bags from boarding the flight at Frankfurt. . . . Stricter application of passenger screening procedures would have increased the likelihood of intercepting any unknowing "dupe" or saboteur from checking a bomb into the plane at either airport. . . .

This Report contains more than 60 detailed recommendations designed to improve the civil aviation security system to deter and prevent terrorist attacks. Before new laws are passed and more regulations are promulgated, existing ones must be fully enforced and properly carried out. The Commission emphasizes that no amount of governmental reorganization or technological developments can ever replace the need for well-trained, highly-motivated people to make the security system work. . . .

At the end of an October 1988 inspection of Pan Am's security operations at Frankfurt, the FAA inspector was troubled by the lack of a tracking system for interline bags transferring from other airlines and the confused state of passenger screening procedures. Overall, the inspector wrote, "the system, trying adequately to control approximately 4,500 passengers and 28 flights per day, is being held together only by a very labor intensive operation and the tenuous threads of luck." Even so, the inspector concluded, "it appears the minimum [FAA] requirements can and are being met."

Passenger/baggage reconciliation is the bedrock of any heightened civil air security system. Under current FAA requirements for international flights, implemented since Pan Am 103, every bag carried on an aircraft must belong to someone who is also on that flight.

A key focus of the Commission's inquiry was the FAA written regulation in effect in December 1988 that unaccompanied baggage should be carried only if it was physically searched.

When Pan Am Flight 103 pushed away from the gate at Frankfurt and again at Heathrow, on December 21, 1988, no one knew whether the plane was carrying an "extra" interline bag that had been checked through to Pan Am from another airline. Months before Pan Am stopped reconciling or searching interline baggage and began simply X-raying this luggage.

Records examined by this Commission indicate that Pan Am Flight 103 might have carried one such interline bag that did not belong to a passenger on a flight. While this extra bag would have been X-rayed, the explosive Semtex cannot be reliably detected by X-ray used at airports.

Pan Am officials told the Commission that the FAA Director of Aviation Security had given the airline verbal approval to X-ray interline bags rather than searching or reconciling them with passengers. The FAA official denied this.

Passenger screening procedures required by FAA at Frankfurt and Heathrow included questioning to identify for additional screening those fitting a "profile" as most likely—knowingly or unknowingly—to be carrying an explosive in any manner, including checked baggage.

The subsequent FAA investigation of Pan Am 103 found that several interline passengers who boarded at Frankfurt were not even initially screened. Several others identified at the check-in counter for further screening did not receive that additional screening at the gate. . . .

The FAA investigation of the Pan Am 103 disaster began immediately and concluded on January 31, 1989. While the results were not announced for over three more months, the FAA proposed fines totaling $630,000 against Pan Am for violations of regulations, both on December 21 and during the five-week period thereafter.

The FAA, significantly, did not cite Pan Am for substituting X-ray for interline passenger/baggage reconciliation. The official FAA report made no reference to the fact that the investigation had found that one interline bag loaded on Flight 103 could not be accounted for in any passenger records. The agency also noted in its announcement that none of the violations cited by its investigation had contributed in any way to the bombing. . . .

The bombing of Flight 103 occurred against the background of warnings that trouble was brewing in the European terrorist community. Nine security bulletins that could have been relevant to the tragedy were issued between June 1, 1988, and December 21, 1988. One described a Toshiba radio cassette player, fully rigged as a bomb with a barometric triggering device, found by the West German police in the automobile of a member of

the Popular Front for the Liberation of Palestine–General Command
(PFLP-GC). The FAA bulletin cautioned that the device "would be very
difficult to detect via normal X-ray," and told U.S. carriers that
passenger/baggage reconciliation procedures should be "rigorously
applied. . . ."

Excerpted from U.S. Executive Office of the President. President's Commission on Aviation Security and Terrorism. *Report to the President by the
President's Commission on Terrorism.* May 15, 1990.

## 38. General Accounting Office Report on the Risk of Terrorist Attacks against Aviation Targets
*January 27, 1994*

### The Threat to Domestic Airports Is Low, but Concerns Exist

Since the early 1970s, FAA has based its domestic security program on
the assumption that hijacking by other than terrorists is the major domestic
threat. Indeed, terrorist acts inside the United States are rare. In 1992, the
last year that the FBI published data on the subject, the United States experienced four incidents; three involved the use of explosive or incendiary
devices. None resulted in the loss of life.

According to FBI officials, networks exist for some terrorist groups inside
the United States that could support terrorist activities. These networks are
important because they supply the necessary equipment, logistics, training,
and financial aid to potential terrorist groups. Because information on these
individuals, groups, and their networks is classified, we are precluded from
discussing these issues in greater detail in this report. Although FAA, airports, and airlines have taken measures to strengthen domestic security,
FAA and FBI officials believe that airports and aircraft will remain an
attractive target for terrorists well into the foreseeable future.

However, the terrorist threat is continually evolving and presenting
unique challenges to FAA and law enforcement agencies. For example, after
FAA responded to the rash of hijackings in the 1970s by deploying metal
detectors at domestic airports, terrorists began to board aircraft and leave
explosive devices in the aircraft via carry-on baggage at various overseas
locations. Similarly, after FAA began examining carry-on baggage, terrorists

were successful in placing explosive devices on board aircraft via checked baggage without actually boarding the aircraft at foreign airports. At each level, terrorists have made it more difficult for FAA and law enforcement authorities to identify the perpetrators. Because of the uncertain nature of terrorist acts, FAA and the FBI have great difficulty in assembling a long-term view of the threat to aviation security, which underscores the need to continually reassess threats to aviation.

## Terrorist Threat Is Greater Overseas

FBI, State Department, FAA, DOT [Department of Transportation], and airline officials maintain that the terrorist threat is still far greater overseas. Terrorists are more comfortable operating closer to home and closer to their infrastructure. According to experts, some terrorist groups seek a high body count. To this end, civil aviation is a tempting target—but one more likely to be located in Europe rather than the United States.

State Department officials point to the terrorist threat emanating from Latin America because of both the growing animosity of so-called "drug lords" to U.S. interdiction policies and their financial wherewithal to sponsor "narco-terrotism." According to the 1992 State Department report on terrorism, the continued threat of international terrorism to Americans and U.S. interests abroad is illustrated by the fact that, while the number of terrorist incidents has declined in recent years, attacks against American targets, both in real terms and as a percentage of the total, have increased. In addition, despite official beliefs that terrorists will continue to operate closer to home (most notably in Europe), the World Trade Center bombing in New York in February 1993 sends a signal that it is possible for terrorists to operate in the United States. . . .

Excerpted from U.S. Congress. General Accounting Office. *Aviation Security: Additional Actions Needed to Meet Domestic and International Challenges.* GAO/RCED-94-38, January 27, 1994. http://archive.gao.gov/t2pbat4/150614.pdf (accessed September 1, 2004).

# 39. General Accounting Office Report on Security Technology for Airports
*May 19, 1994*

## Background

The Aviation Security Improvement Act set a goal for FAA to have new explosive detection equipment in place by November 1993. . . .

## Results in Brief

FAA has made little progress toward meeting the act's goal for deploying new explosive detection systems. Although several devices show promise, technical problems are slowing the development and approval of the devices. FAA's Aviation Security Research and Development Scientific Advisory Panel estimates it could take FAA 2 to 5 years to approve new devices for airlines' use. . . . In addition, despite recommendations from the National Academy of Sciences and others, FAA does not plan to test new explosive detection systems at airports during the certification process. GAO identified several other weaknesses in FAA's security research program. For example, FAA does not (1) conduct software reviews to evaluate system designs, (2) emphasize integrating different technologies into total systems, and (3) focus sufficient attention on human factors issues. . . .

### FAA Needs an Implementation Strategy
FAA does not have a strategy that articulates important milestones, sets realistic expectations, and identifies resources to guide efforts for implementing new explosive detection technology. . . .

## Principal Findings

### Approved Technology Is Not Available for Industry's Use
Technical problems are slowing the development of new technology, and it may be several years before new security devices are in use that can meet FAA's requirements for screening checked baggage. FAA has 40 detection projects but has conducted laboratory tests on only 7; none fully meets FAA's performance requirements. In the interim, FAA is considering pur-

chasing commercially available devices, but such devices have limitations. . . .

### *FAA Can Take Steps to Improve Technology Development*

Since explosive detection technology is evolving, FAA will be conducting security research well into the foreseeable future. GAO identified several weaknesses whose resolution would enhance FAA's current and future efforts. For example, FAA's process for certifying new explosive detection devices does not ensure that the technology can perform reliably in day-to-day use. FAA plans to rely on tests conducted at its own laboratory—not at a major domestic airport—before approving new technology for airlines' use. FAA officials believe that conducting such tests would, among other things, add time and cost to the certification process. However, the airline industry and others disagree with FAA's approach and believe that operational testing should be part of the certification process.

In addition, FAA does not evaluate the effectiveness and/or performance of the software for the new devices even though the devices rely heavily on automation to reduce dependence on human operators. Also, despite recommendations from the Office of Technology Assessment and the Aviation Security Research and Development Scientific Advisory Panel, FAA has made little progress in integrating (linking) various technologies to maximize the strengths of each. FAA, the National Academy of Sciences, and others agree that no single device can meet all of FAA's requirements for screening checked baggage; therefore, devices will have to be used in combination. However, FAA plans to rely largely on the airlines to combine various devices into explosive detection systems. GAO believes a more prudent approach would be to address systems integration early in the development process to reduce development costs and delays and ensure that devices can work together effectively. Furthermore, although the devices rely heavily on automation, they are unlikely, in the near term, to eliminate the need for screeners. Yet FAA does not pay sufficient attention to human factors associated with using the new devices, such as how screeners understand alarms and make decisions about suspicious objects. . . .

Excerpted from U.S. Congress. General Accounting Office. *Aviation Security: Development of New Security Technology Has Not Met Expectations.* GAO/RCED-94-142, May 19, 1994. http://archive.gao.gov/t2pbat3/151682.pdf (accessed September 1, 2004).

## 40. General Accounting Office Congressional Testimony on Security Vulnerabilities in the Aviation System
*September 11, 1996*

Protecting civil aviation from a terrorist attack is an urgent national issue. We appreciate the opportunity to testify before this Committee on the serious vulnerabilities that exist within the nation's air transportation system and ways to address them. Experts on terrorism within the government intelligence agencies believe that the threat to civil aviation is increasing. . . .

### The Threat of Terrorists' Attacks on U.S. Civil Aviation Has Increased

. . . Until the early 1990s, the threat of terrorism was considered far greater overseas than in the United States. However, the threat of international terrorism within the United States has increased. Events such as the World Trade Center bombing have revealed that the terrorists' threat in the United States is more serious and extensive than previously believed.

Terrorists' activities are continually evolving and present unique challenges to FAA and law enforcement agencies. We reported in March 1996 that the bombing of Philippine Airlines flight 434 in December 1994 illustrated the potential extent of terrorists' motivation and capabilities as well as the attractiveness of aviation as a target for terrorists. According to information that was accidentally uncovered in January 1995, this bombing was a rehearsal for multiple attacks on specific U.S. flights in Asia.

### Aviation Security System and Its Vulnerabilities

Even though FAA has increased security procedures as the threat has increased, the domestic and international aviation system continues to have numerous vulnerabilities. According to information provided by the intelligence community, FAA makes judgments about the threat and decides which procedures would best address the threat. The airlines and airports are responsible for implementing the procedures and paying for them. For example, the airlines are responsible for screening passengers and property, and the airports are responsible for the security of the airport environment. FAA and the aviation community rely on a multifaceted approach that includes information from various intelligence and law enforcement agencies, contingency plans to meet a variety of threat levels, and the use of screening equipment, such as conventional X-ray devices and metal detectors.

For flights within the United States, basic security measures include the use of walk-through metal detectors for passengers and X-ray screening of carry-on baggage—measures that were primarily designed to avert hijackings during the 1970s and 1980s, as opposed to the more current threat of attacks by terrorists that involve explosive devices. These measures are augmented by additional procedures that are based on an assessment of risk. Among these procedures are passenger profiling and passenger-bag matching.

Because the threat of terrorism had previously been considered greater overseas, FAA mandated more stringent security measures for international flights. Currently, for all international flights, FAA requires U.S. carriers, at a minimum, to implement the International Civil Aviation Organization's standards that include the inspection of carry-on bags and passenger-bag matching. FAA also requires additional, more stringent measures—including interviewing passengers that meet certain criteria, screening every checked bag, and screening carry-on baggage—at all airports in Europe and the Middle East and many airports elsewhere. . . .

Providing effective security is a complex problem because of the size of the U.S. aviation system, the differences among airlines and airports, and the unpredictable nature of terrorism. In our previous reports and testimonies on aviation security, we highlighted a number of vulnerabilities in the overall security system, such as checked and carry-on baggage, mail, and cargo. We also raised concerns about unauthorized individuals gaining access to critical parts of an airport and the potential use of sophisticated weapons, such as surface-to-air missiles, against commercial aircraft. According to FAA officials, more recent concerns include smuggling bombs aboard aircraft in carry-on bags and on passengers themselves.

Specific information on the vulnerabilities of the nation's aviation security system is classified and cannot be detailed here, but we can provide you with unclassified information. Nearly every major aspect of the system—ranging from the screening of passengers, checked and carry-on baggage, mail, and cargo as well as access to secured areas within airports and aircraft—has weaknesses that terrorists could exploit. FAA believes that the greatest threat to aviation is explosives placed in checked baggage. For those bags that are screened, we reported in March 1996 that conventional X-ray screening systems (comprising the machine and operator who interprets the image on the X-ray screen) have performance limitations and offer little protection against a moderately sophisticated explosive device. . . .

In 1993, the Department of Transportation's Office of the Inspector General also reported weaknesses in security measures dealing with (1) access to restricted airport areas by unauthorized persons and (2) carry-on baggage. A follow-on review in 1996 indicated that these weaknesses continue to persist and have not significantly improved. . . .

## Initiatives to Address Vulnerabilities Should Be Coordinated

Addressing the vulnerabilities in the nation's aviation security system is an urgent national issue. . . . [N]o agreement currently exists among all the key players, namely, the Congress, the administration—specifically FAA and the intelligence community, among others—and the aviation industry, on the steps necessary to improve security in the short and long term to meet the threat. In addition, who will be responsible in the long term for paying for new security initiatives has not been addressed. . . .

In our August 1, 1996, testimony before the Senate Committee on Commerce, Science, and Transportation, we emphasized the importance of informing the American public of and involving them in this effort. Furthermore, we recommended that the following steps be taken immediately:

- Conduct a comprehensive review of the safety and security of all major domestic and international airports and airlines to identify the strengths and weaknesses of their procedures to protect the traveling public.
- Identify vulnerabilities in the system.
- Establish priorities to address the system's identified vulnerabilities.
- Develop a short-term approach with immediate actions to correct significant security weaknesses.
- Develop a long-term and comprehensive national strategy that combines new technology, procedures, and better training for security personnel. . . .

Given the persistence of long-standing vulnerabilities and the increased threat to civil aviation, we believe corrective actions need to be undertaken immediately. These actions need a unified effort from the highest levels of the government to address this national issue. . . .

Excerpted from U.S. Congress. General Accounting Office. *Aviation Security: Urgent Issues Need to Be Addressed.* Prepared testimony of Keith O. Fultz for a hearing by the Subcommittee on Aviation of the House Committee on Transportation and Infrastructure. GAO/T-RCED/NSIAD-96-251, September 11, 1996. http://www.gao.gov/archive/1996/rc96251t.pdf (accessed September 1, 2004).

# 41. White House Commission on Aviation Safety and Security Report

*February 12, 1997*

## Chapter Three: Improving Security for Travelers

. . . The Federal Bureau of Investigation, the Central Intelligence Agency, and other intelligence sources have been warning that the threat of terrorism is changing in two important ways. First, it is no longer just an overseas threat from foreign terrorists. People and places in the United States have joined the list of targets, and Americans have joined the ranks of terrorists. The bombings of the World Trade Center in New York and the Federal Building in Oklahoma City are clear examples of the shift, as is the conviction of Ramzi Yousef for attempting to bomb twelve American airliners out of the sky over the Pacific Ocean. The second change is that in addition to well-known, established terrorist groups, it is becoming more common to find terrorists working alone or in ad-hoc groups, some of whom are not afraid to die in carrying out their designs.

Although the threat of terrorism is increasing, the danger of an individual becoming a victim of a terrorist attack—let alone an aircraft bombing—will doubtless remain very small. But terrorism isn't merely a matter of statistics. We fear a plane crash far more than we fear something like a car accident. One might survive a car accident, but there's no chance in a plane at 30,000 feet. This fear is one of the reasons that terrorists see airplanes as attractive targets. And, they know that airlines are often seen as national symbols.

When terrorists attack an American airliner, they are attacking the United States. . . .

Today's aviation security is based in part on the defenses erected in the 1970s against hijackers and on recommendations made by the Commission on Aviation Security and Terrorism, which was formed in the wake of the bombing of Pan Am 103 over Lockerbie, Scotland. Improvements in aviation security have been complicated because government and industry often found themselves at odds, unable to resolve disputes over financing, effectiveness, technology, and potential impacts on operations and passengers.

Americans should not have to choose between enhanced security and efficient and affordable air travel. Both goals are achievable if the federal government, airlines, airports, aviation employees, local law enforcement agencies, and passengers work together to achieve them. Accordingly, the

Commission recommends a new partnership that will marshal resources more effectively, and focus all parties on achieving the ultimate goal: enhancing the security of air travel for Americans.

The Commission considered the question of whether or not the FAA is the appropriate government agency to have the primary responsibility for regulating aviation security. The Commission believes that, because of its extensive interactions with airlines and airports, the FAA is the appropriate agency, with the following qualifications: first, that the FAA must improve the way it carries out its mission; and second, that the roles of intelligence and law enforcement agencies in supporting the FAA must be more clearly defined and coordinated. The Commission's recommendations address those conditions.

The terrorist threat is changing and growing. Therefore, it is important to improve security not just against familiar threats, such as explosives in checked baggage, but also to explore means of assessing and countering emerging threats, such as the use of biological or chemical agents, or the use of missiles. While these do not present significant threats at present, it would be short-sighted not to plan for their possible use and take prudent steps to counter them.

The Commission believes that aviation security should be a system of systems, layered, integrated, and working together to produce the highest possible levels of protection. . . .

Excerpted from U.S. Executive Office of the President. White House Commission on Aviation Safety and Security. *Final Report to President Clinton.* February 12, 1997. http://www.fas.org/irp/threat/212fin~1.html (accessed September 1, 2004).

---

# 42. Department of Transportation Inspector General's Report on Airport Access Control
*November 18, 1999*

### Objective and Scope

In 1993, we reported that FAA oversight of airport security systems and programs was not adequate, and that FAA inspection and testing of airport security systems and programs were not aggressive. We concluded that, at the airports reviewed, FAA could not rely on existing security systems and programs for safeguarding aircraft, passengers, and property in secure areas and terminals. . . .

We concentrated our work on FAA's efforts to implement corrective actions planned in response to our 1993 report on airport security. . . .

### Results-in-Brief

Airport access control has been, and continues to be, an area of great concern due to increased threat to U.S. airport facilities, aircraft, and most importantly, the flying public. However, FAA has been slow to take actions necessary to strengthen access control requirements and adequately oversee the implementation of existing controls.

We tested access control from December 1998 through April 1999 at eight major U.S. airports and found airport operators and air carriers operating at those airports had not successfully implemented procedures for limiting access to and within secure airport areas to only authorized persons. . . .

We successfully penetrated secure areas on 117 (68 percent) of 173 attempts from the non-sterile and sterile areas of the airport. The non-sterile area is an area to which access is *not* controlled by the inspection of people and property in accordance with an approved security program, i.e. the area before passenger screening. For example, airport terminal areas that include ticketing and baggage claim are usually non-sterile areas. Once a person passes through passenger screening he/she enters the sterile area. Airport concourses that include the gates for aircraft departures and arrivals are sterile areas.

. . . [W]e piggybacked (followed) employees through doors located in non-sterile areas, penetrated other access points in sterile and non-sterile areas by riding unguarded elevators, and walking through concourse doors, gates and jetbridges; walked through cargo facilities unchallenged; and drove through unmanned vehicle gates.

Once we penetrated secure areas, we boarded aircraft operated by 35 different air carriers 117 times. . . .

### Principal Findings

*Airport Operators and Air Carriers Had Not Successfully Implemented Procedures for Controlling Access*

. . . [F]or the 117 aircraft boarded as a result of penetrating into secure areas:

- in 43 (37 percent) boardings, no air carrier personnel were onboard to ensure the security of the aircraft as required by security programs;
- in 43 (37 percent) boardings, employees (flight crews, maintenance

staff, food service workers, and other vendor personnel) were onboard but did not challenge us as required;

- in 13 (11 percent) boardings, air carrier personnel were present and challenged us inside the aircraft more than 3 minutes after we boarded; and

- in only 18 (15 percent) boardings, air carrier personnel were present and properly challenged us inside the aircraft within 3 minutes [FAA uses 3 minutes as the threshold for determining whether an aircraft was successfully penetrated].

In addition, passengers were onboard 18 of the aircraft we boarded. In 12 instances, we were seated and ready for departure at the time we concluded our tests.

*Employees Often Did Not Meet Their Responsibilities for Airport Security*

At each of the eight airports we reviewed, employees authorized for access in secure areas are responsible for, and a part of, airport access control. Employee responsibilities include requirements to: display identification, challenge others not displaying identification, and prohibit other employees and unauthorized individuals from piggybacking when entering secure areas. We frequently found that employees did not meet their responsibilities for airport security, and as a result, they are the primary reason for access control system weaknesses.

The majority of our penetrations (99 of 117) into secure areas that resulted in testers boarding aircraft would not have occurred if employees had (1) ensured the door closed behind them after entering the secure area (68 times); (2) challenged us for following them into secure areas (3 times); or (3) taken other steps required to restrict entry into secure areas (28 times), such as control pedestrian access through cargo facilities and vehicle gates.

In addition to our tests to penetrate secure areas, we performed two specific tests to identify weaknesses in employees' compliance with requirements to challenge and properly display identification in the secure area. The results of our tests found that:

- 283 (72 percent) of the 392 employees we encountered in secure areas failed to challenge testers for unauthorized access; and

- 116 (19 percent) of 625 employees we observed in secure areas did not display identification.

We reported the same weaknesses in 1993. In response to our 1993 recommendations, FAA disclosed that new rules to increase individual accountability for airport security were underway. The proposed rule was issued on August 1, 1997, but was not finalized. According to FAA, the final rule is scheduled to be issued March 1, 2000. . . .

Each of the eight airports reviewed required training for employees seeking authorization to secure airport areas. However, we found the training was not adequate to inform employees of their access control responsibilities, and it was generally one-time rather than recurring training. . . .

*FAA Had Not Fully Implemented Its Oversight Program to Ensure Compliance with Airport Access Control Requirements*
FAA has not adequately assessed and accurately reported on airport operator and air carrier compliance with access control requirements. We found FAA's airport assessments of compliance with access control requirements were limited in scope, included little testing, did not use a testing protocol, and failed to identify violations. Also, assessment data maintained in FAA's security database were inaccurate due to data reporting, entry, and administration errors. Further, FAA has not fully implemented its quality control program to ensure the adequacy and accuracy of compliance assessments. We reported similar conditions in 1993. . . .

Excerpted from U.S. Department of Transportation. Office of Inspector General. *Airport Access Control.* Report No. AV-2000-017, November 18, 1999. http://news.findlaw.com/cnn/docs/terrorism/faaairport111899.pdf (accessed September 1, 2004).

# 43. General Accounting Office Congressional Testimony on Airport Screeners
*March 16, 2000*

. . . Events over the past decade have shown that the threat of terrorism against the United States is an ever-present danger. Aviation is an attractive target for terrorists, and because the air transportation system is critical to the nation's well-being, protecting it is an important national issue. A single lapse in aviation security can result in hundreds of deaths, destruction of equipment worth hundreds of millions of dollars, and have immeasurable negative impacts on the economy and the public's confidence in air travel.

Concerns have been raised for many years by GAO and others about the effectiveness of screeners and the need to improve their performance. Two Presidential commissions—established after the bombing of Pan Am Flight 103 in 1988 and the then-unexplained crash of TWA Flight 800 in 1996—as well as numerous GAO and Department of Transportation Inspector

General reports have highlighted problems with screening and the need for improvements. This situation still exists. . . .

## Background

Screening checkpoints and the screeners who operate them are a key line of defense against the introduction of a dangerous object into the aviation system. Over 2 million passengers and their baggage must be checked each day for weapons, explosives, or other dangerous articles that could pose a threat to the safety of an aircraft and those aboard it. . . .

Screeners use metal detectors, X-ray machines, and physical bag searches to identify dangerous objects. However, because equipment at checkpoints does not automatically detect threats, the effectiveness of the screening depends heavily on the performance of the screeners themselves. It can be a difficult, stressful, yet monotonous job, requiring sustained attention to the task of identifying faint indications of infrequently appearing targets. The screeners detect thousands of dangerous objects each year. Over the last 5 years, screeners detected nearly 10,000 firearms being carried through checkpoints. Nevertheless, screeners do not identify all threats—instances occur each year in which weapons were discovered to have passed through a checkpoint.

## Screener Performance Problems Are Attributed to Rapid Turnover and Inattention to Human Factors

There is no single reason why screeners fail to identify dangerous objects. Two conditions—rapid screener turnover and inadequate attention to human factors—are believed to be important causes. The rapid turnover among screeners has been a long-standing problem, having been singled out as a concern in FAA and GAO reports dating back to at least 1979. We reported in 1987 that turnover among screeners was about 100 percent a year at some airports, and today, the turnover is considerably higher. From May 1998 through April 1999, screener turnover averaged 126 percent at the nation's 19 largest airports, with five airports reporting turnover of 200 percent or more and one reporting turnover of 416 percent. At one airport we visited, of the 993 screeners trained at that airport over about a 1-year period, only 142, or 14 percent, were still employed at the end of that year. Such rapid turnover can seriously affect the level of experience among screeners operating a checkpoint.

Both FAA and the aviation industry attribute the rapid turnover to the low wages screeners receive, the minimal benefits, and the daily stress of the job. Generally, screeners get paid at or near the minimum wage. We found that some of the screening companies at 14 of the nation's 19 largest airports paid screeners a starting salary of $6.00 an hour or less and, at 5 of these airports, the starting salary was the minimum wage—$5.15 an hour. It is common for the starting wages at airport fast-food restaurants to be higher than the wages screeners receive. . . .

Human factors associated with screening—those work-related issues that are influenced by human capabilities and constraints—have also been noted by FAA as problems affecting performance for over 20 years. Screening duties require repetitive tasks as well as intense monitoring for the very rare event when a dangerous object might be observed. Too little attention has been given to factors such as (1) individuals' aptitudes for effectively performing screener duties, (2) the sufficiency of the training provided to the screeners and how well they comprehend it, and (3) the monotony of the job and the distractions that reduce the screeners' vigilance. As a result, screeners are being placed on the job who do not have the necessary abilities, do not have adequate knowledge to effectively perform the work, and who then find the duties tedious and unstimulating.

## FAA is Making Efforts to Address Causes of Screeners' Performance Problems, but Progress Has Been Slow

FAA has demonstrated that it is aware of the need to improve the screeners' performance by conducting efforts intended to address the turnover and human factors problems and establishing goals with which to measure the agency's success in improving screener performance. . . .

### The Threat Image Projection System
FAA is deploying an enhancement to the X-ray machines used at the checkpoints called the threat image projection (TIP) system. As screeners routinely scan passengers' carry-on bags, TIP occasionally projects images of threat objects like guns and explosives on the X-ray machines' screens. Screeners are expected to spot the threat objects and signal for the bags to be manually searched. Once prompted, TIP indicates whether an image is of an actual object in a bag or was generated by the system and also records the screeners' responses, providing a measure of their performance while keeping them more alert. By frequently exposing screeners to what a variety of threat images look like on screen, TIP will also provide continuous on-the-job training.

FAA is behind schedule in deploying this system. . . .

### The Certification of Screening Companies
In response to a mandate in the Federal Aviation Reauthorization Act of 1996 and a recommendation from the 1997 White House Commission on Aviation Safety and Security, FAA is creating a program to certify the security companies that staff the screening checkpoints. The agency plans to

establish performance standards—an action we recommended in 1987—
that the screening companies will have to meet in order to earn and retain
certification. . . . FAA believes that the need to meet certification standards
will give the security companies a greater incentive to retain their best
screeners longer and so will indirectly reduce turnover by raising the screeners' wages and improving training. . . .

The agency plans to use data from the TIP system to guide it in setting
its performance standards, but because the system will not be at all airports
before the end of fiscal year 2003, the agency is having to explore additional
ways to set standards. FAA plans to issue the regulation establishing the certification program by May 2001, over 2 years later than its original deadline. . . .

## Screening Practices in Five Other Countries Differ from U.S. Practices

We visited five countries—Belgium, Canada, France, the Netherlands,
and the United Kingdom—viewed by FAA and industry as having effective
screening operations to identify screening practices that differ from those in
the United States. . . .

First, screening operations in some countries are more stringent. For
example, Belgium, the Netherlands, and the United Kingdom routinely
touch or "pat down" passengers in response to metal detector alarms. Additionally, all five countries allowed only ticketed passengers through the
screening checkpoints, thereby allowing the screeners to more thoroughly
check fewer people. Some countries also had a greater police or military
presence near checkpoints. . . .

Second, the screeners' qualifications are usually more extensive. In contrast to the United States, Belgium requires screeners to be citizens; France
requires screeners to be citizens of a European Union country. In the
Netherlands, screeners do not have to be citizens, but they must have been
residents of the country for 5 years. Four of the countries we visited had
greater training requirements for screeners. While FAA requires that screeners in this country have 12 hours of classroom training, Belgium, Canada,
France, and the Netherlands require more. For example, France requires
60 hours of training and Belgium requires at least 40 hours of training with
an additional 16 to 24 hours for each activity, such as x-ray machine operations, the screener will conduct.

Third, screeners receive relatively better pay and benefits in most of these
countries. While in the United States screeners receive wages that are at or
slightly above minimum wage, screeners in some countries receive wages
that are viewed as being at the "middle income" level by screeners. In the
Netherlands, for example, screeners receive at least the equivalent of about
$7.50 per hour. This wage is about 30 percent higher than wages at fast-

food restaurants. In Belgium, screeners receive about $14 per hour. Not only is pay higher, but the screeners in some countries receive some benefits, such as health care or vacations—in large part because it is required under the laws of these countries.

Finally, the responsibility for screening in most of these countries is placed with the airport or with the government, not with the air carriers as it is in the United States. . . .

## Summary

The message I bring here today is not new. The performance problems affecting airport screeners are longstanding. Yet, as we enter the new millennium, not only do the same problems continue to exist but in the case of turnover among the screeners, it is even getting worse. . . .

> Excerpted from U.S. Congress. General Accounting Office. *Aviation Security: Slow Progress in Addressing Longstanding Screener Performance Problems.* Prepared testimony of Gerald L. Dillingham for a hearing by the Subcommittee on Aviation of the House Committee on Transportation and Infrastructure. GAO/T-RCED-00-125, March 16, 2000. http://www.gao.gov/archive/2000/rc00125t.pdf (accessed September 1, 2004).

# 44. Department of Transportation Inspector General's Press Release on Sentences in Background Check Case

*October 25, 2000*

Argenbright Holdings Limited was placed on 36 months' probation and ordered by a U.S. District Court judge in Philadelphia to pay a $1 million fine, $350,000 in restitution and $200,000 in investigative costs, for failing to conduct background checks on employees staffing security checkpoints at the Philadelphia Airport between 1995 and 1999. Steven Saffer, former district manager for Argenbright, was sentenced on October 20 to 30 months' incarceration for falsely certifying to the FAA that training and background checks of 1,300 security checkers at Philadelphia had been completed. Argenbright employee Sandra Lawrence was fined $15,000 and placed on 60 months' probation. As a result, Argenbright hired convicted felons and improperly trained workers to provide airport security. OIG [Office of Inspector General] investigated this case with the FAA.

U.S. Department of Transportation. Office of Inspector General. *Argenbright Fined $1 Million in Falsification Case.* October 25, 2000. http://www.oig.dot.gov/item_details.php?item=570 (accessed March 7, 2004).

# The 1993 Bombing of the World Trade Center

**45. New York City Police Commissioner Raymond Kelly's Congressional Testimony on the 1993 World Trade Center Bombing, March 9, 1993**

## INTRODUCTION

The plan was carefully designed: in the garage underneath the 110-story World Trade Center in New York City, park a van filled with explosives in a specific spot. The blast would topple one of the twin towers into the other, knocking down both and killing tens of thousands of people.

The bomb exploded at 12:18 p.m. on February 26, 1993. Even though it was strong enough to blast a crater six stories deep, the bomb failed to topple the New York City landmarks. Nonetheless, the explosion killed six people, injured more than 1,000 others, and caused property damage alone of nearly $300 million.

Less than two weeks later, a subcommittee of the House Judiciary Committee conducted the first public hearing into the bombing on March 9, 1993. Law enforcement officials said they suspected a terrorist group was responsible, although they did not name any particular group. William Sessions, the director of the Federal Bureau of Investigation (FBI), tried to calm public fears. "This suspected act of terrorism should not be viewed as an opening act of a coming wave of terror," Sessions said. Raymond Kelly, the New York City police commissioner, provided riveting testimony about efforts by firefighters, police officers, and emergency medical services personnel to treat the injured and evacuate more than 50,000 people from the buildings [Document 45].

The plot's mastermind was Ramzi Yousef, a terrorist with links to Osama bin Laden and his al Qaeda network. Yousef fled the United States the night of the attack. Later he developed a plan to bomb a dozen American airliners as they flew over the Pacific Ocean on their way from the Far East. The bombing was only days away from occurring when a fire broke out on January 6, 1995, in the Philippines apartment where Yousef and another terrorist were mixing chemicals, attracting the attention of authorities. Yousef escaped again, but FBI agents and diplomatic security officers from the State Department captured him on February 7, 1995, in Islamabad, Pakistan, and immediately flew him to the United States for trial.

Yousef was convicted of bombing the World Trade Center and conspiring to blow up the airliners, and on January 8, 1998, a judge sentenced him to life in prison plus 240 years. The judge recommended that Yousef spend the entire sentence in solitary confinement. At the sentencing Yousef said, "Yes, I am a terrorist and proud of it as long as it is against the U.S. government," and denounced U.S. support for Israel. Five other Islamic extremists also were convicted in the World Trade Center bombing.

Eight years after the 1993 bombing, other Islamic terrorists associated with al Qaeda attacked the World Trade Center again, this time by slamming two hijacked commercial airliners into the twin towers. Raging fires fed by thousands of gallons of aviation fuel caused both buildings to collapse, killing nearly 3,000 people (*see* Bush Condemns Terrorist Attacks Against the United States, p. 241).

---

## 45. New York City Police Commissioner Raymond Kelly's Congressional Testimony on the 1993 World Trade Center Bombing
*March 9, 1993*

. . . As you know, the World Trade Center includes two of the tallest office buildings in the world. Up until February, approximately 90,000 people worked and visited there every weekday. At least five of them were killed as a result of the bombing. A thousand more were injured, and the lives of tens of thousands more were severely disrupted. Estimates vary, but the loss incurred by businesses and individuals at the World Trade Center are in the neighborhood of $1 billion.

The World Trade Center bombing was the largest such attack experienced within the borders of the United States. As such, it has implications far beyond the New York metropolitan area. It has implications that Congress certainly will want to address. But before I touch on that let me tell you what happened, how the police department and other agencies responded to the immediate emergency, and how our joint investigation with the FBI and other federal agencies is going forward.

On Friday, February 26th, at 12:18 p.m. an explosion ripped through six underground parking levels of the World Trade Center located immediately underneath the Vista Hotel and between the two twin towers. Within minutes of the explosion, the street in front of the World Trade Center was filled with responding emergency equipment from the New York City Police Department, the New York City Fire Department, emergency medical services, and of course the Port Authority of New York and New Jersey, which owns the center.

As hundreds of victims suffering from smoke inhalation streamed out of the twin towers and the Vista Hotel, emergency equipment and personnel were already on hand to treat them at the scene, or to evacuate them to nearby hospitals.

Over 450 people were sent to area hospitals.

Another 170 were treated at the scene. Four hundred more walked into nearby hospitals on their own. Four New York City Police Department helicopters made 40 rooftop landings on towers one and two of the World Trade Center between 12:30 p.m. and 11:00 p.m.

During these first flights 25 New York City police officers rappelled from helicopters to the roof of tower one, where a landing zone was established and where immediate search and rescue efforts were launched.

Fighting high winds and nightfall, police department pilots delivered a total of 125 rescue personnel to the roofs. Over 30 people were evacuated to safety aboard the helicopters. . . .

A host of police, fire, and EMS equipment was deployed, including mobile light generators, gasoline and diesel refueling trucks, large electrical generators, decontamination vehicles, 125 ambulances, and 119 pieces of firefighting apparatus.

Uniformed officers from our police task forces scattered throughout the five boroughs were mobilized and brought to bear in the emergency. In all, 2,000 police, fire, and EMS personnel were on the scene. The search of the twin towers and the Vista Hotel by police, fire, and Port Authority personnel began immediately and continued through the night. Between 9:30 p.m. and 2:50 a.m. both towers of the World Trade Center were searched for a second time, floor by floor, to make certain no one was left behind.

The fire department and Port Authority personnel searched the first 50 floors of the twin towers, and the police department searched from the 51st floor to the roofs.

While search and rescue were still underway, the simultaneous turning of our attention to the blast site took place. Working with agents of the FBI and ATF [Bureau of Alcohol, Tobacco, and Firearms], here is what we found.

The explosion took place on the B-2 level of the underground garage. The blast was so strong that it produced a crater six stories deep and about 200 feet wide. . . .

You can see in the pictures of these twisted wrecks [of cars in the parking garage] that a tremendous amount of heat was produced at the center of the blast and the heat was one of the factors that led us to the conclusion early on that a bomb had been exploded.

The chassis of a van used in the blast was blown away from the center of the crater. It contained the partial vehicle identification number that eventually led to the arrest of Mohammed Salameh at a truck rental agency in New Jersey.

From the pictures you can get a good idea of how the vertical beams, as we said, were left without any lateral support, and workers are now welding lateral supports in place so that we can go forward with our search for evidence and for the missing employee, Wilfredo Mercado, Jr.

The successes in the investigation to date extend directly in my judgment from the fact that the New York City Police Department and the Federal Bureau of Investigation have a long working relationship. Our joint bank robbery task force was the first cooperative effort in the nation, and remains a national model. Our joint terrorist task force is now 13 years old and we work cooperatively every day of the year. We share resources. . . .

As police commissioner, I certainly welcome the chairman's efforts to seek legislation to strengthen the federal role in combating terrorism. Certainly anything that can help us prevent a single terrorist act from occurring, or in apprehending those responsible, merits serious examination by Congress.

While obviously we would never welcome such attacks, we know that in New York City we are prepared to deal with them. Anyone contemplating such an act should know that the best law enforcement personnel in the world will be on their case for as long as it takes.

We are in the business of tracking down killers and locking them up, and we don't forget. New York City will never forget. . . .

Excerpted from U.S. Congress. House. Committee on the Judiciary. Subcommittee on Crime and Criminal Justice. *World Trade Center Bombing: Terror Hits Home.* Testimony of Raymond Kelly. 103rd Cong., 1st sess., March 9, 1993.

# Bombing of
# the Federal Building in
# Oklahoma City, Oklahoma

## INTRODUCTION

In the later decades of the twentieth century, nations in the Middle East, Europe, and elsewhere suffered frequent terrorist attacks. Terrorists sometimes targeted Americans overseas. Two of the most prominent examples were the 1983 bombing of the Marine headquarters in Beirut, Lebanon, by pro-Iranian Muslim extremists that killed 241 U.S. service personnel and the 1988 bombing of Pan Am Flight 103 by a Libyan agent that killed 270 people—including 189 Americans—as the plane flew from Frankfurt to New York City. But only a few small, isolated terrorist incidents had occurred in the United States, so Americans felt they were safe from terrorism. American counterterrorism officials agreed and concentrated much of their efforts on protecting U.S. targets overseas. These views dominated even after the 1993 bombing of the World Trade Center in New York by Muslim extremists made it clear terrorists could strike the American homeland (*see* The 1993 Bombing of the World Trade Center, p. 125).

Americans forever lost their sense of security a few minutes after 9 a.m. on April 19, 1995, when a massive truck bomb blew up in front of the Alfred P. Murrah Federal Building in Oklahoma City, Oklahoma. The bomb contained at least two tons of fuel oil, fertilizer, and other explosives and destroyed much of the nine-story structure. The blast killed 168 people, including 19 children in the building's day-care center, and injured more than 500 others.

In a brief statement that evening, President Bill Clinton denounced the "evil cowards" who had attacked "innocent children and defenseless citizens." He announced that teams from various federal agencies had been sent to Oklahoma to help the stricken city and find those responsible for the attack. "Let there be no room for doubt: We will find the people who did this," the president said. "When we do, justice will be swift, certain, and severe" [Document 46].

Much of the initial speculation focused on foreign terrorists as the most likely culprits. However, investigators quickly determined that two former Army buddies—Timothy McVeigh and Terry Nichols—were responsible. Government officials identified McVeigh as the plot's mastermind and the person who drove the bomb-laden truck to the Murrah Building, and they said Nichols bought many of the bomb's components. Both men were believed to profoundly hate the federal government, and the Federal Bureau of Investigation (FBI) said McVeigh was particularly upset about the government's handling of a 1993 incident in Waco, Texas, where seventy-two members of an armed religious cult led by David Koresh died in a fire while their compound was under siege by the FBI. The Oklahoma bombing occurred on the second anniversary of the Waco disaster.

Four days after the Oklahoma bombing, more than 10,000 people gathered at the state fairgrounds for a prayer service. "Never in the history of our country have Americans witnessed such senseless barbarism," Gov. Frank Keating told the mourners. President Clinton, who attended the service with his wife, said that to honor the victims the nation must eliminate "the dark forces which gave rise to this evil. They are forces that threaten our common peace, our freedom, our way of life" [Keating's remarks, Document 47; Clinton's remarks, Document 48].

Meanwhile, on April 20 Clinton asked Attorney General Janet Reno to review security measures at all federal buildings, and he later ordered all federal agencies to implement the fifty-two standards for minimum security recommended by the Justice Department. As an additional security precaution, Clinton announced in his weekly radio address on May 20 that the two blocks of Pennsylvania Avenue in front of the White House were being closed immediately to all vehicular traffic [Document 49]. Clinton noted that Pennsylvania Avenue, which was known as "America's Main Street" because it ran in front of the White House, had been open to traffic for the nation's entire history:

Through four Presidential assassinations and eight unsuccessful attempts on the lives of Presidents, it's been open; through a civil war, two world wars and the Gulf War, it was open. And now it must be closed. . . . Clearly, this closing is necessary because of the changing nature and scope of the threat of terrorist actions.

The action helped set off a massive effort in Washington to surround federal buildings and memorials with concrete barriers, chain-link fences, cast-iron posts, and other large objects that could block trucks carrying bombs. Residents and visitors alike lamented that Washington was becoming more ugly and less open with each barrier. The number of barriers and other security measures vastly increased after the terrorist attacks of September 2001. "Though the new urbanscape is meant to enhance security, many places look as though a small bomb already had gone off," wrote *Washington Post* reporter Fred Hiatt in December 2001. "Ditches, concrete barriers, unsightly guard huts, hastily erected fences, barricaded streets: The message is fear."

On August 10, 1995, a federal grand jury in Oklahoma City indicted McVeigh and Nichols on eleven counts: conspiring to use a weapon of mass destruction, destroying federal property, using a truck bomb to kill people, and murdering eight federal law enforcement officials who died in their offices at the Murrah Building. On June 2, 1997, a federal jury in Denver convicted McVeigh on all counts, and on June 13 the same jury said he should receive the death penalty. At his formal sentencing on August 14, McVeigh's only comment was to quote former Supreme Court Justice Louis D. Brandeis: "Our government is the hope, the omnipresent teacher, for good or for ill. It teaches people by its example."

Just five days before McVeigh was scheduled to die on May 16, 2001, Attorney General John Ashcroft took the extraordinary step of postponing the execution after it was revealed that the FBI had failed to share thousands of pages of evidence with McVeigh's attorneys. Government officials said the documents had no bearing on McVeigh's guilt, and two different courts agreed. McVeigh was finally executed by lethal injection in the early morning hours of June 11, 2001, at the U.S. Penitentiary in Terre Haute, Indiana. Harley Lappin, the penitentiary's warden, told reporters that McVeigh cooperated throughout the process [Document 50].

In a separate trial, a federal jury on December 23, 1997, convicted Nichols of conspiracy and involuntary manslaughter. He was sentenced to life in prison without parole after jurors deadlocked on the issue of whether he should be executed. The federal charges only applied to the eight federal law enforcement officers who died.

On March 29, 1999, the Oklahoma County district attorney charged Nichols with 161 state counts of first-degree murder that covered the remaining bombing victims and a fetus. The district attorney announced that he would seek the death penalty.

After a lengthy trial, a jury convicted Nichols of all the charges on May 26, 2004. Like the federal jury, it deadlocked on whether Nichols should be executed. On August 9, 2004, State District Judge Steven Taylor ordered Nichols to serve 161 consecutive life sentences without the possibility of parole.

# 46. President Bill Clinton's Remarks on the Oklahoma City Bombing
*April 19, 1995*

The bombing in Oklahoma City was an attack on innocent children and defenseless citizens. It was an act of cowardice, and it was evil. The United States will not tolerate it. And I will not allow the people of this country to be intimidated by evil cowards.

I have met with our team, which we assembled to deal with this bombing. And I have determined to take the following steps to assure the strongest response to this situation:

First, I have deployed a crisis management team under the leadership of the FBI, working with the Department of Justice, the Bureau of Alcohol, Tobacco and Firearms, military and local authorities. We are sending the world's finest investigators to solve these murders.

Second, I have declared an emergency in Oklahoma City. And at my direction, James Lee Witt, the Director of the Federal Emergency Management Agency, is now on his way there to make sure we do everything we can to help the people of Oklahoma deal with the tragedy.

Third, we are taking every precaution to reassure and to protect people who work in or live near other Federal facilities.

Let there be no room for doubt: We will find the people who did this. When we do, justice will be swift, certain, and severe. These people are killers, and they must be treated like killers.

Finally, let me say that I ask all Americans tonight to pray—to pray for the people who have lost their lives, to pray for the families and the friends of the dead and the wounded, to pray for the people of Oklahoma City.

May God's grace be with them. Meanwhile, we will be about our work. Thank you.

U.S. Executive Office of the President. "Remarks on the Oklahoma City Bombing." April 19, 1995. *Weekly Compilation of Presidential Documents* 31, no. 16 (April 24, 1995): 662. http://frwebgate4.access.gpo.gov/cgi-bin/ waisgate.cgi?WAISdocID=49477729796+2+0+0&WAISaction=retrieve (accessed September 1, 2004).

# 47. Oklahoma Governor Frank Keating's Speech at the Memorial Service for the Oklahoma City Bombing Victims

*April 23, 1995*

The tragedy of April 19th shocked America. Its unspeakable evil sickened the world. Never in the history of our country have Americans witnessed such senseless barbarism. It has been suggested that those who committed this act of mass murder chose us as their victims because we were supposedly immune—the heartland of America.

Well, we are the heartland of America. Today we stand before the world, and before our God, together—our hearts and hands linked in a solidarity these criminals can never understand. We stand together in love. . . .

Through all of this—through the tears, the righteous anger, the soul-rending sorrow of immeasurable loss—we have sometimes felt alone. But we are never truly alone. We have God, and we have each other. . . .

Our pain is vast. Our loss is beyond measure. We cannot fathom this act, but we can reach beyond its horrible consequences.

The thousands of us gathered here today are multiplied by God's love, anointed by His gentle mercy. Today we are one with Him, and with one another.

It is right for us to grieve. We have all been touched by an immense tragedy, and our sorrow is part of the healing process. For some of us stricken with intense personal losses, it will be a long and tortured path. For all of us it is a journey through darkness.

But darkness ends in morning light. That is God's promise, and it is our hope. . . .

Excerpted from State of Oklahoma. Office of the Governor. *Remarks of Governor Frank Keating [at] Oklahoma City Prayer Service*. April 23, 1995. http://www.state.ok.us/osfdocs/nr4-24a.html (accessed September 1, 2004).

# 48. President Bill Clinton's Remarks at the Oklahoma City Memorial Service
*April 23, 1995*

. . . I am honored to be here today to represent the American people. But I have to tell you that Hillary and I also come as parents, as husband and wife, as people who were your neighbors for some of the best years of our lives.

Today our nation joins with you in grief. We mourn with you. We share your hope against hope that some may still survive. We thank all those who have worked so heroically to save lives and to solve this crime, those here in Oklahoma and those who are all across this great land and many who left their own lives to come here to work hand in hand with you.

We pledge to do all we can to help you heal the injured, to rebuild this city, and to bring to justice those who did this evil.

This terrible sin took the lives of our American family, innocent children in that building, only because their parents were trying to be good parents as well as good workers; citizens in the building going about their daily business and many there who served the rest of us—who worked to help the elderly and the disabled, who worked to support our farmers and our veterans, who worked to enforce our laws and to protect us. Let us say clearly, they served us well, and we are grateful.

But for so many of you they were also neighbors and friends. You saw them at church or the PTA meetings, at the civic clubs, at the ball park. You know them in ways that all the rest of America could not.

And to all the members of the families here present who have suffered loss, though we share your grief, your pain is unimaginable, and we know that. We cannot undo it. That is God's work. . . .

To all my fellow Americans beyond this hall, I say, one thing we owe those who have sacrificed is the duty to purge ourselves of the dark forces which gave rise to this evil. They are forces that threaten our common peace, our freedom, our way of life. . . .

Yesterday Hillary and I had the privilege of speaking with some children of other Federal employees—children like those who were lost here. And one little girl said something we will never forget. She said, we should all plant a tree in memory of the children. So this morning before we got on the plane to come here, at the White House, we planted that tree in honor of the children of Oklahoma. It was a dogwood with its wonderful spring flower and its deep, enduring roots. It embodies the lesson of the Psalms: that the life of a good person is like a tree whose leaf does not wither.

My fellow Americans, a tree takes a long time to grow, and wounds take a long time to heal. But we must begin. Those who are lost now belong to God. Some day we will be with them. But until that happens, their legacy must be our lives.

Thank you all, and God bless you.

Excerpted from U.S. Executive Office of the President. "Remarks at a Memorial Service for the Bombing Victims in Oklahoma City, Oklahoma." April 23, 1995. *Weekly Compilation of Presidential Documents* 31, no. 17 (May 1, 1995): 688–689. http://frwebgate2.access.gpo.gov/cgi-bin/ waisgate.cgi?WAISdocID=494902500166+2+0+0&WAISaction=retrieve (accessed September 1, 2004.

## 49. President Bill Clinton's Announcement of the Closing of Pennsylvania Avenue in Front of the White House
*May 20, 1995*

Today, the Secretary of the Treasury, who oversees the Secret Service, will announce that from now on the two blocks of Pennsylvania Avenue in front of the White House will be closed to motor vehicle traffic.

Pennsylvania Avenue has been routinely open to traffic for the entire history of our Republic. Through four Presidential assassinations and eight unsuccessful attempts on the lives of Presidents, it's been open; through a civil war, two world wars and the Gulf War, it was open.

And now, it must be closed. This decision follows a lengthy review by the Treasury Department, the Secret Service and independent experts, including distinguished Americans who served in past administrations of both Democratic and Republican Presidents.

This step is necessary in the view of the Director of the Secret Service and the panel of experts to protect the President and his family, the White House itself, all the staff and others who work here, and the visitors and distinguished foreign and domestic guests who come here every day. . . .

Clearly, this closing is necessary because of the changing nature and scope of the threat of terrorist actions. It should be seen as a responsible security step necessary to preserve our freedom, not part of a long-term restriction of our freedom. . . .

What we do today is a practical step to preserve freedom and peace of mind. It should be seen as a step in a long line of efforts to improve security in the modern world, that began with the installation of airport metal detectors. I remember when that started, and a lot of people thought that it might be seen as a restriction on our freedom, but most of us take it for granted now and after all, hijackings have gone way down. The airport metal detectors increased the freedom of the American people and so can this. . . .

. . . [W]e must all fight terrorism by fighting the fear that terrorists sow. Today, the Secret Service is taking a necessary precaution, but let no one mistake, we will not relinquish our fundamental freedoms. We will secure the personal safety of all Americans to live and move about as they please; to think and to speak as they please; to follow their beliefs and their conscience, as our founding fathers intended. . . .

Excerpted from U.S. Executive Office of the President. *The President's Radio Address.* May 20, 1995. *Weekly Compilation of Presidential Documents* 31, no. 21 (May 29, 1995): 871–872. http://frwebgate5.access. gpo.gov/cgi-bin/waisgate.cgi?WAISdocID=494937491024+0+0+0& WAISaction=retrieve (accessed September 1, 2004).

---

# 50. Warden Harley Lappin Remarks on the Execution of Timothy McVeigh
### *July 11, 2001*

I am Harley Lappin, the warden here at the United States Penitentiary, Terre Haute. The U.S. marshal is still on the execution facility completing his protocol responsibilities.

The court order to execute inmate Timothy James McVeigh has been fulfilled. Pursuant to the sentence of the United States District Court in the District of Colorado, Timothy James McVeigh has been executed by lethal injection. He was pronounced dead at 7:14 a.m., Central Daylight Time. McVeigh's body will be released to a representative of his family. . . .

Inmate McVeigh did not make a final statement. . . .

Inmate McVeigh was calm throughout the entire process. He cooperated entirely during the time he was restrained in the execution holding cell to the time he walked into the execution room. He stepped up on to a small step and sat down on the table where . . . he then positioned himself for us to apply the restraints. He cooperated throughout this entire process.

As you've heard me say before, I anticipated this to be a very difficult thing to do and it was. But I think today my thoughts and prayers are with the many victims of this tragedy in Oklahoma City.

Excerpted from *Statement by Warden of the U.S. Penitentiary in Terre Haute, Indiana, following the Execution of Timothy McVeigh.* July 11, 2001. In *Historic Documents of 2001* (Washington, D.C.: CQ Press, 2002). Also available at http://www.washingtonpost.com/wp-srv/nation/transcripts/lappin.html (accessed September 1, 2004).

# Weapons of Mass Destruction Draw Increased Attention

## INTRODUCTION

In the latter half of the 1990s concerns in the United States that terrorists might acquire or build weapons of mass destruction rose sharply. These concerns about biological, chemical, nuclear, and radiological weapons grew for many reasons: the breakup of the former Soviet Union had left hundreds of tons of nuclear materials poorly guarded; the Japanese cult Aum Shinrikyo had killed twelve people and injured 5,000 others during a 1995 chemical weapons attack on Toyko's subway system; information about how to build the weapons became widely available through the Internet and other sources; many individuals and small groups had been arrested in Europe for possessing slight amounts of nuclear materials; some terrorist groups seemed focused on killing as many people as possible in an attack; and terrorists had openly expressed their interest in acquiring the weapons.

In an interview with ABC News on December 24, 1998, al Qaeda leader Osama bin Laden was asked about suspicions that he was trying to acquire weapons of mass destruction. "If I seek to acquire such weapons, this is a religious duty," bin Laden said. "How we use them is up to us."

More than two years earlier, on April 11, 1996, a report by the Department of Defense heralded the end of the cold war and its risk of global nuclear war, but the report also warned of a "new threat" arising from the worldwide spread of nuclear, biological, and chemical weapons. The Defense Department had examined many types of groups that might use such weapons and concluded that terrorists posed the greatest threat to the United States. "The bottom line is, unlike during the Cold War, those who possess nuclear, biological, and chemical weapons may actually come to use them," the report said [Document 51].

In March 1998 the Defense Department published a paper that examined the threat posed by radiological dispersal devices (RDDs). RDDs are conventional explosives laced with radioactive materials, with the explosion designed to scatter radioactive debris across a wide area. The paper concluded that the explosion of most RDDs would cause minimal numbers of deaths and injuries, but that the psychological and political impact could be overwhelming [Document 52].

On July 14, 1999, a commission created by Congress reported that the federal government was poorly organized to combat the proliferation of weapons of mass destruction. The commission noted that a large number of federal offices and agencies had some role in countering proliferation but said their efforts needed better coordination. "There is no proliferation-related architecture—an end-to-end plan for policy development, program planning, and budget formulation—nor does any person or staff have the power or responsibility to develop one," the commission reported [Document 53].

The United States Air Force Counterproliferation Center in September 1999 published a paper asserting that terrorist groups would be more likely to use biological or chemical weapons than nuclear devices. The paper quoted terrorism experts as saying the materials and technology for biological and chemical weapons were readily available, and that creating some types of weapons was quite easy. It also included an ominous warning: "Counterproliferation experts now agree, the terrorist use of weapons of mass destruction is no longer a question of 'if' but a question of 'when?' "[Document 54].

A month later, a senior official from the General Accounting Office (GAO)— the investigative arm of Congress—testified at a hearing that in most cases, it was much harder than commonly believed to build a biological or chemical weapon that would kill large numbers of people. Terrorists faced "serious technical and operational challenges" in building any kind of biological weapon, said Assistant Comptroller General Henry L. Hinton Jr. The same challenges existed for building most types of chemical weapons, but Hinton acknowledged that some were easy. "Some chemical agents are commercially available and require little sophistication or expertise to obtain or use," he said. Hinton added that the federal government needed to conduct a formal risk assessment of chemical and biological terrorism so priorities and funding could be properly established [Document 55].

On January 10, 2001, the Secretary of Energy Advisory Board released a report that examined the nation's numerous programs to combat nuclear proliferation in Russia. The programs focused on removing nuclear materials from Russia wherever possible, improving security for the materials that remained, and creating employment opportunities for Russian nuclear scientists so they would not be tempted to sell their expertise to a rogue nation or terrorist group. The report concluded that although federal efforts had achieved "impressive results," the United States urgently needed to provide more funding and better coordination of the nonproliferation efforts [Document 56].

A month later, a GAO report specifically focused on the security of Russia's nuclear materials. The GAO said Russia had 603 metric tons of weapons-grade nuclear materials that were at risk of theft. By February 2001 the Department of Energy had completely or partially installed security systems that protected about 32 percent of Russia's nuclear materials. However, hundreds of metric tons of nuclear materials remained unprotected because Russia's Ministry of Atomic Energy had denied the Energy Department access to more than 100 nuclear weapons laboratories and civilian sites, the GAO reported [Document 57].

Testimony at a congressional hearing on July 23, 2001, focused on the recent "Dark Winter" war game that was aimed at determining how the United States would respond to a bioterrorism attack. Participants in the scenario included the president, a role played by former Sen. Sam Nunn, D-Ga.; a National Security Council (NSC) entirely composed of people who had actually served on the NSC, state officials, and journalists. At the beginning of the exercise participants were told that 3,000 people had been infected with smallpox virus—which is highly contagious, takes more than a week to incubate, and has no cure—during simultaneous covert attacks on shopping malls in Oklahoma City, Philadelphia, and Atlanta. The participants then had to develop strategies and make policy decisions to cope with the attacks. The exercise simulated events over thirteen days, and the results were grim. By the game's end, 1,000 people were dead, another 5,000 were expected to die within weeks, and the nation's medical system was completely overwhelmed. The game's planners projected that in a worst-case scenario, by the fourth generation of cases that resulted from the virus's continued spread there could be three million cases and one million people dead [Document 58].

# 51. Proliferation: Threat and Response, Department of Defense Report
*April 11, 1996*

## The New Threat from Nuclear, Biological, and Chemical Weapons

. . . The end of the Cold War has reduced the threat of global nuclear war, but today a new threat is rising from the global spread of nuclear, biological, and chemical [NBC] weapons. Hostile groups and nations have tried—or have been able—to obtain these weapons, the technology, and homegrown ability to make them or ballistic missiles that can deliver the massive annihilation, poison, and death of these weapons hundreds of miles away. . . .

. . . [I]n this era the simple threat of retaliation that worked during the Cold War may not be enough to deter terrorists or aggressive regimes from using nuclear, biological, and chemical weapons. Terrorists operate in a shadowy world in which they can detonate a device and disappear, as the [1995] poison gas attack in Tokyo illustrates. . . . The bottom line is, unlike during the Cold War, those who possess nuclear, biological, and chemical weapons may actually come to use them. . . .

## The Transnational Threat: Dangers from Terrorism, Insurgencies, Civil Wars, and Organized Crime

Transnational groups of proliferation concern include terrorists, insurgents, opposing factions in civil wars, and members of organized criminal groups. Such groups are not generally bound by the same constraints and mores or motivated by the same factors as are nation-states, but pose significant threats to the interests of the United States and our allies and friends worldwide. Terrorist acts pose an especially potent threat to U.S. interests. When carried out by small, close-knit groups, these attacks are difficult to detect in advance, despite diligent intelligence efforts. . . .

### Terrorist Groups
Terrorist groups that acquire NBC weapons and stridently oppose U.S. policies could pose significant potential dangers to U.S. interests. Terrorists armed with these weapons can gain leverage for their demands because of the weapons' nature. . . .

Most terrorist groups do not have the financial and technical resources necessary to acquire nuclear weapons, but could gather materials to make radiological dispersion devices and some biological and chemical agents. Some groups have state sponsors that possess or can obtain NBC weapons. . . .

### Organized Criminal Groups

The potential for international organized criminal groups to obtain, use, or sell NBC weapons has grown in the last few years. In the wake of the Cold War, some of these groups have emerged as a growing threat to U.S. interests. This situation is particularly critical in the former Soviet Union. . . .

Beginning in 1991, multiple incidents involving criminal activity and the theft of nuclear material surfaced in Europe. During a 1994 appearance before the Permanent Subcommittee on Investigations, the head of the German Federal Criminal Police (the Federal Bureau of Investigation's German counterpart) offered his insight into criminal trafficking of nuclear material. He reported that the number of incidents involving nuclear materials within Germany was increasing over time: from 41 in 1991, to 158 in 1992, to 241 in 1993, and to 267 in 1994. . . .

### Implications for Regional Security

. . . Of the transnational groups discussed above . . . the greatest dangers to U.S. interests stem from terrorists and, to a lesser extent, organized criminal groups. One of the most volatile and frightening scenarios for U.S. defense planning posits a terrorist group, whose actions are directed principally against the United States, with nuclear material or an actual NBC weapon. . . .

Excerpted from U.S. Department of Defense. Office of the Secretary of Defense. *Proliferation: Threat and Response.* April 11, 1996. http://www.defenselink.mil/pubs/prolif (accessed September 1, 2004).

# 52. Radiological Dispersal Devices: Assessing the Transnational Threat, Department of Defense Paper
*March 1998*

## Radiological Dispersal Devices Defined

. . . Almost any radioactive material can be used to construct an RDD [radiological dispersal device], including fission products, spent fuel from nuclear reactors, and relatively low-level materials, such as medical, industrial and research waste. Weapons grade materials (i.e., highly enriched uranium or plutonium) are not needed although they could be used.

An RDD is designed to scatter radioactive debris over a wide area, thereby contaminating it and possibly causing casualties through radiation sickness, as well as denying its use to military forces or others for some period of time. According to a recent DOD [Department of Defense] report, the RDD threat is threefold: the blast and fragmentation effects from the conventional explosive, the radiation exposure from the radioactive material used, and the fear and panic that its use would spread among the target group or population. . . .

## How the Experts See It

Notwithstanding popular perceptions, the physical effects of an RDD are dependent on several factors, but the *type* and the *amount* of radioactive material used in any device are especially critical. Current DOD studies underscore the vast difference in lethality produced by different types of radioactive materials. For instance, compare the effects of two different RDDs detonated at the Washington Monument with 100 pounds of high explosives. One device, a man-pack RDD, contains 5,000 curies of cobalt-60 (Co-60); the second device, a truck-delivered RDD, carrying 50 kilograms of bundled . . . one-year-old spent fuel rods.

An RDD constructed using Co-60 would produce a maximum dosage at the point of detonation of 12 rem (Roentgen Man Equivalent), resulting in no radiation related deaths. In marked contrast, the RDD made from spent reactor fuel would result in a maximum dosage at the point of detonation of 3,064 rem (six times the lethal dosage). The detonation could produce a circle of potential lethal dosage extending about a kilometer to the Washington waterfront, and, a significant amount of radioactive material would remain at the detonation site. . . .

## The Threat: Perceptions Versus Reality

The perception that practically any state or non-state actor can build and detonate RDDs may well be coming true. However, the perception that all RDDs will have major *physical* effects is flawed. Experts contend that public commentators have overstated the ease of constructing and deploying an RDD that could cause mass casualties and deny an area's use for a lengthy period of time. Acquiring a sufficient amount of highly radioactive material (such as spent reactor fuel), constructing the device without overexposure to radiation in the process, effectively delivering the device on target, and achieving the necessary lethality to kill targeted personnel in the area are tasks beyond the capability of most non-state actors. U.S. research and experimentation over 50-plus years indicate that lethal RDDs are not easy to build. Most RDDs that non-state actors are likely to build would not be effective in producing mass casualties or denying area use. . . .

On the other hand, it is true that almost any use of an RDD could have a tremendous psychological—and therefore political—impact. Thus, even crude RDDs might meet some state's or terrorist group's objective, particularly if that objective were to create panic, to disrupt (or slow down) military operations, or to bring public pressure on political leaders to change a course of action. . . .

Excerpted from Ford, James L. *Radiological Dispersal Devices: Assessing the Transnational Threat.* National Defense University. *Strategic Forum.* No. 136, March 1998. http://www.ndu.edu/inss/strforum/SF136/forum136.html (accessed September 1, 2004).

---

# 53. Combating Proliferation of Weapons of Mass Destruction, Congressional Commission Report

*July 14, 1999*

## Executive Summary

Every American should understand that weapons of mass destruction (WMD)—nuclear, biological, and chemical weapons and their means of delivery—pose a grave threat to the United States and to our military forces and our vital interests abroad. . . .

These threats define a chilling new reality for our country. Their magnitude and reality require a new strategy focused not just on prevention, but also on *combating all aspects of proliferation,* to include impeding the spread of capability, responding to proliferation as it occurs, strengthening our capacity to defend against such weapons, and preparing to respond if these weapons are used against us at home or abroad. . . .

The Commission finds that *the US Government is not effectively organized to combat proliferation.* . . .

## Chapter 1. A Grave Threat to the United States

*. . .Terrorist acquisition or use of nuclear, chemical, or biological weapons:*

At least a dozen terrorist groups have expressed an interest in or have actively sought nuclear, chemical, or biological weapons capabilities. On March 20, 1995, the Japanese cult group, Aum Shinrikyo, released the nerve agent sarin into the Tokyo subway system, killing 12 people and injuring more than 5,000. A successful nuclear, chemical, or biological attack against the United States would be devastating. Even a credible threat of such an attack could dramatically undermine America's sense of security, constrain our ability to support allies abroad, and cause major disruptions. . . .

*Diversion of nuclear, chemical, or biological weapons, technology, materials, or expertise from Russia:*

We know of seven instances since 1992 in which weapons-usable fissile materials were stolen from Russian facilities. The continuing economic meltdown in Russia has heightened the risk of both further material leakage and the "brain drain" of technical expertise. Russia has no reliable inventory of its fissile material, and Russian vulnerability to an "insider" threat is increased by power outages at Russian nuclear installations, by the need for unpaid guards and technicians to forage for food, and by sporadic violence both by and against personnel from the Ministries of Defense and Atomic Energy. Many dangerous state and sub-national actors would like to exploit Russia's troubles in order to acquire nuclear weapons or small quantities of weapons-usable materials. . . .

## Chapter 2. Combating Proliferation: What the Federal Government Should Do

Successfully combating the proliferation of weapons of mass destruction requires leadership. It requires organization. It requires coordination. . . .

*We do not have a comprehensive approach to combating the proliferation of weapons of mass destruction.* . . .

### Organizing to Combat Proliferation

*How we organize the Federal Government to combat proliferation will have a profound impact on our prospects for success.*

While organization will not by itself determine the overall success or failure of our efforts to combat proliferation, it is a critical component. Organization governs the establishment of priorities, the assignment of tasks, and the allocation of resources. It influences the flow of information and analysis. It affects how the work of government is done and who is accountable for the results.

Many offices and agencies have a role in countering the proliferation threat. These include several White House offices; traditional national security elements in the Intelligence Community and at the Departments of State, Defense, and Energy (including the national laboratories); as well as the Departments of Justice, Commerce, Treasury, Health and Human Services, and Agriculture. . . .

*Ensuring that these diverse elements work effectively during both crises and non-crisis times requires more than coordination. It requires strong and timely direction to establish policy, set program priorities, and allocate resources.* It requires a clear delineation of responsibilities. It requires specific mechanisms to plan and execute operational responses to the threat or use of weapons of mass destruction. . . .

Many present and past officials have indicated that the coordination of proliferation-related programs has often failed to meet these standards. The Commission has identified several areas in which interagency activities are deficient. These have common features:

- *overlapping responsibility and resource requirements:* When a new problem involves identifying available resources or the development of a coordinated response from several agencies, the process is cumbersome and slow, and is further hampered by a lack of resource flexibility. . . .
- *no end-to-end interagency plan for addressing proliferation:* There is no proliferation-related architecture—an end-to-end plan for policy development, program planning, and budget formulation—nor does any person or staff have the power or responsibility to develop one.
- *absence of a cross-cutting budget for program elements related to proliferation:* Neither the President, Congress, nor any executive branch official knows how much the various agencies have spent on these efforts or how much they plan to spend in the future. The private sector has an apt expression: "If you don't measure it, you can't manage it." Without an explicit financial plan tied to programmatic objectives, individual agencies and the corresponding sub-committees on Capitol Hill make their program and resource decisions independently of any overall plan or objective. The result is not only inefficiency and duplication but also potentially catastrophic delay. . . .

Excerpted from U.S. Congress. Commission to Assess the Organization of the Federal Government to Combat the Proliferation of Weapons of Mass Destruction. *Combating Proliferation of Weapons of Mass Destruction.* July 14, 1999. http://www.msiac.dmso.mil/wmd_documents/11910book.pdf (accessed September 1, 2004).

# 54. The Military Role in Countering Terrorist Use of Weapons of Mass Destruction, U.S. Air Force Counterproliferation Center Paper

*September 1999*

## I. Introduction

. . . To many nations and groups, their only means to counter the United States are with weapons of mass destruction (WMD). . . . This threat is not from a regional force, rogue state, or specific terrorist group. As Secretary [of Defense William] Cohen says "A lone madman or nest of fanatics with a bottle of chemicals, a batch of plague-inducing bacteria, or a crude nuclear bomb can threaten or kill tens of thousands of people in a single act of malevolence. . . ."

## II. What Terrorist Threat?

. . . Counterproliferation experts now agree, the terrorist use of weapons of mass destruction is no longer a question of "if," but a question of "when?" It is only a matter of time before another terrorist group uses a weapon of mass destruction. The threat is real, the technology available, agents relatively inexpensive, with attacks that are difficult to prevent. . . .

### Why Weapons of Mass Destruction?

. . . Most experts agree terrorist groups are more likely to use chemical or biological weapons versus a nuclear weapon. This is due to the ease of acquisition, inexpense, and easier methods of delivery. Bruce Hoffman, Director of the Centre for the Study of Terrorism and Political Violence, says, "previously, terrorism was not just a matter of having the will and motivation to act, but of having the capability to do so—the requisite training, access to weaponry, and operational knowledge. . . . Today, however, the means and methods of terrorism can be easily obtained at bookstores, from mail-order publishers, on CD-ROM, or even over the Internet. Relying on such commercially published or readily accessible . . . manuals and operational guides . . . the 'amateur' terrorist can be just as deadly and destructive as his more professional counterpart."

In an Advanced Concept Research Report, B. J. Berkowitz summarizes, "the chief advantages of CB [chemical and biological] weapons are the unrestricted availability of the necessary information, the relatively small resources needed, and the ability to test the product. There are no meaningful controls on the availability of chemicals, and what little control exists over pathogenic cultures can be overcome in a variety of ways. Perhaps most important is the fact that the chemical and biological materials can be produced under the cover of an apparently legitimate commercial venture such as a small research company, fine chemical manufacturer, or biomedical laboratory."

Other scholars point out weapons of mass destruction limit selective targeting and pose a risk to the user. When assessing the terrorist threat, national security analyst Anthony Fainberg says, "Most of them will almost certainly continue to avoid the use of such weapons for a variety of reasons: the old-fashioned methods were suitable for the goals of most; there may be a reluctance to experiment with new and dangerous methods; the nature of the acts might alienate the terrorists from their base of support; the use of such weapons might bring down the wrath of governments and, indeed, most of the world upon the terrorists heads." Would this be enough to persuade groups not to use them?

[Terrorism expert Walter] Laqueur contends religious fanatical elements are the most likely to use WMD. These extremist groups consider the religious cause justification for taking lives. He concludes, "proliferation of the weapons of mass destruction does not mean that most terrorist groups are likely to use them in the foreseeable future, but some almost certainly will, in spite of all the reasons militating against it. . . ."

### Types of Weapons

. . . Chemical warfare agents are readily available and simple to produce. Procedures are based on old technology (used prior to World War I) and within reach of any terrorist group. A CIA threat assessment says, "newer agents, particularly the nerve agents, are more difficult to produce; however, the technology for these agents is widely available in the public domain. In many ways, production of chemical warfare agents is like that of legitimate commercial compounds. . . . The greatest similarities occur between pesticide and nerve agent production units because these compounds are so closely related. . . ."

Biological agents are of great concern because all the equipment needed for production is dual-use [can be used for legitimate purposes or for terrorism] and available on the open market. You can produce biological agents from naturally occurring pathogens such as bacteria and viruses, which are often self-replicating. . . . The OTA [Office of Technology Assessment, a former congressional agency] report states, "Biological warfare agents are easier to produce than either nuclear materials or chemical warfare agents because they require a much smaller and cheaper industrial infrastructure and because the necessary technology and know how is widely available."

Robert Kupperman and David Smith state in a Georgetown University Center for Strategic and International Studies report that terrorists could produce many biological agents in sufficient quantities for their use. They consider anthrax, botulinum toxin, and the plant toxin, ricin, as typical biological agents. Anthrax grows aerobically, a product of fermentation, much the same as brewing beer. Preparing it for dissemination as spores requires some expertise, but the terrorist can practice disseminating species that are not pathogenic to humans. Botulinum toxin is a bacteria found virtually everywhere. Improperly handling food can cause botulinum toxin poisoning. The toxin, when crystallized, is extremely lethal and is easy to produce and dispense. Another easy procedure is extracting ricin from the castor bean which produces a deadly toxin. When inhaled, this toxin causes death in hours. Extracting the protein toxin is a well-documented, easy two-step procedure.

Brigadier General John Doesburg, the former Director of the Joint Program Office for Biological Defense, says, "Anyone who makes home-brewed beer can make anthrax. Anthrax is a deadly toxin that, depending on the quantities used, can disable and kill thousands of people within hours or days. . . ."

The most effective means of delivering toxic agents is through aerosol clouds. Kupperman and Smith state, "aerosol dispersal technology is easy to obtain from open literature and commercial sources, and equipment to aerosolize biological agents is available as virtually off-the-shelf systems produced for legitimate industrial, medical, and agricultural applications. With access to a standard machine shop, it would not be difficult to fabricate aerosol generators and integrate components to produce reliable systems for dispersing microorganisms or toxins." Others suggest dispersing agents with crop dusters or through building air ventilation systems. . . .

Excerpted from Dickinson, Lansing E. *The Military Role in Countering Terrorist Use of Weapons of Mass Destruction.* United States Air Force Counterproliferation Center, Air War College, Air University, Maxwell Air Force Base. *Counterproliferation Paper No. 1.* September 1999. http://www.au.af.mil/au/awc/awcgate/cpc-pubs/dickinson.htm (accessed September 1, 2004).

## 55. Combating Terrorism: Observations on the Threat of Chemical and Biological Terrorism, General Accounting Office Congressional Testimony

*October 20, 1999*

### Summary

According to the experts we consulted, in most cases terrorists would have to overcome significant technical and operational challenges to successfully make and release chemical or biological agents of sufficient quality and quantity to kill or injure large numbers of people without substantial assistance from a state sponsor. . . .

### Production and Delivery of Chemical and Biological Agents Generally Requires Specialized Knowledge

Terrorists face serious technical and operational challenges at different stages of the process of producing and delivering most chemical and all biological agents. The Special Assistant to the Director of Central Intelligence for Nonproliferation testified in March 1999 that "the preparation and effective use of BW [biological weapons] by both potentially hostile states and by non-state actors, including terrorists, is harder than some popular literature seems to suggest." We agree. A number of obstacles exist for terrorists. . . .

Some chemical agents are commercially available and require little sophistication or expertise to obtain or use, but other chemical agents are technically challenging to make and deliver. Toxic industrial chemicals such as chlorine, phosgene, and hydrogen cyanide are used in commercial manufacturing and could be easily acquired and adapted as terrorist weapons. In contrast, most chemical nerve agents such as tabun (GA), sarin (GB), soman (GD), and VX are difficult to produce. To begin with, developing nerve agents requires the synthesis of multiple chemicals that, according to the experts we consulted, are very difficult to obtain in large quantities due to the provisions of the 1993 Chemical Weapons Convention, which has been in force since April 1997. In addition, a 1993 Office of Technology

Assessment report on the technologies underlying weapons of mass destruction indicated that some steps in the production process of these nerve agents are difficult and hazardous. For example, although tabun is one of the easier chemical agents to make, containment of the highly toxic hydrogen cyanide gas that is produced during the process is a technical challenge. . . . Even if chemical agents can be produced successfully, they must be released effectively as a vapor, or aerosol, for inhalation exposure, or they need to be in a spray of large droplets or liquid for skin penetration. . . .

Causing mass casualties with biological agents also presents extraordinary technical and operational challenges for terrorists without the assistance of a state-sponsored program. . . . The only known sources of the smallpox virus, for example, are within government-controlled facilities in the United States and Russia. Ricin, a biological toxin, is easy to obtain and produce but requires such large quantities to cause mass casualties that the risk of arousing suspicion or detection prior to dissemination would be great.

Although most biological agents are easy to grow if the seed stock can be obtained, they are difficult to process into a lethal form and successfully deliver to achieve large scale casualties. Processing biological agents into the right particle size and delivering them effectively requires expertise in a wide range of scientific disciplines. . . .

Terrorists have additional hurdles to overcome. For example, outdoor delivery of chemical and biological agents can be disrupted by environmental (e.g., pollution) and meteorological (e.g., sun, rain, mist, and wind) conditions. . . . Indoor dissemination of an agent could be affected by the air exchange rate of the building. In addition, terrorists risk capture and personal safety in acquiring and processing materials, disposing byproducts, and releasing the agent. Many agents are dangerous to handle. . . .

## National-Level Assessment of the Risk of Chemical and Biological Terrorism Is Needed to Focus Resources

. . . By combining an FBI estimate of the domestic-origin threat with existing intelligence estimates and assessments of the foreign-origin threat, analysts could provide policymakers with a better understanding of the threat from terrorists' use of chemical or biological weapons. A national-level risk assessment based in part on the threat estimates would better enable federal agencies to establish soundly defined program requirements and prioritize and focus the nation's investments to combat terrorism. For example, in March 1999 we testified that the Department of Health and Human Services is establishing a national pharmaceutical and vaccine stockpile to prepare medical responses for possible terrorist use of chemical or biological weapons. We pointed out that the Department's effort was initiated without the benefit of a sound threat and risk assessment process. We also found that some of the items the Department plans to procure do not match intelligence agencies' judgments of the more likely chemical and biological agents that terrorists might use and seem to be based on worst-case scenarios. We questioned whether stockpiling for the items listed in the Department's plan was the best approach for investing in medical preparedness. . . .

Excerpted from U.S. Congress. General Accounting Office. *Combating Terrorism: Observations on the Threat of Chemical and Biological Terrorism.* Prepared testimony of Henry L. Hinton Jr. for a hearing by the Subcommittee on National Security, Veterans Affairs, and International Relations of the House Committee on Government Reform. GAO/T-NSIAD-00-50, October 20, 1999. http://www.gao.gov/archive/2000/ns00050t.pdf (accessed September 1, 2004).

# 56. A Report Card on the Department of Energy's Nonproliferation Programs with Russia, Secretary of Energy Advisory Board Report

*January 10, 2001*

## Executive Summary

### Introduction

Since the breakup of the Soviet Union, we have witnessed the dissolution of an empire having over 40,000 nuclear weapons, over a thousand metric tons of nuclear materials, vast quantities of chemical and biological weapons materials, and thousands of missiles. This Cold War arsenal is spread across 11 time zones and lacks the Cold War infrastructure that provided the control and financing necessary to assure that chains of command remain intact and nuclear weapons and materials remain securely beyond the reach of terrorists and weapons-proliferating states. This problem is compounded by the existence of thousands of weapons scientists who, not always having the resources necessary to adequately care for their families, may be tempted to sell their expertise to countries of proliferation concern.

. . . [T]he Task Force reached the following conclusions and recommendations.

1. *The most urgent unmet national security threat to the United States today is the danger that weapons of mass destruction or weapons-usable mate-*

*rial in Russia could be stolen and sold to terrorists or hostile nation states and used against American troops abroad or citizens at home.*

This threat is a clear and present danger to the international community as well as to American lives and liberties.

*2. Current nonproliferation programs in the Department of Energy, the Department of Defense, and related agencies have achieved impressive results thus far, but their limited mandate and funding fall short of what is required to address adequately the threat. . . .*

The Task Force concludes that the current budget levels are inadequate and the current management of the U.S. Government's response is too diffuse. The Task Force believes that the existing scope and management of the U.S. programs addressing this threat leave an unacceptable risk of failure and the potential for catastrophic consequences.

*3. The new President and leaders of the 107th Congress face the urgent national security challenge of devising an enhanced response proportionate to the threat.*

The enhanced response should include: a net assessment of the threat; a clear achievable mission statement; the development of a strategy with specific goals and measurable objectives; a more centralized command of the financial and human resources required to do the job; and an identification of criteria for measuring the benefits for Russia, the United States, and the entire world.

The Task Force offers one major recommendation to the President and the Congress. *The President, in consultation with Congress and in cooperation with the Russian Federation, should quickly formulate a strategic plan to secure and/or neutralize in the next eight to ten years all nuclear weapons-usable material located in Russia and to prevent the outflow from Russia of scientific expertise that could be used for nuclear or other weapons of mass destruction. Accomplishing this task will be regarded by future generations as one of the greatest contributions the United States and Russia can make to their long-term security and that of the entire world. . . .*

. . . [T]he Task Force report outlines an enhanced national security program. . . . This program could be carried out for less than one percent of the U.S. defense budget, or up to a total of $30 billion over the next eight to ten years. The Russian Government would, of course, be expected to make a significant contribution commensurate with its own financial ability. The national security benefits to U.S. citizens from securing and/or neutralizing the equivalent of more than 80,000 nuclear weapons and potential nuclear weapons would constitute the highest return on investment in any current U.S. national security and defense program. . . .

### Background

. . . Former President Bush negotiated and President Clinton implemented what some have called the "contract of the century" with President Yeltsin. Under this agreement, the U.S. is purchasing 500 metric tons of

HEU [highly enriched uranium] removed from former Soviet nuclear weapons, and this material is being converted to low enriched uranium fuel that is then used in civilian power reactors. To date, more than 110 metric tons of HEU, enough to build some 5,000 nuclear weapons, have been blended down and rendered impotent for nuclear weapons use. In its blended-down form, this material has been delivered to the international market to fuel civilian power reactors. Through close cooperation among the U.S., Russia, and other countries of the former Soviet Union, we have also succeeded in eliminating strategic nuclear arsenals left in Ukraine, Kazakhstan, and Belarus. . . .

Since the Nunn-Lugar legislative initiative of 1991 [PL 102-228, the "Soviet Nuclear Threat Reduction Act of 1991," sponsored by senators Sam Nunn and Richard Lugar] the U.S. Government has established an array of threat reduction programs in both the Departments of Defense and Energy to assist in dismantling Russian nuclear and other weapons of mass destruction and to improve significantly the security of such weapons and materials. Together, these programs have helped to protect, secure, and begin disposition of strategic weapons delivery systems as well as hundreds of metric tons of nuclear weapons-usable material—preventing the emergence of a virtual "Home Depot" for would-be proliferators. Additional work, under the aegis of the Department of State, has addressed what is known as the 'brain drain problem' both in Russia and other countries of the former Soviet Union through programs such as the International Science and Technology Center (ISTC) Program. This program, together with DOE's Initiatives for Proliferation Prevention and its Nuclear Cities Initiative, has helped to redirect weapons scientists and engineers from defense work to civilian employment.

These U.S. programs have reduced the threat of diversion of nuclear weapons materials. To the best of our knowledge, no nuclear weapons or quantity of nuclear weapons-usable material have been successfully stolen and exported, while many efforts to steal weapons-usable material have been intercepted by Russian and international police operations.

Much more remains to be done, however. The Task Force observes that while we know a good deal about the size and state of the Russian weapons complex, there is still much that we do not know. More than 1,000 metric tons of HEU and at least 150 metric tons of weapons-grade plutonium exist in the Russian weapons complex. . . . In addition, many of the Russian nuclear sites remain vulnerable to insiders determined to steal enough existing material to make several nuclear weapons and to transport these materials to Iran, Iraq, or Afghanistan. At some sites, one well-placed insider would be enough. The Task Force was advised that buyers from Iraq, Iran and other countries have actively sought nuclear weapons-usable material from Russian sites.

In a worst-case scenario, a nuclear engineer graduate with a grapefruit-sized lump of HEU or an orange-sized lump of plutonium, together with material otherwise readily available in commercial markets, could fashion a nuclear device that would fit in a van like the one the terrorist Yosif parked in the World Trade Center in 1993. The explosive effects of such a device would destroy every building in the Wall Street financial area and would level lower Manhattan. . . .

### The Threat Today

. . . Democracies like ours are inherently messy, frequently distracted, and often bogged down in partisanship. Our government historically finds it difficult to mobilize without the catalyst of an actual incident. The new President and leaders of the 107th Congress face no larger challenge than to mobilize the nation to precautionary action *before* a major disaster strikes.

## Assessing Current DOE Nonproliferation Programs

. . . Unquestionably, much has been accomplished by the array of programs now being operated by DOE and other U.S. Government agencies. Nonetheless, the Task Force believes it is time for the U.S. Government to perform a risk assessment based on input from all relevant agencies to estimate the total magnitude of the threat posed to U.S. national security. The Task Force also believes there is a strong need to create greater synergies among the existing nonproliferation programs . . . .

## Task Force Assessment

### Need to Improve Coordination and Support

At several levels, the Task Force observed that DOE programs need *improved government-wide coordination and support* for successful, long-term implementation. . . .

Coordination within and among U.S. Government agencies is insufficient and must be improved. . . .

The Task Force believes a high-level position in the White House is needed to coordinate policy and budget for threat reduction and nonproliferation programs across the U.S. Government. . . .

Excerpted from U.S. Department of Energy. The Secretary of Energy Advisory Board. *A Report Card on the Department of Energy's Nonproliferation Programs with Russia.* January 10, 2001. http://www.seab.energy.gov/ publications/rusrpt.pdf (accessed September 1, 2004).

# 57. Nuclear Nonproliferation: Security of Russia's Nuclear Material Improving; Further Enhancements Needed, General Accounting Office Report

*February 28, 2001*

## Results in Brief

The security systems installed by the Department of Energy are reducing the risk of theft of nuclear material in Russia, but hundreds of metric tons of nuclear material still lack improved security systems, and the Department has no mechanism in place to monitor the effectiveness of the systems once they are installed. As of February 2001, the Department had installed completed or partially completed security systems in 115 buildings protecting about 32 percent of the 603 metric tons of weapons-usable nuclear material identified as being at risk of theft or diversion from Russia. . . . According to the Department, the program has work underway on an additional 130 metric tons of nuclear material. The Department's Technical Survey Team found that the majority of the security systems are being installed in a manner that is reducing the risk of nuclear material theft. During our visits to nine sites, we observed, among other things, nuclear material storage vaults equipped with strengthened doors, locks, video surveillance systems, and alarms that can detect and delay thieves as they attempt to steal nuclear material. We also observed instances where systems were not operated properly. For example, at one nuclear facility that we visited, an entrance gate to a building containing nuclear material was left open and unattended by guards. While the Department has made progress in installing security systems at Russian sites, hundreds of metric tons of nuclear material remain unprotected. Because the Russian Ministry of Atomic Energy has restricted the Department's access to some nuclear weapons laboratories and civilian sites, the Department is not installing security systems in 104 buildings containing hundreds of metric tons of material that it has identified as needing improved security systems. . . .

The Department also has projects under way to help Russia's Ministry of Atomic Energy and nuclear regulatory authority develop (1) a nuclear material accounting database that will enable Russia to track its total inventory of nuclear material; (2) regulations to ensure effective operations and maintenance of the systems; and (3) an inspection and enforcement system to ensure that sites comply with regulations. In addition, the Department is supporting security improvements for trains and trucks that transport nuclear material between and within sites and for nuclear material security training centers. While some progress has been made on these projects, the Department does not expect them to be completed before 2020. . . .

Excerpted from U.S. Congress. General Accounting Office. *Nuclear Non-proliferation: Security of Russia's Nuclear Material Improving; Further Enhancements Needed.* GAO-01-312, February 28, 2001. http://www.gao.gov/new.items/d01312.pdf (accessed September 1, 2004).

# 58. The Dark Winter Exercise, Congressional Testimony
*July 23, 2001*

Mr. SHAYS [Rep. Christopher Shays, R-Conn.]: . . . The focus of our hearing today is a recent terrorism response exercise ominously named Dark Winter, during which the unimaginable had to be imagined, a multi-site smallpox attack on an unvaccinated American populace.

The scenario called upon those playing the President, the National Security Council, and State officials to deal with the crippling consequences of what quickly became a massive public health and national security crisis.

The lessons of Dark Winter add to the growing body of strategic and tactical information needed to support coordinated counterterrorism policies and programs. Coming to grips with the needs of first responders, the role of the Governors, use of the National Guard, and the thresholds for Federal intervention in realistic exercises vastly increases our chances of responding effectively when the unthinkable but some say inevitable outbreak is upon us. The costs of an uncoordinated, ineffective response will be paid in human lives, civil disorder, loss of civil liberties and economic disruption that could undermine both national security and even national sovereignty. . . .

Mr. HAMRE [Dr. John Hamre, president and chief executive officer of the Center for Strategic and International Studies]: . . . Dark Winter was meant to be an exercise to see how would the United States cope with a catastrophic event, in this case a bioterrorism event. We thought that we were going to be spending our time with the mechanisms of government. We ended up spending our time saying, how do we save democracy in America? Because it is that serious, and it is that big. . . .

This is what happened on the first day. . . . some two dozen patients were reporting into Oklahoma City hospitals with signs of smallpox. It was quickly spreading around the town, and the Centers for Disease Control quickly confirmed that it was indeed smallpox.

Smallpox was eradicated in the United States in 1978 . . . . It is a very contagious disease and highly lethal; 30 percent of the people that get it will die. And once you get it, you simply have to ride it out. There is no real therapy for it. There is a vaccine that you can take, but you must get the vaccine before you have demonstrated symptoms. So it is a very tough problem to work with. . . .

. . . [W]e thought we had 12 million doses [of vaccine], but as you will see shortly, its exposure in this exercise was in communities where there were more than 12 million people living.

The National Security Council, one of its initial challenges was to decide how do we administer or strategically how do we allocate these scarce numbers of doses to the American public? . . .

We clearly knew that smallpox was now being reported in three States. It was reported in Oklahoma, in Atlanta, and in Pennsylvania. It was presumed to be a deliberate release, because smallpox is no longer natural in the environment, and so it was probably caused, but we did not know how. . . .

On the first night, [the Council] decided to try to accelerate the production of vaccines. There is ongoing production, but emergency production would be required, and you would need to waive a fair amount of regulation. . . . That even meant 6 to 8 weeks before we could get it. . . .

The infection rate was showing up first in the cities where it was released, and they were released in three locations. Deliberate attack in Oklahoma, where it was successful, and two botched attempts, one in Atlanta and one in Philadelphia.

The participants did not know that at the time of the first evening. So this was the scope of the infection that was not even understood when people were having to make initial decisions. This would be very typical of a bioterrorism incident. . . .

Remember, this occurred in the scenario at the start of the shopping season before the Christmas holidays. It occurred in a shopping center. And that is why you don't know if it was a single point event or if was widespread—

Senator NUNN [former Sen. Sam Nunn, D-Ga.]: . . . [T]here was no clarity. We kept asking, do we know that it hasn't already spread all over? And the answer was, it could have spread everywhere, because we didn't know for 10 or 12 days that it had even happened.

And those people that were in those shopping centers had dispersed in all directions. So when you start basically impinging on their civil liberties and telling people they forcefully have to be kept in their homes that may have been exposed, and when you call out the National Guard to do that, and you at gunpoint put your own citizens under, in effect, house arrest, and you don't even know that you are catching the right spot or that you're dealing with the right people. . . .

Mr. HAMRE: . . . We were now at the 6th day in the exercise. Here is what the National Security Council was confronting, that they had—over 2,000 people had been infected. The medical care system had been over-whelmed.

You know, we have cut back medical care so that it is to the least amount of excess capacity in peacetime as possible, because we can't afford it. And of course when you have a catastrophic event like this, it overwhelms the medical care system very quickly for all practical purposes. Vaccine is now gone, because you are trying to contain it in each location. It is now in over 20 States, we are out of vaccine.

Still the Council does not know where it came from or how widespread it is. It is clear that it was probably deliberate, but it is unclear if this was terrorism or really an act of war. . . .

At the time the participants came to realize that vaccine was no longer going to be an effective solution. We were out of it. And we now had to deal with the issues of how do you constrain it by constraining peoples' movement and behavior. . . .

On the 12th day of the scenario . . . is the first time that we are starting to see the second wave of infections. That is the infections of people that came in that caught from people who were exposed in the very first hour.

In the last 48 hours there were 14,000 cases. We now have over 1,000 dead, another 5,000 that we expected to be dead within weeks. There are 200 people who died from the vaccination. . . . At this stage the medical system is overwhelmed completely.

. . . [A]t the end of the first generation of infections, this is approximately December 17th, there were 3,000 infected, and there were 1,000 expected to be dead.

At the end of the second generation . . . it would be 30,000 infected, and 10,000 dead. We were forecasting within 2 weeks to 3 weeks that we would have 300,000 who would be infected and 100,000 dead. It goes off the charts.

It was roughly by the fourth generation that we would expect to be get-ting vaccine produced in the emergency production.

It was at this stage that we were confronting the reality that forcible con-straint of citizens' behavior was probably going to be required to be able to stop that fourth generation of infections. . . .

I think we felt that this would cripple the United States if it were to occur. We have a population that is no longer inoculated.

For all practical purposes, 80 percent of the population has been born or is no longer affected by the vaccines when they stopped [being given] back in 1978. So the country is now vulnerable. Local attack quickly becomes a national crisis, and we saw that very quickly once it spread.

The government response becomes very problematic when it comes to civil liberties. How do you protect democracy at the same time that you are trying to save the Nation? . . .

Excerpted from U.S. Congress. House. Committee on Government Reform. *Combating Terrorism: Federal Response to a Biological Weapons Attack.* A hearing by the Subcommittee on National Security, Veterans Affairs and International Relations. 107th Cong., 1st sess., July 23, 2001. Serial No. 107-99. http://frwebgate.access.gpo.gov/cgi-bin/useftp.cgi?IPaddress=162.140.64.21&filename=81593.wais&directory=/diskc/wais/data/107_house_hearings (accessed September 1, 2004).

# Computer Security Problems Said to Threaten Homeland Security

## INTRODUCTION

The increasing growth of interconnected computers and the Internet in the mid-1990s focused increased attention on computer security problems in the federal government and the private sector. Nobody knew how many attacks occurred or how much damage they did, but federal officials considered these attacks a serious threat to homeland security. The threat was particularly acute because computers controlled elements of the nation's physical infrastructure ranging from banking transactions to electricity transmission to dam operations.

In June 1996 John M. Deutch, the director of the Central Intelligence Agency (CIA), told a Senate subcommittee that he considered attacks on computers the second most serious threat to national security, exceeded only by the worldwide proliferation of nuclear, chemical, and biological weapons. He warned that a sustained and coordinated attack by terrorists or a foreign country on the nation's computer systems could seriously damage the economy.

A month before Deutch testified, the General Accounting Office (GAO)—the investigative arm of Congress—said in a report released May 22, 1996, that computers at the Department of Defense were extremely vulnerable to attacks. It quoted the Defense Information Systems Agency (DISA) as estimating that Pentagon computers were attacked about 250,000 times in 1995. The report also noted that when DISA tested Pentagon computer defenses, 65 percent of the attacks gained access to the computers and few of the attacks were detected [Document 59].

On October 20, 1997, a report by the President's Commission on Critical Infrastructure Protection said that the rapid integration of telecommunications and computer systems had created "a new dimension of vulnerability" that, when combined with increased threats against the United States, posed an "unprecedented national risk." The commission said it had not discovered any imminent threat but added that the nation's vulnerabilities were steadily increasing and the resources needed to conduct a cyber attack consisted simply of a personal computer and a telephone connection to the Internet [Document 60].

In response to the commission's report, on May 22, 1998, President Bill Clinton issued Presidential Decision Directive (PDD) 63 about protecting critical infrastructures. The document, which primarily focused on cyber threats, was the first effort at formulating a policy about protecting the nation's infrastructure. PDD 63 authorized the Federal Bureau of Investigation (FBI) to expand its new National Infrastructure Protection Center (NIPC) to coordinate federal activities, sought to create partnerships regarding cyber issues between the federal government and the private sector, and required federal agencies to improve security in their computer systems, among other actions. The document remains classified, but the White House issued a white paper that explained its major provisions [Document 61].

Almost three years later, a senior GAO official vented his frustration about the lack of progress in improving federal computer security at a congressional hearing on April 5, 2001. "Since 1996, our analyses of information security at major federal agencies have shown that federal systems were not being adequately protected from [computer] threats, even though these systems process, store, and transmit enormous amounts of sensitive data and are indispensable to many federal agency operations," said Robert F. Dacey, the GAO's director of information security issues. Dacey proposed a number of complex solutions but added that many simple yet important fixes—such as ensuring that computers had the latest software patches—could be implemented immediately [Document 62].

A little more than a month later, on May 22, 2001, Dacey returned to Capitol Hill to testify about problems in developing analytical, information sharing, and warning capabilities at the FBI's National Infrastructure Protection Center (NIPC), which Clinton had expanded in 1998 with PDD 63. Dacey said several issues contributed to the problems, such as federal agencies not supplying adequate employees to the NIPC, but that a more fundamental problem was the ongoing evolution of federal plans to protect critical infrastructures from cyber attacks. As a consequence, other federal agencies involved in infrastructure protection had different views of the NIPC's role and responsibilities, it was unclear who was authorized to set the NIPC's priorities and provide oversight, and the NIPC's plans for improving its analytical and warning capabilities were "fragmented and incomplete" [Document 63].

The terrorist attacks of September 11, 2001, in New York City and Washington, D.C., showed how fragile the nation's infrastructure could be. The attacks disrupted telephone service, networked computers, and other critical systems in both cities, leading to increased public and federal attention on the need to better protect the nation's critical infrastructures.

# 59. Information Security: Computer Attacks at Department of Defense Pose Increasing Risks, General Accounting Office Report

*May 22, 1996*

## Executive Summary

### Results in Brief

Attacks on Defense computer systems are a serious and growing threat. . . .

At a minimum, these attacks are a multimillion dollar nuisance to Defense. At worst, they are a serious threat to national security. Attackers have seized control of entire Defense systems, many of which support critical functions, such as weapons systems research and development, logistics, and finance. Attackers have also stolen, modified, and destroyed data and software. In a well-publicized attack on Rome Laboratory, the Air Force's premier command and control research facility, two hackers took control of laboratory support systems, established links to foreign Internet sites, and stole tactical and artificial intelligence research data.

The potential for catastrophic damage is great. . . .

Defense is taking action to address this growing problem, but faces significant challenges in controlling unauthorized access to its computer systems. Currently, Defense is attempting to react to successful attacks as it learns of them, but it has no uniform policy for assessing risks, protecting its systems, responding to incidents, or assessing damage.

Training of users and system and network administrators is inconsistent and constrained by limited resources. . . .

### Principal Findings

#### Computer Attacks Are an Increasing Threat

In preventing computer attacks, Defense has to protect a vast and complex information infrastructure: currently, it has over 2.1 million computers, 10,000 local networks, and 100 long-distance networks. Defense also critically depends on information technology—it uses computers to help design weapons, identify and track enemy targets, pay soldiers, mobilize reservists, and manage supplies. Indeed, its very warfighting capability is dependent on computer-based telecommunications networks and information systems. . . .

#### Attacks Are Costly and Damaging

. . . According to Defense officials, attackers have obtained and corrupted sensitive information—they have stolen, modified, and destroyed both data and software. They have installed unwanted files and "back doors" which circumvent normal system protection and allow attackers unauthorized access in the future. They have shut down and crashed entire systems and networks, denying service to users who depend on automated systems to help meet critical missions. Numerous Defense functions have been adversely affected, including weapons and supercomputer research, logistics, finance, procurement, personnel management, military health, and payroll. . . .

#### Potential Threat to National Security

There is mounting evidence that attacks on Defense computer systems pose a serious threat to national security. Internet connections make it possible for enemies armed with less equipment and weapons to gain a competitive edge at a small price. As a result, this will become an increasingly attractive way for terrorists or adversaries to wage attacks against Defense. For example, major disruptions to military operations and readiness could threaten national security if attackers successfully corrupted sensitive information and systems or denied service from vital communications backbones or power systems.

The National Security Agency has acknowledged that potential adversaries are developing a body of knowledge about Defense's and other U.S. systems and about methods to attack these systems. According to Defense officials, these methods, which include sophisticated computer viruses and automated attack routines, allow adversaries to launch untraceable attacks from anywhere in the world. In some extreme scenarios, studies show that terrorists or other adversaries could seize control of Defense information systems and seriously degrade the nation's ability to deploy and sustain military forces. Official estimates show that more than 120 countries already have or are developing such computer attack capabilities.

### Challenges in Countering Attacks

. . . Defense is taking actions to strengthen information systems security and counter computer attacks, but increased resources and management commitment are needed. Currently, many of Defense's policies relating to computer attacks are outdated and inconsistent. They do not set standards or mandate specific actions for important security activities such as vulnerability assessments, internal reporting of attacks, correction of vulnerabilities, and damage assessments. Many of Defense's policies were developed when computers were physically and electronically isolated and do not reflect today's "networked" environment. Computer users are often unaware of system vulnerabilities and weak security practices. The majority of system and network administrators are not adequately trained in security and do not have sufficient time to perform their duties.

Technical solutions to security show promise, but these alone do not ensure security. While Defense is attempting to react to attacks as it becomes aware of them, it will not be in a strong position to deter them until it develops and implements more aggressive, proactive detection and reaction programs. . . .

Excerpted from U.S. Congress. General Accounting Office. *Information Security: Computer Attacks at Department of Defense Pose Increasing Risks.* GAO/AIMD-96-84, May 22, 1996. http://www.gao.gov/archive/1996/ai96084.pdf (accessed September 1, 2004).

## 60. Critical Foundations: Protecting America's Infrastructures, President's Commission on Critical Infrastructure Protection Report

*October 20, 1997*

## Executive Summary

### Introduction

Our national defense, economic prosperity, and quality of life have long depended on the essential services that underpin our society. These critical infrastructures—energy, banking and finance, transportation, vital human services, and telecommunications—must be viewed in a new context in the Information Age. The rapid proliferation and integration of telecommunications and computer systems have connected infrastructures to one another in a complex network of interdependence. This interlinkage has created a new dimension of vulnerability, which, when combined with an emerging constellation of threats, poses unprecedented national risk. . . .

### The Case for Action

A satchel of dynamite and a truckload of fertilizer and diesel fuel are known terrorist tools. Today, the right command sent over a network to a power generating station's control computer could be just as devastating as a backpack full of explosives, and the perpetrator would be more difficult to identify and apprehend. . . .

. . . [T]he resources necessary to conduct a cyber attack have shifted in the past few years from the arcane to the commonplace. A personal computer and a telephone connection to an Internet Service Provider anywhere in the world are enough to cause harm. . . .

The Commission has not discovered an immediate threat sufficient to warrant a fear of imminent national crisis. However, we are convinced that our vulnerabilities are increasing steadily, that the means to exploit those weaknesses are readily available and that the costs associated with an effective attack continue to drop. What is more, the investments required to improve the situation—now still relatively modest—will rise if we procrastinate.

We should attend to our critical foundations before we are confronted with a crisis, not after. Waiting for disaster would prove as expensive as it would be irresponsible. . . .

## Chapter 1: Acting Now to Protect the Future

. . . Terrorist attacks have typically been against single targets—individuals, buildings, or institutions. Today, more sophisticated physical attacks may also exploit the emerging vulnerabilities associated with the complexity and interconnectedness of our infrastructures. Bombs—even homemade ones—have always been able to damage a pipeline, electrical power transformer, telecommunications switching station, or microwave relay antenna. In the networked world of today, the effects of such physical attacks could spread far beyond the radius of a bomb blast. Adding to our physical vulnerability is the fact that information readily available on the World Wide Web (WWW) may disclose to a terrorist the best place to set explosive charges for maximum disruptive effects. . . .

Physical means to exploit physical vulnerabilities probably remain the most worrisome threat to our infrastructures *today.* But almost every group we met voiced concerns about the new cyber vulnerabilities and threats. They emphasized the importance of developing approaches to protecting our infrastructures against cyber threats *before* they materialize and produce major system damage. . . .

## Chapter 2: The New Geography

. . . [N]ew technologies have appeared that render physical geography less relevant and our domestic sanctuary less secure. Today, a computer can cause switches or valves to open and close, move funds from one account to another, or convey a military order almost as quickly over thousands of miles as it can from next door, and just as easily from a terrorist hideout as from an office cubicle or military command center. . . .

Vulnerability to an adversary using cyber tools was examined during a military exercise conducted in early summer of 1997. The scenario featured "scripted" attacks on the energy and telecommunications infrastructures (controllers injected incidents into the scenario; military commands and government agencies reacted as though the reported incidents were real). Companies providing electrical power in selected cities were subjected to scripted attack by cyber means, over time, in a way that made the resulting simulated outages appear to be random and unrelated. Concurrently, a "Red Team" used hacker techniques available on the Internet to attempt to penetrate Department of Defense (DoD) computers. With no insider information, and constrained by US law, the team spent three months probing the vulnerabilities of several hundred unclassified computer networks. They were able to penetrate many of these networks, and even gained system administrator level privileges in some.

Simulated cyber attacks on nearby privately owned energy companies and telecommunications service providers and successful penetrations into

DoD computers were assessed by controllers as sufficient to have disrupted operations at selected military bases—creating a situation in which our ability to deploy and sustain military forces was degraded. Was this exercise an overstatement of today's vulnerabilities or a glimpse at future forms of terrorism and war? The experience to date, the known vulnerabilities, and the continuing pace of change suggest the latter. . . .

## Chapter 3: New Vulnerabilities, Shared Threats, Shared Responsibility

### Information Warfare

. . . For an adversary willing to take greater risks, cyber attacks could be combined with physical attacks, against facilities or against human targets, in an effort to paralyze or panic large segments of society, damage our capability to respond to incidents (by disabling the 911 system or emergency communications, for example), hamper our ability to deploy conventional military forces, and otherwise limit the freedom of action of our national leadership.

Terrorists frequently choose prominent targets that produce little physical impact beyond the target itself, but widespread psychological impact. For a physical attack on infrastructures, less spectacular targets could be chosen, such as switching stations, communications antennas, pipelines, transformers, pumping stations, and underground cables. Many facilities whose physical damage or destruction would have a disruptive effect on an infrastructure are purposely located in sparsely populated or even unpopulated areas. If they are physically attacked it may take some time to discover the nature of the damage, and in the absence of casualties it may be some time before the attacks are reported. . . .

The chances of immediately discovering that a concerted cyber attack is in progress are today even slimmer. Computer intrusions do not announce their presence the way a bomb does. Depending on the skill of the intruder and the technology and training available to their own system administrators, individual companies whose networks are penetrated may or may not detect an intrusion. Intrusions that are discovered may or may not be reported to law enforcement authorities, who may or may not have the resources to investigate them and conclude whether they are the work of an insider, a hacker, a criminal, or someone truly bent on harming the infrastructure. It sometimes takes months, even years, to determine the significance of individual computer attacks. . . .

Excerpted from U.S. Executive Office of the President. President's Commission on Critical Infrastructure Protection. *Critical Foundations: Protecting America's Infrastructures.* October 20, 1997. http://purl. access.gpo.gov/GPO/LPS15260 (accessed September 1, 2004).

# 61. White Paper—The Clinton Administration's Policy on Critical Infrastructure Protection: Presidential Decision Directive 63, White House Press Release

*May 22, 1998*

## I. A Growing Potential Vulnerability

. . . Critical infrastructures are those physical and cyber-based systems essential to the minimum operations of the economy and government. They include, but are not limited to, telecommunications, energy, banking and finance, transportation, water systems and emergency services, both governmental and private. . . .

Because of our military strength, future enemies, whether nations, groups or individuals, may seek to harm us in non-traditional ways including attacks within the United States. Our economy is increasingly reliant upon interdependent and cyber-supported infrastructures and non-traditional attacks on our infrastructure and information systems may be capable of significantly harming both our military power and our economy. . . .

## III. A National Goal

No later than the year 2000, the United States shall have achieved an initial operating capability and no later than five years from the day the President signed Presidential Decision Directive 63 the United States shall have achieved and shall maintain the ability to protect our nation's critical infrastructures from intentional acts that would significantly diminish the abilities of:

- the Federal Government to perform essential national security missions and to ensure the general public health and safety;
- state and local governments to maintain order and to deliver minimum essential public services;
- the private sector to ensure the orderly functioning of the economy and the delivery of essential telecommunications, energy, financial and transportation services.

Any interruptions or manipulations of these critical functions must be brief, infrequent, manageable, geographically isolated and minimally detrimental to the welfare of the United States.

## IV. A Public-Private Partnership to Reduce Vulnerability

Since the targets of attacks on our critical infrastructure would likely include both facilities in the economy and those in the government, the elimination of our potential vulnerability requires a closely coordinated effort of both the public and the private sector. To succeed, this partnership must be genuine, mutual and cooperative. . . .

For each of the major sectors of our economy that are vulnerable to infrastructure attack, the Federal Government will appoint from a designated Lead Agency a senior officer of that agency as the Sector Liaison Official to work with the private sector. Sector Liaison Officials, after discussions and coordination with private sector entities of their infrastructure sector, will identify a private sector counterpart (Sector Coordinator) to represent their sector.

Together these two individuals and the departments and corporations they represent shall contribute to a sectoral National Infrastructure Assurance Plan by:

- assessing the vulnerabilities of the sector to cyber or physical attacks;
- recommending a plan to eliminate significant vulnerabilities;
- proposing a system for identifying and preventing attempted major attacks;
- developing a plan for alerting, containing and rebuffing an attack in progress and then, in coordination with FEMA [Federal Emergency Management Agency] as appropriate, rapidly reconstituting minimum essential capabilities in the aftermath of an attack. . . .

## Warning and Information Centers

As part of a national warning and information sharing system, the President immediately authorizes the FBI to expand its current organization to a full scale National Infrastructure Protection Center (NIPC). . . .

National Infrastructure Protection Center (NIPC): The NIPC will include FBI, USSS [U.S. Secret Service], and other investigators experienced in computer crimes and infrastructure protection, as well as representatives detailed from the Department of Defense, the Intelligence Community and [federal] Agencies. It will be linked electronically to the rest of the Federal Government, including other warning and operations centers, as well as any private sector sharing and analysis centers. Its mission will include providing timely warnings of intentional threats, comprehensive analyses and law enforcement investigation and response. . . .

The NIPC, in conjunction with the information originating agency, will sanitize law enforcement and intelligence information for inclusion into analyses and reports that it will provide, in appropriate form, to relevant federal, state and local agencies; the relevant owners and operators of critical infrastructures; and to any private sector information sharing and analysis entity. . . . The NIPC will issue attack warnings or alerts to increases in threat condition to any private sector information sharing and analysis entity and to the owners and operators. These warnings may also include guidance regarding additional protection measures to be taken by owners and operators. . . .

The NIPC will provide a national focal point for gathering information on threats to the infrastructures. Additionally, the NIPC will provide the principal means of facilitating and coordinating the Federal Government's response to an incident, mitigating attacks, investigating threats and monitoring reconstitution efforts. . . .

Excerpted from U.S. Executive Office of the President. Office of the Press Secretary. *White Paper—The Clinton Administration's Policy on Critical Infrastructure Protection: Presidential Decision Directive 63.* May 22, 1998. http://clinton6.nara.gov/1998/05/1998-05-22-the-white-paper-on-critical-infrastructure-protection-pdd.html (accessed September 1, 2004).

## 62. Computer Security: Weaknesses Continue to Place Critical Federal Operations and Assets at Risk, General Accounting Office Congressional Testimony

*April 5, 2001*

### Background

Dramatic increases in computer interconnectivity, especially in the use of the Internet, are revolutionizing the way our government, our nation, and much of the world communicate and conduct business. . . .

. . . [T]his widespread interconnectivity poses significant risks to our computer systems and, more important, to the critical operations and infrastructures they support. For example, telecommunications, power distribution, water supply, public health services, and national defense—including the military's warfighting capability—law enforcement, government services, and emergency services all depend on the security of their computer operations. . . .

Government officials are increasingly concerned about attacks from individuals and groups with malicious intent, such as crime, terrorism, foreign intelligence gathering, and acts of war. According to the FBI, terrorists, transnational criminals, and intelligence services are quickly becoming aware of and using information exploitation tools such as computer viruses, Trojan horses, worms, logic bombs, and eavesdropping sniffers that can destroy, intercept, or degrade the integrity of and deny access to data. As greater amounts of money are transferred through computer systems, as more sensitive economic and commercial information is exchanged electronically, and as the nation's defense and intelligence communities increasingly rely on commercially available information technology, the likelihood that information attacks will threaten vital national interests increases. . . .

Since 1996, our analyses of information security at major federal agencies have shown that federal systems were not being adequately protected from these threats, even though these systems process, store, and transmit enormous amounts of sensitive data and are indispensable to many federal agency operations. In September 1996, we reported that serious weaknesses had been found at 10 of the 15 largest federal agencies, and we concluded that poor information security was a widespread federal problem with potentially devastating consequences. In 1998 and in 2000, we analyzed audit results for 24 of the largest federal agencies: both analyses found that all 24 agencies had significant information security weaknesses. . . .

## Improved Security Program Management Is Essential

. . . Agencies have taken steps to address problems and many have good remedial efforts underway. However, these efforts will not be fully effective and lasting unless they are supported by a strong agencywide security management framework. . . .

While instituting this framework is essential, there are several steps that agencies can take immediately. Specifically, they can (1) increase awareness, (2) ensure that existing controls are operating effectively, (3) ensure that software patches are up-to-date, (4) use automated scanning and testing tools to quickly identify problems, (5) propagate their best practices, and (6) ensure that their most common vulnerabilities are addressed. None of these actions alone will ensure good security. However, they take advantage of readily available information and tools and, thus, do not involve significant new resources. As a result, they are steps that can be made without delay. . . .

Excerpted from U.S. Congress. General Accounting Office. *Computer Security: Weaknesses Continue to Place Critical Federal Operations and Assets at Risk.* Prepared testimony of Robert F. Dacey, director of information security issues, for a hearing by the Subcommittee on Oversight and Investigations of the House Committee on Energy and Commerce. GAO-01-600T, April 5, 2001. http://www.gao.gov/archive/2000/d01600t.pdf (accessed September 1, 2004).

# 63. Critical Infrastructure Protection: Significant Challenges in Developing Analysis, Warning, and Response Capabilities, General Accounting Office Congressional Testimony

*May 22, 2001*

. . . Overall, progress in developing the analysis, warning, and information-sharing capabilities called for in PDD 63 [Presidential Decision Directive 63, issued by President Bill Clinton in May 1998] has been mixed. The NIPC [National Infrastructure Protection Center] has initiated a variety of critical infrastructure protection efforts that have laid a foundation for future governmentwide efforts. In addition, it has provided valuable support and coordination related to investigating and otherwise responding to attacks on computers. However, the analytical and information-sharing capabilities that PDD 63 asserts are needed to protect the nation's critical infrastructures have not yet been achieved, and the NIPC has developed only limited warning capabilities. . . .

The NIPC is aware of the challenges it faces and has taken some steps to address them. In addition, the administration is reviewing the federal critical infrastructure protection strategy, including the way the federal government is organized to manage this effort. . . .

## Multiple Factors Have Limited Development of Analysis and Warning Capabilities

. . . Since its establishment in 1998, the NIPC has issued a variety of analytical products, most of which have been tactical analyses pertaining to individual incidents. These analyses have included (1) situation reports related to law enforcement investigations, including denial-of-service attacks that affected numerous Internet-based entities, such as eBay and Yahoo and (2) analytical support of a counterintelligence investigation. In addition, the NIPC has issued a variety of publications, most of which were compilations of information previously reported by others with some NIPC analysis.

Strategic analysis to determine the potential broader implications of individual incidents has been limited. Such analysis looks beyond one specific incident to consider a broader set of incidents or implications that may indicate a potential threat of national importance. Identifying such threats assists in proactively managing risk, including evaluating the risks associated with possible future incidents and effectively mitigating the impact of such incidents.

Three factors have hindered the NIPC's ability to develop strategic analytical capabilities.

- First, there is no generally accepted methodology for analyzing strategic cyber-based threats. For example, there is no standard terminology, no standard set of factors to consider, and no established thresholds for determining the sophistication of attack techniques. According to officials in the intelligence and national security community, developing such a methodology would require an intense interagency effort and dedication of resources.
- Second, the NIPC has sustained prolonged leadership vacancies and does not have adequate staff expertise, in part because other federal agencies had not provided the originally anticipated number of detailees. For example, as of the close of our review in February, the position of Chief of the Analysis and Warning Section, which was to be filled by the Central Intelligence Agency, had been vacant for about half of the NIPC's 3-year existence. In addition, the NIPC had been operating with only 13 of the 24 analysts that NIPC officials estimate are needed to develop analytical capabilities.
- Third, the NIPC did not have industry-specific data on factors such as critical system components, known vulnerabilities, and interdependencies. Under PDD 63, such information is to be developed for each of eight industry segments by industry representatives and the designated federal lead agencies. However, at the close of our work in February, only three industry assessments had been partially completed, and none had been provided to the NIPC. . . .

However, I want to emphasize a more fundamental impediment. Specifically, evaluating the NIPC's progress in developing analysis and warning capabilities is difficult because the federal government's strategy and related plans for protecting the nation's critical infrastructures from computer-based attacks, including the NIPC's role, are still evolving. The entities involved in the government's critical infrastructure protection efforts do not share a common interpretation of the NIPC's roles and responsibilities. Further, the relationships between the NIPC, the FBI, and the National Coordinator for

Security, Infrastructure Protection, and Counter-Terrorism at the National Security Council are unclear regarding who has direct authority for setting NIPC priorities and procedures and providing NIPC oversight. In addition, the NIPC's own plans for further developing its analytical and warning capabilities are fragmented and incomplete. As a result, there are no specific priorities, milestones, or program performance measures to guide NIPC actions or provide a basis for evaluating its progress. . . .

## Progress in Establishing Information-Sharing Relationships Has Been Mixed

Information sharing and coordination among private-sector and government organizations are essential to thoroughly understanding cyber threats and quickly identifying and mitigating attacks. However, as we testified in July 2000, establishing the trusted relationships and information-sharing protocols necessary to support such coordination can be difficult.

NIPC efforts in this area have met with mixed success. . . .

. . . [T]he NIPC and the FBI had made only limited progress in developing a database of the most important components of the nation's critical infrastructures—an effort referred to as the Key Asset Initiative. While FBI field offices had identified over 5,000 key assets, the entities that own or control the assets generally had not been involved in identifying them. As a result, the key assets recorded may not be the ones that infrastructure owners consider to be the most important. Further, the Key Asset Initiative was not being coordinated with other similar federal efforts at the Departments of Defense and Commerce.

In addition, the NIPC and other government entities had not developed fully productive information-sharing and cooperative relationships. For example, federal agencies have not routinely reported incident information to the NIPC, at least in part because guidance provided by the federal Chief Information Officers Council, which is chaired by the Office of Management and Budget, directs agencies to report such information to the General Services Administration's Federal Computer Incident Response Capability. Further, NIPC and Defense officials agreed that their information-sharing procedures need improvement, noting that protocols for reciprocal exchanges of information had not been established. In addition, the expertise of the U.S. Secret Service regarding computer crime had not been integrated into NIPC efforts. . . .

Excerpted from U.S. Congress. General Accounting Office. *Critical Infrastructure Protection: Significant Challenges in Developing Analysis, Warning, and Response Capabilities.* Prepared testimony of Robert F. Dacey, director of information security issues, for a hearing by the Subcommittee on Technology, Terrorism, and Government Information of the Senate Committee on the Judiciary. GAO-01-769T, May 22, 2001. http://www.gao.gov/new.items/d01769t.pdf (accessed September 1, 2004).

# Analysis of Osama bin Laden Threat Changed over Time

## INTRODUCTION

Terrorist leader Osama bin Laden first gained the world's attention as a friend of the United States. In the 1980s guerrillas in Afghanistan backed by the Central Intelligence Agency (CIA) fought to drive out occupying Soviet forces. With a fortune estimated at $300 million, bin Laden spent millions of dollars recruiting and training thousands of foreign fighters who traveled to Afghanistan to help with the jihad, or Islamic holy war, against the Soviets. "His religious fervor, and his role in organizing thousands of Arab volunteers to battle the Soviets in Afghanistan in the 1980s, made him legendary throughout the Islamic world," the *Wall Street Journal* reported on August 10, 1998. "Children have been named after him in Pakistan."

When the Soviets withdrew from Afghanistan in 1989, bin Laden returned to his native Saudi Arabia. According to U.S. intelligence officials, he started funding militant Islamic groups that sought to overthrow Islamic governments they considered too moderate.

American officials believe bin Laden's hatred of the United States began on August 7, 1990, when U.S. soldiers—who would eventually total 500,000—began arriving in Saudi Arabia in preparation for a war to drive Iraq out of Kuwait. He considered the Americans infidels, and he was reportedly enraged by their presence in the country that contained Islam's two holiest mosques in Mecca and Medina. But in 1991 American intelligence agencies largely lost track of bin Laden, according to an unnamed "senior official" quoted by the

*New York Times* in a story published April 13, 1999. The official told the newspaper that the intelligence coverage remained spotty until 1996.

In a fact sheet about bin Laden released on August 14, 1996 [Document 64], the U.S. State Department called him "one of the most significant financial sponsors of Islamic extremist activities in the world today." Just over a week later, bin Laden and several other radical leaders issued a "fatwa," or religious ruling, calling on Muslims to launch terrorist attacks against Americans and their allies—military personnel and civilians alike—around the world. The State Department stuck with its description of bin Laden as a "terrorist financier" in a document released on March 3, 1998. The view that bin Laden only financed terrorism abruptly changed on August 7, 1998, when Islamic extremists almost simultaneously bombed U.S. embassies in Kenya and Tanzania. American officials quickly announced that bin Laden had masterminded the attacks, which killed more than 200 people—including twelve Americans—and wounded more than 4,000. U.S. officials also noted that the bombings occurred exactly eight years after the first United States troops landed in Saudi Arabia.

Less than two weeks after the bombings, on August 20, 1998, the United States launched seventy cruise missiles aimed at terrorist training camps in Afghanistan and a factory in Sudan that American officials insisted was linked to bin Laden and produced precursor chemicals for a deadly nerve gas. The missiles were timed to hit when bin Laden and many other top al Qaeda leaders were meeting at one of the camps. However, bin Laden reportedly left the camp hours before the missiles fell. The missile strikes backfired, as their failure to kill the terrorist leader greatly heightened bin Laden's stature in the Muslim world. The strikes also called into question the strength of American intelligence, because the Sudanese government insisted afterwards that the destroyed factory only produced medicines.

On November 4, 1998, federal prosecutors charged bin Laden and a senior aide with conspiring to blow up the embassies and plotting to kill Americans in foreign countries. That same day the State Department announced a $5 million reward for information leading to bin Laden's arrest or conviction.

In a widely circulated September 1999 report prepared for the CIA, researchers at the Library of Congress warned that bin Laden "most likely will retaliate in a spectacular way" for the 1998 missile strikes on his terrorist training camps. The report said that based on a foiled al Qaeda plot in 1995, suicide bombers might crash aircraft packed with high explosives into the Pentagon, the CIA headquarters, or the White House [Document 65].

Following the September 11, 2001, attacks on the Pentagon and the World Trade Center, Bush administration officials said no one had ever imagined that terrorists would crash planes into buildings. "I don't think that anybody could have predicted that these people . . . would try to use an airplane as a missile," said Condoleezza Rice, Bush's national security adviser, on May 16, 2002. Two days later numerous media outlets reported on the existence of the 1999 study. Later that day Ari Fleischer, the White House press secretary, said the administration had only learned of the study in the morning.

On February 7, 2001—seven months before al Qaeda members used passenger planes to destroy the World Trade Center and damage the Pentagon—CIA Director George J. Tenet gave his annual briefing to Congress about threats against the United States and its interests abroad. "Usama bin Ladin and his global network of lieutenants and associates remain the most immediate and serious threat," Tenet said [Document 66].

The most controversial document about bin Laden was an item titled "Bin Ladin Determined to Strike in US" from the highly classified President's Daily Brief for August 6, 2001. "After US missile strikes on his base in Afghanistan in 1998, Bin Ladin told followers he wanted to retaliate in Washington, according to a [redacted] [foreign intelligence] service," the document said. It also reported that al Qaeda members had resided in or traveled to the United States for years and had developed a support structure that could aid attacks. "FBI information since [1998] indicates patterns of suspicious activity in this country consistent with preparations for hijackings or other types of attacks, including recent surveillance of federal buildings in New York," the document said [Document 67].

The White House had refused to declassify the seventeen-sentence document for two years, contending that it contained sensitive intelligence information. The National Commission on Terrorist Attacks Upon the United States urged the White House to make the document public, and it was finally released on April 10, 2004. In a story the next day, the Associated Press quoted Bush as saying the document contained "nothing about an attack on America." But critics, including some members of the commission, said the document was a dire warning of upcoming attacks upon the United States that should have prompted Bush to act immediately. Left unanswered was the key question: Even if Bush had acted immediately on August 6, could he have stopped the attacks that occurred a month later?

# 64. State Department Fact Sheet on Osama bin Laden

*August 14, 1996*

Usama bin Muhammad bin Awad Bin Ladin is one of the most significant financial sponsors of Islamic extremist activities in the world today. One of some 20 sons of wealthy Saudi construction magnate Muhammad Bin Ladin—founder of the Kingdom's Bin Ladin Group business empire—Usama joined the Afghan resistance movement following the 26 December 1979 Soviet invasion of Afghanistan. "I was enraged and went there at once," he claimed in a 1993 interview. "I arrived within days, before the end of 1979."

Bin Ladin gained prominence during the Afghan war for his role in
financing the recruitment, transportation, and training of Arab nationals
who volunteered to fight alongside the Afghan mujahedin. By 1985, Bin
Ladin had drawn on his family's wealth, plus donations received from sym-
pathetic merchant families in the Gulf region, to organize the Islamic Salva-
tion Foundation, or al-Qaida, for this purpose.

- A network of al-Qaida recruitment centers and guesthouses in Egypt,
  Saudi Arabia, and Pakistan has enlisted and sheltered thousands of
  Arab recruits. This network remains active.
- Working in conjunction with extremist groups like the Egyptian al-
  Gama'at al-Islamiyyah, also known as the Islamic Group, al-Qaida
  organized and funded camps in Afghanistan and Pakistan that provided new recruits paramilitary training in preparation for the fighting
  in Afghanistan.
- Under al-Qaida auspices, Bin Ladin imported bulldozers and other
  heavy equipment to cut roads, tunnels, hospitals, and storage depots
  through Afghanistan's mountainous terrain to move and shelter fighters and supplies.

After the Soviets withdrew from Afghanistan in 1989, Bin Ladin
returned to work in the family's Jeddah-based construction business. However, he continued to support militant Islamic groups that had begun targeting moderate Islamic governments in the region. Saudi officials held
Bin Ladin's passport during 1989–1991 in a bid to prevent him from
solidifying contacts with extremists whom he had befriended during the
Afghan war.

Bin Ladin relocated to Sudan in 1991, where he was welcomed by
National Islamic Front (NIF) leader Hasan al-Turabi. . . .

Bin Ladin's work force grew to include militant Afghan war veterans
seeking to avoid a return to their own countries, where many stood accused
of subversive and terrorist activities. In May 1993, for example, Bin Ladin
financed the travel of 300 to 480 Afghan war veterans to Sudan after
Islamabad launched a crackdown against extremists lingering in Pakistan. In
addition to safehaven in Sudan, Bin Ladin has provided financial support to
militants actively opposed to moderate Islamic governments and the West:

- Islamic extremists who perpetrated the December 1992 attempted
  bombings against some 100 U.S. servicemen in Aden (billeted there to
  support U.N. relief operations in Somalia) claimed that Bin Ladin
  financed their group.
- A joint Egyptian-Saudi investigation revealed in May 1993 that Bin
  Ladin business interests helped funnel money to Egyptian extremists,
  who used the cash to buy unspecified equipment, printing presses, and
  weapons.

- By January 1994, Bin Ladin had begun financing at least three terrorist training camps in northern Sudan (camp residents included Egyptian, Algerian, Tunisian and Palestinian extremists) in cooperation with the NIF. . . .
- Pakistani investigators have said that Ramzi Ahmed Yousef, the alleged mastermind of the February 1993 World Trade Center bombing, resided at the Bin Ladin-funded Bayt Ashuhada (house of martyrs) guesthouse in Peshawar during most of the three years before his apprehension in February 1995.
- A leading member of the Egyptian extremist group al-Jihad claimed in a July 1995 interview that Bin Ladin helped fund the group and was at times witting of specific terrorist operations mounted by the group against Egyptian interests.
- Bin Ladin remains the key financier behind the "Kunar" camp in Afghanistan, which provides terrorist training to al-Jihad and al-Gama'at al-Islamiyyah members, according to suspect terrorists captured recently by Egyptian authorities. . . .

Excerpted from U.S. Department of State. *Usama Bin Ladin: Islamic Extremist Financier.* August 14, 1996. NEA307, Accession Number 452291. Available by searching http://pdq.state.gov (accessed September 1, 2004).

# 65. The Sociology and Psychology of Terrorism: Who Becomes a Terrorist and Why? Library of Congress Report for the Central Intelligence Agency
*September 1999*

## Executive Summary: Mindsets of Mass Destruction

### New Types of Post-Cold War Terrorists
   . . . When the conventional terrorist groups and individuals of the early 1970s are compared with terrorists of the early 1990s, a trend can be seen: the emergence of religious fundamentalist and new religious groups espousing the rhetoric of mass-destruction terrorism. In the 1990s, groups moti-

vated by religious imperatives, such as Aum Shinrikyo, Hizballah, and al-Qaida, have grown and proliferated. These groups have a different attitude toward violence—one that is extranormative and seeks to maximize violence against the perceived enemy, essentially anyone who is not a fundamentalist Muslim or an Aum Shinrikyo member. Their outlook is one that divides the world simplistically into "them" and "us." . . .

New breeds of increasingly dangerous religious terrorists emerged in the 1990s. The most dangerous type is the Islamic fundamentalist. A case in point is Ramzi Yousef, who brought together a loosely organized, ad hoc group, the so-called Liberation Army, apparently for the sole purpose of carrying out the WTC [World Trade Center] operation on February 26, 1993. Moreover, by acting independently the small self-contained cell led by Yousef prevented authorities from linking it to an established terrorist organization, such as its suspected coordinating group, Osama bin Laden's al-Qaida, or a possible state sponsor. . . .

Ramzi Yousef's plot to blow up the WTC [in 1993] might have killed an estimated 50,000 people had his team not made a minor error in the placement of the bomb. . . .

Increasingly, terrorist groups are recruiting members with expertise in fields such as communications, computer programming, engineering, finance, and the sciences. Ramzi Yousef graduated from Britain's Swansea University with a degree in engineering. . . .

Osama bin Laden also recruits highly skilled professionals in the fields of engineering, medicine, chemistry, physics, computer programming, communications, and so forth. Whereas the skills of the elite terrorist commandos of the 1960s and 1970s were often limited to what they learned in training camp, the terrorists of the 1990s who have carried out major operations have included biologists, chemists, computer specialists, engineers, and physicists.

### New Forms of Terrorist-Threat Scenarios

The number of international terrorist incidents has declined in the 1990s, but the potential threat posed by terrorists has increased. The increased threat level, in the form of terrorist actions aimed at achieving a larger scale of destruction than the conventional attacks of the previous three decades of terrorism, was dramatically demonstrated with the bombing of the WTC. The WTC bombing illustrated how terrorists with technological sophistication are increasingly being recruited to carry out lethal terrorist bombing attacks. The WTC bombing may also have been a harbinger of more destructive attacks of international terrorism in the United States. . . .

The threat to U.S. interests posed by Islamic fundamentalist terrorists in particular was underscored by al-Qaida's bombings of the U.S. Embassies in Kenya and Tanzania in August 1998. With those two devastating bombings, Osama bin Laden resurfaced as a potent terrorist threat to U.S. interests worldwide. Bin Laden is the prototype of a new breed of terrorist—the private entrepreneur who puts modern enterprise at the service of a global terrorist network. . . .

If Iran's mullahs or Iraq's Saddam Hussein decide to use terrorists to attack the continental United States, they would likely turn to bin Laden's al-Qaida. Al-Qaida is among the Islamic groups recruiting increasingly skilled professionals, such as computer and communications technicians, engineers, pharmacists, and physicists, as well as Ukrainian chemists and biologists, Iraqi chemical weapons experts, and others capable of helping to develop WMD [Weapons of Mass Destruction]. Al-Qaida poses the most serious terrorist threat to U.S. security interests, for al-Qaida's well-trained terrorists are actively engaged in a terrorist jihad against U.S. interests worldwide. . . .

Al-Qaida's expected retaliation for the U.S. cruise missile attack against al-Qaida's training facilities in Afghanistan on August 20, 1998, could take several forms of terrorist attack in the nation's capital. Al-Qaida could detonate a Chechen-type building-buster bomb at a federal building. Suicide bomber(s) belonging to al-Qaida's Martyrdom Battalion could crash-land an aircraft packed with high explosives (C-4 and semtex) into the Pentagon, the headquarters of the Central Intelligence Agency (CIA), or the White House. Ramzi Yousef had planned to do this against the CIA headquarters. In addition, both al-Qaida and Yousef were linked to a plot to assassinate President Clinton during his visit to the Philippines in early 1995. Following the August 1998 cruise missile attack, at least one Islamic religious leader called for Clinton's assassination, and another stated that "the time is not far off" for when the White House will be destroyed by a nuclear bomb. A horrendous scenario consonant with al-Qaida's mindset would be its use of a nuclear suitcase bomb against any number of targets in the nation's capital. Bin Laden allegedly has already purchased a number of nuclear suitcase bombs from the Chechen Mafia. Al-Qaida's retaliation, however, is more likely to take the lower-risk form of bombing one or more U.S. airliners with time-bombs. Yousef was planning simultaneous bombings of 11 U.S. airliners prior to his capture. Whatever form an attack may take, bin Laden will most likely retaliate in a spectacular way for the cruise missile attack against his Afghan camp in August 1998. . . .

Excerpted from U.S. Congress. Library of Congress. Federal Research Division. *The Sociology and Psychology of Terrorism: Who Becomes a Terrorist and Why?* September 1999. http://www.loc.gov/rr/frd/pdf-files/Soc_Psych_of_Terrorism.pdf (accessed September 1, 2004).

## 66. Worldwide Threat 2001: National Security in a Changing World, CIA Director George J. Tenet Congressional Testimony

*February 7, 2001*

. . . Never in my experience . . . has American intelligence had to deal with such a dynamic set of concerns affecting such a broad range of US interests. Never have we had to deal with such a high quotient of uncertainty. With so many things on our plate, it is important always to establish priorities. For me, the highest priority must invariably be on those things that threaten the lives of Americans or the physical security of the United States. With that in mind, let me turn first to the challenges posed by international terrorism.

We have made considerable progress on terrorism against US interests and facilities, Mr. Chairman, but it persists. The most dramatic and recent evidence, of course, is the loss of 17 of our men and women on the USS Cole at the hands of terrorists.

The threat from terrorism is real, it is immediate, and it is evolving. State sponsored terrorism appears to have declined over the past five years, but transnational groups—with decentralized leadership that makes them harder to identify and disrupt—are emerging. We are seeing fewer centrally controlled operations, and more acts initiated and executed at lower levels.

Terrorists are also becoming more operationally adept and more technically sophisticated in order to defeat counterterrorism measures. For example, as we have increased security around government and military facilities, terrorists are seeking out "softer" targets that provide opportunities for mass casualties. Employing increasingly advanced devices and using strategies such as simultaneous attacks, the number of people killed or injured in international terrorist attacks rose dramatically in the 1990s, despite a general decline in the number of incidents. Approximately one-third of these incidents involved US interests.

Usama bin Ladin and his global network of lieutenants and associates remain the most immediate and serious threat. Since 1998, Bin Ladin has declared all US citizens legitimate targets of attack. As shown by the bombing of our Embassies in Africa in 1998 and his Millennium plots last year, he is capable of planning multiple attacks with little or no warning.

His organization is continuing to place emphasis on developing surrogates to carry out attacks in an effort to avoid detection, blame, and retaliation. As a result it is often difficult to attribute terrorist incidents to his group, Al Qa'ida. . . .

Excerpted from U.S. Central Intelligence Agency. *Worldwide Threat 2001: National Security in a Changing World.* Prepared testimony of CIA Director George J. Tenet for a hearing by the Senate Select Committee on Intelligence. February 7, 2001. http://www.cia.gov/cia/public_affairs/speeches/2001/UNCLASWWT_02072001.html (accessed September 1, 2004).

# 67. Bin Ladin Determined to Strike in US, President's Daily Brief

*August 6, 2001*

Bin Laden Determined to Strike in US

*Clandestine, foreign government, and media reports indicate Bin Ladin since 1997 has wanted to conduct foreign terrorist attacks on the US.* Bin Ladin implied in US television interviews in 1997 and 1998 that his followers would follow the example of World Trade Center bomber Ramzi Yousef and "bring the fighting to America."

After US missile strikes on his base in Afghanistan in 1998, Bin Ladin told followers he wanted to retaliate in Washington, according to a [redacted] [foreign intelligence] service.

An Egyptian Islamic Jihad (EIJ) operative told an [redacted] [foreign intelligence] service at the same time that Bin Ladin was planning to exploit the operative's access to the US to mount a terrorist strike.

*The millennium plotting in Canada in 1999 may have been part of Bin Ladin's first serious attempt to implement a terrorist strike in the US.* Convicted plotter Ahmed Ressam has told the FBI that he conceived the idea to attack Los Angeles International Airport himself, but that Bin Ladin lieutenant Abu Zubaydah encouraged him and helped facilitate the operation. Ressam also said that in 1998 Abu Zubaydah was planning his own US attack.

Ressam says Bin Ladin was aware of the Los Angeles operation.

*Although Bin Ladin has not succeeded, his attacks against the US Embassies in Kenya and Tanzania in 1998 demonstrate that he prepares operations years in advance and is not deterred by setbacks.* Bin Ladin associates surveilled our Embassies in Nairobi and Dar es Salaam as early as 1993, and some members of the Nairobi cell planning the bombings were arrested and deported in 1997.

*Al Qa'ida members—including some who are US citizens—have resided in or traveled to the US for years, and the group apparently maintains a support structure that could aid attacks.* Two al-Qa'ida members found guilty in the conspiracy to bomb our Embassies in East Africa were US citizens, and a senior EIJ member lived in California in the mid-1990s.

A clandestine source said in 1998 that a Bin Ladin cell in New York was recruiting Muslim-American youth for attacks.

*We have not been able to corroborate some of the more sensational threat reporting, such as that from a [redacted] service in 1998 saying that Bin Ladin wanted to hijack a US aircraft to gain the release of "Blind Shaykh" Umar 'Abd al-Rahman and other US-held extremists.*

Nevertheless, FBI information since that time indicates patterns of suspicious activity in this country consistent with preparations for hijackings or other types of attacks, including recent surveillance of federal buildings in New York.

The FBI is conducting approximately 70 full field investigations throughout the US that it considers Bin Ladin-related. CIA and the FBI are investigating a call to our Embassy in the UAE [United Arab Emirates] in May saying that a group of Bin Ladin supporters was in the US planning attacks with explosives.

U.S. Central Intelligence Agency. *Bin Ladin Determined To Strike in US.* Excerpt from the *President's Daily Brief,* August 6, 2001. Declassified and released on April 10, 2004. http://usembassy-australia.state.gov/hyper/ 2004/0412/epf104.htm (accessed September 1, 2004).

# Immigration Agency Reviews and Reforms

## INTRODUCTION

Before it merged into the Department of Homeland Security on March 1, 2003, the Immigration and Naturalization Service (INS) was a key line of defense against terrorists entering the United States. When foreign nationals arrived at the border or got off flights that originated outside the United States, INS inspectors typically examined their passports, visas, or other identifying documents; asked questions if anything seemed out of the ordinary; and then decided whether they should be allowed to enter the country. Inspectors typically had sixty to ninety seconds to process each person. The INS was also charged with removing illegal aliens from the United States and helping foreign nationals become U.S. citizens.

The INS suffered repeated management failures and scandals for more than a decade before it merged into the Department of Homeland Security. In a September 1997 report, the Justice Department's inspector general said the INS had no way to know how many people entered the United States legally and then stayed past the departure dates listed on their visas—as did two of the pilots who hijacked planes on September 11, 2001. The INS estimated that five million illegal aliens lived in the United States, and that more than two million of them were "overstays." The INS also estimated that the overstay population grew by 125,000 people annually. The inspector general said the INS had no enforcement program specifically aimed at identifying, apprehending, and removing overstays [Document 68].

Congress was at least partially to blame for the overstay problem. In 1996 it passed the Illegal Immigration Reform and Immigrant Responsibility Act, which required the INS to develop a computerized system that would track aliens whose visas had expired so the aliens could be removed. But business groups on the nation's borders, along with the governments of Canada and Mexico, complained that the system would cause huge tie-ups at the borders and result in millions of dollars in lost trade. American businesses also welcomed the steady flow of illegal aliens who gladly accepted low-wage, unskilled positions that Americans shunned. In response, Congress never appropriated enough money to build the system and later watered down the law under which it was mandated.

Also in September 1997, the same month as the inspector general's report about overstays, the U.S. Commission on Immigration Reform recommended that the INS be abolished and its duties transferred to other agencies. "Some of the agencies that implement the immigration laws have so many responsibilities that they have proved unable to manage all of them effectively," said the commission, which was created by Congress. "Between Congressional mandates and administrative determinations, these agencies must give equal weight to more priorities than any one agency can handle." Congress, however, did not take up the commission's recommendations.

In January 1999 the General Accounting Office (GAO)—the investigative arm of Congress—reported that the INS had many management problems, some of which had been identified for years but not corrected. The GAO reported—as it had previously done in 1991 and 1997—that the INS suffered from poor communications. In addition, in both 1995 and 1997 nearly 2,000 criminal aliens were released from prisons into American communities without the INS determining whether they posed a danger. The GAO said some of the released aliens were later arrested for new crimes, including felonies [Document 69].

Six months later, on July 29, 1999, the Justice Department's inspector general appeared at a congressional hearing to summarize his office's recent reports about the INS. The studies found that many of the INS's automation efforts were behind schedule for undocumented reasons and there was no assurance they would work when completed; that the INS's automated biometric identification system was underutilized and contained invalid data because there was no quality control; and that the INS could not verify that many illegal aliens who after being caught volunteered to leave the United States had actually done so [Document 70].

In July 2000 the Justice Department's inspector general issued a report about a program the INS implemented in 1995 to speed up processing of applications for citizenship. The INS undertook the effort because the number of applications had doubled since the previous year and showed no signs of slowing, and its backlog in processing the forms had forced some applicants to wait two or three years before becoming citizens. A little more than one million people became citizens under the sped-up program. But a scandal arose when the INS discovered that about 180,000 of the new citizens had not undergone required FBI criminal background checks, meaning that an unknown number of people were naturalized whose serious criminal backgrounds made them ineligible for citizenship. The inspector general found that the INS had subsequently improved some aspects of the naturalization procedure, but that it still lacked any standards for deciding which applicants qualified for citizenship [Document 71].

On August 21, 2001, less than three weeks before the hijackings, the new INS commissioner announced a planned restructuring of the agency from top to bottom. James W. Ziglar, who previously served as the Senate sergeant at arms, inherited an agency with 34,000 employees and a $4.8 billion budget.

In the early morning of September 11, 2001—just hours before the hijackings—the *Washington Times* and other newspapers published a story by United Press International that said Republicans in Congress were split about how to reform the immigration process. "Inattention by Congress and several administrations has left [INS] a bureaucratic nightmare," the story said. "The INS is just now getting effective computer operations. The quick retrieval of information is vital not only to the smooth processing of immigrants, but also to national security."

---

# 68. Inspector General Report on Aliens Who Overstay Their Visas

*September 1997*

## Introduction

The large number of foreign visitors who legally enter the United States and then do not leave presents a disturbing and persistent problem. . . .

INS estimates the current illegal alien population to be approximately 5 million. The common perception of illegal immigration is that illegal aliens enter the United States by surreptitiously crossing the Southwest border. In fact, INS officials have testified before Congress that 40 to 50 percent of the illegal alien population entered the United States legally as temporary visitors but simply failed to depart when required. INS commonly refers to these illegal aliens as overstays.

Each year, millions of aliens enter the United States as temporary visitors, i.e., nonimmigrants (227 million in FY 1996). Over 90 percent are tourists or business visitors, but nonimmigrants also include students, temporary workers and diplomats. Most of these individuals leave the United States, but some do not. INS estimates that the resident illegal alien population in the United States increases by 125,000 overstays annually. . . .

*Dimensions of the Overstay Problem Are Difficult to Determine*

*INS Estimates of the Illegal Alien Population*
. . . INS' latest estimate [which only counted illegal aliens who had been in the United States for more than 12 months] is that, as of October 1996, the illegal alien population residing in the United States was about 5 million and was growing by about 275,000 per year. INS estimated that 41 percent of the resident illegal alien population consisted of aliens who had entered the country legally and failed to depart, i.e., overstays. The remaining 59 percent were EWIs [Entered Without Inspection, which are people who entered the United States illegally]. . . .

## INS Has No Complete and Reliable System to Track Overstays

The principal INS record-keeping system for nonimmigrants is the Nonimmigrant Information System (NIIS). By design, NIIS only captures data on about 10 percent of all nonimmigrant entries—those entering through airports and seaports, and some of those entering through land border ports of entry. Because Canadians and Mexicans crossing at land borders are generally exempt from the Form I-94 requirement, and because they constitute 90 percent of nonimmigrant entries, NIIS contains arrival and departure information on only a small portion of nonimmigrants. . . . In FY 1995, INS counted approximately 236 million nonimmigrant entries into the United States. Of these, NIIS contains information on only 22.9 million entries. Furthermore, the NIIS data on nonimmigrant entries is incomplete and unreliable due to missing departure records and incomplete records processing.

INS created NIIS in 1983 to automate the storage and retrieval of nonimmigrant information. Total NIIS operating costs are over $20 million each year. . . . INS employees query NIIS, as well as other INS systems, to determine an alien's status. . . .

In FY 1992, the last year for which the INS Statistics Division considers NIIS data reliable for overstay calculations, INS collected 20.5 million arrival records. At the time INS made its computations, the period of legal admission had ended for 19.9 million of these aliens and they should have departed the United States. However, INS was able to match departure records to only 18.2 million of the arrival records. The difference between 19.9 million and 18.2 million is, in theory, the number of individuals who failed to depart from the United States. INS refers to these individuals as "apparent overstays." INS estimated, however, that in FY 1992 only 300,000, and not 1.7 million nonimmigrants overstayed. The remaining 1.4 million nonimmigrants were individuals who INS believed left the United States, but for whom no departure record was matched to an arrival record. The number of apparent overstays has increased significantly since FY 1992. . . .

INS redesigned NIIS in 1996 to make the system more user friendly and address a number of problems. While it is too early to fully evaluate the redesigned system, incomplete records processing appears to be a continuing problem. . . .

### INS Has No Specific Overstay Enforcement Program

INS has no specific enforcement program to identify, locate, apprehend, and remove overstays. INS' approach is to locate and remove illegal aliens through its existing interior enforcement programs, regardless of their method of arrival. Currently INS focuses the majority of its interior enforcement resources on criminal aliens and worksite enforcement. These programs identify and remove illegal aliens, including some nonimmigrant overstays. While INS estimates that overstays comprise 41 percent of the illegal alien population, INS data shows that only 11 percent of the deportable aliens apprehended by INS investigators in FY 1996 were overstays. . . .

Excerpted from U.S. Department of Justice. Office of the Inspector General. *Immigration and Naturalization Service Monitoring of Nonimmigrant Overstays.* Report Number I-97-08, September 1997. http://www.usdoj.gov/oig/inspection/INS/9708/index.htm (accessed September 1, 2004).

# 69. General Accounting Office Report on Continuing Management Problems at the Immigration and Naturalization Service (INS)

*January 1999*

## Overview

### INS Management Challenges Persist

INS' functions are multilayered and complex. . . . Effective performance of INS' functions requires skills in a wide range of areas, including leadership, program development, coordination and communication between headquarters and field offices, service delivery, and enforcement. To enable INS to better implement and enforce immigration laws, the Congress significantly increased its resources during the past several years. For example, between fiscal years 1993 and 1998, the number of on-board staff at INS increased from about 19,000 to nearly 31,000. During the same period, INS' budget more than doubled from $1.5 billion in fiscal year 1993 to about $3.8 billion in fiscal year 1998. . . .

*Challenges with Internal Communications and Coordination*

Although INS' Commissioner stated that the 1994 INS reorganization would build communication capabilities, communication continued to be a challenge in INS. We reported in 1997, as we did in 1991, that INS' headquarters and field managers generally viewed headquarters as not being in touch with events, problems, and concerns in the field. . . . Headquarters' efforts to resolve concerns about roles, responsibilities, and communication processes were not successful. For example, instances occurred in which key stakeholders were excluded from decision meetings affecting them, and various inconsistent versions of guidance on naturalization procedures were distributed to field offices. . . .

Lack of up-to-date policies and procedures also have contributed to communications challenges. For example, field manuals containing policies and procedures on how to implement immigration laws were out-of-date at the time of our 1991 report and had not been updated by the time of our 1997 report. As a result, INS employees were burdened with having to search for information on immigration laws or regulations in multiple sources; this sometimes resulted in their obtaining conflicting information. The lack of current manuals also led some field officers to create policy locally, thus compounding coordination difficulties. However, during the past 2 years, INS has published an administrative manual and established a timetable through January 2001 for issuing five field manuals. . . .

## Challenges With Implementation of INS' Programs

*Process for Removing Criminal Aliens Needs Improvement*

In accordance with the Attorney General's strategy, one of INS' priorities has been to remove deportable criminal aliens from this country. However, we and the Department's Inspector General have issued several reports noting that INS has been challenged in implementing this priority,

INS' Institutional Hearing Program (IHP) is the Department's main vehicle for placing aliens who are incarcerated in state and federal prisons into deportation proceedings so that they can be expeditiously deported . . . . We reported in 1997 on the 1995 performance results of the IHP, and in 1998 we reported on 1997 IHP results. In each year, covering a 6-month period, we found that INS failed to identify nearly 2,000 potentially deportable aliens before they completed their prison sentences. As a result, the criminal aliens were released into communities in the United States without INS determining whether they posed a risk to public safety. Hundreds of these criminal aliens were aggravated felons who, by law, should have been placed in removal proceedings while in prison and taken into INS custody upon release. Some of these aliens were subsequently rearrested for new crimes, including felonies . . .

> Excerpted from U.S. Congress. General Accounting Office. *Major Management Challenges and Program Risks: Department of Justice.* GAO/OCG-99-10, January 1999. http://www.gao.gov/archive/1999/cg99010.pdf (accessed September 1, 2004).

## 70. Inspector General Congressional Testimony on Reviews of the Immigration and Naturalization Service (INS)
*July 29, 1999*

### I. Introduction

. . . As you are well aware given my prior appearances before this Subcommittee, the OIG [Office of Inspector General at the Justice Department] expends significant resources to investigate, audit, and inspect INS programs and personnel. In fact, given the importance of the issues, the amount of taxpayer money appropriated to INS, and, frankly, the concern many in the Department of Justice and the Congress express with respect to INS's management of its programs and personnel, the OIG spends more than half of its total resources on INS-related matters. . . .

### II. Highlights of Recent OIG Reviews

The OIG Audit, Inspection, and Investigations Divisions are all involved in examining systems and the conduct of personnel to identify waste, fraud, and abuse in INS programs. We also routinely make recommendations in an effort to assist INS in improving its operations. . . .

#### B. INS Automation Initiatives

INS plans to spend approximately $2.8 billion on its automation programs through 2001 and beyond, but our reviews have found that they fail to adequately manage these programs. In September 1995, we first notified INS of our concerns regarding systemic problems in their automation program. Based on extensive audit work during 1990 through 1995, we identified ten risk areas in INS's management of automation programs requiring close attention by agency managers.

In March 1998, we reported on a comprehensive audit of INS's management of its automation programs. We noted a failure to monitor contractor activities, lack of comprehensive performance measures, insufficient tracking of projects, and numerous other deficiencies. We concluded that INS did not adequately manage its automation programs and risked completed projects not meeting overall goals, significant delays in completing the programs, and unnecessary cost increases.

In July of this year we issued a follow-up report and again found that INS does not adequately manage its automation programs. In the most recent audit, we noted that INS could not sufficiently track the status of its automation projects to determine whether progress was acceptable given the amount of time and funds already spent. As a result, INS continued to spend hundreds of millions of dollars on automation projects for which there were inadequate budgeted costs or explanations for how the funds were spent. In addition, projects were running behind schedule with no documented explanations as to what was causing the delays. We also found serious deficiencies in compliance with the system development life-cycle process. As a result, INS had no assurance that systems will meet performance and functional requirements. . . .

We also found that INS had not implemented adequate safeguards to ensure the accuracy of existing data to be used by systems currently being developed or re-engineered. Moreover, INS had not implemented adequate safeguards to ensure the adequacy of future data inputs. As a result, existing or new INS systems could rely on inaccurate or unreliable data.

### C. Automated Biometric Identification System (IDENT)

. . . In a report issued in March 1998, the OIG assessed INS's implementation of its IDENT system that uses fingerprints and other biometrics to enhance its law enforcement and benefits processing operations. Border Patrol agents and inspectors at ports of entry historically have relied upon the name given by individuals or listed on identification documents to identify individuals they encounter. Such name-based identification has inherent problems. Along the Southwest border, apprehended aliens usually do not carry identification and often provide false names. Consequently, existing records relating to these individuals cannot be located. INS's solution is to use biometrics—individually unique biological measurements such as fingerprints, hand geometry, facial recognition, retinal patterns or other characteristics.

Our inspection found that INS was enrolling less than two-thirds of the aliens apprehended along the U.S.-Mexico border into IDENT. In addition,

INS had entered the fingerprints in the IDENT lookout database of only 41 percent of the aliens deported and excluded in FY 1996; of these, only 24 percent had accompanying photographs even though INS relies on photographs to confirm identification. These failures hamper INS's ability to make consistent and effective use of IDENT as a tool for border enforcement.

We found virtually no controls in place to ensure the quality of data entered into the IDENT lookout database. As a result, we found duplicate records and invalid data. . . .

### E. Visa Waiver Pilot Program

Several of our reviews identified problems in INS programs that concern how and when citizens of other countries may enter or stay in the United States. We found that some of these problems could result in aliens, criminals, or terrorists illegally entering or remaining in the country.

In one of our more significant inspections, the OIG assessed INS efforts to minimize illegal immigration and security threats posed by abuse of the Visa Waiver Pilot Program (VWPP), a program that waives visa requirements for citizens of 26 participating countries. Visitors traveling for business or pleasure under the VWPP do not have to obtain visas and therefore are not screened in any way prior to their arrival at U.S. ports of entry. Instead, VWPP applicants present their passports and other inspection documents to INS inspectors on arrival. The inspectors observe the applicants, examine their passports, and conduct checks against a computerized lookout system to decide whether to allow applicants entry into the United States. This review by INS inspectors is the principal and, in many cases, the only means of preventing illegal entry. INS inspectors have, on average, less than one minute to check and decide on each applicant. In fiscal year 1997, 14.5 million visitors entered the United States under the VWPP.

We found that INS inspectors do not query all VWPP passport numbers against the computerized lookout system (machine-readable passports are queried automatically). In addition, our inspection found that terrorists, criminals, and alien smugglers have attempted to gain entry into the United States through the VWPP. We also found that VWPP visitors violate their nonimmigrant status by staying beyond the allowed 90-day limit; however, sufficient reliable data does not exist to gauge the extent of the problem. . . .

### F. Voluntary Departures

Voluntary departure is a process by which an illegal alien agrees to leave the United States voluntarily, thus avoiding the penalties and stigma of removal. . . .

Our inspection found that aliens were granted the privilege of voluntary departure when, in some cases, they were not eligible because they were aggravated felons. INS district officers performed few criminal checks prior to granting voluntary departure to apprehended aliens and immigration judges frequently issued decisions without completed checks.

The inspection also revealed that INS could not verify that many aliens granted voluntary departure had left the country. We found no evidence of departure in 54 percent of the cases that we reviewed. INS district officers seldom seek or apprehend aliens who violate voluntary departure orders, and immigration judges do not fully utilize voluntary departure bonds or conditions to assist INS in the enforcement of voluntary departure orders. . . .

Excerpted from U.S. Department of Justice. Office of the Inspector General. *Immigration Reorganization and Improvement Act of 1999.* Prepared testimony of Michael R. Bromwich, inspector general at the U.S. Department of Justice, for a hearing by the Subcommittee on Immigration and Claims of the House Judiciary Committee. July 29, 1999. http://www.justice.gov/oig/testimony/9907.htm (accessed September 1, 2004).

# 71. Inspector General Report on Improper Handling of Citizenship Applications
*July 2000*

## Executive Summary

### I. Introduction

Beginning in 1993, the demand for naturalization began to increase at a staggering rate and application backlogs developed at INS offices throughout the country. By June 1995, INS was receiving applications for naturalization at a rate twice as high as it had the previous year. INS projected that without a serious effort to reduce this application backlog, by the summer of 1996 an eligible applicant would have to wait three years from the date of application to be naturalized as a U.S. citizen.

On August 31, 1995, INS Commissioner Doris M. Meissner announced "Citizenship USA" (CUSA), an initiative to reduce the backlog of pending naturalization applications to the point where an eligible applicant would be naturalized within six months of application. The goal of the initiative was to reach this level of processing "currency" within one year. The effort focused on the workload in the five districts in the country—dubbed "Key Cities" for CUSA—which then had the largest application backlogs: Los

Angeles, New York, San Francisco, Miami, and Chicago. To reach the CUSA goal, INS dramatically increased its naturalization workforce in the Key Cities, opened new offices dedicated to naturalization adjudication, and engaged new processing strategies in an effort to "streamline" the naturalization process.

In the spring of 1996, however, just as CUSA moved into its most aggressive phase, media reports began to question the integrity of INS naturalization processing. . . .

Of particular concern were reports that some INS offices were naturalizing applicants so quickly that applicant criminal history reports—generated by the Federal Bureau of Investigation (FBI) after INS submitted applicant fingerprint cards for analysis—were arriving in INS offices only *after* the applicant had been sworn in as a United States citizen. These and other allegations of flaws in naturalization processing suggested that INS had sacrificed naturalization processing integrity in the name of processing applicants more quickly. . . .

In the meantime, in response to congressional requests the Justice Management Division (JMD) of the Department of Justice engaged an outside accounting firm, KPMG Peat Marwick, to oversee a systematic review of CUSA naturalizations that INS would conduct using INS employees. The KPMG-supervised review first concentrated on determining whether each person naturalized during CUSA had a fingerprint check conducted by the FBI. . . . The KPMG-supervised review continued over the course of the next two years, but even its preliminary results were troubling. In March 1997, JMD reported to Congress that of the 1,049,867 persons INS had then identified as having naturalized between August 31, 1995, and September 30, 1996, the fingerprint cards of 124,111 had been returned by the FBI as "unclassifiable," meaning that the fingerprints submitted had not been suitable for comparison. For an additional 61,366 persons, the FBI had no record of having conducted any fingerprint check. This data, therefore, indicated that for 18 percent of those persons naturalized during CUSA, INS had not conducted a complete criminal history background check.

This information was troubling to Congress not only because of what it reflected about criminal history checking procedures and thus the integrity of CUSA adjudications, but also because it suggested that INS had done little to improve its fingerprint processing procedures since 1994, when both the OIG and the General Accounting Office (GAO) had issued reports critical of those procedures and had recommended specific improvements that INS had agreed to undertake. . . .

## II. Summary of OIG Findings and Conclusions

. . . Naturalization processing before CUSA already displayed significant weaknesses that compromised the quality of adjudications. The central standard governing the naturalization adjudication inquiry—whether the applicant was a person of "good moral character"—was subject to varying interpretations in the Field. Administrative files or "A-files," the mechanism by which INS maintained an applicant's immigrant history, were often unavailable to adjudicators and thus not subject to review. As had been documented in both the OIG and GAO reports of 1994, INS' criminal history checking procedures were poorly administered. All of these factors were known to Commissioner Meissner and her staff, and yet INS decided to launch CUSA and thus accelerate a processing system that already was in need of considerable repair. . . .

They represented to the public and to Congress that INS would reduce the naturalization backlog within one year, an ambitious goal under the best of circumstances. However, they failed to address known system weaknesses before implementing a program that they knew would tax that system as it never had been taxed before. Given the known weaknesses in the system and the lack of commitment to repair the deficiencies, the promise of backlog reduction within one year also meant a certain recklessness about the quality of the resulting adjudications. . . .

INS Headquarters encouraged efforts to "streamline" the naturalization process, including methods of reducing the length of interviews. The length of time during which offices had been, at least by policy, expected to wait before adjudicating an application without the applicant's permanent file was reduced from six months to 30 days.

Although we found no explicit instruction from INS Headquarters to ignore standards that had previously existed, neither did we find any instructions concerning how to ensure quality during this period of heightened production. Once INS had rededicated itself to the goal of CUSA, the principle of increased production was pursued at the expense of accuracy in the determination of applicant eligibility, and a process previously regarded as lacking safeguards became even more vulnerable. . . .

### VI. Recommendations

In the wake of CUSA, INS has made some significant improvements and has asserted that it is less tolerant of error in the naturalization process. INS has made obvious improvements in its procedures for ensuring that applicants' fingerprints are checked by the FBI and that the results of those checks are available to adjudicators. It has also markedly improved its procedures for ordering and transferring applicant files so that they, too, are available at interview. Finally, it has implemented standardized checklists and other processing forms that allow it to monitor whether cases are adjudicated in a manner consistent with these new procedures. INS' "Naturalization Quality Procedures," first published in November 1996 and since revised several times, enhance the integrity of naturalization processing.

However, INS has not made progress toward developing and implementing adjudicative standards, including . . . the evaluation of an applicant's "good moral character." There has been little progress toward ensuring that adjudicators, once they have the requisite tools (like the results of criminal history checks or the applicant's file), know how to use them. . . .

Of greatest concern is that INS had not taken steps to identify and promulgate standards that INS itself had recognized as crucial but lacking even before CUSA. The absence of these standards influenced CUSA adjudications and continues to influence INS' current naturalization work. Although Commissioner Meissner announced as early as March 1997 that such standards would be published in an Adjudicator's Manual that would be available throughout the Field, INS has not drafted any portion of that Manual concerning the adjudication of naturalization applications. . . .

INS has made the greatest strides in the area of criminal history checking procedures, the area that was, as Commissioner Meissner called it in her interview with the OIG, CUSA's "fatal flaw." Definitive responses to fingerprint checks are now required for every naturalization applicant. However, INS had not completely eradicated the belief that thorough fingerprint processing in every case is worth the cost. Recently, citing the low risk and burden of other options, INS proposed a policy that permits the adjudication of a naturalization application without further criminal history checks of an applicant whose fingerprints have twice been rejected by the FBI as unclassifiable. We recommend that INS obtain classifiable prints from every naturalization applicant (excluding those exempted by age) unless it certifies that the applicant cannot—because of a physical condition—be fingerprinted in a manner that yields classifiable prints. . . .

Excerpted from U.S. Department of Justice. Office of the Inspector General. *An Investigation of the Immigration and Naturalization Service's Citizenship USA Initiative.* Executive Summary. July 2000. http://www.justice.gov/oig/special/0007/exec.htm (accessed September 1, 2004).

# Defense Science Board Examines Transnational Threats

## INTRODUCTION

Between late 1997 and early 1998 the highly regarded Defense Science Board, which advises the Department of Defense, issued an extraordinary series of reports that analyzed transnational threats to the United States and its troops overseas. The board defined the threats as "any transnational activity that threatens the national security of the United States," including international terrorism, drug trafficking, organized crime, and the proliferation of weapons of mass destruction.

The final report of the twenty-member board said the risk from transnational threats was rising and that groups often sought to inflict maximum casualties and damage. It urged the Defense Department and other agencies to make step-by-step progress in addressing transnational threats instead of deciding they were "too hard" to even consider.

The panel also highlighted three seemingly unconnected incidents—some of which were not initially identified as terrorism—that turned out to be parts of long-term campaigns against the United States. Putting together the pieces to identify such campaigns required more cooperation among government agencies at all levels, it said. "At the present time there are no formal process, infrastructure, and security mechanisms to facilitate the sharing and analysis of transnational threat information" within and between various levels of government, the board said [Document 72].

Globalization had allowed international organized crime and drug-trafficking organizations to develop working relationships with insurgent and terrorist groups, according to a supplemental report released by the board in February 1998. These new arrangements allowed organizations "to take advantage of one another's strengths," the board said, thereby increasing the danger to the United States.

The panel said it wanted to rank the likelihood of various transnational threats to help policymakers make decisions about allocating scarce resources. However, any effort to categorize transnational threats was "all speculative." Part of the reason, the board said, was that federal intelligence agencies devoted insufficient resources to investigating transnational threats and failed to share with other agencies information they obtained [Document 73].

---

# 72. Defense Science Board Final Report on Transnational Threats to the United States
## *September 1997*

## Executive Summary

With the change in the geopolitical structure of the Cold War, we are facing increased threats to the United States and its interests by organizations and individuals with motives and methods quite different than those posed to the nation during its confrontation with the Soviet Union. Among such threats are *transnational threats:* any transnational activity that threatens the national security of the United States—including international terrorism, narcotics trafficking, the proliferation of weapons of mass destruction and the delivery systems for such weapons, and organized crime—or any individual or group that engages in any such activity.

There is a new and ominous trend to these threats: a proclivity towards much greater levels of violence. Transnational groups have the means, through access to weapons of mass destruction and other instruments of terror and disruption, and the motives to cause great harm to our society. For example, the perpetrators of the [1993] World Trade Center bombing and the Tokyo Subway nerve gas attack were aiming for tens of thousands of fatalities. . . .

### *Organizing a DoD Response*

#### *A Major DoD Mission*
Examples of the transnational threat are familiar to us all. Events such as the 1983 attack on the US Marine Corps barracks in Beirut, Lebanon, and the 1996 bombing of Khobar Towers in Saudi Arabia are recent cases of significant consequence. The task force believes that the transnational threat

will escalate in the future and be increasingly characterized by planned campaigns designed to inflict maximum damage and casualties. . . .

### Existing Structures and Processes

. . . Civilian protection begins with the local and state first responder community—law enforcement, fire and rescue, medical, and emergency management personnel. Both the Department of Defense and civilian communities can benefit from improving the integration between the local, state, and federal agencies. Improvements in communication, training, information sharing, operations, and resource transfers would help to streamline emergency response operations and interfaces across all levels of responders. . . .

DoD can and should respond to the escalating transnational threat challenge using the existing national security structure and processes. But within this structure, the Secretary of Defense should clarify responsibilities throughout the organization for policy coordination, operations, and research and development. Today, multiple offices within the Department are involved in each mission area, with no one effectively positioned to ensure the most effective DoD posture against the threat. . . .

### Technical Challenges

An important part of improving DoD's capability to respond to the transnational threat includes drawing on and incorporating technological advances into the Department's response arsenal. In the case of this unique threat, this may mean taking on problems that have long been viewed as too difficult—either bureaucratically or technically. . . .

### Addressing the "Too Hard" Problems

There are a number of challenges that have historically been regarded as "too hard" to solve: the nuclear terrorism challenge, defense against the biological and chemical warfare threat, and defense against the information warfare threat. This task force believes that these challenges should be addressed and that doing so will make a substantive difference in the nation's ability to respond to these distinctly different and serious threats.

In addressing these challenges, the United States must avoid being trapped into inaction because the problems are difficult. Measuring the effectiveness of actions against only the most stressful threat or embracing only the "perfect" solution can stand in the way of important progress. An incremental approach for improving America's capabilities to deal with the nuclear, chemical, and biological transnational threats is prudent and is ardently needed to reduce the enormous potential consequences from such attacks.

*The Nuclear Challenge.* If the required fissile material is available, it is not difficult to design and build a primitive nuclear explosive device. Knowledge about the design and use of nuclear weapons is available in the public domain to an ever-widening clientele. Insuring the security of nuclear weapons and materials in Russia and the states of the Former Soviet Union is crucial . . . .

*The Chemical and Biological Warfare Threat.* Chemical and biological warfare agents share characteristics that make them an especially grave threat. They are relatively easy to obtain, can be developed and produced with modest facilities and equipment, can be lethal even in small quantities, and can be delivered by a variety of means. But they also have substantial differences which must be taken into account when devising strategies and postures to deal with the threat. For example, biological agents can be far more toxic while the lethal effects of chemical agents typically occur more rapidly than biological warfare agents. A focus on incremental steps to mitigate this threat and raise the price to potential attackers will require a sustainable and productive defense effort for the long term. While there are many promising steps to take, there is no silver bullet. . . .

*Information Warfare Threat.* The transnational information warfare threat also poses significant technical challenges. Tools and techniques for penetrating networks illicitly are rapidly becoming more sophisticated and varied, the associated software tools are available, and there is a community eager to share and exploit these tools. The intended effects of an information warfare attack probably will not be subtle, particularly in the context of a carefully orchestrated information warfare campaign. Such a campaign will become increasingly likely. Probable scenarios could couple an attack using chemical or biological weapons with information disruption of the warning and response processes.

DoD's current network security posture is inadequate and the Department's unclassified networks have been compromised on a number of occasions over the last decade. The Department must build the capability to improve its information protection abilities faster than the threat can create new methods for attack. . . .

# Chapter 1. Setting the Stage

### Introduction

. . . The motives and methods of the transnational threat are different from those of traditional nation states. The technology of today, and that which is emerging, allows a small number of people to threaten others with consequences heretofore achievable only by nation states. The United States' homeland, allies, and interests are vulnerable. In the judgment of this task force, the likelihood and consequences of attacks from transnational threats can be as serious, if not more serious, than those of a major military conflict. Defense against transnational threats is part of DoD's core business, and must command the attention of the nation's leaders. . . .

An effective response to these threats requires the interaction of the federal, state, and local law enforcement and emergency response agencies; the broader national security community; and the international community—agencies and parts of society that have had little history of integrated planning, strategy, or action. . . .

## Chapter 2. Organizing a DoD Response

### A Major DoD Mission
#### The Threat

Examples of transnational attacks over the past decade are familiar to all. Looking carefully at these events and their motivations, three lessons emerge. *First, some transnational attacks reflect attempts by transnational adversaries to influence American foreign policy.* The 1983 attack on the US Marine Corps barracks in Beirut, Lebanon; the attack on US forces in Somalia in 1993; and the 1996 bombing of Khobar Towers in Saudi Arabia are recent examples.

*Second, other incidents illustrate the many capabilities in the hands of transnational adversaries: explosives, chemical, and biological agents.* In 1995, the world witnessed the release of the chemical agent sarin in the Tokyo subway. While the chemical release killed a dozen people, well over 5,000 were injured and the release had the potential for far more devastating loss of life. In fact, the plan was for tens of thousands of deaths. And closer to home, incidents like the 1993 World Trade Center bombing, the 1996 bombing of the Murrah Building in Oklahoma City . . . demonstrate that the United States is no longer a sanctuary and is vulnerable on its own soil as well.

A third lesson is that *transnational adversaries, in contrast to traditional terrorists, are motivated to inflict massive destruction and casualties.* In the past, analysts believed one of the key "tenets of terrorism" was that terrorists calculated thresholds of pain and tolerance, so that their cause was not irrevocably compromised by their actions. While US government officials worried about terrorists "graduating" to the use of weapons of mass destruction (almost exclusively nuclear), they believed—based on reports from terrorists themselves—that most terrorist groups thought mass casualties were counterproductive. Mass casualties were believed to delegitimize the terrorists' cause, generate strong governmental responses, and erode terrorist group cohesion. In essence, terrorists were ascribed a certain logic and morality beyond which they would not tread. The world has changed and this mentality is no longer the case. . . .

Transnational groups are increasingly linked in new and more cooperative ways that threaten the stability of governments, the financial and information infrastructure, and international trade and peace agreements. Increasing cooperation among crime, narcotics, and terrorist groups has provided transnational adversaries with new, more creative ways to raise money and with a marketplace to shop for weapons and high technology equipment.

*An increasing number of world actors devoted to political, economic, and ethnic disruption* also contributes to a growing threat environment. Transnational groups include classic terrorists, ethnic groups, religious extremists, anti-government militia, narcotic traffickers, and global criminals. Attacks without attribution are on the rise, and hate groups and religious extremists are growing in numbers. US policies in the Middle East have become the basis for violent retaliation from many groups. . . .

In addition, *the United States is more vulnerable to transnational threats today* than in the past, and this is likely to grow. This vulnerability has increased as critical infrastructure is consolidated and becomes more interdependent. . . .

As part of its global super power position, the United States is called upon frequently to respond to international causes and deploy forces around the world. America's position in the world invites attack simply because of its presence. Historical data show a strong correlation between US involvement in international situations and an increase in terrorist attacks against the United States. . . .

The transnational threat is real, as has been revealed through many international incidents. The United States has been warned. Three examples serve to illustrate the nature and severity of this threat. Each case—the Libyan retaliation campaign, the World Trade Center bombing, and the Aum Shinrikyo subway sarin release—helps to explain the many facets of the threat and the changing nature of motivations of transnational adversaries.

*Libya Retaliation Campaign.* When evidence pointed to Libya as the culprit behind the LaBelle Disco bombing in Berlin, which killed two US soldiers and injured many, the United States retaliated with an air strike in April 1986 against specific Libyan targets in Tripoli. The popular belief for years was that this US attack suppressed Libyan activity in support of terrorism. However, an examination of events in subsequent years paints a different picture. Instead, Libya continued, through transnational actors, to wage a revenge campaign over a number of years.

Three days after the US attack, Libyan retaliation began. An American hostage in Lebanon was sold to Libya and executed. In September 1987, Abu Nidal, working for Libya, hijacked Pan Am 73 causing the death of several Americans. The following April, the Japanese Red Army, under contract to Nidal, bombed the USO in Naples, killing a US soldier. While attempting to coordinate activities, a member of that group was arrested in New Jersey with pipe bombs targeted for New York City. The December 1988 bombing of Pan Am 103—killing 270 people, 200 of whom were Americans—was a Libyan-sponsored act. A year later, in September 1989, a UTA French airliner was destroyed over Chad by the same group. During this period, this group was also responsible for various assassinations of dissident Libyans in the United States. It also recruited a Chicago street gang to attack US airliners with shoulder-fired weapons—a move that was interdicted.

Qadhafi sponsored this series of attacks, using surrogates for plausible denial. While these acts involved the backing of a nation state, Libya, it did not involve traditional military force. It illustrates the ability and willingness of transnational adversaries to wage a continued campaign against the United States, one that the United States, in this case, was only partially successful in countering.

*World Trade Center Bombing.* The motive for the religious extremists involved was to punish the United States for its policies in the Middle East. Their goal was to create maximum casualties and damage.

In May 1990, a small band of religious extremists headed by Ramzi Yousef assassinated Rabbi Meir Kahane. At the time, the rabbi's death was treated as a homicide, unrelated to national security. It was only later that this assassination was discovered to be part of a larger revenge campaign against US foreign policy that included the World Trade Center bombing in February 1993. Six people were killed and five thousand were injured, but the terrorists' plans were to kill 250,000 through the collapse of the towers. Fortunately the building structure was far more robust than they calculated. They also considered augmenting the explosion with radiological materials or chemical agents, which would have pushed the number of casualties far higher.

In addition to the World Trade Center event, this transnational group had planned a massive infrastructure attack on New York City on the Fourth of July that would have included attacks on the George Washington Bridge, Lincoln and Holland Tunnels, the United Nations Headquarters, and the Federal Building in New York. These acts were interdicted through intelligence and surveillance.

The architect of this campaign, Ramzi Yousef, evaded capture for two years, but is now in the hands of US officials and standing trial. His plans were not limited to attacks on New York City, but involved a series of follow-on events to include an attack on thirteen international flights using explosives smuggled aboard. This particular activity was tested on a Philippine airliner where a modified bomb was successfully smuggled on board the aircraft and exploded, killing one passenger. Had the broader plan been successfully executed, several thousand people could have died. . . .

*Aum Shinrikyo.* The Tokyo subway event in 1995, involving the release of the chemical agent sarin, represents a third class of motivation—the desire to create chaos for political purposes. In this case, it was to bring down the existing Japanese government and install a new government. The events that took place seem simple, but the organization behind them is surprisingly large.

In June 1994, sarin was sprayed from a truck, killing 7 and injuring 200 people in Matsumoto, Japan. The motive and organization of the attackers was not understood until nearly a year later when, in March 1995, sarin was released in seven locations in the Tokyo subway system. This attack killed 12 and injured 5,500. Though a dramatic event as executed, the sarin did not disperse as planned, or casualties could have neared 10,000. That same month, the group also attempted the assassination of Japan's National Police Chief. Plans for attacks in the United States in Disneyland and against petrochemical facilities in Los Angeles existed as well. . . .

The group behind these events had impressive membership, size, resources, and capabilities. With 30,000 people involved—10,000 of whom were in Russia—this group resembled a small nation. It operated in Japan, Russia, Korea, Australia, Sri Lanka, and the United States with an asset base estimated at $1.2 billion. The group had independent capabilities to produce sarin, VX, anthrax, botulism, and radiological weapons. Aum Shinrikyo still exists today in Japan and perhaps elsewhere. They are actively recruiting members, raising money, and organizing as before. More important, they are likely to have learned lessons from their past failures to achieve planned results.

The different types of motivation, consequence, and style of the transnational threat are evident from the three cases described. The capability for a few individuals or groups to produce major damage and loss of life exists today. Events that we have already witnessed could well have resulted in far graver consequences had they been executed with better precision or more effective agents. . . .

### A Priority for DoD

. . . *The task force believes there is evidence that the transnational threat will escalate in the future and that the threat will be dealing with extensive campaigns and greater use of weapons of mass destruction.* The Libya retaliation campaign, the World Trade Center bombing, and the Aum Shinrikyo subway sarin release are examples of incidents that were part of an orchestrated, longer-term "campaign" which went unrecognized at the time these events unfolded. . . .

*The task force recommends that to effectively counter this escalating threat, the President must raise the national consciousness across the government—at the federal, state, and local levels—as well as with our principal allies and coalition partners. In turn, the Department of Defense must treat countering transnational threats as a major DoD mission, with the same emphasis as major military conflicts.* This involves including transnational threats in departmental guidance and strategy, in the planning and budgeting processes, and in training and exercises. This is not a new mission for DoD, but a different and difficult challenge to the traditional mission. . . .

# Chapter 3. Technical Challenges

### *A Global Information Infrastructure*

The United States must get smarter about transnational threat groups—their motives, organization, sources of support, and operational means. As such, there is a need for an interactive, two-way global information system that would expand the available sources of information. This system would support gathering more data from the bottom up, exploiting international information sources, and two-way sharing of critical information with state, local, and international partners. . . .

The World Trade Center transnational threat campaign is an example of how better sharing of information between federal, state, and civilian agencies might have prevented the bombing of the tower. The task force believes that sharing and correlation of information could, in fact, help to prevent and even deter future transnational threat activities.

At the present time there are no formal processes, infrastructure, and security mechanisms to facilitate the sharing and analysis of transnational threat information collected by organizations such as local law enforcement, National Guard, Immigration and Naturalization Service, Department of Energy, Central Intelligence Agency, Federal Bureau of Investigation, the Department of Defense, and other organizations. Individually, these organizations collect data that, when viewed independently, may not provide knowledge about plans for an activity or campaign by a transnational adversary. However, correlation of diverse data sources would likely enhance our ability to identify key indicators and provide warning.

Furthermore, other sources of data that could be exploited to provide indicators and warning of transnational threat activities largely remain underutilized. Examples of such sources include the real-time data on international border crossings, real-time cargo manifests, global financial transactions, and the global network carrying international airline ticket manifests. . . .

Excerpted from U.S. Department of Defense. Office of the Under Secretary of Defense for Acquisition & Technology. *The Defense Science Board 1997 Summer Study Task Force on DOD Responses to Transnational Threats.* Vol. I, Final Report. October 1997. http://www.acq.osd.mil/dsb/reports/trans.pdf (accessed September 1, 2004).

# 73. Defense Science Board Supplemental Report on Transnational Threats

*February 1998*

## Executive Summary

The Threats and Scenarios Panel of the Defense Science Board's Summer Study of Transnational Threats reviewed the transnational threat in the context of changes in the motivations, goals, capabilities, and trends of states, groups, and individuals. We concluded that the transnational threat is more difficult and dangerous today and in the future than it has been in the past based on a variety of new ingredients. These new ingredients, or "enablers," include the easy availability of information and technology, the proliferation of weapons of mass destruction and delivery systems, the presence of more technically proficient actors, and the increasing linkages of convenience and cooperation between rouge states, organized crime and narcotics groups, extremists, and terrorists. . . .

The Panel also identified several shortfalls in capabilities to identify the threat. Most critical was the requirement for a focused collection strategy as well as the need for a more comprehensive analytical approach, complete with an interactive information system that crosses the government's stovepiped structures. . . .

## Transnational Threats: The Face of the Future

### Coping with Transnational Threats

*The Globalization of Proliferants, Organized Crime Groups, and Drug Lords*
. . . One of the outcomes of the globalization of economies and technologies is the relatively new linking and intermingling of disparate crime and narcotics organizations with terrorists. Analysts have been dismayed to find that even the most notorious crime groups with global reach—such as the Italian Mafias, the Russian crime groups, the Nigerian enterprises, the Japanese Yakaso, and the Chinese triads—are developing new working relationships, cooperative arrangements, and networking with one another, with drug cartels, and with insurgent and terrorist organizations to take advantage of one another's strengths and to make inroads into previously denied regions. This has allowed terrorists a new means to raise money as well as

provide them with a marketplace to purchase sophisticated weaponry and other high tech equipment. . . .

### Conclusions About Transnational Threat Trends

. . . [T]he United States will remain a significant target for terrorists; almost half of all known international terrorist groups consider the enemy worthy of attack. . . . Traditional modes of terrorism will remain, and the use of high explosives is still the overwhelming choice of tools for terrorists, because it does the job effectively, it can be relatively low cost, and can avoid the galvanizing issue of mass destruction for those groups who care about such things. This being said, however, the trend towards less numbers of incidents, but bigger bombs and higher lethality, appears here to stay. . . .

Internationally financed and supported terrorist groups are capable of mounting a WMD attack of almost any kind. . . .

### Which Transnational Threat Is More Likely? (Where Do We Put the Money?)

All can agree that the nature of transnational threats travels largely in uncharted waters. However, the agreement ends there. Some believe that the most likely future scenario entails the use of a radiological weapon stolen or purchased from East European stockpiles. Others postulate that the "real" threat (the most likely high damage one) is the improvised use of chemical weaponry. Still others firmly defend the notion that the biological threat is the greatest, due to its high lethality, high casualty rate, relative ease of procurement or manufacture, and difficult detectability. Even within our own group, we would categorize the transnational threat differently. . . .

It is all speculative. For that reason, while we would like to be helpful in determining where scarce dollars should be invested, the truth is the proclamation or mathematical formulation of one favored method of terrorism over another is probably a disservice. If history teaches nothing, it is that we are forever wrong about our assumptions. . . .

Excerpted from U.S. Department of Defense. Office of the Under Secretary of Defense for Acquisition & Technology. *The Defense Science Board 1997 Summer Study Task Force on DOD Responses to Transnational Threats.* Vol. III, Supporting Reports. February 1998. http://handle.dtic.mil/100.2/ADA342133 (accessed October 19, 2004).

# General Accounting Office Urges Better Coordination of Federal Terrorism Efforts

74. Combating Terrorism: Observations on Crosscutting Issues, General Accounting Office Congressional Testimony, April 23, 1998

75. Chemical and Biological Defense: Observations on Non-medical Chemical and Biological R&D Programs, General Accounting Office Congressional Testimony, March 22, 2000

76. Combating Terrorism: Comments on Counterterrorism Leadership and National Strategy, General Accounting Office Congressional Testimony, March 27, 2001

## INTRODUCTION

In 1985 the Vice President's Task Force on Terrorism called for improved coordination among the numerous federal agencies and departments that had some role in fighting terrorism and protecting the American homeland. More than a decade later, the General Accounting Office (GAO)—the investigative arm of Congress—started issuing increasingly dire warnings that the continued lack of coordination threatened homeland security.

In testimony on Capitol Hill on April 23, 1998, Richard Davis, director of national security analysis for the GAO, said the need for better coordination was more critical than ever because the number of federal terrorism programs had increased substantially. More than forty federal agencies, bureaus, and offices had some role in combating terrorism, he said, and they were spending billions of dollars annually with little oversight. Because the federal government had not established terrorism priorities or assessed the threat of terrorist attack, "there is no basis to have a reasonable assurance that funds are being spent on the right programs in the right amounts and that unnecessary program and funding duplication, overlap, misallocation, fragmentation, and gaps have not occurred," Davis said [Document 74].

Nearly two years later, Kwai-Cheung Chan, a director in GAO's national security and international affairs division, testified before Congress on March 22, 2000, about the overlaps and possible gaps in research and development efforts by four federal agencies aimed at battling biological and chemical weapons. Program officials also did not know which biological and chemical threats were most important or what capabilities to fight the threats were needed, Chan testified. Information existed regarding these issues, Chan said, but the programs did not formally use it in deciding which projects to fund [Document 75].

On March 27, 2001—less than six months before the terrorist hijackings—Raymond J. Decker, director of defense capabilities and management at the GAO, testified that leadership and management of terrorism programs were "fragmented within the federal government." The fragmentation occurred, Decker said, because no single person was in charge of federal terrorism efforts. He emphasized the critical need to develop a national terrorism strategy in coordination with state and local governments. Although various presidents had issued directives assigning specific roles to federal agencies and departments to deter, interdict, or respond to a terrorist attack, no overall terrorism strategy existed when passenger jets started slamming into the World Trade Center, the Pentagon, and a Pennsylvania field on September 11, 2001 [Document 76].

# 74. Combating Terrorism: Observations on Crosscutting Issues, General Accounting Office Congressional Testimony

*April 23, 1998*

## Summary

. . . More than a decade ago, the Vice President's Task Force on Terrorism highlighted the need for improved, centralized interagency coordination. Our work suggests that the government should continue to strive for improved interagency coordination today. The need for effective interagency coordination—both at the federal level and among the federal, state, and local levels—is paramount. The challenges of efficient and effective management and focus for program investments are growing as the terrorism issue draws more attention from the Congress and as there are more players and more programs and activities to integrate and coordinate. The United States is spending billions of dollars annually to combat terrorism without assurance that federal funds are focused on the right programs or in the right amounts. . . .

## Origins and Principles of U.S. Policy and Strategy to Combat Terrorism

U.S. policy and strategy have evolved since the 1970s, along with the nature and perception of the terrorist threat. The basic principles of the policy continue, though, from the 1970s to today: make no concessions to terrorists, pressure state sponsors of terrorism, and apply the rule of law to terrorists as criminals. U.S. policy on terrorism first became formalized in 1986 with the Reagan administration's issuance of National Security Decision Directive 207. This policy resulted from the findings of the 1985 Vice President's Task Force on Terrorism, which highlighted the need for improved, centralized interagency coordination of the significant federal assets to respond to terrorist incidents. The directive reaffirmed lead agency responsibilities, with the State Department responsible for international terrorism policy, procedures, and programs, and the FBI, through the Department of Justice, responsible for dealing with domestic terrorist acts.

Presidential Decision Directive (PDD) 39—issued in June 1995 following the bombing of the federal building in Oklahoma City—builds on the previous directive and contains three key elements of national strategy for combating terrorism: (1) reduce vulnerabilities to terrorist attacks and prevent and deter terrorist acts before they occur; (2) respond to terrorist acts that do occur—crisis management—and apprehend and punish terrorists; and (3) manage the consequences of terrorist acts, including restoring capabilities to protect public health and safety and essential government services and providing emergency relief. This directive also further elaborates on agencies' roles and responsibilities and some specific measures to be taken regarding each element of the strategy. . . .

## Observations on Crosscutting Terrorism Issues

Based on the reports and work we have performed to date, we would like to make three observations. First, in certain critical areas, just as the Vice President's Task Force on Terrorism noted in 1985, improvements are needed in interagency coordination and program focus. Since that time—and even since PDD-39 was issued in June 1995—the number of players involved in combating terrorism has increased substantially. In our September 1997 report, we noted that more than 40 federal agencies, bureaus, and offices were involved in combating terrorism. . . .

In a second, related observation, more money is being spent to combat terrorism without any assurance of whether it is focused on the right programs or in the right amounts. Our December 1997 report showed that seven key federal agencies spent more than an estimated $6.5 billion in fiscal year 1997 on federal efforts to combat terrorism, excluding classified programs and activities. Some key agencies' spending on terrorism-related programs has increased dramatically. For example, between fiscal year 1995 and 1997, FBI terrorism-related funding and staff-level authorizations tripled, and Federal Aviation Administration spending to combat terrorism tripled.

We also reported that key interagency management functions were not clearly required or performed. For example, neither the National Security Council nor the Office of Management and Budget (OMB) was required to regularly collect, aggregate, and review funding and spending data relative to combating terrorism on a crosscutting, governmentwide basis. Further, neither agency had established funding priorities for terrorism-related programs within or across agencies' individual budgets or ensured that individual agencies' stated requirements had been validated against threat and risk criteria before budget requests were submitted to the Congress.

Because governmentwide priorities have not been established and funding requirements have not necessarily been validated based on an analytically sound assessment of the threat and risk of terrorist attack, there is no basis to have a reasonable assurance that funds are being spent on the right programs in the right amounts and that unnecessary program and funding duplication, overlap, misallocation, fragmentation, and gaps have not occurred. . . .

Many challenges are ahead as we continue to see the need for (1) governmentwide priorities to be set; (2) agencies' programs, activities, and requirements to be analyzed in relation to those priorities; and (3) resources to be allocated based on the established priorities and assessments of the threat and risk of terrorist attack. As an example of my last point, if an agency spends $20 million without a risk assessment on a security system for terrorism purposes at a federal building, and the risk of an attack is extremely low, the agency may have misspent the $20 million, which could have been allocated to higher risk items. . . .

Our third observation is that there are different sets of views and an apparent lack of consensus on the threat of terrorism—particularly WMD [weapons of mass destruction] terrorism. In our opinion, some fundamental questions should be answered before the federal government builds and expands programs, plans, and strategies to deal with the threat of WMD terrorism: How easy or difficult is it for terrorists (rather than state actors) to successfully use chemical or biological WMDs in an attack causing mass casualties? And if it is easy to produce and disperse chemical and biological agents, why have there been no WMD terrorist attacks before or since the [1995] Tokyo subway incident? What chemical and biological agents does the government really need to be concerned about? We have not yet seen a thorough assessment or analysis of these questions. It seems to us that, without such an assessment or analysis and consensus in the policy-making community, it would be very difficult—maybe impossible—to properly shape programs and focus resources. . . .

Excerpted from U.S. Congress. General Accounting Office. *Combating Terrorism: Observations on Crosscutting Issues.* Prepared testimony of Richard Davis for a hearing by the Subcommittee on National Security, International Affairs, and Criminal Justice of the House Committee on Government Reform and Oversight. GAO/T-NSIAD-98-164, April 23, 1998. http://www.gao.gov/archive/1998/ns98164t.pdf (accessed September 15, 2004).

## 75. Chemical and Biological Defense: Observations on Nonmedical Chemical and Biological R&D Programs, General Accounting Office Congressional Testimony

*March 22, 2000*

In the last decade, concerns about the possible use of chemical and biological weapons in both military and civilian settings led Congress and federal agencies to implement new or expanded programs to address these threats. Overall funding in this area increased significantly from 1996 to date. Today, several civilian and military agencies are now conducting research and development programs designed to counter these threats. Without effective coordination among the different agencies, efforts might be unnecessarily duplicated and important questions might be overlooked. . . .

Nonmedical research and development [R&D] focuses on developing techniques for detecting, identifying, or protecting against chemical and biological agents as well as for decontaminating personnel and equipment. The scope of our work was limited to federal programs that fund unclassified research and development. We examined four programs: (1) the Department of Defense's Chemical and Biological Defense Program, (2) the Defense Advanced Research Projects Agency's Biological Warfare Defense Program, (3) the Department of Energy's Chemical and Biological Nonproliferation Program, and (4) the Counterterror Technical Support Program conducted by an interagency working group called the Technical Support Working Group. The intended users of the technologies developed in these programs may be a single military service (such as the Army), multiple services, or organizations that are responsible for addressing threats to civilians (e.g., federal, state, and local emergency response personnel).

# Summary

Each of the federally funded programs conducting nonmedical research and development on threats from chemical and biological agents has its own mission objective. However, we found many similarities among these programs in terms of the research and development activities they engage in, the threats they intend to address, the types of capabilities they seek to develop, the technologies they pursue in developing those capabilities, and the organizations they use to conduct the work. For example, these programs conduct a similar range of research and development activities, such as evaluating the feasibility or showing the practical utility of a technology. With regard to threat, two of the programs (those in the Department of Defense and Defense Advanced Research Projects Agency) focus on threats to the military, and the other two (those in the Department of Energy and the Technical Support Working Group) focus on threats to civilians. However, the military and civilian user communities are concerned about many of the same chemical and biological substances (such as nerve agents) and possible perpetrators (such as foreign terrorists). In addition, we found that these programs are seeking to develop many of the same capabilities, such as detection and identification of biological agents. Furthermore, the types of technologies (such as mass spectroscopy) they pursue to achieve those capabilities may overlap. Finally, these programs may contract with the same groups of laboratories to perform research and development work.

Although the four programs we examined currently use both formal and informal mechanisms for coordination, we found several problems that may hamper their coordination efforts. First, participation in formal and informal coordination mechanisms is inconsistent. For instance, several of these mechanisms do not include representatives of the civilian user community. Second, program officials cited a lack of comprehensive information on which chemical and biological threats to the civilian population are the most important and on what capabilities for addressing these threats are most needed. Third, several programs do not formally incorporate existing information on chemical and biological threats or needed capabilities in deciding what research and development projects to fund. Having and using detailed information on civilian chemical and biological threats and the capabilities needed to respond to those threats would enable coordination mechanisms to better assess whether inefficient duplication or critical research gaps exist, and if so, what changes should be made in federal research and development programs. . . .

## *Potential Benefits from Improving Coordination*

As a result of these problems, R&D programs may not be developing the most important capabilities and addressing the highest priority threats. To eliminate duplication, these programs need detailed information on civilian chemical and biological threats and the capabilities needed to respond to those threats. For example, after the four military services— which have such detailed information—began coordinating their chemical and biological defense efforts in fiscal year 1994 through DOD's Chemical and Biological Defense Program, they were able to consolidate 44 service-specific developmental efforts in the program's contamination avoidance research into 10 joint-service projects. Having comprehensive information can also help program officials determine whether critical gaps in research exist that could be filled by refocusing one or more programs. . . .

Excerpted from U.S. Congress. General Accounting Office. *Chemical and Biological Defense: Observations on Nonmedical Chemical and Biological R&D Programs.* Prepared testimony of Kwai-Cheung Chan for a hearing by the Subcommittee on National Security, Veterans' Affairs, and International Relations of the House Committee on Government Reform. GAO/T-NSIAD-00-130, March 22, 2000. http://www.gao.gov/archive/2000/ns00130t.pdf (accessed September 15, 2004).

# 76. Combating Terrorism: Comments on Counterterrorism Leadership and National Strategy, General Accounting Office Congressional Testimony

*March 27, 2001*

## Summary

Based on our prior and ongoing work, two key issues emerge that the new President and Congress will face concerning programs to combat terrorism. First, the overall leadership and management of such programs are fragmented within the federal government. No single entity acts as the federal government's top official accountable to both the President and Congress. Fragmentation exists in both coordination of domestic preparedness programs and in efforts to develop a national strategy. The Department of Justice worked with other agencies to develop the Attorney General's Five-Year Interagency Counterterrorism and Technology Crime Plan. While this plan is the current document that most resembles a national strategy, we believe it still lacks some critical elements to include measurable desired outcomes, linkage to resources, and a discussion of the role of state and local governments.

## Addressing Overall Leadership and Management

Overall leadership and management efforts are fragmented because there is no single leader in charge of the many functions conducted by different federal departments and agencies. The President appointed a National Coordinator for Security, Infrastructure Protection and Counterterrorism within the National Security Council in May 1998 who was tasked to oversee a broad portfolio of policies and programs related to counterterrorism. However, this position had no budget authority over areas in which essential decisions were being made on federal efforts in combating terrorism. Furthermore, despite the creation of the National Coordinator, no single entity acts as the federal government's top official accountable to both the President and Congress.

Coordinating domestic preparedness programs is another example of fragmented leadership and management with the federal government. Our past work has concluded that the multiplicity of federal assistance programs requires focus and attention to minimize redundancy of efforts and eliminate confusion at the state and local level. Both the Federal Emergency Management Agency and Department of Justice provide liaison and assistance to state and local governments.

The Federal Emergency Management Agency provides grant assistance to the states to support state and local terrorism consequence management planning, training, and exercises. In addition, states work with two offices in the Department of Justice—the National Domestic Preparedness Office and the Office of State and Local Domestic Preparedness. Justice's National Domestic Preparedness Office was authorized by Congress in 1999 and established for the purpose of coordinating federal terrorism crisis and consequence preparedness programs for the state and local emergency response community. The Office of State and Local Domestic Preparedness currently assists states in the development of their State Domestic Preparedness Strategic Plans. This effort includes funding, training, equipment acquisition, technical assistance, and exercise planning and execution. The overlap of federal efforts and lack of a single federal focal point for state and local assistance have highlighted the need for improved leadership and management.

Efforts to develop a national strategy provide additional evidence that there is fragmented leadership and management. In addition to the existing Attorney General's 5-year plan, the National Security Council and the Department of Justice's National Domestic Preparedness Office are each planning to develop national strategies. The danger in this proliferation of strategies is that state and local governments—which are already confused about the multitude of federal domestic preparedness agencies and programs—may become further frustrated about the direction, execution, and management of the overall effort. . . .

## Developing a National Strategy

Combating terrorism requires our nation to focus on a comprehensive national strategy. A national strategy should articulate a clear vision statement that defines what the nation hopes to achieve through its combating terrorism programs. Key aspects of the national strategy should include (1) roles and missions of federal, state, and local entities and (2) establish objectives, priorities, outcome-related goals with milestones, and performance measures to achieve those goals. Ultimately, a national strategy should serve as an effective mechanism for ensuring that all elements of the national effort are clearly integrated and properly focused to eliminate gaps and duplication in programs to combat terrorism. Furthermore, this will provide a framework to guide top-level decisions affecting programs, priorities, and funding considerations.

In December 1998, the Department of Justice issued the Attorney General's Five-Year Plan as mandated by Congress. Congress intended the plan to serve as a baseline for the coordination of a national strategy and operational capabilities to combat terrorism. This classified plan, which represents a substantial interagency effort, includes goals, objectives, performance indicators and recommends specific agency actions to resolve interagency problems. In March 2000, the Department of Justice released an update on the plan, which reported on the accomplishments made by various agencies during fiscal year 1999 on their assigned tasks. The Department of Justice contends that this plan, taken in combination with related presidential decision directives, represents a comprehensive national strategy. We agree that the Attorney General's Five-Year Plan is the current document that most resembles a national strategy. However, we believe that additional work is needed to build upon the progress the plan represents and develop a comprehensive national strategy. Specifically, additional progress should be made in the following areas.

- Based upon our review, the Five-Year Plan does not have measurable desired outcomes. We have reported that a national strategy should provide goals that are related to clearly defined outcomes. For example, the national strategy should include a goal to improve state and local response capabilities. Desired outcomes should be linked to a level of preparedness that response teams should achieve. Without this specificity in a national strategy, the nation will continue to miss opportunities to focus and shape combating terrorism programs to meet the threat.

- Also based upon our review, the Five-Year Plan also lacks linkage to budget resources. We have reported that the nation lacks a coherent framework to develop and evaluate budget requirements for combating terrorism programs since no national strategy exists with clearly defined outcomes. The establishment of a single focal point within the federal government for combating terrorism can provide a mechanism to direct and oversee combating terrorism funding. Moreover, this focal point could ensure that adequate funding is applied to key priorities while eliminating unnecessary spending in duplication efforts to combat terrorism.
- Other experts . . . suggest that a national strategy should be developed in close coordination with state and local governments since they play a major role in preparing against and responding to acts of terrorism. Based upon our preliminary analysis, we agree with this position. Local responders will be the first response to mitigate terrorist incidents. Therefore, they should participate in the development of a national strategy and their roles and responsibilities should be clearly defined. . . .

Excerpted from U.S. Congress. General Accounting Office. *Combating Terrorism: Comments on Counterterrorism Leadership and National Strategy.* Prepared testimony of Raymond J. Decker for a hearing by the Subcommittee on National Security, Veterans Affairs, and International Relations of the House Committee on Government Reform. GAO-01-556T, March 27, 2001. http://www.gao.gov/new.items/d01556t.pdf (accessed September 15, 2004).

# Experts Warn of Increasing Threats to the American Homeland

77. New World Coming: American Security in the 21st Century, United States Commission on National Security/21st Century Report, September 15, 1999

78. Assessing the Threat, Advisory Panel to Assess Domestic Response Capabilities for Terrorism Involving Weapons of Mass Destruction Report, December 15, 1999

79. Countering the Changing Threat of International Terrorism, National Commission on Terrorism Report, June 5, 2000

80. Toward a National Strategy for Combating Terrorism, Advisory Panel to Assess Domestic Response Capabilities for Terrorism Involving Weapons of Mass Destruction Report, December 15, 2000

81. Road Map for National Security: Imperative for Change, United States Commission on National Security/21st Century Report, February 15, 2001

## INTRODUCTION

In the years immediately preceding the terrorist attacks of September 11, 2001, three different blue-ribbon commissions issued reports warning that threats against the American homeland were increasing, many of the threats were difficult to detect because they came from small groups instead of foreign countries, and the federal government needed to develop a national terrorism strategy to pull together fragmented efforts spread across more than forty agencies and departments.

Some of the bluntest warnings came from the United States Commission on National Security/21st Century, commonly known as the Hart-Rudman commission because former senators Gary Hart, a Democrat, and Warren Rudman, a Republican, served as its chairmen. The panel, which was appointed by the Department of Defense to assess the national security system's role in the twenty-first century, included other notable members such as former defense secretary James Schlesinger, former House Speaker Newt Gingrich, and former House Foreign Affairs Committee chairman Lee Hamilton.

In a report released September 15, 1999, the commission said the American homeland would become increasingly vulnerable to attack and "our military superiority will not entirely protect us." The threats would differ significantly from those of the past, the panel said, and one of the biggest would come from terrorists or other groups that acquired biological, chemical, or nuclear weapons. "States, terrorists, and other disaffected groups will acquire weapons of mass destruction and mass disruption, and some will use them," the commission said. "Americans will likely die on American soil, possibly in large numbers." It called for development of "a coherent strategy to deal with both the dangers and the opportunities ahead" [Document 77].

A second commission, charged with examining the nation's vulnerability to weapons of mass destruction, said the threat was real and that an attack would kill and injure people, damage structures and the environment, and threaten "our civil liberties, our economy, and indeed our democratic ideals." But in a report issued December 15, 1999, the Advisory Panel to Assess Domestic Response Capabilities for Terrorism Involving Weapons of Mass Destruction said the federal government should not devote all its time and money preparing for a massive attack that would kill thousands of people. The panel, commonly called the Gilmore commission because Virginia Gov. James Gilmore served as its chairman, said the nation was far more likely to suffer smaller-scale attacks with conventional explosives, biological weapons, or chemical weapons, and needed to devote more attention and resources to these threats. As with the Hart-Rudman commission, the Gilmore panel also called for development of a national preparedness strategy. "The country's seeming inability to develop and implement a clear, comprehensive, and truly integrated national domestic preparedness strategy means that we may still remain fundamentally incapable of responding effectively to a serious terrorist attack," it said [Document 78].

The need to focus attention on smaller-scale threats was reinforced the day before the Gilmore commission issued its report. On December 14 federal authorities arrested an Algerian man as he attempted to cross into the United States from Canada. The trunk of the man's rental car was filled with bomb-making materials, and authorities believed he had planned to strike Los Angeles International Airport during upcoming millennium celebrations.

On June 5, 2000, the National Commission on Terrorism, a group mandated by Congress, said the United States needed to step up its activities to counter international terrorism. The panel was known as the Bremer commission because its chairman was L. Paul Bremer, who later became the U.S. administrator in Iraq. In its report, the commission said the federal government needed to spend even more money on counterterrorism, loosen restrictions on federal agencies that investigated terrorists, improve the collection of intelligence, and—equally important—improve its abilities to analyze the intelligence for useful information. The commission also urged the president and Congress to "reform the system for reviewing and funding departmental counterterrorism programs to ensure that the activities and programs of various agencies are part of a comprehensive plan" [Document 79].

The Gilmore commission issued a second report on December 15, 2000, that emphasized the need to develop a national terrorism strategy with participation by federal, state, and local officials. "The United States has no coherent, functional national strategy for combating terrorism," the commission said. It urged the incoming administration of George W. Bush to establish a National Office for Combating Terrorism in the Executive Office of the President that would review agency programs and budgets for terrorism and decertify those that failed to comply with the national strategy. The commission did not spare Congress. It blasted the congressional system under which at least eleven full committees in the Senate and fourteen full committees in the House—along with a host of subcommittees—claimed oversight over various portions of federal terrorism efforts. It said Congress should consolidate its authority by creating a Special Committee for Combating Terrorism and tell the other committees to back off [Document 80].

On February 15, 2001—less than seven months before the September 11 attacks—the Hart-Rudman commission issued a second report that again emphasized the need for a national terrorism strategy. "The combination of unconventional weapons proliferation with the persistence of international terrorism will end the relative invulnerability of the U.S. homeland to catastrophic attack. . . . In the face of this threat, our nation has no coherent or integrated governmental structures," it said. The panel made many recommendations, but the most important one called for creating an independent National Homeland Security Agency that would plan, coordinate, and integrate federal efforts. The new agency would be built on the Federal Emergency Management Agency, and three agencies responsible for border security—the Coast Guard, the Customs Service, and the Border Patrol—would be transferred to it [Document 81].

Less than two weeks later, Bremer—who had served as chairman of the National Commission on Terrorism—said in a speech that the Bush administration was "paying no attention" to terrorism, according to an Associated Press (AP) article published in April 2004. "What we will do is stagger along until there's a major incident and then suddenly say, 'Oh my God, shouldn't we be organized to deal with this,'" the AP quoted Bremer as saying at a terrorism conference on February 26, 2001.

On May 8, 2001, President George W. Bush announced that Vice President Dick Cheney would chair an examination of national preparedness problems, with special attention on preparations for managing an attack using weapons of mass destruction. That effort was "just getting underway" when the September 11 attack occurred, according to a March 24, 2004, report by staff of the National Commission on Terrorist Attacks Upon the United States.

# 77. New World Coming: American Security in the 21st Century, United States Commission on National Security/21st Century Report

*September 15, 1999*

1. *America will become increasingly vulnerable to hostile attack on our homeland, and our military superiority will not entirely protect us.*

The United States will be both absolutely and relatively stronger than any other state or combination of states. Although a global competitor to the United States is unlikely to arise over the next 25 years, emerging powers—either singly or in coalition—will increasingly constrain U.S. options regionally and limit its strategic influence. As a result, we will remain limited in our ability to impose our will, and we will be vulnerable to an increasing range of threats against American forces and citizens overseas as well as at home. American influence will increasingly be both embraced and resented abroad, as U.S. cultural, economic, and political power persists and perhaps spreads. States, terrorists, and other disaffected groups will acquire weapons of mass destruction and mass disruption, and some will use them. Americans will likely die on American soil, possibly in large numbers.

2. *Rapid advances in information and biotechnologies will create new vulnerabilities for U.S. security.* Governments or groups hostile to the United States and its interests will gain access to advanced technologies. They will seek to counter U.S. military advantages through the possession of these technologies and their actual use in non-traditional attacks. . . .

11. *The essence of war will not change.*

Despite the proliferation of highly sophisticated and remote means of attack, the essence of war will remain the same. There will be casualties, carnage, and death; it will not be like a video game. What will change will be the kinds of actors and the weapons available to them. While some societies will attempt to limit violence and damage, others will seek to maximize them, particularly against those societies with a lower tolerance for casualties.

12. *U.S. intelligence will face more challenging adversaries, and even excellent intelligence will not prevent all surprises.*

Micro-sensors and electronic communications will continue to expand intelligence collection capabilities around the world. As a result of the proliferation of other technologies, however, many countries and disaffected groups will develop techniques of denial and deception in an attempt to thwart U.S. intelligence efforts—despite U.S. technological superiority. In any event, the United States will continue to confront strategic shocks, as intelligence analysis and human judgments will fail to detect all dangers in an ever-changing world. . . .

14. *The emerging security environment in the next quarter century will require different military and other national capabilities.*

The United States must act together with its allies to shape the future of the international environment, using all the instruments of American diplomatic, economic, and military power. The type of conflict in which this country will generally engage in the first quarter of the 21st century will require sustainable military capabilities characterized by stealth, speed, range, unprecedented accuracy, lethality, strategic mobility, superior intelligence, and the overall will and ability to prevail. It is essential to maintain U.S. technological superiority, despite the unavoidable tension between acquisition of advanced capabilities and the maintenance of current capabilities. The mix and effectiveness of overall American capabilities need to be rethought and adjusted, and substantial changes in non-military national capabilities will also be needed. Discriminating and hard choices will be required.

In many respects, the world ahead seems amenable to basic American interests and values. A world pried open by the information revolution is a world less hospitable to tyranny and more friendly to human liberty. A more prosperous world is, on balance, a world more conducive to democracy and less tolerant of fatalism and the dour dogmas that often attend it. A less socially rigid, freer, and self-regulating world also accords with our deepest political beliefs . . . .

Nevertheless, a world amenable to our interests and values will not come into being by itself. Much of the world will resent and oppose us, if not for . . . our preeminence, then for the fact that others often perceive the United States as exercising its power with arrogance and self-absorption. . . .

As a result, for many years to come Americans will become increasingly less secure, and much less secure than they now believe themselves to be. That is because many of the threats emerging in our future will differ significantly from those of the past, not only in their physical but also in their psychological effects. While conventional conflicts will still be possible, the most serious threat to our security may consist of unannounced attacks on American cities by sub-national groups using genetically engineered pathogens. Another may be a well-planned cyber-attack on the air traffic control system on the East Coast of the United States, as some 200 commercial aircraft are trying to land safely in a morning's rain and fog. . . .

Taken together, the evidence suggests that threats to American security will be more diffuse, harder to anticipate, and difficult to neutralize than ever before. Deterrence will not work as it once did; in many cases it may not work at all. There will be a blurring of boundaries: between homeland defense and foreign policy; between sovereign states and a plethora of protectorates and autonomous zones; between the pull of national loyalties on individual citizens and the pull of loyalties both more local and more global in nature.

While the likelihood of major conflicts between powerful states will decrease, conflict itself will likely increase. The world that lies in store for us over the next 25 years will surely challenge our received wisdom about how to protect American interests and advance American values. In such an environment the United States needs a sure understanding of its objectives, and a coherent strategy to deal with both the dangers and the opportunities ahead. . . .

Excerpted from United States Commission on National Security/21st Century. *New World Coming: American Security in the 21st Century.* Phase I report, September 15, 1999. http://govinfo.library.unt.edu/nssg/Reports/NWC.pdf (accessed September 15, 2004).

# 78. Assessing the Threat, Advisory Panel to Assess Domestic Response Capabilities for Terrorism Involving Weapons of Mass Destruction Report
*December 15, 1999*

The possibility that terrorists will use "weapons of mass destruction (WMD)" in this country to kill and injure Americans, including those responsible for protecting and saving lives, presents a genuine threat to the United States. As we stand on the threshold of the twenty-first century, the stark reality is that the face and character of terrorism are changing and that previous beliefs about the restraint on terrorist use of chemical, biological, radiological, and nuclear (CBRN) devices may be disappearing. Beyond the potential loss of life and the infliction of wanton casualties, and the structural or environmental damage that might result from such an attack, our civil liberties, our economy, and indeed our democratic ideals could also be threatened. The challenge for the United States is first to deter and, failing that, to be able to detect and interdict terrorists before they strike. Should an attack occur, we must be confident that local, state, and Federal authorities are well prepared to respond and to address the consequences of the entire spectrum of violent acts.

In recent years, efforts have clearly been focused on more preparations for such attacks. The bombings of the World Trade Center in New York [in 1993] and Alfred P. Murrah Federal Building in Oklahoma City [in 1995], coupled with the 1995 sarin nerve gas attack in Tokyo and the U.S. embassy bombings this past summer, have heightened American concern and have already prompted an array of responses across all levels of government. At the same time, the country's seeming inability to develop and implement a clear, comprehensive, and truly integrated national domestic preparedness strategy means that we may still remain fundamentally incapable of responding effectively to a serious terrorist attack.

The vast array of CBRN weapons conceivably available to terrorists today can be used against humans, animals, crops, the environment, and physical structures in many different ways. The complexity of these CBRN terrorist threats, and the variety of contingencies and critical responses that they suggest, requires us to ensure that preparedness efforts are carefully planned, implemented, and sustained among all potential responders, with all levels of government operating as partners. These threats, moreover, will require new ways of thinking throughout the entire spectrum of local, state, and Federal agencies. Effecting true change in the culture of a single government agency, much less achieving fundamental changes throughout and among all three, presents formidable hurdles. Nonetheless, the nature of these threats and their potential consequences demands the full commitment of officials at all levels to achieve these goals. . . .

. . . CBRN terrorism has emerged as a U.S. national security concern for several reasons:

- There has been a trend toward increased lethality in terrorism in the past decade.
- There is an increasing focus on the apparent dangers posed by potential CBRN terrorism.
- Terrorists may now feel less constrained to use a CBRN device in an attempt to cause mass casualties, especially following the precedent-setting attack in 1995 by the Aum Shinrikyo.

The reasons terrorists may perpetrate a WMD attack include a desire to kill as many people as possible as a means "to annihilate their enemies," to instill fear and panic to undermine a governmental regime, to create a means of negotiating from a position of unsurpassed strength, or to cause great social and economic impact.

Given any of those potential motives, the report identifies the "most likely terrorists groups" to use CBRN as fundamentalist or apocalyptic religious organizations, cults, and extreme single-issue groups but suggests that such a group may resort to a smaller-scale attack to achieve its goal. . . .

The Panel concludes that the Nation must be prepared for the entire spectrum of potential terrorist threats—both the unprecedented higher-consequence attack, as well as the historically more frequent, lesser-consequence terrorist attack, which the Panel believes is more likely in the near term. Conventional explosives, traditionally a favorite tool of the terrorist, will likely remain the terrorist weapon of choice in the near term as well. Whether smaller-scale CBRN or conventional, any such lower-consequence event—at least in terms of casualties or destruction—could, nevertheless, accomplish one or more terrorist objectives: exhausting response capabilities, instilling fear, undermining government credibility, or provoking an overreaction by the government. With that in mind, the Panel's report urges a more balanced approach, so that not only higher-consequence scenarios will be considered, but that increasing attention must now also be paid to the historically more frequent, more probable, lesser-consequence attack, especially in terms of policy implications for budget priorities or the allocation of other resources, to optimize local response capabilities. A singular focus on preparing for an event potentially affecting thousands or tens of thousands may result in a smaller, but nevertheless lethal attack involving dozens failing to receive an appropriate response in the first critical minutes and hours.

While noting that the technology currently exists that would allow terrorists to produce one of several lethal CBRN weapons, the report also describes the current difficulties in acquiring or developing and in maintaining, handling, testing, transporting, and delivering a device that truly has the capability to cause "mass casualties." Those difficulties include the requirement, in almost all cases, for highly knowledgeable personnel, significant financial resources, obtainable but fairly sophisticated production facilities and equipment, quality control and testing, and special handling. In many cases, the personnel of a terrorist organization run high personal safety risks, in producing, handling, testing, and delivering such a device. Moreover, the report notes, the more sophisticated a device, or the more personnel, equipment, facilities, and the like involved, the greater the risk that the enterprise will expose itself to detection and interdiction by intelligence and law enforcement agencies—particularly in light of the increasing attention focused on terrorism today. . . .

The report contains several conclusions and recommendations, as a result of the threat analysis and other information provided to the Panel and the collective expertise and experience of its members:

- The conclusion that the United States needs to have a viable national strategy to guide the development of clear, comprehensive, and truly integrated national domestic preparedness plans to combat terrorism, one that recognizes that the Federal role will be defined by the nature and severity of the incident but will generally be supportive of state and local authorities, who traditionally have the fundamental responsibility for response, and the recommendation for promulgation of a national-level strategy, with a "bottom-up" perspective—a strategy that clearly delineates and distinguishes Federal, state, and local roles and responsibilities and articulates clear direction for Federal priorities and programs to support local responders; and a comprehensive, parallel public education effort.

- The conclusion that initial and continuing, comprehensive and articulate assessments of potential, credible, terrorist threats within the United States, and the ensuing risk and vulnerability assessments are critical for policymakers and the recommendation that more attention be paid to assessments of the higher-probability/lower-consequence threats—not at the expense of, but in addition to, assessments of the lower-probability/higher-consequence threats.

- The conclusion that the complex nature of current Federal organizations and programs makes it very difficult for state and local authorities to obtain Federal information, assistance, funding, and support; that a Federal focal point and "clearinghouse" for related preparedness information and for directing state and local entities to appropriate Federal agencies, is needed; and that the *concept* behind the National Domestic Preparedness Office is fundamentally sound.

- The conclusion that congressional decisions for authority and funding to address the issue appear to be uncoordinated, and the recommendation that Congress consider forming an *ad hoc* Joint Special or Select Committee, to provide more efficiency and effectiveness in Federal efforts.

- The conclusion that much more needs to be and can be done to obtain and share information on potential terrorist threats at all levels of government, to provide more effective deterrence, prevention, interdiction, or response, using modern information technology. . . .

- The conclusion that national standards for responders at all levels, particularly for planning, training, and equipment, are critical, and the recommendation that more emphasis be placed on research, development, testing, and evaluation in the adoption of such standards.

- The conclusion that, despite recent improvements, too much ambiguity remains about the issue of "who's in charge" if an incident occurs, and the recommendation that efforts be accelerated to develop and to test agreed-on templates for command and control under a wide variety of terrorist threat scenarios. . . .

Excerpted from U.S. Advisory Panel to Assess Domestic Response Capabilities for Terrorism Involving Weapons of Mass Destruction. *Assessing the Threat: First Annual Report to the President and the Congress of the Advisory Panel to Assess Domestic Response Capabilities for Terrorism Involving Weapons of Mass Destruction*. December 15, 1999. http://purl.access. gpo.gov/GPO/LPS16552 (accessed September 15, 2004).

# 79. Countering the Changing Threat of International Terrorism, National Commission on Terrorism Report

*June 5, 2000*

## Executive Summary

*International terrorism poses an increasingly dangerous and difficult threat to America.* This was underscored by the December 1999 arrests in Jordan and at the U.S./Canadian border of foreign nationals who were allegedly planning to attack crowded millennium celebrations. Today's terrorists seek to inflict mass casualties, and they are attempting to do so both overseas and on American soil. They are less dependent on state sponsorship and are, instead, forming loose, transnational affiliations based on religious or ideological affinity and a common hatred of the United States. This makes terrorist attacks more difficult to detect and prevent.

*Countering the growing danger of the terrorist threat requires significantly stepping up U.S. efforts.* The government must immediately take steps to reinvigorate the collection of intelligence about terrorists' plans, use all available legal avenues to disrupt and prosecute terrorist activities and private sources of support, convince other nations to cease all support for terrorists, and ensure that federal, state, and local officials are prepared for attacks that may result in mass casualties. The Commission has made a number of recommendations to accomplish these objectives:

*Priority one is to prevent terrorist attacks. U.S. intelligence and law enforcement communities must use the full scope of their authority to collect intelligence regarding terrorist plans and methods.*

- CIA guidelines adopted in 1995 restricting recruitment of unsavory sources should not apply when recruiting counterterrorism sources.
- The Attorney General should ensure that FBI is exercising fully its authority for investigating suspected terrorist groups or individuals, including authority for electronic surveillance.
- Funding for counterterrorism efforts by CIA, NSA [National Security Agency], and FBI must be given higher priority to ensure continuation of important operational activity and to close the technology gap that threatens their ability to collect and exploit terrorist communications.
- FBI should establish a cadre of reports officers to distill and disseminate terrorism-related information once it is collected. . . .

*Private sources of financial and logistical support for terrorists must be subjected to the full force and sweep of U.S. and international laws.*

- All relevant agencies should use every available means, including the full array of criminal, civil, and administrative sanctions to block or disrupt nongovernmental sources of support for international terrorism.
- Congress should promptly ratify and implement the International Convention for the Suppression of the Financing of Terrorism to enhance international cooperative efforts.
- Where criminal prosecution is not possible, the Attorney General should vigorously pursue the expulsion of terrorists from the United States through proceedings which protect both the national security interest in safeguarding classified evidence and the right of the accused to challenge that evidence.

*A terrorist attack involving a biological agent, deadly chemicals, or nuclear or radiological material, even if it succeeds only partially, could profoundly affect the entire nation. The government must do more to prepare for such an event.*

- The President should direct the preparation of a manual to guide the implementation of existing legal authority in the event of a catastrophic terrorist threat or attack. The President and Congress should determine whether additional legal authority is needed to deal with catastrophic terrorism.
- The Department of Defense must have detailed plans for its role in the event of a catastrophic terrorist attack, including criteria for decisions on transfer of command authority to DoD in extraordinary circumstances. . . .

*The President and Congress should reform the system for reviewing and funding departmental counterterrorism programs to ensure that the activities and programs of various agencies are part of a comprehensive plan.*

- The executive branch official responsible for coordinating counterterrorism efforts across the government should be given a stronger hand in the budget process.
- Congress should develop mechanisms for a comprehensive review of the President's counterterrorism policy and budget.

Excerpted from U.S. National Commission on Terrorism. *Countering the Changing Threat of International Terrorism.* June 5, 2000. http://purl.access.gpo.gov/GPO/LPS4710 (accessed September 15, 2004).

## 80. Toward a National Strategy for Combating Terrorism, Advisory Panel to Assess Domestic Response Capabilities for Terrorism Involving Weapons of Mass Destruction Report

*December 15, 2000*

### Executive Summary

We have been fortunate as a nation. The terrorist incidents in this country—however tragic—have occurred so rarely that the foundations of our society or our form of government have not been threatened. Nevertheless, the potential for terrorist attacks inside the borders of the United States is a serious emerging threat. There is no guarantee that our comparatively secure domestic sanctuary will always remain so. Because the stakes are so high, our nation's leaders must take seriously the possibility of an escalation of terrorist violence against the homeland. . . .

To prepare to manage the consequences of such attacks effectively, the United States needs changes in the relationships among all levels of government. Our ability to respond cannot depend on a single level or agency of government. Rather we need a *national* approach, one that recognizes the unique individual skills that communities, States, and the Federal government possess and that, collectively, will give us the "total package" needed to address all aspects of terrorism. . . .

In its second year, the Advisory Panel . . . addressed specific programs for combating terrorism and larger questions of national strategy and Federal organization. While the Advisory Panel found much to commend, it also found problems at all levels of government and in virtually every functional discipline relevant to combating terrorism. The Panel believes these problems are particularly acute at high levels of the Federal Executive Branch. Hence, the present report highlights the related issues of national strategy and Federal organization, and recommends solutions for these and other problems.

*Finding 1: The United States has no coherent, functional national strategy for combating terrorism.*

The United States needs a functional, coherent national strategy for domestic preparedness against terrorism. The nation has a loosely coupled set of plans and specific programs that aim, individually, to achieve certain specific preparedness objectives. The Executive Branch portrays as its strategy a compilation of broad policy statements, and various plans and programs already under way. Many programs have resulted from specific Congressional earmarks in various appropriations bills and did not originate in Executive Branch budget requests; they are the initiatives of activist legislators. Although Federal agencies are administering programs assigned to them, the Executive Branch has not articulated a broad functional national strategy that would synchronize the existing programs and identify future program priorities needed to achieve national objectives for domestic preparedness for terrorism. Given the structure of our national government, only the Executive Branch can produce such a national strategy.

*Recommendation 1: The next President should develop and present to the Congress a national strategy for combating terrorism within one year of assuming office.*

A national strategy is a high-level statement of national objectives coupled logically to a statement of the means that will be used to achieve these objectives. In a coherent strategy, program details are analytically derived from the statement of goals. The next Administration should begin a process of developing a national strategy by a thoughtful articulation of national goals, encompassing deterrence, prevention, preparedness, and response.

*Ends.* The first step in developing a coherent national strategy is for the Executive Branch to define a meaningful, measurable expression of what it is trying to achieve in combating terrorism. To date, the Federal government's goals have been expressed primarily in terms of program execution. Rather, the national strategy must express goals in terms of the "end state" toward which the program strives. Since there exists no ready-made measure of a country's preparedness for terrorism (especially domestically), the Executive Branch must develop objective measurements for its program to combat terrorism, to track its progress, to determine priorities and appropriate funding levels, and to know when the desired "end state" has been achieved.

*Means.* With meaningful objectives, logical priorities and appropriate policy prescriptions can be developed. That is the essence of any coherent strategy. Setting priorities is essential and can only be done after specific objectives have been clearly defined. For instance, should the nation seek a higher level of preparedness for its large urban centers than for its rural areas and, if so, how much higher? In the broad area of terrorism preparedness, what should be the relative importance of preparing for conventional terrorism, radiological incidents, chemical weapons, or biological weapons? With respect to biological weapons, which pathogens deserve priority? What priority and commensurate resources need to be devoted to defending against cyber attacks? A proper national strategy will provide a clear answer to these and many other questions. With these answers in hand it will be possible to design and manage an appropriate set of programs. The country is at a disadvantage, of course, in that a large number of programs have already been established and may have to be reconfigured—an inevitable consequence of their ad hoc origins.

*Finding 2: The organization of the Federal government's programs for combating terrorism is fragmented, uncoordinated, and politically unaccountable.*

The lack of a national strategy results in part from the fragmentation of Executive Branch programs for combating terrorism. These programs cross an extraordinary number of jurisdictions and substantive domains: national security, law enforcement, intelligence, emergency management, fire protection, public health, medical care, as well as parts of the private sector.

No one, at any level, is "in charge" of all relevant capabilities, most of which are not dedicated exclusively to combating terrorism. The lack of a national strategy is inextricably linked to the fact that no entity has the authority to direct all of the entities that may be engaged. At the Federal level, no entity has the authority even to direct the coordination of relevant Federal efforts.

*Recommendation 2: The next President should establish a National Office for Combating Terrorism in the Executive Office of the President, and should seek a statutory basis for this office.*

The office should have a broad and comprehensive scope, with responsibility for the full range of deterring, preventing, preparing for, and responding to international as well as domestic terrorism. . . .

The National Office for Combating Terrorism should exercise program and budget authority over Federal efforts to combat terrorism. It should have the authority to conduct a review of Federal agency programs and budgets to ensure compliance with the priorities established in the national strategy, as well as the elimination of conflicts and unnecessary duplication among agencies. The National Office should administer a budget certification/decertification process with the authority to determine whether an agency's budget complies with the national strategy and to appeal ultimately to the President to resolve disputes. . . .

The National Office for Combating Terrorism should not be an operational entity in the sense of exerting direct control over Federal assets in operations to combat terrorism. . . .

*Finding 3: The Congress shares responsibility for the inadequate coordination of programs to combat terrorism.*

The Congress's strong interest in, and commitment to, U.S. efforts to combat terrorism is readily apparent. The Congress took the initiative in 1995 to improve the nation's domestic preparedness against terrorism. But the Congress has also contributed to the Executive Branch's problems. Over the past five years, there have been a half-dozen Congressional attempts to reorganize the Executive Branch's efforts to combat terrorism, all of which failed. None enjoyed the support of the Executive Branch. At least 11 full committees in the Senate and 14 full committees in the House—as well as their numerous subcommittees—claim oversight or some responsibility for various U.S. programs for combating terrorism. Earmarks in appropriations bills created many of the Federal government's specific domestic preparedness programs without authorizing legislation or oversight. The rapidly growing U.S. budget for combating terrorism is now laced with such earmarks, which have proliferated in the absence of an Executive Branch strategy. The Executive Branch cannot successfully coordinate its programs for combating terrorism alone. Congress must better organize itself and exercise much greater discipline.

*Recommendation 3: The Congress should consolidate its authority over programs for combating terrorism into a Special Committee for Combating Terrorism—either a joint committee between the Houses or separate committees in each House—and Congressional leadership should instruct all other committees to respect the authority of this new committee and to conform strictly to authorizing legislation.*

The creation of a new joint committee or separate committees in each House is necessary to improve the nation's efforts to fight terrorism. . . . We recognize that this task is no less daunting than the Executive Branch reorganization that we propose above, but it is no less needed.

*Finding 4: The Executive Branch and the Congress have not paid sufficient attention to State and local capabilities for combating terrorism and have not devoted sufficient resources to augment these capabilities to enhance the preparedness of the nation as a whole.*

The foundation of the nation's domestic preparedness for terrorism is the network of emergency response capabilities and disaster management systems provided by State and local governments. "Local" response personnel—community and State law enforcement officers, firefighters, emergency medical technicians, hospital emergency personnel, public health officials, and emergency managers—will be the "first responders" to virtually any terrorist attack anywhere in the nation. Federal resources may not arrive for many hours—if not days— after the attack. A disproportionately small amount of the total funds appropriated for combating terrorism is being allocated to provide direct or indirect assistance to State and local response efforts. . . .

*Recommendation 4: The Executive Branch should establish a strong institutional mechanism for ensuring the participation of high-level State and local officials in the development and implementation of a national strategy for terrorism preparedness.*

To be consistent with the Federal structure of our government, the President should work in closer partnership with State and local governments as they collectively strive to achieve higher levels of domestic preparedness for terrorism. The domestic portion of a national strategy for combating terrorism should emphasize programs and initiatives that build appropriately on existing State and local capabilities for other emergencies and disasters. The Executive Branch, therefore, should develop the national strategy in close partnership with high-level State and local officials drawn from key professional communities: elected officials, law enforcement, fire protection, emergency medical technicians, public health officials, hospital medical care providers, and emergency managers.

State and local officials should, in particular, have substantial responsibility for the detailed design and oversight of the Federal training, equipment, and exercise programs. . . .

*Finding 5: Federal programs for domestic preparedness to combat terrorism lack clear priorities and are deficient in numerous specific areas. . . .*

The lack of clear priorities is an obvious byproduct of the lack of a strategy. . . .

Excerpted from U.S. Advisory Panel to Assess Domestic Response Capabilities for Terrorism Involving Weapons of Mass Destruction. *Toward a National Strategy for Combating Terrorism: Second Annual Report to the President and the Congress of the Advisory Panel to Assess Domestic Response Capabilities for Terrorism Involving Weapons of Mass Destruction.* December 15, 2000. http://purl.access.gpo.gov/GPO/LPS16576 (accessed September 15, 2004).

## 81. Road Map for National Security: Imperative for Change, United States Commission on National Security/21st Century Report

*February 15, 2001*

### Executive Summary

. . . We have taken a broad view of national security. In the new era, sharp distinctions between "foreign" and "domestic" no longer apply. We do not equate national security with "defense." We *do* believe in the centrality of strategy, and of seizing opportunities as well as confronting dangers. If the structures and processes of the U.S. government stand still amid a world of change, the United States will lose its capacity to shape history, and will instead be shaped by it.

### Securing the National Homeland

The combination of unconventional weapons proliferation with the persistence of international terrorism will end the relative invulnerability of the U.S. homeland to catastrophic attack. A direct attack against American citizens *on American soil* is likely over the next quarter century. The risk is not only death and destruction but also a demoralization that could undermine U.S. global leadership. In the face of this threat, our nation has no coherent or integrated governmental structures.

*We therefore recommend the creation of an independent National Homeland Security Agency (NHSA) with responsibility for planning, coordinating, and integrating various U.S. government activities involved in homeland security.* NHSA would be built upon the Federal Emergency Management Agency, with the three organizations currently on the front line of border security—the Coast Guard, the Customs Service, and the Border Patrol—transferred to it. NHSA would not only protect American lives, but also assume responsibility for overseeing the protection of the nation's critical infrastructure, including information technology.

The NHSA Director would have Cabinet status and would be a statutory advisor to the National Security Council. . . .

The potentially catastrophic nature of homeland attacks necessitates our being prepared to use the extensive resources of the Department of Defense (DoD). Therefore, the department needs to pay far more attention to this mission in the future. . . .

New priorities also need to be set for the U.S. armed forces in light of the threat to the homeland. *We urge, in particular, that the National Guard be given homeland security as a primary mission, as the U.S. Constitution itself ordains.* The National Guard should be reorganized, trained, and equipped to undertake that mission.

Finally, *we recommend that Congress reorganize itself to accommodate this Executive Branch realignment, and that it also form a special select committee for homeland security to provide Congressional support and oversight in this critical area.*

### Recapitalizing America's Strengths in Science and Education

Americans are living off the economic and security benefits of the last three generations' investment in science and education, but we are now consuming capital. Our systems of basic scientific research and education are in serious crisis, while other countries are redoubling their efforts. In the next quarter century, we will likely see ourselves surpassed, and in relative decline, unless we make a conscious national commitment to maintain our edge. . . .

The United States can remain the world's technological leader *if it makes the commitment to do so.* But the U.S. government has seriously underfunded basic scientific research in recent years. The quality of the U.S. education system, too, has fallen behind those of scores of other nations. . . .

In this Commission's view, the inadequacies of our systems of research and education pose a greater threat to U.S. national security over the next quarter century than any potential conventional war that we might imagine. American national leadership must understand these deficiencies as threats to national security. If we do not invest heavily and wisely in rebuilding these two core strengths, America will be incapable of maintaining its global position long into the 21st century.

*We therefore recommend doubling the federal research and development budget by 2010, and instituting a more competitive environment for the allotment of those funds.*

*We recommend further that the role of the President's Science Advisor be elevated to oversee these and other critical tasks, such as the resuscitation of the national laboratory system and the institution of better inventory stewardship over the nation's science and technology assets.*

*We also recommend a new National Security Science and Technology Education Act to fund a comprehensive program to produce the needed numbers of science and engineering professionals as well as qualified teachers in science and math.* This Act should provide loan forgiveness incentives to attract those who have graduated and scholarships for those still in school and should provide these incentives in exchange for a period of K-12 teaching in science and math, or of military or government service. . . .

### Institutional Redesign

The dramatic changes in the world since the end of the Cold War have not been accompanied by any major institutional changes in the Executive Branch of the U.S. government. Serious deficiencies exist that only a significant organizational redesign can remedy. Most troublesome is the lack of an overarching strategic framework guiding U.S. national security policymaking and resource allocation. Clear goals and priorities are rarely set. Budgets are prepared and appropriated as they were during the Cold War.

The Department of State, in particular, is a crippled institution, starved for resources by Congress because of its inadequacies, and thereby weakened further. Only if the State Department's internal weaknesses are cured will it become an effective leader in the making and implementation of the nation's foreign policy. Only then can it credibly seek significant funding increases from Congress. . . .

For this and other reasons, the power to determine national security policy has steadily migrated toward the National Security Council (NSC) staff. The staff now assumes policymaking roles that many observers have warned against. Yet the NSC staff's role as policy coordinator is more urgently needed than ever, given the imperative of integrating the many diverse strands of policymaking.

Meanwhile, the U.S. intelligence community is adjusting only slowly to the changed circumstances of the post-Cold War era. . . .

Finally, the Department of Defense needs to be overhauled. The growth in staff and staff activities has created mounting confusion and delay. . . . The programming and budgeting process is not guided by effective strategic planning. . . .

In light of such serious and interwoven deficiencies, the Commission's initial recommendation is that *strategy should once again drive the design and implementation of U.S. national security policies.* That means that *the President should personally guide a top-down strategic planning process and that process should be linked to the allocation of resources throughout the government.* When submitting his budgets for the various national security departments, the President should also present an overall national security budget, focused on the nation's most critical strategic goals. Homeland security, counterterrorism, and science and technology should be included. . . .

As for the Department of Defense, resource issues are also very much at stake in reform efforts. The key to success will be direct, sustained involvement and commitment to defense reform on the part of the President, Secretary of Defense, and Congressional leadership. . . .

The processes by which the Defense Department develops its programs and budgets as well as acquires its weapons also need fundamental reform. *The most critical first step is for the Secretary of Defense to produce defense policy and planning guidance that defines specific goals and establishes relative priorities.* . . .

The Commission has concluded that the basic structure of the intelligence community does not require change. . . .

### The Human Requirements for National Security

As it enters the 21st century, the United States finds itself on the brink of an unprecedented crisis of competence in government. The declining orientation toward government service as a prestigious career is deeply troubling. Both civilian and military institutions face growing challenges, albeit of different forms and degrees, in recruiting and retaining America's most promising talent. This problem derives from multiple sources—ample private sector opportunities with good pay and fewer bureaucratic frustrations, rigid governmental personnel procedures, the absence of a single overarching threat like the Cold War to entice service, cynicism about the worthiness of government service, and perceptions of government as a plodding bureaucracy falling behind in a technological age of speed and accuracy.

These factors are adversely affecting recruitment and retention in the Civil and Foreign Services and particularly throughout the military, where deficiencies are both widening the gap between those who serve and the rest of American society and putting in jeopardy the leadership and professionalism necessary for an effective military. *If we allow the human resources of government to continue to decay, none of the reforms proposed by this or any other national security commission will produce their intended results.* . . .

. . . [W]e recommend *substantial enhancements to the Montgomery GI Bill and strengthening recently passed and pending legislation that supports enhanced benefits—including transition, medical, and homeownership—for qualified veterans.* The GI Bill should be restored as a pure entitlement, be transferable to dependents if desired by career service members, and should equal, at the very least, the median tuition cost of four-year U.S. colleges. . . . In addition, Title 38 authority for veterans benefits should be modified to restore and substantially improve medical, dental, and VA home ownership benefits for all who qualify, but especially for career and retired service members. Taken as a package, such changes will help bring the best people into the armed service and persuade quality personnel to serve longer in order to secure greater rewards for their service. . . .

### The Role of Congress

While Congress has mandated many changes to a host of Executive Branch departments and agencies over the years, it has not fundamentally reviewed its own role in national security policy. Moreover, it has not reformed its own structure since 1949. At present, for example, every major defense program must be voted upon no fewer than eighteen times each year by an array of committees and subcommittees. This represents a very poor use of time for busy members of the Executive and Legislative Branches.

To address these deficiencies, *the Commission first recommends that the Congressional leadership conduct a thorough bicameral, bipartisan review of the Legislative Branch's relationship to national security and foreign policy.* . . .

From that basis, *Congressional and Executive Branch leaders must build programs to encourage members to acquire knowledge and experience in national security.* These programs should include ongoing education, greater opportunities for serious overseas travel, more legislature-to-legislature exchanges, and greater participation in war games.

Greater fluency in national security matters must be matched by structural reforms. *A comprehensive review of the Congressional committee structure is needed* to ensure that it reflects the complexity of 21st century security challenges and of U.S. national security priorities. . . .

An effective Congressional role in national security also requires ongoing Executive- Legislative consultation and coordination. The Executive Branch must ensure a sustained effort in consultation and devote resources to it. For its part, Congress must make consultation a higher priority, in part by *forming a permanent consultative group composed of the Congressional leadership and the Chairpersons and Ranking Members of the main committees involved in national security.* This will form the basis for sustained dialogue and greater support in times of crisis. . . .

Finally, *we strongly urge the new President and the Congressional leadership to establish some mechanism to oversee the implementation of the recommendations proffered here.* Once some mechanism is chosen, the President must ensure that responsibility for implementing the recommendations of this Commission be given explicitly to senior personnel in both the Executive and Legislative Branches of government. The press of daily obligations is such that unless such delegation is made, and those given responsibility for implementation are held accountable for their tasks, the necessary reforms will not occur. The stakes are high. We of this Commission believe that many thousands of American lives, U.S. leadership among the community of nations, and the fate of U.S. national security itself are at risk unless the President and the Congress join together to implement the recommendations set forth in this report. . . .

Excerpted from United States Commission on National Security/21st Century. *Road Map for National Security: Imperative for Change.* Phase III Report, February 15, 2001. http://govinfo.library.unt.edu/nssg/PhaseIIIFR.pdf (accessed September 15, 2004).

# Bush Condemns Terrorist Attacks against the United States

## INTRODUCTION

At 8:46 a.m. on September 11, 2001, a beautiful, clear day on the East Coast, an American Airlines plane loaded with passengers, crew members, and thousands of gallons of aviation fuel slammed into the 110-story north tower of New York's World Trade Center, exploding in a massive fireball. Seventeen minutes later, at 9:03 a.m., millions of horrified people watching live television coverage saw a United Airlines plane cross their screens, bank sharply, and smash into the 110-story south tower, exploding in another inferno that blew flames and debris out the other side of the building.

At the time, President George W. Bush was in Sarasota, Florida, meeting with children at Emma Booker Elementary School. After the second plane struck, an aide whispered in Bush's ear that the nation was under attack. Before leaving the school, Bush made a brief statement at 9:30 a.m. confirming what everyone watching TV already knew: two planes had crashed into the World Trade Center "in an apparent terrorist attack on our country" [Document 82].

The day's horrors had just begun. At 9:37 a.m., less than ten minutes after Bush spoke, another American Airlines plane crashed into the Pentagon, just across the Potomac River from Washington, D.C. Twenty-two minutes later, at 9:59 a.m., the unthinkable happened: the World Trade Center's south tower collapsed, the top floors smashing through lower floors as they fell. Just four minutes later, at 10:03 a.m., a second United plane crashed nose-first into a field in Pennsylvania. Some passengers on that flight had called loved ones on cell phones after the hijacking started and learned of the earlier attacks.

They then apparently attempted in vain to wrestle control of their plane from the hijackers. The terrorists had reportedly planned to crash the plane into the White House or the U.S. Capitol. Finally, at 10:28 a.m.—twenty-five minutes after the Pennsylvania crash—the World Trade Center's north tower collapsed in a billowing cloud of dust and ash. By 10:30 a.m., 2,973 people were dead or dying in the worst assault on the United States since the Japanese attacked Pearl Harbor sixty years earlier. The dead included 343 New York City firefighters, thirty-seven police officers with the Port Authority of New York and New Jersey, and twenty-three officers from the New York City Police Department.

After the Pentagon crash, for the first time in history the Federal Aviation Administration shut down the nation's airspace and ordered all airborne planes to immediately land at the nearest airport. The commercial planes were quickly replaced by fighter jets streaking across the sky above the nation's largest cities. The pilots were ordered to shoot down any planes that did not land.

Investigators eventually determined that a total of nineteen Middle Eastern men—fifteen of them from Saudi Arabia—had hijacked the four planes in a plot developed over many years. All of the men were tied to the al Qaeda terrorist network run by Osama bin Laden. They apparently commandeered the planes by using box cutters or other short knives to kill or incapacitate the pilots and some flight attendants. Hijackers who had trained as pilots, largely in the United States, then took over the controls and deliberately crashed the planes.

That night, Bush gave a televised address from the White House aimed at reassuring a stunned nation and world. "These acts of mass murder were intended to frighten our nation into chaos and retreat, but they have failed," the president said [Document 83].

Three days later, as fires continued raging at the World Trade Center and the Pentagon, Bush spoke again during a service at Washington's National Cathedral marking a National Day of Prayer and Remembrance. "War has been waged against us by stealth and deceit and murder," Bush said. "This nation is peaceful, but fierce when stirred to anger. This conflict was begun on the timing and terms of others. It will end in a way, and at an hour, of our choosing" [Document 84].

Not knowing whether further attacks were imminent, law enforcement officials scurried in the hours and days after the airliners crashed to increase security at everything from airports to the White House. Whether they could actually protect the United States from further attacks was unclear, but one thing was certain: life in the homeland would never again be the same.

## 82. President George W. Bush's Remarks on the Terrorist Attack on New York City's World Trade Center in Sarasota, Florida

*September 11, 2001*

Ladies and gentlemen, this is a difficult moment for America. I, unfortunately, will be going back to Washington after my remarks. Secretary [of Education] Rod Paige and the Lieutenant Governor will take the podium and discuss education. I do want to thank the folks here at Booker Elementary School for their hospitality.

Today we've had a national tragedy. Two airplanes have crashed into the World Trade Center in an apparent terrorist attack on our country. I have spoken to the vice president, to the governor of New York, to the director of the FBI, and have ordered that the full resources of the federal government go to help the victims and their families and to conduct a full-scale investigation to hunt down and to find those folks who committed this act.

Terrorism against our nation will not stand.

And now if you would join me in a moment of silence. May God bless the victims, their families, and America.

Thank you very much.

U.S. Executive Office of the President. "Remarks on the Terrorist Attack on New York City's World Trade Center in Sarasota, Florida." September 11, 2001. *Weekly Compilation of Presidential Documents* 37, no. 37 (Sept. 17, 2001): 1300. http://www.gpoaccess.gov/wcomp/v37no37.html (accessed September 15, 2004).

## 83. President George W. Bush's Address to the Nation on the Terrorist Attacks

*September 11, 2001*

Good evening. Today, our fellow citizens, our way of life, our very freedom came under attack in a series of deliberate and deadly terrorist acts. The victims were in airplanes, or in their offices; secretaries, businessmen and women, military and federal workers; moms and dads, friends and neighbors. Thousands of lives were suddenly ended by evil, despicable acts of terror.

The pictures of airplanes flying into buildings, fires burning, huge structures collapsing, have filled us with disbelief, terrible sadness, and a quiet, unyielding anger. These acts of mass murder were intended to frighten our nation into chaos and retreat. But they have failed; our country is strong.

A great people has been moved to defend a great nation. Terrorist attacks can shake the foundations of our biggest buildings, but they cannot touch the foundation of America. These acts shattered steel, but they cannot dent the steel of American resolve.

America was targeted for attack because we're the brightest beacon for freedom and opportunity in the world. And no one will keep that light from shining.

Today, our nation saw evil, the very worst of human nature. And we responded with the best of America—with the daring of our rescue workers, with the caring for strangers and neighbors who came to give blood and help in any way they could.

Immediately following the first attack, I implemented our government's emergency response plans. Our military is powerful, and it's prepared. Our emergency teams are working in New York City and Washington, D.C., to help with local rescue efforts.

Our first priority is to get help to those who have been injured, and to take every precaution to protect our citizens at home and around the world from further attacks.

The functions of our government continue without interruption. Federal agencies in Washington which had to be evacuated today are reopening for essential personnel tonight, and will be open for business tomorrow. Our financial institutions remain strong, and the American economy will be open for business, as well.

The search is underway for those who are behind these evil acts. I've directed the full resources of our intelligence and law enforcement communities to find those responsible and to bring them to justice. We will make no distinction between the terrorists who committed these acts and those who harbor them.

I appreciate so very much the members of Congress who have joined me in strongly condemning these attacks. And on behalf of the American people, I thank the many world leaders who have called to offer their condolences and assistance.

America and our friends and allies join with all those who want peace and security in the world, and we stand together to win the war against terrorism. Tonight, I ask for your prayers for all those who grieve, for the children whose worlds have been shattered, for all whose sense of safety and security has been threatened. And I pray they will be comforted by a power greater than any of us, spoken through the ages in Psalm 23: "Even though

I walk through the valley of the shadow of death, I fear no evil, for You are with me."

This is a day when all Americans from every walk of life unite in our resolve for justice and peace. America has stood down enemies before, and we will do so this time. None of us will ever forget this day. Yet, we go forward to defend freedom and all that is good and just in our world.

Thank you. Good night, and God bless America.

U.S. Executive Office of the President. "Address to the Nation on the Terrorist Attacks." September 11, 2001. *Weekly Compilation of Presidential Documents* 37, no. 37 (Sept. 17, 2001): 1301–1302. http://www.gpoaccess.gov/wcomp/v37no37.html (accessed September 15, 2004).

# 84. President George W. Bush's Remarks at the National Day of Prayer and Remembrance Service

*September 14, 2001*

We are here in the middle hour of our grief. So many have suffered so great a loss, and today we express our nation's sorrow. We come before God to pray for the missing and the dead, and for those who love them.

On Tuesday, our country was attacked with deliberate and massive cruelty. We have seen the images of fire and ashes, and bent steel.

Now come the names, the list of casualties we are only beginning to read. They are the names of men and women who began their day at a desk or in an airport, busy with life. They are the names of people who faced death, and in their last moments called home to say, be brave, and I love you.

They are the names of passengers who defied their murderers, and prevented the murder of others on the ground. They are the names of men and women who wore the uniform of the United States, and died at their posts.

They are the names of rescuers, the ones whom death found running up the stairs and into the fires to help others. We will read all these names. We will linger over them, and learn their stories, and many Americans will weep.

To the children and parents and spouses and families and friends of the lost, we offer the deepest sympathy of the nation. And I assure you, you are not alone.

Just three days removed from these events, Americans do not yet have the distance of history. But our responsibility to history is already clear: to answer these attacks and rid the world of evil.

War has been waged against us by stealth and deceit and murder. This nation is peaceful, but fierce when stirred to anger. This conflict was begun on the timing and terms of others. It will end in a way, and at an hour, of our choosing.

Our purpose as a nation is firm. Yet our wounds as a people are recent and unhealed, and lead us to pray. In many of our prayers this week, there is a searching, and an honesty. At St. Patrick's Cathedral in New York on Tuesday, a woman said, "I prayed to God to give us a sign that He is still here." Others have prayed for the same, searching hospital to hospital, carrying pictures of those still missing.

God's signs are not always the ones we look for. We learn in tragedy that His purposes are not always our own. Yet the prayers of private suffering, whether in our homes or in this great cathedral, are known and heard, and understood.

There are prayers that help us last through the day, or endure the night. There are prayers of friends and strangers, that give us strength for the journey. And there are prayers that yield our will to a will greater than our own.

This world He created is of moral design. Grief and tragedy and hatred are only for a time. Goodness, remembrance, and love have no end. And the Lord of life holds all who die, and all who mourn.

It is said that adversity introduces us to ourselves. This is true of a nation as well. In this trial, we have been reminded, and the world has seen, that our fellow Americans are generous and kind, resourceful and brave. We see our national character in rescuers working past exhaustion; in long lines of blood donors; in thousands of citizens who have asked to work and serve in any way possible.

And we have seen our national character in eloquent acts of sacrifice. Inside the World Trade Center, one man who could have saved himself stayed until the end at the side of his quadriplegic friend. A beloved priest died giving the last rites to a firefighter. Two office workers, finding a disabled stranger, carried her down sixty-eight floors to safety. A group of men drove through the night from Dallas to Washington to bring skin grafts for burn victims.

In these acts, and in many others, Americans showed a deep commitment to one another, and an abiding love for our country. Today, we feel what Franklin Roosevelt called the warm courage of national unity. This is a unity of every faith, and every background.

It has joined together political parties in both houses of Congress. It is evident in services of prayer and candlelight vigils, and American flags, which are displayed in pride, and wave in defiance.

Our unity is a kinship of grief, and a steadfast resolve to prevail against our enemies. And this unity against terror is now extending across the world.

America is a nation full of good fortune, with so much to be grateful for. But we are not spared from suffering. In every generation, the world has produced enemies of human freedom. They have attacked America, because we are freedom's home and defender. And the commitment of our fathers is now the calling of our time.

On this national day of prayer and remembrance, we ask almighty God to watch over our nation, and grant us patience and resolve in all that is to come. We pray that He will comfort and console those who now walk in sorrow. We thank Him for each life we now must mourn, and the promise of a life to come.

As we have been assured, neither death nor life, nor angels nor principalities nor powers, nor things present nor things to come, nor height nor depth, can separate us from God's love. May He bless the souls of the departed. May He comfort our own. And may He always guide our country.

God bless America.

U.S. Executive Office of the President. "Remarks at the National Day of Prayer and Remembrance Service." September 14, 2001. *Weekly Compilation of Presidential Documents* 37, no. 37 (Sept. 17, 2001): 1309–1310. http://www.gpoaccess.gov/wcomp/v37no37.html (accessed September 15, 2004).

# America Prepares for War against al Qaeda and in Afghanistan

85. Senate Joint Resolution 23 (Authorization for Use of Military Force), September 14, 2001

86. President George W. Bush's Speech to a Joint Session of Congress, September 20, 2001

87. U.S. Ambassador John D. Negroponte's Letter to the United Nations Security Council, October 7, 2001

88. President George W. Bush's Address to the Nation on the Beginning of the Afghan War, October 7, 2001

## INTRODUCTION

Almost as soon as the second plane smashed into the World Trade Center on September 11, 2001—making it clear that the homeland was under terrorist attack—a widespread cry arose among Americans of all political persuasions demanding that the United States take military action to punish those responsible and prevent further attacks.

Congress and the administration of President George W. Bush quickly started negotiating over language for a resolution authorizing the use of military force. Bush had asked for such a resolution to demonstrate unity. The Constitution gave him broad powers as commander-in-chief to defend the nation against attacks, but it gave Congress the power to actually declare war. Bush wanted a wide-ranging resolution authorizing the use of force to "deter and preempt any future acts of terrorism or aggression against the United States." Many members of Congress from both political parties thought that language went too far, effectively empowering the president to attack anyone at any time. The final language approved by Congress on September 14, 2001, authorized the president to take military action against "those nations, organizations, or persons he determines planned, authorized, committed, or aided the terrorist attacks that occurred on September 11, 2001, or harbored such organizations or persons." The Senate approved the resolution 98–0, and the House of Representatives passed it 420–1. Rep. Barbara Lee, D-Calif., was the lone dissenter. She warned that "we must be careful not to embark on an open-ended war with neither an exit strategy nor a focused target."

By any measure, the resolution was extraordinary. As one of its architects, Sen. Carl Levin, D-Mich., said on the Senate floor shortly before it was approved: "I believe it is important to note that this joint resolution would authorize the use of force even before the president or the Congress knows with certainty which nations, organizations, or persons were involved in the September 11 terrorist acts. This is a truly noteworthy action and a demonstration of our faith in the ability of our government to determine the facts and in the president to act upon them" [Document 85].

Six days after Congress approved the use of force, Bush announced before a joint session of Congress on September 20, 2001, the beginning of a "war on terrorism" to prevent further attacks on the American homeland. He warned that the war would be "a lengthy campaign, unlike any other we have ever seen" [Document 86].

Bush also announced that Gov. Tom Ridge of Pennsylvania would head a new Office of Homeland Security. Ridge's job was to coordinate efforts by thousands of local, state, and federal agencies that had various responsibilities for homeland security, Bush said. Ridge was made a cabinet-level member of the White House staff, not the head of a new federal department as many members of Congress, past government commissions, and other experts had advocated (*see* General Accounting Office Urges Better Coordination of Federal Terrorism Efforts, p. 210; Experts Warn of Increasing Threats to the American Homeland, p. 220).

In an interview the next day with the British Broadcasting Corp., Secretary of State Colin Powell was asked how the government would judge that it had won the war on terrorism. The United States would declare victory, Powell said, when there were no more attacks like those that occurred on September 11. "Now, will we ever get there?" he said. "I don't know." So how long would the war on terrorism last? "I can't predict that," Powell said. "I think it will certainly be years and I think it's a campaign that will probably continue as long as I can imagine."

On October 7, 2001, U.S. Ambassador to the United Nations (UN) John D. Negroponte announced in a letter to the UN Security Council that the United States "together with other States" had launched military strikes against Afghanistan. Negroponte said the attacks were acts of "self-defence" allowed under the UN Charter and were designed "to prevent and deter further attacks on the United States."

One sentence in Negroponte's letter caused consternation among many Arab governments and at the United Nations. "We may find," Negroponte wrote, "that our self-defence requires further actions with respect to other organizations and other States." Many Arab leaders believed this meant the United States would attack other countries at will that it believed harbored or otherwise helped terrorists, using "self-defense" as justification for a broad war against Muslim nations. Iraq, Iran, Syria, and Sudan, among other countries, were thought to be possible future targets [Document 87].

As American and British bombs and missiles started falling on Afghanistan that same day, in a televised address Bush said the "carefully targeted actions" were aimed at al Qaeda terrorist training camps and military installations operated by Afghanistan's Taliban government, which provided sanctuary to the terrorists. He did nothing to calm fears that military attacks on other countries might be forthcoming. "Today we focus on Afghanistan, but the battle is broader," Bush said. "Every nation has a choice to make. In this conflict, there is no neutral ground. If any government sponsors the outlaws and killers of innocents, they have become outlaws and murderers, themselves. And they will take that lonely path at their own peril" [Document 88].

According to a Gallup Poll, 90 percent of Americans supported the strikes against Afghanistan. Yet the same poll found that 83 percent of Americans feared they would provoke retaliatory terrorist attacks against the United States. Only a week before the Afghanistan war started, Attorney General John Ashcroft had warned that more attacks against the United States were likely and terrorists might use biological or chemical weapons.

The Taliban government collapsed two months after the war began, and thousands of Taliban and al Qaeda fighters simply melted back into the population or fled to neighboring Pakistan. American forces failed to capture or kill Osama bin Laden, the al Qaeda leader, and many of his senior associates during these first few months. Their best chance came late in 2001 when intelligence indicated that bin Laden, other top al Qaeda leaders, and hundreds of fighters had hidden in an enormous cave complex in the rugged Tora Bora mountains. Following intense bombing of the caves, U.S. commanders sent in Afghan warlords and their forces to undertake the tedious and dangerous process of flushing out survivors. It was suspected that the warlords, who were known for frequently switching sides in any dispute, allowed bin Laden and his men to escape. As of September 2004, bin Laden and many other al Qaeda leaders remained at large and Taliban forces were regrouping in Afghanistan.

---

# 85. Senate Joint Resolution 23 (Authorization for Use of Military Force)
## September 14, 2001

Whereas, on September 11, 2001, acts of treacherous violence were committed against the United States and its citizens; and

Whereas, such acts render it both necessary and appropriate that the United States exercise its rights to self-defense and to protect United States citizens both at home and abroad, and

Whereas, in light of the threat to the national security and foreign policy of the United States posed by these grave acts of violence, and

Whereas, such acts continue to pose an unusual and extraordinary threat to the national security and foreign policy of the United States,

Whereas, the President has authority under the Constitution to take action to deter and prevent acts of international terrorism against the United States.

*Resolved by the Senate and House of Representatives of the United States of America in Congress assembled,*

## SECTION 1. Short Title

This joint resolution may be cited as the "Authorization for Use of Military Force."

## SEC. 2. Authorization for Use of United States Armed Forces

(a) That the President is authorized to use all necessary and appropriate force against those nations, organizations, or persons he determines planned, authorized, committed, or aided the terrorist attacks that occurred on September 11, 2001, or harbored such organizations or persons, in order to prevent any future acts of international terrorism against the United States by such nations, organizations or persons.

(b) WAR POWERS RESOLUTION REQUIREMENTS.—

(1) SPECIFIC STATUTORY AUTHORIZATION.—Consistent with section 8(a)(1) of the War Powers Resolution, the Congress declares that this section is intended to constitute specific statutory authorization within the meaning of section 5(b) of the War Powers Resolution.

(2) APPLICABILITY OF OTHER REQUIREMENTS.—Nothing in this resolution supercedes any requirement of the War Powers Resolution.

U.S. Congress. Senate. *Authorization for Use of Military Force,* S.J. Res. 23, 107th Cong., 1st sess. *Congressional Record* 147, no. 120, daily ed. (September 14, 2001): S 9421. http://frwebgate.access.gpo.gov/cgi-bin/getpage.cgi?dbname=2001_record&page=S9421&position=all (accessed September 15, 2004).

# 86. President George W. Bush's Speech to a Joint Session of Congress
*September 20, 2001*

In the normal course of events, Presidents come to this Chamber to report on the state of the Union. Tonight, no such report is needed. It has already been delivered by the American people. . . .

We have seen the State of our Union in the endurance of rescuers, working past exhaustion. We have seen the unfurling of flags, the lighting of candles, the giving of blood, the saying of prayers in English, Hebrew, and Arabic. We have seen the decency of a loving and giving people who have made the grief of strangers their own.

My fellow citizens, for the last nine days, the entire world has seen for itself the state of our Union—and it is strong.

Tonight we are a country awakened to danger and called to defend freedom. Our grief has turned to anger and anger to resolution. Whether we bring our enemies to justice, or bring justice to our enemies, justice will be done. . . .

On September 11th, enemies of freedom committed an act of war against our country. . . . All of this was brought upon us in a single day and night fell on a different world, a world where freedom itself is under attack.

Americans have many questions tonight. Americans are asking, who attacked our country? The evidence we have gathered all points to a collection of loosely affiliated terrorist organizations known as Al Qaida. They are the same murderers indicted for bombing American embassies in Tanzania and Kenya, and responsible for bombing the *U.S.S. Cole.*

Al Qaida is to terror what the mafia is to crime. But its goal is not making money. Its goal is remaking the world and imposing its radical beliefs on people everywhere.

The terrorists practice a fringe form of Islamic extremism that has been rejected by Muslim scholars and the vast majority of Muslim clerics, a fringe movement that perverts the peaceful teachings of Islam. The terrorists' directive commands them to kill Christians and Jews, to kill all Americans, and make no distinction among military and civilians, including women and children.

This group and its leader, a person named Usama bin Laden, are linked to many other organizations in different countries, including the Egyptian Islamic Jihad and the Islamic Movement of Uzbekistan. There are thousands of these terrorists in more than 60 countries. They are recruited from their own nations and neighborhoods and brought to camps in places like Afghanistan, where they are trained in the tactics of terror. They are sent back to their homes or sent to hide in countries around the world to plot evil and destruction.

The leadership of Al Qaida has great influence in Afghanistan and supports the Taliban regime in controlling most of that country. In Afghanistan, we see Al Qaida's vision for the world.

Afghanistan's people have been brutalized. Many are starving and many have fled. Women are not allowed to attend school. You can be jailed for owning a television. Religion can be practiced only as their leaders dictate. A man can be jailed in Afghanistan if his beard is not long enough.

The United States respects the people of Afghanistan—after all, we are currently its largest source of humanitarian aid—but we condemn the Taliban regime. It is not only repressing its own people, it is threatening people everywhere by sponsoring and sheltering and supplying terrorists. By aiding and abetting murder, the Taliban regime is committing murder.

And tonight, the United States of America makes the following demands on the Taliban: Deliver to United States authorities all the leaders of Al Qaida who hide in your land. Release all foreign nationals, including American citizens, you have unjustly imprisoned. Protect foreign journalists, diplomats, and aid workers in your country. Close immediately and permanently every terrorist training camp in Afghanistan, and hand over every terrorist and every person in their support structure to appropriate authorities. Give the United States full access to terrorist training camps, so we can make sure they are no longer operating.

These demands are not open to negotiation or discussion. The Taliban must act and act immediately. They will hand over the terrorists, or they will share in their fate.

I also want to speak tonight directly to Muslims throughout the world. We respect your faith. It's practiced freely by many millions of Americans and by millions more in countries that America counts as friends. Its teachings are good and peaceful, and those who commit evil in the name of Allah blaspheme the name of Allah. The terrorists are traitors to their own faith, trying, in effect, to hijack Islam itself. The enemy of America is not our many Muslim friends; it is not our many Arab friends. Our enemy is a radical network of terrorists and every government that supports them.

Our war on terror begins with Al Qaida, but it does not end there. It will not end until every terrorist group of global reach has been found, stopped, and defeated. . . .

Our response involves far more than instant retaliation and isolated strikes. Americans should not expect one battle, but a lengthy campaign, unlike any other we have ever seen. It may include dramatic strikes, visible on TV, and covert operations, secret even in success. We will starve terrorists of funding, turn them one against another, drive them from place to place, until there is no refuge or no rest. And we will pursue nations that provide aid or safe haven to terrorism. Every nation, in every region, now has a decision to make. Either you are with us, or you are with the terrorists. From this day forward, any nation that continues to harbor or support terrorism will be regarded by the United States as a hostile regime.

Our Nation has been put on notice: We are not immune from attack. We will take defensive measures against terrorism to protect Americans. Today dozens of Federal departments and agencies, as well as State and local governments, have responsibilities affecting homeland security. These efforts must be coordinated at the highest level. So tonight I announce the creation of a Cabinet-level position reporting directly to me, the Office of Homeland Security.

And tonight I also announce a distinguished American to lead this effort to strengthen American security, a military veteran, an effective Governor, a true patriot, a trusted friend, Pennsylvania's Tom Ridge. He will lead, oversee, and coordinate a comprehensive national strategy to safeguard our country against terrorism and respond to any attacks that may come.

These measures are essential. But the only way to defeat terrorism as a threat to our way of life is to stop it, eliminate it, and destroy it where it grows.

Many will be involved in this effort, from FBI agents to intelligence operatives to the reservists we have called to active duty. All deserve our thanks, and all have our prayers. And tonight, a few miles from the damaged Pentagon, I have a message for our military: Be ready. I've called the Armed Forces to alert, and there is a reason. The hour is coming when America will act, and you will make us proud.

This is not, however, just America's fight, and what is at stake is not just America's freedom. This is the world's fight. This is civilization's fight. This is the fight of all who believe in progress and pluralism, tolerance and freedom. . . .

The civilized world is rallying to America's side. They understand that if this terror goes unpunished, their own cities, their own citizens may be next. Terror, unanswered, cannot only bring down buildings, it can threaten the stability of legitimate governments. And you know what? We're not going to allow it. . . .

After all that has just passed, all the lives taken and all the possibilities and hopes that died with them, it is natural to wonder if America's future is one of fear. Some speak of an age of terror. I know there are struggles ahead and dangers to face. But this country will define our times, not be defined by them. As long as the United States of America is determined and strong, this will not be an age of terror; this will be an age of liberty, here and across the world. . . .

I will not forget this wound to our country and those who inflicted it. I will not yield; I will not rest; I will not relent in waging this struggle for freedom and security for the American people.

The course of this conflict is not known, yet its outcome is certain. Freedom and fear, justice and cruelty have always been at war, and we know that God is not neutral between them.

Fellow citizens, we'll meet violence with patient justice, assured of the rightness of our cause and confident of the victories to come. In all that lies before us, may God grant us wisdom, and may He watch over the United States of America.

Thank you.

Excerpted from U.S. Executive Office of the President. "Address Before a Joint Session of the Congress on the United States Response to the Terrorist Attacks of September 11." *Weekly Compilation of Presidential Documents* 37, no. 38 (September 24, 2001): 1347–1351. http://www.gpoaccess.gov/wcomp/v37no38.html (accessed September 15, 2004).

# 87. U.S. Ambassador John D. Negroponte's Letter to the United Nations Security Council
## October 7, 2001

In accordance with Article 51 of the Charter of the United Nations, I wish, on behalf of my Government, to report that the United States of America, together with other States, has initiated actions in the exercise of its inherent right of individual and collective self-defence following the armed attacks that were carried out against the United States on 11 September 2001.

On 11 September 2001, the United States was the victim of massive and brutal attacks in the states of New York, Pennsylvania and Virginia. These attacks were specifically designed to maximize the loss of life; they resulted in the death of more than 5,000 persons, including nationals of 81 countries, as well as the destruction of four civilian aircraft, the World Trade Center towers and a section of the Pentagon. Since 11 September, my Government has obtained clear and compelling information that the Al-Qaeda organization, which is supported by the Taliban regime in Afghanistan, had a central role in the attacks. There is still much we do not know. Our inquiry is in its early stages. We may find that our self-defence requires further actions with respect to other organizations and other States. . . .

In response to these attacks, and in accordance with the inherent right of individual and collective self-defence, United States armed forces have initiated actions designed to prevent and deter further attacks on the United States. . . .

Excerpted from United Nations Security Council. Letter Dated 7 October 2001 from the Permanent Representative of the United States of America to the United Nations Addressed to the President of the Security Council. S/2001/946, October 7, 2001. http://www.un.int/usa/s-2001-946.htm (accessed September 15, 2004).

# 88. President George W. Bush's Address to the Nation on the Beginning of the Afghan War

*October 7, 2001*

Good afternoon. On my orders, the United States military has begun strikes against Al Qaida terrorist training camps and military installations of the Taliban regime in Afghanistan. These carefully targeted actions are designed to disrupt the use of Afghanistan as a terrorist base of operations and to attack the military capability of the Taliban regime.

We are joined in this operation by our staunch friend, Great Britain. Other close friends, including Canada, Australia, Germany, and France, have pledged forces as the operation unfolds. More than 40 countries in the Middle East, Africa, Europe, and across Asia have granted air transit or landing rights. Many more have shared intelligence. We are supported by the collective will of the world. . . .

Initially, the terrorists may burrow deeper into caves and other entrenched hiding places. Our military action is also designed to clear the way for sustained, comprehensive, and relentless operations to drive them out and bring them to justice.

At the same time, the oppressed people of Afghanistan will know the generosity of America and our allies. As we strike military targets, we'll also drop food, medicine, and supplies to the starving and suffering men and women and children of Afghanistan.

The United States of America is a friend to the Afghan people, and we are the friends of almost a billion worldwide who practice the Islamic faith. The United States of America is an enemy of those who aid terrorists and of the barbaric criminals who profane a great religion by committing murder in its name.

This military action is a part of our campaign against terrorism, another front in a war that has already been joined through diplomacy, intelligence, the freezing of financial assets, and the arrests of known terrorists by law enforcement agents in 38 countries. Given the nature and reach of our enemies, we will win this conflict by the patient accumulation of successes, by meeting a series of challenges with determination and will and purpose.

Today we focus on Afghanistan, but the battle is broader. Every nation has a choice to make. In this conflict, there is no neutral ground. If any government sponsors the outlaws and killers of innocents, they have become outlaws and murderers, themselves. And they will take that lonely path at their own peril. . . .

I know many Americans feel fear today. And our government is taking strong precautions. All law enforcement and intelligence agencies are working aggressively around America, around the world, and around the clock. At my request, many Governors have activated the National Guard to strengthen airport security. We have called up Reserves to reinforce our military capability and strengthen the protection of our homeland.

In the months ahead, our patience will be one of our strengths: patience with the long waits that will result from tighter security; patience and understanding that it will take time to achieve our goals; patience in all the sacrifices that may come.

Today those sacrifices are being made by members of our Armed Forces who now defend us so far from home, and by their proud and worried families. A Commander in Chief sends America's sons and daughters into a battle in a foreign land only after the greatest care and a lot of prayer. . . . We ask them to leave their loved ones, to travel great distances, to risk injury, even to be prepared to make the ultimate sacrifice of their lives. They are dedicated; they are honorable; they represent the best of our country. And we are grateful.

To all the men and women in our military, every sailor, every soldier, every airman, every coastguardsman, every marine, I say this: Your mission is defined; your objectives are clear; your goal is just; you have my full confidence; and you will have every tool you need to carry out your duty. . . .

The battle is now joined on many fronts. We will not waver; we will not tire; we will not falter; and we will not fail. Peace and freedom will prevail.

Thank you. May God continue to bless America.

Excerpted from U.S. Executive Office of the President. "Address to the Nation Announcing Strikes Against Al Qaida Training Camps and Taliban Military Installations in Afghanistan." *Weekly Compilation of Presidential Documents* 37, no. 41 (October 15, 2001): 1432-1433. http://www. gpoaccess.gov/wcomp/v37no41.html (accessed September 15, 2004).

# President Bush Creates the Office of Homeland Security

## INTRODUCTION

When he declared a "war on terrorism" during a speech before a joint session of Congress on September 20, 2001, President George W. Bush devoted only two paragraphs of the thirty-two-paragraph address to announcing that he would create a new Office of Homeland Security and appoint Gov. Tom Ridge, R-Penn., to direct it. "He will lead, oversee, and coordinate a comprehensive national strategy to safeguard our country against terrorism, and respond to any attacks that may come," Bush said. The president added that the cabinet-level position would report directly to him (*see* America Prepares for War Against al Qaeda and Afghanistan, p. 248).

Bush's move to create a vehicle for coordinating efforts by the more than forty federal agencies and departments that played some role in fighting terrorism drew unanimous praise from members of both political parties. At the time the agencies spent more than $11 billion annually, and they were expected to receive tens of billions more in new appropriations. Bush's choice of Ridge, who had served six terms in the House of Representatives before becoming Pennsylvania's governor, also was widely cheered.

For several years, a variety of federal commissions, members of Congress, and terrorism experts had warned that the lack of coordination in federal terrorism efforts severely limited the nation's ability to prevent attacks and respond to any that occurred (*see* Defense Science Board Examines Transnational Threats, p. 199; General Accounting Office Urges Better Coordination of Federal Terrorism Efforts, p. 210; Experts Warn of Increasing Threats to the American Homeland, p. 220).

Two schools of thought existed regarding the best way to defend the nation and respond to any attacks, although differences over details existed within each school. The first advocated creating a new office in the White House to oversee and coordinate efforts among the existing federal departments and agencies that had terrorism responsibilities. The second held that a new federal department should be created that would join together some or all of the existing agencies and departments—ranging from the Department of Agriculture to the U.S. Border Patrol—that played some role in fighting terrorism.

Ironically, on the same day that Bush announced his plan to create an Office of Homeland Security within the White House, the General Accounting Office (GAO)—the investigative arm of Congress—issued a report recommending a similar approach. However, Bush and the GAO differed sharply on how the new office should be created. Bush planned to establish it through an executive order, effectively shutting Congress out of the process. The GAO, by contrast, said the office should be established by legislation "to provide it with legitimacy and authority," guarantee accountability, and ensure continuity across administrations [Document 89].

Accountability was a key theme on September 21, 2001—the day after Bush's speech—at a hearing by the Senate Committee on Governmental Affairs titled "Responding to Homeland Threats: Is Our Government Organized for the Challenge?" Experts testifying at the hearing unanimously agreed it was not. "Our panel's review of the federal bureaucratic structure, spread across numerous agencies vested with some responsibilities for combating terrorism, revealed a structure that is uncoordinated, complex, and confusing," said Gov. James Gilmore, R-Va., chairman of the Advisory Panel to Assess the Capabilities for Domestic Response to Terrorism Involving Weapons of Mass Destruction. Gilmore's panel recommended creating a White House office similar to the one announced by Bush but emphasized that the office must have strong authority over budgets, programs, and other areas to be effective [Document 90].

On October 8, 2001, the details of Bush's plan finally became public when he issued Executive Order 13228, which created the Office of Homeland Security. The order said the office's overall job "shall be to coordinate the executive branch's efforts to detect, prepare for, prevent, protect against, respond to, and recover from terrorist attacks within the United States." However, the order did not give the office direct authority over budgets and programs at federal agencies and departments involved in homeland security [Document 91].

As Bush issued the order, the nation was on high alert for terrorist attacks that might be launched in reprisal for the military assault on Afghanistan by U.S. and British forces that had started the day before. National Guard troops patrolled airports across the country, and Vice President Dick Cheney worked at a secret location away from Washington, D.C., to separate him from Bush and thus help ensure the government's continuity if terrorists targeted the president. The day after Ridge took office, the North Atlantic Treaty Organization (NATO) started dispatching AWACS surveillance planes to patrol the skies over the United States—the first time that NATO had ever helped protect the continental United States. "America has moved to the highest stage of alert at home since World War II," proclaimed a story in *The Wall Street Journal.*

On October 12, 2001—four days after Ridge was sworn in—a stream of terrorism experts testified before the Senate Committee on Governmental Affairs that Bush's executive order did not give Ridge enough power and doomed him to failure. Retired Gen. Barry R. McCaffrey, former director of the White House Office of National Drug Control Policy, was the most blunt. "Notwithstanding [Ridge's] superb credentials, clear access to the Cabinet and to the senior leadership of Congress, within one year, with a small staff of detailees [from other federal agencies], with no federal legislation, with no separate budget, no budget certification, he will be relegated to running the Speaker's Bureau on Counterterrorism Operations," he said [Document 92]. The White House was invited to testify at the hearing but did not appear.

Amid a growing clamor on Capitol Hill to increase Ridge's power or create a new Department of Homeland Security, at a press briefing on October 24, 2001, White House spokesperson Ari Fleischer said Bush opposed both ideas. "Governor Ridge has everything he needs to be able to get his job done," Fleischer said [Document 93].

At a hearing on November 7, 2001, by the House Budget Committee, Comptroller General David M. Walker—the head of the GAO—disagreed with Fleischer. Walker praised Bush's executive order as "a good first step." But he added: "The long-term, expansive nature of the homeland security issue suggests the need for a more sustained and institutionalized approach" [Document 94].

As the debate continued, bills to create a homeland security department were introduced in Congress. Finally, on June 6, 2002, Bush reversed course and announced his own plan to establish a new Department of Homeland Security (*see* Executive Branch, Congress Restructure for Homeland Security, p. 429).

# 89. Combating Terrorism: Selected Challenges and Related Recommendations, General Accounting Office Report

*September 20, 2001*

. . . U.S. policy and strategy for dealing with terrorism, along with the nature and perception of the terrorist threat, have been evolving over the past 30 years. A complex framework of programs and activities across more than 40 federal agencies, bureaus, and offices are in place to combat terrorism. The evolution of these programs came from a variety of Presidential decision directives, implementing guidance, executive orders, interagency agreements, and legislation. . . .

For fiscal year 2002, the federal government's proposed budget for these programs is over $12.8 billion, of which about $8.6 billion is to combat terrorism, about $1.8 billion is to combat weapons of mass destruction, and about $2.6 billion is for critical infrastructure protection (CIP). Compared with the fiscal year 1998 funding level of about $7.2 billion, this proposed budget represents about a 78-percent increase in total funding to combat terrorism. In addition, the Congress recently approved the President's request for $20 billion in emergency assistance and provided an additional $20 billion to supplement existing contingency funds. . . .

Because of the interagency and intergovernmental nature of programs to combat terrorism, certain leadership and coordination functions are needed above the level of individual agencies. These include, among others, overseeing a threat and risk assessment, developing a national strategy, monitoring governmentwide budgets, and coordinating agency implementation. . . .

Based upon years of evaluations, the fragmentation of leadership and coordination . . . and our assessment of the various proposals, our analysis indicates there needs to be a single focal point with responsibility for all critical functions to lead and coordinate these programs. Furthermore, the focal point should be in the Executive Office of the President and be independent of any existing federal agency. Such a position would allow the focal point to be outside the interests of any individual agency. Proposals to create a focal point within a lead agency—whether the Department of Justice or FEMA [Federal Emergency Management Agency]—would not allow the focal point to have the governmentwide perspective needed. Specifically, the focal point needs to be above both crisis and consequence management. In addition, creating a new agency to combine functions currently in several agencies—such as the proposed National Homeland Security

Agency—still would not contain all the government agencies and functions needed to combat terrorism. . . .

We recommend that the President . . . appoint a single focal point that has the responsibility and authority for all critical leadership and coordination functions to combat terrorism. The focal point should have the following characteristics and responsibilities.

- The focal point should be in the Executive Office of the President, outside individual agencies, and encompass activities to include prevention, crisis management, and consequence management.
- The focal point should oversee a national-level authoritative threat and risk assessment on the potential use of weapons of mass destruction by terrorists on U.S. soil. Such assessments should be updated regularly.
- The focal point also should lead the development of a national strategy for combating terrorism. . . .
- The focal point should coordinate implementation of the national strategy among the various federal agencies. This would entail reviewing agency and interagency programs to ensure that they are being implemented in accordance with the national strategy and do not constitute duplication of effort.
- The focal point should analyze and prioritize governmentwide budgets and spending to combat terrorism to eliminate gaps and duplication of effort. The focal point's role will be to provide advice or to certify that the budgets are consistent with the national strategy, not to make final budget decisions. . . .
- The focal point should be established by legislation to provide it with legitimacy and authority and its head should be appointed by the President with the advice and consent of the U.S. Senate. This would provide accountability to both the President and the Congress. Also, it would provide continuity across administrations. . . .

Excerpted from U.S. Congress. General Accounting Office. *Combating Terrorism: Selected Challenges and Related Recommendations.* GAO-01-822, September 20, 2001. http://www.gao.gov/docdblite/summary.php? recflag=&accno=A01496&rptno=GAO-01-822 (accessed September 15, 2004).

## 90. Responding to Homeland Threats: Is Our Government Organized for the Challenge? Senate Committee on Governmental Affairs Hearing

*September 21, 2001*

Senator RUDMAN [former Sen. Warren Rudman, R-N.H., co-chair of the U.S. Commission on National Security/21st Century]: . . . The President has moved quickly to establish an office of homeland security. We do not know yet the details of the office, but [it] would appear to be what is generally called the czar approach. We have had drug czars and others. . . . It is a very good method to bring attention to a recognized problem. Moreover, it is a very good way in time of crisis to encourage improved coordination between disparate agencies which, in normal times, tend to pursue their own bureaucratic purposes.

We applaud the President's initiative and heartily endorse Governor Ridge, who is known to all of us. It is a great choice. For an enduring solution to what we feel certain will be a long-term problem, we believe the President must move beyond this White House office and establish a major department with homeland security, with a seat at the cabinet table, as its singular mission.

We believe that without budget authority, command authority, accountability, and responsibility to the Congress and to the President, nothing in this government ever works very well, but we applaud this step, and we believe that the Congress and the President can build on it. . . .

Senator HART [former Sen. Gary Hart, D-Colo., co-chair of the U.S. Commission on National Security/21st Century]: . . . No homeland czar can possibly hope to coordinate the almost hopeless dispersal of authority that currently characterizes the 40 or 50 agencies or elements of agencies with some piece of responsibility for protecting our homeland. . . .

Governor GILMORE [Gov. James Gilmore, R-Va., chairman of the Advisory Panel to Assess the Capabilities for Domestic Response to Terrorism Involving Weapons of Mass Destruction]: . . . Our panel's review of the federal bureaucratic structure, spread across numerous agencies vested with some responsibilities for combating terrorism, revealed a structure that is uncoordinated, complex, and confusing. . . . Our research indicated that attempts to create a federal focal point for coordination with state and local officials—such as the National Domestic Preparedness Office—have met with little success. Moreover, many state and local officials believe that federal programs intended to assist at their levels are often created and implemented without sufficient consultation. We concluded that the current bureaucratic structure lacks the requisite authority and accountability to make policy changes and impose the discipline necessary among the numerous federal agencies involved. . . .

Our proposal is an office located in the White House, reporting directly to the President of the United States—not a separate agency that competes for turf against other agencies and even Cabinet Secretaries. . . .

[T]he director [of the proposed National Office for Combating Terrorism] must be politically accountable and responsible. Therefore, he must be vested with sufficient authority to accomplish the office's goals. . . . That is why we have recommended the director be appointed by the President, confirmed by the Senate, and serve in a "cabinet-level" position.

The office should have sufficient budget authority and programmatic oversight to influence the resource allocation process and ensure program compatibility and effectiveness. The best way to instill this attribute is to give the director a "certification" power—a process by which he could formally "decertify" all or part of an agency's budget as "non-compliant" with a national strategy. . . .

Senator HART: I think it gets down to one word, and that is accountability. If a White House office has authority to coordinate, the agencies that it has authority to coordinate are not necessarily accountable to that office. They are accountable to their department head, cabinet secretary or whatever. They will accept the coordination recommendations. There will be a lot of task forces and working groups and so forth, but no one is accountable. No one is accountable today. . . .

Excerpted from U.S. Congress. Senate. *Responding to Homeland Threats: Is Our Government Organized for the Challenge? Hearing before the Senate Committee on Governmental Affairs.* 107th Cong., 1st sess. S. Hrg. 107-207, September 21, 2001. http://frwebgate.access.gpo.gov/cgi-bin/useftp.cgi?IPaddress=162.140.64.88&filename=76801.pdf&directory=/diskc/wais/data/107_senate_hearings (accessed September 15, 2004).

# 91. Executive Order 13228: Establishment of the Office of Homeland Security and the Homeland Security Council

*October 8, 2001*

By the authority vested in me as President by the Constitution and the laws of the United States of America, it is hereby ordered as follows:

*Section 1. Establishment.* I hereby establish within the Executive Office of the President an Office of Homeland Security (the "Office") to be headed by the Assistant to the President for Homeland Security.

*Sec. 2. Mission.* The mission of the Office shall be to develop and coordinate the implementation of a comprehensive national strategy to secure the United States from terrorist threats or attacks. . . .

*Sec. 3. Functions.* The functions of the Office shall be to coordinate the executive branch's efforts to detect, prepare for, prevent, protect against, respond to, and recover from terrorist attacks within the United States.

(a) *National Strategy.* The Office shall work with executive departments and agencies, State and local governments, and private entities to ensure the adequacy of the national strategy for detecting, preparing for, preventing, protecting against, responding to, and recovering from terrorist threats or attacks within the United States and shall periodically review and coordinate revisions to that strategy as necessary.

(b) *Detection.* The Office shall identify priorities and coordinate efforts for collection and analysis of information within the United States regarding threats of terrorism against the United States and activities of terrorists or terrorist groups within the United States. The Office also shall identify, in coordination with the Assistant to the President for National Security Affairs, priorities for collection of intelligence outside the United States regarding threats of terrorism within the United States. . . .

(c) *Preparedness.* The Office of Homeland Security shall coordinate national efforts to prepare for and mitigate the consequences of terrorist threats or attacks within the United States. In performing this function, the Office shall work with Federal, State, and local agencies, and private entities, as appropriate, to:

(i) review and assess the adequacy of the portions of all Federal emergency response plans that pertain to terrorist threats or attacks within the United States;

(ii) coordinate domestic exercises and simulations designed to assess and practice systems that would be called upon to respond to a terrorist threat or attack within the United States and coordinate programs and activities for training Federal, State, and local employees who would be called upon to respond to such a threat or attack;

(iii) coordinate national efforts to ensure public health preparedness for a terrorist attack, including reviewing vaccination policies and reviewing the adequacy of and, if necessary, increasing vaccine and pharmaceutical stockpiles and hospital capacity;

(iv) coordinate Federal assistance to State and local authorities and nongovernmental organizations to prepare for and respond to terrorist threats or attacks within the United States;

(v) ensure that national preparedness programs and activities for terrorist threats or attacks are developed and are regularly evaluated under appropriate standards and that resources are allocated to improving and sustaining preparedness based on such evaluations; and

(vi) ensure the readiness and coordinated deployment of Federal response teams to respond to terrorist threats or attacks, working with the Assistant to the President for National Security Affairs, when appropriate.

(d) *Prevention.* The Office shall coordinate efforts to prevent terrorist attacks within the United States. In performing this function, the Office shall work with Federal, State, and local agencies, and private entities, as appropriate, to:

(i) facilitate the exchange of information among such agencies relating to immigration and visa matters and shipments of cargo; and, working with the Assistant to the President for National Security Affairs, ensure coordination among such agencies to prevent the entry of terrorists and terrorist materials and supplies into the United States and facilitate removal of such terrorists from the United States, when appropriate;

(ii) coordinate efforts to investigate terrorist threats and attacks within the United States; and

(iii) coordinate efforts to improve the security of United States borders, territorial waters, and airspace in order to prevent acts of terrorism within the United States, working with the Assistant to the President for National Security Affairs, when appropriate.

(e) *Protection.* The Office shall coordinate efforts to protect the United States and its critical infrastructure from the consequences of terrorist attacks. In performing this function, the Office shall work with Federal, State, and local agencies, and private entities, as appropriate, to:

(i) strengthen measures for protecting energy production, transmission, and distribution services and critical facilities; other utilities; telecommunications; facilities that produce, use, store, or dispose of nuclear material; and other critical infrastructure services and critical facilities within the United States from terrorist attack;

(ii) coordinate efforts to protect critical public and privately owned information systems within the United States from terrorist attack;

(iii) develop criteria for reviewing whether appropriate security measures are in place at major public and privately owned facilities within the United States;

(iv) coordinate domestic efforts to ensure that special events determined by appropriate senior officials to have national significance are protected from terrorist attack;

(v) coordinate efforts to protect transportation systems within the United States, including railways, highways, shipping, ports and waterways, and airports and civilian aircraft, from terrorist attack;

(vi) coordinate efforts to protect United States livestock, agriculture, and systems for the provision of water and food for human use and consumption from terrorist attack; and

(vii) coordinate efforts to prevent unauthorized access to, development of, and unlawful importation into the United States of, chemical, biological, radiological, nuclear, explosive, or other related materials that have the potential to be used in terrorist attacks.

(f) *Response and Recovery.* The Office shall coordinate efforts to respond to and promote recovery from terrorist threats or attacks within the United States. . . .

(g) *Incident Management.* The Assistant to the President for Homeland Security shall be the individual primarily responsible for coordinating the domestic response efforts of all departments and agencies in the event of an imminent terrorist threat and during and in the immediate aftermath of a terrorist attack within the United States and shall be the principal point of contact for and to the President with respect to coordination of such efforts. . . .

(h) *Continuity of Government.* The Assistant to the President for Homeland Security, in coordination with the Assistant to the President for National Security Affairs, shall review plans and preparations for ensuring the continuity of the Federal Government in the event of a terrorist attack that threatens the safety and security of the United States Government or its leadership.

(i) *Public Affairs.* The Office, subject to the direction of the White House Office of Communications, shall coordinate the strategy of the executive branch for communicating with the public in the event of a terrorist threat or attack within the United States. The Office also shall coordinate the development of programs for educating the public about the nature of terrorist threats and appropriate precautions and responses.

(j) *Cooperation with State and Local Governments and Private Entities.* The Office shall encourage and invite the participation of State and local governments and private entities, as appropriate, in carrying out the Office's functions.

(k) *Review of Legal Authorities and Development of Legislative Proposals.* The Office shall coordinate a periodic review and assessment of the legal authorities available to executive departments and agencies to permit them to perform the functions described in this order. . . .

(l) *Budget Review.* The Assistant to the President for Homeland Security, in consultation with the Director of the Office of Management and Budget (the "Director") and the heads of executive departments and agencies, shall identify programs that contribute to the Administration's strategy for homeland security and, in the development of the President's annual budget submission, shall review and provide advice to the heads of departments and agencies for such programs. . . .

Excerpted from U.S. Executive Office of the President. Executive Order 13228—Establishing the Office of Homeland Security and the Homeland Security Council. *Weekly Compilation of Presidential Documents* 37, no. 41 (October 15, 2001): 1434-1439. http://www.gpoaccess.gov/wcomp/ v37no41.html (accessed September 15, 2004).

# 92. Legislative Options to Strengthen Homeland Defense, Senate Committee on Governmental Affairs Hearing

*October 12, 2001*

Senator [Robert] BENNETT [R-Utah]: . . . I entered the executive branch in the first of the Nixon administrations in 1969 at the Department of Transportation [as it was being created]. . .

It took the FAA [Federal Aviation Administration], which was an independent agency, the Urban Mass Transit Administration, which was part of HUD [Department of Housing and Urban Development], the Federal Highway Administration, which was in [the Department of] Commerce, the Coast Guard, which was in [the Department of the] Treasury, the St. Lawrence Seaway, and I have forgotten where it was, and the Federal Rail Administration that was created de novo to be part of this Department of Transportation—and all this was done in the Johnson Administration, and the Department was 18 months old when President Nixon was elected, and I was part of the team that went in to take over that Department.

I saw firsthand . . . how badly it was struggling to come together and how difficult those 18 months were. In the next 2 years . . . we struggled mightily just to pull the thing together and make it work. It was one of the most difficult, exhilarating, educational management experiences of my young life, to go through that. I just want to sound a note of caution, having been through that experience, that the idea of pulling together a group of existing agencies, ripping them out of the roots that they have established in the departments where they exist, and then putting them together on what looks like a very clean piece of paper, in terms of an organizational chart, is a very difficult reality . . . .

Ms. HARMAN [Rep. Jane Harman, D-Calif., ranking member of the House Intelligence Committee and a member of the National Commission on Terrorism]: . . . According to President Bush's Executive Order, Governor Ridge's mission is to "develop and coordinate the implementation" of a comprehensive national strategy against terrorism. But he is not directed to actually *develop* the strategy itself—in fact, no one appears to be.

Ridge is directed to "advise" the Office of Management and Budget on the appropriateness of other agencies' budgets for homeland security. But he is not given real budget authority.

He is authorized to "review" plans and preparations for ensuring the continuity of government.

He is directed to "work" with executive departments and agencies to "ensure" the adequacy of the national strategy for detecting, preparing for, preventing, protecting against, responding to, and recovering from terrorist threats or attacks.

He is directed to "encourage" and "invite" the participation of state and local governments and private entities to carry out his office's duties.

And he is subject to the White House Office of Communications in "coordinating" the strategy of communicating with the public in the event of a terrorist attack.

Governor Ridge has been told to do a lot of things, but has to rely on the cooperation of the various departments and agencies to succeed.

Beyond his persuasive abilities and his close relationship with the President, Ridge has none of the tools required to force coordination of efforts or to win turf battles.

And the turf battles have already begun. . . .

Mr. HAMILTON [former Rep. Lee Hamilton, D-Ind., member of the U.S. Commission on National Security/21st Century and director of the Woodrow Wilson International Center for Scholars]: . . . In the view of the Hart-Rudman Commission, terrorism is the number one threat to the national security of the United States. If that is true, and we believe that unanimously—if it is true, then that has profound implications as to how the government should be organized and how the resources of the government should be allocated. . . .

The administration has emphasized that Governor Ridge will have access to the President and strong support from him. I do not doubt that, but it is not enough. There are dozens of people who have access to the President of the United States, and without a legislative framework providing budgetary authority and staff, his power will be uncertain and subject to the vagaries of future Presidents and their attention to homeland security. It looks to me like, as I understand it, Governor Ridge will have borrowed staff, uncertain power over department budgets, and have very little control over counter-terrorism budgets of the more than 40 agencies that he is to oversee. He will lack the tools necessary to force those agencies to carry out his plans and work together. . . .

General MCCAFFREY [Gen. (Ret.) Barry R. McCaffrey, former director of the White House Office of National Drug Control Policy]: . . . Governor Ridge's attempt to organize what I would primarily see as the domestic aspect of that problem is one that is vitally needed, and I applaud the President for identifying such a superb public servant and for giving him his initial authority. Nothing but good can come out of that.

Let me, if I may, however, offer a notion that if you skim-read the Presidential order that set up his effort, there is no mention of the Armed Forces. There is no adviser from the Chairman of the Joint Staff or the armed forces on this council. It is a coordinating, not a directing, authority. It does not mention missile defense, cyber warfare, counter-drug, economic warfare, information warfare, civil disturbances, national disasters, or any other aspect except a narrow definition of counterterrorism. . . .

[Ridge] lacks budgetary authority. There will be no unity of effort in supporting exercises, training and directing the responsible use of monies in the current bureaucratic format. More importantly . . . it lacks the force of law. . . .

He is not charged with developing a national strategy, with articulating it. He has not been given budget certification authority or decertification authority. He has not been specifically identified as a policy coordination authority. There is no requirement to develop a performance measure-of-effectiveness system. . . . There is no requirement on him to report to the Congress. . . .

There is no authority to call interagency meetings. He does not have his own staff and budget. . . .

In sum, I would argue that notwithstanding this man's superb credentials, clear access to the Cabinet and to the senior leadership of Congress, within one year, with a small staff of detailees, with no federal legislation, with no separate budget, no budget certification, he will be relegated to running the Speaker's Bureau on Counterterrorism Operations. . . .

General BOYD [Gen. (Ret.) Charles G. Boyd, director of the Washington office of the Council on Foreign Relations and executive director of the U.S. Commission on National Security/21st Century]: . . . The recent initiative taken by the Bush administration is a good "First Step," a step hopefully that will not become the last step. Our Commission believed another step, creation of an agency or department, is critical to success. Some believe that the National Homeland Security Agency is a "great idea," but that the time is not right to reorganize the government—not now, in the middle of a crisis. I strongly disagree. Were the crisis likely to be a short one, I might say wait. But, if this is to be, as our President believes, and certainly I believe, a very protracted struggle lasting years or perhaps decades, why would we want to continue indefinitely with a dysfunctional system, or even a sub-optimal one?

As long as a sense of urgency exists, former governor Ridge may be partially successful in his new office. I am thankful for that. However, as soon as the level of fear declines even slightly, old bureaucratic prerogatives will resurface—possibly aided by Congressional committees trying to guard their oversight responsibilities—and current organizations vested with different aspects of homeland security will ultimately move to regain control of resources and missions. . . .

Excerpted from U.S. Congress. Senate. *Legislative Options to Strengthen Homeland Defense. Hearing before the Senate Committee on Governmental Affairs.* 107th Cong., 1st sess. S. Hrg. 107-212, October 12, 2001. http://purl.access.gpo.gov/GPO/LPS22107 (accessed September 15, 2004).

# 93. White House Press Secretary Ari Fleischer's Press Briefing
*October 24, 2001*

[Response to a question about a meeting earlier in the day between selected members of Congress, President George W. Bush, and Gov. Tom Ridge, director of the Office of Homeland Security].

One of the purposes of the meeting . . . was it's no secret that there are a number of members of Congress—some of whom came down to the White House today—who believe that legislation is necessary to give Governor Ridge more power, the power that they think he may need. And they received a very strong message from the President today that no legislation is necessary; that Governor Ridge has all the power that he needs; that Governor Ridge, by virtue of the fact that he is in such proximity to the President, has the ear of the President, has the respect of the President, Governor Ridge has everything he needs to be able to get his job done. And that was the message that the President and the Governor gave to members of Congress earlier today.

Excerpted from U.S. Executive Office of the President. Office of the Press Secretary. Press Briefing by Ari Fleischer on October 24, 2001. Available by searching http://pdq.state.gov (accessed September 15, 2004).

# 94. Homeland Security: Challenges and Strategies in Addressing Short- and Long-Term National Needs, General Accounting Office Congressional Testimony

*November 7, 2001*

. . . Both the focus of the executive order and the appointment of a coordinator within the Executive Office of the President fit the need to act rapidly in response to the threats that surfaced in the events of September 11 and the anthrax issues we continue to face. Although this was a good first step, a number of important questions related to institutionalizing and sustaining the effort over the long term remain, including:

- What will be included in the definition of homeland security? What are the specific homeland security goals and objectives?
- How can the coordinator identify and prioritize programs that are spread across numerous agencies at all levels of government? What criteria will be established to determine whether an activity does or does not qualify as related to homeland security?
- How can the coordinator have a real impact in the budget and resource allocation process?
- Should the coordinator's roles and responsibilities be based on specific statutory authority? And if so, what functions should be under the coordinator's control?
- Depending on the basis, scope, structure, and organizational location of this new position and entity, what are the implications for the Congress and its ability to conduct effective oversight? . . .

The long-term, expansive nature of the homeland security issue suggests the need for a more sustained and institutionalized approach. . . .

Excerpted from U.S. Congress. General Accounting Office. *Homeland Security: Challenges and Strategies in Addressing Short- and Long-Term National Needs.* Prepared testimony of David M. Walker, Comptroller General of the United States, for a hearing by the House Committee on the Budget. GAO-02-160T, November 7, 2001. http://www.gao.gov/docdblite/getrpt.php?rptno=GAO-02-160T (accessed September 15, 2004).

# Aviation Security on
# September 11, 2001

## INTRODUCTION

On September 11, 2001, nineteen hijackers passed through security checkpoints at airports in Boston, Newark, and Washington, D.C., with no significant problems. After they smashed two commercial airplanes into New York's World Trade Center and a third into the Pentagon just outside Washington, D.C., at 9:42 a.m. the Federal Aviation Administration (FAA) ordered all planes in American airspace to land immediately at the nearest airport. The unprecedented order came too late to save United Airlines Flight 93, which hijackers already controlled and crashed into a Pennsylvania field at 10:03 a.m. after passengers stormed the cockpit. The hijackers of Flight 93 had reportedly planned to crash the plane into the White House or the U.S. Capitol.

As the tragedy unfolded, two questions immediately arose: How did the hijackers take over the planes? If they used weapons, how did they get the weapons past airport security screeners?

Nine days after the hijackings, on September 20, 2001, an expert from the General Accounting Office (GAO) testified before the Senate Commerce Committee about some of the aviation security problems his agency had uncovered before September 11. Gerald Dillingham, director of physical infrastructure issues for the GAO, said the problems included poor security for the FAA's air traffic control computer systems; a lack of controls limiting access to secure areas at airports, including aircraft; and continuing poor performance by airport security screeners. For more than a decade before September 2001, the GAO—the investigative arm of Congress—the inspector general at the Department of Transportation, and federal commissions had repeatedly documented a wide range of flaws in the nation's aviation security system [Document 95].

On May 22, 2003, the Department of Transportation's inspector general testified before the National Commission on Terrorist Attacks Upon the United States, more commonly known as the 9/11 Commission. Kenneth Mead said that before September 11, the aviation security system suffered from "significant weaknesses," many of which "existed for years." He added that the aviation security model then in place "was mostly based on reacting to known security threats instead of being proactive against potential threats" [Document 96].

The staff of the 9/11 Commission issued a statement on January 27, 2004, that said there was no evidence the FAA possessed "any credible and specific intelligence" indicating that Osama bin Laden, al Qaeda, or any other terrorists were "actually plotting" to hijack commercial planes and use them as weapons. But it found that at least as far back as March 1998, the FAA's Office of Civil Aviation Security had "officially considered" the potential for terrorist suicide hijackings in the United States. "However," the staff wrote, "in a presentation the agency made to air carriers and airports in 2000 and early 2001 the FAA discounted the threat because, 'fortunately, we have no indication that any group is currently thinking in that direction.' "

The staff also criticized the FAA for setting vague standards regarding what items passengers were banned from carrying aboard planes. FAA rules banned knives with blades four inches or longer but let the airlines decide whether to allow shorter knives. The airlines decided that shorter knives were fine, and the hijackers on September 11 used such knives to kill or incapacitate pilots and others when they seized control of the four planes [Document 97].

One of the most startling findings in the Final Report issued by the 9/11 Commission on July 22, 2004, was that—contrary to government accounts at the time and later—fighter aircraft had absolutely no chance to intercept and shoot down any of the four hijacked planes. According to the commission's minute-by-minute account of events on September 11, the FAA notified the North American Aerospace Defense Command (NORAD), which is charged with protecting U.S. airspace, just nine minutes before the first aircraft—American Airlines Flight 11—struck the World Trade Center. That notification occurred only because officials at the FAA's Boston Control Center deviated from protocols and the chain of command by contacting NORAD themselves. For the other three planes, the FAA failed to notify NORAD at all or notified NORAD as the hijacked planes were striking their targets, according to the commission [Document 98].

# 95. Aviation Security: Terrorist Acts Illustrate Severe Weaknesses in Aviation Security, General Accounting Office Congressional Testimony

*September 20, 2001*

A safe and secure civil aviation system is a critical component of the nation's overall security, physical infrastructure, and economic foundation. Billions of dollars and a myriad of programs and policies have been devoted to achieving such a system. Although it is not fully known at this time what actually occurred or what all the weaknesses in the nation's aviation security apparatus are that contributed to the horrendous events of last week, it is clear that serious weaknesses exist in our aviation security system and that their impact can be far more devastating than previously imagined.

We are here today to discuss the vulnerabilities that we have identified throughout the nation's aviation system. . . .

In summary:

- As we reported last year, our reviews of the Federal Aviation Administration's (FAA) oversight of air traffic control (ATC) computer systems showed that FAA had not followed some critical aspects of its own security requirements. Specifically, FAA had not ensured that ATC buildings and facilities were secure, that the systems themselves were protected, and that the contractors who access these systems had undergone background checks. As a result, the ATC system was susceptible to intrusion and malicious attacks. FAA is making some progress in addressing the 22 recommendations we made to improve computer security, but most have yet to be completed.
- Controls for limiting access to secure areas, including aircraft, have not always worked as intended. As we reported in May 2000, our special agents used fictitious law enforcement badges and credentials to gain access to secure areas, bypass security checkpoints at two airports, and walk unescorted to aircraft departure gates. The agents, who had been issued tickets and boarding passes, could have carried weapons, explosives, or other dangerous objects onto aircraft. FAA is acting on the weaknesses we identified and is implementing improvements to more closely check the credentials of law enforcement officers. The Department of Transportation's Inspector General has also documented

numerous problems with airport access controls, and in one series of tests, the Inspector General's staff successfully gained access to secure areas 68 percent of the time.

- As we reported in June 2000, tests of screeners revealed significant weaknesses as measured in their ability to detect threat objects located on passengers or contained in their carry-on luggage. In 1987, screeners missed 20 percent of the potentially dangerous objects used by FAA in its tests. At that time, FAA characterized this level of performance as unsatisfactory. More recent results have shown that as testing gets more realistic—that is, as tests more closely approximate how a terrorist might attempt to penetrate a checkpoint—screeners' performance declines significantly. A principal cause of screeners' performance problems is the rapid turnover among screeners. Turnover exceeded over 100 percent a year at most large airports, leaving few skilled and experienced screeners, primarily because of the low wages, limited benefits, and repetitive, monotonous nature of their work. Additionally, too little attention has been given to factors such as the sufficiency of the training given to screeners. FAA's efforts to address these problems have been slow. We recommended that FAA develop an integrated plan to focus its efforts, set priorities, and measure progress in improving screening. FAA is addressing these recommendations, but progress on one key effort—the certification of screening companies—is still not complete because the implementing regulation has not been issued. It is now nearly 2 1/2 years since FAA originally planned to implement the regulation.
- Screening operations in Belgium, Canada, France, the Netherlands, and the United Kingdom—countries whose systems we have examined—differ from this country's in some significant ways. Their screening operations require more extensive qualifications and training for screeners, include higher pay and better benefits, and often include different screening techniques, such as "pat-downs" of some passengers. Another significant difference is that most of these countries place responsibility for screening with airport authorities or the government instead of air carriers. The countries we visited had significantly lower screener turnover, and there is some evidence they may have better screener performance; for example, one country's screeners detected over twice as many test objects as did U.S. screeners in a 1998 joint screener testing program conducted with FAA. . . .

It has been observed that previous tragedies have resulted in congressional hearings, studies, recommendations, and debates, but little long-term resolve to correct flaws in the system as the memory of the crisis recedes. The future of aviation security hinges in large part on overcoming this cycle of limited action that has too often characterized the response to aviation security concerns. . . .

Excerpted from U.S. Congress. General Accounting Office. *Aviation Security: Terrorist Acts Illustrate Severe Weaknesses in Aviation Security.* Prepared testimony of Gerald L. Dillingham for a hearing by the Subcommittees on Transportation of the Senate and House Committees on Appropriations. GAO-01-1166T, September 20, 2001. http://www.gao.gov/new.items/d011166t.pdf (accessed September 15, 2004).

## 96. Statement before the National Commission on Terrorist Attacks Upon the United States on Aviation Security, Department of Transportation Inspector General's Testimony

*May 22, 2003*

. . . The aviation security system in place before September 11th had undergone some incremental improvements over the years, such as deployment of explosives detection machines, and probably provided a deterrent value to certain types of threats. However, neither the system nor the model on which it was based worked very well, and there were significant weaknesses in the protection it provided—even for the type of threat the model was designed to prevent. . . .

Before September 11th, the aviation security model was mostly based on reacting to known security threats instead of being proactive against potential threats. The model, dating back to the early 1970's, was implemented through a system of shared responsibilities. Industry provided and paid for the security; FAA's role was to establish security requirements and ensure compliance with these requirements.

Within the model were counter pressures to control security costs and limit the impact of security on aviation operations, so that industry could concentrate on its primary mission of moving passengers seamlessly and safely through the system. In our opinion, these counter pressures manifested themselves as significant weaknesses in the security system that we and others repeatedly found during audits and investigative work. Many of these weaknesses, even for the threats the model was designed to prevent, existed for years, such as underutilization of bulk explosives detection machines, lack of performance standards for screening companies and their employees, inadequate controls to prevent unauthorized access to secure areas of the airport, ineffective background investigation requirements for employees working at the airport, and deficiencies in the cargo security program. For example:

- Air carriers were required to screen passengers and their carry-on baggage but would typically award the screening contract to the lowest bidder. Employees of these screening companies typically received only the minimum required security training (15 hours) and usually received prevailing minimum wages—it was not unusual for the starting wages at airport fast-food restaurants to be higher than the wages screeners received. These conditions, along with others, resulted in screener turnover rates as high as 400 percent annually.

  Our 1996 report on efforts to improve airport security, and audits going back nearly a decade before this, found that screeners frequently failed to detect threat items—firearms and mock explosives—at security checkpoints. However, FAA never issued a final rule on the certification of screening companies to address the deficiencies in screening operations, even though the rule was required by the Federal Aviation Reauthorization Act of 1996. In early 1997, FAA issued an Advanced Notice of Proposed Rulemaking (ANPRM) on certification of screening companies. It was withdrawn in May 1998 and re-issued in January 2000. FAA was prepared to issue its final rule on the certification of screening companies the week of September 10, 2001.

- In 1998, we found that air carriers were significantly underutilizing explosives detection systems (EDS) already deployed and that continued low use would affect operator proficiency and prevent effective measurement of how dependable the equipment was in actual operations. Overriding reasons that EDS was underutilized were that air carriers were only required to use the machines to screen the baggage of passengers selected by Computer-Assisted Passenger Prescreening System (CAPPS) and the machine had a high false alarm rate. The requirement to screen only selectees' bags addressed the air carriers' concerns that screening more than selectees' checked baggage would compound the delays air carriers were already experiencing in their operations. Therefore, equipment with a demonstrated ability to improve airport security often sat idle in airport lobbies.

- Criminal investigations we conducted before and after September 11th showed serious weaknesses in background checks of contract screener and airport workers. In October 2000, one of the Nation's largest private security companies pled guilty and paid more than $1 million in fines and restitutions for falsifying criminal history checks and screener qualification records at one of the Nation's largest airports. Before September 11th, little public attention was given to the seriousness of this issue. . . .

Excerpted from U.S. Department of Transportation. Office of the Inspector General. *Statement Before the National Commission on Terrorist Attacks Upon the United States on Aviation Security.* May 22, 2003. http://www.oig. dot.gov/item_details.php?item=1101 (accessed September 15, 2004).

# 97. The Aviation Security System and the 9/11 Attacks, National Commission on Terrorist Attacks Upon the United States Staff Statement

*January 27, 2004*

## Intelligence

The first layer of defense was intelligence. While the FAA was not a member of the U.S. Intelligence Community, the agency maintained a civil aviation intelligence division that operated 24 hours per day. The intelligence watch was the collection point for a flow of threat related information from federal agencies, particularly the FBI, CIA, and State Department. . . .

While the staff has not completed its review and analysis as to what the FAA knew about the threat posed by al Qaeda to civil aviation, including the potential use of aircraft as weapons, we can say:

First, no documentary evidence reviewed by the Commission or testimony we have received to this point has revealed that any level of the FAA possessed any credible and specific intelligence indicating that Usama Bin Ladin, al Qaeda, al Qaeda affiliates or any other group were actually plotting to hijack commercial planes in the United States and use them as weapons of mass destruction.

Second, the threat posed by Usama Bin Ladin, al Qaeda, and al Qaeda affiliates, including their interest in civil aviation, was well known to key civil aviation security officials. The potential threat of Middle Eastern terrorist groups to civil aviation security was acknowledged in many different official FAA documents. The FAA possessed information claiming that associates with Usama Bin Ladin in the 1990s were interested in hijackings and the use of an aircraft as a weapon.

Third, the potential for terrorist suicide hijacking in the United States was officially considered by the FAA's Office of Civil Aviation Security dating back to at least March 1998. However in a presentation the agency made to air carriers and airports in 2000 and early 2001 the FAA discounted the threat because, "fortunately, we have no indication that any group is currently thinking in that direction."

It wasn't until well after the 9/11 attacks that the FAA learned of the "Phoenix EC"—an internal FBI memo written in July of 2001 by an FBI agent in the Phoenix field office suggesting steps that should be taken by the Bureau to look more closely at civil aviation education schools around the country and the use of such programs by individuals who may be affiliated with terrorist organizations.

Fourth, the FAA was aware prior to September 11, 2001, of the arrest of Zacarias Moussaoui in Minnesota, a man arrested by the INS [Immigration and Naturalization Service] in August of 2001 following reports of suspicious behavior in flight school and the determination that he had overstayed his visa waiver period. Several key issues remain regarding what the FAA knew about Moussaoui, when they knew it, and how they responded to the information supplied by the FBI, which we are continuing to pursue.

Fifth, the FAA did react to the heightened security threat identified by the Intelligence Community during the summer of 2001, including issuing alerts to air carriers about the potential for terrorist acts against civil aviation. In July 2001, the FAA alerted the aviation community to reports of possible near-term terrorist operations . . . particularly on the Arabian Peninsula and/or Israel. The FAA informed the airports and air carriers that it had no credible evidence of specific plans to attack U.S. civil aviation. The agency said that some of the currently active groups were known to plan and train for hijackings and had the capability to construct sophisticated improvised explosive devices concealed inside luggage and consumer products. The FAA encouraged all U.S. Carriers to exercise prudence and demonstrate a high degree of alertness.

Although several civil aviation security officials testified that the FAA felt blind when it came to assessing the domestic threat because of the lack of intelligence on what was going on in the American homeland as opposed to overseas, FAA security analysts did perceive an increasing terrorist threat to U.S. civil aviation at home. FAA documents, including agency accounts published in the Federal Register on July 17, 2001, expressed the FAA's understanding that terrorist groups were active in the United States and maintained an historic interest in targeting aviation, including hijacking. While the agency was engaged in an effort to pass important new regulations to improve checkpoint screener performance, implement anti-sabotage measures, and conduct ongoing assessments of the system, no major increases in anti-hijacking security measures were implemented in response to the heightened threat levels in the spring and summer of 2001, other than general warnings to the industry to be more vigilant and cautious. . . .

## Prescreening

. . . The hijackers purchased their tickets for the 9/11 flights in a short period of time at the end of August 2001, using credit cards, debit cards, or cash. The ticket record provides the FAA and the air carrier with passenger information for the prescreening process.

The first major prescreening element in place on 9/11 was the FAA listing of individuals known to pose a threat to commercial aviation. Based on information provided by the Intelligence Community, the FAA required air carriers to prohibit listed individuals from boarding aircraft or, in designated cases, to assure that the passenger received enhanced screening before boarding. None of the names of the 9/11 hijackers were identified by the FAA to the airlines in order to bar them from flying or subject them to extra security measures. In fact, the number of individuals subject to such special security instructions issued by the FAA was less than 20 compared to the tens of thousands of names identified in the State Department's TIPOFF watch list.

The second component of prescreening was a program to identify those passengers on each flight who may pose a threat to aviation. In 1998, the FAA required air carriers to implement a FAA-approved computer-assisted passenger prescreening program (CAPPS) designed to identify the pool of passengers most likely in need of additional security scrutiny. The program employed customized, FAA-approved criteria derived from a limited set of information about each ticketed passenger in order to identify "selectees."

FAA rules required that the air carrier only screen each selectee's checked baggage for explosives using various approved methods. However, under the system in place on 9/11, selectees—those who were regarded as a risk to the aircraft—were not required to undergo any additional screening of their person or carry-on baggage at the checkpoint.

The consequences of selection reflected FAA's view that non-suicide bombing was the most substantial risk to domestic aircraft. Since the system in place on 9/11 confined the consequences of selection to the screening of checked bags for explosives, the application of CAPPS did not provide any defense against the weapons and tactics employed by the 9/11 hijackers. . . .

## Checkpoint Screening

. . . As of 2001 any confidence that checkpoint screening was operating effectively was belied by numerous publicized studies by the General Accounting Office and the Department of Transportation's Office of Inspector General. Over the previous twenty years they had documented repeatedly serious, chronic weaknesses in the systems deployed to screen passengers and baggage for weapons or bombs. Shortcomings with the screening process had also been identified internally by the FAA's assessment process.

Despite the documented shortcomings of the screening system, the fact that neither a hijacking nor a bombing had occurred domestically in over a decade was perceived by many within the system as confirmation that it was working. . . .

The evolution of checkpoint screening illustrates many of the systemic problems that faced the civil aviation security system in place on 9/11. The executive and legislative branches of government, and the civil aviation industry were highly reactive on aviation security matters. Most of the aviation security system's features had developed in response to specific incidents, rather than in anticipation. Civil aviation security was primarily accomplished through a slow and cumbersome rulemaking process—a reflection of the [FAA's] conflicting missions of both regulating and promoting the industry. A number of FAA witnesses said this process was the "bane" of civil aviation security. For example, the FAA attempted to set a requirement that it would certify screening contractors. The FAA Aviation Reauthorization Act of 1996 directed the FAA to take such action, which the 1997 Gore Commission endorsed. But the process of implementing this action had still not been completed by September 11, 2001.

Those are systemic observations. But, to analyze the 9/11 attack, we had to focus on which items were prohibited and which were allowed to be carried into the cabin of an aircraft. FAA guidelines were used to determine what objects should not be allowed into the cabin of an aircraft. Included in the listing were knives with blades 4 inches long or longer and/or knives considered illegal by local law; and tear gas, mace, and similar chemicals.

These guidelines were to be used by screeners, to make a reasonable determination of what items in the possession of a person should be considered a deadly or dangerous weapon. The FAA told the air carriers that common sense should prevail.

Hence the standards of what constituted a deadly or dangerous weapon were somewhat vague. Other than for guns, large knives, explosives and incendiaries, determining what was prohibited and what was allowable was up to the common sense of the carriers and their screening contractors.

To write out what common sense meant to them, the air carriers developed, through their trade associations, a Checkpoint Operations Guide. This document was approved by the FAA. The edition of this guide in place on September 11, 2001, classified "box cutters," for example as "Restricted" items that were not permitted in the passenger cabin of an aircraft. The checkpoint supervisor was required to be notified if an item in this category was encountered. Passengers would be given the option of having those items transported as checked baggage. "Mace," "pepper spray," as well as "tear gas" were categorized as hazardous materials and passengers could not take items in that category on an airplane without the express permission of the airline.

On the other hand, pocket utility knives (less than 4 inch blade) were allowed. The Checkpoint Operations Guide provided no further guidance on how to distinguish between "box cutters" and "pocket utility knives." . . .

In practice, we believe the FAA's approach of admonishing air carriers to use common sense about what items should not be allowed on an aircraft, while also approving the air carrier's checkpoint operations guidelines that defined the industry's "common sense," in practice, created an environment where both parties could deny responsibility for making hard and most likely unpopular decisions. . . .

Return again to the perspective of the enemy. The plan required all of the hijackers to successfully board the assigned aircraft. If several of their number failed to board, the operational plan might fall apart or their operational security might be breached. To have this kind of confidence, they had to develop a plan they felt would work anywhere they were screened, regardless of the quality of the screener. We believe they developed such a plan and practiced it in the months before the attacks, including in test flights, to be sure their tactics would work. In other words, we believe they did not count on a sloppy screener. All 19 hijackers were able to pass successfully through checkpoint screening to board their flights. They were 19 for 19. They counted on beating a weak system. . . .

Excerpted from U.S. National Commission on Terrorist Attacks Upon the United States. *The Aviation Security System and the 9/11 Attacks.* Staff Statement No. 3. January 27, 2004. http://www.9-11commission.gov/ hearings/hearing7/staff_statement_3.pdf (accessed September 15, 2004).

# 98. Chapter 1: "We Have Some Planes," Final Report of the National Commission on Terrorist Attacks Upon the United States
*July 22, 2004*

## 1.2 Improvising a Homeland Defense

### The FAA and NORAD
On 9/11, the defense of U.S. airspace depended on close interaction between two federal agencies: the FAA [Federal Aviation Administration]

and the North American Aerospace Defense Command (NORAD). The most recent hijacking that involved U.S. air traffic controllers, FAA management, and military coordination had occurred in 1993. . . .

*FAA Mission and Structure.* As of September 11, 2001, the FAA was mandated by law to regulate the safety and security of civil aviation. . . .

*NORAD Mission and Structure.* NORAD is a binational command established in 1958 between the United States and Canada. Its mission was, and is, to defend the airspace of North America and protect the continent. That mission does not distinguish between internal and external threats; but because NORAD was created to counter the Soviet threat, it came to define its job as defending against external attacks.

The threat of Soviet bombers diminished significantly as the Cold War ended, and the number of NORAD alert sites was reduced from its Cold War high of 26. . . . NORAD perceived the dominant threat to be from cruise missiles. Other threats were identified during the late 1990s, including terrorists' use of aircraft as weapons. Exercises were conducted to counter this threat, but they were not based on actual intelligence. In most instances, the main concern was the use of such aircraft to deliver weapons of mass destruction. . . .

Exercise planners also assumed that the aircraft would originate from outside the United States, allowing time to identify the target and scramble interceptors. The threat of terrorists hijacking commercial airliners within the United States—and using them as guided missiles—was not recognized by NORAD before 9/11.

Notwithstanding the identification of these emerging threats, by 9/11 there were only seven alert sites left in the United States, each with two fighter aircraft on alert. This led some NORAD commanders to worry that NORAD was not postured adequately to protect the United States. . . .

*Interagency Collaboration.* The FAA and NORAD had developed protocols for working together in the event of a hijacking. As they existed on 9/11, the protocols for the FAA to obtain military assistance from NORAD required multiple levels of notification and approval at the highest levels of government.

FAA guidance to controllers on hijack procedures assumed that the aircraft pilot would notify the controller via radio or by "squawking" a transponder code of "7500"—the universal code for a hijack in progress. Controllers would notify their supervisors, who in turn would inform management all the way up to FAA headquarters in Washington. Headquarters had a hijack coordinator, who was the director of the FAA Office of Civil Aviation Security or his or her designate.

If a hijack was confirmed, procedures called for the hijack coordinator on duty to contact the Pentagon's National Military Command Center (NMCC) and to ask for a military escort aircraft to follow the flight, report anything unusual, and aid search and rescue in the event of an emergency. The NMCC would then seek approval from the Office of the Secretary of

Defense to provide military assistance. If approval was given, the orders would be transmitted down NORAD's chain of command.

The NMCC would keep the FAA hijack coordinator up to date and help the FAA centers coordinate directly with the military. NORAD would receive tracking information for the hijacked aircraft either from joint use radar or from the relevant FAA air traffic control facility. Every attempt would be made to have the hijacked aircraft squawk 7500 to help NORAD track it.

The protocols did not contemplate an intercept. They assumed the fighter escort would be discreet, "vectored to a position five miles directly behind the hijacked aircraft," where it could perform its mission to monitor the aircraft's flight path. . . .

On the morning of 9/11, the existing protocol was unsuited in every respect for what was about to happen.

### American Airlines Flight 11

*FAA Awareness.* . . . At 8:14, when the flight failed to heed [instructions to climb from the FAA's Boston Control Center], the controller repeatedly tried to raise the flight. He reached out to the pilot on the emergency frequency. Though there was no response, he kept trying to contact the aircraft.

At 8:21, American 11 turned off its transponder, immediately degrading the information available about the aircraft. The controller told his supervisor that he thought something was seriously wrong with the plane, although neither suspected a hijacking. The supervisor instructed the controller to follow standard procedures for handling a "no radio" aircraft.

The controller checked to see if American Airlines could establish communication with American 11. He became even more concerned as its route changed, moving into another sector's airspace. Controllers immediately began to move aircraft out of its path, and asked other aircraft in the vicinity to look for American 11.

At 8:24:38, the following transmission came from American 11:

> *American 11: We have some planes. Just stay quiet, and you'll be okay.*
> *We are returning to the airport.*

The controller only heard something unintelligible; he did not hear the specific words "we have some planes." The next transmission came seconds later:

> *American 11: Nobody move. Everything will be okay. If you try to make*
> *any moves, you'll endanger yourself and the airplane. Just stay quiet.*

The controller told us that he then knew it was a hijacking. He alerted his supervisor, who assigned another controller to assist him. He redoubled his efforts to ascertain the flight's altitude. Because the controller didn't understand the initial transmission, the manager of Boston Center instructed his quality assurance specialist to "pull the tape" of the radio transmission, listen to it closely, and report back.

Between 8:25 and 8:32, in accordance with the FAA protocol, Boston Center managers started notifying their chain of command that American 11 had been hijacked. At 8:28, Boston Center called the [FAA's Central] Command Center in Herndon [Virginia] to advise that it believed American 11 had been hijacked and was heading toward New York Center's airspace.

By this time, American 11 had taken a dramatic turn to the south. At 8:32, the Command Center passed word of a possible hijacking to the Operations Center at FAA headquarters. The duty officer replied that security personnel at headquarters had just begun discussing the apparent hijack on a conference call with the New England regional office. FAA headquarters began to follow the hijack protocol but did not contact the NMCC [National Military Command Center] to request a fighter escort. . . .

*Military Notification and Response.* Boston Center did not follow the protocol in seeking military assistance through the prescribed chain of command. In addition to notifications within the FAA, Boston Center took the initiative, at 8:34, to contact the military . . . . At 8:37:52, Boston Center reached NEADS [NORAD's Northeast Defense Sector]. This was the first notification received by the military—at any level—that American 11 had been hijacked. . . .

F-15 fighters were scrambled at 8:46 from Otis Air Force Base [in Falmouth, Massachusetts]. But NEADS did not know where to send the alert fighter aircraft . . . . Because the hijackers had turned off the plane's transponder, NEADS personnel spent the next minutes searching their radar scopes for the primary radar return. American 11 struck the North Tower at 8:46. Shortly after 8:50, while NEADS personnel were still trying to locate the flight, word reached them that a plane had hit the World Trade Center. . . .

In summary, NEADS received notice of the hijacking nine minutes before it struck the North Tower. That nine minutes' notice before impact was the most the military would receive of any of the four hijackings.

### United Airlines Flight 175

*FAA Awareness.* . . . [When the FAA's Boston Control Center learned that a second plane had hit the World Trade Center, it] immediately advised the New England Region that it was going to stop all departures at airports under its control. At 9:05, Boston Center confirmed for both the FAA Command Center and the New England Region that the hijackers aboard American 11 said "we have *planes*." At the same time, New York Center declared "ATC zero"—meaning that aircraft were not permitted to depart from, arrive at, or travel through New York Center's airspace until further notice.

Within minutes of the second impact, Boston Center instructed its controllers to inform all aircraft in its airspace of the events in New York and to advise aircraft to heighten cockpit security. Boston Center asked the Herndon [National] Command Center to issue a similar cockpit security alert nationwide. We have found no evidence to suggest that the Command Center acted on this request or issued any type of cockpit security alert.

*Military Notification and Response.* The first indication that the NORAD air defenders had of the second hijacked aircraft, United 175, came in a phone call from New York Center to NEADS at 9:03. The notice came at about the time the plane was hitting the South Tower. . . .

### United Airlines Flight 93

*FAA Awareness.* . . . By 9:34, word of the hijacking had reached FAA headquarters. . . .

At approximately 9:36, Cleveland [Control Center] advised the [FAA's National] Command Center that it was still tracking United 93 and specifically inquired whether someone had requested the military to launch fighter aircraft to intercept the aircraft. Cleveland even told the Command Center it was prepared to contact a nearby military base to make the request. . . .

At 9:42, the Command Center learned from news reports that a plane had struck the Pentagon. The Command Center's national operations manager, Ben Sliney, ordered all FAA facilities to instruct all aircraft to land at the nearest airport. This was an unprecedented order. The air traffic control system handled it with great skill, as about 4,500 commercial and general aviation aircraft soon landed without incident. . . .

Despite the discussions about military assistance, no one from FAA headquarters requested military assistance regarding United 93. Nor did any manager at FAA headquarters pass any of the information it had about United 93 to the military. . . .

### Clarifying the Record

The defense of U.S. airspace on 9/11 was not conducted in accord with preexisting training and protocols. It was improvised by civilians who had never handled a hijacked aircraft that attempted to disappear, and by a military unprepared for the transformation of commercial aircraft into weapons of mass destruction. As it turned out, the NEADS air defenders had nine minutes' notice on the first hijacked plane, no advance notice on the second, no advance notice on the third, and no advance notice on the fourth.

We do not believe that the true picture of that morning reflects discredit on the operational personnel at NEADS or FAA facilities. NEADS commanders and officers actively sought out information, and made the best judgments they could on the basis of what they knew. Individual FAA controllers, facility managers, and Command Center managers thought outside the box in recommending a nationwide alert, in ground-stopping local traffic, and, ultimately, in deciding to land all aircraft and executing that unprecedented order flawlessly.

More than the actual events, inaccurate government accounts of those events made it appear that the military was notified in time to respond to two of the hijackings, raising questions about the adequacy of the response. Those accounts had the effect of deflecting questions about the military's capacity to obtain timely and accurate information from its own sources. In addition, they overstated the FAA's ability to provide the military with timely and useful information that morning. . . .

## 1.3 National Crisis Management

. . . In Sarasota, Florida, the presidential motorcade was arriving at the Emma E. Booker Elementary School, where President Bush was to read to a class and talk about education. White House Chief of Staff Andrew Card told us he was standing with the President outside the classroom when Senior Advisor to the President Karl Rove first informed them that a small, twin-engine plane had crashed into the World Trade Center. The President's reaction was that the incident must have been caused by pilot error.

At 8:55, before entering the classroom, the President spoke to National Security Advisor Condoleezza Rice, who was at the White House. She recalled first telling the President it was a twin-engine aircraft—and then a commercial aircraft—that had struck the World Trade Center . . . .

*The FAA and White House Teleconferences.* The FAA, the White House, and the Defense Department each initiated a multiagency teleconference before 9:30. Because none of these teleconferences—at least before 10:00— included the right officials from both the FAA and Defense Department, none succeeded in meaningfully coordinating the military and FAA response to the hijackings. . . .

### The President and the Vice President

The President was seated in a classroom when, at 9:05, Andrew Card whispered to him: "A second plane hit the second tower. America is under attack." The President told us his instinct was to project calm, not to have the country see an excited reaction at a moment of crisis. The press was standing behind the children; he saw their phones and pagers start to ring. The President felt he should project strength and calm until he could better understand what was happening. The President remained in the classroom for another five to seven minutes while the children continued reading. . . .

Excerpted from U.S. National Commission on Terrorist Attacks Upon the United States. *The 9/11 Commission Report: Final Report of the National Commission on Terrorist Attacks Upon the United States.* Chapter 1. July 22, 2004. http://www.9-11commission.gov (accessed September 15, 2004).

# More Than 1,200 People Detained in September 11 Investigation

## INTRODUCTION

In the weeks and months following the terrorist attacks on September 11, 2001, law enforcement officials had two goals: stop any other imminent attacks and find anyone who had helped the hijackers. As part of this effort, officers arrested more than 1,200 people—almost all of them men of Middle Eastern or South Asian descent—on suspicions they were terrorists or were witnesses to terrorist activities. The administration of President George W. Bush released little information about the detainees. Administration officials said the secrecy was necessary to keep terrorists from gaining valuable information about the scope of their investigation, but civil liberties advocates and some detainee lawyers said the secrecy violated the U.S. Constitution.

Many of the men arrested were illegal immigrants. They were typically jailed for violating immigration laws, such as overstaying their visas. Previously, immigration laws were rarely enforced inside the United States, and the nation had hundreds of thousands of "overstays."

Under federal law before the post–September 11 arrests began, the Immigration and Naturalization Service (INS) had twenty-four hours after taking an immigrant into custody to decide whether to file criminal charges. But on September 17, 2004, INS Commissioner Jim Ziglar—acting under orders from Attorney General John Ashcroft—issued a rule that significantly expanded the detention law. Under the new law, which took effect immediately, the INS was given forty-eight hours to decide whether to file criminal charges against an immigrant "except in the event of an emergency or other extraordinary circumstance in which case a determination will be made within an additional reasonable period of time." The change effectively authorized the INS to detain immigrants indefinitely [Document 99].

On September 21, 2001, Chief Immigration Judge Michael Creppy—again acting at Ashcroft's direction—ordered that all deportation hearings for detainees of "special interest" in the government's investigation be held in secret. News organizations and civil liberties groups said the blanket order was unconstitutional because it closed all hearings without a case-by-case determination whether security concerns required the information blackout.

Exactly two weeks after the attacks—on September 25, 2001—Ashcroft told the House Judiciary Committee that 352 people had been arrested in the nationwide dragnet for suspects and witnesses, and that authorities were seeking 400 others. Ashcroft said the INS was holding ninety-eight people for allegedly violating immigration laws, and that the other 254 were being held as "material witnesses" or had been charged with minor crimes such as traffic offenses. "We are conducting this effort with a total commitment to protect the rights and privacy of all Americans and the constitutional protections we hold dear," Ashcroft told the committee.

At a press conference on November 27, 2001, Ashcroft said slightly more than 600 people remained in custody. He refused to disclose any information regarding the 548 people who were being held on immigration charges. "We're removing suspected terrorists who violate the law from our streets to prevent further terrorist attack," Ashcroft said. "We believe we have al Qaeda membership in custody, and we will use every constitutional tool to keep suspected terrorists locked up." Ashcroft noted that some people had accused the Justice Department of barring detainees from contacting attorneys or their families, but he denied the charges. "I would hope that those who make allegations about something as serious as a violation of an individual's civil rights would not do so lightly or without specificity or without facts," Ashcroft said [Document 100].

A week later, an attorney who represented one of the detainees provided the specificity and facts that Ashcroft had demanded. Gerald H. Goldstein, a San Antonio attorney and former president of the National Association of Criminal Defense Attorneys, testified before the Senate Committee on the Judiciary about his efforts to represent Al-Badr Al Hazmi, a fifth-year radiology resident at the University of Texas Health Science Center. Federal agents seized Al Hazmi and searched his home early in the morning of September 12, 2001. After Al Hazmi made a brief phone call to Goldstein that was cut off by an INS agent, Goldstein and a quickly hired immigration lawyer tried unsuccessfully for days to find out why and where their client was being held. During this period, Goldstein testified, Al Hazmi made repeated requests to consult with his attorney that were ignored. On September 14, agents from the

Federal Bureau of Investigation (FBI) took Al Hazmi to New York, and three days later Goldstein finally learned where he was. On September 24, the FBI cleared and released Al Hazmi. "While my client has been completely absolved of any wrongdoing or connection to the acts of terrorism," Goldstein said, "I am still prohibited by court order from discussing certain aspects of the case." He also criticized the "extraordinary secrecy" that surrounded the post–September 11 investigation. "Many of my colleagues who represent past or current detainees share my view that this veil of secrecy serves only to shield the government from criticism," he said [Document 101].

Shortly after the arrests began, allegations that the detainees were being mistreated started appearing in the media. On June 2, 2003, the Justice Department's internal watchdog confirmed many of the allegations in a report that focused on the 762 illegal immigrants who had been arrested. Inspector General Glenn A. Fine found "significant problems" with the treatment of the detainees after their arrests, including physical and verbal abuse; harsh jail conditions; long delays in informing detainees of the charges against them; improper limits on access to lawyers and family members; and lengthy delays in deporting detainees who had no ties to terrorism [Document 102].

Ashcroft avoided questions about the report after its release. However, Justice Department spokesperson Barbara Comstock said: "We make no apologies for finding every legal way possible to protect the American public from further terrorist attacks."

On January 13, 2004, the *Boston Globe* reported that the government had not disclosed how many detainees remained in custody. But at least three were released during the year:

- In April 2004 a federal judge ordered the release of a Palestinian activist who had been held for nearly two years. The government had charged him with overstaying his visa and sought to deport him after his release.
- In May 2004 a former San Diego State student was deported to his home country of Yemen after spending nearly three years in jail. Following his arrest shortly after the 2001 attacks, federal investigators said Mohdar Abdullah was friends with three of the hijackers and may have helped them. But he was only charged with lying on an asylum application.
- On June 29, 2004, a Pakistani man who was a legal permanent resident lost his final deportation appeal after being jailed for nearly three years. Ansar Mahmood, who delivered pizzas, was arrested in October 2001 while taking autumn photographs near a reservoir in upstate New York. Federal officials initially thought he was scouting the reservoir for an attack, but they ultimately decided his picture taking was innocent. However, when federal agents searched his home, they found that Mahmood had cosigned for an apartment and registered a car for friends who were illegal immigrants. Those were deportable crimes.

Detainees, news organizations, civil liberties groups, and others filed numerous lawsuits regarding the detentions. Three cases made it to the U.S. Supreme Court by early fall 2004:

- On May 27, 2003, the Court declined without comment to hear a case challenging the secret deportation hearings. The U.S. Court of Appeals for the Third Circuit had upheld the secret proceedings, while the U.S. Court of Appeals for the Sixth Circuit had ruled that closed hearings violated the First Amendment. The Supreme Court's rejection of the case left both rulings by the lower courts standing even though they conflicted. The previous month, the Justice Department had announced that the government designated 766 detainees to be of "special interest," and 611 of them had one or more hearings in secret.
- On January 12, 2004, the Court declined without comment to hear an appeal of a lower-court ruling that upheld the government's decision to keep secret the names of detainees and details about their cases.
- On February 23, 2004, the Court declined to hear a challenge to the total secrecy imposed by the government in a case involving an Algerian who worked as a waiter and may have served meals to some of the September 11 hijackers. Mohamed Kamel Bellahouel had filed a habeas corpus petition challenging his detention, but the proceedings were conducted in secret and all documents kept under seal. The mere existence of his case became public only by accident, and he was released without being charged.

On April 13, 2004, the Department of Homeland Security announced new rules aimed at preventing the prolonged detention of immigrants without evidence. Under the new rules, an immigrant could be held without charge more than forty-eight hours only if the FBI proclaimed a national security emergency and a high-ranking FBI official approved the detention. The rules also required periodic reviews of cases so that detainees who were cleared of criminal charges did not remain jailed indefinitely.

By September 2004, not a single person arrested in the post-September 11 sweep had been charged with any crime related to the attacks. The vast bulk of the detainees who were illegal immigrants were deported after spending anywhere from hours to nearly three years in jail. Other detainees were charged with minor crimes or released without charge. The one person the government had charged in connection with the attacks, Zacarias Moussaoui, was arrested the month before the hijackings.

## 99. New Immigration and Naturalization Service Rule Regarding Alien Detentions

*September 17, 2001*

### Background

The current rule provides that unless voluntary departure is granted, the Service must make determinations within 24 hours of an alien's arrest whether to continue the alien in custody or to release the alien on bond or recognizance and whether to issue a notice to appear and a warrant of arrest. However, this 24-hour period is not mandated by constitutional requirements. The interim rule provides the Service 48 hours to make these determinations, except in the event of emergency or other extraordinary circumstance in which case the Service must make such determinations within an additional reasonable period of time.

### Explanation of Changes

. . . The immediate implementation of this interim rule without public comment is necessary to ensure that the Service has sufficient time, personnel, and resources to process cases—including establishing true identities and communicating with other law enforcement agencies—that arise in connection with the emergency posed by the recent terrorist activities perpetrated on United States soil. This rule does not alter the standards for issuing charging documents or determining the issue of custody or release, but simply extends the period by which the Service must make such determinations. For this reason, the Service has determined that there is good cause to publish this interim rule and to make it effective immediately, because the delays inherent in the regular notice and comment process would be "impracticable, unnecessary and contrary to the public interest". . . .

Excerpted from U.S. Department of Justice. Immigration and Naturalization Service. *8 CFR Part 287, Custody Procedures.* September 17, 2001. *Federal Register* 66:48334–48335. http://www.access.gpo.gov/su_docs/fedreg/a010920c.html (accessed September 15, 2004).

# 100. Press Conference by Attorney General John Ashcroft

*November 27, 2001*

As I've discussed previously, the Department of Justice is now focused on two important priorities: first, finding those responsible for the horrific acts of September the 11th, and second and more importantly, making sure that we prevent any further terrorist activity. Through dozens of warnings to law enforcement, a delicate campaign and a deliberate campaign of terrorist disruption, tighter security around potential targets, with arrests and detentions, we have avoided further major terrorist attacks, and we've avoided these further major terrorist attacks despite threats and videotape tauntings. America's defenses have grown stronger.

We are standing firm in our commitment to protect American lives. The Department of Justice is waging a deliberate campaign of arrest and detention to protect American lives. We're removing suspected terrorists who violate the law from our streets to prevent further terrorist attack. We believe we have al Qaeda membership in custody, and we will use every constitutional tool to keep suspected terrorists locked up.

The department has charged 104 individuals on federal criminal charges. Fifty-five of these individuals are currently in custody on federal criminal charges. Although some of the indictments or complaints are filed under seal by order of the court, the department has made available the public complaints.

For example, Luis Martinez Flores was charged with helping hijackers Hani Hanjour and Khalid al-Midhar obtain fraudulent Virginia identification cards. Mohammed Adbi was charged with forging a housing subsidy check. Adbi's phone number and name were found on a map retrieved from hijacker Alhamzi's car that was left at the Dulles airport on September the 11th.

Osama al-Adallah was charged with making false statements to the grand jury. His name was also found in Alhamzi's car left at Dulles. Faisal al-Samni was charged with giving false statements to the FBI in connection with the investigation into the September 11th attacks. Al-Samni lied about his association with Hani Hanjour, one of the hijackers. . . .

There are currently 548 individuals who are in custody on immigration charges. . . . For those detained by the INS, I do not think it is responsible for us, in a time of war, when our objective is to save American lives, to advertise to the opposing side that we have al Qaeda membership in custody. When the United States is at war, I will not share valuable intelligence with our enemies. We might as well mail this list to the Osama bin Laden al Qaeda network as to release it. The al Qaeda network may be able to get information about which terrorists we have in our custody, but they'll have to get it on their own and get it from someone other than me.

These detainees do have a right to counsel. The . . . 554, I believe it is, in INS custody—but they do not have a right to taxpayer-funded counsel. The INS assists detainees with information about how to obtain free counsel, which is available. In addition, they have the right to make phone calls to family or attorneys. Also, they can make their identity public, if they wish to. There is no gag order preventing them from doing so.

There are other individuals who have been detained who are currently being detained on material-witness warrants. Those proceedings are being conducted under seal as related to grand juries and, therefore, the department cannot provide the number or identity of those individuals. . . .

While I am aware of various charges being made by organizations and individuals about the actions of the Justice Department, I have yet to be informed of a single lawsuit filed against the government charging a violation of someone's civil rights as a result of this investigation.

One of the accusations suggests that detainees are not able to be represented by an attorney or to contact their families. As you have just heard me discuss, this is simply not true. I would hope that those who make allegations about something as serious as a violation of an individual's civil rights would not do so lightly or without specificity or without facts. This does a disservice to our entire justice system . . . .

Q: . . Yesterday, you explicitly [said] the law prevents us [from releasing the names of detainees]. . . . What law did you have in mind?

Ashcroft: Well, we're dealing with different categories of detainees, and these—

Q: Not the ones under seal, but all the others I ask about—

Ashcroft: The law relating to Immigration and Naturalization Service detainees is different from the law relating to people detained pursuant to criminal charges. The names which I gave today are those names which are already public as a result of the publicity given to criminal charges that are filed and that are not under seal. . . .

I do not believe that it's appropriate for us to provide a list, nor do I believe the law provides that we should provide a list of the INS detainees, and therefore, I haven't used their names. We have provided, in compliance with the law, certain information about those kinds of detainees with the names redacted.

Now, it's very possible that some individuals that we think might be terrorists might someday, by further investigation, be shown not to be terrorists. I think it would be inappropriate for us to either advertise the fact of their detention or to provide the suggestion that they are terrorists in a way which would be prejudicial to their not only privacy interest but personal interest. And for that reason, we are not going to do that. The law is simply different in the area of criminal complaints than it is from INS detentions. The department is following that law scrupulously. . . .

Q: Is there any specific law that prevents you from releasing the names of the INS detainees?

Ashcroft: We believe that the rules regarding INS detentions would provide that it's improper for us to release those names. And we not only think that it's improper in terms of the legal sense—and that's why when we've released documents, we've released documents with the names redacted—but we believe that it would be inappropriate for us at a time of war to provide that information, as well. . . .

Q: Would you be willing to have like a bipartisan commission, civil liberties commission, perhaps appointed by Congress, oversee the conduct of this massive investigation to ensure that there aren't any civil liberty violations?

Ashcroft: Well, that's an interesting and novel idea. In one respect, it's novel. In another respect, it sounds like the Justice—or the Judiciary Committee of the House or Senate. We already have bipartisan committees whose responsibility it is to oversee the Justice Department. . . .

Q: But the Judiciary Committee has other responsibilities. What about—

Ashcroft: Do you think there would be other groups that wouldn't have any other responsibilities?

Q: Well, what about a full-time commission, civil liberties commission, that basically has the confidence of Congress, that could assure the American people that civil liberties are not—

Ashcroft: Maybe you ought to make that your platform when you run for president next time!

Excerpted from U.S. Department of Justice. Office of the Attorney General. "Attorney General Ashcroft Provides Total Number of Federal Criminal Charges and INS Detainees." Press release, November 27, 2001. http://www.justice.gov/ag/speeches/2001/agcrisisremarks11_27.htm (accessed September 15, 2004).

# 101. Testimony of Attorney Gerald H. Goldstein at a Hearing by the Senate Committee on the Judiciary

*December 4, 2001*

In the early morning hours of September 12, 2001, Dr. Al-Badr Al Hazmi, a fifth-year radiology resident at the University of Texas Health Science Center in San Antonio, Texas, was studying for his upcoming medical board exams, when federal law enforcement agents entered his home, searched the premises for some six hours, and took Dr. Al Hazmi into custody. Immigration authorities transported Dr. Al Hazmi to the nearby Comal County Jail.

Later that afternoon, Dr. Al Hazmi was allowed a brief telephone call to my office, at which time he explained that he was being held by United States Immigration authorities and inquired as to the reasons for his detention. Almost immediately, an Immigration and Naturalization Agent took the telephone and told me that he could provide no information regarding the reason for my client's detention, nor his whereabouts; he then referred me to his "supervisor."

After my numerous telephone calls to the supervising agent on September 12th and 13th went unanswered, I wrote a letter to the Immigration and Naturalization Service, seeking to ascertain the whereabouts of my client and requesting an opportunity to communicate with him. . . .

Dr. Al Hazmi's repeated requests to consult with his attorney were ignored, as authorities continued to interrogate him. . . .

On September 13, 2001, my office retained an immigration attorney, and both counsel filed formal "Notice[s] of Entry of Appearance as Attorney" on INS Form G–28.

When I was finally able to reach the "supervising" INS agent, on September 14, 2001, he advised that he too was unable to provide me with access to, or any information regarding my client, referring me instead to an attorney with the Immigration Services' Trial Litigation Unit.

However, when I reached the Immigration Services' attorney, he advised that he could not speak to me about Dr. Al Hazmi and would not provide any information regarding the whereabouts of my client.

On that same day, Mr. Shivers, the immigration attorney hired by our firm, sent a letter to the District Director of the Immigration Service, detailing counsels' repeated attempts to determine the whereabouts of our client, again requesting an opportunity to consult with Dr. Al Hazmi, and expressing his concern that "misrepresentations were knowingly made to prevent our consulting with our client."

I then sent a letter to the acting United States Attorney for our district (copying the Assistant United States Attorney whom I had been advised was assigned the case), again attempting to ascertain the whereabouts of my client and making a "formal demand" for an opportunity to consult with him. . . .

Earlier that day, Dr. Al Hazmi had been taken by FBI agents to New York, and held in a lower Manhattan detention facility, without an opportunity to contact his family as to his whereabouts or have any contact or consult with his attorney.

The following sequence of events brought this Kafkaesque experience to a conclusion:

On September 17, 2001, almost a week after my client had been taken into custody, I was advised that he was being detained by Federal authorities in New York City.

On September 18, 2001, local New York counsel, hired by my office, was advised by the detention facility authorities that he would not be permitted to visit with Dr. Al Hazmi, because the court had appointed a different lawyer to represent him, without Dr. Al Hazmi's knowledge.

On September 19, 2001, the local counsel hired by my office was permitted to visit with Dr. Al Hazmi at the Manhattan detention facility. On September 24, 2001, the FBI cleared and released Dr. Al Hazmi. He returned home to San Antonio the following day.

The Department of Justice has denied that any of the detainees are being held incommunicado, suggesting that any interference with the right to counsel was due to time compression and administrative shortcomings. However, as the above scenario demonstrates, Dr. Al Hazmi was not someone who simply "slipped through the cracks." Dr. Al Hazmi was represented by retained counsel who had filed formal notices of appearance on behalf of their client. Moreover, Dr. Al Hazmi's attorneys had notified the appropriate law enforcement agencies and the Department of Justice in writing, requesting the whereabouts of their client and expressing their desire to communicate with him. Despite these efforts—and despite Dr. Al Hazmi's repeated requests to consult with his counsel—Federal authorities stonewalled and continued to interrogate Dr. Al Hazmi in the absence of his counsel.

By denying Dr. Al Hazmi access to his retained counsel, Federal law enforcement officials not only violated my client's rights, they deprived themselves of valuable information and documentation that would have eliminated many of their concerns. Their obstructionism prolonged the investigative process, wasting valuable time and precious resources. . . .

The right to the assistance of counsel is the cornerstone of our adversarial system. One need only read *Miranda v. Arizona,* which recounts the widespread abuses that plagued our nation's interrogation rooms, to fully appreciate the risks that accompany any abrogation of the right to counsel. . . .

These are among the concerns that mandate a right to representation not only when one is charged with a crime, but when one is subjected to custodial interrogation as well. It is well-established that once an individual in custody requests counsel, all further questioning must cease. . . .

The government's current dragnet-style investigation—characterized by ethnic profiling, selective enforcement of criminal and immigration laws, and pretrial detention for petty offenses—heightens the important role counsel plays from the very inception of custody.

The interests protected by defense counsel go beyond the procedural protections guaranteed by the Bill of Rights. As recognized by the Innocence Protection Act, introduced by Chairman Leahy and supported by NACDL [National Association of Criminal Defense Lawyers], without the effective representation of counsel, not only are innocent persons incarcerated or worse, but the guilty go free.

The right to counsel also serves as an invaluable check on the illegitimate or indiscriminate use of government power. At no time is this right more important than when the government has acquired or claimed sweeping new powers. . . .

While my client has been completely absolved of any wrongdoing or connection to the acts of terrorism, I am still prohibited by court order from discussing certain aspects of the case. The extraordinary secrecy which has characterized the post–9/11 investigation has made it difficult for defense lawyers to discuss the facts surrounding their clients' detentions and impossible for the public to gain a complete picture of the government's tactics. Many of my colleagues who represent past or current detainees share my view that this veil of secrecy serves only to shield the government from criticism. . . .

Excerpted from U.S. Congress. Senate. *Department of Justice Oversight: Preserving Our Freedoms While Defending Against Terrorism.* Prepared testimony of Gerald H. Goldstein for a hearing by the Committee on the Judiciary. 107th Cong., 1st sess, serial J-107-50, December 4, 2001. http://purl.access.gpo.gov/GPO/LPS25921 (accessed September 15, 2004).

---

# 102. Justice Department Inspector General's Report about Alien Detentions, June 2, 2003

*June 2, 2003*

## Chapter One: Introduction

. . . The Federal Bureau of Investigation (FBI) immediately initiated a massive investigation, called "PENTTBOM," into this coordinated terrorist attack [on September 11]. The FBI investigation focused on identifying the terrorists who hijacked the airplanes and anyone who aided their efforts. In addition, the FBI worked with other federal, state, and local law enforcement agencies to prevent follow-up attacks in this country and against U.S. interests abroad.

Shortly after the attacks, the Attorney General directed the FBI and other federal law enforcement personnel to use "every available law enforcement tool" to arrest persons who "participate in, or lend support to, terrorist activities." One of the principal responses by law enforcement authorities after the September 11 attacks was to use the federal immigration laws to detain aliens suspected of having possible ties to terrorism. Within 2 months of the attacks, law enforcement authorities had detained, at least for questioning, more than 1,200 citizens and aliens nationwide. Many of these individuals were questioned and subsequently released without being charged with a criminal or immigration offense. Many others, however, were arrested and detained for violating federal immigration law.

Our review determined that the Immigration and Naturalization Service (INS) detained 762 aliens as a result of the PENTTBOM investigation. Of these 762 aliens, 24 were in INS custody on immigration violations prior to the September 11 attacks. The remaining 738 aliens were arrested between September 11, 2001, and August 6, 2002, as a direct result of the FBI's PENTTBOM investigation. . . .

The Government held these aliens in a variety of federal, local, and private detention facilities across the United States while the FBI investigated them for ties to the September 11 attacks or terrorism in general. . . .

Soon after these detentions began, the media began to report allegations of mistreatment of the detainees. For example, detainees and their attorneys alleged that the detainees were not informed of the charges against them for extended periods of time; were not permitted contact with attorneys, their families, and embassy officials; remained in detention even though they had no involvement in terrorism; or were physically abused, verbally abused, and mistreated in other ways while detained. . . .

We focused our review on INS detainees housed at two facilities—the BOP's [federal Bureau of Prison's] Metropolitan Detention Center (MDC) in Brooklyn and the Passaic County Jail (Passaic) in Paterson, New Jersey. We chose these two facilities because they held the majority of September 11 detainees and were the focus of many complaints about detainee mistreatment. . . .

## Chapter Ten: Conclusions

. . . In conducting our review, we were mindful of the circumstances confronting the Department [of Justice] and the country as a result of the September 11 attacks, including the massive disruptions they caused. The Department was faced with monumental challenges, and Department employees worked tirelessly and with enormous dedication over an extended period to meet these challenges.

It is also important to note that nearly all of the 762 aliens we examined violated immigration laws, either by overstaying their visas, by entering the country illegally, or some other immigration violation. In other times, many of these aliens might not have been arrested or detained for these violations. However, the September 11 attacks changed the way the Department, particularly the FBI and the INS, responded when encountering aliens who were in violation of their immigration status. It was beyond the scope of this review to examine the specific law enforcement decisions regarding who to arrest or detain. Rather, we focused primarily on the treatment of the aliens who were detained.

While recognizing the difficult circumstances confronting the Department in responding to the terrorist attacks, we found significant problems in the way the September 11 detainees were treated. The INS did not serve notices of the immigration charges on these detainees within the specified timeframes. This delay affected the detainees in several ways, from their ability to understand why they were being held, to their ability to obtain legal counsel, to their ability to request a bond hearing.

In addition, the Department instituted a policy that these detainees would be held until cleared by the FBI. Although not communicated in writing, this "hold until cleared" policy was clearly understood and applied throughout the Department. The policy was based on the belief—which turned out to be erroneous—that the FBI's clearance process would proceed quickly. Instead of taking a few days as anticipated, the clearance process took an average of 80 days, primarily because it was understaffed and not given sufficient priority by the FBI.

We also found that the FBI and the INS in New York City made little attempt to distinguish between aliens who were subjects of the PENTTBOM investigation and those encountered coincidentally to a PENTTBOM lead. Even in the chaotic aftermath of the September 11 attacks, we believe the FBI should have taken more care to distinguish between aliens who it actually suspected of having a connection to terrorism from those aliens who, while possibly guilty of violating federal immigration law, had no connection to terrorism but simply were encountered in connection with a PENTTBOM lead. Alternatively, by early November 2001, when it became clear that the FBI could not complete its clearance investigations in a matter of days or even weeks, the Department should have reviewed those cases and kept on the list of September 11 detainees only those for whom it had some basis to suspect a connection to terrorism.

The FBI's initial classification decisions and the untimely clearance process had enormous ramifications for the September 11 detainees. The Department instituted a "no bond" policy for all September 11 detainees. The evidence indicates that the INS raised concerns about this blanket "no bond" approach, particularly when it became clear that the FBI's clearance process was slow and the INS had little information in many individual cases on which to base its continued opposition to bond. The INS also raised concerns about the legality of holding aliens to conduct clearance investigations after they had received final orders of removal or voluntary departure orders. We found that the Department did not address these legal issues in a timely way.

The FBI's classification of the detainees and the slow clearance process also had important ramifications on their conditions of confinement. Many aliens characterized by the FBI as "of high interest" to the September 11 investigation were detained at the MDC under highly restrictive conditions. While the FBI's classification decisions needed to be made quickly and were based on less than complete information, we believe the FBI should have exercised more care in the process, since it resulted in the MDC detainees being kept in the highest security conditions for a lengthy period. At the least, the FBI should have conducted more timely clearance checks, given the conditions under which the MDC detainees were held.

Our review also raised various concerns about the treatment of these detainees at the MDC. For example, we found that MDC staff frequently—and mistakenly—told people who inquired about a specific September 11 detainee that the detainee was not held at the facility when, in fact, the opposite was true. In addition, the MDC's restrictive and inconsistent policies on telephone access for detainees prevented them from obtaining legal counsel in a timely manner.

With regard to allegations of abuse, the evidence indicates a pattern of physical and verbal abuse by some correctional officers at the MDC against some September 11 detainees, particularly during the first months after the attacks. Although most correctional officers denied any such physical or verbal abuse, our interviews and investigation of specific complaints developed evidence that abuse had occurred.

We also concluded that, particularly at the MDC, certain conditions of confinement were unduly harsh, such as illuminating the detainees' cells for 24 hours a day. Further, we found that MDC staff failed to inform MDC detainees in a timely manner about the process for filing complaints about their treatment.

The September 11 detainees held at Passaic had much different, and significantly less harsh, experiences than the MDC detainees. The Passaic detainees were housed in the facility's general population and treated like other INS detainees held at the facility. Although we received some allegations of physical and verbal abuse, we did not find evidence of a pattern of abuse at Passaic as we did at the MDC. However, we found that the INS did not conduct sufficient and regular visits to Passaic to ensure the conditions of confinement were appropriate.

In sum, while the chaotic situation and the uncertainties surrounding the detainees' connections to terrorism explain some of these problems, they do not explain them all. . . .

Excerpted from U.S. Department of Justice. Office of the Inspector General. *The September 11 Detainees: A Review of the Treatment of Aliens Held on Immigration Charges in Connection with the Investigation of the September 11 Attacks.* June 2, 2003. http://www.usdoj.gov/oig/special/0306/index.htm (accessed September 15, 2004).

# U.S. and Foreign Governments Attempt to Cut Off Terrorist Funds

## INTRODUCTION

To help prevent further terrorist attacks in the United States, on September 24, 2001, President George W. Bush signed an executive order requiring U.S. banks and other financial institutions to freeze any assets of Osama bin Laden, al Qaeda, and twenty-five other individuals and groups that he said financed terrorism. Executive Order 13224 also banned any foreign financial institutions that did business with terrorist groups from participating in U.S. financial markets. The second provision was necessary because, as Bush acknowledged, terrorists "don't have much money in the United States" [Document 103].

On October 25, 2001, top officials at the Treasury Department announced the creation of a new multiagency enforcement program led by the U.S. Customs Service. Operation Green Quest sought to break up terrorists' financial networks and hurt their ability to raise funds. More than a month earlier—on September 13, 2001—the Federal Bureau of Investigation (FBI) had launched a similar multiagency effort of its own. Evidence later showed that turf battles erupted almost immediately between Operation Green Quest and the FBI, hampering federal efforts to track terrorist money.

By February 11, 2002, the United States had frozen the assets of 168 people or groups, 147 countries had issued blocking orders of their own, and a total of $104 million in terrorist assets had been frozen around the world, according to a State Department press release. While the blocking orders drew headlines, investigators soon found that methodically tracking the movements of terrorist assets was more useful because it often led them to individual terrorists or terrorist cells.

In a progress report released on September 10, 2002, the Treasury Department said that although the fight against terrorist financing was "an immense undertaking," there had been many successes. "We have frozen dollars and the assets of organizations, stopping acts of terror before they can occur . . . ," the report said. "Al-Qaida and other terrorist organizations are suffering financially as a result of our actions" [Document 104].

On October 16, 2002, a prestigious task force sponsored by the nonpartisan Council on Foreign Relations dropped a bombshell in a report about terrorist financing:

> It is worth stating clearly and unambiguously what official U.S. government spokespersons have not: For years, individuals and charities based in Saudi Arabia have been the most important source of funds for al-Qaeda; and for years, Saudi officials have turned a blind eye to this problem.

The task force also blasted U.S. officials for repeatedly saying Saudi Arabia was fully cooperating in blocking terrorist financing when they knew it was not true. The group added that the United States had to crack down on Saudi Arabia to help stem the flow of terrorist money.

The report came at a particularly delicate moment in the complicated relationship between the United States and Saudi Arabia. American law enforcement officials had conclusively proven that fifteen of the nineteen hijackers on September 11 were Saudi citizens, which several senior Saudi officials denied nonetheless. Most important, the United States needed Saudi Arabia's cooperation for the war it was planning against Iraq.

"The last thing this administration wants right now is a big controversy over terrorist financing," Doug Bandow, a foreign policy expert at the conservative Cato Institute, told the *Christian Science Monitor*. "For Bush, it would raise the question of what do you care more about: the terrorists that attacked us or Saddam Hussein? That's a debate this administration can't win."

The *New York Times* quoted Rob Nichols, a spokesperson for the Treasury Department, as saying that the administration was "pleased with the cooperation with the Saudis," including recent efforts to regulate charities. Saudi officials declined to comment on the report.

On January 9, 2003, Customs Service officials announced they were nearly doubling the size of Operation Green Quest because it had developed a backlog of leads and evidence in terrorist financing cases. Customs officials said they were dedicating another 150 agents and analysts to the multiagency task force, which the *New York Times* reported brought the total number of employees to 460. The same article said unnamed FBI officials "hinted that the move could inflame tensions" between Operation Green Quest and the FBI's terrorist financing task force.

A report on June 26, 2003, by the United Nations Security Council's Committee on al-Qaeda Sanctions said that despite many successes in fighting al Qaeda, the terrorist network remained a "significant threat" and was adapting its operations when necessary. "The success of clamping down on the formal banking system has driven the terrorist groups . . . to use other information means," said Michael Chandler, chairman of the committee's monitoring group.

> We found that many of the cells that were broken up in Europe were actually self-sufficient in many ways. They were able to survive and able to raise quite considerable sums of cash purely by petty street crime, small drug sales, credit card fraud, and other similar scams which are quite common.

Saudi Arabia attracted attention again on June 26, 2003, when a top Treasury Department official testified before Congress that the country was the "epicenter" of terrorist financing. David Aufhauser, the department's general counsel and supervisor of its Office of Terrorist Financing and Financial Crimes, said individuals and charities in Saudi Arabia were a significant source of funds for terrorism generally, although most of the money went to al Qaeda [Document 105].

The controversy over Saudi Arabia exploded on July 24, 2003, when the House and Senate intelligence committees issued a joint report based on a lengthy investigation of the September 11 attacks. At issue was a twenty-eight-page section of the report that the White House demanded be classified and deleted from the public version. The section discussed the role of foreign governments in the hijackings and reportedly centered on Saudi Arabia. "Some people who have read the classified chapter said it represented a searing indictment of how Saudi Arabia's ruling elite have, under the guise of support for Islamic charities, distributed millions of dollars to terrorists through an informal network of Saudi nationals, including some in the United States," the *New York Times* reported on July 26. "But other officials said the stricken chapter retraces Saudi Arabia's well-documented support for Islamic charitable groups and said the report asserts without convincing evidence that Saudi officials knew that recipient groups used the money to finance terror."

At a news conference on July 30, 2003, Bush said he would not declassify the chapter "because there's an ongoing investigation into the 9/11 attacks, and we don't want to compromise that investigation." Bush also said "declassification of that part of a 900-page document would reveal sources and methods that would make it harder for us to win the war on terror." Saudi officials said their government did not finance terrorist groups and had nothing to do with the hijackings.

The subject was turf battles between the FBI and Operation Green Quest when a top official from the General Accounting Office (GAO)—the investigative arm of Congress—testified at a congressional hearing on May 11, 2004. "Law enforcement officials told us that the lack of clearly defined roles and coordination procedures contributed to duplication of efforts and disagreements over which agency should pursue investigations," said Richard M. Stana, director of homeland security and justice issues at the GAO. In May 2003 Attorney General John Ashcroft and Tom Ridge, secretary of the Department of Homeland Security, had signed a Memorandum of Agreement that gave the FBI lead responsibility for terrorist financing investigations, Stana said. The former Operation Green Quest, which two months earlier had become part of U.S. Immigration and Customs Enforcement (ICE) at the Homeland Security Department, was left to investigate other types of financial crimes. However, the agreement said ICE could investigate suspicious financial activities that had a potential but unconfirmed connection to terrorism. Once a terrorism connection was confirmed, Stana said, ICE and the FBI were supposed to follow an elaborate procedure to determine which agency would pursue the investigation [Document 106].

In its final report issued on July 22, 2004, the National Commission on Terrorist Attacks Upon the United States—known more commonly as the 9/11 Commission—said intelligence and law enforcement agencies had killed or captured several key people who raised and delivered money for al Qaeda. This careful targeting had decreased the amount of money available to al Qaeda, made it harder for al Qaeda to raise money, and resulted in "a windfall of intelligence that can be used to continue the cycle of disruption," the commission said. However, the commission added that terrorists "have shown considerable creativity in their methods of moving money" and warned that if al Qaeda broke up into small, decentralized terrorist groups it would be much harder to trace terrorist money [Document 107].

A supplemental report issued by the 9/11 Commission staff on August 21, 2004, said the September 11 hijacking plot cost al Qaeda only $400,000 to $500,000. It also said that al Qaeda attacks in Saudi Arabia in May and November 2003 had helped rouse the Saudi government to take action against terrorist financing. The report concluded: "It remains to be seen whether they will (and are able to) do enough, and whether the U.S. government will push them hard enough, to substantially eliminate al Qaeda financing by Saudi citizens and institutions. . . ." [Document 108].

# 103.  Remarks by President George W. Bush about New Terrorist Financing Order

*September 24, 2001*

At 12:01 this morning, a major thrust of our war on terrorism began with the stroke of a pen. Today we have launched a strike on the financial foundation of the global terror network. . . .

I've signed an Executive order that immediately freezes United States financial assets of and prohibits United States transactions with 27 different entities. They include terrorist organizations, individual terrorist leaders, a corporation that serves as a front for terrorism, and several nonprofit organizations. . . .

We know that many of these individuals and groups operate primarily overseas, and they don't have much money in the United States. So we've developed a strategy to deal with that. We're putting banks and financial institutions around the world on notice. We will work with their governments, ask them to freeze or block terrorists' ability to access funds in foreign accounts. If they fail to help us by sharing information or freezing accounts, the Department of the Treasury now has the authority to freeze their banks' assets and transactions in the United States.

We have developed the international financial equivalent of law enforcement's "Most Wanted" list. And it puts the financial world on notice. If you do business with terrorists, if you support or sponsor them, you will not do business with the United States of America.

I want to assure the world that we will exercise this power responsibly. But make no mistake about it, we intend to, and we will, disrupt terrorist networks. I want to assure the American people that in taking this action and publishing this list, we're acting based on clear evidence, much of which is classified, so it will not be disclosed. . . .

And by the way, this list is just a beginning. We will continue to add more names to the list. We will freeze the assets of others as we find that they aid and abet terrorist organizations around the world. We've established a foreign terrorist asset tracking center at the Department of the Treasury to identify and investigate the financial infrastructure of the international terrorist networks. It will bring together representatives of the intelligence, law enforcement, and financial regulatory agencies to accomplish two goals: to follow the money as a trail to the terrorists—to follow their money so we can find out where they are—and to freeze the money to disrupt their actions. . . .

Excerpted from U.S. Executive Office of the President. "Remarks on United States Financial Sanctions Against Foreign Terrorists and Their Supporters and an Exchange With Reporters." *Weekly Compilation of Presidential Documents* 37, no. 39 (October 1, 2001): 1364–1368. http://www.gpoaccess.gov/wcomp/v37no39.htm (accessed September 15, 2004).

# 104. Treasury Department Report about the Financial War on Terrorism
*September 10, 2002*

## Executive Summary

. . . The war on terrorist financing is an immense undertaking. The openness of our modern financial system, which allows savers and investors to fuel economic growth, also creates opportunities for terrorist parasites to hide in the shadows. Our challenge in this front of the war is to protect the freedom and flexibility the world's financial systems while driving our enemies into the sunlight, where we and our allies can sweep them up. We have enjoyed success, but much more remains to be done.

The United States took six principal steps in the fall of 2001 to pursue financial underwriters of terrorism:

1. President Bush signed Executive Order 13224 giving the United States greater power to freeze terrorist-related assets;
2. The United States won the adoption of UN [United Nations] Security Council Resolutions 1373 and 1390, which require member nations to join in the effort to disrupt terrorist financing;
3. We are implementing the USA PATRIOT Act to broaden and deepen information sharing and the regulatory net for our financial system;
4. We are engaging multilateral institutions such as the Financial Action Task Force and the international financial institutions (IFIs) to focus on terrorist financing;
5. We established Operation Green Quest—an inter-agency task force which has augmented existing counter-terrorist efforts by bringing the full scope of the government's financial expertise to bear against systems, individuals, and organizations that serve as sources of terrorist funding; and
6. We are sharing information across the federal government, with the private sector, and among our allies to crack down on terrorist financiers. . . .

Over the past year, we have seen successes in the financial war on terrorism.

For example, we exposed and dismantled the al Barakaat financial network. Al Barakaat's worldwide network and its owners were channeling several million dollars a year to and from al Qaida. Last November, Treasury agents shut down eight al Barakaat offices in the United States, and took possession of evidence that will be investigated for further leads in the terrorist money trail. Millions of dollars have moved through these U.S. offices of al Barakaat. At its core, it was a conglomerate operating in 40 countries around the world with business ventures in telecommunications, construction, and currency exchange. They were a source of funding and money transfers for bin Laden. Our allies around the world are joining us in cutting al Barakaat out of the world financial system. . . .

Our war on terror is working—both here in the U.S. and overseas. We are harvesting information, and we are putting it to good use. We are seeing progress. We have frozen dollars and the assets of organizations, stopping acts of terror before they can occur, and forcing terrorist backers to riskier, more vulnerable positions.

Our efforts are having real-world effects. Al-Qaida and other terrorist organizations are suffering financially as a result of our actions. . . .

Excerpted from U.S. Department of the Treasury. Office of Public Affairs. *Contributions by the Department of the Treasury to the Financial War on Terrorism: Fact Sheet.* September 10, 2002. http://www.ustreas.gov/press/releases/reports/2002910184556291211.pdf (accessed September 15, 2004).

# 105. Treasury Department Congressional Testimony about Saudi Arabia's Role in Financing Terrorism
*June 26, 2003*

## Opening Statement of Hon. Jon Kyl, [R], a U.S. Senator from the State of Arizona

. . . Nearly 22 months have passed since the atrocity of September 11th. Since then, many questions have been asked about the role in that day's terrible events and in other challenges we face in the war against terror of Saudi Arabia and its official sect, a separatist, exclusionary and violent form of Islam known as Wahhabism.

It is widely recognized that all of the 19 suicide pilots were Wahhabi followers. In addition, 15 of the 19 were Saudi subjects. Journalists and experts, as well as spokespeople of the world, have said that Wahhabism is the source of the overwhelming majority of terrorist atrocities in today's world, from Morocco to Indonesia, via Israel, Saudi Arabia, Chechnya. . . .

The extreme nature of Wahhabism is well established. As the great scholar of Islam, Bernard Lewis, has noted, "Saudi oil revenues have allowed the Saudis to spread this fanatical, destructive form of Islam all over the Muslim World and among the Muslims in the West. Without oil and the creation of the Saudi kingdom, Wahhabism would have remained a lunatic fringe. . . ."

[Questioning of David Aufhauser, general counsel for the Department of the Treasury and supervisor of the Office for Terrorist Financing and Financial Crimes]

Senator KYL: . . . Are the Saudis part of the general terrorist threat against the United States?

Mr. AUFHAUSER: People within Saudi Arabia are, yes.

Senator KYL: Is there still a significant al Qaeda terrorist threat here in the United States?

Mr. AUFHAUSER: Yes. . . .

Senator KYL:. With regard to the trail of money I should have asked you, Mr. Aufhauser, specifically about the trail of money and whether it leads in some cases to Saudi Arabia.

Mr. AUFHAUSER: In many cases it is the epicenter.

Senator KYL:. Does that trail of money also show money going to al Qaeda?

Mr. AUFHAUSER: Yes.

Senator KYL: Is the money from Saudi Arabia a significant source of funding for terrorism generally?

Mr. AUFHAUSER: Yes. Principally al Qaeda but many other recipients as well. . . .

Excerpted from U.S. Congress. Senate. Committee on the Judiciary. Subcommittee on Terrorism, Technology, and Homeland Security. *Terrorism: Growing Wahhabi Influence in the United States.* 108th Cong., 1st sess., serial J-108-21, June 26, 2003. http://frwebgate.access.gpo.gov/cgi-bin/getdoc.cgi?dbname=108_senate_hearings&docid=f:91326.wais (accessed September 15, 2004).

# 106. General Accounting Office Congressional Testimony about Challenges in Coordinating Terrorist Financing Investigations
*May 11, 2004*

## Background

. . . The former U.S. Customs Service, which is now part of ICE [U.S. Immigration and Customs Enforcement, a division in the Department of Homeland Security], and the FBI both have a long history of investigating money laundering and other financial crimes. In response to the terrorist attacks of September 11, [the Department of the] Treasury and [the Department of] Justice both established multiagency task forces dedicated to combating terrorist financing. Treasury established Operation Green Quest, led by Customs, to augment existing counterterrorist efforts by targeting current terrorist funding sources and identifying possible future sources. In addition to targeting individuals and organizations, Operation Green Quest was designed to attack the financial systems that may be used by terrorists to raise and move funds, such as fraudulent charities and the shipment of bulk currency. . . . In March 2003, Operation Green Quest was transferred to ICE, within the Department of Homeland Security.

On September 13, 2001, the FBI formed a multiagency task force— which is now known as the Terrorist Financing Operations Section (TFOS)—to combat terrorist financing. The mission of TFOS has evolved into a broad role to identify, investigate, prosecute, disrupt, and dismantle all terrorist-related financial and fundraising activities. The FBI also took action to expand the antiterrorist financing focus of its Joint Terrorism Task Forces (JTTF)—teams of local and state law enforcement officials, FBI agents, and other federal agents and personnel whose mission is to investigate and prevent acts of terrorism. In 2002, the FBI created a national JTTF in Washington, D.C., to collect terrorism information and intelligence and funnel it to the field JTTFs, various terrorism units within the FBI, and partner agencies.

The attacks of September 11 emphasized the need for federal agencies to wage a coordinated campaign against sources of terrorist financing. Following September 11, representatives of the FBI and Operation Green Quest met on several occasions to attempt to delineate antiterrorist financing roles and responsibilities. However, such efforts were largely unsuccessful until May 2003, when the Attorney General and the Secretary of Homeland Security signed a Memorandum of Agreement that contained a number of provisions designed to resolve jurisdictional issues and enhance interagency coordination of terrorist financing investigations. According to the Agreement, the FBI is to lead terrorist financing investigations and operations, using the intergovernmental and intra-agency national JTTF at FBI headquarters and the JTTFs in the field. . . . Further, to increase information sharing and coordination of terrorist financing investigations, the Agreement required the FBI and ICE to (1) detail appropriate personnel to each other's agency and (2) develop specific collaborative procedures to determine whether applicable ICE investigations or financial crimes leads may be related to terrorism or terrorist financing. . . .

## Most Key Memorandum of Agreement Provisions Have Been Implemented, but Terrorist Financing Investigations Still Present Operational and Organizational Challenges

The NMLS [National Money Laundering Strategy] was adjusted in 2002 to reflect new federal priorities in the aftermath of the September 11 attacks, including a goal to combat terrorist financing. However, due to difficulties in reaching agreement over which agency should lead investigations, the 2002 NMLS did not address agency and task force roles and interagency coordination procedures for investigating terrorist financing. Law enforcement officials told us that the lack of clearly defined roles and coordination procedures contributed to duplication of efforts and disagreements over which agency should lead investigations. To help resolve these long-standing jurisdictional issues, in May 2003, the Attorney General and the Secretary of Homeland Security signed a Memorandum of Agreement regarding roles and responsibilities in investigating terrorist financing.

In our February 2004 report, we noted that most of the key Memorandum of Agreement provisions had been implemented or were in the process of being implemented. . . .

The Memorandum of Agreement, by granting the FBI the lead role in investigating terrorist financing, altered ICE's role in investigating terrorism-related financial crimes. However, while the Agreement specified that the FBI has primary investigative jurisdiction over confirmed terrorism-related financial crimes, the Agreement does not preclude ICE from investigating suspicious financial activities that have a potential (unconfirmed) nexus to terrorism—which was the primary role of the former Operation Green Quest. . . .

Our February 2004 report noted that—while the Memorandum of Agreement represents a partnering commitment by the FBI and ICE— continued progress in implementing the Agreement will depend largely on the ability of these law enforcement agencies to meet various operational and organizational challenges. For instance, the FBI and ICE face challenges in ensuring that the implementation of the Agreement does not create a disincentive for ICE agents to initiate or support terrorist financing investigations. That is, ICE agents may perceive the Agreement as minimizing their role in terrorist financing investigations. Additional challenges involve ensuring that the financial crimes expertise and other investigative competencies of the FBI and ICE are effectively utilized and that the full range of the agencies' collective authorities—intelligence gathering and analysis as well as law enforcement actions, such as executing search warrants and seizing cash and other assets—are effectively coordinated. Inherently, efforts to meet these challenges will be an ongoing process. Our interviews with FBI and ICE officials at headquarters and three field locations indicated that long-standing jurisdictional and operational disputes regarding terrorist financing investigations may have strained interagency relationships to some degree and could pose an obstacle in fully integrating investigative efforts. . . .

Excerpted from U.S. Congress. General Accounting Office. *Investigating Money Laundering and Terrorist Financing: Federal Law Enforcement Agencies Face Continuing Coordination Challenges.* Prepared testimony of Richard M. Stana for a hearing by the Subcommittee on Criminal Justice, Drug Policy, and Human Resources of the House Committee on Government Reform. GAO-04-710T, May 11, 2004. http://www.gao.gov/new.items/d04710t.pdf (accessed September 15, 2004).

# 107. 9/11 Commission on Terrorist Financing
*July 22, 2004*

## Targeting Terrorist Money

The general public sees attacks on terrorist finance as a way to "starve the terrorists of money." So, initially, did the U.S. government. After 9/11, the United States took aggressive actions to designate terrorist financiers and freeze their money, in the United States and through resolutions of the United Nations. These actions appeared to have little effect and, when confronted by legal challenges, the United States and the United Nations were often forced to unfreeze assets.

The difficulty, understood later, was that even if the intelligence community might "link" someone to a terrorist group through acquaintances or communications, the task of tracing the money from that individual to the terrorist group, or otherwise showing complicity, was far more difficult. It was harder still to do so without disclosing secrets.

These early missteps made other countries unwilling to freeze assets or otherwise act merely on the basis of a U.S. action. Multilateral freezing mechanisms now require waiting periods before being put into effect, eliminating the element of surprise and thus virtually ensuring that little money is actually frozen. Worldwide asset freezes have not been adequately enforced and have been easily circumvented, often within weeks, by simple methods.

But trying to starve the terrorists of money is like trying to catch one kind of fish by draining the ocean. A better strategy has evolved since those early months, as the government learned more about how al Qaeda raises, moves, and spends money.

*Recommendation: Vigorous efforts to track terrorist financing must remain front and center in U.S. counterterrorism efforts. The government has recognized that information about terrorist money helps us to understand their networks, search them out, and disrupt their operations. Intelligence and law enforcement have targeted the relatively small number of financial facilitators—individuals al Qaeda relied on for their ability to raise and deliver money—at the core of al Qaeda's revenue stream. These efforts have worked. The death or capture of several important facilitators has decreased the amount of money available to al Qaeda and has increased its costs and difficulty in raising and moving that money. Captures have additionally provided a windfall of intelligence that can be used to continue the cycle of disruption.*

The U.S. financial community and some international financial institutions have generally provided law enforcement and intelligence agencies with extraordinary cooperation, particularly in supplying information to support quickly developing investigations. Obvious vulnerabilities in the U.S. financial system have been corrected. The United States has been less successful in persuading other countries to adopt financial regulations that would permit the tracing of financial transactions.

Public designation of terrorist financiers and organizations is still part of the fight, but it is not the primary weapon. Designations are instead a form of diplomacy, as governments join together to identify named individuals and groups as terrorists. They also prevent open fundraising. Some charities that have been identified as likely avenues for terrorist financing have seen their donations diminish and their activities come under more scrutiny, and others have been put out of business, although controlling overseas branches of Gulf-area charities remains a challenge. The Saudi crackdown after the May 2003 terrorist attacks in Riyadh has apparently reduced the funds available to al Qaeda—perhaps drastically—but it is too soon to know if this reduction will last.

Though progress apparently has been made, terrorists have shown considerable creativity in their methods of moving money. If al Qaeda is replaced by smaller, decentralized terrorist groups, the premise behind the government's efforts—that terrorists need a financial support network—may become outdated. Moreover, some terrorist operations do not rely on outside sources of money and may now be self-funding, either through legitimate employment or low-level criminal activity. . . .

Excerpted from U.S. National Commission on Terrorist Attacks Upon the United States. *The 9/11 Commission Report: Final Report of the National Commission on Terrorist Attacks Upon the United States.* July 22, 2004. http://www.9-11commission.gov/report/911Report_Ch12.pdf (accessed September 15, 2004).

# 108. 9/11 Commission Staff Report about Terrorist Financing
*August 21, 2004*

## Introduction

After the September 11 attacks, the highest-level U.S. government officials publicly declared that the fight against al Qaeda financing was as critical as the fight against al Qaeda itself. It has been presented as one of the keys to success in the fight against terrorism: if we choke off the terrorists' money, we limit their ability to conduct mass casualty attacks. In reality, completely choking off the money to al Qaeda and affiliated terrorist groups has been essentially impossible. At the same time, tracking al Qaeda financing has proven a very effective way to locate terrorist operatives and supporters and to disrupt terrorist plots. . . .

## Findings

### The Funding of the Hijackers

- The 9/11 plot cost al Qaeda approximately $400,000–500,000, of which approximately $300,000 was deposited into U.S. bank accounts of the 19 hijackers. . . . Once here, all of the hijackers used the U.S. banking system to store their funds and facilitate their transactions.

- The hijackers and their financial facilitators used the anonymity provided by the vast international and domestic financial system to move and store their money through a series of unremarkable transactions. The existing mechanisms to prevent abuse of the financial system did not fail. They were never designed to detect or disrupt transactions of the type that financed 9/11.
- Virtually all of the plot funding was provided by al Qaeda. There is no evidence that any person in the United States, or any foreign government, provided any substantial funding to the hijackers. . . .

### Raising and Moving Money for al Qaeda

- Contrary to public opinion, Bin Ladin did not have access to any significant amounts of personal wealth (particularly after his move from Sudan to Afghanistan) and did not personally fund al Qaeda, either through an inheritance or businesses he owned in Sudan. Rather, al Qaeda relied on diversions from Islamic charities and on well-placed financial facilitators who gathered money from both witting and unwitting donors, primarily in the Gulf region.
- The nature and extent of al Qaeda fund-raising and money movement make intelligence collection exceedingly difficult, and gaps appear to remain in the intelligence community's understanding of the issue. Because of the complexity and variety of ways to collect and move small amounts of money in a vast worldwide financial system, gathering intelligence on al Qaeda financial flows will remain a hard target for the foreseeable future.

### Intelligence Gathering on al Qaeda

- Within the United States, although FBI street agents had gathered significant intelligence on specific suspected fund-raisers before 9/11, the FBI did not systematically gather and analyze the information its agents developed. The FBI as an organization failed to understand the nature and extent of the problem or to develop a coherent strategy for confronting it. As a result the FBI could not fulfill its role to provide intelligence on domestic terrorist financing to government policymakers and did not contribute to national policy coordination.
- Outside the United States, the U.S. intelligence community before 9/11 devoted relatively few resources to collecting financial intelligence on al Qaeda. This limited effort resulted in an incomplete understanding of al Qaeda's methods to raise, move, and store money, and thus hampered the effectiveness of the overall counterterrorism strategy.
- Since 9/11 the intelligence community (including the FBI) has created significant specialized entities, led by committed and experienced individuals and supported by the leadership of their agencies, focused on

both limiting the funds available to al Qaeda and using financial information as a powerful investigative tool. The FBI and CIA meet regularly to exchange information, and they have cross-detailed their agents into positions of responsibility.

### Economic Disruption of al Qaeda

- Before 9/11 the limited U.S. and UN [United Nations] efforts to freeze assets of and block transactions with Bin Ladin were generally ineffective. . . .
- The United States engaged in a highly visible series of freezes of suspected terrorist assets after 9/11. Although few funds have been frozen since the first few months after 9/11, asset freezes are useful diplomatic tools in engaging other countries in the war on terror and have symbolic and deterrence value. . . .
- The financial provisions enacted after September 11, particularly those contained in the USA PATRIOT Act and subsequent regulations, have succeeded in addressing obvious vulnerabilities in our financial system. Vigilant enforcement is crucial in ensuring that the U.S. financial system is not a vehicle for the funding of terrorists. . . .
- Although the government can often show that certain fund-raising groups or individuals are "linked" to terrorist groups (through common acquaintances, group affiliations, historic relationships, phone communications, or other such contacts), it is far more difficult to show that a suspected NGO [non-governmental organization] or individual actually funds terrorist groups. In assessing both the domestic efforts of the U.S. government and the overseas efforts of other nations, we must keep in mind this fundamental and inherently frustrating challenge of combating terrorist financing. . . .

### Diplomatic Efforts and Saudi Arabia

- Before the September 11 attacks, the Saudi government resisted cooperating with the United States on the al Qaeda financing problem, although the U.S. government did not make this issue a priority or provide the Saudis with actionable intelligence about al Qaeda fundraising in the Kingdom.
- Notwithstanding a slow start, since the al Qaeda bombings in Saudi Arabia in May and November of 2003 and the delivery of a more consistent and pointed U.S. message, it appears that the Saudis have accepted that terrorist financing is a serious issue and are making progress in addressing it. It remains to be seen whether they will (and are able to) do enough, and whether the U.S. government will push them hard enough, to substantially eliminate al Qaeda financing by Saudi citizens and institutions. . . .

## *Overall Effectiveness of the U.S. Government's Efforts on Terrorist Financing since 9/11*

- All relevant elements of the U.S. government—intelligence, law enforcement, diplomatic, and regulatory (often with significant assistance from the U.S. and international banking community)—have made considerable efforts to identify, track, and disrupt the raising and movement of al Qaeda funds.
- While definitive intelligence is lacking, these efforts have had a significant impact on al Qaeda's ability to raise and move funds, on the willingness of donors to give money indiscriminately, and on the international community's understanding of and sensitivity to the issue. Moreover, the U.S. government has used the intelligence revealed through financial information to understand terrorist networks, search them out and disrupt their operations.
- While a perfect end state—the total elimination of money flowing to al Qaeda—is virtually impossible, current government efforts to raise the costs and risks of gathering and moving money are necessary to limit al Qaeda's ability to plan and mount significant mass casualty attacks. We should understand, however, that success in these efforts will not of itself immunize us from future terrorist attacks. . . .

Excerpted from U.S. National Commission on Terrorist Attacks Upon the United States. *Monograph on Terrorist Financing: Staff Report to the Commission.* August 21, 2004. http://www.9-11commission.gov/staff_statements/911_TerrFin_Monograph.pdf (accessed September 15, 2004)

# Bioterrorism Strikes the United States

## INTRODUCTION

As the nation continued reeling from the terrorist attacks of September 11, 2001, Tommy Thompson, secretary of health and human services, testified at a congressional hearing only weeks later about the nation's preparedness for a bioterrorism attack. "Let me characterize our status this way," he told a Senate subcommittee on October 3. "We are prepared to respond. But there is more we can do—and must do—to strengthen our response."

Just how unprepared the United States was for a biological attack started becoming clear the next day when the Centers for Disease Control and Prevention (CDC)—an agency that Thompson oversaw—issued a press release confirming reports that it was investigating the case of a Florida man who had contracted anthrax. "Sporadic cases of anthrax do occur in the United States, so a single case is not an indication of an outbreak," the CDC said. "The last case of anthrax reported in the United States was earlier this year in Texas" [Document 109]. The CDC did not mention that the Texas case resulted from skin contact with anthrax, while the Florida man had a far more rare and deadly form caused by inhaling anthrax. The CDC also did not say that only eighteen causes of inhalation anthrax had been reported in the United States during the twentieth century, the last in 1976.

On October 5, 2001, Thompson said at a press conference that the Florida case of Bob Stevens, a 63-year-old photo editor for a supermarket tabloid based in Boca Raton, was "isolated" and that anthrax was not contagious. Thompson added: "There is no evidence of terrorism." Hours after Thompson spoke, Stevens died.

Two days later, a second man who worked in the same building as Stevens was diagnosed with anthrax. He survived following antibiotic treatment. In announcing the second case, the CDC said it had found evidence anthrax was present in the building where the two men worked. Public health officials sealed the building and provided antibiotics to everyone who worked there. Because the two cases of the extremely rare disease occurred in such close proximity, the Federal Bureau of Investigation (FBI) launched a massive investigation.

In just two months—October and November 2001—the anthrax attacks killed five people, including two postal workers; sickened eighteen others; caused more than 30,000 people who might have been exposed to anthrax to take powerful antibiotics at the urging of public health officials; forced Congress and the Supreme Court to temporarily close their buildings for testing; made the Hart Senate Office Building—the largest Senate building in Washington, D.C.—uninhabitable for more than three months after tests showed it was contaminated with anthrax; and resulted in the U.S. Postal Service closing twenty-three facilities for cleaning.

Investigators ultimately determined that the anthrax was mailed in envelopes postmarked in Trenton, New Jersey. The first wave of attacks had been aimed at the news media; the second, at prominent politicians. The two postal workers apparently died because high-speed mail processing equipment allowed some of the anthrax spores to escape from their envelopes, while many of the others who died or were injured received mail that was contaminated in the postal system by the anthrax letters.

A report released on October 15, 2003, by the General Accounting Office (GAO)—the investigative arm of Congress—said the effects of the attacks spread far beyond the areas where people were killed or injured:

> Although the anthrax incidents were limited to six epicenters on the East Coast, the incidents had national implications. Because mail processed at contaminated postal facilities could be cross-contaminated and end up anywhere in the country, the localized incidents generated concern about white powders found in locations beyond the epicenters and created a demand throughout the nation for public health resources at the local, state, and federal levels.

Throughout the anthrax scare, the government's response was marked by uncertainty and confusion. "The response to the incidents has been characterized by several public officials, academics, and other commentators as problematic and an indication that the country was unprepared for a bioterrorist attack," said the GAO report released in October 2003. For most people, the most frightening aspects were the inability of investigators to identify the source of the anthrax or to say whether the attacks were part of a broad terrorist strike against the United States.

Nonetheless, fast actions by physicians in Florida and by local, state, and federal public health authorities undoubtedly saved lives. So did actions by the Postal Service to quickly close facilities once public health officials corrected their initial underestimates of the threat posed to postal workers.

Congress responded to the anthrax scare by including $2.9 billion in a supplemental appropriations bill in January 2002 for programs "countering potential biological, disease, and chemical threats to civilian populations." The measure included $1.1 billion for purchasing pharmaceuticals, including smallpox vaccines, for government stockpiles. The bill also included $1.1 billion to help states improve their public health systems to respond to a bioterrorism attack.

A classified study prepared in April 2002 by the Defense Threat Reduction Agency and the Center for Strategic and International Studies offered a harsh assessment of the government's bioterrorism preparedness at the time of the anthrax attacks. A redacted version of the report released on March 15, 2004, said:

> *Bacillus anthracis* [anthrax] is the most studied pathogen of possible biological agents, the use of mailed letters as a delivery mechanism provided a readily identifiable, overt means of attack; and the areas attacked were for the most part easy to isolate. Despite this, the anthrax attacks revealed weaknesses in almost every aspect of U.S. biopreparedness and response. The attacks exposed deficiencies in our public health infrastructure and in our laboratory, forensic, and diagnostic capabilities. They uncovered gaps in our scientific base. . . .

On June 12, 2002, President George W. Bush signed the Public Health Security and Bioterrorism Preparedness and Response Act of 2002. The bill gave the government broader authority to track biological materials at laboratories in the United States, provided states with another $1.5 billion to help them prepare for a biological attack, gave the Centers for Disease Control and Prevention $300 million to improve its physical infrastructure, and increased inspections of imported foods, among other provisions.

In January 2003 the Department of Homeland Security began upgrading Environmental Protection Agency (EPA) air-monitoring systems around the country so they could detect biological attacks. The new system was designed to alert public health officials when an attack occurred so they could act quickly to minimize casualties. Overall, federal spending on biodefense skyrocketed. It grew from just $294 million in fiscal year 2001 to $5.2 billion in fiscal year 2004.

Yet testimony at a congressional hearing on October 7, 2003, revealed that the government was failing to take some of the most basic precautions to protect the nation against bioterrorism. Gregory Kutz, director of the financial management and assurance team at the GAO, testified that the agency had created a fictitious company that purchased excess Defense Department property over the Internet. For just $4,100, Kutz said, the GAO had purchased a wide variety of advanced biological equipment and protective gear "that could be used to produce and disseminate anthrax."

Kutz acknowledged that terrorists would also need to obtain the biological source agent to make anthrax, but said that wasn't hard. "Subsequent to the anthrax attacks of 2001, GAO and agency IGs [inspector generals] assessed controls at laboratories that handle biological source agents," he said. "Substantial problems were identified such as inventory control, physical control and transfer controls. As a result, biological agents may have fallen into the wrong hands" [Document 110].

In April 2004 Bush signed a classified directive that outlined the specific responsibilities of various federal agencies in protecting the nation against bioterrorism. Three months later, on July 21, 2004, he signed the Project BioShield Act, which was designed to further bolster the nation's bioterrorism defenses.

Bush had first proposed Project BioShield in his 2003 State of the Union address. Administration officials said the law was needed because no vaccines or drugs to prevent or treat infections were available for many biological agents that terrorists might use. In other cases, vaccines and drugs existed but were not entirely effective. Pharmaceutical companies were not developing new vaccines and drugs to fight bioterrorism because, the officials said, no commercial market existed for the products.

The Project BioShield Act was designed to create that market. It authorized the government to spend $5.6 billion over ten years to purchase and stockpile vaccines and drugs to fight anthrax, smallpox, and other biological agents. "By acting as a willing buyer for the best new medical technologies, the government ensures that our drug stockpile remains safe, effective and advanced," Bush said when he signed the bill [Document 111].

Meanwhile, DNA tests had found that the anthrax in the letters was developed from stocks at U.S. military laboratories. The FBI's continuing criminal investigation focused on those laboratories and their current and former employees—especially at Fort Detrick in Maryland, home to the Army's biological defense program. Yet despite offering a $2.5 million reward for information in the case, by the end of October 2004 the FBI had made no arrests.

# 109. Public Health Message Regarding Anthrax Case, a Press Release from the Centers for Disease Control and Prevention

*October 4, 2001*

## Public Health Message Regarding Anthrax Case

The Florida State Department of Health and the CDC [Centers for Disease Control and Prevention] are investigating a case of anthrax in a 63-year-old male Florida resident. The diagnosis is confirmed by CDC's laboratory. So far this appears to be an isolated case.

Anthrax is not contagious. The illness is not transmitted person to person.

Sporadic cases of anthrax do occur in the United States, so a single case is not an indication of an outbreak. The last case of anthrax reported in the United States was earlier this year in Texas.

The rapid identification of this single case is the result of the heightened level of disease monitoring being done by the public health and medical community. This is the disease monitoring system in action.

Right now, there is no suggestion of other possible cases, but we are aggressively checking to see if other people are similarly ill.

The Florida State Health Department and a team from CDC are aggressively investigating the source of infection. They are reconstructing the patient's schedule for the last few weeks to attempt to determine the location where the patient may have been exposed.

A team of CDC epidemiologists were sent to Florida to look for any indications of exposure to this disease. Medical teams and supplies are prepared to be moved quickly if needed.

CDC and state health officials are alerting health care providers to look for unusual cases of respiratory disease. Although anthrax starts out with flu-like symptoms, it rapidly progresses to severe illnesses, including pneumonia and meningitis.

If anyone has been exposed, antibiotics are the appropriate preventive treatment. CDC has an emergency supply of antibiotics readily available for distribution. If the investigation of the cause of this illness indicated that you need antibiotics, your state and local health department will notify you and your physician and will assure you receive the drugs.

Based on what we know right now, there is no need for people to take any extraordinary actions or steps. They should not go to a doctor or hospital unless they are sick. They should not buy and horde medicines or antibiotics. They should not buy gas masks.

The public needs to understand that our public health system is on a heightened sense of alert for any diseases that may come from a biological attack. So we may have more reports of what may appear to be isolated cases. We're going to respond more aggressively to these cases than in the past.

> U.S. Department of Health and Human Services. Centers for Disease Control and Prevention. Office of Communication. *Public Health Message Regarding Anthrax Case.* October 4, 2001. http://www.cdc.gov/od/oc/media/pressrel/r011004.htm (accessed October 15, 2004).

# 110. Congressional Testimony about Government Sales of Equipment that Could Be Used in a Bioterrorism Attack

*October 7, 2003*

. . . [O]ur bottom line is that DOD [Department of Defense] is selling excess property that could be used to produce and disseminate anthrax or other biological agents.

My testimony has three parts. First, background on controls over biological source agents and the expertise needed to produce anthrax. Second, the sale of excess DOD biological equipment and protective clothing. And third, controls over public sales of these items.

First, the anthrax attacks of 2001 have heightened the public's awareness to the risk of a biological attack on the United States. Experts advised us that the production of biological agents for use as a weapon of mass destruction would require substantial expertise and sophisticated equipment. However, they told us it was more likely that terrorists could produce and disseminate a crude form of anthrax that could be used to cause fear, significant economic consequences and some deaths.

The biological source agent is also needed to produce anthrax. Subsequent to the anthrax attacks of 2001, GAO and agency IGs [inspector generals] assessed controls at laboratories that handle biological source agents. Substantial problems were identified such as inventory control, physical control and transfer controls. As a result, biological agents may have fallen into the wrong hands.

Moving on to my second point, we found that DOD is selling excess property that could be used to produce and disseminate anthrax. Similar property is available from other sources such as medical industry suppliers, indicating a broader problem.

As you requested, we established a fictitious company and purchased excess DOD property over the Internet from govliquidation.com. We spent $4,100 to purchase these new and usable items. We have with us today the biological equipment and some of the chem/bio suits and related protective gear that we purchased. The biological equipment currently has no restrictions for sales to the public.

Let me walk you through the six exhibits. First, we purchased a biological safety cabinet. We found that at least 18 similar cabinets were sold by DOD over the last 3½ years. Although purchased by DOD several years ago, this cabinet appears to be unused.

Second, a bacteriological incubator. We found that DOD sold at least 199 similar incubators over the last 3½ years, including larger versions.

Third, a laboratory centrifuge. We found that DOD sold at least 521 centrifuges over the last 3½ years.

Fourth, a laboratory evaporator. We found that DOD sold at least 65 laboratory evaporators over the last 3½ years.

Experts told us that the final two [items], chem/bio suits and related protective gear, would be critical to the protection of terrorists during the production, handling and dissemination of anthrax.

Unlike biological equipment, DOD's policy is that the chem/bio suits and protective gear should not be sold to the public. However, as our fifth exhibit clearly shows, this policy has not been effective.

In June and August 2003 we purchased two DOD bid lots that included over 500 chem/bio suits. We found that DOD sold at least 286,000 chem/bio suits over the last 3½ years.

Several of the suits you see exhibited are unused in sealed packages and have not exceeded their expiration date for effectiveness. To purchase these suits, we submitted fictitious information to DOD and had an end use certificate issued for these purchases.

In addition, 379 of the suits we purchased were defective battle dress overgarments. As you may recall from prior hearings of this subcommittee, DOD has been unable to account for about 250,000 of these defective suits. Our investigation found that all 379 of the defective suits that we purchased had previously been issued to local law enforcement agencies. In addition, 4,700 suits that may be defective were also issued to local law enforcement.

In addition to chem/bio suits, DOD was selling restricted protective gear similar to our sixth exhibit. We found that DOD sold several hundred thousand pieces of protective gear over the last 3½ years.

Because protective gear was only available in large bid lots at the time we made our purchases, we bought these items from a private sector vendor that sells them to DOD. We paid $190 for the items, including a mask, filters, hood, gloves and boot covers.

We also found that DOD excess property is feeding a robust secondary market. The purchase and sale of DOD excess property appears to be a profitable venture with many individuals and businesses involved. We investigated 42 buyers of our case study items. We found that 15 of these buyers exported used laboratory equipment to countries such as the United Arab Emirates and the Philippines. Individuals in these countries are known to be involved in transshipments to terrorist-supporting countries.

One of the buyers we investigated had been contacted previously by the FBI as part of the anthrax investigations from 2001. The FBI contacted this buyer about the disposition of several micromilling machines purchased originally from DOD.

My third point is that Federal regulations and policies do not restrict DOD from selling our case study biological equipment to the general public. Initiatives exist to monitor and control exports of the type of items that we purchased, such as Customs Operation Shield America and the Australia Group Agreement. However, there are no Federal regulations for control of domestic sales of any of these items.

In summary, sales of biological equipment and protective clothing is a much broader issue than DOD excess property. The biological equipment and protective gear being sold by DOD are available from a number of sources worldwide. However, uncontrolled public sale of DOD excess property increases the risk that terrorists could obtain and use these items to produce and deliver anthrax within the United States. . . .

Excerpted from U.S. Congress. House of Representatives. Committee on Government Reform. Subcommittee on National Security, Emerging Threats and International Relations. *Emerging Threats: Assessing DoD Control of Surplus Chemical and Biological Equipment and Material.* Testimony by Gregory Kutz, director of the financial management and assurance team at the General Accounting Office. 108th Cong., 1st sess., serial 108-121, October 7, 2003. http://purl.access.gpo.gov/GPO/LPS49083 (accessed October 15, 2004).

# 111. President George W. Bush's Remarks on Signing the Project BioShield Act

*July 21, 2004*

. . . On September the 11th, 2001, America saw the destruction and grief terrorists could inflict with commercial airlines turned into weapons of mass murder. Those attacks revealed the depth of our enemies' determination but not the extent of their ambitions. We know that the terrorists seek an even deadlier technology. And if they acquire chemical, biological, or nuclear weapons, we have no doubt they will use them to cause even greater harm.

The bill I am about to sign is an important element in our response to that threat. By authorizing unprecedented funding and providing new capabilities, Project BioShield will help America purchase, develop, and deploy cutting-edge defenses against catastrophic attack.

This legislation represents the collective foresight and considered judgment of United States Senators and Members of the House of Representatives from both political parties, many of whom experienced bioterror firsthand when anthrax and ricin were found on Capitol Hill. It reflects 18 months of hard work and cooperation by many dedicated public servants in Congress and in the White House. It sends a message about our direction in the war on terror: We refuse to remain idle while modern technology might be turned against us; we will rally the great promise of American science and innovation to confront the greatest danger of our time. . . .

Project BioShield will transform our ability to defend the Nation in three essential ways. First, Project BioShield authorizes $5.6 billion over 10 years for the Government to purchase and stockpile vaccines and drugs to fight anthrax, smallpox, and other potential agents of bioterror. The Department of Health and Human Services has already taken steps to purchase 75 million doses of an improved anthrax vaccine for the Strategic National Stockpile. Under Project BioShield, HHS is moving forward with plans to acquire a safer, second-generation smallpox vaccine, an antidote to botulinum toxin, and better treatments for exposure to chemical and radiological weapons.

Private industry plays a vital role in our biodefense efforts by taking risks to bring new treatments to the market, and we appreciate those efforts.

By acting as a willing buyer for the best new medical technologies, the Government ensures that our drug stockpile remains safe, effective, and advanced. The Federal Government and our medical professionals are working together to meet the threat of bioterrorism; we're making the American people more secure in doing so.

Second, Project BioShield gives the Government new authority to expedite research and development on the most promising and time-sensitive medicines to defend against bioterror. We will waste no time putting those new powers to use. Today [Health and Human Services] Secretary [Tommy] Thompson will direct the NIH [National Institutes of Health] to launch two initiatives, one to speed the development of new treatments for victims of a biological attack and another to expedite development of treatments for victims of a radiological or nuclear attack. Under the old rules, grants of this kind of research often took 18 to 24 months to process. Under Project BioShield, HHS expects the process to be completed in about 6 months. Our goal is to translate today's promising medical research into drugs and vaccines to combat a biological attack in the future, and now we will not let bureaucratic obstacles stand in the way.

Third, Project BioShield will change the way the Government authorizes and deploys medical defenses in a crisis. When I sign this bill, the Food and Drug Administration will be able to permit rapid distribution of promising new drugs and antidotes in the most urgent circumstances. This will allow patients to quickly receive the best treatments in an emergency. Secretary Thompson has directed the FDA to prepare guidelines and procedures for implementing this new authority. By acting today, we are making sure we have the best medicine possible to help the victims of a biological attack.

Project BioShield is part of a broader strategy to defend America against the threat of weapons of mass destruction. Since September the 11th, we've increased funding for the Strategic National Stockpile by a factor of 5, increased funding for biodefense research at NIH by a factor of 30, secured enough smallpox vaccine for every American, worked with cities on plans to deliver antibiotics and chemical antidotes in an emergency, improved the safety of our food supply, and deployed advanced environmental detectors under the BioWatch Program to provide the earliest possible warning of a biological attack.

The threat of bioterrorism has brought new challenges to our Government, to our first-responders, and to our medical personnel. We are grateful for their service. Not long ago, few of these men and women could have imagined duties like monitoring the air for anthrax or delivering antibiotics on a massive scale. Yet, this is the world as we find it. This Nation refuses to let our guard down. . . .

Excerpted from U.S. Executive Office of the President. "Remarks on Signing the Project BioShield Act of 2004." *Weekly Compilation of Presidential Documents* 40, no. 30 (July 26, 2004): 1346–1348. http://www.gpoaccess.gov/wcomp/v40no30.html (accessed October 15, 2004).

# Supporters, Critics Face Off over Parts of USA Patriot Act

## INTRODUCTION

The terrorist attacks on September 11, 2001, caused a massive wave of fear and anger to sweep across the United States. The scope and intensity of these emotions had few precedents. In modern American history, the only previous instances where public fear and anger reached such heights may have been during the Cuban missile crisis in 1962 or after the Japanese attack on Pearl Harbor in 1941.

A Gallup Poll conducted only days after the attacks found that nearly 60 percent of respondents feared they could be victims of terrorist strikes. A *Los Angeles Times* poll found that a similar percentage of people thought the attacks would "dramatically alter everyday living." Americans wanted President George W. Bush and Congress to do something to restore their sense of safety. In the *Times* poll 61 percent of the respondents said reducing civil liberties was a necessary sacrifice. Nearly seven in ten favored letting police use racial profiling to randomly stop people who shared the physical characteristics of the September 11 hijackers.

Within days of the attacks, Attorney General John Ashcroft said federal law enforcement agencies needed expanded intelligence and surveillance powers to fight terrorism. At a press conference on September 17, 2001, Ashcroft announced that the Justice Department would finish work on a "comprehensive" package of antiterrorism legislation within two days, and he urged Congress to approve it by the week's end. The Justice Department gave Congress its bill on September 19, leaving lawmakers just three days to approve it if they were to meet the attorney general's deadline.

Congress did not. The *Wall Street Journal* reported on September 20 that the Justice Department bill was "significantly more far-reaching than the department previously had suggested." Many members of Congress, both liberals and conservatives, said parts of Ashcroft's legislation violated civil liberties guaranteed by the U.S. Constitution. One of the most criticized sections authorized the attorney general to indefinitely jail any noncitizen that he believed was a risk to national security. The section was reminiscent of the Alien Act of 1798, which authorized the president to deport all aliens that he judged were "dangerous to the peace and safety of the United States" (*see* Laws Provide Broad Powers to Deport Aliens and Penalize Speech, p. 1).

Nonetheless, a September 22 article in *CQ Weekly* summed up the prevailing mood in the Capitol: "The horror of the terrorist attacks has left official Washington desperate to respond. As a result, Congress is preparing to debate new anti-terrorism legislation, proposed by Ashcroft, with provisions that just weeks ago would never have been seriously considered."

Some members of Congress had drafted their own antiterrorism bills, and intense negotiations with the administration ensued behind closed doors. The House Judiciary Committee was a key player, and the Republican-led panel soon started meeting without its Democratic members as White House pressure increased. House Speaker J. Dennis Hastert, R-Ill., used his considerable power behind the scenes on behalf of the White House.

As the Bush administration and Congress wrangled over the secret legislation, administration officials issued frequent warnings of imminent terrorist attacks. An editorial published October 2, 2001, in the *Atlanta Journal-Constitution* wondered whether the warnings were really aimed at pressuring Congress to pass the administration's bill. "The attorney general would have a much stronger case for speedy passage if his proposed measures would have prevented Sept. 11," the newspaper said. "In truth, law enforcement and intelligence officials failed to detect the worst attack on this country in 60 years despite existing capabilities, not for a lack of investigative reach."

Meanwhile, on October 14, an aide to Senate Majority Leader Tom Daschle, D-S.D., opened a letter that contained millions of anthrax spores. Emergency officials quarantined Daschle's office, and within days more than two dozen congressional staff members tested positive for anthrax exposure. On October 17, the House and Senate shut all of their office buildings for anthrax tests, and the Hart Senate Office Building—the largest of the Senate buildings—remained closed for more than three months as officials tried various decontamination strategies. The apparent terrorist attack at their door prompted a new urgency among members of Congress to pass an antiterrorism bill (*see* Bioterrorism Strikes the United States, p. 319).

A newly drafted bill was introduced in the House on October 23, 2001. It carried the unwieldy title "Uniting and Strengthening America by Providing Appropriate Tools Required to Intercept and Obstruct Terrorism." The title's purpose was to create an acronym: the USA Patriot Act. The bill moved swiftly through the legislative process after it was introduced. The House passed it the morning of October 24 by a vote of 357–66, despite complaints by some members that the fast vote gave them no time to read the new bill.

The Senate moved quickly, too, but not before giving Sen. Patrick Leahy, D-Vt., then-chairman of the Senate Judiciary Committee, the honor of opening and closing the Senate debate on October 25. Leahy had drafted his own bill immediately after the attacks, and he was intimately involved in the tough negotiations over several competing proposals that followed. Leahy said of the Patriot Act in his closing statement, "We will enhance our security in this bill, but we will preserve our liberties." The bill contained some "tough measures," Leahy acknowledged, some of which "may even push the envelope to the extent that we worry." But Leahy said lawmakers had built many civil liberties protections into the bill, and he promised that the Senate Judiciary Committee would provide close oversight of government actions. [Document 112].

The Senate approved the bill 98–1, with Sen. Russ Feingold, D-Wis., casting the sole dissenting vote. "There is no doubt that if we lived in a police state, it would be easier to catch terrorists," he said during the Senate debate.

> If we lived in a country that allowed the police to search your home at any time for any reason; if we lived in a country that allowed the government to hold people in jail indefinitely based on what they write or think, or based on mere suspicion that they are up to no good, then the government would no doubt discover and arrest more terrorists. But that probably would not be a country in which we would want to live.

Bush signed the legislation on October 26. The new law granted nearly every power that the White House had requested. However, it placed limits on the attorney general's ability to jail noncitizens that he thought posed a risk to national security.

The Patriot Act contained more than 150 sections that amended more than a dozen other federal laws, sometimes by changing just one word. Although the Patriot Act was touted as an antiterrorism measure, a number of its provisions applied to all types of crime—not just terrorism.

For example, the bill drew widespread praise for toughening the nation's money-laundering laws. Section 312 required all U.S. financial institutions that did business with foreign banks or persons to establish detailed policies and controls to detect and report money laundering that occurred through the accounts [Document 113]. Section 312, like the other money-laundering provisions in the Patriot Act, was aimed at detecting and stopping money laundering by terrorists, drug traffickers, corrupt foreign officials, and others.

Some other parts of the law also were not controversial. Examples included sections that made it easier for the FBI to quickly hire more translators, improved security on the 4,000-mile border the United States shared with Canada, provided grants to state and local governments to respond to bioterrorism attacks, and increased payments to families of fallen firefighters, police officers, and other public safety workers.

A few parts simply updated laws to keep pace with technology. For example, a law written back when telephones had wires that connected them to physical places required investigators to obtain separate court orders authorizing wiretaps for each phone the suspect used. To keep up with technology that allowed terrorists and others to easily buy and throw away cell phones at will, the Patriot Act allowed investigators to obtain a single court order that authorized wiretaps on all phones a suspect might use.

But some sections of the law aroused intense opposition across the political spectrum, from the liberal American Civil Liberties Union (ACLU) to the conservative Eagle Forum. Individual groups and people often focused on different sections of the law that caused them particular concern. They generally agreed, however, that the Patriot Act gave the federal government too much power, lacked enough checks and balances, and severely infringed on civil liberties. The administration responded that the law contained numerous oversight provisions to guard against misuse of the new powers, and that the additional authority it provided was essential if the nation was to win the war against terrorism.

Two parts of the law that drew some of the broadest opposition were:

- Section 213, which allowed federal agents to engage in "sneak-and-peek" searches of dwellings and other places where a search warrant was required. Before the Patriot Act, law enforcement officers had to knock or otherwise announce their presence and give the person named in the warrant a copy before entering. If no one was present, officers left the warrant behind so the person named knew that the premises had been searched. The new law provided a broad range of circumstances under which officers could conduct searches and then at a later date provide notification that a search had occurred. The law said notification must occur "within a reasonable period" after officers executed the warrant, but it did not define "a reasonable period." A judge could also extend the reasonable period, the law said, "for good cause shown." The section applied to all types of crimes [Document 114].
- Section 215, under which FBI agents could request a court order allowing them to require a person, business, or other entity to turn over "any tangible things" if the purpose of their investigation was "to protect against international terrorism or clandestine intelligence activities." The judge was required to issue the order, the new law said, if the FBI agent said

the investigation met the purpose test and that it was "not conducted solely upon the basis of activities protected by the first amendment to the Constitution." Previously, the law said courts could only approve orders if there were "specific and articulable facts giving reason to believe that the person to whom the records pertain is a foreign power or an agent of a foreign power." The new law also barred the person who complied with the order from telling anyone about it [Document 115].

Some sections of the Patriot Act contained "sunset" causes, which meant they expired at the end of 2005 unless Congress reauthorized them. The idea was to let Congress reconsider at a calmer time some of the provisions that had the greatest impact on civil liberties. Most of these sections expanded law enforcement powers. For example, Section 215—which broadened the FBI's authority to require a person, business, or other entity to turn over "any tangible things" if the investigation was aimed at international terrorism or clandestine intelligence activities—had a sunset clause. But other parts of the law such as Section 213, which allowed sneak-and-peek searches, did not have sunset clauses and were permanent unless Congress specifically repealed them.

Ashcroft steadfastly defended the Justice Department's actions against terrorism in general and its use of the Patriot Act in particular during a Senate Judiciary Committee hearing on December 6, 2001, titled "Department of Justice Oversight: Preserving Our Freedoms While Defending Against Terrorism." Ashcroft said the Justice Department had "waged a deliberate campaign of arrest and detention to remove suspected terrorists who violate the law from our streets," although all departmental efforts had been "carefully crafted to avoid infringing on constitutional rights while saving American lives" [Document 116].

The attorney general said that only hours after Congress passed the Patriot Act in October, the Justice Department started using some of its provisions to fight terrorism. He had harsh words for critics of the Patriot Act and his department:

We need honest, reasoned debate; not fearmongering. To those who pit Americans against immigrants and citizens against non-citizens, to those who scare peace-loving people with phantoms of lost liberty, my message is this: Your tactics only aid terrorists, for they erode our national unity and diminish our resolve. They give ammunition to America's enemies and pause to America's friends.

In subsequent speeches and congressional testimony, Ashcroft repeatedly hailed the Patriot Act as a "key weapon" in fighting terrorism. Groups that tried to monitor how the government used the Patriot Act frequently found themselves frustrated because the law or Ashcroft shrouded so many government actions in secrecy.

The Patriot Act drew renewed attention on February 7, 2003, when the Center for Public Integrity—an ethics watchdog in Washington—posted on its Web site an eighty-six-page draft bill written by the Justice Department that sought new, expanded powers to fight terrorism. The leaked bill, which was quickly dubbed Patriot II, sought broad new surveillance powers, access to consumer credit reports and library records without a warrant, creation of a DNA database that would collect genetic information on suspected terrorists, and an expansion of the definition of domestic terrorism that some said had the potential to result in Americans who engaged in civil disobedience losing their citizenship. The Justice Department downplayed the importance of the document, which it acknowledged was genuine. "During our internal deliberations, many ideas are considered, some are discarded, and new ideas emerge in the process, along with numerous discussion drafts," the department said in a statement.

Many lawmakers were angered by the draft—especially those who had been assured by the Justice Department that no such document existed—but Ashcroft repeatedly said the original Patriot Act did not go far enough to protect the nation against terrorist attack. In a speech on September 10, 2003, the day before the two-year anniversary of the terrorist attacks, President Bush called on Congress to pass legislation to "untie the hands of our law enforcement officials" by expanding federal police powers. He advocated allowing authorities to issue administrative subpoenas in terrorism investigations, holding suspects without bail, and pressing for the death penalty more frequently in terrorism cases.

In November 2003 Congress approved an intelligence spending bill that contained a provision straight out of the Patriot II draft bill, leading civil liberties advocates to fear that members would insert sections of the bill bit-by-bit into other legislation until the whole bill was effectively adopted.

In early December 2003 a federal judge in Detroit heard arguments in a lawsuit filed by the ACLU challenging Section 215 of the Patriot Act. The next month a federal judge in Los Angeles declared unconstitutional a provision in the law that barred providing expert advice or assistance to groups that the government had designated as foreign terrorist organizations. U.S. District Judge Audrey Collins ruled that the provision was so vague that it risked infringing on rights protected by the First Amendment. It appeared virtually certain that this case and other legal challenges to the Patriot Act would eventually end up before the U.S. Supreme Court.

On February 4, 2004, the city council in New York City—the largest city in the nation and the one that suffered most heavily in the 2001 terrorist attacks—passed a resolution that condemned the Patriot Act [Document 117]. New York City thus joined a list of more than 250 state and local governing bodies around the country that had passed a variety of measures expressing concern about the act. The resolutions were similar in many ways to resolutions passed in 1798 by the Virginia and Kentucky legislatures opposing the

Alien and Sedition Acts (*see* Laws Provide Broad Powers to Deport Aliens and Penalize Speech, p. 1).

In its final report released on July 24, 2004, the National Commission on Terrorist Attacks Upon the United States—known more commonly as the 9/11 Commission—added its voice to the Patriot Act debate. "In wartime," the commission wrote, "government calls for greater powers, and then the need for those powers recedes after the war ends. This struggle [against terrorism] will go on. Therefore, while protecting our homeland, Americans should be mindful of threats to vital personal and civil liberties." Any power granted to the government during wartime must have "adequate guidelines and oversight to properly confine its use," the commission said.

The commission did not take a formal position regarding the Patriot Act. However, it said: "Because of concerns regarding the shifting balance of power to the government, we think that a full and informed debate on the Patriot Act would be healthy" [Document 118].

# 112. Statements by Sen. Patrick Leahy, D-Vt., Chairman of the Senate Judiciary Committee, during Debate on the USA Patriot Act

*October 25, 2001*

## Opening Statement

. . . Today we consider H.R. 3162, the second House-passed version of the "Uniting and Strengthening of America Act" or "USA Act of 2001." Senate passage of this measure without amendment will amount to final passage of this important legislation, and the bill will be sent to the President for his signature. We complete our work six weeks after the September 11 attacks and months ahead of final action following the destruction of the Federal Building in Oklahoma City in 1995. The American people and the Members of this body deserve fast work and final action. . . .

Let me outline just ten ways in which we in the bicameral, bipartisan negotiations were able to supplement and improve this legislation from the original proposal we received from the Administration.

We improved security on the Northern Border;

We added money laundering;

We added programs to enhance information sharing and coordination with State and local law enforcement, grants to State and local governments to respond to bioterrorism, and to increase payments to families of fallen firefighters, police officers and other public safety workers;

We added humanitarian relief to immigrant victims of the September 11 terrorist attacks;

We added help to the FBI to hire translators;

We added more comprehensive victims assistance;

We added measures to fight cybercrime;

We added measures to fight terrorism against mass transportation systems;

We added important measures to use technology to make our borders more secure;

Finally, and most importantly, we were able to include additional important checks on the proposed expansion of government powers contained in the Attorney General's initial proposal.

In negotiations with the Administration, I did my best to strike a reasonable balance between the need to address the threat of terrorism, which we all keenly feel at the present time, and the need to protect our constitutional freedoms. Despite my misgivings, I acquiesced in some of the Administration's proposals to move the legislative process forward. That progress has been rewarded by a bill we have been able to improve further during discussions over the last two weeks. . . .

I do believe that some of the provisions contained both in this bill and the original USA Act will face difficult tests in the courts, and that we in Congress may have to revisit these issues at some time in the future when the present crisis has passed, the sunset has expired or the courts find an infirmity in these provisions. I also intend as Chairman of the Judiciary Committee to exercise careful oversight of how the Department of Justice, the FBI and other executive branch agencies are using the newly-expanded powers that this bill will give them. . . .

The negotiations on anti-terrorism legislation have not been easy. Within days of the September 11 attacks, I began work on legislation to address security needs on the Northern Border, the needs of victims and State and local law enforcement, and criminal law improvements. A week after the attack, on September 19, the Attorney General and I exchanged the outlines of the legislative proposals and pledged to work together toward our shared goal of putting tools in the hands of law enforcement that would help prevent another terrorist attack.

Let me be clear: No one can guarantee that Americans will be free from the threat of future terrorist attacks, and to suggest that this legislation—or any legislation—would or could provide such a guarantee would be a false promise. I will not engage in such false promises, and those who make such assertions do a disservice to the American people. . . .

## Closing Statement

Mr. President, we are about to vote and we will vote in a matter of minutes. I want us to think just for a moment why we are here. We have all shared the sadness, the horror of September 11. We are seeing Members of Congress and staffs threatened, tragic deaths in the Postal Service, those who died in the Pentagon, those who died at the Twin Towers.

It is also almost a cliche to say America is under attack, but that is what it is. Each of us has a job helping to respond to that. We are not Republicans or Democrats in that, we are Americans preserving our Nation and preserving our democracy. But, you know, we preserve it not just for today, we preserve it for the long run. That presents the kind of questions we have to answer in a bill such as this.

I suspect terrorist threats against the United States will exist after all of us, all 100 of us, are no longer serving in the Senate. It is a fact of life. It will come from people who hate our democracy, hate our diversity, hate our success. But that doesn't mean we are going to stop our democracy, our diversity, or our success.

Think what we cherish in this Nation. Our first amendment, for example, giving us the right to speak out about what we want—as we want. How many countries even begin to give that freedom?

Also, in that same first amendment, the right to practice any religion we want, or none if we want.

The leaders of the Judiciary Committee, Senator [Orrin] Hatch [R-Utah] and I, belong to different religions which we hold deeply. I think we gain a great deal of inner strength from our respective faiths. But we know we are not judged by our religion. That is something we must protect and hold. We are judged by how well we do in representing our States and our Nation.

Because we face terrible terrorist attacks today, we should not succumb tomorrow by giving up what makes us a great nation. That has been my benchmark throughout the work I have done in this bill. . . .

There was a rush, an understandable and even, some may say, justifiable rush, to pass legislation immediately after these terrible events. I understand that, the United States having been attacked within our borders for the first time, really, by an outside power since the War of 1812—attacked terribly, devastatingly. Who can forget the pictures we saw over and over again on television?

So I can understand the rush to do something, anything. But I used every bit of credibility I had as a Senator to say, wait, let us take time. I applaud people such as Senator [Thomas] Daschle [D-S.D.] who, using his great power as majority leader, said we will take the time to do this right, and backed me up on this. Other Senators from both sides of the aisle said, OK, let's work together.

I know the Senator from Utah [Hatch] shared the same anger that I did at the terrorists, and perhaps had been reluctant at first to join with me on that. But then the Senator from Utah and I worked day and night, weekends, evenings, and everything else to put together the best possible bill.

We worked with our friends and our colleagues in both parties in the other body [the House of Representatives]. Ultimately, we do nothing to protect America if we pass a bill which for short-term solutions gives us long-term pain by destroying our Constitution or our rights as Americans.

There are tough measures in this legislation. Some may even push the envelope to the extent that we worry. That is why we put in a four-year sunset. We have also built in constitutional checks and balances within the court system and within even some of the same agencies that will be given new enforcement powers. But we also will not forget our rights and responsibilities and our role as U.S. Senators.

We will not forget our role and our responsibilities as Senators to do oversight. Senator Hatch and I are committed to that. We will bring the best people from both sides of the aisle, across the political spectrum, to conduct effective oversight.

I have notified Attorney General Ashcroft and [Federal Bureau of Investigation] Director [Robert] Mueller that we will do that to make sure these powers are used within the constitutional framework to protect all of us. I said earlier on this floor what Benjamin Franklin said: that the people who would trade their liberties for security deserve neither.

We will enhance our security in this bill, but we will preserve our liberties. How could any one of us who have taken an oath of office to protect the Constitution do otherwise? . . .

I want to be able to look back at my time in the U.S. Senate and be able to tell my children, my grandchildren, and my friends and neighbors in Vermont—the State I love so much—that I came home having done my best.

We have so much in this country—so much. But it is our rights and our Constitution that give us everything we have, which allows us to use the genius of so many people who come from different backgrounds and different parts of the world. That makes us stronger. We become weak if we cut back on those rights.

We have had some difficult times in our Nation where we have not resisted the temptation to cut back. Here we have. The American people will know that this Congress has worked hard to protect us with this bill.

I will vote for this legislation knowing that we will continue to do our duty, and to follow it carefully to make sure that these new powers are used within our Constitution.

I suggest that all time be yielded, and that we be prepared to vote. I ask for the yeas and nays.

Excerpted from U.S. Congress. Senate. *USA Patriot Act of 2001,* Senate
Debate. Statements of Sen. Patrick Leahy (D-Vt.). 107th Cong., 1st sess.
*Congressional Record* 147, no. 144, daily ed. (October 25, 2001):
S10990–10991, S11058-9. http://www.gpoaccess.gov/crecord/index.html
(accessed October 15, 2004).

# 113. Section 312 of the USA Patriot Act (Money Laundering)

*October 26, 2001*

## SEC. 312. Special Due Diligence for Correspondent Accounts and Private Banking Accounts

(a) IN GENERAL.—Section 5318 of title 31, United States Code, is amended by adding at the end the following:

"(i) DUE DILIGENCE FOR UNITED STATES PRIVATE BANKING AND CORRESPONDENT BANK ACCOUNTS INVOLVING FOREIGN PERSONS.—

"(1) IN GENERAL.—Each financial institution that establishes, maintains, administers, or manages a private banking account or a correspondent account in the United States for a non-United States person, including a foreign individual visiting the United States, or a representative of a non-United States person shall establish appropriate, specific, and, where necessary, enhanced, due diligence policies, procedures, and controls that are reasonably designed to detect and report instances of money laundering through those accounts.

"(2) ADDITIONAL STANDARDS FOR CERTAIN CORRESPONDENT ACCOUNTS.—

"(A) IN GENERAL.—Subparagraph (B) shall apply if a correspondent account is requested or maintained by, or on behalf of, a foreign bank operating—

"(i) under an offshore banking license; or

"(ii) under a banking license issued by a foreign country that has been designated—

"(I) as noncooperative with international anti-money laundering principles or procedures by an intergovernmental group or organization of which the United States is a member, with which designation the United States representative to the group or organization concurs; or

"(II) by the Secretary of the Treasury as warranting special measures due to money laundering concerns.

"(B) POLICIES, PROCEDURES, AND CONTROLS.—The enhanced due diligence policies, procedures, and controls required under paragraph (1) shall, at a minimum, ensure that the financial institution in the United States takes reasonable steps—

"(i) to ascertain for any such foreign bank, the shares of which are not publicly traded, the identity of each of the owners of the foreign bank, and the nature and extent of the ownership interest of each such owner;

"(ii) to conduct enhanced scrutiny of such account to guard against money laundering and report any suspicious transactions under subsection (g); and

"(iii) to ascertain whether such foreign bank provides correspondent accounts to other foreign banks and, if so, the identity of those foreign banks and related due diligence information, as appropriate under paragraph (1).

"(3) MINIMUM STANDARDS FOR PRIVATE BANKING ACCOUNTS.—If a private banking account is requested or maintained by, or on behalf of, a non-United States person, then the due diligence policies, procedures, and controls required under paragraph (1) shall, at a minimum, ensure that the financial institution takes reasonable steps—

"(A) to ascertain the identity of the nominal and beneficial owners of, and the source of funds deposited into, such account as needed to guard against money laundering and report any suspicious transactions under subsection (g); and

"(B) to conduct enhanced scrutiny of any such account that is requested or maintained by, or on behalf of, a senior foreign political figure, or any immediate family member or close associate of a senior foreign political figure that is reasonably designed to detect and report transactions that may involve the proceeds of foreign corruption. . . .

Excerpted from U.S. Congress. *Uniting and Strengthening America By Providing Appropriate Tools Required to Intercept and Obstruct Terrorism (USA Patriot) Act of 2001,* Sec. 312. 107th Congress, 1st sess. October 26, 2001. Public Law 107-56, 115 Stat. 272. http://frwebgate.access.gpo.gov/cgi-bin/getdoc.cgi?dbname=107_cong_public_laws&docid=f:publ056.107.pdf (accessed October 15, 2004).

# 114. Section 213 of the USA Patriot Act (Search Warrants)

*October 26, 2001*

## SEC. 213. Authority for Delaying Notice of the Execution of a Warrant

Section 3103a of title 18, United States Code, is amended—. . .

(2) by adding at the end the following:

"(b) DELAY.—With respect to the issuance of any warrant or court order under this section, or any other rule of law, to search for and seize any property or material that constitutes evidence of a criminal offense in violation of the laws of the United States, any notice required, or that may be required, to be given may be delayed if—

"(1) the court finds reasonable cause to believe that providing immediate notification of the execution of the warrant may have an adverse result (as defined in section 2705);

"(2) the warrant prohibits the seizure of any tangible property, any wire or electronic communication (as defined in section 2510), or, except as expressly provided in chapter 121, any stored wire or electronic information, except where the court finds reasonable necessity for the seizure; and

"(3) the warrant provides for the giving of such notice within a reasonable period of its execution, which period may thereafter be extended by the court for good cause shown."

Excerpted from U.S. Congress. *Uniting and Strengthening America By Providing Appropriate Tools Required to Intercept and Obstruct Terrorism (USA Patriot) Act of 2001,* Sec. 213. 107th Congress, 1st sess. October 26, 2001. Public Law 107-56, 115 Stat. 272. http://frwebgate.access. gpo.gov/cgi-bin/getdoc.cgi?dbname=107_cong_public_laws&docid= f:publ056.107.pdf (accessed October 15, 2004).

# 115. Section 215 of the USA Patriot Act (Access to Records)

*October 26, 2001*

## SEC. 215. Access to Records and Other Items Under the Foreign Intelligence Surveillance Act

Title V of the Foreign Intelligence Surveillance Act of 1978 (50 U.S.C. 1861 et seq.) is amended by striking sections 501 through 503 and inserting the following:

## "SEC. 501. Access to Certain Business Records for Foreign Intelligence And International Terrorism Investigations

"(a)(1) The Director of the Federal Bureau of Investigation or a designee of the Director (whose rank shall be no lower than Assistant Special Agent in Charge) may make an application for an order requiring the production of any tangible things (including books, records, papers, documents, and other items) for an investigation to protect against international terrorism or clandestine intelligence activities, provided that such investigation of a United States person is not conducted solely upon the basis of activities protected by the first amendment to the Constitution.

"(2) An investigation conducted under this section shall—

"(A) be conducted under guidelines approved by the Attorney General under Executive Order 12333 (or a successor order); and

"(B) not be conducted of a United States person solely upon the basis of activities protected by the first amendment to the Constitution of the United States.

"(b) Each application under this section—

"(1) shall be made to—

"(A) a judge of the court established by section 103(a); or

"(B) a United States Magistrate Judge under chapter 43 of title 28, United States Code, who is publicly designated by the Chief Justice of the United States to have the power to hear applications and grant orders for the production of tangible things under this section on behalf of a judge of that court; and

"(2) shall specify that the records concerned are sought for an authorized investigation conducted in accordance with subsection (a)(2) to obtain foreign intelligence information not concerning a United States person or to protect against international terrorism or clandestine intelligence activities.

"(c)(1) Upon an application made pursuant to this section, the judge shall enter an ex parte order as requested, or as modified, approving the release of records if the judge finds that the application meets the requirements of this section.

"(2) An order under this subsection shall not disclose that it is issued for purposes of an investigation described in subsection (a).

"(d) No person shall disclose to any other person (other than those persons necessary to produce the tangible things under this section) that the Federal Bureau of Investigation has sought or obtained tangible things under this section.

"(e) A person who, in good faith, produces tangible things under an order pursuant to this section shall not be liable to any other person for such production. Such production shall not be deemed to constitute a waiver of any privilege in any other proceeding or context.

## "SEC. 502. Congressional Oversight

"(a) On a semiannual basis, the Attorney General shall fully inform the Permanent Select Committee on Intelligence of the House of Representatives and the Select Committee on Intelligence of the Senate concerning all requests for the production of tangible things under section 402.

"(b) On a semiannual basis, the Attorney General shall provide to the Committees on the Judiciary of the House of Representatives and the Senate a report setting forth with respect to the preceding 6-month period—

"(1) the total number of applications made for orders approving requests for the production of tangible things under section 402; and

"(2) the total number of such orders either granted, modified, or denied.".

U.S. Congress. *Uniting and Strengthening America By Providing Appropriate Tools Required To Intercept and Obstruct Terrorism (USA Patriot) Act of 2001,* Sec. 215. 107th Congress, 1st sess. October 26, 2001. Public Law 107-56, 115 Stat. 272. http://frwebgate.access.gpo.gov/cgi-bin/getdoc.cgi?dbname=107_cong_public_laws&docid=f:publ056.107.pdf (accessed September 15, 2004).

# 116. Congressional Testimony by Attorney General John Ashcroft

*December 6, 2001*

. . . On the morning of September 11, as the United States came under attack, I was in an airplane with several members of the Justice Department en route to Milwaukee, in the skies over the Great Lakes. By the time we could return to Washington, thousands of people had been murdered at the World Trade Center. One hundred eighty-nine were dead at the Pentagon. Forty-four had crashed to the ground in Pennsylvania. From that moment, at the command of the President of the United States, I began to mobilize the resources of the Department of Justice toward one single, over-arching and over-riding objective: to save innocent lives from further acts of terrorism.

America's campaign to save innocent lives from terrorists is now 87 days old. It has brought me back to this committee to report to you in accordance with Congress's oversight role. I welcome this opportunity to clarify for you and the American people how the Justice Department is working to protect American lives while preserving American liberties. . . .

Under the leadership of President Bush, America has made the choice to fight terrorism—not just for ourselves but for all civilized people. Since September 11, through dozens of warnings to law enforcement, a deliberate campaign of terrorist disruption, tighter security around potential targets, and a preventative campaign of arrest and detention of lawbreakers, America has grown stronger—and safer—in the face of terrorism.

Thanks to the vigilance of law enforcement and the patience of the American people, we have not suffered another major terrorist attack. Still, we cannot—we must not—allow ourselves to grow complacent. The reasons are apparent to me each morning. My day begins with a review of the threats to Americans and American interests that were received in the previous 24 hours. If ever there were proof of the existence of evil in the world, it is in the pages of these reports. They are a chilling daily chronicle of hatred of America by fanatics who seek to extinguish freedom, enslave women, corrupt education and to kill Americans wherever and whenever they can.

The terrorist enemy that threatens civilization today is unlike any we have ever known. It slaughters thousands of innocents—a crime of war and a crime against humanity. It seeks weapons of mass destruction and threatens their use against America. No one should doubt the intent, nor the depth, of its consuming, destructive hatred.

Terrorist operatives infiltrate our communities—plotting, planning and waiting to kill again. They enjoy the benefits of our free society even as they commit themselves to our destruction. They exploit our openness—not randomly or haphazardly—but by deliberate, premeditated design.

This is a seized al Qaeda training manual—a "how-to" guide for terrorists—that instructs enemy operatives in the art of killing in a free society. Prosecutors first made this manual public in the trial of the al Qaeda terrorists who bombed U.S. embassies in Africa. We are posting several al Qaeda lessons from this manual on our website today so Americans can know our enemy.

In this manual, al Qaeda terrorists are told how to use America's freedom as a weapon against us. They are instructed to use the benefits of a free press—newspapers, magazines and broadcasts—to stalk and kill their victims. They are instructed to exploit our judicial process for the success of their operations. Captured terrorists are taught to anticipate a series of questions from authorities and, in each response, to lie—to lie about who they are, to lie about what they are doing and to lie about who they know in order for the operation to achieve its objective. Imprisoned terrorists are instructed to concoct stories of torture and mistreatment at the hands of our officials. They are directed to take advantage of any contact with the outside world to, quote, "communicate with brothers outside prison and exchange information that may be helpful to them in their work. The importance of mastering the art of hiding messages is self-evident here."

Mr. Chairman and members of the committee, we are at war with an enemy who abuses individual rights as it abuses jet airliners: as weapons with which to kill Americans. We have responded by redefining the mission of the Department of Justice. Defending our nation and its citizens against terrorist attacks is now our first and overriding priority.

We have launched the largest, most comprehensive criminal investigation in world history to identify the killers of September 11 and to prevent further terrorist attacks. Four thousand FBI [Federal Bureau of Investigation] agents are engaged with their international counterparts in an unprecedented worldwide effort to detect, disrupt and dismantle terrorist organizations.

We have created a national task force at the FBI to centralize control and information sharing in our investigation. This task force has investigated hundreds of thousands of leads, conducted over 500 searches, interviewed thousands of witnesses and obtained numerous court-authorized surveillance orders. Our prosecutors and agents have collected information and evidence from countries throughout Europe and the Middle East.

Immediately following the September 11 attacks, the Bureau of Prisons acted swiftly to intensify security precautions in connection with all al Qaeda and other terrorist inmates, increasing perimeter security at a number of key facilities.

We have sought and received additional tools from Congress. Already, we have begun to utilize many of these tools. Within hours of passage of the USA PATRIOT Act, we made use of its provisions to begin enhanced information sharing between the law-enforcement and intelligence communities. We have used the provisions allowing nationwide search warrants for e-mail and subpoenas for payment information. And we have used the Act to place those who access the Internet through cable companies on the same footing as everyone else.

Just yesterday, at my request, the State Department designated 39 entities as terrorist organizations pursuant to the USA PATRIOT Act.

We have waged a deliberate campaign of arrest and detention to remove suspected terrorists who violate the law from our streets. Currently, we have brought criminal charges against 110 individuals, of whom 60 are in federal custody. The INS has detained 563 individuals on immigration violations.

We have investigated more than 250 incidents of retaliatory violence and threats against Arab Americans, Muslim Americans, Sikh Americans and South Asian Americans. . . .

We have embarked on a wartime reorganization of the Department of Justice. We are transferring resources and personnel to the field offices where citizens are served and protected. The INS [Immigration and Naturalization Service] is being restructured to better perform its service and border security responsibilities. Under Director Bob Mueller, the FBI is undergoing an historic reorganization to put the prevention of terrorism at the center of its law enforcement and national security efforts.

Outside Washington, we are forging new relationships of cooperation with state and local law enforcement.

We have created 93 Anti-Terrorism Task Forces—one in each U.S. Attorney's district—to integrate the communications and activities of local, state and federal law enforcement.

In all these ways and more, the Department of Justice has sought to prevent terrorism with reason, careful balance and excruciating attention to detail. Some of our critics, I regret to say, have shown less affection for detail. Their bold declarations of so-called fact have quickly dissolved, upon inspection, into vague conjecture. Charges of "kangaroo courts" and "shredding the Constitution" give new meaning to the term, "the fog of war."

Since lives and liberties depend upon clarity, not obfuscation, and reason, not hyperbole, let me take this opportunity today to be clear: Each action taken by the Department of Justice, as well as the war crimes commissions considered by the President and the Department of Defense, is carefully drawn to target a narrow class of individuals—terrorists. Our legal powers are targeted at terrorists. Our investigation is focused on terrorists. Our prevention strategy targets the terrorist threat.

Since 1983, the United States government has defined terrorists as those who perpetrate premeditated, politically motivated violence against noncombatant targets. My message to America this morning, then, is this: If you fit this definition of a terrorist, fear the United States, for you will lose your liberty.

We need honest, reasoned debate; not fearmongering. To those who pit Americans against immigrants, and citizens against non-citizens; to those who scare peace-loving people with phantoms of lost liberty; my message is this: Your tactics only aid terrorists—for they erode our national unity and diminish our resolve. They give ammunition to America's enemies, and pause to America's friends. They encourage people of good will to remain silent in the face of evil.

Our efforts have been carefully crafted to avoid infringing on constitutional rights while saving American lives. We have engaged in a deliberate campaign of arrest and detention of law breakers. All persons being detained have the right to contact their lawyers and their families. Out of respect for their privacy, and concern for saving lives, we will not publicize the names of those detained.

We have the authority to monitor the conversations of 16 of the 158,000 federal inmates and their attorneys because we suspect that these communications are facilitating acts of terrorism. Each prisoner has been told in advance his conversations will be monitored. None of the information that is protected by attorney-client privilege may be used for prosecution. Information will only be used to stop impending terrorist acts and save American lives.

We have asked a very limited number of individuals—visitors to our country holding passports from countries with active Al Qaeda operations—to speak voluntarily to law enforcement. We are forcing them to do nothing. We are merely asking them to do the right thing: to willingly disclose information they may have of terrorist threats to the lives and safety of all people in the United States.

Throughout all our activities since September 11, we have kept Congress informed of our continuing efforts to protect the American people. Beginning with a classified briefing by Director Mueller and me on the very evening of September 11, the Justice Department has briefed members of the House, the Senate and their staffs on more than 100 occasions.

We have worked with Congress in the belief and recognition that no single branch of government alone can stop terrorism. We have consulted with members out of respect for the separation of powers that is the basis of our system of government. However, Congress' power of oversight is not without limits. The Constitution specifically delegates to the President the authority to "take care that the laws are faithfully executed." And perhaps most importantly, the Constitution vests the President with the extraordinary and sole authority as Commander-in-Chief to lead our nation in times of war.

Mr. Chairman and members of the committee, not long ago I had the privilege of sitting where you now sit. I have the greatest reverence and respect for the constitutional responsibilities you shoulder. I will continue to consult with Congress so that you may fulfill your constitutional responsibilities. In some areas, however, I cannot and will not consult you.

The advice I give to the President, whether in his role as Commander-in-Chief or in any other capacity, is privileged and confidential. I cannot and will not divulge the contents, the context, or even the existence of such advice to anyone—including Congress—unless the President instructs me to do so. I cannot and will not divulge information, nor do I believe that anyone here would wish me to divulge information, that will damage the national security of the United States, the safety of its citizens or our efforts to ensure the same in an ongoing investigation.

As Attorney General, it is my responsibility—at the direction of the President—to exercise those core executive powers the Constitution so designates. The law enforcement initiatives undertaken by the Department of Justice, those individuals we arrest, detain or seek to interview, fall under these core executive powers. In addition, the President's authority to establish war-crimes commissions arises out of his power as Commander in Chief. For centuries, Congress has recognized this authority and the Supreme Court has never held that any Congress may limit it.

In accordance with over two hundred years of historical and legal precedent, the executive branch is now exercising its core Constitutional powers in the interest of saving the lives of Americans. I trust that Congress will respect the proper limits of Executive Branch consultation that I am duty-bound to uphold. I trust, as well, that Congress will respect this President's authority to wage war on terrorism and defend our nation and its citizens with all the power vested in him by the Constitution and entrusted to him by the American people.

Thank you.

Excerpted from U.S. Congress. Senate. Committee on the Judiciary. *Department of Justice Oversight: Preserving Our Freedoms While Defending Against Terrorism.* Prepared Testimony of Attorney General John Ashcroft. 107th Cong., 1st sess. S. Hrg. 107-704, serial J-107-50, December 6, 2001. http://purl.access.gpo.gov/GPO/LPS25921 (accessed October 15, 2004).

# 117. New York City Council Resolution about the USA Patriot Act

*February 4, 2004*

*Whereas,* The protection of civil rights and civil liberties is essential to the well being of a free and democratic society; and

*Whereas,* The City of New York has a diverse population, including immigrants and students, whose contributions to the city are vital to its economy, culture and civic character; and

*Whereas,* The members of the Council of the City of New York believe that there is no inherent conflict between national security and the preservation of liberty—Americans can be both safe and free; and

*Whereas,* Government security measures that undermine fundamental rights do damage to the American institutions and values that the residents of the City of New York hold dear; and

*Whereas,* Federal, state and local governments should protect the public from terrorist attacks, such as those that occurred on September 11, 2001, but should do so in a rational and deliberative fashion in order to ensure that security measures enhance the public safety without impairing constitutional rights or infringing on civil liberties; and

*Whereas,* Certain federal policies adopted since September 11, 2001, including certain provisions in the USA PATRIOT Act (Public Law 107-56) and related federal actions, unduly infringe upon fundamental rights and liberties; and

*Whereas,* These new policies include the power to authorize the indefinite incarceration of non-citizens based on mere suspicion of terrorist activity, and the indefinite incarceration of citizens designated as "enemy combatants" without access to counsel or meaningful recourse to the federal courts; limitations on the traditional authority of federal courts to curb law enforcement abuse of electronic surveillance in anti-terrorism investigations and ordinary criminal investigations; the expansion of the authority of federal agents to conduct so-called "sneak and peek" or "black bag" searches, in which the subject of the search warrant is unaware that his property has been searched; grants to law enforcement and intelligence agencies of broad access to personal medical, financial, library and education records with little if any judicial oversight; and

*Whereas,* These new policies may undermine trust between immigrant communities and the government and, in particular, pose a threat to the civil rights and liberties of the residents of our city who are or who appear to be of Arab, Muslim or South Asian descent; and

*Whereas,* The federal government has drafted new legislation entitled the Domestic Security Enhancement Act (DSEA) (also known as

PATRIOT II), which may further compromise constitutional rights and our government's unique system of checks and balances; and

*Whereas,* Three states and more than 200 communities throughout the country have enacted resolutions that reaffirm support for civil rights and civil liberties and that demand accountability from law enforcement agencies regarding the exercise of the extraordinary new powers referred to herein; now, therefore, be it

*Resolved,* That the Council of the City of New York calls upon federal, state and local officials, and upon New York City agencies and institutions, to affirm and protect civil rights and civil liberties; and be it further

*Resolved,* That the Council of the City of New York affirms its strong support for the rights of immigrants and opposes measures that single out individuals for legal scrutiny or enforcement activity based primarily upon their country of origin; and be it further

*Resolved,* That the Council of the City of New York affirms its commitment to uphold civil rights and civil liberties, and therefore expresses its opposition to:

(a) investigation of individuals or groups of individuals based on their participation in activities protected by the First Amendment, such as political advocacy or the practice of a religion, without reasonable suspicion of criminal activity unrelated to the activity protected by the First Amendment;

(b) racial, religious or ethnic profiling;

(c) participation in the enforcement of federal immigration laws, except as directed by New York City Executive Order 41;

(d) deployment of biometric identification technology that is unreliable;

(e) establishment of a network of general surveillance cameras unless such a network is subject to regulations that provide reasonable and effective protections of privacy and due process rights of individuals who appear in recorded material; and

(f) "sneak and peek" searches, pursuant to Section 213 of the Patriot Act, unless the search is authorized and conducted in accordance with New York State law; and

(g) establishment or maintenance of an anti-terrorism reporting system that creates an electronic record on an individual unless subject to regulations that provide for the protection of individuals who are the subject of unfounded reports; and be it further

*Resolved,* That the Council of the City of New York opposes requests by federal authorities that, if granted, would cause agencies of the City of New York to exercise powers or cooperate in the exercise of powers in apparent violation of any city ordinance or the laws or Constitution of this State or the United States; and be it further

*Resolved,* That the Council of the City of New York opposes the secret detention of persons and the detention of persons without charges or access to a lawyer; and be it further

*Resolved*, That the Council of the City of New York urges each of the City's public libraries to inform library patrons that Section 215 of the USA PATRIOT Act gives the government new authority to monitor book-borrowing and Internet activities without patrons' knowledge or consent and that this law prohibits library staff from informing patrons if federal agents have requested patrons' library records; and be it further

*Resolved*, That in order to assess the effect of antiterrorism initiatives on the residents of the City of New York, the City Council calls upon federal officials to make periodic reports, consistent with the Freedom of Information Act, that include:

(a) the number of New York City residents who have been arrested or otherwise detained by federal authorities as a result of terrorism investigations since September 11, 2001;

(b) the number of search warrants that have been executed in the City of New York without notice to the subject of the warrant pursuant to section 213 of the USA PATRIOT Act;

(c) the number of electronic surveillance actions carried out in the City of New York under powers granted in the USA PATRIOT Act;

(d) the number of investigations undertaken by federal authorities to monitor political meetings, religious gatherings or other activities protected by the First Amendment within the City of New York;

(e) the number of times education records have been obtained from public schools and institutions of higher learning in the City of New York under section 507 of the USA PATRIOT Act;

(f) the number of times library records have been obtained from libraries in the City of New York under section 215 of the USA PATRIOT Act;  and

(g) the number of times that records of the books purchased by store patrons have been obtained from bookstores in the City of New York under section 215 of the USA PATRIOT Act; and be it further

*Resolved*, That the Council of the City of New York calls upon our United States Representatives and Senators to monitor the implementation of the USA PATRIOT Act and related federal actions and to actively work for the repeal of those sections of the USA PATRIOT Act and related federal actions that unduly infringe upon fundamental rights and liberties as recognized in the U.S. Constitution and its Amendments; and be it further

*Resolved*, That the Council of the City of New York calls upon our United States Representatives and Senators to take a lead in Congressional action to prohibit passage of the Domestic Security Enhancement Act, known as "Patriot II"; and be it further

*Resolved*, That the Council of the City of New York calls upon Governor George Pataki, Senate Majority Leader Joseph Bruno and Assembly Speaker Sheldon Silver and the members of the State Legislature to ensure that state anti-terrorism laws and policies are implemented in a manner that does not infringe upon fundamental rights and liberties as recognized in the U.S. Constitution and its Amendments and in the New York State Constitution.

New York City. Council of the City of New York. *Resolution Calling upon Federal, State and Local Officials, and upon New York Agencies and Institutions, to Affirm and Uphold Civil Rights and Civil Liberties.* Res. 60-2004, February 4, 2004. http://webdocs.nyccouncil.info/textfiles/Res%200060-2004.htm?CFID=170449&CFTOKEN=28019366 (accessed October 15, 2004).

# 118. 9/11 Commission on the USA Patriot Act and Civil Liberties

*July 22, 2004*

## The Protection of Civil Liberties

Many of our recommendations call for the government to increase its presence in our lives—for example, by creating standards for the issuance of forms of identification, by better securing our borders, by sharing information gathered by many different agencies. We also recommend the consolidation of authority over the now far-flung entities constituting the intelligence community. The Patriot Act vests substantial powers in our federal government. We have seen the government use the immigration laws as a tool in its counterterrorism effort. Even without the changes we recommend, the American public has vested enormous authority in the U.S. government.

At our first public hearing on March 31, 2003, we noted the need for balance as our government responds to the real and ongoing threat of terrorist attacks. The terrorists have used our open society against us. In wartime, government calls for greater powers, and then the need for those powers recedes after the war ends. This struggle will go on. Therefore, while protecting our homeland, Americans should be mindful of threats to vital personal and civil liberties. This balancing is no easy task, but we must constantly strive to keep it right.

This shift of power and authority to the government calls for an enhanced system of checks and balances to protect the precious liberties that are vital to our way of life. We therefore make three recommendations.

First, to open up the sharing of information across so many agencies and with the private sector, the President should take responsibility for determining what information can be shared by which agencies and under what conditions. Protection of privacy rights should be one key element of this determination.

*Recommendation: As the President determines the guidelines for information sharing among government agencies and by those agencies with the private sector, he should safeguard the privacy of individuals about whom information is shared.*

Second, Congress responded, in the immediate aftermath of 9/11, with the Patriot Act, which vested substantial new powers in the investigative agencies of the government. Some of the most controversial provisions of the Patriot Act are to "sunset" at the end of 2005. Many of the act's provisions are relatively noncontroversial, updating America's surveillance laws to reflect technological developments in a digital age. Some executive actions that have been criticized are unrelated to the Patriot Act. The provisions in the act that facilitate the sharing of information among intelligence agencies and between law enforcement and intelligence appear, on balance, to be beneficial. Because of concerns regarding the shifting balance of power to the government, we think that a full and informed debate on the Patriot Act would be healthy.

*Recommendation: The burden of proof for retaining a particular governmental power should be on the executive, to explain (a) that the power actually materially enhances security and (b) that there is adequate supervision of the executive's use of the powers to ensure protection of civil liberties. If the power is granted, there must be adequate guidelines and oversight to properly confine its use.*

Third, during the course of our inquiry, we were told that there is no office within the government whose job it is to look across the government at the actions we are taking to protect ourselves to ensure that liberty concerns are appropriately considered. If, as we recommend, there is substantial change in the way we collect and share intelligence, there should be a voice within the executive branch for those concerns. Many agencies have privacy offices, albeit of limited scope. The Intelligence Oversight Board of the President's Foreign Intelligence Advisory Board has, in the past, had the job of overseeing certain activities of the intelligence community.

*Recommendation: At this time of increased and consolidated government authority, there should be a board within the executive branch to oversee adherence to the guidelines we recommend and the commitment the government makes to defend our civil liberties.*

We must find ways of reconciling security with liberty, since the success of one helps protect the other. The choice between security and liberty is a false choice, as nothing is more likely to endanger America's liberties than the success of a terrorist attack at home. Our history has shown us that insecurity threatens liberty. Yet, if our liberties are curtailed, we lose the values that we are struggling to defend.

Excerpted from U.S. National Commission on Terrorist Attacks Upon the United States. *The 9/11 Commission Report: Final Report of the National Commission on Terrorist Attacks Upon the United States.* July 22, 2004: 393–395. Washington, D.C.: Government Printing Office. http://www. gpoaccess.gov/911/index.html (accessed October 15, 2004).

# Federal Actions Aimed at Preserving Continuity of Government

## INTRODUCTION

The horrific terrorist attacks of September 11, 2001, could have been even worse. Without a bit of good work, some luck, and a lot of heroism, United Flight 93 probably would have smashed into the White House or the U.S. Capitol in Washington, D.C. A successful attack on either building could have destroyed an important symbol of the nation's government; killed hundreds or even thousands of high-ranking government officials, staff members, and others; and strained the continuity of government, which the Congressional Research Service defines as "the continued functioning of constitutional government under all circumstances."

The good work came a month before the attacks when an immigration inspector in Orlando denied admittance to Mohamed al Kahtani, a Saudi Arabian man who aroused his suspicions. Kahtani probably would have been the fifth hijacker on Flight 93, but the inspector's action left Flight 93 with four hijackers instead of the five aboard the three planes that hit their targets. The luck occurred when Flight 93's departure was delayed about twenty-five minutes because of heavy traffic at Newark's airport. The delay meant that when passengers and crew members on Flight 93 called loved ones and colleagues after the plane was hijacked, they learned that two planes had already struck the World Trade Center. The passengers then heroically attacked the hijackers. With a battle raging just outside the cockpit door, the hijacker at the plane's controls turned the control wheel hard to the right and the plane slammed into a Pennsylvania field. At that point, Flight 93 was only about twenty minutes in flying time from Washington.

"The nation owes a debt to the passengers of United 93," the National Commission on Terrorist Attacks Upon the United States—better known as the 9/11 Commission—wrote in its final report. "Their actions saved the lives of countless others, and may have saved either the Capitol or the White House from destruction."

The September 11 attacks focused attention on the need to ensure the government could continue functioning even if Washington was attacked. On December 28, 2001, President George W. Bush signed executive orders that extensively detailed the lines of succession at key federal agencies [Document 119]. He signed orders for other agencies in mid-2002.

But the Bush administration had secretly taken more dramatic action within hours of the hijackings. Under a contingency plan first developed by the Eisenhower administration when Washington faced a possible nuclear attack during the cold war, the administration sent about 100 top civilian managers in the executive branch to a pair of underground locations on the East Coast. Many were transported by helicopter. It was later revealed that the administration took the unprecedented action because it feared that al Qaeda might explode a suitcase nuclear bomb in Washington that would destroy the city. If that happened and the government was wiped out, the senior administrators—who lived and worked underground in rotations that usually lasted ninety days—were to restore public services and then create a new government.

The *Cleveland Plain Dealer* and *U.S. News & World Report* revealed the existence of the "shadow government" in October 2001. Nonetheless, the issue went unnoticed until the *Washington Post* published an article about the shadow government on March 1, 2002. Senior administration officials confirmed that the contingency plan had been implemented but refused to provide details. During a presidential trip to Des Moines, Iowa, on the day the *Post* story appeared, a reporter asked Bush if there really was a shadow government. Bush did not directly answer the question, but said:

[W]e take the continuity-of-government issue very seriously, because our nation was under attack. And I still take the threats that we receive from Al Qaida killers and terrorists very seriously. I have an obligation as the President, and my administration has an obligation to the American people to provide—to put measures in place that, should somebody be successful in attacking Washington, DC, there's an ongoing government. That's one reason why the vice president was going to undisclosed locations. This is serious business, and we take it seriously.

The next day, the *New York Times* reported that Congress and the Supreme Court also had classified contingency plans. The military had already been rotating senior officials to secure locations for years.

Some top congressional leaders complained that they only learned of the shadow government by reading newspaper articles. "None of us knew about the secret government," Senate Majority Leader Tom Daschle, D-S.D., said on *Fox News Sunday.* "Not knowing things as basic as that is a pretty profound illustration of the chasm that exists sometimes with information." Republican lawmakers said the secrecy was justified by events, and the administration quickly scheduled a round of briefings for senior members of Congress.

The Constitution prohibits either house of Congress from meeting in any other place "than that in which the two Houses shall be sitting" without the consent of the other chamber. The House of Representatives dealt with this by passing a concurrent resolution on January 7, 2003, that authorized the Speaker of the House and the majority leader of the Senate or their designees to notify their respective members "to assemble at a place outside the District of Columbia whenever, in their opinion, the public interest shall warrant it." The Senate approved the measure in February, but it did not have the force of law because concurrent resolutions are not submitted to the president for approval [Document 120].

On June 4, 2003, the independent Continuity of Government Commission released a report that said the Constitution should be amended so Congress could pass laws creating procedures for replacing members who were killed or incapacitated. The laws should allow for emergency temporary appointments of House members until special elections could be held, the commission said. The commission was a project of two think tanks in Washington, D.C.—the Brookings Institution and the American Enterprise Institute—and the twenty-member panel included prominent political leaders such as former House Speakers Newt Gingrich, R-Ga., and Thomas S. Foley, D-Wash. The commission noted that current law allowed governors to name replacements for senators who died, but the Constitution required that House vacancies be filled by election. Arranging special elections usually took at least three months, and the commission said the nation could not wait that long if hundreds of members of Congress were killed or incapacitated by an attack [Document 121]. However, many lawmakers strongly opposed amending the Constitution and allowing anything other than direct election of House members. Lawmakers also were naturally reluctant to consider the possibility that they would die in a terrorist attack.

On February 27, 2004, the General Accounting Office (GAO)—the investigative arm of Congress—reported that it found serious flaws in many continuity of operations (COOP) plans that federal agencies had in place on October 1, 2002. For example, agencies were supposed to identify their essential functions so continuity efforts could center on them. Five of the thirty-four plans that the GAO examined did not list any essential functions, and the remaining plans listed anywhere from three to 399 functions as essential, although the GAO said that some of the functions listed "appeared to be of secondary importance." The congressional investigators cited one plan that included providing "speeches and articles for the Secretary and Deputy Secretary" among the department's essential functions, leaving out nine of the ten departmental programs that the Office of Management and Budget had previously identified as having a high impact on the public. The GAO placed much of the blame for the poor plans on the Federal Emergency Management Agency (FEMA), which was supposed to oversee development of the plans and provide guidance to federal agencies. "If FEMA does not address these shortcomings," the GAO concluded, "agency COOP plans may not be effective in ensuring that the most vital government services can be maintained in an emergency" [Document 122].

In April 2004 the House passed a bill by a 306–97 margin that would require states to hold special elections within forty-five days after the Speaker of the House certified that at least 100 of the 435 representatives had died in a catastrophic event. Opponents said states would not be able to hold elections that quickly, especially if the nation had suffered a major terrorist attack. They also said that even reconstituting the House within forty-five days was far too long a period after a major terrorist strike and pointed out that within days of the September 11 attacks Congress passed major legislation, including appropriations bills, to help the nation recover. Near the end of the year, however, it appeared likely the bill would die because the Senate showed no interest in considering it. Two months after approving the special elections bill, the House voted overwhelmingly to reject a proposed constitutional amendment that would have allowed governors to temporarily appoint House members if an attack killed a majority of them.

---

# 119. Executive Order Regarding State Department Succession
### *December 28, 2001*

By the authority vested in me as President by the Constitution and laws of the United States of America, including the Federal Vacancies Reform Act of 1998, 5 U.S.C. 3345 *et seq.*, it is hereby ordered that:

*Section 1.* Subject to the provisions of section 3 of this order, the officers named in section 2, in the order listed, shall act as, and perform the duties of, the office of Secretary of State (Secretary) during any period in which the Secretary has died, resigned, or otherwise become unable to perform the functions and duties of the office of Secretary.

*Sec. 2. Order of Succession.*

(a) Deputy Secretary of State;

(b) Deputy Secretary of State for Management and Resources;

(c) Under Secretary of State designated for political affairs pursuant to section 2651a(b) of title 22, United States Code;

(d) Under Secretary of State designated for management affairs pursuant to section 2651a(b) of title 22, United States Code;

(e) The remaining Under Secretaries of State, in the order in which they shall have taken the oath of office as such;

(f) Assistant Secretaries of State designated for regional bureaus pursuant to section 2651a(c) of title 22, United States Code, in the order in which they shall have taken the oath of office as such;

(g) The following officers, in the order in which they shall have taken the oath of office as such:

(1) Remaining Assistant Secretaries of State;

(2) Coordinator for Counterterrorism;

(3) Director General of the Foreign Service; and

(4) Legal Adviser;

(h) United States Representative to the United Nations (New York);

(i) Deputy United States Representative to the United Nations (New York);

(j) The following other United States Representatives to the United Nations (New York), in the order in which they shall have taken the oath of office as such:

United States Representative to the United Nations for United Nations Management and Reform; United States Representative to the United Nations on the Economic and Social Council of the United Nations; and Alternate United States Representative to the United Nations for Special Political Affairs in the United Nations;

(k) The following Chiefs of Mission, in the order listed:

(1) United States Ambassador to the United Kingdom;

(2) United States Ambassador to Canada;

(3) United States Ambassador to Australia;

(4) United States Ambassador to Mexico;

(5) United States Ambassador to Japan; and

(6) United States Ambassador to India;

(l) The following officers, in the order in which they shall have taken the oath of office as such:

(1) United States Ambassadors at Large;

(2) Counselor; and

(3) Special Representatives of the President; and

(m) The remaining Chiefs of Mission, in the order in which they shall have taken the oath of office as such.

*Sec. 3. Exceptions.*

(a) No individual who has not been appointed by the President by and with the consent of the Senate shall act as Secretary pursuant to this order.

(b) No individual who is serving in an office listed in section 2(a)-(m) in an acting capacity shall act as Secretary pursuant to this order.

(c) Notwithstanding the provisions of this order, the President retains discretion, to the extent permitted by the Federal Vacancies Reform Act of

1998, 5 U.S.C. 3345 *et seq.*, to depart from this order in designating an acting Secretary.

(d) A successor office, intended to be the equivalent of an office identified in section 2 of this order, shall be deemed to be the position identified in section 2 for purposes of this order.

*Sec. 4.* Executive Order 12343 of January 27, 1982, is hereby revoked.

George W. Bush
The White House
December 28, 2001

U.S. Executive Office of the President. Executive Order—Providing an Order of Succession within the Department of State. December 28, 2001. *Weekly Compilation of Presidential Documents* 37, no. 52 (December 31, 2001): 1841–1842. http://www.gpoaccess.gov/wcomp/v37no52.html (accessed October 15, 2004).

# 120. House Concurrent Resolution 1
### *January 7, 2003*

## Concurrent Resolution

*Resolved by the House of Representatives (the Senate concurring),* That pursuant to clause 4, section 5, article I of the Constitution, during the One Hundred Eighth Congress the Speaker of the House and the Majority Leader of the Senate or their respective designees, acting jointly after consultation with the Minority Leader of the House and the Minority Leader of the Senate, may notify the Members of the House and the Senate, respectively, to assemble at a place outside the District of Columbia whenever, in their opinion, the public interest shall warrant it.

Passed the House of Representatives January 7, 2003.

U.S. Congress. House of Representatives. *House Concurrent Resolution 1,* 108th Cong., 1st sess. *Congressional Record 149, no. 1,* daily ed. (January 7, 2003): H20–H21. http://frwebgate.access.gpo.gov/cgi-bin/getdoc.cgi?dbname=108_cong_bills&docid=f:hc1eh.txt.pdf (accessed October 15, 2004).

# 121. The Congress: Preserving Our Institutions, a Report by the Continuity in Government Commission

*June 4, 2003*

## Preface: The Continuity of Government

It is 11:30 a.m., inauguration day. Thousands await the noon hour when a new president will take the oath of office in the presence of members of Congress, the Supreme Court, family, and supporters. The outgoing president is meeting at the White House with his cabinet and top aides for a final farewell before attending the swearing in ceremony where the reins of power will switch hands. Television networks have their cameras trained on the West Front of the Capitol, beaming live coverage of the event into millions of homes around the world.

Suddenly the television screens go blank! Al Qaeda operatives have detonated a small nuclear device on Pennsylvania Avenue halfway between the White House and the Capitol. A one-mile-radius circle of Washington is destroyed. Everyone present at the Capitol, the White House, and in between is presumed dead, missing, or incapacitated. The death toll is horrific, the symbolic effect of the destruction of our national symbols is great, but even worse, the American people are asking who is in charge, and there is no clear answer.

The incoming president and vice president are surely dead, so the presidency passes through the line of succession to the Speaker of the House and then to the President Pro Tempore of the Senate. But both of them were at the inaugural ceremony, as protocol requires, so the presidency passes to the cabinet officers—but which cabinet? The president-elect never took office and never confirmed a cabinet. The presidency passes through the line of succession to the cabinet officers of the departing administration, assuming they have not resigned by January 20th, as is standard procedure, and assuming that they were not at the White House bidding farewell to the outgoing president. Perhaps the Secretary of Veterans Affairs, or another lesser-known cabinet member, was not in the area; then he or she would become president. Or maybe no one in the line of succession is alive, and a number of generals, undersecretaries, and governors claim that they are in charge.

Congress has been annihilated as well, with only a few members who did not attend the ceremony remaining. It will be many months before Congress can function. Our Constitution requires a majority of each house of Congress to constitute a quorum to do business, and no such majority of the House or Senate exists. In addition, because of a series of past parliamentary rulings, there is confusion about whether there are enough members to proceed. The House's official interpretation of the quorum requirement is a majority of the living members, a proposition that scholars have questioned. Under this interpretation, if only five House members survive, a group of three might proceed with business and elect a new Speaker who would become president of the United States, bumping any cabinet member who had assumed the presidency and remaining in office for the rest of the four-year term.

Because the House of Representatives can fill vacancies only by special election, the House might go on for months with a membership of only five. On average, states take four months to hold special elections, and in the aftermath of a catastrophic attack, elections would likely take much longer. Under the Seventeenth Amendment governors can fill [Senate] vacancies within days by temporary appointment, therefore the Senate would reconstitute itself much more quickly than the House.

Imagine in this chaotic situation that all these events are taking place without access to normal organization, procedure, and communication channels. The confusion might very well lead to a conflict over who would be president, Speaker of the House, or commander in chief, and a cloud of illegitimacy would likely hang over all government action. The institution that might resolve such disputes is the Supreme Court. However, it is likely that the entire Court would be killed in such an attack, leaving no final tribunal to appeal to for answers to questions about succession and legislative and executive action. A new court could be appointed by a new president and confirmed by a new Senate, but which president, which Senate, and how soon? Further, would we want the entire Supreme Court appointed for life tenure by a disputed or unelected president?

As terrible as the events of September 11th were, we were fortunate that in the aftermath, our government was able to function through normal constitutional channels. It almost was not so. In interviews broadcast on the Al-Jazeera network, the 9/11 plotters have claimed that the fourth plane, United Flight 93, was headed for the Capitol. This fourth plane took off forty-one minutes late, which allowed the passengers to contact loved ones by cell phone and learn that their flight was on a suicide mission. Passengers stormed the cockpit, ultimately bringing down the plane and preventing it from hitting its target.

If United Flight 93 had departed on time and the hijackers had flown to Washington without interference, the plane might have hit the Capitol between 9:00 and 9:30 A.M. At nine o'clock the House met with Speaker J. Dennis Hastert (R-IL) presiding and recognized Representative Earl Blumenauer (D-OR), who spoke about the World Health Organization. Representative Tim Johnson (R-IL) took over the chair and recognized Representative Cass Ballenger (R-NC), who discussed the budget surplus. The chair then recognized Representative Peter DeFazio (D-OR), who talked about the Social Security Trust Fund. The floor was not heavily populated that Tuesday morning, with most business scheduled later that day, but there were still a number of members on the floor and many others in leadership offices or in private meetings in the Capitol. How many members of the House were in the building that morning is difficult to calculate, but it is clear that many would have perished. Had the attacks occurred a little later in the day, the toll would have been even greater. What if the plane had hit the Capitol the week before, on September 6, 2001, when Mexican President Vicente Fox addressed a joint session of Congress with the vice president and the president's cabinet in attendance? What if the attack had been carried out during a major vote when almost all members were present?

The inauguration scenario described above is admittedly dire, but even less calamitous scenarios could plunge our constitutional government into chaos. Imagine a House of Representatives hit by an attack killing more than half the members and unable to reconstitute itself for months. Imagine any attack killing the president and vice president, subjecting us to a new president who had not been elected by the people. Imagine a biological attack that prevented Congress from convening for fear of spreading infectious agents. A few years ago, these were fanciful notions, the stuff of action movies and Tom Clancy novels. Now they are all too realistic.

### The Continuity of the Three Branches of Government

The mission of the Continuity of Government Commission is to make recommendations to ensure the continuity of our three branches of government after a terrorist attack on Washington. While we hope and pray that the United States never faces such an attack, we believe it is imperative to plan for such a scenario. Given the events of September 11th, we must prepare for an orderly and legitimate succession of governance after a catastrophic event.

What are the problems of continuity associated with the three branches of government?

*Congress.* The greatest hole in our constitutional system is the possibility of an attack that would kill or injure many members of Congress, thereby preventing the branch from operating or alternatively, causing it to operate with such a small number that many people would question its legitimacy. The problem is acute in the House of Representatives. Because the House can only fill vacancies by special election, not by temporary appointment, it would take over four months to reconstitute the full membership of the House. In the interim, the House might be unable to meet its quorum requirement and would be unable to proceed with business. Alternatively, due to ambiguities regarding the definition of a quorum, a very small number of representatives might be able to conduct business for many months, possibly electing a Speaker who could become the president of the United States. A House consisting of only a few members would raise serious questions of legitimacy. Finally, it is possible that an attack, severely injuring but not killing large numbers of members, would threaten the continuity of both the House and the Senate. Because it is very difficult to replace incapacitated members, many House and Senate seats would remain effectively vacant until the next general election. If anyone doubts the importance of Congress in times of crisis, it is helpful to recall that in the days after September 11th, Congress authorized the use of force in Afghanistan; appropriated funds for reconstruction of New York and for military preparations; and passed major legislation granting additional investigative powers and improving transportation security. In a future emergency, Congress might also be called upon to confirm a new vice president, to elect a Speaker of the House who might become president of the United States, or to confirm Supreme Court justices for lifetime appointments. In the event of a disaster that debilitated Congress, the vacuum could be filled by unilateral executive action—perhaps a benign form of martial law. The country might get by, but at a terrible cost to our democratic institutions.

*The President.* Presidential succession is the most visible aspect of continuity of government. Nothing is more important than having a credible and legitimate president leading the nation in the aftermath of a catastrophic attack. In this area, the country has some existing protection in the Constitution and in the Presidential Succession Act of 1947, which provide for the transfer of power to legitimate authorities. But the law defining presidential succession is by no means perfect, and there are a number of scenarios that would leave doubt as to who is president or elevate an obscure claimant to the office. There are at least seven significant issues with our presidential succession law that warrant attention. First, all figures in the current line of succession work and reside in the Washington, D.C. area. In the nightmare scenario of a nuclear attack, there is a possibility that everyone in the line of succession would be killed. Second, a number of constitutional scholars doubt that it is constitutional to have the Speaker of the House and the President Pro Tempore of the Senate in the line of succession, because they do not meet the constitutional definition of "Officers" of the United States. Third, regardless of its constitutionality, some question the wisdom of putting the President Pro Tempore of the Senate in the line of succession, because this largely honorific post is traditionally held by the longest serving senator of the majority party. Fourth, some suggest that congressional leaders of the president's party should be in the line of succession; the current law allows for a switch in party control of the presidency if the Speaker of the House or President Pro Tempore of the Senate is from a different party than the president. Fifth, the line of succession proceeds through the cabinet members in order of the dates of creation of the departments that they head. While several of the most significant departments are also the oldest, it may not make sense to rely simply on historical accident rather than an evaluation based on present circumstances in appointing a successor. For example, should the Secretary of the Interior be ahead of the Secretaries of Commerce, Energy, or Education? Sixth, if the line of succession passes to a cabinet member, the law allows for the House of Representatives to elect a new Speaker (or the Senate a new President Pro Tempore) who could bump the cabinet member and assume the presidency at any time. Seventh, the Twenty-fifth Amendment provides for several instances of presidential disability when the vice president can act as president, but it does not cover circumstances when the president is disabled and the vice presidency is vacant. In this case, the Presidential Succession Act allows congressional leaders and cabinet officers to act as president for a short time, but only if they resign their posts. . . .

It is not acceptable to face a situation when no one in the line of succession survives or when there are competing rivals for the presidency or a presidency that shifts numerous times from one individual to another.

*The Supreme Court.* The deliberative schedule of the Supreme Court of the United States is generally predictable and measurable over a period of months: from the time petitions are filed, to the time a case might be argued, to the time a decision would be delivered by the Court. There have been, however, extraordinary cases that require the Court's immediate attention. If such a case arose during a national crisis involving, for example, separation of powers issues or presidential succession issues, the Supreme Court might be needed to make a prompt ruling. Thus, the continuity of the Supreme Court during a period of crisis also deserves attention.

Congress has provided that a quorum of the Supreme Court is six justices. In the absence of a quorum, there are provisions for sending cases to the lower courts. Additionally, lower courts routinely rule on constitutional issues. If the entire Supreme Court were eliminated, however, there would be no final arbiter to resolve differences in the lower courts' opinions for a period of time. This situation could add to feelings of instability in the country. Moreover, the appointment process of an entirely new Court by a potentially un-elected president (serving in the line of succession) presents other issues that need to be addressed. . . .

Excerpted from American Enterprise Institute and Brookings Institution. Continuity of Government Commission. *The Congress: Preserving Our Institutions—The First Report of the Continuity of Government Commission.* June 4, 2003. http://www.continuityofgovernment.org/pdfs/ FirstReport.pdf (accessed October 15, 2004).

## 122. General Accounting Office Report on Continuity of Operations Planning
*February 27, 2004*

### Results in Brief

Twenty-nine of the 34 COOP [Continuity of Operations] plans that we reviewed identified at least one essential function. However, the functions identified in these plans varied widely in number—ranging from 3 to 399—and included functions that appeared to be of secondary importance. At the same time, the plans omitted many programs that OMB [Office of Management and Budget] had previously identified as having a high impact on the public. Agencies did not list among their essential functions 20 of the 38 high-impact programs that had been identified at those agencies. For example, one department included "provide speeches and articles for the Secretary and Deputy Secretary" among its essential functions, but it did not include 9 of its 10 high-impact programs. In addition, although many agency functions rely on the availability of resources or functions controlled by another organization, more than three-fourths of the plans did not fully identify such dependencies. Several factors contributed to these government-wide shortcomings: FPC [Federal Preparedness Circular] 65 does not provide specific criteria for identifying essential functions, nor does it address interdependencies; FEMA [Federal Emergency Management Agency] did not review the essential functions identified in its assessments of COOP planning or follow up with agencies to determine whether they addressed previously identified weaknesses; and it did not conduct tests or exercises that could confirm that the identified essential functions were correct. Although FEMA has begun efforts to develop additional guidance and conduct a governmentwide exercise, these actions have not yet been completed. Without better oversight, agencies are likely to continue to base their COOP plans on ill-defined assumptions that may limit the utility of the resulting plans.

While all but three of the agencies that we reviewed had developed and documented some elements of a COOP plan, none of the agencies provided documentation sufficient to show that they were following all the guidance in FPC 65. A contributing cause for the deficiencies in agency COOP plans is the level of FEMA oversight. In 1999, FEMA conducted an assessment of agency compliance with FPC 65, but it has not conducted oversight that is sufficiently regular and extensive to ensure that agencies correct deficiencies identified. FEMA officials told us that they plan to improve oversight by providing more detailed guidance and developing a system to collect data from agencies on their COOP readiness. However, FEMA has not yet determined how it will verify the agency-reported data, assess the essential functions and interdependencies identified, or use the data to conduct regular oversight. If FEMA does not address these short-comings, agency COOP plans may not be effective in ensuring that the most vital government services can be maintained in an emergency.

In light of the essential need for agencies to develop viable COOP plans and FEMA's responsibility for overseeing the development of such plans, we are recommending that the Secretary of Homeland Security direct the Under Secretary for Emergency Preparedness and Response to take steps to ensure that agencies have plans in place and improve FEMA's oversight of existing plans. . . .

## Background

Federal operations and facilities have been disrupted by a range of events, including the terrorist attacks on September 11, 2001; the Oklahoma City bombing; localized shutdowns due to severe weather conditions, such as the closure of federal offices in Denver for 3 days in March 2003 due to snow; and building-level events, such as asbestos contamination at the Department of the Interior's headquarters. Such disruptions, particularly if prolonged, can lead to interruptions in essential government services. Prudent management, therefore, requires that federal agencies develop plans for dealing with emergency situations, including maintaining services, ensuring proper authority for government actions, and protecting vital assets.

Until relatively recently, continuity planning was generally the responsibility of individual agencies. In October 1998, PDD [Presidential Decision Directive] 67 identified FEMA—which is responsible for responding to, planning for, recovering from, and mitigating against disasters—as the executive agent for federal COOP planning across the federal executive branch. FEMA was an independent agency until March 2003, when it became part of the Department of Homeland Security, reporting to the Under Secretary for Emergency Preparedness and Response.

PDD 67 is a Top Secret document controlled by the National Security Council. FPC 65 states that PDD 67 made FEMA, as executive agent for COOP, responsible for:

- formulating guidance for agencies to use in developing viable plans;
- coordinating interagency exercises and facilitating interagency coordination, as appropriate; and:

- overseeing and assessing the status of COOP capabilities across the executive branch.

According to FEMA officials, PDD 67 also required that agencies have COOP plans in place by October 1999.

In July 1999, FEMA issued FPC 65 to assist agencies in meeting the October 1999 deadline. FPC 65 states that COOP planning should address any emergency or situation that could disrupt normal operations, including localized emergencies. FPC 65 also determined that COOP planning is based first on the identification of essential functions—that is, those functions that enable agencies to provide vital services, exercise civil authority, maintain safety, and sustain the economy during an emergency. FPC 65 gives no criteria for identifying essential functions beyond this definition.

Although FPC 65 gives no specific criteria for identifying essential functions, a logical starting point for this process would be to consider programs that had been previously identified as important. For example, in March 1999, as part of the efforts to address the Y2K computer problem, the Director of OMB identified 42 programs with a high impact on the public:

- Of these 42 programs, 38 were the responsibility of the 23 major departments and agencies that we reviewed.
- Of these 23 major departments and agencies, 16 were responsible for at least one high-impact program; several were responsible for more than one.

Programs that were identified included weather service, disease monitoring and warnings, public housing, air traffic control, food stamps, and Social Security benefits. . . .

## Agency COOP Plans Addressed Some, but Not All, of FEMA's Guidance

As of October 1, 2002, almost 3 years after the planning deadline established by PDD 67, 3 of the agencies we reviewed had not developed and documented a COOP plan. The remaining 20 major federal civilian agencies had COOP plans in place. . . .

### *Limitations in FEMA's Oversight Contribute to Noncompliance*

The lack of compliance shown by many COOP plans can be largely attributed to FEMA's limited guidance and oversight of executive branch COOP planning. First, FEMA has issued little guidance to assist agencies in developing plans that address the goals of FPC 65. Following FPC 65, FEMA issued more detailed guidance in April 2001 on two of FPC 65's eight topic areas: FPC 66 provides guidance on developing viable test, training, and exercise programs, and FPC 67 provides guidance for acquiring alternate facilities. However, FEMA did not produce any detailed guidance on the other six topic areas.

In October 2003, FEMA began working with several members of the interagency COOP working group to revise FPC 65. FEMA officials expect this revised guidance, which was still under development as of January 2004, to incorporate the guidance from the previous FPCs and to address more specifically what agencies need to do to comply with the guidance.

Second, as part of FEMA's oversight responsibilities, its Office of National Security Coordination is tasked with conducting comprehensive assessments of the federal executive branch COOP programs. With the assistance of contractors, the office has performed assessments, on an irregular schedule, of federal agencies' emergency planning capabilities. . . .

According to FEMA officials, the system it is developing to collect agency-reported data on COOP plan readiness will improve FEMA's oversight. The system is based on a database of information provided by agencies for the purpose of determining if they are prepared to exercise their COOP plans, in part by assessing compliance with FPC 65. However, according to FEMA officials, while they recognize the need for some type of verification, FEMA has not yet determined a method of verifying these data.

Without regular assessments of COOP plans that evaluate individual plans for adequacy, FEMA will not be able to provide information to help agencies improve their COOP plans. Further, if FEMA does not verify the data provided by the agencies or follow up to determine whether agencies have improved their plans in response to such assessments, it will have no assurance that agencies' emergency procedures are appropriate. . . .

## Conclusions

While most of the federal agencies we reviewed had developed COOP plans, three agencies did not have documented plans as of October 2002. Those plans that were in place exhibited weaknesses in the form of widely varying determinations about what functions are essential and inconsistent compliance with guidance that defines a viable COOP capability. The weaknesses that we identified could cause the agencies to experience difficulties in delivering key services to citizens in the aftermath of an emergency.

A significant factor contributing to this condition is FEMA's limited efforts to fulfill its responsibilities first by providing guidance to help agencies develop effective plans and then by assessing those plans. Further, FEMA has done very little to help agencies identify those functions that are truly essential or to identify and plan for interdependencies among agency functions. FEMA has begun taking steps to improve its oversight, by developing more specific guidance and a system to track agency-provided COOP readiness information, and it is planning a governmentwide exercise. However, although the proposed guidance and exercise may help agencies improve their plans, the system that FEMA is developing to collect data on COOP readiness is weakened by a lack of planning to verify agency-submitted data, validate agency-identified essential functions, or identify interdependencies with other activities. Without this level of active oversight, continuity planning efforts will continue to fall short and increase the risk that the public will not be able to rely upon the continued delivery of essential government programs and services following an emergency. . . .

Excerpted from U.S. Congress. General Accounting Office. *Continuity of Operations: Improved Planning Needed to Ensure Delivery of Essential Government Services.* GAO-04-160, February 27, 2004. http://purl.access. gpo.gov/GPO/LPS52026 (accessed October 15, 2004).

# FBI Transforms Itself to Fight Terrorism

On September 3, 2001, Robert S. Mueller became director of the Federal Bureau of Investigation (FBI), an agency that had a proud history of capturing criminals, including the most infamous in U.S. history. However, when he arrived agents were using vintage 1987 desktop computers, the agency lacked full e-mail capabilities, and its database was so dysfunctional that agents typically wrote their reports on paper.

Eight days after Mueller took over, terrorists hijacked four passenger planes and smashed them into the World Trade Center in New York, the Pentagon outside Washington, D.C., and a field in Pennsylvania. The FBI immediately launched an investigation that became the largest in world history. The agency also took primary responsibility for protecting the nation from further attacks, a new and somewhat uncomfortable role. The FBI throughout its history had been mostly reactive, coming in after a crime was committed and solving it. Now it had to be proactive—to use its intelligence capabilities to identify and arrest terrorists before they could strike. To complicate matters, a recent internal assessment had found that two-thirds of the FBI's intelligence analysts were unqualified.

Mueller started a massive effort to transform the FBI—everything from its culture to its computer systems. Part of his effort included championing the Patriot Act, which increased the FBI's intelligence powers (*see* Supporters, Critics Face Off Over Parts of USA Patriot Act, p. 329). He received assistance on May 30, 2002, when Attorney General John Ashcroft announced new guidelines for FBI investigations. The new rules largely overturned restrictions on domestic surveillance that were imposed in the 1970s after congressional investigations documented widespread abuses of civil liberties by the FBI and other intelligence agencies (*see* Intelligence Agencies and Civil Liberties, p. 80).

In announcing the new rules, Ashcroft said the old restrictions hampered agents' abilities to prevent terrorism. As an example, he cited a previous rule that generally barred FBI agents from visiting political meetings, churches, mosques, libraries, and similar public places unless they had evidence a crime was being committed. The new rule said: "For the purpose of detecting or preventing terrorist activities, the FBI is authorized to visit any place and attend any event that is open to the public on the same terms and conditions as members of the public generally" [Document 123]. Some leading members of Congress and others said the changes paved the way to resuming abuses of civil liberties.

As more details about the terrorist attacks became public, however, the FBI and other intelligence agencies came under withering criticism for failing to stop them. Investigations by Congress and the National Commission on Terrorist Attacks Upon the United States—commonly known as the 9/11 Commission—found that numerous clues existed before the attacks, but no one at any intelligence agency had put together the pieces to uncover the plot. This failure partly occurred, the investigations concluded, because the clues were spread among the FBI and other intelligence agencies and none of them shared information with each other.

When the Justice Department's inspector general audited the FBI's counterterrorism program in September 2002, some FBI managers used the word "broken" to describe the agency's intelligence analysis capability. Critics who served on terrorism-related commissions or in Congress "suggested that the FBI's intelligence capability was more than broken; it had been virtually nonexistent," the inspector general said. The FBI began hiring more intelligence analysts and improving their training. The agency even offered bonuses of $10,000 to attract top candidates for the jobs.

Meanwhile, efforts to transform the FBI continued. "Refocusing the FBI to preventing terrorist acts and developing the set of skills required to collect, analyze, and disseminate intelligence strategically as well as tactically has required a change in the FBI's culture that has not been easy or quick," the Justice Department's inspector general reported on December 22, 2003. By March 2004 the FBI had shifted 674 field agents to counterterrorism and counterintelligence from their previous positions tackling drugs, white-collar crime, or violent crime. But a series of reports and congressional testimony in 2004 provided varying perspectives on whether the transformation efforts were succeeding.

On March 23, 2004, two senior officials from the General Accounting Office (GAO)—the investigative arm of Congress—focused part of their joint congressional testimony on the FBI's continuing computer troubles. The FBI's largest computer project was Trilogy, a system that was designed to replace the agency's computer infrastructure and provide new tools for managing cases. The GAO officials said cost overruns for Trilogy totaled $120 million, and development of the system was nearly two years behind schedule. The problems were partly caused by rapid turnover in the bureau's key information technology (IT) leadership and management positions [Document 124].

The Congressional Research Service (CRS) released the next major report, titled "FBI Intelligence Reform Since September 11, 2001: Issues and Options for Congress," on April 6, 2004. The CRS, which is part of the Library of Congress, prepares in-depth, impartial reports for lawmakers on important public policy issues. Its report on the FBI traced the agency's transformation efforts in detail and concluded there were two "fundamentally opposing views" about the best method for preventing terrorist acts and clandestine foreign intelligence activities directed against the United States:

> Adherents to one school of thought believe there are important synergies to be gained from keeping intelligence and law enforcement functions combined as they are currently under the FBI. They argue that the two disciplines share the goal of terrorism prevention; that prevention within the U.S. will invariably require law enforcement to arrest and prosecute alleged terrorists; and, that the decentralized nature of terrorist cells is analogous to that of organized crime. A second school of thought counters that the chasm between the exigencies of the two disciplines, both cultural and practical, is simply too broad to effectively bridge, and, therefore, that the two should be bureaucratically separated [Document 125].

On May 10, 2004, a National Research Council committee that studied the Trilogy project released a detailed review. "The FBI has made significant progress in certain areas of its IT modernization program in the last year or so," the committee's report said. "For example, it has achieved the modernization of the computing hardware and baseline software on the desktops of agents and other personnel and has taken major strides forward in the deployment of its networking infrastructure. Nevertheless, in a number of key areas, the FBI's progress has fallen significantly short of what it, and the nation, require."

In a July report, the Justice Department's inspector general examined the FBI's difficulties in translating all of the texts, videotapes, and audiotapes it obtained in terrorism investigations. "The FBI's collection of material requiring translation has continued to outpace its translation capabilities," the inspector general said. "In fact, despite the infusion of more than 620 additional linguists since September 11, 2001, the FBI reported that nearly 24 percent of ongoing FISA [Foreign Intelligence Surveillance Act] counterintelligence and counterterrorism intercepts are not being monitored" [Document 126].

In its final report released July 22, 2004, the 9/11 Commission praised the FBI's "significant progress in improving its intelligence capabilities." The commission also commended Mueller for recognizing that the FBI's reforms were far from complete. It made a dozen recommendations "to ensure that the Bureau's shift to a preventive counterterrorism posture is more fully institutionalized so that it survives beyond Director Mueller's tenure" [Document 127].

However, the report also helped prompt Congress to consider making major changes in the nation's intelligence system. The outcome of those debates was expected to determine whether the FBI retained its intelligence responsibilities—and thus its critical role in homeland security (*see* 9/11 Commission Primarily Focuses on Intelligence Reforms, p. 456).

# 123. Attorney General John Ashcroft Announces New FBI Guidelines

*May 30, 2002*

. . . On September 11, a stunned nation turned once again to the brave men and women of the FBI, and they, once again, answered the call. I spent the hours, days, and most of the first weeks after the attack in the FBI's Strategic Information and Operations Center with [FBI] Director [Robert] Mueller. Even today, eight months later, it is difficult to convey the professionalism, dedication and quiet resolve I witnessed in those first, 24-hour days. I saw men and women work themselves beyond fatigue to prevent new terrorist attacks. I witnessed individuals put aside their personal lives, personal agendas and personal safety to answer our nation's call.

From the first moments we spent together, launching the largest investigation in history, we understood that the mission of American justice and law enforcement had changed. That day, in those early hours, the prevention of terrorist acts became the central goal of the law enforcement and national security mission of the FBI. And from that time forward, we in the leadership of the FBI and the Department of Justice began a concerted effort to free the field agents—the brave men and women on the front lines—from the bureaucratic, organizational, and operational restrictions and structures that hindered them from doing their jobs effectively.

As we have heard recently, FBI men and women in the field are frustrated because many of our own internal restrictions have hampered our ability to fight terrorism. The current investigative guidelines have contributed to that frustration. In many instances, the guidelines bar FBI field agents from taking the initiative to detect and prevent future terrorist acts unless the FBI learns of possible criminal activity from external sources.

Under the current guidelines, FBI investigators cannot surf the web the way you or I can. Nor can they simply walk into a public event or a public place to observe ongoing activities. They have no clear authority to use commercial data services that any business in America can use. These restrictions are a competitive advantage for terrorists who skillfully utilize sophisticated techniques and modern computer systems to compile information for targeting and attacking innocent Americans.

That is why the Attorney General's guidelines and procedures relating to criminal investigations and national security were high on the list of action items for reform. Beginning in the 1970s, guidelines have been developed to inform agents of the circumstances under which investigations may be opened, the permissible scope of these investigations, the techniques that may be used, and the objectives that should be pursued. These guidelines provide limitations and guidance over and above all requirements and safeguards imposed by the Constitution and beyond the legal framework established by federal statutes enacted by Congress. Promulgated for different purposes and revised at various times, the guidelines currently cover FBI investigations, undercover operations, the use of confidential informants, and consensual monitoring of verbal communications.

The guidelines defining the general rules for FBI investigations, for example, were first issued over 20 years ago. They derive from a period in which Soviet communism was the greatest threat to the United States, in which the Internet did not exist, and in which concerns over terrorist threats to the homeland related mainly to domestic hate groups.

Shortly after September 11, I took two steps to free FBI field agents to prevent additional terrorist attacks. First, I authorized the FBI to waive the guidelines, with headquarters approval, in extraordinary cases to prevent and investigate terrorism. That authority has been used, but I am disappointed that it was not used more widely. This experience over the past few months reinforces my belief that greater authority to investigate more vigorously needs to be given directly to FBI field agents.

Second, I directed a top-to-bottom review of the guidelines to ensure that they provide front-line field agents with the legal authority they need to protect the American people from future terrorist attacks. That comprehensive review showed that the guidelines mistakenly combined timeless objectives—the enforcement of the law and respect for civil rights and liberties—with outdated means.

Today, I am announcing comprehensive revisions to the Department's investigative guidelines. As revised, the guidelines reflect four overriding principles.

First, the war against terrorism is the central mission and highest priority of the FBI. This principle is stated explicitly in the revised guidelines, and it is facilitated and reinforced through many specific reforms. The guidelines emphasize that the FBI must not be deprived of using all lawful authorized methods in investigations, consistent with the Constitution and statutory authority, to pursue and prevent terrorist actions.

Second, terrorism prevention is the key objective under the revised guidelines. Our philosophy today is not to wait and sift through the rubble following a terrorist attack. Rather, the FBI must intervene early and investigate aggressively where information exists suggesting the possibility of terrorism, so as to prevent acts of terrorism. The new guidelines advance this strategy of prevention by strengthening investigative authority at the early stage of preliminary inquiries. Also, even absent specific investigative predicates, FBI agents under the new guidelines are empowered to scour public sources for information on future terrorist threats.

Third, unnecessary procedural red tape must not interfere with the effective detection, investigation, and prevention of terrorist activities. To this end, the revised guidelines allow Special Agents in Charge of FBI field offices to approve and renew terrorism enterprise investigations, rather than having to seek and wait for approval from headquarters. I believe this responds to a number of concerns we have heard from our field agents. The guidelines expand the scope of those investigations to the full range of terrorist activities under the USA Patriot Act. These major changes will free field agents to counter potential terrorist threats swiftly and vigorously without waiting for headquarters to act.

Fourth, the FBI must draw proactively on all lawful sources of information to identify terrorist threats and activities. It cannot meet its paramount responsibility to prevent acts of terrorism if FBI agents are required, as they were in the past, to blind themselves to information that everyone else is free to see. Under the revised guidelines, the FBI can identify and track foreign terrorists by combining its investigative results with information obtained from other lawful sources, such as foreign intelligence and commercial data services. To detect and prevent terrorist activities, the FBI under the revised guidelines will also be able to enter and observe public places and forums just as any member of the public might.

Let me pause here for a moment. What I am saying is this: FBI field agents have been inhibited from attending public events, open to any other citizen—not because they are barred by the U.S. Constitution, or barred by any federal law enacted by Congress, but because of the lack of clear authority under administrative guidelines issued decades ago. Today, I am clarifying that, for the specific purpose of detecting or preventing terrorist activities, FBI field agents may enter public places and attend events open to other citizens, unless they are barred from attending by the Constitution or federal law.

Our new guideline reads, "For the purpose of detecting or preventing terrorist activities, the FBI is authorized to visit any place and attend any event that is open to the public, on the same terms and conditions as members of the public generally."

I believe in the principle of community policing, in which an active, visible law enforcement presence is linked to communities and neighborhoods. Local police can enter public places and attend public events in their communities, and they detect and prevent crime by doing so. To protect our communities from terrorism, the FBI must be free to do the same. . . .

Excerpted from U.S. Department of Justice. Office of the Attorney General. *Remarks of Attorney General Ashcroft: Attorney General Guidelines.* Prepared Statement. May 30, 2002. http://www.justice.gov/ag/speeches/2002/53002agpreparedremarks.htm (accessed October 22, 2004).

# 124. General Accounting Office Testimony about Continuing Computer Problems at the FBI
*March 23, 2004*

. . . Our research of private and public sector organizations that effectively manage IT [information technology] shows that they have adopted an agencywide approach to managing IT under the sustained leadership of a CIO [chief information officer] or comparable senior executive who has the responsibility and the authority for managing IT across the agency. According to the research, these executives function as members of the leadership team and are instrumental in developing a shared vision for the role of IT in achieving major improvements in business processes and operations to effectively optimize mission performance. In this capacity, leading organizations also provide these individuals with the authority they need to carry out their diverse responsibilities by providing budget management control and oversight of IT programs and initiatives.

Over the last several years, the FBI has not sustained IT management leadership. Specifically, the bureau's key leadership and management positions, including the CIO, have experienced frequent turnover. For instance, the CIO has changed five times in the past 24 months. The current CIO, who is also the CIO at the Department of Justice's Executive Office of the U.S. Attorneys (EOUSA), is temporarily detailed to the FBI for 6 months and is serving in an acting capacity while also retaining selected duties at EOUSA. In addition, the IT official responsible for developing the bureau's enterprise architecture, the chief architect, has changed five times in the past 16 months. As a result, development and implementation of key management controls, such as enterprise architecture, have not benefited from sustained management attention and leadership and thus have lagged.

In addition, the FBI has not provided its CIO with bureauwide IT management authority and responsibility. Rather, the authority and responsibility for managing IT is diffused across and vested in the bureau's divisions. As our research and work at other agencies has shown, managing IT in this manner results in disparate, stove-piped environments that are unnecessarily expensive to operate and maintain. In the FBI's case, it resulted, as

reported by Justice's Inspector General in December 2002, in 234 noninte-
grated applications, residing on 187 different servers, each of which had its
own unique databases, unable to share information with other applications
or with other government agencies. According to the acting CIO, the FBI is
considering merging bureauwide authority and responsibility for IT in the
CIO's office with the goal of having this in place in time to formulate the
bureau's fiscal year 2006 budget request. In our view, this proposal, if properly defined and implemented, is a good step toward implementing the
practices of leading organizations. However, until it is implemented, we
remain concerned that the bureau will not be positioned to effectively leverage IT as a bureauwide resource. . . .

Excerpted from U.S. Congress. General Accounting Office. *FBI Transforma-
tion: FBI Continues to Make Progress in Its Efforts to Transform and
Address Priorities.* Prepared testimony of Laurie E. Ekstrand and Randolph
C. Hite for a hearing by the Senate Appropriations Committee's Subcom-
mittee on Commerce, Justice, State, and the Judiciary. GAO-04-578T,
March 23, 2004. http://purl.access.gpo.gov/GPO/LPS48415 (accessed
October 22, 2004).

# 125. Congressional Research Service Report about FBI Intelligence Reform

*April 6, 2004*

## Introduction

The September 11, 2001 terrorist attacks on the United States have been
labeled as a major intelligence failure, similar in magnitude to that associated with the Japanese attack on Pearl Harbor. In response to criticisms of
its role in this failure, the Federal Bureau of Investigation (FBI) has introduced a series of reforms to transform the Bureau from a largely reactive law
enforcement agency focused on criminal investigations into a more mobile,
agile, flexible, intelligence-driven agency that can prevent acts of terrorism.

FBI Director Robert S. Mueller, III initiated changes that were sparked by
congressional charges that the Intelligence Community (IC), including the
FBI, missed opportunities to prevent, or at least, disrupt the September 11

attacks on New York City and Washington. In a sweeping indictment of the FBI's intelligence activities relating to counterterrorism, the [congressional] Joint Inquiry Into Intelligence Community Activities Before and After the Terrorist Attacks of September 11, 2001, (JIC) criticized the FBI for failing to focus on the terrorist threat domestically; collect useful intelligence; strategically analyze intelligence, and to share intelligence internally, and with the rest of the IC. According to the congressional inquiry, the FBI was incapable of producing significant intelligence products, and was seriously handicapped in its efforts to identify, report on and defend against the foreign terrorist threat to the United States.

Observers believe successful FBI reform will depend in large measure on whether the FBI can strengthen what critics have characterized as its historically neglected and weak intelligence program, particularly in the area of strategic analysis. They contend the FBI must improve its ability to collect, analyze and disseminate domestic intelligence so that it can help federal, state and local officials stop terrorists before they strike. If the FBI is viewed as failing this fundamental litmus test, they argue, confidence in any beefed up intelligence program will quickly erode.

Critics contend the FBI's intelligence reforms are moving too slowly and are too limited. They argue that the FBI's deeply rooted law enforcement culture and its reactive practice of investigating crimes after the fact, will undermine efforts to transform the FBI into a proactive agency able to develop and use intelligence to prevent terrorism. . . .

Critics also question whether Director Mueller, who has an extensive background in criminal prosecution but lacks experience in the intelligence field, sufficiently understands the role of intelligence to be able to lead an overhaul of the FBI's intelligence operation.

Supporters counter that they believe the FBI can change, that its shortcomings are fixable, and that the Director's intelligence reforms are appropriate, focused and will produce the needed changes. They also argue that a successful war against terrorism demands that law enforcement and intelligence are closely linked. And they maintain that the FBI is institutionally able to provide an integrated approach, because it already combines both law enforcement and intelligence functions. . . .

## FBI Intelligence Reforms

The FBI is responding to the numerous shortcomings outlined by the JIC by attempting to transform itself into an agency that can prevent terrorist acts, rather than react to them as criminal acts. The major component of this effort is the restructuring and upgrading of its various intelligence support units into a formal and integrated intelligence program. . . .

### Business Process Changes

. . . FBI officials say their objective is to better focus intelligence collection against terrorists operating in the U.S. through improved strategic analysis that can identify gaps in their knowledge. . . .

*Centralized Headquarters Authority.* Following September 11, Director Mueller announced that henceforth, the FBI's top three priorities would be counterterrorism, counterintelligence and cyber crime, respectively. He signaled his intention to improve the FBI's intelligence program by, among other measures, consolidating and centralizing control over fragmented intelligence capabilities, both at FBI Headquarters and in the FBI's historically autonomous field offices. He restated that intelligence had always been one of the FBI's core competencies and organic to the FBI's investigative mission, and asserted that the organization's intelligence efforts had and would continue to be disciplined by the intelligence cycle of intelligence requirements, collection, analysis, and dissemination. . . .

### Implementation Challenges

The FBI is likely to confront significant challenges in implementing its reforms. Its most fundamental challenge, some assert, will be to transform the FBI's deeply entrenched law enforcement culture, and its emphasis on criminal convictions, into a culture that emphasizes the importance that intelligence plays in counterterrorism and counterintelligence. Although observers believe that FBI Director Mueller is identifying and communicating his counterterrorism and intelligence priorities, they caution that effective reform implementation will be the ultimate determinant of success. The FBI, they say, must implement programs to recruit intelligence professionals with operational and analytical expertise; develop formal career development paths, including defined paths to promotion; and continue to improve information management and technology. These changes, they say, should be implemented in a timely fashion, as over two and a half years have passed since the attacks of September 11, 2001. They also contend the FBI must improve intelligence sharing within the FBI and with other IC agencies, and with federal, state and local agencies.

*Technology.* Inadequate information technology, in part, contributed to the FBI being unable to correlate the knowledge possessed by its components prior to September 11, according to the congressional joint inquiry. GAO [Government Accounting Office, the investigative arm of Congress] and the Department of Justice Office of Inspector General reports conclude that the FBI still lacks an enterprise architecture, a critical and necessary component, they argue, to successful IT modernization. In addition to lacking an enterprise architecture plan, according to the GAO, the FBI has also not had sustained information technology leadership and management. . . .

*FBI Field Leadership.* An important issue is whether the FBI's field leadership is able and willing to support Director Mueller's reforms. Critics argue that the lack of national security experience among the existing cadre of Special Agents-in-Charge (SACs) of the FBI's field offices represents a significant impediment to change. According to one former senior FBI official, ". . . over 90 percent of the SACs have very little national security experience. . . ." He suggested that lack of understanding and experience would result in continued field emphasis on law enforcement rather than an intelligence approach to terrorism cases.

Supporters counter that Director Mueller has made it inalterably clear that his priorities are intelligence and terrorism prevention. Some SACs who have been uncomfortable with the new priorities have chosen to retire. But critics also contend that it will require a number of years of voluntary attrition before field leadership more attuned to the importance of intelligence is in place. . . .

*Funding and Personnel Resources to Support Intelligence Reform.* Prior to September 11, FBI analytic resources—particularly in strategic analysis—were severely limited. The FBI had assigned only one strategic analyst exclusively to Al-Qaeda prior to September 11. Of its approximately 1,200 intelligence analysts, 66% were unqualified, according to the FBI's own assessment. The FBI also lacked linguists competent in the languages and dialects spoken by radicals linked to Al-Qaeda. . . .

Supporters of the ongoing FBI intelligence reform describe a "dramatic increase" in intelligence analysts, both at headquarters and in the field—from 159 in 2001, to 347 planned in 2003, . . . Moreover, the FBI intends to hire 900 intelligence analysts in 2004. Supporters also point to the Daily Presidential Threat Briefings the FBI drafts, and 30 longer-term analyses and a comprehensive national terrorist threat assessment that have been completed. But even supporters caution that institutional change now underway at the FBI "does not occur overnight and involves major cultural change." They estimate that with careful planning, the commitment of adequate resources and personnel, and hard work, the FBI's "transformation" will be well along in three to five years, though it will take longer to fully accomplish its goals. . . .

Skeptics of the ongoing FBI intelligence reform argue—and supporters concede—that this is not the first time the FBI has singled out intelligence for additional resources. The FBI did so in the wake of the 1993 World Trade Center bombing and the 1995 Oklahoma City bombing, only to allow those resources to revert to the FBI's traditional priorities—violent and organized crime, drug trafficking, and infrastructure protection. Additional intelligence analysts also were hired, but they were viewed as poorly trained, limited in experience, and lacking in needed information technology tools. They also were easily diverted to support the FBI's traditional anti-crime operations, even though efforts were made during the intervening years to protect resources intended to support the agency's national security efforts, including intelligence. . . .

Skeptics also question whether the FBI is prepared to recruit the type of individual needed to effectively collect and analyze intelligence. The FBI's historic emphasis on law enforcement has encouraged and rewarded agents who gather as many facts as legally possible in their attempt to make a criminal case. Because a successful case rests on rules of criminal procedure, the FBI draws largely from the top talent in state and local law enforcement agencies, and the military; in short, some say, those individuals who focus on discrete facts rather than on the connections between them. . . .

*Are Analytical Capabilities Sufficient?* Some observers contend that the FBI has made notable progress in professionalizing its analytical program since September 11, and, indeed, over the past two decades. During this period, they assert that the FBI's analytic cadre, particularly at Headquarters, has evolved from a disjointed group of less than qualified individuals into a group of professionals which understands the role analysis plays in advancing national security investigations and operations. The majority of intelligence analysts at Headquarters possesses advanced degrees and has expert knowledge in various functional and geographic areas. Over the last two decades, they also cite the FBI's progress in internally promoting analysts to analytic management positions. . . .

Critics, however, remain largely unpersuaded and argue that analysis remains a serious FBI vulnerability in the war on terrorism. The Congressional Joint Inquiry on September 11 urged the FBI, among other steps, to

> . . . significantly improve strategic analytical capabilities by assuring qualification, training, and independence of analysts coupled with sufficient access to necessary information and resources.

Although they applaud the FBI's new focus on analysis, critics question its effectiveness and point to a number of trends. For example, they cite the continuing paucity of analysts in the FBI's senior national security ranks, even more than two years after the September 11 attacks. This, they say, reflects the FBI's continuing failure to treat analysis as a priority and more fundamentally to understand how to leverage analysis in the war on terror. They also point to the FBI's own internal study that found 66 percent of its analytic corps unqualified and question whether the FBI's changes are sufficiently broad to address this legacy problem. . . .

FBI supporters give the FBI high marks since the September 11th attacks for sharing threat information, building information bridges to the intelligence agencies and state and local law enforcement, collaborating with foreign law enforcement components, and opening itself up to external reviewers. But even supporters believe that maintaining this commendable record will be a continuing management challenge, one which will require constant reinforcement. They emphasize that the traditional values of FBI agents as independent and determined must give way to include values of information sharing and cooperation. . . .

Although these changes undoubtedly will improve intelligence sharing between FBI's criminal and intelligence components, the question remains whether the information will be shared with other agencies and state and local law officials. Some critics do not dispute that Director Mueller's decision will enhance intelligence sharing within the FBI. They agree it will. Rather, they are concerned that more innocent people will become the targets of clandestine surveillance. . . .

## Congressional Oversight Issues

. . . One oversight issue is whether the current congressional structure is sufficiently focused to monitor effectively the FBI's intelligence reforms. In the wake of the September 11 terrorist attacks, the FBI has been criticized for failing to more effectively collect, analyze and disseminate intelligence. The congressional committees principally responsible for conducting FBI oversight—the Intelligence, Judiciary and Appropriations Committees—on the other hand, have been subject to little or no criticism. Some critics argue that those responsible for conducting oversight should be held accountable as well. They have questioned the diligence of the committees and, in the case of the Intelligence Committees, the committees' structure. . . .

*Oversight Effectiveness.* According to Representative David Obey, congressional oversight, at times, has been "miserable."

> I've been here 33 years and I have seen times when Congress exercised adequate oversight, with respect to [the FBI], and I've seen times when I thought Congress' actions in that regard were miserable. . . . I can recall times when members of the committee seemed to be more interested in getting the autographs of the FBI director than they were in doing their job asking tough questions. And I don't think the agency was served by that any more than the country was. . . .

Some observers agree, and have singled out the oversight exercised by the two congressional intelligence committees for particular criticism. According to Loch Johnson, a former congressional staff member and intelligence specialist at the University of Georgia, "They [the intelligence committees] didn't press hard enough [with regard to 9/11]. There's all the authority they need. They didn't press hard enough [for change]." Another observer commented, "They should be held as accountable as the intelligence agencies. . . ."

## Options

The debate over Congressional options on FBI reform centers on two fundamentally opposing views on how best to prevent terrorist acts and other clandestine foreign intelligence activities directed against the United

States before they occur. Adherents to one school of thought believe there are important synergies to be gained from keeping intelligence and law enforcement functions combined as they are currently under the FBI. They argue that the two disciplines share the goal of terrorism prevention; that prevention within the U.S. will invariably require law enforcement to arrest and prosecute alleged terrorists; and, that the decentralized nature of terrorist cells is analogous to that of organized crime.

A second school of thought counters that the chasm between the exigencies of the two disciplines, both cultural and practical, is simply too broad to effectively bridge, and, therefore, that the two should be bureaucratically separated.

These two opposing views raise several options for Congress, including the following:

- Option 1: Support Director Mueller's reform package.
- Option 2: Create a semi-autonomous National Security Intelligence Service within the FBI.
- Option 3: Establish a separate domestic intelligence agency within the Department of Homeland Security.
- Option 4: Establish a separate domestic intelligence agency under the authority of the DCI, but subject to oversight of the Attorney General.
- Option 5: Create an entirely new stand-alone domestic intelligence service. . . .

Excerpted from U.S. Congress. Library of Congress. Congressional Research Service. *FBI Intelligence Reform Since September 11, 2001: Issues and Options for Congress.* RL32336, April 6, 2004. http://www.au. af.mil/au/awc/awcgate/crs/rl32336.pdf (accessed October 22, 2004).

# 126. Justice Department Inspector General's Report about the FBI's Translation Capabilities

*July 2004*

## Executive Summary

Critical to the Federal Bureau of Investigation's (FBI) success in protecting national security is its ability to prioritize, translate, and understand in a timely fashion the information to which it has access. In this regard, the Foreign Language Program's support to the FBI's law enforcement function is substantial. In addition to supporting the FBI's two highest priorities of counterterrorism and counterintelligence, increasing demands have been placed on the Foreign Language Program to support the FBI's criminal and cyber-crimes programs, international training, international deployments, and interpreting/interviewing assignments.

Prior reviews of the FBI's Foreign Language Program revealed severe shortages of linguists that resulted in the accumulation of thousands of hours of audio and videotapes and thousands of pages of text going unreviewed or untranslated. As the FBI continues to focus its priorities on counterterrorism and counterintelligence, it must rely heavily on linguistic capabilities for interview support and surveillance activities.

The FBI's linguists play a critical role in developing effective intelligence and counterterrorism information. Linguists are the first line of analysis for information collected in a language other than English. Linguists must use their judgment in filtering the information to ensure that information of potential intelligence value is passed along to agents or analysts. Linguists must sort through the thousands of hours and pages of intercepted telephone conversations and documents to identify pertinent foreign intelligence information. Information of intelligence value is often subtle, because the parties to the conversation may suspect they are being monitored. For example, linguists must be able to recognize coded words or the implications of a conversation when the parties refer to issues cryptically. This requires high standards of language proficiency and cultural knowledge.

The Foreign Language Program presents significant management challenges for the FBI, including prioritizing workload and balancing limited resources. . . .

### FBI Linguistic Capabilities

The FBI's approximately 1,200 linguists are stationed across the United States in 52 field offices and Headquarters. They are connected via secure communications networks that allow a linguist in one FBI office to work on projects for any other office. As of April 2004, the 1,200 linguists consisted of about 800 contract linguists and 400 language specialists. Functionally, there is little difference between contract linguists and language specialists. Language specialists are employees of the FBI, while contract linguists are contractors. In addition, unlike language specialists, contract linguists are not under an obligation to be available for work. According to the FBI, contract linguists assigned to counterterrorism and counterintelligence matters work an average of 29 hours per week. FBI officials told us that the lack of contract linguist full-time availability can disrupt the normal course of investigations and an office's ability to monitor FISA lines [wiretaps authorized under the Foreign Intelligence Surveillance Act] on a near-live basis.

Since September 11, 2001, the FBI's Foreign Language Program has experienced a large influx of funding and linguists. Language program funding increased from $21.5 million in fiscal year (FY) 2001 to nearly $70 million in FY 2004; the number of linguists has grown from 883 in 2001 to 1,214 as of April 2004. According to the FBI, its linguist growth occurred at the maximum rate that the FBI's congressionally earmarked funding would allow. The FBI has increased its linguist capabilities in languages associated with counterterrorism and counterintelligence activities. . . .

### The FBI's Ability to Translate All Critical Foreign Language Material

. . . The FBI's electronic surveillance collection in languages primarily related to counterterrorism activities (i.e., Arabic, Farsi, Urdu, and Pashto) has increased by 45 percent, when comparing total collection in FY 2003 to total collection in FY 2001. Text collection in these languages has increased 566 percent, increasing from 2 percent of total collection in FY 2001, when combining audio and text collection, to 10 percent in FY 2003. Translation growth rates in these languages are expected to trend upward by at least 15 percent annually. . . .

The FBI cannot translate all the foreign language counterterrorism and counterintelligence material it collects. The FBI's collection of material requiring translation has continued to outpace its translation capabilities. In fact, despite the infusion of more than 620 additional linguists since September 11, 2001, the FBI reported that nearly 24 percent of ongoing FISA counterintelligence and counterterrorism intercepts are not being monitored.

With respect to unreviewed material, the FBI currently only tracks backlog for counterterrorism FISA cases, and the FBI only does so by case, not by language. Using available foreign language program data, we compiled the following statistics which show that since September 11, 2001, more than 89,000 hours of [Classified information redacted] audio and 30,000 hours of audio in other counterterrorism languages have not been reviewed. Additionally, over 370,000 hours of audio in languages associated with counterintelligence activities have not been reviewed, including over 116,000 hours in [Classified information redacted] and 88,000 hours in [Classified information redacted]. . . .

We attributed the FBI's backlog of unreviewed material to its difficulties in hiring sufficient numbers of linguists and limitations in the FBI's translation information technology systems.

### Difficulties in Hiring Linguists

At a news conference with the Attorney General on September 17, 2001, the FBI Director announced the FBI's critical need for additional Arabic, Farsi, Pashto, and Mandarin contract linguists. According to the FBI, more than 20,000 applications spanning the foreign language spectrum were received by its on-line employment application collection system within the next 30 days. The FBI estimates that the contract linguist vetting process eliminates over 90 percent of the applicants processed for hiring. The ratio of contract linguist applicants selected for processing to hires is as follows: FY 2002—one hire for every 14 applicants, FY 2003—one hire for every 13 applicants, first half of FY 2004—one hire for every 19 applicants. For those applicants who pass the vetting process and are hired, the applicant processing cycle is about 13 months.

As previously mentioned, from September 11, 2001, through April 1, 2004, the FBI hired 626 linguists—548 contract linguists and 78 language specialists. Nonetheless, the FBI has difficulty hiring linguists because it must compete with other Intelligence Community agencies as well as private firms. Despite the fact that the government has employed thousands of linguists, these numbers are not sufficient to keep abreast of the changing requirements of the Community's intelligence mission. Because Intelligence Community agencies are responding to similar threats, linguists in the same languages are in high demand at each agency.

### System Limitations

In addition to hiring difficulties, we also found that system limitations contributed to the FBI's backlog of unreviewed material. The FBI's digital collection systems have limited storage capacity. Because of this, audio sessions resident on a system are sometimes deleted through an automatic file deletion procedure to make room for incoming audio sessions. Although sessions are automatically deleted in a set order, we found that sessions which are unreviewed are sometimes included in those that are deleted, especially in offices with a high volume of audio to review. Because these sessions have not been reviewed, they will continue to be reflected in backlog statistics.

The FBI has been aware of problems regarding audio sessions being automatically deleted and the inability of the digital collection systems to identify or quantify the volume of deleted audio. Yet, necessary system controls have not been established to prevent critical audio material from being automatically deleted, such as protecting sessions of the highest priority on digital collection systems' active on-line storage until linguists review them. The results of our tests showed that three of eight offices tested had Al Qaeda sessions that potentially were deleted by the system before linguists had reviewed them. . . .

Excerpted from U.S. Department of Justice. Office of the Inspector General. *The Federal Bureau of Investigation's Foreign Language Program: Translation of Counterterrorism and Counterintelligence Foreign Language Material.* Executive Summary, Redacted and Unclassified. July 2004, Report No. 04-25. http://www.justice.gov/oig/audit/FBI/0425/index.htm (accessed October 22, 2004).

# 127. 9/11 Commission Recommendations Regarding the FBI

*July 22, 2004*

. . . Under Director Robert Mueller, the Bureau has made significant progress in improving its intelligence capabilities. It now has an Office of Intelligence, overseen by the top tier of FBI management. Field intelligence groups have been created in all field offices to put FBI priorities and the emphasis on intelligence into practice. Advances have been made in improving the Bureau's information technology systems and in increasing connectivity and information sharing with intelligence community agencies.

Director Mueller has also recognized that the FBI's reforms are far from complete. He has outlined a number of areas where added measures may be necessary. Specifically, he has recognized that the FBI needs to recruit from a broader pool of candidates, that agents and analysts working on national security matters require specialized training, and that agents should specialize within programs after obtaining a generalist foundation. The FBI is developing career tracks for agents to specialize in counterterrorism/counterintelligence, cyber crimes, criminal investigations, or intelligence. It is establishing a program for certifying agents as intelligence officers, a certification that will be a prerequisite for promotion to the senior ranks of the Bureau. New training programs have been instituted for intelligence-related subjects.

The Director of the FBI has proposed creating an Intelligence Directorate as a further refinement of the FBI intelligence program. This directorate would include units for intelligence planning and policy and for the direction of analysts and linguists.

We want to ensure that the Bureau's shift to a preventive counterterrorism posture is more fully institutionalized so that it survives beyond Director Mueller's tenure. We have found that in the past the Bureau has announced its willingness to reform and restructure itself to address transnational security threats, but has fallen short—failing to effect the necessary institutional and cultural changes organization-wide. We want to ensure that this does not happen again. Despite having found acceptance of the Director's clear message that counterterrorism is now the FBI's top priority, two years after 9/11 we also found gaps between some of the announced reforms and the reality in the field. We are concerned that management in the field offices still can allocate people and resources to local concerns that diverge from the national security mission. This system could revert to a focus on lower-priority criminal justice cases over national security requirements.

*Recommendation: A specialized and integrated national security workforce should be established at the FBI consisting of agents, analysts, linguists, and surveillance specialists who are recruited, trained, rewarded, and retained to ensure the development of an institutional culture imbued with a deep expertise in intelligence and national security.*

- The president, by executive order or directive, should direct the FBI to develop this intelligence cadre.
- Recognizing that cross-fertilization between the criminal justice and national security disciplines is vital to the success of both missions, all new agents should receive basic training in both areas. Furthermore, new agents should begin their careers with meaningful assignments in both areas.
- Agents and analysts should then specialize in one of these disciplines and have the option to work such matters for their entire career with the Bureau. Certain advanced training courses and assignments to other intelligence agencies should be required to advance within the national security discipline.
- In the interest of cross-fertilization, all senior FBI managers, including those working on law enforcement matters, should be certified intelligence officers.
- The FBI should fully implement a recruiting, hiring, and selection process for agents and analysts that enhances its ability to target and attract individuals with educational and professional backgrounds in intelligence, international relations, language, technology, and other relevant skills.
- The FBI should institute the integration of analysts, agents, linguists, and surveillance personnel in the field so that a dedicated team approach is brought to bear on national security intelligence operations.
- Each field office should have an official at the field office's deputy level for national security matters. This individual would have management oversight and ensure that the national priorities are carried out in the field.
- The FBI should align its budget structure according to its four main programs—intelligence, counterterrorism and counterintelligence, criminal, and criminal justice services—to ensure better transparency on program costs, management of resources, and protection of the intelligence program.
- The FBI should report regularly to Congress in its semiannual program reviews designed to identify whether each field office is appropriately addressing FBI and national program priorities.
- The FBI should report regularly to Congress in detail on the qualifications, status, and roles of analysts in the field and at headquarters. Congress should ensure that analysts are afforded training and career

opportunities on a par with those offered analysts in other intelligence community agencies. . . .

Excerpted from U.S. National Commission on Terrorist Attacks Upon the United States. *The 9/11 Commission Report: Final Report of the National Commission on Terrorist Attacks Upon the United States.* July 22, 2004: 425–427. Washington, D.C.: Government Printing Office. http://www.gpoaccess.gov/911/index.html (accessed October 22, 2004).

# Congressional Investigations Fault Intelligence Agencies in Terrorist Attacks

128. Report by the House Subcommittee on Terrorism and Homeland Security, July 17, 2002

129. Report of the Joint Congressional Investigation into the September 11, 2001, Terrorist Attacks, July 24, 2003

## INTRODUCTION

Questions quickly arose after the terrorist attacks on September 11, 2001, about whether failures by U.S. intelligence agencies played a role. Congress launched two different investigations to find answers.

The first results were released July 17, 2002, in a report by the House Sub-committee on Terrorism and Homeland Security. The panel's full report of more than one hundred pages was classified, but a ten-page executive summary released to the public sharply criticized three of the nation's leading intelligence agencies: the Central Intelligence Agency (CIA), the Federal Bureau of Investigation (FBI), and the National Security Agency (NSA). The panel faulted the agencies for responding to events instead of anticipating them, devoting insufficient attention to terrorism, failing to share information, and failing to hire sufficient staff with the needed foreign language skills [Document 128].

The second investigation was an unprecedented joint inquiry by the Senate Select Committee on Intelligence and the House Permanent Select Committee on Intelligence. The committees completed their ten-month investigation in December 2002, but declassification reviews delayed public release of the full report until July 24, 2003. The committees concluded that U.S. intelligence agencies knew in mid-2001 that a major attack by al Qaeda terrorists against American interests was imminent somewhere in the world, yet the agencies failed to put together bits of information that might have prevented the assault on September 11, 2001. The report cited a host of reasons for the failures, including a lack of collaboration both within and between individual intelligence agencies, "outdated and inefficient technical systems," "insufficient analytic focus and quality," and the "absence of any collective national strategy" to fight terrorism [Document 129]. To fix the problems, the committees recommended creating a cabinet-level position to oversee and coordinate all U.S. intelligence efforts.

Key portions of the nearly nine-hundred-page report were classified and deleted before it was publicly released. A twenty-eight-page section that was almost entirely deleted discussed foreign support for the hijackers. It was widely reported that much of the deleted material referred to Saudi Arabia. For example, in a July 26, 2003, story headlined "Classified Section of Sept. 11 Report Faults Saudi Rulers," the *New York Times* reported: "Senior officials of Saudi Arabia have funneled hundreds of millions of dollars to charitable groups and other organizations that may have helped finance the September 2001 attacks, a still-classified section of a Congressional report on the hijackings says, according to people who have read it. Fifteen of the nineteen hijackers were Saudi nationals. Saudi Arabian officials denounced the report and joined with some members of Congress in demanding that the twenty-eight pages be released. President George W. Bush denied the request. Bush said that releasing the information could compromise "'an ongoing investigation into the 9/11 attacks.'"

Meanwhile, an independent commission that Congress created in November 2002 continued its investigation of the terrorist attacks. Congress gave the National Commission on Terrorist Attacks Upon the United States, which became known as the 9/11 Commission, a broad mandate to examine all issues related to the September 11 hijackings (*see* 9/11 Commission Primarily Focuses on Intelligence Reforms, p. 456).

---

# 128. Report by the House Subcommittee on Terrorism and Homeland Security

*July 17, 2002*

## Executive Summary

The principal objective of this report and the work of the Subcommittee has been to review the counterterrorism capabilities and performance of the Intelligence Community before 9-11 in order to assess intelligence deficiencies and reduce the risks from acts of terrorism in the future.

The terrorist attacks perpetrated on September 11, 2001 constituted a significant strategic surprise for the United States. The failure of the Intelligence Community (IC) to provide adequate forewarning was affected by resource constraints and a series of questionable management decisions related to funding priorities. Prophetically, IC leadership concluded at a

high-level offsite on September 11, 1998 that "failure to improve operations management, resource allocation, and other key issues within the
[IC], including making substantial and sweeping changes in the way the
nation collects, analyzes, and produces intelligence, will likely result in a
catastrophic systemic intelligence failure."

The Subcommittee has found that practically every agency of the United
States Government (USG) with a counterterrorism mission uses a different
definition of terrorism. All USG agencies charged with the counterterrorism
mission should agree on a single definition, so that it would be clear what
activity constitutes a terrorist act and who should be designated a terrorist.
Without a standard definition, terrorism might be treated no differently
than other crimes. The Subcommittee supports a standard definition as follows: *"Terrorism is the illegitimate, premeditated use of politically motivated
violence or the threat of violence by a sub-national group against persons or
property with the intent to coerce a government by instilling fear amongst the
populace. . . ."*

## CIA

The summary finding regarding CIA is that *CIA needs to institutionalize
its sharp reorientation toward going on the offensive against terrorism.* This
report also arrived at the findings and recommendations that follow.

- *Keep HUMINT [human intelligence] Mission Central.* CIA is the government's national HUMINT organization—it has to keep this mission at its center. CIA did not sufficiently penetrate the al-Qa'ida
  organization before September 11th. Because of the perceived reduction in the threat environment in the early to mid 1990s, and the con-
  comitant reduction in resources for basic human intelligence
  collection, there were fewer operations officers, fewer stations, fewer
  agents, and fewer intelligence reports produced. This likely gave CIA
  fewer opportunities for accessing agents useful in the counterterrorism
  campaign and eroded overall capabilities. Several management decisions also likely degraded CIA's CT [counterterrorism] capabilities by,
  for example, redirecting funds earmarked for core field collection and
  analysis to headquarters; paying insufficient attention to CIA's unilateral CT capability; relying too much on liaison for CT; and neglecting
  sufficient investment of foreign language training and exploitation.
  The dramatic increase in resources for intelligence since 9-11 improves
  the outlook for CIA's CT capabilities, but only if CIA management
  acknowledges and deals with the systemic problems outlined in this
  report. . . .
- *Build New Platforms.* CIA needs to make long-term investments in
  new platforms to collect on the al-Qa'ida target. Using both unilateral
  and liaison resources will be necessary. Recognizing that liaison partners may have different interests, maintaining a unilateral capability is

of key importance. More attention to individual al-Qa'ida network presence worldwide is necessary. . . .

- *Forewarning of Terrorist Intentions.* There were a number of pre-9-11 successes, including a number of takedowns during the Millennium. There was also, however, intelligence acquired prior to 9-11 that, in retrospect, proved to be directly relevant to 9-11. The ability to watch-list terrorist suspects by CIA and in other agencies proved inadequate. Fixing some of the structural issues identified in this report might have put CIA in a better position to make use of such warning information. . . .

- *Additional Attention to Foreign Language Training and Document Exploitation.* CIA has paid insufficient attention to foreign language training and document exploitation efforts requiring linguists. In the most recent class of new case officers in training, less than one-third had any language expertise. CIA also needs to focus on finding ways to provide clearances for people with the right language skills in less commonly taught languages for document exploitation and other linguist needs. . . .

- *Additional Institutional Support for the CT career path.* CTC [Counterterrorist Center] more than doubled in size from September 2001 to Spring 2002, but these officers were not all experienced in the counterterrorism mission. CIA needs to ensure that all training incorporates skill development to support the counterterrorism mission, and that home basing for CTC case officers is a viable option and is career-enhancing. . . .

- *Balance CIA's no threshold terrorist threat reporting policy.* It has been increasingly difficult for consumers to determine the reliability of source reporting amidst the large volumes of reporting provided. One example of a CTC summer 2001 threat report, entitled "Threat of Impending al-Qa'ida Attack to Continue Indefinitely" illustrates the point. . . .

- *Recruiting Assets.* The availability and allocation of resources, including the redirection by CIA managers of funds earmarked for core field collection and analysis to headquarters, likely negatively impacted CIA's CT capabilities. The excessive caution and burdensome vetting process resulting from the guidelines on the recruitment of foreign assets and sources issued in 1995 undermined the CIA's ability and willingness to recruit assets, especially those who would provide insights into terrorist organizations and other hard targets. Despite a statutory requirement in December 2001 to rescind the 1995 guidelines the DCI [Director of Central Intelligence] still had not done so at the time this report was completed. . . .

- CIA's problems require more than just *expressed* commitment from senior CIA managers. They require sustained attention, and the subcommittee will be looking for deeds rather than words. As a start, CIA should begin to develop and implement a strategic plan to address the shortcomings identified in this report.

- CIA may not be capable of providing information useful in preventing every 9-11 type incident, but it can certainly manage its resources more efficiently and effectively to enhance its CT capabilities and thereby reduce the likelihood that future 9-11s will occur. HUMINT is one of out best hopes. We must not squander this historic opportunity to effect lasting positive change.

### *FBI*

The summary finding regarding FBI is that *FBI's main problem going forward is to overcome its information sharing failures.* This report also arrived at the findings and recommendations that follow.

- *Enhance FBI's prevention mission.* The Subcommittee has found that FBI focus has been investigating terrorist acts, but it has placed less emphasis on preventing such acts. FBI identified many of its CT program shortcomings prior to 9-11, but was slow to implement necessary changes. FBI's policy to decentralize investigations was inefficient for CT operations, especially against the international terrorist target. FBI's CT Program was most negatively impacted by the reticence of senior FBI managers to institute broader information-sharing initiatives; a failure to leverage FBI's ability to perform joint financial operations with other U.S. government agencies against terrorists until after 9-11; an ineffective FBI headquarters-based CT analytical capability prior to 9-11; the failure to share field office CT expertise with the FBI community-at-large; and critical staffing shortages of translators, interpreters, and Special Agents with proficiency in languages native to most terrorists. Since accepting the position as FBI Director just a few days prior to the 9-11 attacks, Robert Mueller has mandated positive, substantive changes in the modus operandi of the FBI's CT Program. . . .
- *Improve intelligence gathering and analytical capabilities.* Significant changes in law were made in the October 2001 USA Patriot Act and the May 2002 changes to the Attorney General's guidelines. While these may improve intelligence gathering, FBI's analytical capabilities remain insufficient, pending the establishment of the new Office of Intelligence.
- *Address foreign language shortfalls.* A January 2002 report noted that FBI projected shortages of permanent translators and interpreters in FY 2002 and 2003, and reported backlogs of thousands of unreviewed and untranslated materials. In key counterterrorism languages, FBI reported having in June 2001 a critical shortage of special agents with some proficiency, and FBI had very few translators and interpreters with native language skills in those languages.

- *Fixing Information Technology Challenges.* The Webster Commission in March 2002 noted in detail many of the information technology challenges of the FBI. FBI has made concerted efforts to implement change to improve technology. . . .

## NSA

The summary finding regarding NSA [National Security Agency] is that *NSA needs to change from a passive gatherer to a proactive hunter—a revolution in how it conducts its work.* This report also arrived at the findings and recommendations that follow.

- *Ensure Appropriate Intelligence Collection Priorities.* The Subcommittee found it troubling that more SIGINT [signals intelligence] resources were not devoted by NSA to CT prior to 9-11, given the prior terrorist attacks against US interests starting in 1983. Also of concern is the fact that NSA hired virtually no new employees for an extended period of time prior to 9-11, resulting in a negative impact in overall capabilities, including CT. . . .
- *Address Analyst and Linguist Shortfalls.* In April 2000, the GAO [General Accounting Office] reported a significant shortfall in linguists at NSA. After the 9-11 attacks, this shortfall actually increased slightly and was well below additional requirements identified since 9-11. A long-term linguist and analyst hiring strategy is required, as well as a methodical program to improve the skills of non-native linguists. The solution should not be agency specific. . . .
- *Support Signals Research and Target Development.* In the art of finding new targets, before 9-11 NSA did not have a comprehensive, focused, counter-terrorism target development effort. Although there were numerous analysts conducting the mission across NSA and its collection sites, NSA claims there were insufficient resources to conduct a focused CT-specific target development effort. NSA needs an aggressive target development focus against CT and other targets that should not be in competition for assets conducting collection against established targets. NSA also needs to strengthen a cultural norm in the organization to encourage target discovery. . . .
- *Need for worldwide collection across the global communications network.* The global communications network is increasingly digital, high-volume fiber optic cable rather than radio frequency, internal rather than telephone, and packet-switched rather than circuit-switched, with customer instruments moving from fixed to mobile. NSA has been unable to organize itself to define and implement an integrated system that can follow the target across the global intelligent network, beyond high-level goals and plans. NSA also needs to develop methodologies to find nongovernmental radical extremists who are associated with international terrorist organizations but might not be in direct contact

with them. NSA also needs to balance modernization funds across its collection systems in order to continue to produce intelligence on CT. . . .

- *Fix Systems Development Deficiencies.* NSA has fundamental acquisition management problems. Technical solutions continue to be solved by tackling isolated, smaller "manageable" projects and lack a larger plan on how these small projects will integrate into a whole. NSA has historically been able to successfully develop quick reaction solutions to address crisis needs, but has been unable to establish an effective requirements process for balancing systems acquisition with available resources. . . .

Excerpted from U.S. Congress. House of Representatives. House Permanent Select Committee on Intelligence. Subcommittee on Terrorism and Homeland Security. *Counterterrorism Intelligence Capabilities and Performance Prior to 9/11.* July 17, 2002. http://www.fas.org/irp/congress/2002_rpt/hpsci_ths0702.html (accessed October 22, 2004).

## 129. Report of the Joint Congressional Investigation into the September 11, 2001, Terrorist Attacks

*July 24, 2003*

*[Editor's note: Brackets [ ] indicate sections that the committees rewrote in whole or in part before public release to remove classified information; brackets enclosing dashes [———] indicate classified sections of the report that were deleted before public release; and angle brackets < > indicate content added by the editor.]*

## Abridged Findings and Conclusions

### Factual Findings

*1. Finding:* While the Intelligence Community had amassed a great deal of valuable intelligence regarding Usama Bin Ladin and his terrorist activities, none of it identified the time, place, and specific nature of the attacks that were planned for September 11, 2001. Nonetheless, the Community did have information that was clearly relevant to the September 11 attacks, particularly when considered for its collective significance.

2. *Finding:* During the spring and summer of 2001, the Intelligence Community experienced a significant increase in information indicating that Bin Ladin and al-Qa'ida intended to strike against U.S. interests in the very near future.

3. *Finding:* Beginning in 1998 and continuing into the summer of 2001, the Intelligence Community received a modest, but relatively steady, stream of intelligence reporting that indicated the possibility of terrorist attacks within the United States. Nonetheless, testimony and interviews confirm that it was the general view of the Intelligence Community, in the spring and summer of 2001, that the threatened Bin Ladin attacks would most likely occur against U.S. interests overseas, despite indications of plans and intentions to attack in the domestic United States.

4. *Finding:* From at least 1994, and continuing into the summer of 2001, the Intelligence Community received information indicating that terrorists were contemplating, among other means of attack, the use of aircraft as weapons. This information did not stimulate any specific Intelligence Community assessment of, or collective U.S. Government reaction to, this form of threat.

5. *Finding:* Although relevant information that is significant in retrospect regarding the attacks was available to the Intelligence Community prior to September 11, 2001, the Community too often failed to focus on that information and consider and appreciate its collective significance in terms of a probable terrorist attack. Neither did the Intelligence Community demonstrate sufficient initiative in coming to grips with the new transnational threats. Some significant pieces of information in the vast stream of data being collected were overlooked, some were not recognized as potentially significant at the time and therefore not disseminated, and some required additional action on the part of foreign governments before a direct connection to the hijackers could have been established. For all those reasons, the Intelligence Community failed to fully capitalize on available, and potentially important, information. The sub-findings below identify each category of this information.

*[Terrorist Communications in 1999]*

5.a. [During 1999, the National Security Agency obtained a number of communications—none of which included specific detail regarding the time, place or nature of the September 11 attacks—connecting individuals to terrorism who were identified, after September 11, 2001, as participants in the attacks that occurred on that day.]

*Malaysia Meeting and Travel of al-Qa'ida Operatives to the United States*

5.b. The Intelligence Community acquired additional, and highly significant, information regarding Khalid al-Mihdhar and Nawaf al-Hazmi <two

of the hijackers> in early 2000. Critical parts of the information concerning al-Mihdhar and al-Hazmi lay dormant within the Intelligence Community for as long as eighteen months, at the very time when plans for the September 11 attacks were proceeding. The CIA missed repeated opportunities to act based on information in its possession that these two Bin Ladin-associated terrorists were traveling to the United States, and to add their names to watchlists.

*[Terrorist Communications in Spring 2000]*
    5.c. [In January 2000, after the meeting of al-Qa'ida operatives in Malaysia, Khalid al-Mihdhar and Nawaf al-Hazmi entered the United States [——].
    Thereafter, the Intelligence Community obtained information indicating that an individual named "Khaled" at an unknown location had contacted a suspected terrorist facility in the Middle East. The Intelligence Community reported some of this information, but did not report all of it. Some of it was not reported because it was deemed not terrorist-related. It was not until after September 11, 2001 that the Intelligence Community determined that these contacts had been made from future hijacker Khalid al-Mihdhar while he was living within the domestic United States.]

*[Two Hijackers Had Numerous Contacts with an Active FBI Informant]*
    5.d. [This Joint Inquiry confirmed that these same two future hijackers, Khalid al- Mihdhar and Nawaf al-Hazmi, had numerous contacts with a long time FBI counterterrorism informant in California and that a third future hijacker, Hani Hanjour, apparently had more limited contact with the informant. In mid- to late- 2000, the CIA already had information indicating that al-Mihdhar had a multiple entry U.S. visa and that al-Hazmi had in fact traveled to Los Angeles, but the two had not been watchlisted and information suggesting that two suspected terrorists could well be in the United States had not yet been given to the FBI. The San Diego FBI field office that handled the informant in question, did not receive that information or any of the other intelligence information pertaining to al-Mihdhar and al-Hazmi, prior to September 11, 2001. As a result, the FBI missed the opportunity to task a uniquely well-positioned informant—who denies having any advance knowledge of the plot—to collect information about the hijackers and their plans within the United States].

*The Phoenix Electronic Communication*
    5.e. On July 10, 2001, an FBI Phoenix field office agent sent an "Electronic Communication" to 4 individuals in the Radical Fundamentalist Unit (RFU) and two people in the Usama Bin Ladin Unit (UBLU) at FBI headquarters, and to two agents on International Terrorism squads in the New York Field Office. In the communication, the agent expressed his con-

cerns, based on his first-hand knowledge, that there was a coordinated effort underway by Bin Ladin to send students to the United States for civil aviation-related training. He noted that there was an "inordinate number of individuals of investigative interest" in this type of training in Arizona and expressed his suspicion that this was an effort to establish a cadre of individuals in civil aviation who would conduct future terrorist activity. The Phoenix EC requested that FBI Headquarters consider implementing four recommendations:

- accumulate a list of civil aviation university/colleges around the country;
- establish liaison with these schools;
- discuss the theories contained in the Phoenix EC with the Intelligence Community; and
- consider seeking authority to obtain visa information concerning individuals seeking to attend flight schools.

However, the FBI headquarters personnel did not take the action requested by the Phoenix agent prior to September 11, 2001. The communication generated little or no interest at either FBI Headquarters or the FBI's New York field office.

### The FBI Investigation of Zacarias Moussaoui

5.f. In August 2001, the FBI's Minneapolis field office, in conjunction with the INS <Immigration and Naturalization Service>, detained Zacarias Moussaoui, a French national who had enrolled in flight training in Minnesota. FBI agents there also suspected that Moussaoui was involved in a hijacking plot. FBI Headquarters attorneys determined that there was not probable cause to obtain a court order to search Moussaoui's belongings under the Foreign Intelligence Surveillance Act (FISA). However, personnel at FBI Headquarters, including the Radical Fundamentalism Unit and the National Security Law Unit, as well as agents in the Minneapolis field office, misunderstood the legal standard for obtaining an order under FISA. As a result, FBI Minneapolis Field Office personnel wasted valuable investigative resources trying to connect the Chechen rebels to al-Qa'ida. Finally, no one at the FBI apparently connected the Moussaoui investigation with the heightened threat environment in the summer of 2001, the Phoenix communication, or the entry of al-Mihdhar and al-Hazmi into the United States.

### Hijackers in Contact with Persons of FBI Investigative Interest in the United States

5.g. The Joint Inquiry confirmed that at least some of the hijackers were not as isolated during their time in the United States as has been previously suggested. Rather, they maintained a number of contacts both in the

United States and abroad during this time period. Some of those contacts were with individuals who were known to the FBI, through either past or, at the time, ongoing FBI inquiries and investigations. Although it is not known to what extent any of these contacts in the United States were aware of the plot, it is now clear that they did provide at least some of the hijackers with substantial assistance while they were living in this country.

### Hijackers' Associates in Germany

5.h. [Since 1995, the CIA had been aware of a radical Islamic presence in Germany, including individuals with connections to Usama Bin Ladin. Prior to September 11, 2001, the CIA had unsuccessfully sought additional information on individuals who have now been identified as associates of some of the hijackers.]

### Khalid Shaykh Mohammad

5.i. Prior to September 11, the Intelligence Community had information linking Khalid Shaykh Mohammed (KSM), now recognized by the Intelligence Community as the mastermind of the attacks, to Bin Ladin, to terrorist plans to use aircraft as weapons, and to terrorist activity in the United States. The Intelligence Community, however, relegated Khalid Shaykh Mohammed (KSM) to rendition target status following his 1996 indictment in connection with the Bojinka Plot <a plan to blow up a dozen American airliners over the Pacific> and, as a result, focused primarily on his location, rather than his activities and place in the al-Qa'ida hierarchy. The Community also did not recognize the significance of reporting in June 2001 concerning KSM's active role in sending terrorists to the United States, or the facilitation of their activities upon arriving in the United States. Collection efforts were not targeted on information about KSM that might have helped better understand al-Qa'ida's plans and intentions, and KSM's role in the September 11 attacks was a surprise to the Intelligence Community.

### [Terrorist Communications in September 2001]

5.j. [In the period from September 8 to September 10, 2001 NSA <National Security Agency> intercepted, but did not translate or disseminate until after September 11, some communications that indicated possible impending terrorist activity.]

### Conclusion—Factual Findings

In short, for a variety of reasons, the Intelligence Community failed to capitalize on both the individual and collective significance of available information that appears relevant to the events of September 11. As a result, the Community missed opportunities to disrupt the September 11 plot by denying entry to or detaining would-be hijackers; to at least try to unravel the plot through surveillance and other investigative work within the

United States; and, finally, to generate a heightened state of alert and thus harden the homeland against attack.

No one will ever know what might have happened had more connections been drawn between these disparate pieces of information. We will never definitively know to what extent the Community would have been able and willing to exploit fully all the opportunities that may have emerged. The important point is that the Intelligence Community, for a variety of reasons, did not bring together and fully appreciate a range of information that could have greatly enhanced its chances of uncovering and preventing Usama Bin Ladin's plan to attack these United States on September 11, 2001.

### Systemic Findings

Our review of the events surrounding September 11 has revealed a number of systemic weaknesses that hindered the Intelligence Community's counterterrorism efforts before September 11. If not addressed, these weaknesses will continue to undercut U.S. counterterrorist efforts. In order to minimize the possibility of attacks like September 11 in the future, effective solutions to those problems need to be developed and fully implemented as soon as possible.

*1. Finding:* Prior to September 11, the Intelligence Community was neither well organized nor equipped, and did not adequately adapt, to meet the challenge posed by global terrorists focused on targets within the domestic United States. Serious gaps existed between the collection coverage provided by U.S. foreign and U.S. domestic intelligence capabilities. The U.S. foreign intelligence agencies paid inadequate attention to the potential for a domestic attack. The CIA's failure to watchlist suspected terrorists aggressively reflected a lack of emphasis on a process designed to protect the homeland from the terrorist threat. As a result, CIA employees failed to watchlist al-Mihdhar and al-Hazmi. At home, the counterterrorism effort suffered from the lack of an effective domestic intelligence capability. The FBI was unable to identify and monitor effectively the extent of activity by al-Qa'ida and other international terrorist groups operating in the United States. Taken together, these problems greatly exacerbated the nation's vulnerability to an increasingly dangerous and immediate international terrorist threat inside the United States.

*2. Finding:* Prior to September 11, 2001, neither the U.S. Government as a whole nor the Intelligence Community had a comprehensive counterterrorist strategy for combating the threat posed by Usama Bin Ladin. Furthermore, the Director of Central Intelligence (DCI) was either unwilling or unable to marshal the full range of Intelligence Community resources necessary to combat the growing threat to the United States.

*3. Finding:* Between the end of the Cold War and September 11, 2001, overall Intelligence Community funding fell or remained even in constant dollars, while funding for the Community's counterterrorism efforts increased considerably. Despite those increases, the accumulation of intelligence priorities, a burdensome requirements process, the overall decline in Intelligence Community funding, and reliance on supplemental appropriations made it difficult to allocate Community resources effectively against an evolving terrorist threat. Inefficiencies in the resource and requirements process were compounded by problems in Intelligence Community budgeting practices and procedures.

4. *Finding:* While technology remains one of this nation's greatest advantages, it has not been fully and most effectively applied in support of U.S. counterterrorism efforts. Persistent problems in this area included a lack of collaboration between Intelligence Community agencies, a reluctance to develop and implement new technical capabilities aggressively, the FBI's reliance on outdated and insufficient technical systems, and the absence of a central counterterrorism database.

5. *Finding:* Prior to September 11, the Intelligence Community's understanding of al-Qa'ida was hampered by insufficient analytic focus and quality, particularly in terms of strategic analysis. Analysis and analysts were not always used effectively because of the perception in some quarters of the Intelligence Community that they were less important to agency counterterrorism missions than were operations personnel. The quality of counterterrorism analysis was inconsistent, and many analysts were inexperienced, unqualified, under-trained, and without access to critical information. As a result, there was a dearth of creative, aggressive analysis targeting Bin Ladin and a persistent inability to comprehend the collective significance of individual pieces of intelligence. These analytic deficiencies seriously undercut the ability of U.S. policymakers to understand the full nature of the threat, and to make fully informed decisions.

6. *Finding:* Prior to September 11, the Intelligence Community was not prepared to handle the challenge it faced in translating the volumes of foreign language counterterrorism intelligence it collected. Agencies within the Intelligence Community experienced backlogs in material awaiting translation, a shortage of language specialists and language-qualified field officers, and a readiness level of only 30% in the most critical terrorism-related languages <used by terrorists>.

7. *Finding:* [Prior to September 11, the Intelligence Community's ability to produce significant and timely signals intelligence on counterterrorism was limited by NSA's failure to address modern communications technology aggressively, continuing conflict between Intelligence Community agencies, NSA's cautious approach to any collection of intelligence relating to activities in the United States, and insufficient collaboration between NSA and the FBI regarding the potential for terrorist attacks within the United States].

8. *Finding:* The continuing erosion of NSA's program management expertise and experience has hindered its contribution to the fight against terrorism. NSA continues to have mixed results in providing timely techni-

cal solutions to modern intelligence collection, analysis, and information sharing problems.

*9. Finding:* The U.S. Government does not presently bring together in one place all terrorism-related information from all sources. While the CTC <CIA's Counterterrorist Center> does manage overseas operations and has access to most Intelligence Community information, it does not collect terrorism-related information from all sources, domestic and foreign. Within the Intelligence Community, agencies did not adequately share relevant counterterrorism information, prior to September 11. This breakdown in communications was the result of a number of factors, including differences in the agencies' missions, legal authorities and cultures. Information was not sufficiently shared, not only between different Intelligence Community agencies, but also within individual agencies, and between the intelligence and the law enforcement agencies.

*10. Finding:* Serious problems in information sharing also persisted, prior to September 11, between the Intelligence Community and relevant non-Intelligence Community agencies. This included other federal agencies as well as state and local authorities. This lack of communication and collaboration deprived those other entities, as well as the Intelligence Community, of access to potentially valuable information in the "war" against Bin Ladin. The Inquiry's focus on the Intelligence Community limited the extent to which it explored these issues, and this is an area that should be reviewed further.

*11. Finding:* Prior to September 11, 2001, the Intelligence Community did not effectively develop and use human sources to penetrate the al-Qa'ida inner circle. This lack of reliable and knowledgeable human sources significantly limited the Community's ability to acquire intelligence that could be acted upon before the September 11 attacks. In part, at least, the lack of unilateral (i.e., U.S.-recruited) counterterrorism sources was a product of an excessive reliance on foreign liaison services.

*12. Finding:* During the summer of 2001, when the Intelligence Community was bracing for an imminent al-Qa'ida attack, difficulties with FBI applications for Foreign Intelligence Surveillance Act (FISA) surveillance and the FISA process led to a diminished level of coverage of suspected al-Qa'ida operatives in the United States. The effect of these difficulties was compounded by the perception that spread among FBI personnel at Headquarters and the field offices that the FISA process was lengthy and fraught with peril.

*13. Finding:* [——].

*14. Finding:* [Senior U.S. military officials were reluctant to use U.S. military assets to conduct offensive counterterrorism efforts in Afghanistan, or to support or participate in CIA operations directed against al-Qa'ida prior to September 11. At least part of this reluctance was driven by the military's view that the Intelligence Community was unable to provide the intelligence needed to support military operations. Although the U.S. military did participate in [———] counterterrorism efforts to counter Usama Bin Ladin's terrorist network prior to September 11, 2001, most of the military's focus was on force protection].

*15. Finding:* The Intelligence Community depended heavily on foreign intelligence and law enforcement services for the collection of counterterrorism intelligence and the conduct of other counterterrorism activities. The results were mixed in terms of productive intelligence, reflecting vast differences in the ability and willingness of the various foreign services to target the Bin Ladin and al-Qa'ida network. Intelligence Community agencies sometimes failed to coordinate their relationships with foreign services adequately, either within the Intelligence Community or with broader U.S. Government liaison and foreign policy efforts. This reliance on foreign liaison services also resulted in a lack of focus on the development of unilateral human sources.

*16. Finding:* [The activities of the September 11 hijackers in the United States appear to have been financed, in large part, from monies sent to them from abroad and also brought in on their persons. Prior to September 11, there was no coordinated U.S. Government-wide strategy to track terrorist funding and close down their financial support networks. There was also a reluctance in some parts of the U.S. Government to track terrorist funding and close down their financial support networks. As a result, the U.S. Government was unable to disrupt financial support for Usama Bin Ladin's terrorist activities effectively.]

### Related Findings

*17. Finding:* Despite intelligence reporting from 1998 through the summer of 2001 indicating that Usama Bin Ladin's terrorist network intended to strike inside the United States, the United States Government did not undertake a comprehensive effort to implement defensive measures in the United States.

*18. Finding:* Between 1996 and September 2001, the counterterrorism strategy adopted by the U. S. Government did not succeed in eliminating Afghanistan as a sanctuary and training ground for Usama Bin Ladin's terrorist network. A range of instruments was used to counter al-Qa'ida, with law enforcement often emerging as a leading tool because other means were deemed not to be feasible or failed to produce results. While generating numerous successful prosecutions, law enforcement efforts were not adequate by themselves to target or eliminate Bin Ladin's sanctuary. While the United States persisted in observing the rule of law and accepted norms of international behavior, Bin Ladin and al-Qa'ida recognized no rules and thrived in the safe haven provided by Afghanistan.

*19. Finding:* Prior to September 11, the Intelligence Community and the U.S. Government labored to prevent attacks by Usama Bin Ladin and his terrorist network against the United States, but largely without the benefit of an alert, mobilized and committed American public. Despite intelligence information on the immediacy of the threat level in the spring and summer of 2001, the assumption prevailed in the U.S. Government that attacks of the magnitude of September 11 could not happen here. As a result, there was insufficient effort to alert the American public to the reality and gravity of the threat.

*20. Finding:* Located in Part Four Entitled "Finding, Discussion and Narrative Regarding Certain Sensitive National Security Matters." <Part 4 was classified.>

Excerpted from U.S. Congress. Senate Select Committee on Intelligence and House Permanent Select Committee on Intelligence. *Joint Inquiry into Intelligence Community Activities before and after the Terrorist Attacks of September 11, 2001.* S. Rept. 107-351 and H. Rept. 107-792. 108th Cong., 1st sess. July 24, 2003. http://www.gpoaccess.gov/serialset/creports/ 911.html (accessed October 22, 2004).

# Immigration and Border Security Receive Renewed Attention after Attacks

130. Attorney General John Ashcroft on Implementation of the National Security Entry-Exit Registration System, November 7, 2002

131. General Accounting Office Report about Terrorist Watch Lists, April 15, 2003

132. General Accounting Office Testimony about Success in Using Counterfeit Identification Documents, May 13, 2003

133. General Accounting Office Testimony about Problems with Tracking Overstays, October 16, 2003

134. 9/11 Commission on Immigration Issues, July 22, 2004

## INTRODUCTION

Many of the hijackers on September 11, 2001, should not have been allowed to enter the United States or violated immigration laws after they arrived, according to a report by staff members of the National Commission on Terrorist Attacks Upon the United States, also known as the 9/11 Commission. For the nineteen hijackers, the January 2004 report listed the following immigration problems:

- At least two and as many as eight of the hijackers used passports to enter the United States that were "clearly doctored" in ways that were associated with al Qaeda.
- At least two and possibly up to five other hijackers used passports containing markings that were "suspicious indicators."
- Three hijackers—including one of the pilots—submitted visa applications containing false statements "that could have been proven to be false at the time they applied."
- At least six hijackers—including two other pilots—violated immigration laws once they were in the United States, the pilots by staying longer than their visas allowed.
- Yet another hijacker listed no address on his I-94 entry form, spoke little English, and had only a one-way ticket and $500 in cash. The immigra-

tion inspector thought the man might intend to illegally immigrate to the United States, but the hijacker convinced him he was a tourist.

Immigration inspectors generally had about 60 to 90 seconds to examine the demeanor of any traveler, to check his or her passport and visa, and decide whether the person should be admitted and how long he or she could stay.

Ever since the attacks on September 11, 2001, top officials in the Bush administration—including the director of the Federal Bureau of Investigation (FBI)—had said that all of the hijackers entered the country legally. "We believe the information we have provided today gives the Commission the opportunity to reevaluate those statements," the staff report said.

Most of the missed opportunities to stop at least some of the hijackers involved the Immigration and Naturalization Service (INS), an agency within the Department of Justice that had experienced serious problems for years before the terrorist attacks. In September 1997 the Justice Department's inspector general had reported that the INS lacked any way to determine how many people entered the United States legally and then stayed past their required departure dates—as did two of the September 11 pilots. That same month the U.S. Commission on Immigration Reform, which was created by Congress, recommended that the INS be abolished and its duties given to other agencies (see Immigration Agency Reviews and Reforms, p. 186).

The new INS commissioner, James W. Ziglar, announced less than three weeks before the hijackings that he planned to restructure the agency, which had 34,000 employees and a $4.8 billion budget. The plan he unveiled on November 14, 2001, called for keeping the agency intact but dividing it into two bureaus: one to enforce immigration laws and the other to provide services to immigrants such as processing applications for naturalization.

The INS suffered more embarrassment when Huffman Aviation International, a flight school in Venice, Florida, announced it had received a notice from the INS on March 11, 2002—exactly six months after the terrorist attacks—approving a change in visa status for two of the September 11 hijackers. Mohamed Atta, the ringleader of the plot, and Marwan Al-Shehhi had arrived at Huffman for flight training in July 2000 on business and tourist visas, respectively. The school's student coordinator submitted applications in August 2000 asking that their visas be changed to student status, as required under INS regulations.

On May 14, 2002, President George W. Bush signed the Enhanced Border Security and Visa Entry Reform Act. The measure increased the number of INS inspectors and investigators, imposed a one-year deadline for developing and certifying a technology standard for authenticating the identities of aliens who sought to enter the United States, and required the State Department to share visa information with the INS before an alien entered the United States. It also called on the attorney general to develop an electronic method for verifying and monitoring foreign students and exchange visitors and set a deadline of October 26, 2004, for implementing an integrated entry and exit data system and for other countries to develop machine-readable passports that contained biometric identifiers.

Less than a month later—on June 6, 2002—Attorney General John Ashcroft announced a new system to track "foreign visitors who may pose a national security concern" to the United States. The National Security Entry-Exit Registration System (NSEERS) applied to all nationals of Iran, Iraq, Libya, Sudan, and Syria; to aliens that the State Department determined posed "an elevated national security risk, based on criteria reflecting current intelligence"; and to aliens that INS inspectors identified at the port of entry as meeting the risk criteria.

Aliens covered under the program were fingerprinted and photographed when they entered the country; had to register with the INS if they stayed in the United States thirty days or more; and had to notify the INS when they departed. Under NSEERS, the fingerprints of aliens who registered at the border were run through a database of known criminals and terrorists. Ashcroft called NSEERS the "crucial first phase" of a system that would eventually track all 35 million aliens who visited the United States annually. The Justice Department said federal law had long required aliens who stayed in the United States for more than thirty days to register and be fingerprinted, but that the requirements had been suspended for decades.

In a speech at Niagara Falls on November 7, 2002, Ashcroft announced that NSEERS was operational at every air, land, and sea port of entry in the United States. During the eight weeks since NSEERS had started operating at selected ports of entry, Ashcroft said, the fingerprint matching technology had led to the arrests of 179 aliens. Those arrested included wanted felons, aliens who were barred from entering the United States because they had serious criminal records, and others who attempted to enter the United States "under false pretenses or with fraudulent documents," Ashcroft said. He added that "if today or tomorrow a suspected terrorist is identified through NSEERS, it will not be the first time that such an apprehension has been made" [Document 130].

On December 11, 2002, the INS issued final rules for the Student and Exchange Visitor Information System (SEVIS), which was designed to track foreign students in the United States. One of the system's major features notified schools when individual students arrived in the United States and required them to report to the INS if any student did not show up within thirty days. One of the September 11 hijackers had entered the United States on a student visa and never attended classes.

NSEERS attracted new controversy when male aliens over age sixteen from Iran, Iraq, Libya, Sudan, and Syria who were already in the United States were ordered to register with the INS by December 18, 2002. A second group of men who were citizens of Afghanistan, Algeria, Bahrain, Eritrea, Lebanon, Morocco, North Korea, Oman, Qatar, Somalia, Tunisia, United Arab Emirates, and Yemen had to register by January 10, 2003. A third group consisting of citizens from Pakistan and Saudi Arabia was ordered to register by February 21, 2003.

Much of the controversy arose because aliens who appeared at INS offices to register were detained if they had committed minor visa violations. Thousands of them were deported, causing Muslim and immigrant groups to charge that the registration program amounted to racial profiling and was a trick designed to ensnare aliens from Arab countries for deportation.

On March 1, 2003, the INS was officially abolished when its employees became part of the new Department of Homeland Security (DHS). They were joined there by employees from two other agencies that had provided border security and investigations: the U.S. Customs Service and the Animal and Plant Health Inspection Service, which had been part of the Agriculture Department.

All of the new registration requirements and the reorganization of border agencies were aimed at keeping terrorists out of the United States. Yet on April 15, 2003, the General Accounting Office (GAO)—the investigative arm of Congress—reported that the government did not have a single "watch list" of suspected terrorists and criminals. Instead, the GAO said, nine federal agencies had created a total of twelve watch lists. Sharing of watch lists was "inconsistent and limited," the GAO said, because each had been developed in isolation from the others and used different computer hardware, software, and data elements. The congressional agency recommended that the watch lists be consolidated to increase their effectiveness and save money, but noted that many agencies opposed the idea [Document 131].

Two weeks later Tom Ridge, secretary of homeland security, announced plans for a new U.S. entry-exit system that would take photographs and fingerprints from all foreign nationals and run them through a database to determine whether an individual had possible ties to terrorism or criminal activity. The U.S. Visitor and Immigrant Status Indication Technology system (US VISIT) would replace the existing NSEERS program and integrate the SEVIS program for students.

When implemented, US VISIT had the potential to overcome the types of problems revealed by the GAO on May 13, 2003. Robert J. Cramer, managing director of the GAO's Office of Special Investigations, testified before a House subcommittee that undercover agents had assumed fake identities, created identification documents using off-the-shelf software, and successfully entered the United States from Barbados, Canada, Jamaica, and Mexico. Cramer said that although immigration inspectors frequently asked the agents to show documents at the border, the inspectors did not detect that the drivers' licenses and birth certificates they examined were fake [Document 132].

Another border control problem involved overstays—aliens who entered the United States legally but then stayed longer than allowed. On October 16, 2003, Nancy R. Kingsbury, managing director of applied research and methods at the GAO, testified before a House subcommittee that the Department of Homeland Security had no way to find overstays. Kingsbury said DHS estimated that 2.3 million overstays were in the United States, although the figure was likely much higher. "Tracking system weaknesses may encourage overstaying on the part of visitors and potential terrorists who legally enter the United States," Kingsbury said [Document 133].

As US VISIT was becoming operational at more U.S. ports of entry in 2004, on July 22 the 9/11 Commission discussed border security weaknesses in its final report:

> Our investigation showed that two systemic weaknesses came together in our border system's inability to contribute to an effective defense against the 9/11 attacks; a lack of well-developed counterterrorism measures as a part of border security and an immigration system not able to deliver on its basic commitments, much less support counterterrorism. These weaknesses have been reduced but are far from being overcome [Document 134].

# 130. Attorney General John Ashcroft on Implementation of the National Security Entry-Exit Registration System
## *November 7, 2002*

It is fitting that this event take place at the edge of Niagara Falls—a majestic setting that has drawn visitors to this land for centuries. But Niagara is more than just a wonder of nature.

The Falls stand as an imposing sentinel on our northern border; a physical reminder of the importance that national boundaries play in securing free peoples. When our nation was founded, the raging waters of the Niagara River served as a barrier that protected Americans against hostile British troops on the other side.

Two and a quarter centuries later, on September 11, 2001, we saw just how much things had changed. The physical borders of the United States are no longer sufficient to prevent our nation's enemies from treading on American soil and endangering our freedoms. We are confronted with a new adversary, one whose platoons seek to enter the country quietly, disguised in the form of legitimate tourists, students, and businessmen. The challenge that we face is to identify and apprehend such individuals while maintaining the free flow of goods and people across the border that is so important to us and to our neighbors.

As part of our ongoing efforts to meet this challenge, five months ago, I announced that the Department of Justice and the Immigration and Naturalization service would develop and deploy the National Security Entry-Exit Registration System, or "NSEERS," as it has come to be called. On September 11, 2002, a year to the day after terrorists declared war on the United States, NSEERS began operation at selected ports of entry.

Today, I am here at Niagara Falls to announce that the NSEERS system is up and running at every port of entry into the United States. We have increased our capacity to intercept terrorists or criminals who attempt to enter the country and to verify that foreign visitors who may present national security concerns stick to their plans while they are here. And we have elevated substantially our ability to know instantly when such visitors overstay their visas. . . .

Today, I am pleased to report that the system is performing extremely well. In the eight weeks since the operation of NSEERS commenced, the INS has fingerprinted and registered more than 14,000 visitors to the United States. A significant portion of those aliens came from those nations that sponsor terrorism, but NSEERS applies to visitors from every corner of the globe. . . .

NSEERS has already paid large dividends in national security and law enforcement. The fingerprint matching technology has provided a basis for the arrest of 179 aliens at the border. Some were wanted felons who fled law enforcement during a prior visit to the United States. Others were aliens who had serious criminal records and were therefore inadmissible. And others were attempting to enter the United States under false pretenses or with fraudulent documents. These arrests would not have occurred without NSEERS. And let me also add that, if today or tomorrow a suspected terrorist is identified through NSEERS, it will not be the first time that such an apprehension has been made. . . .

Excerpted from U.S. Department of Justice. Office of the Attorney General. *Attorney General's Remarks: Implementation of NSEERS.* November 7, 2002. http://www.justice.gov/ag/speeches/2002/110702agremarksnseers_niagarafalls.htm (accessed November 1, 2004).

## 131. General Accounting Office Report about Terrorist Watch Lists
*April 15, 2003*

### Results in Brief

Generally, the federal government's approach to developing and using terrorist and criminal watch lists in performing its border security mission is diffuse and nonstandard, largely because these lists were developed and have evolved in response to individual agencies' unique mission needs and the agencies' respective legal, cultural, and technological environments. More specifically, nine federal agencies—which spanned the Departments of Defense, Justice, State, Transportation, and the Treasury—have developed and maintain 12 watch lists. These lists contain a wide variety of data; most contain biographical data, such as name and date of birth, and a few contain biometric data, such as fingerprints. Beyond the nine agencies that have developed and maintain these watch lists, about 50 other federal agencies and many state and local government entities have access to one or more of these lists.

Nonstandardization also extends to the policies and procedures governing whether and how agencies share watch lists. Specifically, two of the nine federal agencies do not have such policies and procedures, and the remaining seven have differing ones. For example, one of the agencies' policies included guidance on sharing with other federal agencies as well as state and local governments, but another addressed sharing only with federal agencies. As a general rule, the federal agencies that have watch lists share the lists among themselves. However, half of these agencies share their respective lists with state and local agencies, and one-fourth share them with private entities. The extent to which such sharing is accomplished electronically is constrained by fundamental differences in watch list system architectures (that is, the hardware, software, network, and data characteristics of the systems).

The number and variability of federal watch lists, combined with the commonality of purpose of these lists, point to opportunities to consolidate and standardize them. Appropriately exploiting these opportunities offers certain advantages—such as faster access, reduced duplication, and increased consistency—which can reduce costs and improve data reliability. Some of the agencies that have developed and maintain watch lists acknowledged these opportunities, as does the President's homeland security strategy. To this end, Office of Homeland Security officials stated in public forums during the course of our review that watch list consolidation activities were under way as part of efforts to develop a set of integrated blueprints—commonly called an enterprise architecture—for the new Department of Homeland Security (DHS). According to DHS's Chief Information Officer, responsibility for the consolidation effort has been transferred to DHS.

To strengthen our nation's homeland security capability, we are recommending that the Secretary of DHS take a series of steps aimed at ensuring that watch lists are appropriately and effectively standardized, consolidated, and shared. . . .

## Background

The President's national strategy for homeland security and the Homeland Security Act of 2002 provide for securing our national borders against terrorists. Terrorist and criminal watch lists are important tools for accomplishing this end. . . .

### Overview of the President's Homeland Security Strategy and the Homeland Security Act

Since the September 11th terrorist attacks, homeland security—including securing our nation's borders—has become a critical issue. To mobilize and organize our nation to secure the homeland from attack, the administration issued, in July 2002, a federal strategy for homeland security. Subsequently, the Congress passed and the President signed the Homeland Security Act, which established DHS in January 2003. Among other things, the strategy provides for performance of six mission areas, each aligned with a strategic objective, and identifies major initiatives associated with these mission areas. One of the mission areas is border and transportation security.

For the border and transportation security mission area, the strategy and the act specify several objectives, including ensuring the integrity of our borders and preventing the entry of unwanted persons into our country. To accomplish this, the strategy provides for, among other things, reform of immigration services, large-scale modernization of border crossings, and consolidation of federal watch lists. It also acknowledges that accomplishing these goals will require overhauling the border security process. This will be no small task, given that the United States shares a 5,525 mile border with Canada and a 1,989 mile border with Mexico and has 95,000 miles of shoreline. Moreover, each year, more than 500 million people legally enter our country, 330 million of them noncitizens. More than 85 percent enter via land borders, often as daily commuters. . . .

### *The Role of Watch Lists in the Border Security Process*

Watch lists are important tools that are used by federal agencies to help secure our nation's borders. These lists share a common purpose—to provide decisionmakers with information about individuals who are known or suspected terrorists and criminals, so that these individuals can either be prevented from entering the country, apprehended while in the country, or apprehended as they attempt to exit the country. . . .

### *President's Strategy Recognizes Problems with Watch Lists and Proposes Improvements*

In addition to highlighting the importance of watch lists for border security, the President's national strategy cites problems with these lists, including limited sharing. According to the July 2002 strategy, in the aftermath of the September 11th attacks it became clear that vital watch list information stored in numerous and disparate federal databases was not available to the right people at the right time. In particular, federal agencies that maintained information about terrorists and other criminals had not consistently shared it. The strategy attributed these sharing limitations to legal, cultural, and technical barriers that resulted in the watch lists being developed in different ways, for different purposes, and in isolation from one another. . . .

## Federal Agency Watch List Data Sharing and Supporting System Architectures Vary

The President's homeland security strategy and recent legislation call for increased sharing of watch lists, not only among federal agencies, but also among federal, state, and local government entities and between government and private-sector organizations. Currently, sharing of watch list data is occurring, but the extent to which it occurs varies, depending on the entities involved. Further, these sharing activities are not supported by systems with common architectures. This is because agencies have developed their respective watch lists, and have managed their use, in isolation from each other, and in recognition of each agency's unique legal, cultural, and technological environments. The result is inconsistent and limited sharing. . . .

## Opportunities Exist for Consolidating Watch Lists and Improving Information Sharing

. . . Most of the agencies that have developed and maintain watch lists did not identify consolidation opportunities. Of the nine federal agencies that operate and maintain watch lists, seven reported that the current state and configuration of federal watch lists meet their mission needs, and that they are satisfied with the level of watch list sharing. However, two agencies supported efforts to consolidate these lists. The State Department's Bureau of Consular Affairs and the Justice Department's U.S. Marshals Service agreed that some degree of watch list consolidation would be beneficial and would improve information sharing. . . .

The President's strategy also recognizes that watch list consolidation opportunities exist and need to be exploited. More specifically, the strategy states that the events of September 11th raised concerns regarding the effectiveness of having multiple watch lists and the lack of integration and sharing among them. To address these problems, the strategy calls for integrating the numerous and disparate systems that support watch lists as a way to reduce the variations in watch lists and remove barriers to sharing them.

To implement the strategy, Office of Homeland Security officials have stated in public settings that they were developing an enterprise architecture for border and transportation security, which is one of the six key mission areas of the newly created DHS. They also reported the following initial projects under this architecture effort: (1) developing a consolidated watch list that brings together information on known or suspected terrorists in the federal agencies' watch lists, and (2) establishing common metadata or data definitions for electronic watch lists and other information that is relevant to homeland security. However, the Office of Homeland Security did not respond to our inquiries about this effort, and thus we could not determine the substance, status, and schedule of any watch list consolidation activities. Since then, the DHS Chief Information Officer told us that DHS has assumed responsibility for these efforts. . . .

Excerpted from U.S. Congress. General Accounting Office. *Information Technology: Terrorist Watch Lists Should Be Consolidated to Promote Better Integration and Sharing.* GAO-03-322, April 15, 2003. http://purl.access.gpo.gov/GPO/LPS36707 (accessed November 1, 2004).

# 132. General Accounting Office Testimony about Success in Using Counterfeit Identification Documents

*May 13, 2003*

I am here today to discuss the results of security tests we performed in which agents of the Office of Special Investigations (OSI), acting in an undercover capacity, entered the United States from various countries in the Western Hemisphere using counterfeit documentation and fictitious identities. . . . The purpose of our tests was to determine whether U. S. government officials conducting inspections at ports of entry would detect the counterfeit identification documents.

I am accompanied this morning by Ronald Malfi, Director for Investigations, and Special Agent Ramon Rodriguez.

In summary, we created counterfeit identification documents in order to establish fictitious identities for our agents by using off-the-shelf computer graphic software that is available to any purchaser. The agents entered the United States from Jamaica, Barbados, Mexico, and Canada using fictitious names, counterfeit driver's licenses and birth certificates. Bureau of Customs & Border Protection (BCBP) staff never questioned the authenticity of the counterfeit documents, and our agents encountered no difficulty entering the country using them. On two occasions, BCBP staff did not ask for any identification when our agents entered the United States from Mexico and Canada. . . .

## Background

Immigration regulations require that all persons who arrive at a U.S. port of entry be inspected by a government official. A U.S. citizen traveling from countries in the Western Hemisphere, such as those we visited for purposes of these tests, is not required to show a passport when entering the United States but is required to prove citizenship. BCBP accepts as proof of citizenship documents, such as a United States' state or federally issued birth certificate or a baptismal record, and photo identification such as a driver's license. However, since the law does not require that U.S. citizens who enter the United States from Western Hemisphere countries present documents to prove citizenship they are permitted to establish U.S. citizenship by oral statements alone.

## Border Crossings

### U.S. Border Crossing from Jamaica

Two of our agents traveling on one-way tickets from Jamaica arrived at an airport in the United States. After landing at the U.S. airport, the two agents proceeded to the immigration checkpoint and presented to BCBP immigration inspectors counterfeit driver's licenses in fictitious names along with fictitious birth certificates purportedly issued by two different states. One BCBP inspector asked one of the agents for his date of birth, and inquired about where and when the agent had obtained the birth certificate. The agent stated that he had obtained the birth certificate about 4 or 5 years earlier. A different BCBP inspector did not question the second agent. The BCBP inspectors did not recognize any of the documents presented as counterfeit and allowed the agents to enter the United States.

### U.S. Border Crossing from Barbados

Barbados immigration officials provide visitors entering Barbados with a two-part immigration form to complete. They collect one part and return the second part to the visitor stamped with the date of entry into Barbados. Visitors are instructed to return the second part to immigration officials upon departing Barbados. In May 2003, two of our agents departed Barbados and provided Barbados immigration officials with unstamped immigration forms in fictitious names. Barbados officials accepted the forms without questioning why they were not stamped.

Two agents traveled on one-way tickets from Barbados and arrived at an airport in the United States. The two agents separately proceeded to the immigration checkpoint and were checked by the same BCBP immigration inspector. One agent was asked for his passport, and he responded that he did not have one. The agent provided a fictitious birth certificate and a Customs declaration form. The BCBP inspector reviewed the documents and asked for picture identification. In response to this request, the agent provided a counterfeit driver's license. The BCBP inspector then asked the agent several questions, reviewed the documents again, asked additional questions, and instructed the agent to proceed through Customs. The agent provided the BCBP customs officer with the Customs form and subsequently left the airport without any further scrutiny.

The second agent had a similar experience. The BCBP immigration inspector asked for a passport. The agent explained that he did not have one and provided a counterfeit birth certificate. The BCBP inspector then asked for picture identification and the agent offered to produce a driver's license. The BCBP inspector did not ask to see the driver's license but asked several questions and then instructed the agent to proceed to Customs. The agent turned in his Customs form to a Customs official and then left the airport without any further scrutiny.

The BCBP immigration inspector did not question any of the counterfeit documents.

### U.S. Border Crossings from Mexico

On two occasions our agents crossed the border from Mexico into the United States. On one occasion, at a land border crossing, a BCBP immigration inspector asked our agent if he was a U.S. citizen and whether he had brought anything across the border from Mexico. After the agent responded that he was a U.S. citizen and that he was not bringing anything into the United States from Mexico, the inspector allowed him to proceed without requiring any proof of identity.

On a subsequent occasion at the same border crossing, two of our agents were asked for identification by separate BCBP inspectors. Both agents presented counterfeit driver's licenses and were allowed to cross into the United States.

### U.S. Border Crossings from Canada

On three occasions our agents crossed the border from Canada into the United States. The first border crossing occurred when two agents entered the United States through a sea port of entry from Canada. On that occasion, the agents were not asked to show identification. On a subsequent occasion, two agents, driving a rented car with Canadian plates, using fictitious names and counterfeit documents, crossed the border into the United States at a Canadian border crossing. A BCBP immigration inspector asked for identification and was provided the counterfeit documents. After the inspector reviewed the documents, the agents were allowed to cross the border.

During the Canadian land border crossing, the agents discovered a further potential security problem. A park straddles the U.S. and Canada at this border crossing. One of our agents was able to walk across this park into the United States from Canada without being stopped or questioned by any U.S. government official. Later, that agent walked back to Canada through this park without being inspected by Canadian authorities.

## Conclusion

. . . Although BCBP inspects millions of people who enter the United States and detects thousands of individuals who attempt to enter illegally each year, the results of our work indicate that BCBP inspectors are not readily capable of detecting counterfeit identification documents. Further, people who enter the United States are not always asked to present identification. While current law does not require that U.S. Citizens who enter the U.S. from Western Hemisphere countries provide documentary proof of U.S. citizenship, this does provide an opportunity for individuals to enter the United States illegally.

Excerpted from U.S. Congress. General Accounting Office. *Counterfeit Documents Used to Enter the United States from Certain Western Hemisphere Countries Not Detected.* Prepared testimony of Robert J. Cramer for a hearing by the Subcommittee on Immigration, Border Security, and Claims of the House Committee on the Judiciary. GAO-03-713T, May 13, 2003. http://purl.access.gpo.gov/GPO/LPS37067 (accessed November 1, 2004).

# 133. General Accounting Office Testimony about Problems with Tracking Overstays

*October 16, 2003*

I am pleased to be here today to discuss overstays—that is, foreign citizens who enter the United States legally but do not leave when their authorized period of admission expires. Overstay issues have gained heightened attention because some of the 9/11 hijackers had overstayed their periods of admission. . . .

While the vast majority of overstays appear to be motivated by economic opportunities, the few who are potential terrorists could represent a significant threat to our domestic security. An effective strategy to address this risk is best developed within the larger context of a layered defense for domestic security. . . .

To summarize the results of our analysis of overstay issues and domestic security, we found that:

- Overstaying is significant and may be understated by DHS's [Department of Homeland Security] recent estimate.
- The current system for tracking foreign visitors has several weaknesses.
- It is more difficult to ensure our domestic security because of the weaknesses in the tracking system and the level of overstaying that apparently occurs. . . .

## Background

. . . Form I-94 is the basis of the current overstay tracking system. For visitors from most countries, the period of admission is authorized (or set) by a DHS inspector when they enter the United States legally and fill out this form. Each visitor is to give the top half to the inspector and to retain the bottom half, which should be collected on his or her departure.

When visiting the United States for business or pleasure, two major groups are exempt from filling out an I-94 form:

- Mexicans entering the United States with a Border Crossing Card (BCC) at the Southwestern border who intend to limit their stay to less than 72 hours and not to travel beyond a set perimeter (generally, 25 miles from the border) and:

- Canadians admitted for up to 6 months without a perimeter restriction. Thus, the majority of Canadian and Mexican visits cannot be tracked by the current system, because the visitors have not filled out Form I-94. Tracking should be possible for almost all other legal temporary visitors, including visitors from visa waiver countries, because they are required to fill out the form.

Terrorists might be better prevented from legally entering the United States if consular officials and DHS inspectors used improved watch lists to screen visa applicants and make border inspections. However, some terrorists may continue to slip through these border defenses. Keeping all dangerous persons and potential terrorist-suspects from legally entering the United States is difficult because some do not match the expected characteristics of terrorists or suspicious persons; in addition, some may not be required to apply for visas (that is, citizens of Canada or one of the 27 visa waiver countries).

Watch lists have been improved somewhat since 9/11, but further improvements are needed. For example, earlier this year we reported that the State Department "with the help of other agencies, almost doubled the number of names and the amount of information" in its Consular Lookout and Support System. We also reported that "the federal watch list environment has been characterized by a proliferation of [terrorist and watch list] systems, among which information sharing is occurring in some cases but not in others. . . ."

## The Extent of Overstaying Is Significant and May Be Understated by DHS's Estimate

Significant numbers of visitors overstay their authorized periods of admission. A recent DHS estimate put the January 2000 resident overstay population at 1/3 of 7 million illegal immigrants, or 2.3 million. The method DHS used to obtain the 1/3 figure is complex and indirect, and we plan to evaluate that estimate further. However, the 2.3 million overstay estimate excludes specific groups, and we believe, therefore, that it potentially understates the extent of overstaying. . . .

## Unresolved Tracking System Weaknesses Heighten the Overstay Problem

### I-94 Tracking System Weaknesses Limit Control Options

One weakness in DHS's system for tracking the paper Form I-94—its limited coverage of Mexican and Canadian visitors—was discussed in the section above. In our previous work, we have pointed to at least three other weaknesses in this tracking system:

- *Failure to update the visitor's authorized period of admission or immigration status.* . . .
- *Lack of reliable address information and inability to locate visitors.* Some visitors do not fill in destination address information on Form I-94 or they do so inadequately. . . .
- *Missing departure forms.* . . .

In our current work, we have identified two further weaknesses in the tracking system. One weakness is the inability to match some departure forms back to corresponding arrival forms. DHS has suggested that when a visitor loses the original departure form, matching is less certain because it can no longer be based on identical numbers printed on the top and bottom halves of the original form. The other weakness is that at land ports (and possibly airports and seaports), the collection of departure forms is vulnerable to manipulation—in other words, visitors could make it appear that they had left when they had not. To illustrate, on bridges where toll collectors accept I-94 departure forms at the Southwestern border, a person departing the United States by land could hand in someone else's I-94 form.

Because of these weaknesses, DHS has no accurate list of overstays to send to consular officials or DHS inspectors. This limits DHS's ability to consider past overstaying when issuing new visas or allowing visitors to reenter.

More generally, the lack of an accurate list limits prevention and enforcement options. For example, accurate data on overstays and other visitors might help define patterns to better differentiate visa applicants with higher overstay risk. And without an accurate list and updated addresses, it is not possible to identify and locate new overstays to remind them of penalties for not departing. Such efforts fall under the category of interior enforcement: As we previously testified, "historically . . . over five times more resources in terms of staff and budget [have been devoted to] border enforcement than . . . [to] interior enforcement. . . . DHS statisticians told us that for fiscal year 2002, the risk of arrest for all overstays was less than 2 percent. . . .

## Overstay Issues May Complicate Efforts to Ensure Domestic Security

### *Tracking System Weaknesses Encourage Overstays and Hamper Some Counterterrorism Efforts*

Tracking system weaknesses may encourage overstaying on the part of visitors and potential terrorists who legally enter the United States. Once here, terrorists may overstay or use other stratagems—such as exiting and reentering (to obtain a new authorized period of admission) or applying for a change of status—to extend their stay. Three of the six pilots and apparent leaders were out of status on or before 9/11, two because of short-term overstaying.

Additionally, a current overstay recently pled guilty to identity document fraud in connection with the 9/11 hijackers. Two others with a history of overstaying were recently convicted of crimes connected to terrorism (money-laundering and providing material support to terrorists); both had overstayed for long periods.

Terrorists who enter as legal visitors are hidden within the much larger populations of all legal visitors, overstays, and other illegals such as border crossers. Improved tracking could help counterterrorism investigators and prosecutors track them and prosecute them, particularly in cases in which suspicious individuals are placed on watch lists after they enter the country. . . . For example, these data—together with additional analysis—can be important in quickly and efficiently determining whether suspected terrorists were in the United States at specific times.

As we reported earlier this year, between "September 11 and November 9, 2001 [that is, over the course of 2 months], . . . INS compiled a list of aliens whose characteristics were similar to those of the hijackers" in types of visa, countries issuing their passports, and dates of entry into the United States. While the list of aliens was part of an effort to identify and locate specific persons for investigative interviews, it contained duplicate names and data entry errors. In other words, poor data hampered the government's efforts to obtain information in a national emergency, and investigators turned to private sector information. . . .

### *Overstays' Employment in Sensitive Airport Jobs Illustrates Potential Effects on Domestic Security*

DHS has declared that combating fraudulent employment at critical infrastructures, such as airports, is a priority for domestic security. DHS has planned and ongoing efforts to identify illegal workers in key jobs at various infrastructures (for example, airport workers with security badges). These sweeps are thought to reduce the nation's vulnerability to terrorism, because, as experts have told us, (1) security badges issued on the basis of fraudulent IDs constitute security breaches, and (2) overstays and other illegals working in such facilities might be hesitant to report suspicious activities for fear of drawing authorities' attention to themselves or they might be vulnerable to compromise.

Operation Tarmac swept 106 airports and identified 4,271 illegal immigrants who had misused Social Security numbers and identity documents in obtaining airport jobs and security badges. A much smaller number of airport employees had misrepresented their criminal histories in order to obtain their jobs and badges. The illegal immigrant workers with access to secure airport areas were employed by airlines (for example, at Washington Dulles International Airport and Ronald Reagan Washington National Airport, this included American, Atlantic Coast, Delta, Northwest, and United Airlines as well as SwissAir and British Airways) and by a variety of other companies (for example, Federal Express and Ogden Services). Job descriptions included, among others, aircraft maintenance technician, airline agent, airline cabin service attendant, airplane fueler, baggage handler, cargo operations manager, electrician, janitorial supervisor, member of a cleaning crew, predeparture screener, ramp agent, and skycap.

In the large majority of these cases, identity fraud or counterfeit IDs were involved; without fraud or counterfeit documents, illegal workers would not have been able to obtain the jobs and badges allowing them access to secure areas.

When we obtained data on the specific immigration status of workers who were arrested or scheduled for deportation at 14 Operation Tarmac airports, we found that a substantial number were overstays. A DHS official told us that Operation Tarmac is likely not to have identified all illegal aliens working in secure areas of airports.

## Conclusion

Weaknesses in DHS's current overstay tracking system and the magnitude of the overstay problem make it more difficult to ensure domestic security. . . . Designing and implementing a viable and effective tracking system is a critical component of the nation's domestic security and continues to be a DHS priority. . . .

Excerpted from U.S. Congress. General Accounting Office. *Homeland Security: Overstay Tracking Is a Key Component of a Layered Defense*. Prepared testimony of Nancy R. Kingsbury for a hearing by the Subcommittee on Immigration, Border Security, and Claims of the House Committee on the Judiciary. GAO-04-170T, October 16, 2003.
http://purl.access.gpo.gov/GPO/LPS53032 (accessed November 1, 2004).

# 134. 9/11 Commission on Immigration Issues

*July 22, 2004*

## Chapter 3: Counterterrorism Evolves

. . . The Immigration and Naturalization Service (INS), with its 9,000 Border Patrol agents, 4,500 inspectors, and 2,000 immigration special agents, had perhaps the greatest potential to develop an expanded role in counterterrorism. However, the INS was focused on the formidable challenges posed by illegal entry over the southwest border, criminal aliens, and a growing backlog in the applications for naturalizing immigrants. The White House, the Justice Department, and above all the Congress reinforced these concerns. In addition, when Doris Meissner became INS Commissioner in 1993, she found an agency seriously hampered by outdated technology and insufficient human resources. Border Patrol agents were still using manual typewriters; inspectors at ports of entry were using a paper watchlist; the asylum and other benefits systems did not effectively deter fraudulent applicants.

Commissioner Meissner responded in 1993 to the World Trade Center bombing by providing seed money to the State Department's Consular Affairs Bureau to automate its terrorist watchlist, used by consular officers and border inspectors. The INS assigned an individual in a new "lookout" unit to work with the State Department in watchlisting suspected terrorists and with the intelligence community and the FBI in determining how to deal with them when they appeared at ports of entry. By 1998, 97 suspected terrorists had been denied admission at U.S. ports of entry because of the watchlist. . . .

Midlevel INS employees proposed comprehensive counterterrorism proposals to management in 1986, 1995, and 1997. No action was taken on them. In 1997, a National Security Unit was set up to handle alerts, track potential terrorist cases for possible immigration enforcement action, and work with the rest of the Justice Department. It focused on the FBI's priorities of Hezbollah and Hamas, and began to examine how immigration laws could be brought to bear on terrorism. For instance, it sought unsuccessfully to require that CIA security checks be completed before naturalization applications were approved. Policy questions, such as whether resident alien status should be revoked upon the person's conviction of a terrorist crime, were not addressed.

Congress, with the support of the Clinton administration, doubled the number of Border Patrol agents required along the border with Mexico to one agent every quarter mile by 1999. It rejected efforts to bring additional resources to bear in the north. The border with Canada had one agent for every 13.25 miles. Despite examples of terrorists entering from Canada, awareness of terrorist activity in Canada and its more lenient immigration laws, and an inspector general's report recommending that the Border Patrol develop a northern border strategy, the only positive step was that the number of Border Patrol agents was not cut any further.

Inspectors at the ports of entry were not asked to focus on terrorists. Inspectors told us they were not even aware that when they checked the names of incoming passengers against the automated watchlist, they were checking in part for terrorists. In general, border inspectors also did not have the information they needed to make fact-based determinations of admissibility. The INS initiated but failed to bring to completion two efforts that would have provided inspectors with information relevant to counterterrorism—a proposed system to track foreign student visa compliance and a program to establish a way of tracking travelers' entry to and exit from the United States.

In 1996, a new law enabled the INS to enter into agreements with state and local law enforcement agencies through which the INS provided training and the local agencies exercised immigration enforcement authority. Terrorist watchlists were not available to them. Mayors in cities with large immigrant populations sometimes imposed limits on city employee cooperation with federal immigration agents. A large population lives outside the legal framework. Fraudulent documents could be easily obtained. Congress kept the number of INS agents static in the face of the overwhelming problem. . . .

## Chapter 12: What to Do? A Global Strategy

. . . More than 500 million people annually cross U.S. borders at legal entry points, about 330 million of them noncitizens. Another 500,000 or more enter illegally without inspection across America's thousands of miles of land borders or remain in the country past the expiration of their permitted stay. The challenge for national security in an age of terrorism is to prevent the very few people who may pose overwhelming risks from entering or remaining in the United States undetected.

In the decade before September 11, 2001, border security—encompassing travel, entry, and immigration—was not seen as a national security matter. Public figures voiced concern about the "war on drugs," the right level and kind of immigration, problems along the southwest border, migration crises originating in the Caribbean and elsewhere, or the growing criminal traffic in humans. The immigration system as a whole was widely viewed as increasingly dysfunctional and badly in need of reform. In national security circles, however, only smuggling of weapons of mass destruction carried weight, not the entry of terrorists who might use such weapons or the presence of associated foreign-born terrorists.

For terrorists, travel documents are as important as weapons. Terrorists must travel clandestinely to meet, train, plan, case targets, and gain access to attack. To them, international travel presents great danger, because they must surface to pass through regulated channels, present themselves to border security officials, or attempt to circumvent inspection points.

In their travels, terrorists use evasive methods, such as altered and counterfeit passports and visas, specific travel methods and routes, liaisons with corrupt government officials, human smuggling networks, supportive travel agencies, and immigration and identity fraud. These can sometimes be detected.

Before 9/11, no agency of the U.S. government systematically analyzed terrorists' travel strategies. Had they done so, they could have discovered the ways in which the terrorist predecessors to al Qaeda had been systematically but detectably exploiting weaknesses in our border security since the early 1990s.

We found that as many as 15 of the 19 hijackers were potentially vulnerable to interception by border authorities. Analyzing their characteristic travel documents and travel patterns could have allowed authorities to intercept 4 to 15 hijackers and more effective use of information available in U.S. government databases could have identified up to 3 hijackers.

Looking back, we can also see that the routine operations of our immigration laws—that is, aspects of those laws not specifically aimed at protecting against terrorism—inevitably shaped al Qaeda's planning and opportunities. Because they were deemed not to be bona fide tourists or students as they claimed, five conspirators that we know of tried to get visas and failed, and one was denied entry by an inspector. We also found that had the immigration system set a higher bar for determining whether individuals are who or what they claim to be—and ensuring routine consequences for violations—it could potentially have excluded, removed, or come into further contact with several hijackers who did not appear to meet the terms for admitting short-term visitors.

Our investigation showed that two systemic weaknesses came together in our border system's inability to contribute to an effective defense against the 9/11 attacks: a lack of well-developed counterterrorism measures as a part of border security and an immigration system not able to deliver on its basic commitments, much less support counterterrorism. These weaknesses have been reduced but are far from being overcome.

*Recommendation: Targeting travel is at least as powerful a weapon against terrorists as targeting their money. The United States should combine terrorist travel intelligence, operations, and law enforcement in a strategy to intercept terrorists, find terrorist travel facilitators, and constrain terrorist mobility.*

Since 9/11, significant improvements have been made to create an integrated watchlist that makes terrorist name information available to border and law enforcement authorities. However, in the already difficult process of merging border agencies in the new Department of Homeland Security—"changing the engine while flying" as one official put it—new insights into terrorist travel have not yet been integrated into the front lines of border security.

The small terrorist travel intelligence collection and analysis program currently in place has produced disproportionately useful results. It should be expanded. Since officials at the borders encounter travelers and their documents first and investigate travel facilitators, they must work closely with intelligence officials.

Internationally and in the United States, constraining terrorist travel should become a vital part of counterterrorism strategy. Better technology and training to detect terrorist travel documents are the most important immediate steps to reduce America's vulnerability to clandestine entry. Every stage of our border and immigration system should have as a part of its operations the detection of terrorist indicators on travel documents. Information systems able to authenticate travel documents and detect potential terrorist indicators should be used at consulates, at primary border inspection lines, in immigration services offices, and in intelligence and enforcement units. All frontline personnel should receive some training. Dedicated specialists and ongoing linkages with the intelligence community are also required. The Homeland Security Department's Directorate of Information Analysis and Infrastructure Protection should receive more resources to accomplish its mission as the bridge between the frontline border agencies and the rest of the government counterterrorism community. . . .

Excerpted from U.S. National Commission on Terrorist Attacks Upon the United States. *The 9/11 Commission Report: Final Report of the National Commission on Terrorist Attacks Upon the United States.* July 22, 2004: 80–81, 383–385. Washington, D.C.: Government Printing Office. http://www.gpoaccess.gov/911/index.html (accessed November 1, 2004).

# Executive Branch, Congress Restructure for Homeland Security

## INTRODUCTION

After the terrorist attacks of September 11, 2001, strong sentiment existed for reorganizing the executive branch so it was better prepared to protect the nation against more attacks. President George W. Bush created the Office of Homeland Security on October 8, 2001, to coordinate the more than forty federal agencies and departments that played some role in fighting terrorism. Many experts were skeptical about its potential for success because Bush's order did not give the new office's director, former Pennsylvania governor Tom Ridge, budget authority over the agencies he was to coordinate (*see* President Bush Creates the Office of Homeland Security, p. 258).

Some Democrats in Congress championed creating a new cabinet-level Department of Homeland Security (DHS) that would bring together all or some of the federal agencies involved in protecting the American homeland. Bush initially opposed the move, contending it was unnecessary. As legislation to create the new department picked up momentum, Bush reversed his position and offered his own plan in June. Congress ultimately passed legislation that closely followed the president's proposal.

Bush signed the Homeland Security Act of 2002, which created the new department, on November 25, 2002. At a signing ceremony, Bush said DHS would do everything from analyzing threats to protecting the nation's borders. "With the Homeland Security Act, we're doing everything we can to protect

America," Bush said. "We're showing the resolve of this great Nation to defend our freedom, our security, and our way of life" [Document 135].

The legislation called for merging all or parts of twenty-two existing agencies into the new department, the biggest reorganization of the federal government since creation of the Defense Department more than fifty years earlier. The new department was to include the Coast Guard, the Immigration and Naturalization Service (INS), the new Transportation Security Administration (TSA), the Federal Emergency Management Agency (FEMA), and the Agriculture Department's Animal and Plant Health Inspection Service, among other agencies. About 170,000 to 180,000 federal workers were to be merged in the new department. In many cases, the day-to-day activities of the agencies and their employees were not expected to change. What would change, Bush said, was the degree of coordination among them.

The biggest surprise was that the new department did not include any intelligence agencies. By then various investigations had revealed failures by agencies such as the Federal Bureau of Investigation (FBI) and the Central Intelligence Agency (CIA) to put together clues that might have revealed the terrorist plot. Many critics said the counterintelligence functions of both agencies should be combined, preferably in the new department. Bush rejected that idea, agreeing with his aides that the intelligence agencies should be left alone.

In January 2003 the General Accounting Office (GAO), the investigative arm of Congress, designated DHS as "high risk," as it had with other federal programs that needed major transformation. "It is well recognized that mergers of this magnitude in the public and private sector carry significant risks, including lost productivity and inefficiencies," the GAO said. "Generally, successful transformations of large organizations, even those undertaking less strenuous reorganizations and with less pressure for immediate results, can take from 5 to 7 years to achieve" [Document 136].

With Ridge at the helm, DHS officially opened for business on March 1, 2003. Its creation led leaders in the House of Representatives to create a new Select Committee on Homeland Security to oversee the department. The new committee had fifty members—many of them among the most powerful members of Congress—making it somewhat unwieldy. The committee was set to expire at the end of 2004 unless it was converted into a permanent panel when the House convened in January 2005. House leaders also reorganized the Appropriations Committee. Eight of its thirteen subcommittees claimed some jurisdiction over homeland security, but leaders created a new Homeland Security Subcommittee to consolidate the jurisdiction. The Senate took no action regarding its committees.

At a hearing by the Select Committee on Homeland Security on July 10, 2003, its chairman—Rep. Christopher Cox, R-Calif.—said eighty-eight committees and subcommittees in the House and Senate claimed jurisdiction over the new department. "This is simply too many," Cox said. "It's not going to work. We need to move beyond jurisdictional turf and partisan politics to establish a central point for substantive jurisdiction over DHS. Without it, we'll have continuing problems with oversight, legislation and authorization for the department."

The key witness at the hearing was James Schlesinger, who had served as chairman of the Atomic Energy Commission, director of the CIA, and secretary of defense under President Richard Nixon, and then secretary of the Department of Energy under President Jimmy Carter. Schlesinger was blunt: "It will be a disaster for the incoming department unless you simplify its obligations to the Congress," he said. Schlesinger called for making the select committee permanent so that a single committee had primary responsibility for DHS [Document 137].

Congressional oversight of intelligence and counterterrorism was "dysfunctional," the National Commission on Terrorist Attacks Upon the United States—more commonly known as the 9/11 Commission—said in its final report on July 22, 2004. It recommended that Congress choose between two alternatives:

- Create a joint congressional committee to oversee intelligence; or
- Create a single intelligence committee in each house that would have far greater powers than the existing committees.

"Tinkering with the existing structure is not sufficient," the commission said. It also recommended choosing a single committee in each house to provide oversight of DHS. The commission said congressional leaders were best able to judge which committee in each chamber should have jurisdiction, but it said the panels should be permanent standing committees with nonpartisan staffs [Document 138].

An article about the report in the *Washington Post* said:

Few in Congress disagree that there are serious problems with the oversight of counterterrorism and intelligence. Responsibility for oversight has been granted to dozens of committees and subcommittees whose jurisdictions overlap and conflict, often resulting in confusion and gridlock.

It was widely acknowledged, however, that getting Congress to approve the commission's recommendations was a tough sell. It was particularly difficult because adopting the recommendations would force many members to give up cherished turf.

Meanwhile, on October 11, 2004, the Senate followed the House in passing a $33.1 billion appropriations bill for DHS in fiscal 2005. The bill boosted funding for the department by $2.8 billion, or 9 percent, over the previous year and gave DHS $896 million more than Bush had requested in his budget.

## 135. President Bush's Remarks on Signing the Homeland Security Act of 2002

*November 25, 2002*

. . . Today we are taking historic action to defend the United States and protect our citizens against the dangers of a new era. With my signature, this act of Congress will create a new Department of Homeland Security, ensuring that our efforts to defend this country are comprehensive and united.

The new Department will analyze threats, will guard our borders and airports, protect our critical infrastructure, and coordinate the response of our Nation to future emergencies. The Department of Homeland Security will focus the full resources of the American Government on the safety of the American people. This essential reform was carefully considered by Congress and enacted with strong bipartisan majorities. . . .

From the morning of September the 11th, 2001, to this hour, America has been engaged in an unprecedented effort to defend our freedom and our security. We're fighting a war against terror with all our resources, and we're determined to win.

With the help of many nations, with the help of 90 nations, we're tracking terrorist activity; we're freezing terrorist finances; we're disrupting terrorist plots; we're shutting down terrorist camps; we're on the hunt one person at a time. Many terrorists are now being interrogated. Many terrorists have been killed. We've liberated a country.

We recognize our greatest security is found in the relentless pursuit of these coldblooded killers. Yet, because terrorists are targeting America, the front of the new war is here in America. Our life changed and changed in dramatic fashion on September the 11th, 2001.

In the last 14 months, every level of our Government has taken steps to be better prepared against a terrorist attack. We understand the nature of the enemy. We understand they hate us because of what we love. We're doing everything we can to enhance security at our airports and powerplants and border crossings. We've deployed detection equipment to look for weapons of mass destruction. We've given law enforcement better tools to detect and disrupt terrorist cells which might be hiding in our own country. . . .

The Homeland Security Act of 2002 takes the next critical steps in defending our country. The continuing threat of terrorism, the threat of mass murder on our own soil, will be met with a unified, effective response. Dozens of agencies charged with homeland security will now be located within one Cabinet Department with the mandate and legal authority to protect our people. America will be better able to respond to any future attacks, to reduce our vulnerability and, most important, prevent the terrorists from taking innocent American lives.

The Department of Homeland Security will have nearly 170,000 employees, dedicated professionals who will wake up each morning with the overriding duty of protecting their fellow citizens. As Federal workers, they have rights, and those rights will be fully protected. And I'm grateful that the Congress listened to my concerns and retained the authority of the President to put the right people in the right place at the right time in the defense of our country.

I've great confidence in the men and women who will serve in this Department and in the man I've asked to lead it. As I prepare to sign this bill into law, I am pleased to announce that I will nominate Governor Tom Ridge as our Nation's first Secretary of Homeland Security. Americans know Tom as an experienced public servant and as the leader of our homeland security efforts since last year. Tom accepted that assignment in urgent circumstances, resigning as the Governor of Pennsylvania to organize the White House Office of Homeland Security and to develop a comprehensive strategy to protect the American people. He's done a superb job. He's the right man for this new and great responsibility.

We're going to put together a fine team to work with Tom. The Secretary of the Navy, Gordon England, will be nominated for the post of Deputy Secretary. And Asa Hutchinson of Arkansas, now the Administrator of the Drug Enforcement Administration, will be nominated to serve as Under Secretary for Border and Transportation Security.

The Secretary-designate and his team have an immense task ahead of them. Setting up the Department of Homeland Security will involve the most extensive reorganization of the Federal Government since Harry Truman signed the National Security Act. To succeed in their mission, leaders of the new Department must change the culture of many diverse agencies, directing all of them toward the principal objective of protecting the American people. The effort will take time and focus and steady resolve. It will also require full support from both the administration and the Congress. Adjustments will be needed along the way. Yet this is pressing business, and the hard work of building a new Department begins today.

When the Department of Homeland Security is fully operational, it will enhance the safety of our people in very practical ways. First, this new Department will analyze intelligence information on terror threats collected by the CIA [Central Intelligence Agency], the FBI [Federal Bureau of Investigation], the National Security Agency, and others. The Department will match this intelligence against the Nation's vulnerabilities and work with other agencies and the private sector and State and local governments to harden America's defenses against terror.

Second, the Department will gather and focus all our efforts to face the challenge of cyberterrorism and the even worse danger of nuclear, chemical, and biological terrorism. This Department will be charged with encouraging research on new technologies that can detect these threats in time to prevent an attack.

Third, State and local governments will be able to turn for help and information to one Federal domestic security agency, instead of more than 20 agencies that currently divide these responsibilities. This will help our local governments work in concert with the Federal Government for the sake of all the people of America.

Fourth, the new Department will bring together the agencies responsible for border, coastline, and transportation security. There will be a coordinated effort to safeguard our transportation systems and to secure the border so that we're better able to protect our citizens and welcome our friends.

Fifth, the Department will work with State and local officials to prepare our response to any future terrorist attack that may come. We have found that the first hours and even the first minutes after the attack can be crucial in saving lives, and our first-responders need the carefully planned and drilled strategies that will make their work effective.

The Department of Homeland Security will also end a great deal of duplication and overlapping responsibilities. Our objective is to spend less on administrators in offices and more on working agents in the field, less on overhead and more on protecting our neighborhoods and borders and waters and skies from terrorists.

With a vast nation to defend, we can neither predict nor prevent every conceivable attack. And in a free and open society, no Department of Government can completely guarantee our safety against ruthless killers who move and plot in shadows. Yet our Government will take every possible measure to safeguard our country and our people.

We're fighting a new kind of war against determined enemies. And public servants long into the future will bear the responsibility to defend Americans against terror. This administration and this Congress have the duty of putting that system into place. We will fulfill that duty. With the Homeland Security Act, we're doing everything we can to protect America. We're showing the resolve of this great Nation to defend our freedom, our security, and our way of life.

It's now my privilege to sign the Homeland Security Act of 2002.

Excerpted from U.S. Executive Office of the President. "Remarks on Signing the Homeland Security Act of 2002." November 25, 2002. *Weekly Compilation of Presidential Documents* 38, no. 48 (December 2, 2002): 2090–2092. http://www.gpoaccess.gov/wcomp/v38no48.html (accessed November 1, 2004).

## 136. General Accounting Office Report Designating the Department of Homeland Security as "High-Risk"

*January 2003*

### Implementing and Transforming the New Department of Homeland Security

We designated implementation and transformation of the new Department of Homeland Security as high risk based on three factors. First, the implementation and transformation of DHS is an enormous undertaking that will take time to achieve in an effective and efficient manner. Second, components to be merged into DHS already face a wide array of existing challenges. Finally, failure to effectively carry out its mission would expose the nation to potentially very serious consequences.

In the aftermath of September 11, invigorating the nation's homeland security missions has become one of the federal government's most significant challenges. DHS, with an anticipated budget of almost $40 billion and an estimated 170,000 employees, will be the third largest government agency; not since the creation of DOD more than 50 years ago has the government sought an integration and transformation of this magnitude. In DOD's case, the effective transformation took many years to achieve, and even today, the department continues to face enduring management challenges and high-risk areas that are, in part, legacies of its unfinished integration.

Effectively implementing and transforming DHS may be an even more daunting challenge. DOD at least was formed almost entirely from agencies whose principal mission was national defense. DHS will combine 22 agencies specializing in various disciplines: law enforcement, border security, biological research, disaster mitigation, and computer security, for instance. Further, DHS will oversee a number of non-homeland-security activities, such as Coast Guard's marine safety responsibilities and the Federal Emergency Management Agency's (FEMA) natural disaster response functions. Yet only in the effective integration and collaboration of these entities will the nation achieve the synergy that can help provide better security against terrorism. The magnitude of the responsibilities, combined with the challenge and complexity of the transformation, underscores the perseverance and dedication that will be required of all DHS's leaders, employees, and stakeholders to achieve success.

Further, it is well recognized that mergers of this magnitude in the public and private sector carry significant risks, including lost productivity and inefficiencies. Generally, successful transformations of large organizations, even those undertaking less strenuous reorganizations and with less pressure for immediate results, can take from 5 to 7 years to achieve. Necessary management capacity and oversight mechanisms must be established. Moreover, critical aspects of DHS's success will depend on well-functioning relationships with third parties that will take time to establish and maintain, including those with state and local governments, the private sector, and other federal agencies with homeland security responsibilities, such as the Department of State, the FBI [Federal Bureau of Investigation] and the Central Intelligence Agency, DOD [Department of Defense], and the Department of Health and Human Services (HHS). Creating and maintaining a structure that can leverage partners and stakeholders will be necessary to effectively implement the national homeland security strategy.

The new department is also being formed from components with a wide array of existing major management challenges and program risks. For instance, one DHS directorate's responsibility includes the protection of critical information systems that we already consider a high risk. In fact, many of the major components merging into the new department, including the Immigration and Naturalization Service (INS), the Transportation Security Administration (TSA), Customs Service, FEMA [Federal Emergency Management Agency], and the Coast Guard, face at least one major problem, such as strategic human capital risks, critical information technology challenges, or financial management vulnerabilities; they also confront an array of challenges and risks to program operations. For example, TSA has had considerable challenges in meeting deadlines for screening baggage, and the agency has focused most of its initial security efforts on aviation security, with less attention to other modes of transportation. INS has had difficulty in tracking aliens due to unreliable address information. Customs must meet challenges from the potential threats of weapons of mass destruction smuggled in cargo arriving at U.S. ports, and the Coast Guard faces the challenges inherent in a massive fleet modernization.

DHS's national security mission is of such importance that the failure to address its management challenges and program risks could have serious consequences on our intergovernmental system, our citizens' health and safety, and our economy. Overall, our designation of the implementation and transformation of DHS as a high-risk area stems from the importance of its mission and the nation's reliance on the department's effectiveness in meeting its challenges for protecting the country against terrorism.

Excerpted from U.S. Congress. General Accounting Office. *High-Risk Series: An Update*. GAO-03-119, January 2003. http://purl.access.gpo.gov/GPO/LPS32133 (accessed November 1, 2004).

# 137. Prepared Testimony of James Schlesinger about Simplifying Congressional Committees

*July 10, 2003*

. . . Let me start with this observation. In the 35 years since I first became a government official, relations between the Congress and executive agencies have changed markedly, indeed, one might say radically. In the earlier era, a senior official was called on far less frequently to testify. There would be a number of budget hearings—and from time to time testimony on some prominent issues. To an extent that may seem surprising today, agencies were left to manage themselves. Inquiries about specific issues tended to be on an informal basis—rather than testimony in public session. When I was Chairman of the Atomic Energy Commission, all issues were handled by the Joint Committee [on Atomic Energy]. When I became the Director of Central Intelligence, the director was rarely called upon to testify—at least up until the time of Watergate—and that was primarily in closed session. In the intervening years, that has changed significantly, as congressional committees have become more deeply involved in the management of executive agencies.

When we created the Department of Energy, in contrast to those older conditions, I found that half my time or more was spent on Capitol Hill testifying before various committees. Of course, the creation of the Department had involved the jurisdictions of several standing committees. In the circumstances of the day, with repeated energy events or "crises" like the shutdown of oil production in Iran, rising gasoline prices, the nuclear trauma at Three Mile Island, these committees legitimately wanted a piece of the action—and testimony. Moreover, in these last twenty-odd years, the continued proliferation of subcommittees has only made the problem worse.

Subsequent to the dramatic terrorist attack on the United States in September of 2001, the decision has been taken to consolidate a whole range of security-related activities into the new Department of Homeland Security. The longer-term benefits should be substantial. In particular, it should gradually reorient the cultures of the agencies coming together in the new department towards the post-9/11 mission of homeland security. But there are always costs of such consolidation, primarily short-term costs. There will be bureaucratic resistance. There are inevitable frictions associated with the movement of agencies. There is a clash of cultures that have to be adjudicated and, of course, the reconciliation of contrasting personnel and acquisition systems. It is not a certainty that the benefits of consolidation will outweigh the costs.

For the Department of Homeland Security, however, that decision is behind us. It is now the duty of all of us to do our best to make this crucial consolidation work effectively. It is a monumental challenge successfully to bring together these rather disparate elements—and efficiently combine them in pursuit of the common mission.

Here is the crucial point to bear in mind. A new government department does not spring, like Athena from the brow of Zeus, full blown and ready for action. Organizing the department is not instantaneous; it takes time. There are many organizational challenges and organizational gaps, especially in the early days of a new department. The Department of Homeland Security is, in a sense, a start-up organization. Contrary to the expectations of too many, there will be unavoidable growing pains—as the overall organization gradually comes together. No such thing as immediate and complete success should be expected. Inevitably, in so complicated an operation, there will be unresolved problems and some setbacks. Consequently, for those inclined to be critical, there will be all too many targets to shoot at. The critics can have a field day.

In the case of the Department of Homeland Security, there are all too many platforms for such criticism. At last count, there were 26 full committees with jurisdiction—and a total of 88 committees including subcommittees. As problems are uncovered or take time to be resolved, the opportunities for criticism will mount. Nonetheless, since the stake is the security of our homeland, the new department deserves support—and not unnecessary carping. To whatever extent the Congress can help by simplifying the overlapping committee structure that oversees the department, that would be a significant contribution.

By comparison, the creation of the Department of Energy was relatively child's play. The Department was far smaller. Most of the budget came from what had been the Atomic Energy Commission. The incorporated entities, by and large, had a common mission either producing energy or weapons. . . .

Some . . . jurisdictional problems will likely afflict the new Department of Homeland Security, though others will not. Nonetheless, I underscore that we all have a vast stake in the mission and the success of this new department. Any weaknesses in the department likely will prolong the activities of potential terrorists. So, I repeat: it is a monumental challenge to integrate the elements that are being brought together in a common mission. Anything that the House can do to help the new department, rather than provide additional perches from which the department can be criticized would serve the national interest. . . .

Excerpted from U.S. Congress. House. Select Committee on Homeland Security. Subcommittee on Rules. *Hearing on Perspectives on House Reform: Committees and the Executive Branch.* 108th Cong., 2nd sess., serial 108-15, July 10, 2003. http://frwebgate.access.gpo.gov/cgi-bin/

useftp.cgi?IPaddress=162.140.64.21&filename=95872.pdf&directory=/disk
b/wais/data/108_house_hearings (accessed November 1, 2004).

# 138. 9/11 Commission on the Need for Congressional Changes

*July 22, 2004*

## Unity of Effort in the Congress

### *Strengthen Congressional Oversight of Intelligence and Homeland Security*

Of all our recommendations, strengthening congressional oversight may be among the most difficult and important. So long as oversight is governed by current congressional rules and resolutions, we believe the American people will not get the security they want and need. The United States needs a strong, stable, and capable congressional committee structure to give America's national intelligence agencies oversight, support, and leadership.

Few things are more difficult to change in Washington than congressional committee jurisdiction and prerogatives. To a member, these assignments are almost as important as the map of his or her congressional district. The American people may have to insist that these changes occur, or they may well not happen. Having interviewed numerous members of Congress from both parties, as well as congressional staff members, we found that dissatisfaction with congressional oversight remains widespread.

The future challenges of America's intelligence agencies are daunting. They include the need to develop leading-edge technologies that give our policymakers and warfighters a decisive edge in any conflict where the interests of the United States are vital. Not only does good intelligence win wars, but the best intelligence enables us to prevent them from happening altogether.

Under the terms of existing rules and resolutions the House and Senate intelligence committees lack the power, influence, and sustained capability to meet this challenge. While few members of Congress have the broad knowledge of intelligence activities or the know-how about the technologies employed, all members need to feel assured that good oversight is happening. When their unfamiliarity with the subject is combined with the need to preserve security, a mandate emerges for substantial change.

Tinkering with the existing structure is not sufficient. Either Congress should create a joint committee for intelligence, using the Joint Atomic Energy Committee as its model, or it should create House and Senate committees with combined authorizing and appropriations powers.

Whichever of these two forms are chosen, the goal should be a structure—codified by resolution with powers expressly granted and carefully limited—allowing a relatively small group of members of Congress, given time and reason to master the subject and the agencies, to conduct oversight of the intelligence establishment and be clearly accountable for their work. The staff of this committee should be nonpartisan and work for the entire committee and not for individual members.

The other reforms we have suggested—for a National Counterterrorism Center and a National Intelligence Director—will not work if congressional oversight does not change too. Unity of effort in executive management can be lost if it is fractured by divided congressional oversight.

*Recommendation: Congressional oversight for intelligence—and counterterrorism—is now dysfunctional. Congress should address this problem. We have considered various alternatives: A joint committee on the old model of the Joint Committee on Atomic Energy is one. A single committee in each house of Congress, combining authorizing and appropriating authorities, is another.*

- The new committee or committees should conduct continuing studies of the activities of the intelligence agencies and report problems relating to the development and use of intelligence to all members of the House and Senate.
- We have already recommended that the total level of funding for intelligence be made public, and that the national intelligence program be appropriated to the National Intelligence Director, not to the secretary of defense.
- We also recommend that the intelligence committee should have a subcommittee specifically dedicated to oversight, freed from the consuming responsibility of working on the budget.
- The resolution creating the new intelligence committee structure should grant subpoena authority to the committee or committees. The majority party's representation on this committee should never exceed the minority's representation by more than one.
- Four of the members appointed to this committee or committees should be a member who also serves on each of the following additional committees: Armed Services, Judiciary, Foreign Affairs, and the Defense Appropriations subcommittee. In this way the other major congressional interests can be brought together in the new committee's work.
- Members should serve indefinitely on the intelligence committees, without set terms, thereby letting them accumulate expertise.

- The committees should be smaller—perhaps seven or nine members in each house—so that each member feels a greater sense of responsibility, and accountability, for the quality of the committee's work.

The leaders of the Department of Homeland Security now appear before 88 committees and subcommittees of Congress. One expert witness (not a member of the administration) told us that this is perhaps the single largest obstacle impeding the department's successful development. The one attempt to consolidate such committee authority, the House Select Committee on Homeland Security, may be eliminated. The Senate does not have even this.

Congress needs to establish for the Department of Homeland Security the kind of clear authority and responsibility that exist to enable the Justice Department to deal with crime and the Defense Department to deal with threats to national security. Through not more than one authorizing committee and one appropriating subcommittee in each house, Congress should be able to ask the secretary of homeland security whether he or she has the resources to provide reasonable security against major terrorist acts within the United States and to hold the secretary accountable for the department's performance.

*Recommendation: Congress should create a single, principal point of oversight and review for homeland security. Congressional leaders are best able to judge what committee should have jurisdiction over this department and its duties. But we believe that Congress does have the obligation to choose one in the House and one in the Senate, and that this committee should be a permanent standing committee with a nonpartisan staff.*

Excerpted from U.S. National Commission on Terrorist Attacks Upon the United States. *The 9/11 Commission Report: Final Report of the National Commission on Terrorist Attacks Upon the United States.* July 22, 2004: 419–421. Washington, D.C.: Government Printing Office. http://www.gpoaccess.gov/911/index.html (accessed November 1, 2004).

# Studies Analyze Federal Allocations for First Responders

139. Emergency Responders: Drastically Underfunded,
     Dangerously Unprepared, Report by the Council on Foreign
     Relations, June 29, 2003.

140. An Analysis of First Responder Grant Funding, Report by the
     House Select Committee on Homeland Security, April 27,
     2004.

141. 9/11 Commission on First Responder Funding, July 22, 2004.

## INTRODUCTION

As part of its report issued in July 2004, the National Commission on Terrorist Attacks Upon the United States—commonly known as the 9/11 Commission—paid tribute to the firefighters and police officers in New York City who struggled against chaos and confusion on September 11, 2001, to evacuate civilians from the World Trade Center:

> Some specific rescues are quantifiable, such as an FDNY [Fire Department of New York] company's rescue of civilians trapped on the 22d floor of the North Tower, or the success of FDNY, PAPD [Port Authority of New York and New Jersey Police Department], and NYPD [New York Police Department] personnel in carrying nonambulatory civilians out of both the North and South Towers. In other instances, intangibles combined to reduce what could have been a much higher death total. It is impossible to measure how many more civilians who descended to the ground floors would have died but for the NYPD and PAPD personnel directing them—via safe exit routes that avoided jumpers and debris—to leave the complex urgently but calmly. It is impossible to measure how many more civilians would have died but for the determination of many members of the FDNY, PAPD, and NYPD to continue assisting civilians after the South Tower collapsed. It is impossible to measure the calming influence that ascending firefighters had on descending civilians or whether but for the firefighters' presence the poor behavior of a very few civilians could have caused a dangerous and panicked mob flight. But

the positive impact of the first responders on the evacuation came at a tremendous cost of first responder lives lost.

A total of 403 first responders died that day—343 from the Fire Department of New York, thirty-seven from the Port Authority of New York and New Jersey Police Department, and twenty-three from the New York Police Department. The 343 deaths suffered by the Fire Department of New York represented the largest loss of life of any emergency response agency in history.

The terrorist attacks focused new attention on the first responders—firefighters, police officers, emergency medical technicians, and others—around the nation who put their lives on the line each day to help others. The attacks also brought to light a serious issue: first responders nationwide were woefully unprepared and ill-equipped to handle a major terrorist attack or other horrific event. The subsequent terrorist attacks using anthrax-laced letters also raised questions about whether first responders could protect themselves and save others when faced with dangers that previously had seemed unthinkable.

Congress and the White House moved quickly to boost the amount of grant money available to states and localities for terrorism preparedness, much of which was destined for first responders. Between the September 11 attacks and April 2004 the federal government allocated $6.3 billion in terrorism preparedness grants, according to a study by the House Select Committee on Homeland Security.

Yet on June 29, 2003—almost two years after the terrorist attacks—a task force convened by the nonpartisan Council on Foreign Relations in partnership with the Concord Coalition and the Center for Strategic and Budgetary Assessments, two leading budget analysis organizations, released a report bearing a title that succinctly summarized its findings: "Emergency Responders: Drastically Underfunded, Dangerously Unprepared." The report cited numerous examples, but one was particularly striking: the average fire department in the United States only had enough radios to equip half the firefighters on a shift. The report called for massive increases in federal aid for first responders. "If the nation does not take immediate steps to better identify and address the urgent needs of emergency responders, the next terrorist incident could have an even more devastating impact than the September 11 attacks," the report said [Document 139].

At about the same time the report was released, many first responders were asking why they had not yet received any federal money. The answer came in a staff report released by the House Select Committee on Homeland Security on April 27, 2004: about $5.2 billion of the $6.3 billion that had been allocated remained "in the administrative pipeline," according to the report. It said the holdup was not at the Department of Homeland Security, which distributed the funds. Instead, it was occurring at the state and local levels for a variety of reasons, the report said. Some states had not passed along federal funds to localities, the report said, because they were still developing state-wide assessments of where the money was most needed. In other cases, state and local procurement regulations slowed down the process.

The report also strongly criticized the federal government's formula for allocating money among the states. Distribution of nearly 40 percent of federal preparedness money in the largest grant program was governed by a provision in the USA Patriot Act, which Congress passed shortly after the attacks. The provision required DHS to give each state 0.75 percent of the total amount appropriated for terrorism preparedness grants. An agency at DHS then apportioned the remaining 60 percent of funding to states based solely on population. "The ramifications of these funding decisions are profound," the report said. "The system has provided small counties across the country with relatively large awards of terrorism preparedness money, while major cities such as New York, Los Angeles, Washington, and Chicago struggle to address their needs in a near-constant heightened alert environment."

As an example of wasteful spending, the report cited a small rural county in Washington state where the principal industries were logging and Christmas tree farming. The county received $132,000 in homeland security money in fiscal year 2003, the report said, and spent $63,000 on a hazardous materials decontamination unit that was stored in a crate. The report called the unit "an expensive item for a county that does not even have a Hazmat team and little, if any, critical infrastructure" [Document 140].

The federal funding formula was also sharply criticized by the 9/11 Commission. In its report released on July 22, 2004, the commission said federal money should be distributed "based strictly on an assessment of risks and vulnerabilities."

Now, in 2004, Washington, D.C., and New York City are certainly at the top of any such list. We understand the contention that every state and city needs to have some minimum infrastructure for emergency response. But federal homeland security assistance should not remain a program for general revenue sharing. It should supplement state and local resources based on the risks or vulnerabilities that merit additional support. Congress should not use this money as a pork barrel.

The federal budget for fiscal year 2005 that Congress approved and President George W. Bush signed in October 2004 moved slightly toward allocating more money based on risk. The budget cut funding for the largest emergency preparedness grant program, under which each state got a share, to $1.1 billion from $1.7 billion the previous year. But it boosted funding for the smaller Urban Area Security Initiative, which provided money to high-risk cities, to $885 million from $725 million in fiscal 2004 [Document 141].

# 139. Emergency Responders: Drastically Underfunded, Dangerously Unprepared, Report by the Council on Foreign Relations
*June 29, 2003*

## Executive Summary

*If we knew that there was going to be a terrorist attack sometime in the next five years but did not know what type of attack it would be, who would carry it out, or where in the United States it would occur, what actions would we take to prepare and how would we allocate our human and financial resources to do so?*

The tragic events of September 11, 2001, brought home to the American people the magnitude of the danger posed by terrorism on U.S. soil. Now, in the aftermath of the September 11 attacks, the United States must assume that terrorists will strike again, possibly using chemical, biological, radiological, or even nuclear materials. The unthinkable has become thinkable.

Although in some respects the American public is now better prepared to address aspects of the terrorist threat than it was two years ago, the United States remains dangerously ill prepared to handle a catastrophic attack on American soil.

- On average, fire departments across the country have only enough radios to equip half the firefighters on a shift, and breathing apparatuses for only one-third. Only 10 percent of fire departments in the United States have the personnel and equipment to respond to a building collapse.
- Police departments in cities across the country do not have the protective gear to safely secure a site following an attack with weapons of mass destruction (WMD).
- Public health laboratories in most states still lack basic equipment and expertise to adequately respond to a chemical or biological attack, and 75 percent of state labs report being overwhelmed by too many testing requests.
- Most cities do not have the necessary equipment to determine what kind of hazardous materials emergency responders may be facing.

If the nation does not take immediate steps to better identify and address the urgent needs of emergency responders, the next terrorist incident could have an even more devastating impact than the September 11 attacks.

According to data provided to the Task Force by emergency responder professional associations and leading emergency response officials from around the country, America will fall approximately $98.4 billion short of meeting critical emergency responder needs over the next five years if current funding levels are maintained.

Currently the federal budget to fund emergency responders is $27 billion for five years beginning in 2004. Because record keeping and categorization of state and local spending varies greatly across states and localities, it is extremely difficult to come up with an estimate for a five-year total for expenditures by state and local governments. According to budget estimates, state and local spending over the same period could be as low as $26 billion or as high as $76 billion. Therefore, total estimated spending for emergency responders by federal, state, and local governments combined would be between $53 billion and $103 billion for five years beginning in FY04.

Because the $98.4 billion unmet-needs budget covers areas not adequately addressed at current funding levels, the total necessary overall expenditure for emergency responders would be $151.4 billion over five years if the United States is currently spending $53 billion, and $201.4 billion if the United States is currently spending $103 billion. Estimated combined federal, state, and local expenditures therefore would need to be as much as tripled over the next five years to address this unmet need. Covering this funding shortfall using federal funds alone would require a fivefold increase from the current level of $5.4 billion per year to an annual federal expenditure of $25.1 billion.

The preliminary figures were based on the critical analysis of needs estimates provided by emergency responder communities and were developed in partnership with the Concord Coalition and the Center for Strategic and Budgetary Assessments, two of the nation's leading budget analysis organizations. While these figures represent the most reliable public numbers to date, the nation urgently needs to develop a better framework and procedures for generating more precise numbers. But the government cannot wait until it has completed this process before increasing funding for emergency responders.

Among other things, additional funds are desperately needed for the following purposes:

- to extend the emergency 911 system nationally to foster effective emergency data collection and accurate local dispatch;
- to significantly enhance urban search and rescue capabilities of major cities and the Federal Emergency Management Agency (FEMA) in

cases where buildings or other large structures collapse and trap individuals;

- to foster interoperable communications systems for emergency responders across the country so that those on the front lines can communicate with each other while at the scene of an attack;
- to enhance public health preparedness by strengthening laboratories, disease tracking, and communications and by training public health professionals for biological, chemical, and radiological events;
- to strengthen emergency operations centers for local public safety coordination;
- to provide protective gear and WMD remediation equipment to firefighters;
- to support an extensive series of national exercises that would allow responders to continually learn and improve on effective response techniques;
- to enhance emergency agricultural and veterinary capabilities for effective response to attacks on the national food supply;
- to help develop surge capacity in the nation's hospitals and to help them better prepare for a WMD attack; and
- to enhance the capacity of emergency medical technicians, paramedics, and others to respond to mass casualty events.

There are two major obstacles hampering America's emergency preparedness efforts. First, it is impossible to know precisely what is needed and how much it will cost due to the lack of preparedness standards. Second, funding for emergency responders has been sidetracked and stalled due to a politicized appropriations process, the slow distribution of funds by federal agencies, and bureaucratic red tape at all levels of government.

To address the lack of standards and good numbers, the Task Force recommends the following measures:

- Congress should require the Department of Homeland Security (DHS) and the Department of Health and Human Services (HHS) to work with state and local agencies and officials as well as emergency responder professional associations to establish clearly defined standards and guidelines for emergency preparedness. These standards must be sufficiently flexible to allow local officials to set priorities based on their needs, provided that they reach nationally determined preparedness levels within a fixed time period.
- Congress should require that DHS and HHS submit a coordinated plan for meeting identified national preparedness standards by the end of FY07.
- Congress should establish within DHS a National Institute for Best Practices in Emergency Preparedness to work with state and local

governments, emergency preparedness professional associations, and other partners to share best practices and lessons learned.

- Congress should make emergency responder grants in FY04 and thereafter on a multiyear basis to facilitate long-term planning and training.

To deal with the problem of appropriations and stalled distribution, the Task Force recommends the following measures:

- Congress should establish a system for allocating scarce resources based less on dividing the spoils and more on addressing identified threats and vulnerabilities. To do this, the federal government should consider such factors as population, population density, vulnerability assessment, and presence of critical infrastructure within each state. State governments should be required to use the same criteria for distributing funds within each state.
- The U.S. House of Representatives should transform the House Select Committee on Homeland Security into a standing committee and give it a formal, leading role in the authorization of all emergency responder expenditures in order to streamline the federal budgetary process.
- The U.S. Senate should consolidate emergency preparedness and response oversight in the Senate Government Affairs Committee.
- Congress should require DHS to work with other federal agencies to streamline homeland security grant programs in a way that reduces unnecessary duplication and establishes coordinated "one-stop shopping" for state and local authorities seeking grants.
- States should develop a prioritized list of requirements in order to ensure that federal funding is allocated to achieve the best return on investments.
- Congress should ensure that all future appropriations bills funding emergency response include strict distribution timelines.
- DHS should move the Office of Domestic Preparedness (ODP) from the Bureau of Border and Transportation Security to the Office of State and Local Government Coordination in order to consolidate oversight of grants to emergency responders within the Office of the Secretary.

The Task Force credits the Bush administration, Congress, governors, and mayors with taking important steps since the September 11 attacks to respond to the risk of catastrophic terrorism, and does not seek to apportion blame for what has not been done or not been done quickly enough. The Task Force is not in a position to argue that meeting the critical needs of emergency responders is more urgent than other demands on government spending, but, without prejudice to other national needs, seeks to point out one important area where more must be done.

America's local emergency responders will always be the first to confront a terrorist incident and will play the central role in managing its immediate consequences. Their efforts in the first minutes and hours following an attack will be critical to saving lives, reestablishing order, and preventing mass panic. Like the police and fire professionals who entered the World Trade Center on September 11, emergency responders will respond to crises with whatever resources they have. The United States has both a responsibility and a critical need to provide them with the equipment, training, and other resources necessary to do their jobs safely and effectively.

Excerpted from Council on Foreign Relations. Independent Task Force on Emergency Responders. *Emergency Responders: Drastically Underfunded, Dangerously Unprepared.* June 29, 2003. http://www.cfr.org/publication. php?id=6085 (accessed November 1, 2004).

---

# 140. An Analysis of First Responder Grant Funding, Report by the House Select Committee on Homeland Security

*April 27, 2004*

## Executive Summary

On September 11, 2001, our Nation's first responders rose to the challenge of the most serious terrorist attack on the American homeland in our history. In the weeks that followed, Congress moved swiftly to appropriate funds to enhance the ability of our first responders to prevent, prepare for, and respond to acts of terrorism. In the two subsequent years, Congress went even further, increasing terrorism preparedness grant programs for first responders more than 2000% over 2001 levels.

Yet, two and one half years later, first responders across the Nation report that they have not yet received the vast majority of the $6.3 billion that Congress and the Administration have allocated in terrorism preparedness grants since September 11. In fact, roughly $5.2 billion in Department of Homeland Security (DHS) grant money remains in the administrative pipeline, waiting to be used by our first responders to, among other things, enhance the interoperability of their communications, purchase protective gear and radiological, biological and chemical agent detectors, and improve training and exercises for responding to terrorist events. Under President Bush's most recent budget proposal, another $2 billion likely will be added to the pipeline by the end of this year.

There also have been numerous reports suggesting that the first responder monies that have been received and spent to date have not necessarily gone to the first responders who need it most, or for projects that materially enhance our homeland security. . . .

Based on a review of the grant data and other information collected, Committee staff found that:

1. DHS awarded homeland security grant funds to States reasonably quickly, but without any real assessment of need or risk (except for the Urban Area Security Initiative).
2. Almost one-third of all States allocated money among their internal jurisdictions without regard to need or risk (other than population), and those that applied risk or need factors did not follow any standard approach to doing so.
3. There were no Federal terrorism preparedness standards or goals to guide expenditure of funds at the state and local levels, leading to numerous examples of questionable spending.
4. Only a very small portion of awarded funds has been utilized to date by state and local recipients. Committee staff found a myriad of explanations for this delay, but identified four common causes: planning to spend the grant, which often occurred late in the grant process, after the grant was awarded and obligated to localities; obtaining local board approval of grant spending; fulfilling state and local procurement regulations; and setting aside funds that could be used to purchase equipment while waiting for reimbursement from DHS.

### I. DHS Awards and the Federal Allocation System

. . . With respect to method of allocation among the States, DHS followed, in part, a formula set by the Congress that provided each State with a guaranteed minimum amount of State formula grants, regardless of risk or need. Specifically, section 1014 of the USA Patriot Act, passed by Congress in the immediate aftermath of the September 11th attacks, guaranteed each State 0.75% of the total amount appropriated to DHS for state terrorism preparedness grants, and provided smaller guaranteed amounts for certain U.S. territories. These guaranteed funds amount to almost 40% of the total funding. At the time the Patriot Act was enacted into law (October 2001), total funding covered by this formula was less than $100 million per year, providing for a guaranteed minimum of less than $1 million per State. However, due to the 20-fold increase in this program between Fiscal Years 2001 and 2003, roughly $800 million of the $2.06 billion appropriated for the state formula grants in FY 2003 was distributed according to this formula, giving each State a minimum of approximately $15 million, regardless of risk or need.

Compared to other formula grants administered by the Federal government, this minimum percentage guarantee is unusually large—of a sampling of the largest Federal grant programs to States in FY 2003, totaling over $200 billion, 75 percent of those funds were free from any minimum guarantees, and even when a minimum guarantee was included in a program's formula, the guaranteed percentage was much lower, typically between 0.25 and 0.5 percent.

After 40% of the State formula grants were divided and distributed as specified in the Patriot Act, ODP [the DHS Office for Domestic Preparedness] then apportioned the remaining 60% of such funds among the States based solely on population, with each State receiving an additional share of funding. For even the smallest State, this approach meant additional funding of $2 million on top of its guaranteed minimum. In FY 2003, the combined ODP allocation method thus resulted in each State receiving at least $17.5 million. In contrast, most grant programs administered by the Federal government that ensure minimum funding for States first allocate funds according to meritorious factors (such as need or risk), and only then "top off" those States that have not reached the guaranteed minimum level. By funding the entire state minimum first and then adding additional funding to every State based on population, the State formula grants allocate an even greater percentage of total funding without any real assessment of risk or need. While Congress mandated the state minimum, Congress did not require that the remaining 60% of the money be apportioned based on population; nor did Congress require that the state minimum serve as a base upon which additional funds would be allocated.

The ramifications of these funding decisions are profound. The system has provided small counties across the country with relatively large awards of terrorism preparedness money, while major cities such as New York, Los Angeles, Washington, and Chicago struggle to address their needs in a near-constant heightened alert environment. For example, a rural county in Wyoming (population 11,500) was awarded $546,000 in 2003 State formula grants. By contrast, Jefferson County, Kentucky (population 693,604), which encompasses the city of Louisville, received just $237,000 more than the Wyoming county in 2003—despite the fact that Jefferson County has 60 times the population, a significant amount of critical infrastructure, and was recently designated by DHS as a high-threat urban area. . . .

## II. State Awards and Allocation Systems

. . . With respect to method of allocation, many States follow the Federal government's example by providing a base amount to each county, with an additional amount based on population. In fact, almost one-third of our Nation's States distributed their Federal first responder funds—totaling over $650 million in FY 2003—by formulas that did not account for either need or risk (other than population). . . .

Some States have recognized the inadequacies of the Federal model and have incorporated threat, vulnerability, and risk factors into their funding decisions. Massachusetts, for example, decided to allocate funds based on identified threats.

The State developed a grant process that relied on competition among grantees for the most compelling projects to be funded, on the theory that not all areas of the State were as equally vulnerable to attack. Wisconsin also incorporated need and threat factors into its funding formula. After the State allocated 50% of grants based on population, it partnered with local communities to allocate 20% based on threat, 10% on vulnerability, and 20% on need.

Other States that have incorporated at least some threat, risk, or vulnerability factors into their funding formulas include Idaho, Oklahoma, Oregon, Louisiana, Iowa, New Mexico, Nevada, and Rhode Island. However, the risk-based approaches of the States varied widely due to a lack of Federal guidance and insufficient sharing of threat and vulnerability information, according to staff interviews. Accordingly, very few States weighted such risk factors heavily in their funding formulas.

In fact, many of the States that followed the Federal formula in FY 2003 told Committee staff in interviews that they plan to move towards a more threat-, vulnerability-, and risk-based approach for the FY 2004 allocation of first responder monies, stressing the need to distribute funding in a more focused and effective manner. . . .

### III. Lack of Federal Terrorism Preparedness Goals

Common sense suggests that a mid-size Midwestern city with a nuclear power plant to the north and a row of chemical facilities to the south has different (and greater) terrorism preparedness needs than a similarly-sized city without such critical infrastructures, or a smaller, rural community without any attractive terrorist targets. But, due to the lack of clear strategic guidance from the Federal level about the definition and objectives of terrorism preparedness, communities across America report that they do not know how best to spend their Federal grant dollars. Based on Committee staff interviews with state and local officials across the country, it is clear that there currently is no consistent methodology for States and localities to determine their terrorism preparedness needs or what their preparedness goals should be. The lack of target goals and guidance has resulted in terrorism preparedness dollars being spent on equipment or projects of only marginal utility to homeland security.

For example, Committee staff interviewed an official from a small rural county of 49,405 people in the State of Washington. Its principal industries are logging and Christmas tree farming. In FY 2003, the county received $132,000 in homeland security funds. With those funds, the county purchased a $63,000 decontamination hazmat unit that is being stored in a crate in a metal warehouse across the street from the county sheriff's office—an expensive item for a county that does not even have a Hazmat team and little, if any, critical infrastructure. In an interview with Committee staff, an official with the county Sheriff's Department wondered at the choices that were being made: "We are a small rural county, not a high-risk threat area. This specialized equipment will go to waste sitting on a shelf collecting dust."

The lack of preparedness goals also has led to miscommunication between States and localities as to what capabilities need to be funded. For example, this same county submitted a request for basic radios to outfit its law enforcement, but the State, purchasing on its behalf, instead delivered six encrypted radios worth $3,856 each, which turned out to be incompatible with the county's existing radio system and could not be used. This mishap led one county official to comment: "This is a lot of money with no forethought. Not a lot of thought has gone into this and how we can best use funds for our particular type of community."

The lack of defined preparedness goals—combined with the breadth of the ODP purchasing guidelines—lead many state officials to confess that the ODP program is treated as a wish list. ODP guidelines include 18 general equipment categories, including protective gear, animal-restraint devices, airplanes, boats, and medications. While flexibility is valuable and allows States and localities to tailor funding to meet the unique needs of their individual communities, flexibility in the absence of target goals for preparedness fails to guarantee that funds will be spent on actual needs. The lack of clear preparedness objectives led Supervisor Mike Thomas of Outgamie County, Wisconsin to equate the array of purchases available through the grant to "a Christmas list . . . from a mail-order catalog." An official from the rural county in Washington discussed above echoed these sentiments: "Some of the equipment on the ODP list we don't even recognize. We think, well this looks good, maybe we'll need it. We're getting stuff we won't use. This equipment could have gone to Seattle where the real threat is." . . .

The establishment of national goals or benchmarks for appropriate levels of terrorism preparedness for different types of communities is a critical first step in ensuring the effectiveness of Federal anti-terrorism grant funds. . . . President Bush, in a Homeland Security Presidential Directive issued last December, has prioritized the development of a national preparedness goal, which "will establish measurable readiness priorities and targets. . . . It will also include readiness metrics and elements that support the national preparedness goal, including standards for preparedness assessments and strategies, and a system for assessing the Nation's overall preparedness to respond." . . .

Excerpted from U.S. Congress. House of Representatives. House Select Committee on Homeland Security. *An Analysis of First Responder Grant Funding.* April 27, 2004. http://homelandsecurity.house.gov/files/First Responder Report.pdf (accessed November 1, 2004)

⬤────────────────────────────────────────────────⬤

# 141. 9/11 Commission on First Responder Funding

*July 22, 2004*

## Setting Priorities for National Preparedness

Before 9/11, no executive department had, as its first priority, the job of defending America from domestic attack. That changed with the 2002 creation of the Department of Homeland Security. This department now has the lead responsibility for problems that feature so prominently in the 9/11 story, such as protecting borders, securing transportation and other parts of our critical infrastructure, organizing emergency assistance, and working with the private sector to assess vulnerabilities.

Throughout the government, nothing has been harder for officials—executive or legislative—than to set priorities, making hard choices in allocating limited resources. These difficulties have certainly afflicted the Department of Homeland Security, hamstrung by its many congressional overseers. In delivering assistance to state and local governments, we heard—especially in New York—about imbalances in the allocation of money. The argument concentrates on two questions.

First, how much money should be set aside for criteria not directly related to risk? Currently a major portion of the billions of dollars appropriated for state and local assistance is allocated so that each state gets a certain amount, or an allocation based on its population—wherever they live.

*Recommendation: Homeland security assistance should be based strictly on an assessment of risks and vulnerabilities. Now, in 2004, Washington, D.C., and New York City are certainly at the top of any such list. We understand the contention that every state and city needs to have some minimum infrastructure for emergency response. But federal homeland security assistance should not remain a program for general revenue sharing. It should supplement state and local resources based on the risks or vulnerabilities that merit additional support. Congress should not use this money as a pork barrel.*

The second question is, Can useful criteria to measure risk and vulnerability be developed that assess all the many variables? The allocation of funds should be based on an assessment of threats and vulnerabilities. That assessment should consider such factors as population, population density, vulnerability, and the presence of critical infrastructure within each state. In addition, the federal government should require each state receiving federal emergency preparedness funds to provide an analysis based on the same criteria to justify the distribution of funds in that state.

In a free-for-all over money, it is understandable that representatives will work to protect the interests of their home states or districts. But this issue is too important for politics as usual to prevail. Resources must be allocated according to vulnerabilities. We recommend that a panel of security experts be convened to develop written benchmarks for evaluating community needs. We further recommend that federal homeland security funds be allocated in accordance with those benchmarks, and that states be required to abide by those benchmarks in disbursing the federal funds. The benchmarks will be imperfect and subjective; they will continually evolve. But hard choices must be made.

Those who would allocate money on a different basis should then defend their view of the national interest. . . .

Excerpted from U.S. National Commission on Terrorist Attacks Upon the United States. *The 9/11 Commission Report: Final Report of the National Commission on Terrorist Attacks Upon the United States.* July 22, 2004: 395–396. Washington, D.C.: Government Printing Office. http://www. gpoaccess.gov/911/index.html (accessed November 1, 2004).

# 9/11 Commission Primarily Focuses on Intelligence Reforms

142. Final Report of the National Commission on Terrorist Attacks Upon the United States, July 22, 2004

## INTRODUCTION

Just months after the terrorist attacks on September 11, 2001, family members of some of the victims started pressuring the White House and Congress to create an independent commission to investigate what went wrong. They wanted to know more about the fate of their loved ones and why the federal government failed to stop hijackers from turning four passenger airliners into missiles that they smashed into the World Trade Center in New York City, the Pentagon just outside Washington, D.C., and a field in Pennsylvania, killing 2,973 people.

The family members were quiet but determined, meeting with anyone who would listen and often carrying framed photographs of their loved ones. Despite their persistent efforts and support from some key members of Congress, they nearly lost their battle for the creation of an independent commission. During their year-long campaign, both houses of Congress passed separate bills to create a commission. President George W. Bush opposed creating a commission on the grounds that it would be a diversion from the U.S. war against terrorism and could potentially intrude into his responsibilities as president.

The White House finally agreed in late September 2002 to support a bipartisan investigation, but negotiations with Congress regarding the details quickly fell apart. With Congress poised to adjourn for the year and hopes for a commission seemingly dashed, the White House accepted a congressional compromise on the evening of November 14, 2002. The House and Senate quickly passed a bill to create the commission, and Bush signed it into law on November 27, 2002.

---

Editor's note: Excerpts from the 9/11 Commission final report also appear in Aviation Security on September 11, 2001, p. 273; U.S. and Foreign Governments Attempt to Cut Off Terrorist Funds, p. 303; Supporters, Critics Face Off Over Parts of USA Patriot Act, p. 329; FBI Transforms Itself to Fight Terrorism, p. 371; Immigration and Border Security Receive Renewed Attention after Attacks, p. 407; Executive Branch, Congress Restructure for Homeland Security, p. 429; Studies Analyze Federal Allocations for First Responders, p. 442.

The agreement created a ten-member commission, with appointments evenly split between Democrats and Republicans. The Senate Republican leader, the Senate Democratic leader, the House Republican leader, and the House Democratic leader would each appoint two members. The White House won the right to appoint the chairman, and congressional Democrats were to appoint the vice chairman. The legislation gave the commission a broad mandate to investigate intelligence and law enforcement agencies, aviation security, border security, the government's antiterrorism policies, and other issues related to homeland security. A key provision in the compromise authorized the commission to issue subpoenas for witnesses or documents. However, agreement by the chairman and vice chairman or six members was required to issue a subpoena.

On the same night that negotiators hammered out the final details for creating the commission, the FBI issued an alert to state and local law enforcement agencies nationwide warning that al Qaeda in the future might be planning "spectacular attacks that meet several criteria: high symbolic value, mass casualties, severe damage to the American economy and maximum psychological trauma."

In November 2002 Bush announced that his choice for chairman was Henry Kissinger, the former secretary of state for Richard Nixon and Gerald R. Ford and winner of the Nobel Peace Prize. Hours later, Democrats said their choice for vice chairman was George J. Mitchell, the former Senate majority leader who after leaving Congress helped broker peace talks in Northern Ireland and the Middle East. Within weeks of their appointments, however, both men resigned because of business conflicts. The White House and congressional Democrats quickly named substitutes. Bush chose former New Jersey governor Thomas Kean, and Democrats selected former representative Lee Hamilton of Indiana. Both men were widely respected in Washington, although they lacked the high profiles of Kissinger and Mitchell.

The National Commission on Terrorist Attacks Upon the United States, usually referred to simply as the 9/11 Commission, began a series of public hearings in April 2003. During its investigation the commission repeatedly clashed with the Bush administration over access to information, who the White House would allow to testify, and the circumstances under which certain witnesses would appear. The White House cited various reasons for its actions, ranging from executive privilege to concerns about protecting national security. The commission issued numerous subpoenas, and in other cases reached compromises with the administration. Max Cleland, a former Democratic senator from Georgia, resigned his seat on the commission in November 2003, saying he was frustrated by the administration's delays in providing necessary information. Former Democratic senator Robert Kerrey of Nebraska replaced him.

The commission's hearings revealed security failures by agencies throughout the federal government during the current Bush administration and during the previous administration of Bill Clinton. Perhaps most important, the hearings made it clear that the nation's intelligence agencies—including the Federal Bureau of Investigation (FBI) and the Central Intelligence Agency (CIA)—did not share information. Witnesses testified that various FBI and CIA agents obtained valuable clues before the September 11 attacks, raising the possibility that the attacks could have been prevented if the agencies had shared information or even followed up on what their agents discovered.

The commission issued a unanimous final report on July 22, 2004, that found no "smoking gun" but described in painstaking detail the events of September 11, 2001, and the failures by top government officials and agencies that allowed them to happen. The 567-page report also criticized Congress for providing poor oversight of the nation's intelligence agencies.

"The 9/11 attacks were a shock, but they should not have come as a surprise," the report said. "Islamist extremists had given plenty of warning that they meant to kill Americans indiscriminately and in large numbers." Despite these warnings, the report said, the government made little effort to secure the American homeland:

> Since the plotters were flexible and resourceful, we cannot know whether any single step or series of steps would have defeated them. What we can say with confidence is that none of the measures adopted by the U.S. government from 1998 to 2001 disturbed or even delayed the progress of the al Qaeda plot. Across the government, there were failures of imagination, policy, capabilities, and management.

The report noted that the United States and its allies had killed or captured a majority of al Qaeda's leadership and "severely damaged" the organization. These actions, combined with efforts to improve homeland security, made the homeland safer than it was on September 11, 2001. "But we are not safe," the report said.

> The problem is that al Qaeda represents an ideological movement, not a finite group of people. It initiates and inspires, even if it no longer directs. In this way it has transformed itself into a decentralized force. Bin Ladin [the al Qaeda leader] may be limited in his ability to organize major attacks from his hideouts. Yet killing or capturing him, while extremely important, would not end terror. His message of inspiration to a new generation of terrorists would continue.

The report included dozens of recommendations, including a call to create a government board to oversee the protection of civil liberties—one item that Bush quickly acted on. He issued an executive order on August 27, 2004, that created the President's Board on Safeguarding Americans' Civil Liberties. Critics, however, said the board would be ineffective because all of its twenty members were officials in the executive branch, and nearly all of them came from the Justice Department, the Homeland Security Department, and federal intelligence agencies—the very agencies that were likely to be subjects of complaints about civil liberties. Some said that a board entrusted with protecting civil liberties needed to be independent of the government.

Many recommendations in the 9/11 Commission's report focused on reforming the nation's intelligence agencies. The report's most controversial recommendation called for creating a new position of national intelligence director to oversee all government intelligence programs. Under existing law, the CIA director was charged with overseeing all of the nation's intelligence activities.The report generated widespread debate in Washington about how best to reform the intelligence agencies. The House and Senate passed competing bills to overhaul intelligence, but by early November 2004 they were unable to reconcile differences between the two measures.

---

## 142. Final Report of the National Commission on Terrorist Attacks Upon the United States
*July 22, 2004*

### 13. How to Do It? A Different Way of Organizing the Government

As presently configured, the national security institutions of the U.S. government are still the institutions constructed to win the Cold War. The United States confronts a very different world today. Instead of facing a few very dangerous adversaries, the United States confronts a number of less visible challenges that surpass the boundaries of traditional nation-states and call for quick, imaginative, and agile responses.

The men and women of the World War II generation rose to the challenges of the 1940s and 1950s. They restructured the government so that it could protect the country. That is now the job of the generation that experienced 9/11. Those attacks showed, emphatically, that ways of doing business rooted in a different era are just not good enough. Americans should not settle for incremental, ad hoc adjustments to a system designed generations ago for a world that no longer exists.

We recommend significant changes in the organization of the government. We know that the quality of the people is more important than the quality of the wiring diagrams. Some of the saddest aspects of the 9/11 story are the outstanding efforts of so many individual officials straining, often without success, against the boundaries of the possible. Good people can overcome bad structures. They should not have to.

The United States has the resources and the people. The government should combine them more effectively, achieving unity of effort. We offer five major recommendations to do that:

- unifying strategic intelligence and operational planning against Islamist terrorists across the foreign-domestic divide with a National Counterterrorism Center;
- unifying the intelligence community with a new National Intelligence Director;
- unifying the many participants in the counterterrorism effort and their knowledge in a network-based information-sharing system that transcends traditional governmental boundaries;
- unifying and strengthening congressional oversight to improve quality and accountability; and
- strengthening the FBI and homeland defenders.

### 13.1 Unity of Effort Across the Foreign-Domestic Divide

*Joint Action*
Much of the public commentary about the 9/11 attacks has dealt with "lost opportunities," . . . These are often characterized as problems of "watchlisting," of "information sharing," or of "connecting the dots.". . . [T]hese labels are too narrow. They describe the symptoms, not the disease. . . .

In our hearings we regularly asked witnesses: Who is the quarterback? The other players are in their positions, doing their jobs. But who is calling the play that assigns roles to help them execute as a team? Since 9/11, those issues have not been resolved. In some ways joint work has gotten better, and in some ways worse. The effort of fighting terrorism has flooded over many of the usual agency boundaries because of its sheer quantity and energy. Attitudes have changed. Officials are keenly conscious of trying to avoid the mistakes of 9/11. They try to share information. They circulate—even to the President—practically every reported threat, however dubious.

Partly because of all this effort, the challenge of coordinating it has multiplied. Before 9/11, the CIA was plainly the lead agency confronting al Qaeda. The FBI played a very secondary role. The engagement of the departments of Defense and State was more episodic.

- Today the CIA is still central. But the FBI is much more active, along with other parts of the Justice Department.
- The Defense Department effort is now enormous. Three of its unified commands, each headed by a four-star general, have counterterrorism as a primary mission: Special Operations Command, Central Com-

mand (both headquartered in Florida), and Northern Command (headquartered in Colorado).

- A new Department of Homeland Security combines formidable resources in border and transportation security, along with analysis of domestic vulnerability and other tasks.
- The State Department has the lead on many foreign policy tasks.
- At the White House, the National Security Council (NSC) now is joined by a parallel presidential advisory structure, the Homeland Security Council.

So far we have mentioned two reasons for joint action—the virtue of joint planning and the advantage of having someone in charge to ensure a unified effort. There is a third: the simple shortage of experts with sufficient skills. The limited pool of critical experts—for example, skilled counterterrorism analysts and linguists—is being depleted. Expanding these capabilities will require not just money, but time.

Primary responsibility for terrorism analysis has been assigned to the Terrorist Threat Integration Center (TTIC), created in 2003, based at the CIA headquarters but staffed with representatives of many agencies, reporting directly to the Director of Central Intelligence. Yet the CIA houses another intelligence "fusion" center: the Counterterrorist Center that played such a key role before 9/11. A third major analytic unit is at Defense, in the Defense Intelligence Agency. A fourth, concentrating more on homeland vulnerabilities, is at the Department of Homeland Security. The FBI is in the process of building the analytic capability it has long lacked, and it also has the Terrorist Screening Center. The U.S. government cannot afford so much duplication of effort. There are not enough experienced experts to go around. The duplication also places extra demands on already hard-pressed single-source national technical intelligence collectors like the National Security Agency.

*Combining Joint Intelligence and Joint Action*

A "smart" government would *integrate* all sources of information to see the enemy as a whole. Integrated all-source analysis should also inform and shape strategies to collect more intelligence. Yet the Terrorist Threat Integration Center, while it has primary responsibility for terrorism analysis, is formally proscribed from having any oversight or operational authority and is not part of any operational entity, other than reporting to the director of central intelligence.

The government now tries to handle the problem of joint management, informed by analysis of intelligence from all sources, in two ways.

- First, agencies with lead responsibility for certain problems have constructed their own interagency entities and task forces in order to get cooperation. The Counterterrorist Center at CIA, for example, recruits liaison officers from throughout the intelligence community. The military's Central Command has its own interagency center, recruiting liaison officers from all the agencies from which it might need help. The FBI has Joint Terrorism Task Forces in 84 locations to coordinate the activities of other agencies when action may be required.

- Second, the problem of joint operational planning is often passed to the White House, where the NSC [National Security Council] staff tries to play this role. The national security staff at the White House (both NSC and new Homeland Security Council staff) has already become 50 percent larger since 9/11. But our impression, after talking to serving officials, is that even this enlarged staff is consumed by meetings on day-to-day issues, sifting each day's threat information and trying to coordinate everyday operations. . . .

Yet a subtler and more serious danger is that as the NSC staff is consumed by these day-to-day tasks, it has less capacity to find the time and detachment needed to advise a president on larger policy issues. That means less time to work on major new initiatives, help with legislative management to steer needed bills through Congress, and track the design and implementation of the strategic plans for regions, countries, and issues. . . .

Much of the job of operational coordination remains with the agencies, especially the CIA. There DCI [Director of Central Intelligence George] Tenet and his chief aides ran interagency meetings nearly every day to coordinate much of the government's day-to-day work. The DCI insisted he did not make policy and only oversaw its implementation. In the struggle against terrorism these distinctions seem increasingly artificial. Also, as the DCI becomes a lead coordinator of the government's operations, it becomes harder to play all the position's other roles, including that of analyst in chief.

The problem is nearly intractable because of the way the government is currently structured. Lines of operational authority run to the expanding executive departments, and they are guarded for understandable reasons: the DCI commands the CIA's personnel overseas; the secretary of defense will not yield to others in conveying commands to military forces; the Justice Department will not give up the responsibility of deciding whether to seek arrest warrants. But the result is that each agency or department needs its own intelligence apparatus to support the performance of its duties. It is hard to "break down stovepipes" when there are so many stoves that are legally and politically entitled to have cast-iron pipes of their own.

Recalling the Goldwater-Nichols legislation of 1986, Secretary [of Defense Donald] Rumsfeld reminded us that to achieve better joint capability, each of the armed services had to "give up some of their turf and authorities and prerogatives." Today, he said, the executive branch is "stove-piped much like the four services were nearly 20 years ago." He wondered if it might be appropriate to ask agencies to "give up some of their existing turf and authority in exchange for a stronger, faster, more efficient government wide joint effort." Privately, other key officials have made the same point to us.

We therefore propose a new institution: a civilian-led unified joint command for counterterrorism. It should combine strategic intelligence and joint operational planning.

In the Pentagon's Joint Staff, which serves the chairman of the Joint Chiefs of Staff, intelligence is handled by the J-2 directorate, operational planning by J-3, and overall policy by J-5. Our concept combines the J-2 and J-3 functions (intelligence and operational planning) in one agency, keeping overall policy coordination where it belongs, in the National Security Council.

*Recommendation: We recommend the establishment of a National Counterterrorism Center (NCTC), built on the foundation of the existing Terrorist Threat Integration Center (TTIC). Breaking the older mold of national government organization, this NCTC should be a center for joint operational planning and joint intelligence, staffed by personnel from the various agencies. The head of the NCTC should have authority to evaluate the performance of the people assigned to the Center. . . .*

Countering transnational Islamist terrorism will test whether the U.S. government can fashion more flexible models of management needed to deal with the twenty-first-century world.

An argument against change is that the nation is at war, and cannot afford to reorganize in midstream. But some of the main innovations of the 1940s and 1950s, including the creation of the Joint Chiefs of Staff and even the construction of the Pentagon itself, were undertaken in the midst of war. Surely the country cannot wait until the struggle against Islamist terrorism is over.

"Surprise, when it happens to a government, is likely to be a complicated, diffuse, bureaucratic thing. It includes neglect of responsibility, but also responsibility so poorly defined or so ambiguously delegated that action gets lost." That comment was made more than 40 years ago, about Pearl Harbor. We hope another commission, writing in the future about another attack, does not again find this quotation to be so apt.

### 13.2 Unity of Effort in the Intelligence Community

In our first section, we concentrated on counterterrorism, discussing how to combine the analysis of information from all sources of intelligence with the joint planning of operations that draw on that analysis. In this section, we step back from looking just at the counterterrorism problem. We reflect on whether the government is organized adequately to direct resources and build the intelligence capabilities it will need not just for countering terrorism, but for the broader range of national security challenges in the decades ahead. . . .

The need to restructure the intelligence community grows out of six problems that have become apparent before and after 9/11:

- *Structural barriers to performing joint intelligence work.* National intelligence is still organized around the collection disciplines of the home agencies, not the joint mission. The importance of integrated, all-source analysis cannot be overstated. Without it, it is not possible to "connect the dots." No one component holds all the relevant information.

  By contrast, in organizing national defense, the Goldwater-Nichols legislation of 1986 created joint commands for operations in the field, the Unified Command Plan. The services—the Army, Navy, Air Force, and Marine Corps—organize, train, and equip their people and units to perform their missions. Then they assign personnel and units to the joint combatant commander, like the commanding general of the Central Command (CENTCOM). The Goldwater-Nichols Act required officers to serve tours outside their service in order to win promotion. The culture of the Defense Department was transformed, its collective mind-set moved from service-specific to "joint," and its operations became more integrated.

- *Lack of common standards and practices across the foreign-domestic divide.* The leadership of the intelligence community should be able to pool information gathered overseas with information gathered in the United States, holding the work—wherever it is done—to a common standard of quality in how it is collected, processed (e.g., translated), reported, shared, and analyzed. A common set of personnel standards for intelligence can create a group of professionals better able to operate in joint activities, transcending their own service-specific mind-sets.

- *Divided management of national intelligence capabilities.* While the CIA was once "central" to our national intelligence capabilities, following the end of the Cold War it has been less able to influence the use of the nation's imagery and signals intelligence capabilities in three national agencies housed within the Department of Defense: the National Security Agency, the National Geospatial-Intelligence Agency, and the National Reconnaissance Office. One of the lessons learned from the 1991 Gulf War was the value of national intelligence systems (satellites in particular) in precision warfare. Since that war, the department has appropriately drawn these agencies into its transformation of the military. Helping to orchestrate this transformation is the under secretary of defense for intelligence, a position established by Congress after 9/11. An unintended consequence of these developments has been the far greater demand made by Defense on technical systems, leaving the DCI less able to influence how these technical resources are allocated and used.

- *Weak capacity to set priorities and move resources.* The agencies are mainly organized around what they collect or the way they collect it. But the priorities for collection are national. As the DCI makes hard choices about moving resources, he or she must have the power to reach across agencies and reallocate effort.
- *Too many jobs.* The DCI now has at least three jobs. He is expected to run a particular agency, the CIA. He is expected to manage the loose confederation of agencies that is the intelligence community. He is expected to be the analyst in chief for the government, sifting evidence and directly briefing the President as his principal intelligence adviser. No recent DCI has been able to do all three effectively. Usually what loses out is management of the intelligence community, a difficult task even in the best case because the DCI's current authorities are weak. With so much to do, the DCI often has not used even the authority he has.
- *Too complex and secret.* Over the decades, the agencies and the rules surrounding the intelligence community have accumulated to a depth that practically defies public comprehension. There are now 15 agencies or parts of agencies in the intelligence community. The community and the DCI's authorities have become arcane matters, understood only by initiates after long study. Even the most basic information about how much money is actually allocated to or within the intelligence community and most of its key components is shrouded from public view.

The current DCI is responsible for community performance but lacks the three authorities critical for any agency head or chief executive officer: (1) control over purse strings, (2) the ability to hire or fire senior managers, and (3) the ability to set standards for the information infrastructure and personnel. . . .

*Combining Joint Work with Stronger Management*
    We have received recommendations on the topic of intelligence reform from many sources. Other commissions have been over this same ground. . . . Past efforts have foundered, because the president did not support them; because the DCI, the secretary of defense, or both opposed them; and because some proposals lacked merit. We have tried to take stock of these experiences, and borrow from strong elements in many of the ideas that have already been developed by others.
    *Recommendation: The current position of Director of Central Intelligence should be replaced by a National Intelligence Director with two main areas of responsibility: (1) to oversee national intelligence centers on specific subjects of interest across the U.S. government and (2) to manage the national intelligence program and oversee the agencies that contribute to it.*

First, the National Intelligence Director should oversee *national intelligence centers* to provide all-source analysis and plan intelligence operations for the whole government on major problems.

- One such problem is counterterrorism. In this case, we believe that the center should be the intelligence entity (formerly TTIC) inside the National Counterterrorism Center we have proposed. . . . Other national intelligence centers—for instance, on counterproliferation, crime and narcotics, and China—would be housed in whatever department or agency is best suited for them.
- The National Intelligence Director would retain the present DCI's role as the principal intelligence adviser to the president. We hope the president will come to look directly to the directors of the national intelligence centers to provide all-source analysis in their areas of responsibility, balancing the advice of these intelligence chiefs against the contrasting viewpoints that may be offered by department heads at State, Defense, Homeland Security, Justice, and other agencies.

Second, the National Intelligence Director should manage the national intelligence program and oversee the component agencies of the intelligence community.

- The National Intelligence Director would submit a unified budget for national intelligence that reflects priorities chosen by the National Security Council, an appropriate balance among the varieties of technical and human intelligence collection, and analysis. He or she would receive an appropriation for national intelligence and apportion the funds to the appropriate agencies, in line with that budget, and with authority to reprogram funds among the national intelligence agencies to meet any new priority (as counterterrorism was in the 1990s). . . .
- The National Intelligence Director would manage this national effort with the help of three deputies, each of whom would also hold a key position in one of the component agencies.
- foreign intelligence (the head of the CIA)
- defense intelligence (the under secretary of defense for intelligence)
- homeland intelligence (the FBI's executive assistant director for intelligence or the under secretary of homeland security for information analysis and infrastructure protection).

Other agencies in the intelligence community would coordinate their work within each of these three areas, largely staying housed in the same departments or agencies that support them now.

Returning to the analogy of the Defense Department's organization, these three deputies—like the leaders of the Army, Navy, Air Force, or

Marines—would have the job of acquiring the systems, training the people, and executing the operations planned by the national intelligence centers.

And, just as the combatant commanders also report to the secretary of defense, the directors of the national intelligence centers—e.g., for counter-proliferation, crime and narcotics, and the rest—also would report to the National Intelligence Director.

- The Defense Department's military intelligence programs—the joint military intelligence program (JMIP) and the tactical intelligence and related activities program (TIARA)—would remain part of that department's responsibility.
- The National Intelligence Director would set personnel policies to establish standards for education and training and facilitate assignments at the national intelligence centers and across agency lines. The National Intelligence Director also would set information sharing and information technology policies to maximize data sharing, as well as policies to protect the security of information.
- Too many agencies now have an opportunity to say no to change. The National Intelligence Director should participate in an NSC executive committee that can resolve differences in priorities among the agencies and bring the major disputes to the president for decision.

The National Intelligence Director should be located in the Executive Office of the President. This official, who would be confirmed by the Senate and would testify before Congress, would have a relatively small staff of several hundred people, taking the place of the existing community management offices housed at the CIA. . . .

We are wary of too easily equating government management problems with those of the private sector. But we have noticed that some very large private firms rely on a powerful CEO who has significant control over how money is spent and can hire or fire leaders of the major divisions, assisted by a relatively modest staff, while leaving responsibility for execution in the operating divisions.

There are disadvantages to separating the position of National Intelligence Director from the job of heading the CIA. For example, the National Intelligence Director will not head a major agency of his or her own and may have a weaker base of support. But we believe that these disadvantages are outweighed by several other considerations:

- The National Intelligence Director must be able to directly oversee intelligence collection inside the United States. Yet law and custom has counseled against giving such a plain domestic role to the head of the CIA.

- The CIA will be one among several claimants for funds in setting national priorities. The National Intelligence Director should not be both one of the advocates and the judge of them all.
- Covert operations tend to be highly tactical, requiring close attention. The National Intelligence Director should rely on the relevant joint mission center to oversee these details, helping to coordinate closely with the White House. The CIA will be able to concentrate on building the capabilities to carry out such operations and on providing the personnel who will be directing and executing such operations in the field.
- Rebuilding the analytic and human intelligence collection capabilities of the CIA should be a full-time effort, and the director of the CIA should focus on extending its comparative advantages.

*Recommendation: The CIA Director should emphasize (a) rebuilding the CIA's analytic capabilities; (b) transforming the clandestine service by building its human intelligence capabilities; (c) developing a stronger language program, with high standards and sufficient financial incentives; (d) renewing emphasis on recruiting diversity among operations officers so they can blend more easily in foreign cities; (e) ensuring a seamless relationship between human source collection and signals collection at the operational level; and (f) stressing a better balance between unilateral and liaison operations.*

The CIA should retain responsibility for the direction and execution of clandestine and covert operations, as assigned by the relevant national intelligence center and authorized by the National Intelligence Director and the president. This would include propaganda, renditions, and nonmilitary disruption. We believe, however, that one important area of responsibility should change.

*Recommendation: Lead responsibility for directing and executing paramilitary operations, whether clandestine or covert, should shift to the Defense Department. There it should be consolidated with the capabilities for training, direction, and execution of such operations already being developed in the Special Operations Command.*

- Before 9/11, the CIA did not invest in developing a robust capability to conduct paramilitary operations with U.S. personnel. It relied on proxies instead, organized by CIA operatives without the requisite military training. The results were unsatisfactory.
- Whether the price is measured in either money or people, the United States cannot afford to build two separate capabilities for carrying out secret military operations, secretly operating standoff missiles, and secretly training foreign military or paramilitary forces. The United States should concentrate responsibility and necessary legal authorities in one entity.

- The post–9/11 Afghanistan precedent of using joint CIA-military teams for covert and clandestine operations was a good one. We believe this proposal to be consistent with it. Each agency would concentrate on its comparative advantages in building capabilities for joint missions. The operation itself would be planned in common.
- . . . The CIA's experts should be integrated into the military's training, exercises, and planning. To quote a CIA official now serving in the field: "One fight, one team."

*Recommendation: Finally, to combat the secrecy and complexity we have described, the overall amounts of money being appropriated for national intelligence and to its component agencies should no longer be kept secret. Congress should pass a separate appropriations act for intelligence, defending the broad allocation of how these tens of billions of dollars have been assigned among the varieties of intelligence work.*

The specifics of the intelligence appropriation would remain classified, as they are today. Opponents of declassification argue that America's enemies could learn about intelligence capabilities by tracking the top-line appropriations figure. Yet the top-line figure by itself provides little insight into U.S. intelligence sources and methods. The U.S. government readily provides copious information about spending on its military forces, including military intelligence. The intelligence community should not be subject to that much disclosure. But when even aggregate categorical numbers remain hidden, it is hard to judge priorities and foster accountability.

### 13.3 Unity of Effort in Sharing Information

*Information Sharing*

We have already stressed the importance of intelligence analysis that can draw on all relevant sources of information. The biggest impediment to all-source analysis—to a greater likelihood of connecting the dots—is the human or systemic resistance to sharing information.

The U.S. government has access to a vast amount of information. When databases not usually thought of as "intelligence," such as customs or immigration information, are included, the storehouse is immense. But the U.S. government has a weak system for processing and using what it has. In interviews around the government, official after official urged us to call attention to frustrations with the unglamorous "back office" side of government operations.

In the 9/11 story, for example, we sometimes see examples of information that could be accessed—like the undistributed NSA information that would have helped identify Nawaf al Hazmi [one of the hijackers] in January 2000. But someone had to ask for it. In that case, no one did. Or . . . the information is distributed, but in a compartmented channel. Or the information is available, and someone does ask, but it cannot be shared.

What all these stories have in common is a system that requires a demonstrated "need to know" before sharing. This approach assumes it is possible to know, in advance, who will need to use the information. Such a system implicitly assumes that the risk of inadvertent disclosure outweighs the benefits of wider sharing. Those Cold War assumptions are no longer appropriate. The culture of agencies feeling they own the information they gathered at taxpayer expense must be replaced by a culture in which the agencies instead feel they have a duty to the information—to repay the taxpayers' investment by making that information available.

Each intelligence agency has its own security practices, outgrowths of the Cold War. We certainly understand the reason for these practices. Counterintelligence concerns are still real, even if the old Soviet enemy has been replaced by other spies.

But the security concerns need to be weighed against the costs. Current security requirements nurture overclassification and excessive compartmentation of information among agencies. Each agency's incentive structure opposes sharing, with risks (criminal, civil, and internal administrative sanctions) but few rewards for sharing information. No one has to pay the long-term costs of overclassifying information, though these costs—even in literal financial terms—are substantial. There are no punishments for *not* sharing information. Agencies uphold a "need-to-know" culture of information protection rather than promoting a "need-to-share" culture of integration.

*Recommendation: Information procedures should provide incentives for sharing, to restore a better balance between security and shared knowledge.*

Intelligence gathered about transnational terrorism should be processed, turned into reports, and distributed according to the same quality standards, whether it is collected in Pakistan or in Texas.

The logical objection is that sources and methods may vary greatly in different locations. We therefore propose that when a report is first created, its data be separated from the sources and methods by which they are obtained. The report should begin with the information in its most shareable, but still meaningful, form. Therefore the maximum number of recipients can access some form of that information. If knowledge of further details becomes important, any user can query further, with access granted or denied according to the rules set for the network—and with queries leaving an audit trail in order to determine who accessed the information. But the questions may not come at all unless experts at the "edge" of the network can readily discover the clues that prompt to them.

We propose that information be shared horizontally, across new networks that transcend individual agencies.

- The current system is structured on an old mainframe, or hub-and-spoke, concept. In this older approach, each agency has its own database. Agency users send information to the database and then can retrieve it from the database.

- A decentralized network model, the concept behind much of the information revolution, shares data horizontally too. Agencies would still have their own databases, but those databases would be searchable across agency lines. In this system, secrets are protected through the design of the network and an "information rights management" approach that controls access to the data, not access to the whole network. . . .

*Recommendation: The president should lead the government-wide effort to bring the major national security institutions into the information revolution. He should coordinate the resolution of the legal, policy, and technical issues across agencies to create a "trusted information network."*

- No one agency can do it alone. Well-meaning agency officials are under tremendous pressure to update their systems. Alone, they may only be able to modernize the stovepipes, not replace them.
- Only presidential leadership can develop government-wide concepts and standards. Currently, no one is doing this job. Backed by the Office of Management and Budget, a new National Intelligence Director empowered to set common standards for information use throughout the community, and a secretary of homeland security who helps extend the system to public agencies and relevant private-sector databases, a government-wide initiative can succeed.
- White House leadership is also needed because the policy and legal issues are harder than the technical ones. The necessary technology already exists. What does not are the rules for acquiring, accessing, sharing, and using the vast stores of public and private data that may be available. When information sharing works, it is a powerful tool. Therefore the sharing and uses of information must be guided by a set of practical policy guidelines that simultaneously empower and constrain officials, telling them clearly what is and is not permitted.

"This is government acting in new ways, to face new threats," the most recent Markle [Foundation] report explains. "And while such change is necessary, it must be accomplished while engendering the people's trust that privacy and other civil liberties are being protected, that businesses are not being unduly burdened with requests for extraneous or useless information, that taxpayer money is being well spent, and that, ultimately, the network will be effective in protecting our security." The authors add: "Leadership is emerging from all levels of government and from many places in the private sector. What is needed now is a plan to accelerate these efforts, and public debate and consensus on the goals." . . .

*Improve the Transitions between Administrations*

In [an earlier chapter], we described the transition of 2000–2001. Beyond the policy issues we described, the new administration did not have its deputy cabinet officers in place until the spring of 2001, and the critical subcabinet officials were not confirmed until the summer—if then. In other words, the new administration—like others before it—did not have its team on the job until at least six months after it took office.

*Recommendation: Since a catastrophic attack could occur with little or no notice, we should minimize as much as possible the disruption of national security policymaking during the change of administrations by accelerating the process for national security appointments. We think the process could be improved significantly so transitions can work more effectively and allow new officials to assume their new responsibilities as quickly as possible.*

- Before the election, candidates should submit the names of selected members of their prospective transition teams to the FBI so that, if necessary, those team members can obtain security clearances immediately after the election is over.
- A president-elect should submit lists of possible candidates for national security positions to begin obtaining security clearances immediately after the election, so that their background investigations can be complete before January 20.
- A single federal agency should be responsible for providing and maintaining security clearances, ensuring uniform standards—including uniform security questionnaires and financial report requirements, and maintaining a single database. This agency can also be responsible for administering polygraph tests on behalf of organizations that require them.
- A president-elect should submit the nominations of the entire new national security team, through the level of under secretary of cabinet departments, not later than January 20. The Senate, in return, should adopt special rules requiring hearings and votes to confirm or reject national security nominees within 30 days of their submission. The Senate should not require confirmation of such executive appointees below Executive Level 3.
- The outgoing administration should provide the president-elect, as soon as possible after election day, with a classified, compartmented list that catalogues specific, operational threats to national security; major military or covert operations; and pending decisions on the possible use of force. Such a document could provide both notice and a checklist, inviting a president-elect to inquire and learn more.

### 13.5 *Organizing America's Defenses in the United States*

*The Future Role of the FBI*

We have considered proposals for a new agency dedicated to intelligence collection in the United States. Some call this a proposal for an "American MI- 5," although the analogy is weak—the actual British Security Service is a relatively small worldwide agency that combines duties assigned in the U.S. government to the Terrorist Threat Integration Center, the CIA, the FBI, and the Department of Homeland Security.

The concern about the FBI is that it has long favored its criminal justice mission over its national security mission. Part of the reason for this is the demand around the country for FBI help on criminal matters. The FBI was criticized, rightly, for the overzealous domestic intelligence investigations disclosed during the 1970s. The pendulum swung away from those types of investigations during the 1980s and 1990s, though the FBI maintained an active counterintelligence function and was the lead agency for the investigation of foreign terrorist groups operating inside the United States.

We do not recommend the creation of a new domestic intelligence agency. It is not needed if our other recommendations are adopted—to establish a strong national intelligence center, part of the NCTC, that will oversee counterterrorism intelligence work, foreign and domestic, and to create a National Intelligence Director who can set and enforce standards for the collection, processing, and reporting of information.

Under the structures we recommend, the FBI's role is focused, but still vital. The FBI does need to be able to direct its thousands of agents and other employees to collect intelligence in America's cities and towns—interviewing informants, conducting surveillance and searches, tracking individuals, working collaboratively with local authorities, and doing so with meticulous attention to detail and compliance with the law. The FBI's job in the streets of the United States would thus be a domestic equivalent, operating under the U.S. Constitution and quite different laws and rules, to the job of the CIA's operations officers abroad. . . .

Our recommendation to leave counterterrorism intelligence collection in the United States with the FBI still depends on an assessment that the FBI—if it makes an all-out effort to institutionalize change—can do the job. We have been impressed by the determination that agents display in tracking down details, patiently going the extra mile and working the extra month, to put facts in the place of speculation. . . .

FBI agents and analysts in the field need to have sustained support and dedicated resources to become stronger intelligence officers. They need to be rewarded for acquiring informants and for gathering and disseminating information differently and more broadly than usual in a traditional criminal investigation. FBI employees need to report and analyze what they have learned in ways the Bureau has never done before. . . .

*Homeland Defense*

At several points in our inquiry, we asked, "Who is responsible for defending us at home?" Our national defense at home is the responsibility, first, of the Department of Defense and, second, of the Department of Homeland Security. They must have clear delineations of responsibility and authority.

We found that NORAD [North American Aerospace Defense Command], which had been given the responsibility for defending U.S. airspace, had construed that mission to focus on threats coming from outside America's borders. It did not adjust its focus even though the intelligence community had gathered intelligence on the possibility that terrorists might turn to hijacking and even use of planes as missiles. We have been assured that NORAD has now embraced the full mission. Northern Command has been established to assume responsibility for the defense of the domestic United States.

*Recommendation: The Department of Defense and its oversight committees should regularly assess the adequacy of Northern Command's strategies and planning to defend the United States against military threats to the homeland.*

The Department of Homeland Security was established to consolidate all of the domestic agencies responsible for securing America's borders and national infrastructure, most of which is in private hands. It should identify those elements of our transportation, energy, communications, financial, and other institutions that need to be protected, develop plans to protect that infrastructure, and exercise the mechanisms to enhance preparedness. This means going well beyond the preexisting jobs of the agencies that have been brought together inside the department.

*Recommendation: The Department of Homeland Security and its oversight committees should regularly assess the types of threats the country faces to determine (a) the adequacy of the government's plans—and the progress against those plans—to protect America's critical infrastructure and (b) the readiness of the government to respond to the threats that the United States might face. . . .*

Excerpted from U.S. National Commission on Terrorist Attacks Upon the United States. *The 9/11 Commission Report: Final Report of the National Commission on Terrorist Attacks Upon the United States,* Chapter 13. July 22, 2004: 399–428. Washington, D.C.: Government Printing Office. http://www.gpoaccess.gov/911/index.html (accessed November 1, 2004).

# Chronology of Documents

# Department of Homeland Security Organizational Chart

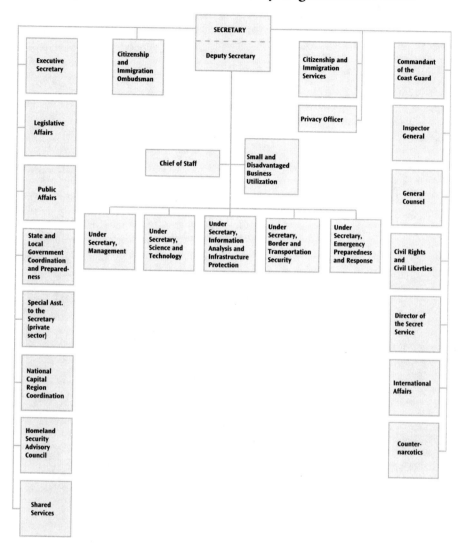

**SECRETARY**

**Deputy Secretary**

**Executive Secretary**

**Citizenship and Immigration Ombudsman**

**Citizenship and Immigration Services**

**Commandant of the Coast Guard**

**Legislative Affairs**

**Privacy Officer**

**Inspector General**

**Public Affairs**

**Chief of Staff**

**Small and Disadvantaged Business Utilization**

**General Counsel**

**State and Local Government Coordination and Preparedness**

**Under Secretary, Management**

**Under Secretary, Science and Technology**

**Under Secretary, Information Analysis and Infrastructure Protection**

**Under Secretary, Border and Transportation Security**

**Under Secretary, Emergency Preparedness and Response**

**Civil Rights and Civil Liberties**

**Special Asst. to the Secretary (private sector)**

**Director of the Secret Service**

**National Capital Region Coordination**

**International Affairs**

**Homeland Security Advisory Council**

**Counter-narcotics**

**Shared Services**

# Bibliography

## Articles, Books, Government Documents, and Reports

Anonymous [Michael Scheuer]. *Imperial Hubris: Why the West Is Losing the War on Terror.* Washington, D.C.: Brassey's, 2004.

Balz, Dan, and Bob Woodward. "Bush's Global Strategy Began to Take Shape in First Frantic Hours After Attack." Part 1 of "America's Chaotic Road to War." *Washington Post,* January 27, 2002. http://www.washingtonpost.com/ac2/wp-dyn?pagename= article&node=&contentId=A42754-2002Jan26 (accessed October 28, 2004).

Bergen, Peter L. *Holy War, Inc.: Inside the Secret World of Osama bin Laden.* New York: Free Press, 2001.

Bovard, James. *Terrorism and Tyranny: Trampling Freedom, Justice, and Peace to Rid the World of Evil.* New York: Palgrave Macmillan, 2003.

Bremer, L. Paul III, and Edwin Meese III. *Defending the American Homeland: A Report of the Heritage Foundation Homeland Security Task Force.* Washington, D.C.: Heritage Foundation, 2002. http://www.heritage.org/Research/Homeland Defense/ loader.cfm?url=/commonspot/security/getfile.cfm&PageID=9713 (accessed October 28, 2004).

Brown, Cynthia, ed. *Lost Liberties: Ashcroft and the Assault on Personal Freedom.* New York: New Press, 2003.

Chafee, Zechariah Jr. *Free Speech in the United States.* Cambridge, Mass.: Harvard University Press, 1967.

Clarke, Richard A. *Against All Enemies: Inside America's War on Terror.* New York: Free Press, 2004.

Dalglish, Lucy A., and Gregg P. Leslie, eds. *Homefront Confidential: How the War on Terrorism Affects Access to Information and the Public's Right to Know.* 5th ed. Arlington, Va.: Reporters Committee for Freedom of the Press, 2004. http://www. rcfp.org/homefrontconfidential (accessed October 29, 2004).

Emerson, Thomas. *The System of Freedom of Expression.* New York: Random House, 1970.

Gellman, Barton. "Broad Effort Launched After '98 Attacks." *Washington Post,* December 19, 2001. http://www.washingtonpost.com/ac2/wp-dyn?pagename= article&node=&contentId=A62725-2001Dec18 (accessed October 29, 2004).

Goldstein, Robert Justin. *Political Repression in Modern America from 1870 to 1976.* Urbana: University of Illinois Press, 2001.

Hersh, Seymour M. "Missed Messages: Why the Government Didn't Know What It Knew." *New Yorker,* June 3, 2002. http://www.newyorker.com/printable/?fact/ 020603fa_FACT (accessed October 29, 2004).

————. *Chain of Command: The Road from 9/11 to Abu Ghraib.* New York: Harper-Collins, 2004.

Hoffman, Bruce. *Inside Terrorism.* New York: Columbia University Press, 1998.

Hofstadter, Richard, and Michael Wallace, eds. *American Violence: A Documentary History.* New York: Knopf, 1970.

Laqueur, Walter. *The New Terrorism: Fanaticism and the Arms of Mass Destruction.* Oxford: Oxford University Press, 1999.

Leone, Richard C., and Greg Anrig Jr., eds. *The War on Our Freedoms: Civil Liberties in an Age of Terrorism.* A Century Foundation Book. New York: Public Affairs, 2003.

Levy, Leonard W. *Emergence of a Free Press.* New York: Oxford University Press, 1985.

Linfield, Michael. *Freedom Under Fire: U.S. Civil Liberties in Times of War.* Boston: South End Press, 1990.

Markle Foundation. Task Force on National Security in the Information Age. *Creating a Trusted Network for Homeland Security.* Washington, D.C.: Markle Foundation, 2003. http://www.markletaskforce.org/Report2_Full_Report.pdf (accessed October 28, 2004).

Miller, John C. *Crisis in Freedom: The Alien and Sedition Acts.* Boston: Little, Brown/ Atlantic Monthly Press, 1951.

Miller, Judith, Jeff Gerth, and Don Van Natta Jr. "Many Say U.S. Planned for Terror but Failed to Take Action." *New York Times,* December 30, 2001. http://www. nytimes.com/2001/12/30/national/30TERR.html (accessed July 30, 2002).

O'Hanlon, Michael E., Peter R. Orszag, Ivo H. Daalder, I. M. Destler, David L. Gunter, James M. Lindsay, Robert E. Litan, and James B. Steinberg. *Protecting the American Homeland: One Year On.* Washington, D.C.: Brookings Institution Press, 2003.

Pillar, Paul R. *Terrorism and U.S. Foreign Policy.* Washington, D.C.: Brookings Institution Press, 2001.

Smolla, Rodney A. *Free Speech in an Open Society.* New York: Knopf, 1992.

Thompson, Paul, and the Center for Cooperative Research. *The Terror Timeline: Chronicle of the Road to 9/11—And America's Response.* New York: Regan Books, 2004.

U.S. Advisory Panel to Assess Domestic Response Capabilities for Terrorism Involving Weapons of Mass Destruction. *Implementing the National Strategy: Fourth Annual Report to the President and the Congress of the Advisory Panel to Assess Domestic Response Capabilities for Terrorism Involving Weapons of Mass Destruction.* December 12, 2002. http://purl.access.gpo.gov/GPO/LPS25391 (accessed October 28, 2004).

————. *Toward a National Strategy for Combating Terrorism: Second Annual Report to the President and the Congress of the Advisory Panel to Assess Domestic Response Capabilities for Terrorism Involving Weapons of Mass Destruction.* December 15, 2000. http://purl.access.gpo.gov/GPO/LPS16576 (accessed October 28, 2004).

U.S. Congress. General Accounting Office. *Homeland Security: Justice Department's Project to Interview Aliens after September 11, 2001.* GAO-03-459, April 11, 2003. http://purl.access.gpo.gov/GPO/LPS32463 (accessed October 28, 2004).

————. *Homeland Security: Selected Recommendations from Congressionally Chartered Commissions and GAO.* GAO-04-591, March 31, 2004. http://purl.access.gpo.gov/GPO/LPS52199 (accessed October 28, 2004).

————. *Major Management Challenges and Program Risks: Department of Homeland Security.* GAO-03-102, January 2003. http://purl.access.gpo.gov/GPO/LPS32147 (accessed October 28, 2004).

U.S. Congress. House. Committee on Government Reform. *Knives, Box Cutters, and Bleach—A Review of Passenger Screening Training, Testing and Supervision: Hearing Before the Committee on Government Reform.* 108th Cong., 1st sess., November 20, 2003. http://purl.access.gpo.gov/GPO/LPS47894 (accessed October 28, 2004).

————. *Out of Many, One: Assessing Barriers to Information Sharing in the Department of Homeland Security: Hearing Before the Committee on Government Reform.* 108th Cong., 1st sess., May 8, 2003. http://purl.access.gpo.gov/GPO/LPS39037 (accessed October 29, 2004).

U.S. Congress. House. Committee on Government Reform. Subcommittee on National Security, Veterans Affairs and International Relations. *Combating Terrorism: In Search of a National Strategy: Hearing Before the Subcommittee on National Security, Veterans Affairs and International Relations of the Committee on Government Reform.* 107th Cong., 1st sess., serial 107-18, March 27, 2001. http://purl.access.gpo.gov/GPO/LPS17320 (PDF);http://purl.access.gpo.gov/GPO/LPS17321 (HTML) (accessed October 28, 2004).

U.S. Congress. House. Committee on the Judiciary. Subcommittee on Crime, Terrorism, and Homeland Security; Select Committee on Homeland Security. Subcommittee on Intelligence and Counterterrorism. *Progress in Consolidating Terrorist Watchlists—The Terrorist Screening Center (TSC): Joint Hearing Before the Subcommittee on Crime, Terrorism, and Homeland Security of the Committee on the Judiciary and the Subcommittee on Intelligence and Counterterrorism of the Select Committee on Homeland Security.* 108th Cong., 2nd sess., March 25, 2004. http://purl/access.gpo.gov/GPO/LPS52823 (accessed October 28, 2004).

U.S. Congress. Library of Congress. Congressional Research Service. *Afghanistan: Post-War Governance, Security, and U.S. Policy.* RL30588, June 15, 2004. http://fpc.state.gov/documents/organization/33748.pdf (accessed October 29, 2004).

————. *Al Qaeda After the Iraq Conflict.* RS21529, May 23, 2003. http://fpc.state.gov/documents/organization/21191.pdf (accessed October 29, 2004).

————. *Border Security: Inspections Practices, Policies, and Issues.* RL32399, May 26, 2004. http://fpc.state.gov/documents/organization/33856.pdf (accessed October 29, 2004).

————. *FBI Intelligence Reform Since September 11, 2001: Issues and Options for Congress.* RL32336, April 6, 2004. http://fpc.state.gov/documents/organization/32038.pdf (accessed October 29, 2004).

————. *First Responder Grant Formulas: The 9/11 Commission Recommendation and Other Options for Congressional Action.* RL32475, August 5, 2004. http://fpc.state.gov/documents/organization/35801.pdf (accessed October 29, 2004).

————. *Information Sharing for Homeland Security: A Brief Overview.* RL32597, September 30, 2004. http://www.fas.org/sgp/crs/RL32597.pdf (accessed October 29, 2004).

————. *Iraq and Al Qaeda: Allies or Not?* RL32217, February 5, 2004. http://fpc.state.gov/documents/organization/34715.pdf (accessed October 29, 2004).

————. *A Joint Committee on Intelligence: Proposals and Options from the 9/11 Commission and Others.* RL32525, August 25, 2004. http://www.fas.org/irp/crs/RL32525.pdf (accessed October 29, 2004).

————. *Military Tribunals: Historical Patterns and Lessons.* RL32458, July 9, 2004. http://www.fas.org/irp/crs/RL32458.pdf (accessed October 29, 2004).

————. *Nuclear Terrorism: A Brief Review of Threats and Responses.* RL32595, September 22, 2004. http://www.fas.org/irp/crs/RL32595.pdf (accessed October 29, 2004).

————. *Pakistan-U.S. Relations.* IB94041, October 8, 2004. http://fpc.state.gov/documents/organization/37133.pdf (accessed October 29, 2004).

————. *The Position of Director of National Intelligence: Issues for Congress.* RL32506, August 12, 2004. http://fpc.state.gov/documents/organization/35458.pdf (accessed October 29, 2004).

————. *Proposals for Intelligence Reorganization: 1949–2004.* RL32500, July 29, 2004. http://www.fas.org/irp/crs/RL32500.pdf (accessed October 29, 2004).

————. *Removing Terrorist Sanctuaries: The 9/11 Commission Recommendations and U.S. Policy.* RL32518, August 10, 2004. http://www.fas.org/irp/crs/RL32518.pdf (accessed October 29, 2004).

————. *Saudi Arabia: Terrorist Financing Issues.* RL32499, October 4, 2004. http://www.fas.org/man/crs/RL32499.pdf (accessed October 29, 2004).

————. *Secrecy Versus Openness: New Proposed Arrangements for Balancing Competing Needs.* RS21895, October 12, 2004. http://www.fas.org/sgp/crs/RS21895.pdf (accessed October 29, 2004).

————. *Terrorism: Key Recommendations of the 9/11 Commission and Recent Major Commissions and Inquiries.* RL32519, August 11, 2004. http://fpc.state.gov/documents/organization/35800.pdf (accessed October 29, 2004).

————. *U.S. Visitor and Immigrant Status Indicator Technology Program (US-VISIT).* RL32234, February 18, 2004. http://fpc.state.gov/documents/organization/35355.pdf (accessed October 29, 2004).

————. *USA Patriot Act Sunset: Provisions That Expire on December 31, 2005.* RL32186, June 10, 2004. http://fpc.state.gov/documents/organization/34499.pdf (accessed October 29, 2004).

————. *Visa Issuances: Policy, Issues, and Legislation.* RL31512, August 4, 2004. http://fpc.state.gov/documents/organization/36284.pdf (accessed October 29, 2004).

U.S. Congress. Senate. Committee on Foreign Relations. *Strategies for Homeland Defense: A Compilation by the Committee on Foreign Relations.* 107th Cong., 1st sess., Committee Print 107-43, September 26, 2001. http://purl.access.gpo.gov/GPO/LPS15541 (HTML); http://purl.access.gpo.gov/GPO/LPS15542 (PDF) (accessed October 29, 2004).

U.S. Congress. Senate Select Committee on Intelligence and House Permanent Select Committee on Intelligence. *Joint Inquiry into Intelligence Community Activities Before and After the Terrorist Attacks of September 11, 2001.* S. Rept. 107-351 and H. Rept. 107-792. 108th Cong., 1st sess., July 24, 2003. http://www.gpoaccess.gov/serialset/creports/911.html (accessed October 28, 2004).

U.S. Congress. Senate. Committee on the Judiciary. Subcommittee on Technology, Terrorism, and Government Information. *America Still Unprepared, America Still in Danger: The October 2002 Hart-Rudman Terrorism Task Force Report: Hearing Before the Committee on the Judiciary.* S. Hrg. 107-978. 107th Cong., 2nd sess., November 14, 2002. http://purl.access.gpo.gov/GPO/LPS36085 (accessed October 29, 2004).

U.S. Department of Defense. Office of the Under Secretary of Defense for Acquisition, Technology, and Logistics. Defense Science Board. *Defense Science Board 2003 Summer Study on DoD Roles and Missions in Homeland Security.* Vol. 1. November 2003. http://purl.access.gpo.gov/GPO/LPS53737 (accessed October 29, 2004).

———. *Defense Science Board 2003 Summer Study on DoD Roles and Missions in Homeland Security.* Vol. II—A: Supporting Reports. May 2004.http://purl.access.gpo.gov/GPO/LPS53736 (accessed October 29, 2004).

U.S. Executive Office of the President. *National Strategy for Combating Terrorism.* February 2003. http://purl.access.gpo.gov/GPO/LPS47951 (accessed October 28, 2004).

———. *National Strategy to Combat Weapons of Mass Destruction.* December 2002. http://purl.access.gpo.gov/GPO/LPS24899 (accessed October 28, 2004).

———. *National Strategy for Homeland Security.* July 2002. http://purl.access.gpo.gov/GPO/LPS20641 (accessed October 28, 2004).

———. *The National Strategy for the Physical Protection of Critical Infrastructures and Key Assets.* February 2003. http://www.whitehouse.gov/pcipb/physical.html (accessed November 18, 2004).

———. *The National Strategy to Secure Cyberspace.* February 2003. http://purl.access.gpo.gov/GPO/LPS28730 (accessed October 28, 2004).

U.S. National Commission on Terrorist Attacks Upon the United States. *The 9/11 Commission Report: Final Report of the National Commission on Terrorist Attacks Upon the United States.* July 22, 2004. http://www.gpoaccess.gov/911/index.html (accessed October 28,2004).

Woodward, Bob. *Bush at War.* New York: Simon & Schuster, 2002.

## Web Sites

### America's War Against Terrorism
http://www.lib.umich.edu/govdocs/usterror.html

The Documents Center at the University of Michigan Library offers links to hundreds of Web sites about virtually every aspect of terrorism through this excellent page. The links are divided into eight major categories: September 11th attack, terrorism suspects and prosecution, counterterrorism, post–September 11 attacks, previous attacks, other countries, background research, and related Web pages.

### Annotated Bibliography of Government Documents Related to the Threat of Terrorism and the Attacks of September 11, 2001
http://www.odl.state.ok.us/usinfo/terrorism/911.htm

This amazing site's title summarizes what it offers: a carefully annotated bibliography of more than 700 pages that lists a huge range of government documents related to terrorism and homeland security. The bibliography is divided into sixteen PDF files by topic for easy downloading. Some of the topics covered include the aftermath of the September 11 attacks, emergency preparedness, homeland security efforts and domestic counterterrorism, U.S. interests and policies in the Middle East, terrorist groups, actions by the executive and legislative branches in the war on terrorism, organizing the government to combat terrorism, Afghanistan, and Iraq. For each document, the bibliography includes a brief but thorough description and a full bibliographic citation (including Superintendent of Documents numbers and Web addresses where available). A librarian at the Oklahoma Department of Libraries created the bibliography, which is already legendary in the government documents community.

### Behind the Homefront
http://www.rcfp.org/behindthehomefront
The Reporters Committee for Freedom of the Press operates this site, which provides links to articles and reports about homeland security and military operations that affect newsgathering, access to information, and the public's right to know. The site is updated frequently.

### CDC Emergency Preparedness & Response
http://www.bt.cdc.gov
The federal Centers for Disease Control and Prevention operates this site, which offers extensive information for the public and health professionals about topics such as anthrax, smallpox, radiation contamination from "dirty bombs," and threats from other chemical and biological agents.

### Central Intelligence Agency: The War on Terrorism
http://www.cia.gov/terrorism/index.html
Selected reports, speeches, and transcripts of congressional testimony about the war on terrorism are available through this site operated by the Central Intelligence Agency.

### Christian Science Monitor: A Changed World—Combating Terrorism
http://www.csmonitor.com/specials/sept11
This site's highlight is its daily updates about the war on terrorism that quote a wide range of media sources from around the world. It also provides free access to all articles the *Christian Science Monitor* published about terrorism and homeland security in the year after the terrorist attacks of September 11, 2001.

### Citizenship and Immigration Services
http://uscis.gov
Citizenship and Immigration Services is a bureau within the Department of Homeland Security.

### Customs and Border Protection
http://cbp.gov

Customs and Border Protection is a bureau within the Department of Homeland Security.

### Defend AMERICA
http://www.defendamerica.mil

Defend AMERICA is the official Department of Defense Web site about the war on terrorism. Its original content is mainly limited to news stories and photographs, but it also has links to lots of other government sites that provide information about terrorism.

### Department of Homeland Security
http://www.dhs.gov

The Department of Homeland Security (DHS), which was formally launched in early 2003, represents the largest restructuring of the U.S. government since World War II. All or parts of twenty-two existing agencies were merged into the department, affecting between 170,000 and 180,000 federal employees. Its Web site provides background information about the department's creation, transcripts of congressional testimony and speeches by DHS officials, and press releases.

### Department of Homeland Security: Inspector General
http://www.dhs.gov/dhspublic/display?theme=89

The inspector general serves as the watchdog at the Department of Homeland Security (DHS). The Web site contains congressional testimony and reports about subjects such as DHS information security programs, training of airport security screeners by the Transportation Security Agency, passenger and baggage screening procedures at U.S. airports, DHS challenges in consolidating terrorist watch list information from numerous federal agencies, progress and challenges in securing cyberspace, the security implications of the visa waiver program, the distribution and spending of "first responder" grants, and management challenges at DHS.

### Department of Justice: Inspector General
http://www.justice.gov/oig/

The inspector general at the Department of Justice conducts investigations that are aimed at improving efficiency and enforcing laws and ethical standards at the Department. The inspector general's Web site has reports about the abuse of detainees who were arrested in the days and weeks after the September 2001 terrorist attacks, the internal impact of new priorities at the Federal Bureau of Investigation (FBI), the FBI's program to translate counter-intelligence and counterterrorism documents, and efforts to integrate fingerprint databases maintained by the FBI and the former Immigration and Naturalization Service, among other subjects.

### Department of State: Counterterrorism Office
http://www.state.gov/s/ct

Highlights at this site operated by the State Department include a list of groups designated as foreign terrorist organizations, chronologies of terrorist incidents, the annual report *Patterns of Global Terrorism*, and other State Department reports and press releases about terrorism.

### Department of State: Foreign Press Center
http://fpc.state.gov/c4564.htm

Through this site the Department of State provides access to hundreds of reports about homeland security, terrorism, and other issues prepared by the Congressional Research Service (CRS), which is part of the Library of Congress. The CRS does not itself place the reports online.

### Dudley Knox Library: Terrorism
http://library.nps.navy.mil/home/terrorism.htm

Among the many excellent collections of links to terrorism information available on the Internet, this list from the Dudley Knox Library at the Naval Postgraduate School is among the best because the links have obviously been carefully selected for their quality. The site has links to a wide range of terrorism bibliographies, presidential directives, terrorism chronologies, reports by the Congressional Research Service and other government agencies, and Web sites.

### Federation of American Scientists
http://www.fas.org

Through its publications, postings of government publications that are otherwise unavailable, and links to other sites, the Federation of American Scientists provides access to a huge collection of resources about homeland security, terrorism, weapons of mass destruction, information security, intelligence programs, and related topics. The site is one of the best places online to obtain Congressional Research Service (CRS) reports, which the agency itself does not make available electronically.

### Google Web Directory: Terrorism
http://directory.google.com/Top/Society/Issues/Terrorism

Links to several thousand Web sites about terrorism are provided on this page at the Google Web Directory. Most of the links are organized into categories such as articles and reports, biological and chemical terrorism, cyber terrorism, incidents, terrorist organizations, U.S. domestic terrorism, and the war on terrorism.

### Government Accountability Office: Airport Security

http://www.gao.gov/docsearch/featured/airptsec.html

The Government Accountability Office (GAO), which is commonly referred to as the investigative arm of Congress, provides links to more than sixty of its reports about airport and aviation security through this page. The GAO was known as the General Accounting Office before its name changed on July 7, 2004.

### Government Accountability Office: Homeland Security

http://www.gao.gov/docsearch/featured/homelandsecurity.html

Links to more than 240 reports about homeland security by the Government Accountability Office (GAO) are provided on this page.

### Government Accountability Office: Terrorism

http://www.gao.gov/docsearch/featured/terrorism.html

This page at the Government Accountability Office's Web site has links to more than 375 reports about terrorism that the agency has released.

### GovExec.com: Homeland Security

http://www.govexec.com/homeland

This site provides an archive of stories about homeland security published in Government Executive.

### Immigration and Customs Enforcement

http://www.ice.gov

Immigration and Customs Enforcement is a bureau within the Department of Homeland Security.

### Librarians' Index to the Internet: September 11 Terrorist Attacks

http://lii.org/search/file/911

The Librarians' Index to the Internet offers hundreds of carefully annotated links to Web sites and documents related to the terrorist attacks, divided under more than three dozen topics. Some of the topics include Afghanistan, anti-Americanism, censorship and freedom of information post–September 11, collapse of the World Trade Center, economic impact and assistance, Islam, magazine and newspaper articles, national security, Osama bin Laden, reading lists and bibliographies, resources for educators, rumors and hoaxes, and timelines.

### Librarians' Index to the Internet: USA Patriot Act Resources

http://lii.org/search/search/file/patriotact

This page at the Librarians' Index to the Internet offers annotated links to more than two dozen Web sites that provide information about the Patriot Act, which Congress passed in October 2001.

### *National Commission on Terrorist Attacks Upon the United States: Hearing Transcripts*

http://govinfo.library.unt.edu/911/hearings/index.htm

This page provides transcripts of all twelve public hearings held by the National Commission on Terrorist Attacks Upon the United States, more commonly known as the 9/11 Commission. The underlying site was created through a partnership between the Government Printing Office and the University of North Texas Libraries to preserve Web sites of defunct government agencies and commissions.

### *National Commission on Terrorist Attacks Upon the United States: Staff Monographs and Statements*

http://govinfo.library.unt.edu/911/staff_statements/index.htm

The seventeen statements issued by the staff of the 9/11 Commission during the commission's public hearings are available through this page. The page also has staff monographs about terrorist financing and terrorist travel that were released after the commission issued its final report.

### *National Security Archive: The September 11th Sourcebooks*

http://www.gwu.edu/~nsarchiv/NSAEBB/sept11

More than one hundred government documents related to the September 2001 terrorist attacks and their aftermath—many of them previously classified and obtained under the Freedom of Information Act—are available at this site. The documents are about topics such as terrorism and U.S. policy, the end of the U.S. biological warfare program, Afghanistan and the Taliban, the hunt for Osama bin Laden, and a deadly anthrax accident at a Russian plant in 1979. The National Security Archive, an independent research institute and library in Washington, D.C., operates the site.

### *Newseum: America Under Attack*

http://www.newseum.org/frontpages/

Stunning images of the front pages from more than 120 newspapers published around the world the day after the September 11 terrorist attacks are available at this site from the Newseum.

### *Open Directory Project: War on Terrorism—News and Media*

http://dmoz.org/Society/Issues/Warfare_and_Conflict/Specific_Conflicts/War_on_Terrorism/News_and_Media/September_11,_2001

This page from the Open Directory Project provides links to nearly 2,000 articles and news media sites about the September 11 terrorist attacks and the subsequent war on terrorism.

### Preserving Life & Liberty

http://www.lifeandliberty.gov

The Justice Department operates this site about the Patriot Act. Documents at the site describe how the Patriot Act has improved counterterrorism efforts, reply to criticisms of the law, provide the full text of the Patriot Act, and offer major speeches about the law by Justice Department officials.

### Response to Terrorism: U.S. Department of State

http://usinfo.state.gov/is/international_security/terrorism.html

This site is an excellent source for current press releases, speech transcripts, and reports about terrorism from a variety of federal agencies and departments.

### September 11, 2001: Attack on America

http://www.yale.edu/lawweb/avalon/sept_11/sept_11.htm

Hundreds of primary source documents about the September 11 attacks and their aftermath are available from this page at Yale Law School's Avalon Project site. The documents, which are arranged by date, include speeches by U.S. and foreign leaders, congressional bills and resolutions, transcripts of press briefings by various federal agencies, transcripts of statements at congressional hearings, executive orders, statements by organizations such as NATO and the Organization of American States, and United Nations resolutions.

### September 11, 2001 Resources

http://poynteronline.org/column.asp?id=49&aid=3401

Links to several dozen news media sites that offer coverage about the September 11 attacks and terrorism highlight this site by the Poynter Institute, a school for journalists in Florida. Best of all, the links take users directly to the section at each site devoted to terrorism instead of taking them to the home page. The site also provides images of newspaper front pages from around the world published on September 11 and 12 and links to several dozen useful sites about the attacks and terrorism.

### September 11 Web Archive

http://september11.archive.org

The Library of Congress has joined with several other organizations to create this archive of reactions to the September 11 attacks from Web sites operated by everyone from individuals to government institutions around the world.

### Strategic Intelligence

http://www.loyola.edu/dept/politics/intel.html

This site provides extensive links to information about intelligence issues. The links lead to Web sites operated by U.S. and foreign intelligence agencies, numerous government documents about intelligence, laws and legislative reports, transcripts of congressional hearings, and historical documents. The political science department at Loyola College in Maryland operates the site.

### *Transportation Security Administration*
http://www.tsa.gov

The Transportation Security Administration, which is part of the Department of Homeland Security, is responsible for the safety of all methods of transportation in the United States, including aviation.

### *The U.S. Intelligence Community: Selected Resources*
http://www.columbia.edu/cu/lweb/indiv/lehman/guides/intell.html

Librarians at Columbia University created this excellent list of Web and print resources about U.S. intelligence agencies. The list includes bibliographies, publications about intelligence reform, executive orders, congressional floor debates, information about the Freedom of Information Act, and publications about specific intelligence agencies.

### *War on Terrorism Resource Guides*
http://www.lib.ecu.edu/govdoc/waronterror.html

This superb site organizes hundreds of annotated links to sites about terrorism into six guides: attack on America; Osama bin Laden and al Qaeda; Saddam Hussein and Iraq; news, commentary, and analysis; Afghanistan and the Taliban; and post-Saddam Iraq. A political science and government documents librarian at East Carolina University operates the site.

### *Washington Post: America at War*
http://www.washingtonpost.com/wp-dyn/nation/specials/attacked

The *Washington Post* provides free access to several thousand articles and editorials about the September 11 attacks and the war on terrorism through this page.

### *Yahoo! News: Afghanistan*
http://story.news.yahoo.com/fc?cid=34&tmpl=fc&in=World&cat=Afghanistan

This page at Yahoo! News provides links to several thousand news reports about Afghanistan dating back to December 1997. Some of the sources include Agence France-Presse (France), the Associated Press, the BBC (United Kingdom), the *Christian Science Monitor,* the *Economist* (United Kingdom), the *Globe and Mail* (Canada), the Guardian (United Kingdom), the *Independent* (United Kingdom), the *Los Angeles Times,* Reuters, National Public Radio, the *New York Times, U.S. News & World Report,* and the *Washington Post.* The page also has links to several dozen major Web sites about Afghanistan.

### *Yahoo! News: Biological and Chemical Weapons*
http://story.news.yahoo.com/fc?cid=34&tmpl=fc&in=World&cat=Biological_and_Chemical_Weapons

Links to hundreds of news stories about biological and chemical weapons from a variety of news sources are available from this page at Yahoo! News. The articles date back to March 1999.

### *Yahoo! News: Civil Liberties*

http://story.news.yahoo.com/fc?cid=34&tmpl=fc&in=US&cat=Civil_
Liberties

Through this page Yahoo! News provides links to several hundred news stories about civil liberties, many of which relate to homeland security and the
war on terrorism. The articles date from August 1999 to the present. The page
also has links to about a dozen related documents and Web sites.

### *Yahoo! News: Guantanamo Detainees*

http://story.news.yahoo.com/fc?cid=34&tmpl=fc&in=World&cat=
Guantanamo_Detainees

More than 100 news stories about the detainees that the United States is
holding at Guantanamo Bay, Cuba, are available through this page at Yahoo!
News. The articles date back to November 2003.

### *Yahoo! News: Iraq Conflict*

http://story.news.yahoo.com/fc?cid=34&tmpl=fc&in=World&cat=Iraq

Links to more than 10,000 news reports about Iraq from a variety of news
sources that date back to November 1997 are available through this page at
Yahoo! News.

### *Yahoo! News: Osama bin Laden & al-Qaida*

http://story.news.yahoo.com/fc?cid=34&tmpl=fc&in=World&cat=
Osama_bin_Laden_and_al_Qaida

More than 1,000 articles about Osama bin Laden and al Qaeda that date
back to August 1998 are available through this page at Yahoo! News. The
articles were published by a variety of domestic and foreign news media.

### *Yahoo! News: Terrorism & 9/11*

http://news.yahoo.com/fc?tmpl=fc&cid=34&in=us&cat=terrorism

Links to more than 5,000 current and archived news stories about terrorism and the attacks on September 11, 2001, can be accessed through this page
at Yahoo! News. The stories, which date back to December 1995, were published by more than two dozen domestic and foreign media outlets. The page
also has links to more than two dozen related documents and Web sites.

### *Yahoo! News: World Trade Center*

http://story.news.yahoo.com/fc?cid=34&tmpl=fc&in=US&cat=World_
Trade_Center

Several hundred articles about New York's World Trade Center, which was
destroyed in the terrorist attacks on September 11, 2001, are available through
links at this page from Yahoo! News. The articles date from the day after the
attacks to the present.

# Index

Note: page numbers in **boldface** indicate document texts.